P. Forrest Talley, PhD
Editor

Handbook
for the Treatment
of Abused and Neglected
Children

Pre-publication
REVIEWS,
COMMENTARIES,
EVALUATIONS . . .

"**F**or child and family therapists who are generalists and do not devote much of their practice to child maltreatment, this book will be an essential guide in developing a comprehensive treatment plan that conforms to our current understanding of 'best practice' for the individual client. For child and family therapists who specialize in maltreatment, they may find four or five chapters that are primarily congruent with aspects of their expertise, while taking delight in the discovery that ten to twelve chapters provide new information that both broadens and deepens their effective practice.

This book provides detailed knowledge about medical and legal issues that range from assessment and medication to expert witness testimony, investigative interviews, and confidentiality. A wide array of clinical understandings is crucial if we therapists are to develop and maintain a comprehensive conceptual intervention framework when we provide treatment for this very vulnerable population. This handbook will greatly aid us in carrying out our varied professional responsibilities, one unique child and family at a time."

Dan Hughes, PhD
Clinician specializing in training
therapists in the treatment of maltreated
children and youth;
Author of *Building the Bonds*
of Attachment

"**T**his timely book is a comprehensive guide to the skills needed to assess and treat maltreated children and their families. The emphasis of this handbook is on clinical practice, so beginning and experienced clinicians alike will find specific tools to enhance their effectiveness with this population."

Charles E. Schaefer, PhD
Professor of Psychology,
Fairleigh Dickinson University

Handbook for the Treatment of Abused and Neglected Children

HAWORTH Social Work Practice with Children and Families
John T. Pardeck, PhD, LCSW
Senior Editor

Social Work Practice with Children and Families: A Family Health Approach edited by Francis K. O. Yuen

Homelessness in Rural America: Policy and Practice by Paul A. Rollinson and John T. Pardeck

Handbook for the Treatment of Abused and Neglected Children edited by P. Forrest Talley

Titles of Related Interest:

From Surviving to Thriving: A Therapist's Guide to Stage II Recovery for Survivors of Childhood Abuse by Mary Bratton

Breaking the Silence: Group Therapy for Childhood Sexual Abuse, A Practitioner's Manual by Judith A. Margolin

Child Maltreatment Risk Assessments: An Evaluation Guide by Sue Righthand, Bruce B. Kerr, and Kerry M. Drach

Effects of and Interventions for Childhood Trauma from Infancy Through Adolescence: Pain Unspeakable by Sandra B. Hutchison

Maltreatment in Early Childhood: Tools for Research-Based Intervention edited by Kathleen Coulborn Faller

The Victimization of Children: Emerging Issues edited by James W. Marquart, Janet L. Mullings, and Deborah J. Hartley

Handbook
for the Treatment
of Abused and Neglected
Children

P. Forrest Talley, PhD
Editor

The Haworth Social Work Practice Press™
The Haworth Reference Press™
Imprints of The Haworth Press, Inc.
New York • London • Oxford

For more information on this book or to order, visit
http://www.haworthpress.com/store/product.asp?sku=5407

or call 1-800-HAWORTH (800-429-6784) in the United States and Canada
or (607) 722-5857 outside the United States and Canada

or contact orders@HaworthPress.com

Published by

The Haworth Social Work Practice Press™ and The Haworth Reference Press™, imprints of
The Haworth Press, Inc., 10 Alice Street, Binghamton, NY 13904-1580.

PUBLISHER'S NOTE
Identities and circumstances of individuals discussed in this book have been changed to protect confidentiality.

Cover design by Marylouise E. Doyle.

Library of Congress Cataloging-in-Publication Data

Handbook for the treatment of abused and neglected children / P. Forrest Talley, editor.
    p. cm.
  Includes bibliographical references and index.
  ISBN-13: 978-0-7890-2677-4 (hc. : alk. paper)
  ISBN-10: 0-7890-2677-5 (hc. : alk. paper)
  ISBN-13: 978-0-7890-2678-1 (pbk. : alk. paper)
  ISBN-10: 0-7890-2678-3 (pbk. : alk. paper)
1. Child abuse—Treatment. 2. Abused children—Rehabilitation. 3. Child psychotherapy. 4. Child
welfare. I. Talley, P. Forrest.
  [DNLM: 1. Child Abuse—therapy. 2. Child Abuse—psychology. 3. Psychotherapy—
methods—Child. WS 350.2 H23515 2005]
  RJ507.A29H36 2005
  362.76'86—dc22
                                                                                          2004028452

Dedicated to my father, Charles O. Talley Jr.,
whose lifelong passion for helping others,
joined with an unquenchable curiosity,
motivates me still.

CONTENTS

PART III: THERAPY FOR ABUSED AND NEGLECTED CHILDREN

ABOUT THE EDITOR

P. Forrest Talley, PhD, is Supervising Psychologist in the Department of Pediatrics at the University of California–Davis Children's Hospital in Sacramento. His work is in the hospital's CAARE Center—a multidisciplinary treatment center for abused and neglected children. Dr. Talley manages the individual component of the Center's psychological services, coteaches a yearlong seminar on individual therapy, supervises psychology interns and staff, and sees children in both group and individual therapy. He received his doctorate in psychology in 1988 from Vanderbilt University, having performed his graduate work with Hans Strupp, PhD. Dr. Talley is a co-editor of *Psychotherapy Research and Practice: Bridging the Gap* (1994).

Contributors

Pamela C. Alexander, PhD, is a senior research investigator at the University of Pennsylvania. She has conducted research in the area of family violence for twenty-five years and is the recipient of several federal grants and contracts. Her primary research interests include the evaluation of family violence prevention and treatment programs, the intergenerational transmission of family violence, attachment theory, and stages of change as applied to family violence. Dr. Alexander completed her doctoral degree in clinical psychology at Emory University.

Catherine L. Anderson, PhD, is a licensed psychologist in full-time private practice in Bethesda, MD. She provides individual therapy to adolescents and adults, forensic psychological assessments, parenting capacity evaluations, and expert testimony for federal, state, and district court systems. She has done research, writing, training, supervision, and consultation in the areas of trauma, developmental psychopathology, psychoanalysis, and attachement theory. Dr. Anderson completed her doctoral degree in clinical psychology at the University of Maryland.

Sandra T. Azar, PhD, is Professor in the Department of Psychology at Pennsylvania State University in State College. She is also Research Associate at the Center for Adoption Research at the University of Massachusetts Medical Center in Worcester. She has published numerous articles and chapters on the theory, assessment, and treatment of child abuse and neglect and legal issues in this area. She conducts research work testing cognitive behavioral models of the etiology of child maltreatment and its treatment.

Dawn M. Blacker, PhD, is a clinical psychologist and Director of Clinical Training at the University of California–Davis Medical Center, Child and Adolescent Abuse Resources and Evaluation (CAARE) Diagnostic Center, in the Department of Pediatrics. Her clinical and research interests include child maltreatment, juvenile sexual offenders, and developmental disorders.

Joaquin Borrego Jr., PhD, is Assistant Professor in the Department of Psychology at Texas Tech University. Dr. Borrego received his degree from the University of Nevada, Reno, and completed his clinical internship at the University of California, San Diego. His research interests include child physical abuse, parent training, and behavioral assessment of parent-child relationships. Dr. Borrego is also interested in working with Spanish-speaking populations and community interventions.

Judianne Chew, MSW, is a clinical social worker at the University of California–Davis Medical Center, CAARE Center, Department of Pediatrics. She provides mental health services to abused and neglected children involved with Child Protective Services. Her interests include therapeutic change using art therapy, specialized groups for maltreated children, and crisis intervention for children at risk.

Linda R. Cote, PhD, is a psychologist for Child and Family Research, National Institute of Child Health and Human Development. Her research examines the influence of adult-child interaction on infants' and young children's development among immigrant families.

Michael De Bellis, MD, is Professor of Psychiatry and Behavioral Sciences at Duke University Medical Center, Director of Healthy Childhood Brain Development and Developmental Traumatology Research Program, Department of Psychiatry and Behavioral Sciences, Duke University Medical Center, and is board certified in child and adolescent psychiatry. Dr. De Bellis has extensive clinical and research experience in the clinical assessment of maltreatment in children, the psychobiology of child abuse, and anatomical MRI brain measurements in children and adolescents. He is the recipient of many professional awards and has authored over sixty publications. He has received several federally funded grants and two NARSAD Young Investigators Awards (1995 and 1998) for studies of brain maturation in maltreated children with post-traumatic stress disorder and in adolescents with alcohol use disorders. He won the 1998 A.E. Bennett Research Award for Original Research in Clinical Science, the 1999 American College of Neuropsychopharmacology (ACNP) Travel Award, and the 1999 Chaim Danieli Young Professional Award from the International Society of Traumatic Stress Studies for his papers on developmental traumatology.

Esther Deblinger, PhD, is Associate Professor of Psychiatry at the University of Medicine and Dentistry of New Jersey–School of Osteopathic Medicine. She serves as the Clinical Director of the Center for Children's Support, a multidisciplinary program that provides medical and mental health services for children who have suffered abuse. Dr. Deblinger has served as principal investigator for research grants from the Foundation of the University of Medicine and Dentistry of New Jersey, the National Center on Child Abuse and Neglect, and the National Institute for Mental Health. She is also a frequent invited speaker and has co-authored numerous publications as well as a book titled *Treating Sexually Abused Children and Their Nonoffending Parents.*

Holly A. Filcheck, PhD, is Assistant Professor of Clinical Psychology at Louisiana State University. Her clinical and research interests are focused on behavior management in preschool classrooms and in the home, and parent-training programs concerning children with disruptive behavior problems as well as developmental disabilities.

Elizabeth Gonzalez, PhD, is a clinical psychologist at the University of California–Davis Medical Center, CAARE Center, Department of Pediatrics. She provides mental health services to abused and neglected children involved with child protective services. Her interests include cross-cultural issues in foster care, special education, and the developmental impact of child maltreatment.

Amy D. Herschell, PhD, is completing a postdoctoral research fellowship at Western Psychiatric Institute and Clinic, University of Pittsburgh School of Medicine. She is pursuing clinical and research work focused on the treatment of child physical abuse and dissemination of evidence-based treatments from university to community settings.

Michele Ornelas Knight, PsyD, is a clinical psychologist at the University of California–Davis Medical Center, CAARE Center, Department of Pediatrics, and the assistant manager of the individual therapy program. She provides mental health services to abused and neglected children involved with Child Protective Services. Her interests include the coping strategies of maltreated children, abused children's perceptions of attachment relationships, and the therapeutic factors of change in treating abused children.

Thomas D. Lyon, JD, PhD, is Professor of Law at the University of Southern California. His PhD is in Developmental Psychology, and his research and writing concern child witnesses and child abuse. He has authored or co-authored half a dozen book chapters and his work has appeared in *Child Development, Law and Human Behavior, Cornell Law Review, Southern California Law Review, Pacific Law Journal, Harvard Women's Law Journal, Psychology, Public Policy and Law, Contemporary Psychology, Applied Developmental Science,* and *Developmental and Behavioral Pediatrics*.

Cheryl B. McNeil, PhD, is Associate Professor of Psychology in the Child Clinical Program at West Virginia University. Her clinical and research interests are focused on program development and evaluation, specifically with regard to abusive parenting practices and managing the disruptive behaviors of young children in both home and school settings. She has co-authored two books *(Parent-Child Interaction Therapy* and *Short-Term Play Therapy for Disruptive Children),* a continuing education audio and video package (Working with Oppositional Defiant Disorder in Children), and a classroom management program.

John E. B. Myers, JD, is Professor of Law at the University of the Pacific in Sacramento, California. John is the author of numerous books, chapters, and articles on legal issues in child abuse.

John T. Pardeck, PhD, was Professor of Social Work in the School of Social Work and a Research Fellow at Southwest Missouri State University. Prior to this position, he was Chair of the Department of Social Work at Southeast Missouri State University. Dr. Pardeck advocated for persons with disabilities and for interpreting the Americans with Disabilities Act to both private and public sector organizations. He authored a number of works, including *Social Work After the Americans with Disabilities Act: New Challenges and Opportunities for Social Services Professionals* (Auburn House, 1998), *Social Work Practice: An Ecological Approach* (Auburn House, 1996), and *Children in Foster Care and Adoption: A Guide to Bibliotherapy* (Greenwood Press, 1998). Dr. Pardeck also published more than 100 articles on disabilities and related topics in journals that include *Social Work, Child Welfare, Families in Society,* and *Research on Social Work Practice.* He was also the Editor in Chief of the *Journal of Social Work in Disability and Rehabilitation*.

Angela J. Rosas, MD, FAAP, is a pediatrician specializing in the field of child abuse and neglect. She is currently the Director of the Bridging Evidence Assessment and Resources (BEAR) Care Center in Sacramento, California, a joint program between Children's Specialist Medical Group and Sutter Children's Center. She has more than ten years of exprience examining patients with all forms of child maltreatment. She has lectured around the country and published several articles, case reports, and book chapters.

Jane F. Silovsky, PhD, is Assistant Professor and the Associate Director of the Center on Child Abuse and Neglect in the Department of Pediatrics at the University of Oklahoma Health Sciences Center. She conducts treatment outcome research with children who have sexual behavior problems and children who have experienced traumatic events, including child maltreatment. Dr. Silovsky also conducts program evaluations of family preservation and family reunification services.

Steven N. Sparta, PhD, ABPP, is Clinical Professor of Psychiatry, University of California–San Diego School of Medicine; Adjunct Professor of Psychology, San Diego State University; and Adjunct Professor of Law, Thomas Jefferson School of Law. He holds diplomas in clinical and forensic psychology, and maintains an independent psychology practice. Dr. Sparta is Chair (2002) of the American Psychological Association's Ethics

Committe. He formerly served on the APA Committee on Professional Practices and Standards, where he helped write the APA Guidelines on Psychological Evaluations in Child Protection Matters. Formerly, he was Chief Psychologist at Children's Hospital San Diego. Dr. Sparta was Commissioner of the Juvenile Justice Commission, San Diego County, and previously served on a committee rewriting a portion of the family law code for the Judicial Council of California.

Lori B. Stauffer, PhD, is the founder and president of Hope for Families, Inc., a company that produces educational materials and presentations regarding sexual abuse and other issues that impact families. Dr. Stauffer is also a part-time faculty instructor at the Center for Children's Support at the University of Medicine and Dentistry of New Jersey–School of Osteopathic Medicine. She has been actively involved in treating children and adolescents who suffered child sexual abuse as well as developing and conducting research examining various aspects of child sexual abuse. Dr. Stauffer has published and presented research at national conferences. Her research has been funded by the National Center on Child Abuse and Neglect and the National Institute of Mental Health. She also works as a staff psychologist at a community mental health agency.

Sherri Y. Terao, EdD, is a senior research associate at the Chapin Hall Center for Children, and Staff Psychologist at the Preschool Behavior Problems Clinic in the Department of Psychiatry at the University of Chicago. Dr. Terao's research interests include cross- cultural issues in mental health, outcomes for youth in foster care, parent-child interventions for children with disruptive behavior problems, and group psychotherapy with abused children.

Anthony J. Urquiza, PhD, is a clinical child psychologist at the CAARE Center and serves on the clinical faculty in the Department of Pediatrics, University of California–Davis. He is Director of Mental Health Services and Clinical Research for the CAARE Center. Dr. Urquiza's primary clinical research interest and publications address all types of violence within the family with an emphasis on child maltreatment. His focus has included treatment approaches to physically abusive families (i.e., parent-child interaction therapy), the dissemination of empirically supported treatments to community mental health agencies, an examination of culture and family violence, the treatment of sexually abused children and survivors of childhood sexual abuse, and psychodiagnostic issues as they apply to child maltreatment.

Foreword

Practical, heartfelt guidance and coordination shared across various disciplines is what excites me professionally. I love knowing that teaching a child to tell a joke and how to play, while he or she is learning to love and be loved, is supported by my esteemed colleagues' research. It pleases me to tell specialists, such as the neurodevelopmental folk, how their work guides therapeutic interventions and has been used in court to support my recommendations for children. Multidisciplinary coordination and planning for a child's best interest is necessary to provide a foundation of stability and security needed for therapy to be effective. Without such planning, children can be further abused by serial placements, multiple changes of schools and therapists, and will not be helped by even the most skillful therapy.

Professional work with maltreated youngsters was simpler, albeit just as heartrending, decades ago. Typically, we just removed them from their family homes when sufficient evidence was present to do so. When not sufficient, we held our collective breaths, secretly prayed for them, and did all we could think of to get the family into counseling. Counseling for the children was limited to social work visits with youngsters in foster care.

But life, and child abuse and its treatment, has become more complex, and those who work in the field must know much more than they did decades ago. Reports of child sexual abuse were rare until the 1970s. The extremely young victim of sexual assault did not appear to exist. Did youngsters lie about abuse or not? How do we know? What relationships now exist between abuse and the disorders of posttraumatic stress, hyperactivity, depression, dissociation, attachment, and learning disabilities? Where are the treatment implications for injuries to a child's emotional, cognitive, social, interpersonal, and moral development?

We keep finding new possible neurophysiological changes in victims and are learning to provide treatment that includes specific educational and sensory remediation. We now look at child safety issues in a different light and our views of what child victims need is constantly changing. Our growth in knowledge is accompanied by growth in the abundance and complexity of related issues. Psychotherapists and social service representatives are not the only persons now involved in doing something about child abuse. Law enforcement, researchers, medical and legal professionals, court systems, ethicists, and many others are now routinely involved in these matters. Our actions are now preemptive as well as reactive.

The *Handbook for the Treatment of Abused and Neglected Children* is an important, much-needed manual for mental health professionals who provide therapy for abused children. The book is rich in detail, research based, practical, suggests useful tools, and provides inspiring case examples. Chapters by experts in various methods of psychotherapy, child welfare services, the law, and medicine provide guidance for therapists and counselors. The information will be helpful when records are subpoenaed, testimony in court is needed, when a partial disclosure of abuse occurs in therapy, and when cultural issues are a concern. The book explains the intricacies of the judiciary and child welfare systems, how to conduct a comprehensive assessment, and what medical examinations can and cannot tell us about abuse and neglect.

This manual promotes confidence and competence among practitioners that will help us to better provide needed services for children and more effectively understand and communicate with professionals from related disciplines. The challenges of working with maltreated children are intense and heartrending; the rewards include having had a significant positive influence in a person's life and an experience of sacred intimacy with another not found elsewhere.

Beverly James, LCSW
Author, Treating Traumatized Children
and Handbook for Treatment of Attachment
Problems in Children

Preface

Working as a child therapist presents a number of challenges. Working with abused and neglected children presents the therapist with even more challenges. To meet these demands, the practitioner must possess skills in a number of domains. It is not enough simply to be a good therapist as that term is generally understood. You must also be knowledgeable about the child protective system (CPS) within which the child and the family's future is held. The court system, which is intimately joined to CPS, must be familiar to the therapist as well, who should also be competent to operate within it as an expert. Frequently, abused and neglected children are found to have traumatic medical histories, or they are in need of psychiatric services—consequently you must be able to work with medical professionals. Developmental delays are common and need to be assessed, as do academic difficulties. Skills in working with schools and developmental specialists are a must. In addition to the clinical skills needed for meeting the challenges found within each of these domains are the more common but essential clinical demands of expert assessment and thoughtful intervention. For all these reasons, the therapist choosing to work with abused and neglected children needs to acquire a very broad base of knowledge and abilities.

Several years ago, after I had already worked with maltreated children for some time and had supervised students, fellows, and colleagues in a variety of settings, it became clear to me that we needed a book that would help teach these sundry skills. Subsequently the project of bringing together the collaborative efforts of professionals from a variety of settings was begun, with the goal of creating a volume that would fill this need. The result is this volume, containing chapters that guide the clinician through myriad aspects of work with maltreated children. This includes understanding the impact of child abuse and neglect, becoming familiar with common medical findings seen in these children, working within the child welfare system, assessing maltreated children, learning how to effectively talk with children, practical advice on how to engage them in various types of therapy, insights into the role of medication in their treatment, clear instruction on how to effectively present yourself in court, and more.

The chapter topics were carefully selected to provide readers with help in building skills in those areas most needed by counselors in this field. Although many of the authors are academicians of national standing, well versed in the theories of their specialty, they have taken particular care to write chapters that are practice oriented. In this spirit, each of the clinical chapters is written with a case vignette that illustrates the major points made by the authors. My goal has been to develop a book that was so practical that it would allow therapists to use in the clinic in the afternoon what they had read just that morning in the office. Does that mean that all of the material covered is easily understood? No. As is true with all advanced learning, certain aspects of this book will be more readily grasped than others, and consequently more readily applied. Nevertheless, the concepts taught herein are generally straightforward, and success at learning and applying them largely is a matter of the effort put to the task.

This is not a book that requires reading chapters in order. Although this may work perfectly well for the classroom, I expect that most clinicians will pick and choose according to their particular needs and interests. That is, after all, one of the reasons handbooks are so named. This is also a practical book oriented to assisting practitioners on a day-to-day basis. One week you may be charged with starting a therapy group for young children and find yourself reading Chapter 9. The next week, however, you may be approaching a court hearing date and find yourself engrossed with reading Chapter 15 on testifying as a therapist in court (forensic work has a way of focusing one's attention in this way). This is exactly as is intended, and I have no doubt that if chapters are read according to the needs within your practice with maltreated children, it will not be long until the entire book is read through and through—for as I mentioned before, the demands of this work are very broad indeed.

Acknowledgments

In January of 1996 I came to work as the treatment coordinator at what is now known as the CAARE Center, a clinic within the Department of Pediatrics at the University of California–Davis Children's Hospital. By accepting this position I made a professional jump from private practice and teaching in the broad sector of child therapy to the more specialized work of helping abused and neglected children. Within a brisk period of time I came to the sober understanding that very few books offered practical guidance for the day-to-day challenges that faced a practitioner in this field. During my frequent meetings with supervisees I was repeatedly impressed with their need for a resource that would address the wide spectrum of questions that arose each week in our meetings. Moreover, as I spoke with others who had worked in this field for a number of years it became clear that the need was not limited to trainees, but extended to just about all therapists who worked with this very challenging population of children.

It is gratifying to now be able to provide just such a reference, one that can benefit both the novice and the veteran therapist. It is likewise gratifying to have this opportunity to express my sincere appreciation for the efforts so generously made by each contributor to this book. Likewise, I have been fortunate to have several colleagues within the CAARE Center who were willing to read the chapters that I authored or co-authored. Thanks go to Judianne Chew, Kim Lundquist, and June Paltzer for their observations and insights. My appreciation also goes to Anthony Urquiza who not only co-authored one of the chapters but also made many helpful suggestions with regard to the selection of contributors, and assisted in the recruitment · of several colleagues. Lavina Kinney and Gina LaTour could always be counted upon to help with manuscript duplication and other matters—thanks again.

A note is due to Les Morey, whom I forgot to thank with regard to his support on an earlier book. Let me now remediate that oversight by noting that I continue to be grateful for the encouragement that led me initially to take on projects such as this one. Thanks likewise go to Steve Sparta, my primary clinical supervisor from an internship many years past, whose emphasis on the primacy of practical interventions when working with children made a lasting impact on me. I should like to also note that I am espe-cially grateful to the late John Pardeck for the encouragement and support he offered in advocating for publication by The Haworth Press.

As always, to my children and wife, my greatest thanks, for the under-standing and support that greeted the demands of time away to work on this book.

PART I:
CONSIDERATIONS IN WORKING WITH MALTREATED CHILDREN

Chapter 1

The Effects of Abuse on Children's Development: An Attachment Perspective

Catherine L. Anderson
Pamela C. Alexander

Although the impact of physical and sexual abuse on children has been the focus of innumerable books and articles over the past three decades (Cicchetti & Carlson, 1989; Perry, 1994; Pynoos, 1993; Terr, 1991), both the clinical literature and the research literature have often failed to reflect the heterogeneity of symptoms and the individual differences that characterize abused children and adolescents (Shahinfar & Fox, 1997). As a result, the clinician or other professional working with abused children may have difficulty matching appropriate interventions to the presenting issues of an individual child. It is well established that abused individuals show a highly variable response (both immediate and long term) to trauma (Alexander & Anderson, 1997). Given that family dynamics and specific aspects of the parent-child relationship account for more of the symptomatology shown by abuse survivors than does the abuse itself (Edwards & Alexander, 1992), attachment theory provides a systematized method for better understanding the presentation and treatment interventions targeted toward these children.

The goal of this chapter is to present attachment theory as a conceptual framework for understanding the impact of abuse and neglect on children across the developmental spectrum. This perspective is well documented in research and has a corresponding applicability within the clinical literature. Of equal importance, such a developmental framework helps to account for the variable symptoms demonstrated by abused and neglected children with apparently similar histories. Attachment theory allows us to assess both the trauma presentation and the potential resiliency of the abused children who appear in our therapy offices, courtrooms, and foster care systems. As a result, it helps us tailor interventions that address more precisely the extraordinary challenges faced by professionals who work with traumatized children.

3

The following sections provide readers with a basic description of attachment theory and the four primary attachment patterns as they are expressed across the developmental spectrum. Case examples of each of the three insecure attachment patterns are presented. Finally, the relevance of developmental trajectories for both abuse and insecure attachment are explored.

ATTACHMENT THEORY

Attachment refers to the way in which the young of a species maintain proximity to the parents (Bowlby, 1969/1982). The evolutionary effect of this proximity is to provide a survival advantage to the young, vulnerable offspring by maximizing the caregiving of the adult during periods of increased stress or threat. Bowlby noted that attachment serves a biological function in which the child is genetically predisposed to seek the parent during times of distress. This need for intimacy does not abate across the life cycle, but merely adapts itself to the interactional style of the primary attachment figures. This predisposition toward relatedness with others is thus seen as a necessary, normal, and healthy characteristic of all people across the developmental life span. Rather than being reflexive in nature, each child's attachment behavior represents the most efficient manner of achieving and maintaining the necessary, consistent, and predictable access to the caregiver (Cassidy, 1999).

The response of the parent to the child's attempts to gain access to the parent during times of perceived threat or significant distress is incorporated slowly into the child's development of an internal working model of caregiving relationships. This internal working model eventually forms the child's sense of self as either deserving of attention and nurturance or not and a sense of others as either trustworthy and supportive or untrustworthy and abandoning (Bowlby, 1980). This cognitive template ultimately determines what information, affects, memories, and behaviors are evoked and expressed within the intimate relationships that the individual develops across the life span (Zeanah & Zeanah, 1989). For example, depending on their history of parenting, infants may either markedly underrespond or overrespond to separation, based on their developing understanding of which response makes it most likely that the attachment figure will provide them the needed comfort and safety. As a result of this cognitive template, secure infants expect optimal responsiveness, while insecurely attached infants modify their responses to maximize their caretaker's engagement with them. Of course, even the parents of securely attached children may at times exhibit less than optimal responsiveness to their children; moreover, all families experience excessive stress at times. However, while even securely attached children may occasionally exhibit insecure behaviors, the prevalence of these behaviors is much lower than that of children with an insecure pattern of attachment, as is illustrated in a later section.

Since attachment behaviors are formed in the earliest primary relationships and operate largely out of conscious awareness, the internal working model tends to be resistant to change and influences subsequent attachment relationships. As a result, research findings show substantial continuities in attachment strategies across the developmental spectrum (Allen & Land, 1999; Waters, Merrick, Treboux, Crowell, & Albersheim, 2000). Movement toward more adaptive attachment strategies is certainly achievable but is a gradual process that occurs either as stress decreases within the caretaking relationship or within subsequent attachment relationships. As such, despite an abused child's placement in a safe environment with securely attached caregivers, the process of developing a secure attachment strategy will be slow and arduous, if it occurs at all.

PATTERNS OF ATTACHMENT STRATEGIES

Researchers have identified three organized attachment strategies that children use to achieve predictable access to the attachment figure and thus to reduce the anxiety that they experience during situations of heightened attachment distress (Ainsworth, Blehar, Waters, & Wall, 1978; Main & Hesse, 1990; Main & Solomon, 1986). These strategies provide the rules that govern how young children and their attachment figures interact to regulate distress (Kobak & Sceery, 1988). In addition to the three primary strategies, a fourth pattern of attachment has been identified that does not represent an organized strategy, but rather reflects the breakdown of an attachment pattern. These four attachment patterns are outlined in the following sections. In addition, case examples illustrate some of the variability · in the presentations and subsequent therapeutic interventions shown across attachment patterns. Demographic information has been changed for some, while others represent aggregated clinical examples. Because the vast majority of seriously abused or neglected children fall into the insecure attachment patterns, no example of a securely attached child is given.

Secure Attachment

Children who learn that their clear expression of negative affect produces an appropriate and adequate response by the parent develop a secure attachment strategy (Main, 1990). In an unknown environment, a securely attached infant will engage in exploration but will repeatedly visually or physically reference the caregiver. If stressed, the secure child will show a clear preference for the caregiver and will be easily soothed. Parents of children with a secure attachment strategy have been observed to respond in an available, appropriately responsive, and emotionally accepting manner (Cassidy, 1988). During the preschool years, secure children have been described as competent, curious, and open and reciprocal in their communication with their parents about their feelings and desires (Crittenden, 1995). Securely attached children use the parent as a secure base from which to explore the environment, develop the capacity for self-soothing, see themselves as deserving of attention, and come to see others as trustworthy and responsive to their needs. They possess the ability to tolerate negative affect while remaining constructively engaged with others (Sroufe, Schork, Frosso, Lawroski, & LaFreniere, 1984) and are popular, resourceful, and empathic toward others (Bohlin, Hagekull, & Rydell, 2000; Sroufe, 1988). In adolescence, secure attachment is a protective factor that helps adolescents achieve an appropriate balance of autonomy and attachment needs within their families, perhaps because they believe that differences of opinion with their parents will not cause significant disruption in these important relationships (Allen & Land, 1999). Despite the intensity of the disagreement, therefore, the secure adolescent's focus tends to remain on resolving the issue by focusing on productive, problem-solving approaches (Kobak, Cole, Ferenz-Gillies, Fleming, & Gamble, 1993).

Almost by definition, it is unlikely that a child who is abused or neglected by the primary attachment figure would be securely attached. However, it is possible that a securely attached child may be abused by someone other than the attachment figure. In such a case, the securely attached child would in most cases quickly and readily make his or her concerns known to the primary attachment figure in order to seek protection and redress. Also in such a case, when the abused child receives the immediate support of the parent upon disclosure of abuse, the effects of the abuse are generally quite minimal (Finkelhor, 1990). Of course, mitigating circumstances (such as a battered woman's inability to quickly leave her abusive husband upon disclosure of her child also having been abused by him) could interfere with the normal responsiveness of a parent of a secure child. In general, however, the secure child's experience of a responsive and attuned parent will protect that child from significant effects of abuse, if not from actual abuse in the first place.

Insecure Attachment

According to Bowlby (1973), the failure to gain comfort from an attachment figure produces feelings of anxiety and anger. Therefore, despite the child's compelling need to stay in proximity to the caregiver during periods of threat or danger, these painful emotional states would be prominent during situations of heightened attachment distress. The two most common forms of insecure attachment found in community samples are avoidant attachment and resistant attachment. These are considered to be organized insecure patterns, in that the child develops a systematic (although somewhat unsatisfactory) strategy for accessing the attachment figure (Main, 2000). However, a majority of children in high-risk samples (such as children involved in the court system) will fall into a third insecure attachment pattern known as disorganized or disoriented attachment (Main & Hesse, 1990): This form of attachment is of particular concern since, unlike the other three attachment patterns, it does not allow the child to predictably access the attachment figure or develop an organized and coherent method of accessing the parent.

Avoidant Attachment

Infants and children with avoidant attachment patterns learn to blunt their negative emotions and remain detached from the parent in order to maintain access to the parent during periods of heightened emotional distress. This strategy develops as the child learns that his or her expression of negative affect is met with parental rejection and/or insensitivity. Therefore, the child inhibits negative affect so as to maximize the responsiveness of the parent (Cassidy & Kobak, 1988; Izard & Kobak, 1991; Troy & Sroufe, 1987). Development of this avoidant attachment strategy suggests that the parent is unable to sustain emotional availability to the child in the presence of the child's strong expressed negative affect (Cummings, 1990). Although this affective cutoff provides a short-term adaptive value by maximizing attention from insensitive or rejecting attachment figures, it results in the child's increasing lack of awareness of his or her own internal state. Thus, avoidantly attached children are characterized by an overreliance on emotional detachment, the maintenance of affective neutrality, and "compulsive self-reliance" (Bowlby, 1973). As toddlers, they will show little, if any, protest or distress during separation from the parent (Crittenden, 1995). Similarly, the avoidant preschooler presents with a cool detachment and avoidance of the parent during events that elicit distress, which he or she subsequently attempts to regulate through an overfocus on toy play as a means of deflecting attention from the importance of the relationship. School-aged children with avoidant attachment have been found to be more hostile or antisocial and less empathic than other children in their peer relationships (Main & Cassidy, 1988; Sroufe, 1988).

Although some research has found avoidant strategies to be associated more with externalizing symptoms such as substance abuse and conduct disorder, especially in girls (Munson, McMahon, & Spieker, 2001; Rosenstein & Horowitz, 1996), other research has found higher rates of internalizing disorders among avoidant children and adolescents, especially in boys (Lyons-Ruth, Easterbrooks, & Cibelli, 1997; Moss et al., 1999). Therefore, gender may interact with attachment in predicting the course of symptoms. Adults with this attachment history exhibit heightened physiological arousal when answering questions about parental rejection and separation (Dozier & Kobak, 1992). However, like their child counterparts, they minimize any expression of distress and instead present as "more normal than normal" (Crittenden, Partridge, & Claussen, 1991).

Case Example of Avoidant Attachment

Billy G. was eight years old when he and his domestically violent parents were ordered into therapy. He was never identified as having been the direct victim of the ongoing domestic violence, but he repeatedly witnessed marital violence and general chaos within the family home. He was loved and indulged by both parents, who were unable to place appropriate expectations on his behavior. Because of the marital violence, Child Protective Services (CPS) was awarded protective supervision and home-based services were implemented. Unfortunately, little compliance or change was noted in the family over the course of CPS's involvement.

Mr. and Mrs. G. proudly described Billy's early developmental milestones as inappropriately autonomous. According to them, he was successfully sleeping through the night by one month of age and did not ever awaken them if he had a bad dream after about age two and a half, instead maintaining that "he just learned to take care of it himself." They started leaving him alone for several hours by the time he was about seven years old. The parents had little understanding of, or willingness to respond to, the developmental needs that he possessed. As a result of this nonprotective stance, Billy was injured on several occasions, which resulted in trips to the emergency room. When Billy was sick or injured, he tended to care for himself. He would rebuff comforting by teachers or other adults when he was hurt or upset, although he could be very demanding at other times.

As Billy became older, his behavior toward his peers worsened. He was shunned by his classmates due to his aggression and failures of empathy. He was often cruel and bullying toward his peers, especially those whom he viewed as more vulnerable than himself. He would frequently instigate fights and was often suspended from his class. By the time Billy was brought to therapy, his peer problems were deeply entrenched. He was placed in a therapy group that focused on developing empathy and impulse control. Medication appeared to help him with his aggressive outbursts. He was also placed in a special education program that identified one highly trained teacher who remained with this small class of conduct-disordered boys throughout their elementary school years. This allowed for the slow development of increased security with this individual over several years. Because of the negative impact of his family, however, Billy was unable to consolidate these gains over an extended period and was ultimately placed in a residential treatment program for young adolescents.

Resistant/Ambivalent Attachment

In marked contrast to the avoidant coping strategy, the resistant/ambivalent child's negative affect is responded to inconsistently by the attachment figure (Mayseless, 1998). Therefore, in an attempt to gain the necessary nurturance and soothing by the attachment figure, these children exaggerate their expression of negative affect (Izard & Kobak, 1991). They tend to maintain proximity to the caregiver through a combination of angry, demanding behaviors or conversely dependent and coy behaviors when the caregiver responds to the child (Crittenden, 1992, 1994a; Greenberg & Speltz, 1988). Their caregivers describe them as fussy and difficult (Moran & Pederson, 1998). The hallmark of the resistantly attached individual is to strongly protest separation, desperately seek contact with the caregiver upon return, and then angrily resist contact once it is achieved. Thus, behavioral and affective ambivalence characterize many of these significant relationships across the developmental spectrum.

Because of their inability to use the caregiver as a secure base, resistantly attached infants are unable to engage in adequate exploration of the environment, become highly distressed during separation, and are unable to utilize the attachment relationship to adequately self-soothe. Resistantly attached preschoolers show a mix of babyish, coy behavior and subtle resistance or anger (Main & Cassidy, 1988). Their interactions are often characterized by exaggerated problems and conflicts and coercive behavior (either threatening or disarming and coy) (Crittenden, 1992, 1994a). Children with a resistant attachment pattern come to see themselves as unworthy and undeserving of attention and nurturance by others and thus become needy, tense, impulsive, passive, and vulnerable to victimization by their peers (Sroufe, 1988; Troy & Sroufe, 1987). In childhood, they exhibit behavior problems (Moss et al., 1999), while in adolescence, they exhibit internalizing symptoms, especially depression (Allen, Moore, Kuperminc, &

Bell, 1998). Resistantly attached adolescents who demonstrate hostile, self-destructive, and apparently deliberately irritating behaviors may have as the goals of these behaviors both parental attention and the expression of anger and resistance (Allen & Land, 1999). These adolescents tend to become overengaged in heightened and unproductive arguments with parents that ultimately undermine the development of age-appropriate autonomy (Allen & Hauser, 1996). Adults with a history of resistant/ambivalent attachment are more likely to experience distress, distrust, intrusive psychological symptoms, difficulty in seeking help, and loneliness (Gittleman, Klein, Smider, & Essex, 1998; Kemp & Neimeyer, 1999; Larose & Bernier, 2001).

Case Example of Resistant Attachment

Shontelle D. is a sixteen-year-old adolescent with a resistant attachment pattern who has been placed in multiple foster homes over the past six years following removal from her mentally ill, drug-abusing, and suicidal mother. The removal occurred after the school reported that the children were not receiving adequate medical care or supervision. Ms. D., who was chronically overwhelmed, was neglectful but not abusive toward Shontelle. Following the children's removal, Ms. D. left the area and did not pursue further contact with them.

When Shontelle initially entered foster care, she was placed in several interim homes. However, because of her intense dependency needs when she was twelve, she was placed in the home of a single older woman, where she remains. Shontelle was described as difficult to soothe and required considerable attention. At the time that she presented to the community mental health center when she was fourteen, her foster mother described her as demanding, needy, and easily upset. When she would engage in power struggles with her foster mother around curfew or homework, she would often deliberately provoke her foster mother by flagrant violations of the rules with escalating complaints about her poor treatment in the foster home or her own suicidal impulses. On two occasions when she was angry about her restrictions, Shontelle filed false reports of physical abuse by her foster mother. These were recanted on both occasions and she admitted that they served as retaliation. However, when her foster mother had to be unexpectedly hospitalized for surgery, she became hysterical and was unwilling to leave the hospital to attend school. Similar neediness was noted by her foster mother who, on multiple occasions, would find Shontelle sleeping on the floor outside her bedroom door. Over the course of therapy when Shontelle became upset, she was able to awaken her foster mother who gave her a cup of warm milk until she was calmer. Knowing that her foster mother was available if needed and having one of her foster mother's old robes to wear for comfort when she was frightened soon resulted in her successfully remaining in her room at night.

Shontelle became promiscuous in her early teens due to her desire to "find someone to love me." She engaged in intense, short-lived relationships with both boys and men, many of whom exploited her both financially and sexually. Shontelle felt unable to set sexual boundaries within these relationships due to her fear that they would abandon her. When she was fifteen, she was repeatedly physically abused by one of her boyfriends. Finally, after she required medical attention following a beating, she was able to extricate herself from the relationship.

Shontelle has developed an increasingly trusting relationship with her foster mother, school counselor, and therapist over the past two years. She remains dependent and emotionally needy but is no longer as willing to accept abusive treatment by others. When she becomes anxious, Shontelle tends to quickly regress to very escalated, demanding behaviors. However, she is developing an increasing ability to self-regulate her mood during most activities.

Disorganized/Disoriented Attachment

By contrast, children who show a disorganized/disoriented pattern of attachment do not possess an organized system for gaining predictable access to the parent as do children in the other three attachment categories. Although it is a relatively rare occurrence within a community sample, this pattern of attachment has been found to predominate in samples of abused and neglected children, depending on the number and type of family risk factors (Lyons-Ruth & Jacobvitz, 1999). For example, in a study of maltreated infants, Carlson, Cicchetti, Barnett, and Braunwald (1989) found that 82 percent of the maltreated infants in their low-income sample demonstrated a disorganized attachment strategy, compared with only 18 percent of a matched low-income control sample. In another sample of abused infants receiving intensive home-based services, 55 percent of the infants were classified as disorganized (Lyons-Ruth, Connell, Grunebaum, & Botein, 1990). Moreover, while half of all infants in a study of middle-class families in which the mother was depressed or bipolar were found to be disorganized (Teti, Gelfand, Messinger, & Isabella, 1995; DeMulder & Radke-Yarrow, 1991), only the most chronic and severe maternal depression appeared to produce a strong association with infant disorganization (Lyons-Ruth & Jacobvitz, 1999). Thus, children's history of abuse, neglect, or unstable parenting, combined with further disruptions of attachment often associated with necessary system intervention, would be expected to lead to a predominance of disorganized attachment among severely abused and neglected children.

Presumably, as a result of the parent's own experiences of unresolved loss or trauma, either the parent's own attachment-related anxieties are triggered by the presence of the child or the parent is otherwise preoccupied (Liotti, 1992). Consequently, the parent relies on the child to control the parent's anxieties (Liotti, 1992). When the child necessarily fails, the parent responds with anger toward the child and/or fear of the child. This "frightened and/or frightening behavior" places the child in the untenable position of needing to approach the attachment figure who is both the source of and solution to the child's anxiety (Main & Hesse, 1990; Main & Solomon, 1986). This frightened and/or frightening behavior has been found to differentiate parents with unresolved loss or trauma whose children develop a disorganized attachment pattern from those whose children do not (Lyons-Ruth & Jacobvitz, 1999; Main & Hesse, 1990).

The disorganized child's obvious inability to develop a predictable behavioral strategy to access the attachment figure results in futile contradictory behaviors with regard to the caregiver. For example, a toddler with disorganized patterns of attachment may approach an attachment figure with his face averted; may indicate a wish to be picked up by the caregiver while simultaneously arching away from the contact; may rise to greet the parent upon reunion before falling prone to the floor; may scream for the parent during separation and then angrily resist or avoid the parent upon return; or may freeze all movement in the presence of the parent (Main & Solomon, 1990). Thus, preschool children with disorganized/disoriented attachment are unable to utilize a coherent strategy to access their attachment figures, resulting in expressions of fear, confusion, and disorganization (Teti & Gelfand, 1997). Consistent with this behavioral research, neurological research suggests that disorganized children are the most likely to exhibit high levels of adrenocortical output, an index of their experience of "fright without solution" (Hesse & Main, 2000; Spangler & Grossman, 1999).

The developmental reliance on incompatible behavioral and emotional strategies to manage overwhelming negative affect results in a confused presentation by children with disorganized attachment. Jacobvitz and Hazen (1999) state that, due to the multiple unintegrated model of their attachment figures that disorganized children possess, they may draw on markedly different, mutually incompatible, internal models with various peers. As such, their behavior with different peers may be quite inconsistent. Preschool children who were disorganized in infancy show more aggression, fearfulness, and odd contradictory behavior when initiating play with their peers (Jacobvitz & Hazen, 1999). Compared with secure children, disorganized/disoriented children are rated as less socially competent (Wartner, Grossman, Fremmer-Bombik, & Suess, 1994) and show more behavior problems, including heightened aggression (Solomon, George, & De Jong, 1995).

As these disorganized/disoriented children reach school age, the role-reversal with the caregiver referred to by Liotti (1992) manifests itself in the form of controlling/caregiving or controlling/punitive strategies (Main & Cassidy, 1988). Controlling/caregiving children utilize nurturance and over-brightness when interacting with their attachment figures in an attempt to repair or maintain a relationship with an abusive or neglectful parent (Teti, 1999). Mothers of these disorganized caregiving children characterize themselves in the relationship with their children as disinvested and express a wish to withdraw, flee, or disappear (George & Solomon, 1998). By contrast, disorganized school-age children who are controlling/punitive make specific strategic use of a mix of punishment, humiliation, and coy/sweet behavior to maintain control over their attachment figures (Solomon et al., 1995). Mothers of disorganized punitive children describe the relationship as mutually combative, adversarial, and confrontational, with both mother and child making repeated attempts to take control of the relationship (George & Solomon, 1998). Moreover, although the behavior of controlling children appears to be more organized in latency age than it was in toddlerhood, their mental representations tend to be chaotic, flooded, fearful, and disoriented (Solomon & George, 1999).

Given the prevalence of disorganized attachment among abused children, it should be no surprise that follow-up research on children originally classified as disorganized is consistent with follow-up research on children who were severely abused. Liotti's (1992) reference to "multiple and incompatible mental models" is confirmed in Macfie, Cicchetti, and Toth's (2001) observation of dissociation in maltreated preschoolers and in Ogawa, Sroufe, Weinfield, Carlson, and Egeland's (1997) finding of severe dissociation at age nineteen among children who were disorganized in toddlerhood and who had experienced intervening trauma. The heightened adrenocortical levels observed in disorganized children (Hertsgaard, Gunnar, Erickson, & Nachmias, 1995; Spangler & Grossman, 1999) are consistent with the increased vulnerability of sexually abused girls to depression, one manifestation of a dysregulation of the hypothalamic-pituitary-adrenocortical axis (Weiss, Longhurst, & Mazure, 1999). Peter Fonagy's analysis of the disorganized child's deficit in mentalizing is consistent with the symptoms of an unstable sense of self, impulsivity, emotional instability and irritability, suicidality, splitting, and feelings of emptiness associated with borderline personality disorder and a history of trauma (Fonagy, Target, & Gergely, 2000). The self-perception of "badness" observed so frequently among abused children is mirrored in disorganized six-year-olds' descriptions of themselves as evil (Cassidy, 1988).

Finally, just as a history of abuse is associated with later increased risk for both aggression toward others (Dutton, 1999) and revictimization by others (Follette, Polusny, Bechtle, & Naugle, 1996), so also disorganized attachment leads to conduct disorders in children (Lyons-Ruth, 1996), increased aggression in adulthood (Lyons-Ruth & Jacobvitz, 1999), and revictimization in adulthood (Liotti, 1999). Lyons-Ruth and Jacobvitz (1999) have stated that the risk for subsequent victimization of and by others observed in Troy and Sroufe's (1987) avoidant preschoolers may be more appropriately inferred to be characteristic of disorganized children. (According to these authors, Troy and Sroufe's "avoidant" children were probably "avoidant/disorganized.")

Indeed, the unbalanced parent-child relationships experienced by disorganized children in which the parent's needs continually take precedence over the child's needs lead to at least two contradictory and unintegrated behavioral outcomes (Lyons-Ruth, Bronfman, & Atwood, 1999). Thus, according to this model, the abused disorganized child may become both a battered spouse and a battering parent, depending on the model in the relationship. Lyons and Block (1996) actually made note of these subtle differences in working models in their comparison of women with a history of physical abuse (some of whom had also been sexually abused) and women with a history of sexual abuse but no history of physical abuse. The former group was more likely to be hostile and the latter group more likely to be withdrawn. Thus, while disorganized abused children overall are more likely to be involved in subsequent unbalanced and aggressive relationships, the particular roles that they exhibit are a function of both their initial internal working models and also of the peer or partner with whom they are subsequently interacting. As would be expected, a history of disorganized attachment in childhood is also associated with such disorders in adulthood as borderline personality disorder (Fonagy et al., 1996) and dissociation (Alexander et al., 1998).

Case Example of Disorganized/Disoriented Attachment

Amber R. is a four-and-a-half-year-old Asian-American child who has been raised by her father since she was three months old. She briefly sees her mother on a regular basis but appears to have no connection with her as a primary caretaker or maternal figure. Her father, who suffers from a religiously based delusional disorder, kept her isolated from others because of a fear that they would "cast a spirit on her." According to the reports of neighbors, police, and CPS, Amber's noncompliant or hesitant behavior produces loud, intense prayer by her father and an anointing with "holy oil." While Mr. R. allows Amber limited play with children in the family or neighborhood, he often "rebukes" other parents or even Amber's preschool peers for allegedly "turning their demons loose on her." This has resulted in several police interventions for disrupting the peace or for assaults on the neighbors. Religious audiotapes play twenty-four hours per day in her house and she has no predictable schedule. Instead, he attempts to completely conform himself to her wishes.

After Amber was taken into CPS custody following her father's failure to provide necessary medical care, I observed the first supervised visit between Amber and Mr. R. When Mr. R. entered the playroom with loud cries of distress and prayerful remonstrations, he moved toward Amber quite forcefully in an attempt to place his oil on her. As he entered the room, moved toward her, and hugged her, she immediately froze with a bright smile and averted gaze. She did not move toward him, attempt to extricate herself from him, or hug him back. As he hugged her around the stomach, her chest and arms fell away from him. At no time during his greeting did her bright smile waver, nor did she engage with him visually, verbally, or physically.

Throughout the visitation, he would periodically weep, loudly cast out demons, and physically intrude on her space without warning. At other times, however, he would attempt to appropriately engage her in play or conversation. She would alternate between periods of normal reciprocal play and attention seeking with her father and episodic freezing when he would intrude on her. Finally, as he called her toward him in preparation for leaving, she advanced in a very physically uncoordinated, jerky manner. She again appeared dissociative, with an overly bright smile and blank stare. Her face remained turned away from him and at no time did she turn her face toward him. Amber stumbled toward him with her stomach extended forward, her back arched, and her shoulders bowed away from him. Her arms swung limply from her sides and she initiated no spontaneous contact with him and did not return his hug.

That night at her temporary foster home, Amber had multiple nightmares, inconsolable crying, and wet her bed. Within forty-eight hours after this visit, Amber began to disclose sexual abuse by her father, which was subsequently verified by physical examination. Based on these findings and her father's unwillingness to pursue sex-offender treatment, his parental rights were ultimately terminated.

DEVELOPMENTAL TRAJECTORIES: RISK AND PROTECTIVE FACTORS ACROSS DEVELOPMENTAL STAGES

Due to the multiple pathways to and from abuse and neglect, it is unlikely that a specific risk factor such as insecure attachment would be directly causally linked to a specific outcome (Sroufe, 1997). For example, insecure attachment has been associated with both internalizing and externalizing disorders. Although one or two risk factors show little predictive value for poor outcomes, there is a marked increase in risk for the development of subsequent disorder as additional risk factors accrue (Sameroff,

Seifer, Barocas, Zax, & Greenspan, 1987). Thus, although insecure attach-ment is not a measure of psychopathology in and of itself, it may result in a developmental trajectory that, when combined with other risk factors, in-creases the risk for later psychopathology. In other words, the acting-out behavior exhibited by disorganized children could be expected to elicit (1) rejection by securely attached peers, (2) association with similarly con-duct-disordered peers, and (3) the reinforcement of bullying behavior by intimidated peers. The effects of these peer relationships could then exacer-bate (or fail to inhibit) subsequent conduct-disordered behavior, thus con-tributing to a trajectory of problem behavior and negative peer influences.

In addition to direct effects of abuse and insecure attachment, some of the long-term effects may be indirect and attributable to the developmental trajectories that follow the abuse. For example, it is clear that childhood sexual abuse has not only a direct effect on increased risk for sexual victim-ization during adolescence (Messman & Long, 1996), but also an indirect effect (Tyler, Hoyt, & Whitbeck, 2000). There are many possible pathways to this increased risk for revictimization. For example, through its effects on attention and cognitive functioning, sexual abuse is associated with poor school performance (Trickett, Noll, Horn, & Putnam, 2001). Both poor school performance and poor social skills (characteristic of insecure attachment) lead to deviant peer associations (Alexander, 2001). Both deviant peer asso-ciations and running away from home due to family conflict contribute to negative developmental trajectories once the adolescent is on the streets (Tyler et al., 2000). Thus, there are many pathways that could account for the observed connection between sexual victimization in childhood and in adulthood.

However, as opposed to viewing this relationship as inevitable, the no-tion of developmental trajectories also suggests that there are many poten-tial points of intervention. For example, focusing on an abused child's po-tential in school appears to provide an important protective effect with regard to peer associations (McCloskey, Bailey, & Herrera, 2001). Simi-larly, while there is certainly evidence of continuity in internal working models, it is important to remember that they are only working models. Re-search on "earned security" (i.e., the development of secure attachment in individuals with a troubled childhood history from which initial insecure at-tachment could reasonably be inferred) suggests that negative developmen-tal trajectories are not inevitable (Pearson, Cohn, Cowan, & Cowan, 1994). Instead, in ideal circumstances, identification of a child's abuse experience could lead to the establishment of supportive therapeutic relationships that could serve to overcome some of the negative effects of family experiences even beyond the effects of the abuse itself.

Finally, the discussion of trajectories of effects is somewhat complicated by the fact that what constitutes a risk factor in some situations or developmental periods may act as a protective factor in others. For example, in addition to negative outcomes associated with avoidant attachment, it also has been observed to function as a protective factor against suicide (Adam, Sheldon-Keller, & West, 1995). Conversely, although in most situations secure attachment would afford significant protection, it is hypothesized, in certain situations, to increase a child's risk of exploitation by a psychopathic adult (Crittenden, 1994b).

Not only does the interaction between the attachment pattern and the context make it difficult for research to predict the functionality of a child's coping strategy, but it also suggests that a child's context must be considered before the goals of an intervention are established. For example, children in foster care usually come into the system with insecure attachment strategies that have helped them navigate treacherous childhoods. It would be naive, and ultimately destructive, to assume that presenting the insecurely attached child with a secure living arrangement would result in an easy adaptation to a secure attachment strategy. It becomes evident that for professionals to anticipate the impact of the court system's interventions on the child, the internal working model associated with each attachment pattern as well as the functionality of symptoms are important to consider in order to understand the child's prior responses to his or her initial caregiving environment and in anticipating the child's responses to subsequent placements.

CONCLUSION

It is clear that the experience of abuse or neglect occurs within an important interpersonal context. The abuser may be the attachment figure or, alternatively, the nonabusive attachment figure may be unable to provide the protection and nurturance necessary for a child to recover from an abusive experience. In either case, attachment theory provides a well-documented conceptual framework for understanding the diversity of experiences of children who are abused and neglected. It accounts for both the cognitive and affective components of symptoms and also highlights the importance of abuse for later interpersonal relationships.

Not only is there diversity in the experiences and parent-child relationships of abused and neglected children, but there is also diversity in the developmental trajectories that follow from the abuse and neglect. Although many pathways to negative outcomes exist, many potential points of intervention also exist. Attention to the particular internal working models and expectations of abused children can help therapists working with parents and foster parents to develop interventions that are attuned to the child's unique attachment patterns and needs.

REFERENCES

Adam, K. S., Sheldon-Keller, A., & West, M. (1995). Attachment organization and vulnerability to loss, separation, and abuse in disturbed adolescents. In S. Goldberg, R. Muir, & J. Kerr (Eds.), *Attachment theory: Social, developmental, and clinical perspectives* (pp. 309-342). Hillsdale, NJ: Analytic Press.

Ainsworth, M. D. S., Blehar, M. C., Waters, E., & Wall, S. (1978). *Patterns of attachment.* Hillsdale, NJ: Erlbaum.

Alexander, P. C. (2001, April). *Discussion of the impact of child sexual abuse on development.* Presentation at the biennial meeting of the Society for Research on Child Development, Minneapolis, MN.

Alexander, P. C., & Anderson, C. L. (1997). Incest, attachment, and developmental psychopathology. In D. Cicchetti & S. L. Toth (Eds.), *Rochester symposium on developmental psychopathology: Vol. 8. Developmental perspectives on trauma: Theory, research, and intervention* (pp. 343-378). Rochester, NY: University of Rochester Press.

Alexander, P. C., Anderson, C. L., Brand, B., Schaeffer, C. M., Grelling, B. Z., & Kretz, L. (1998). Adult attachment and longterm effects in survivors of incest. *Child Abuse and Neglect, 22,* 45-81.

Allen, J. P., & Hauser, S. T. (1996). Autonomy and relatedness in adolescent-family interactions as predictors of young adults' states of mind regarding attachment. *Development and Psychopathology, 8,* 793-809.

Allen, J. P., & Land, D. (1999). Attachment in adolescence. In J. Cassidy & P. R. Shaver (Eds.), *Handbook of attachment: Theory, research, and clinical applications* (pp. 319-335). New York: Guilford Press.

Allen, J. P., Moore, C. M., Kuperminc, G. P., & Bell, K. L. (1998). Attachment and adolescent psychosocial functioning. *Child Development, 69,* 1406-1419.

Bohlin, G., Hagekull, B., & Rydell, A. M. (2000). Attachment and social functioning: A longitudinal study from infancy to middle childhood. *Social Development, 9,* 24-39.

Bowlby, J. (1973). *Attachment and loss: Vol. 2. Separation.* New York: Basic Books.

Bowlby, J. (1980). *Attachment and loss: Vol. 3. Loss, sadness, and depression.* New York: Basic Books.

Bowlby, J. (1982). *Attachment and loss: Vol. 1. Attachment.* New York: Basic Books. (Original work published 1969.)

Carlson, V., Cicchetti, D., Barnett, D., & Braunwald, K. (1989). Disorganized/disoriented attachment relationships in maltreated infants. *Developmental Psychology, 25,* 525-531.

Cassidy, J. (1988). Child-mother attachment and the self in six-year-olds. *Child Development, 59,* 121-135.

Cassidy, J. (1999). The nature of the child's ties. In J. Cassidy & P. R. Shaver (Eds.), *Handbook of attachment: Theory, research, and clinical applications* (pp. 3-20). New York: Guilford Press.

Cassidy, J., & Kobak, R. (1988). Avoidance and its relation to other defensive processes. In J. Belsky & T. Nezworski (Eds.), *Clinical implications of attachment* (pp. 300-323). Hillsdale, NJ: Erlbaum.

Cicchetti, D., & Carlson, V. (1989). *Child maltreatment: Theory and research on the causes and consequences of child abuse and neglect.* New York: Cambridge University Press.

Crittenden, P. M. (1992). Quality of attachment in the preschool years. *Development and Psychopathology, 4,* 209-241.

Crittenden, P. M. (1994a). Peering into the black box: An exploratory treatise on the development of self in young children. In D. Cicchetti & S. L. Toth (Eds.), *Rochester symposium on developmental psychopathology: Vol. 8. Developmental perspectives on trauma: Theory, research, and intervention* (pp. 33-84). Rochester, NY: University of Rochester Press.

Crittenden, P. M. (1994b, October). *Trauma: Effects on memory systems, internal representational models, and behavior.* Paper presented at the Rochester Symposium on Developmental Psychopathology, Rochester, New York.

Crittenden, P. M. (1995). *Coding manual: Classification of quality of attachment for preschool-aged children.* Miami, FL: Family Relations Institute.

Crittenden, P. M., Partridge, M. F., & Claussen, A. H. (1991). Family patterns of relationship in normative and dysfunctional families. *Development and Psychopathology, 3,* 491-512.

Cummings, M. (1990). Classification of attachment on a continuum of felt security: Illustrations from the study of children of depressed parents. In M. Greenberg, D. Cicchetti, & M. Cummings (Eds.), *Attachment in the preschool years* (pp. 311-338). Chicago: University of Chicago Press.

DeMulder, E. K., & Radke-Yarrow, M. (1991). Attachment with affectively ill and well mothers: Concurrent behavioral correlates. *Development and Psychopathology, 3,* 227-242.

Dozier, M., & Kobak, R. (1992). Psychophysiology in attachment interviews: Converging evidence for deactivating strategies. *Child Development, 63,* 1473-1480.

Dutton, D. G. (1999). Traumatic origins of intimate rage. *Aggression and Violent Behavior, 4,* 431-447.

Edwards, J., & Alexander, P. C. (1992). The contributions of family background to the long-term adjustment of women sexually abused as children. *Journal of Interpersonal Violence, 7*(3), 306-320.

Finkelhor, D. (1990). Early and long-term effects of child sexual abuse: An update. *Professional Psychology: Research and Practice, 21,* 325-330.

Follette, V. M., Polusny, M. A., Bechtle, A. E., & Naugle, A. E. (1996). Cumulative trauma: The impact of child sexual abuse, adult sexual assault, and spouse abuse. *Journal of Traumatic Stress, 9,* 25-35.

Fonagy, P., Leigh, T., Steele, M., Steele, H., Kennedy, R., Mattoon, G., Target, M., & Gerber, A. (1996). The relation of attachment status, psychiatric classification, and response to psychotherapy. *Journal of Consulting and Clinical Psychology, 64,* 22-31.

Fonagy, P., Target, M., & Gergely, G. (2000). Attachment and borderline personality disorder: A theory and some evidence. *Psychiatric Clinics of North America, 23,* 103-122.

George, C., & Solomon, J. (1998). *Attachment disorganization at age six: Differences in doll play between punitive and caregiving children.* Paper presented at the meeting of the International Society for the Study of Behavioural Development, Bern, Switzerland.

Gittleman, M. G., Klein, M. H., Smider, N. A., & Essex, M. J. (1998). Recollections of parental behaviour, adult attachment and mental health: Mediating and moderating effects. *Psychological Medicine, 28,* 1443-1455.

Greenberg, M. T., & Speltz, M. (1988). Attachment and the ontogeny of conduct problems. In J. Belsky & T. Nezworski (Eds.), *Clinical implications of attachment* (pp. 177-218). Hillsdale, NJ: Erlbaum.

Hertsgaard, L., Gunnar, M., Erickson, M. F., & Nachmias, M. (1995). Adrenocortical responses to the strange situation in infants with disorganized/disoriented attachment relationships. *Child Development, 66,* 1100-1106.

Hesse, E., & Main, M. (2000). Disorganized infant, child, and adult attachment: Collapse in behavioral and attentional strategies. *Journal of the American Psychoanalytic Association, 48,* 1097-1127.

Izard, C., & Kobak, R. (1991). Emotion system functioning and emotion regulation. In J. Garber & K. Dodge (Eds.), *The development of affect regulation* (pp. 303-321). Cambridge: Cambridge University Press.

Jacobvitz, D., & Hazen, N. (1999). Developmental pathways from infant disorganization to childhood peer relationships. In J. Solomon & C. George (Eds.), *Attachment disorganization* (pp. 127-159). New York: Guilford Press.

Kemp, M. A., & Neimeyer, G. J. (1999). Interpersonal attachment: Experiencing, expressing, and coping with stress. *Journal of Counseling Psychology, 46,* 388-394.

Kobak, R. R., Cole, H. E., Ferenz-Gillies, R., Fleming, W. S., & Gamble, W. (1993). Attachment and emotional regulation during mother-teen problem-solving: A control theory analysis. *Child Development, 64,* 231-245.

Kobak, R. R., & Sceery, A. (1988). Attachment in late adolescence: Working models, affect regulation, and representations of the self and others. *Child Development, 59,* 135-146.

Larose, S., & Bernier, A. (2001). Social support processes: Mediators of attachment state of mind and adjustment in late adolescence. *Attachment and Human Development, 3,* 96-120.

Liotti, G. (1992). Disorganized/disoriented attachment in the etiology of the dissociative disorders. *Dissociation, 5,* 196-204.

Liotti, G. (1999). Understanding the dissociative processes: The contribution of attachment theory. *Psychoanalytic Inquiry, 19,* 757-783.

Lyons-Ruth, K. (1996). Attachment relationships among children with aggressive behavior problems: The role of disorganized early attachment patterns. *Journal of Consulting and Clinical Psychology, 64,* 64-73.

Lyons-Ruth, K., & Block, D. (1996). The disturbed caregiving system: Relations among childhood trauma, maternal caregiving, and infant affect and attachment. *Infant Mental Health Journal, 17,* 257-275.

Lyons-Ruth, K., Bronfman, E., & Atwood, G. (1999). A relational diathesis model of hostile-helpless states of mind: Expressions in mother-infant interaction. In J. Solomon & C. George (Eds.), *Attachment disorganization* (pp. 33-70). New York: Guilford Press.

Lyons-Ruth, K., Connell, D., Grunebaum, H., & Botein, S. (1990). Infants at social risk: Relations among infant maltreatment, maternal behavior, and infant attachment behavior. *Developmental Psychology, 23,* 223-232.

Lyons-Ruth, K., Easterbrooks, M. A., & Cibelli, C. D. (1997). Infant attachment strategies, infant mental lag, and maternal depressive symptoms: Predictors of internalizing and externalizing problems at age 7. *Developmental Psychology, 33,* 681-692.

Lyons-Ruth, K., & Jacobvitz, D. (1999). Attachment disorganization: Unresolved loss, relational violence, lapses in behavioral and attentional strategies. In J. Cassidy & P. R. Shaver (Eds.), *Handbook of attachment: Theory, research, and clinical applications* (pp. 520-554). New York: Guilford Press.

Macfie, J., Cicchetti, D., & Toth, S. L. (2001). The development of dissociation in maltreated preschool-aged children. *Development and Psychopathology, 13,* 233-254.

Main, M. (1990). Cross-cultural studies of attachment organization: Recent studies, changing methodologies and the concept of conditional strategies. *Human Development, 33,* 48-61.

Main, M. (2000). The organized categories of infant, child, and adult attachment: Flexible vs inflexible attention under attachment-related stress. *Journal of the American Psychoanalytic Association, 48,* 1055-1096.

Main, M., & Cassidy, J. (1988). Categories of response to reunion with the parent at age 6: Predictable from infant attachment classifications and stable over a 1-month period. *Developmental Psychology, 24*(3), 415-426.

Main, M., & Hesse, E. (1990). Parents' unresolved traumatic experiences are related to infant disorganized attachment status: Is frightened and/or frightening parental behavior the linking mechanism? In M. T. Greenberg, D. Cicchetti, & E. M. Cummings (Eds.), *Attachment in the preschool years* (pp. 161-182). Chicago: University of Chicago Press.

Main, M., & Solomon, J. (1986). Discovery of an insecure-disorganized attachment pattern. In T. B. Brazelton & M. Yogman (Eds.), *Affective development in infancy* (pp. 95-124). Norwood, NJ: Ablex.

Main, M., & Solomon, J. (1990). Procedures for identifying infants as disorganizing/disoriented during the Ainsworth strange situation. In M. T. Greenberg, D. Cicchetti, & E. M. Cummings (Eds.), *Attachment in the preschool years* (pp. 121-160). Chicago: University of Chicago Press.

Mayseless, O. (1998). Maternal caregiving strategy: A distinction between the ambivalent and the disorganized profile. *Infant Mental Health Journal, 19,* 20-33.

McCloskey, L., Bailey, J., & Herrera, V. (2001, April). *The impact of child sexual abuse on adolescent risk-taking.* Presentation at the biennial meeting of the Society for Research on Child Development, Minneapolis, MN.

Messman, T. L., & Long, P. J. (1996). Child sexual abuse and its relationship to revictimization in adult women: A review. *Clinical Psychology Review, 16,* 397-420.

Moran, G., & Pederson, D. R. (1998). Proneness to distress and ambivalent relationships. *Infant Behavior and Development, 21,* 493-503.

Moss, E., St-Laurent, D., Rousseau, D., Parent, S., Gosselin, C., & Saintonge, J. (1999). L'attachment a l'age scolaire et le developpement des troubles de comportement. *Canadian Journal of Behavioural Science, 31,* 107-118.

Munson, J. A., McMahon, R. J., & Spieker, S. J. (2001). Structure and variability in the developmental trajectory of children's externalizing problems: Impact of infant attachment, maternal depressive symptomatology, and child sex. *Development and Psychopathology, 13,* 277-296.

Ogawa, J. R., Sroufe, L. A., Weinfield, N. S., Carlson, E., & Egeland, B. (1997). Development and the fragmented self: A longitudinal study of dissociative symptomatology in a nonclinical sample. *Development and Psychopathology, 9,* 855-879.

Pearson, J. L., Cohn, D. A., Cowan, P. A., & Cowan, C. P. (1994). Earned- and continuous-security in adult attachment: Relation to depressive symptomatology and parenting style. *Development and Psychopathology, 6,* 359-373.

Perry, B. D. (1994). Neurobiological sequelae of childhood trauma: Post-traumatic stress disorders in children. In M. Murberg (Ed.), *Catecholamine function in post-traumatic stress disorder: Emerging concepts* (pp. 233-255). Washington, DC: American Psychiatric Press.

Pynoos, R. S. (1993). Traumatic stress and developmental psychopathology in children and adolescents. In J. Oldham, M. Riba, & A. Tasman (Eds.), *American Psychiatric Press review of psychiatry* (Vol. 12, pp. 205-238). Washington, DC: American Psychiatric Press.

Rosenstein, D. S., & Horowitz, H. A. (1996). Adolescent attachment and psychopathology. *Journal of Consulting and Clinical Psychology, 64,* 244-253.

Sameroff, A. J., Seifer, R., Barocas, R., Zax, M., & Greenspan, S. (1987). Intelligence quotient scores of 4-year-old children: Social-environmental risk factors. *Pediatrics, 79,* 343-350.

Shahinfar, A., & Fox, N. A. (1997). The effects of trauma on children: Conceptual and methodological issues. In D. Cicchetti & S. L. Toth (Eds.), *Rochester symposium on developmental psychopathology: Vol. 8. Developmental perspectives on trauma: Theory, research, and intervention.* Rochester, NY: University of Rochester Press.

Solomon, J., & George, C. (1999). The place of disorganization in attachment theory: Linking classic observations with contemporary findings. In J. Solomon & C. George (Eds.), *Attachment disorganization* (pp. 3-32). New York: Guilford Press.

Solomon, J., George, C., & De Jong, A. (1995). Children classified as controlling at age six: Evidence of disorganized representational strategies and aggression at home and at school. *Development and Psychopathology, 7*(3), 447-464.

Spangler, G., & Grossmann, K. (1999). Individual and physiological correlates of attachment disorganization in infancy. In J. Solomon & C. George (Eds.), *Attachment disorganization* (pp. 95-124). New York: Guilford Press.

Sroufe, L. A. (1988). The role of infant caregiver attachment in development. In J. Belsky & T. Neworski (Eds.), *Clinical applications of attachment* (pp. 18-40). Hillsdale, NJ: Erlbaum.

Sroufe, L. A. (1997). Psychopathology as an outcome of development. *Development and Psychopathology, 9,* 251-268.

Sroufe, L. A., Schork, E., Frosso, M., Lawroski, N., & LaFreniere, P. (1984). The role of affect in social competence. In C. Izard, J. Kagan, & R. Zajonc (Eds.), *Emotions, cognitions and behavior* (pp. 289-319). New York: Cambridge University Press.

Terr, L. C. (1991). Childhood traumas: An outline and overview. *American Journal of Psychiatry, 148,* 10-20.

Teti, D. M. (1999). Conceptualizations of disorganization in the preschool years: An integration. In J. Solomon & C. George (Eds.), *Attachment disorganization* (pp. 213-242). New York: Guilford Press.

Teti, D. M., & Gelfand, D. M. (1997). The Preschool Assessment of Attachment: Construct validity in a sample of depressed and nondepressed families. *Development and Psychopathology, 9,* 517-536.

Teti, D., Gelfand, D. M., Messinger, D. S., & Isabella, R. (1995). Maternal depression and the quality of early attachment classification at 4.5 years. *Child Development, 66,* 583-596.

Trickett, P., Noll, J., Horn, J., & Putnam, F. (2001, April). *Classroom performance and cognitive abilities of sexually abused females.* Presentation at the biennial meeting of the Society for Research in Child Development, Minneapolis, MN.

Troy, M., & Sroufe, L. A. (1987). Victimization among preschoolers: Role of attachment relationship history. *Journal of the American Academy of Child and Adolescent Psychiatry, 26,* 166-172.

Tyler, K. A., Hoyt, D. R., & Whitbeck, L. B. (2000). The effects of early sexual abuse on later sexual victimization among female homeless and runaway adolescents. *Journal of Interpersonal Violence, 15,* 235-250.

Wartner, U. G., Grossman, K., Fremmer-Bombik, E., & Suess, G. (1994). Attachment patterns at age six in south Germany: Predictability from infancy and implications for preschool behavior. *Child Development, 65,* 1014-1027.

Waters, E., Merrick, S., Treboux, D., Crowell, J., & Albersheim, L. (2000). Attachment security in infancy and early adulthood: A twenty-year longitudinal study. *Child Development, 71,* 684-689.

Weiss, E. L., Longhurst, J. G., & Mazure, C. M. (1999). Childhood sexual abuse as a risk factor for depression in women: Psychosocial and neurobiological correlates. *American Journal of Psychiatry, 156,* 816-828.

Zeanah, C., & Zeanah, P. (1989). Intergenerational transmission of maltreatment: Insights from attachment theory and research. *Psychiatry, 52,* 177-196.

Chapter 2

The Child Welfare System:
A Map for the Bold Traveler

Michele Ornelas Knight
Judianne Chew
Elizabeth Gonzalez

INTRODUCTION

In 1999 an estimated 2,974,000 referrals were received nationwide for suspected child abuse or neglect. Of those an estimated 826,000 children were found to be victims of child maltreatment (U.S. Department of Health and Human Services, 2004b). As defined by the Federal Child Abuse Prevention and Treatment Act (CAPTA) (42 U.S.C.A. 5106g), child abuse and neglect includes any recent act or failure to act on the part of parent or caretaker that results in death, serious physical or emotional harm, or sexual abuse or exploitation, or presents an imminent risk of serious harm. Across this nation, hundreds of thousands of children are removed from their parents each year to protect them from suffering further abuse and neglect. The maltreatment that leads to their removal often results in the children developing cognitive, behavioral, and emotional difficulties. Considering the variety of problems that these children present, it is not surprising to find a number of professionals involved in their care. These include psychologists, social workers, law enforcement personnel, school personnel, medical professionals, and others. The work of each of these individuals, regardless of their specific role, will occur under the umbrella of the child welfare system (CWS).

The CWS includes regulations governing the child and family such as where the child lives and goes to school, the parents' rights, the plans for eventually reuniting the child with family, time frames for making decisions about permanently severing ties with parents, and whether the child will remain with siblings, in foster care, or be adopted separately. The regulations guiding these decisions are all made and executed under this system. To be an effective advocate for a child involved with the CWS, the clinician needs to understand how this system operates. Under these circumstances, good clinical skills are not enough. The clinician needs to have a broader understanding of not only the child's family system but of the larger, more complex system in which the child is embedded. As an analogy, to go backpacking, good camping skills are not enough. Without a map of the woods, you will walk in circles. The purpose of this chapter is to provide a map by giving you a general overview of the CWS. With this map in mind, you will be better equipped to navigate the system (avoiding some pitfalls) and use your clinical skills to their best advantage.

REASONS FOR REMOVAL

Children are removed from their parents' home most often as a result of severe maltreatment. The specific reasons that prompt this type of drastic action on the part of the state are numerous, but generally fall under four categories: physical abuse, neglect, sexual abuse, and emotional abuse. Each state has its own definitions of child abuse within the civil and criminal context. The civil statutes describe the circumstances and conditions that require mandated reporters to report known or suspected cases of abuse. The statutes also provide the definitions from which juvenile and family courts determine whether a child will become a dependent of the court. Although legal definitions of child maltreatment vary across states, the following provides a general definition of the four major types of child maltreatment.

Physical abuse is defined as any act that results in nonaccidental physical injury. Inflicted physical injury most often represents unreasonably severe corporal punishment or unjustifiable punishment. Legal definitions vary but general types of physical abuse include damage to the skin and surface tissue that results in bruising, abrasions or lacerations, bite marks, burns, head injuries, internal injuries, and fractures. State law differentiates between abuse and reasonable, age-appropriate spanking of a child's buttocks where no serious physical injury has occurred. When it has been determined that the child is at substantial risk of suffering serious physical, nonaccidental injury, this is also considered child abuse. For example, California law indicates that substantial risk of future harm may be determined by the manner in which a less serious injury was obtained, a history of repeated injuries to the child, and/or a history of repeated injuries to his or her siblings (Legislative Counsel California, 2005).

Sexual abuse includes sexual assault (i.e., rape, statutory rape), incest, sodomy, lewd or lascivious acts upon a child, oral copulation, sexual penetration, and sexual exploitation. Legal definitions vary but generally include any penetration of the vagina or anus of the child by the penis of another person or intrusion of an object. In addition, any sexual contact between the genitals or anal opening of one person and the mouth or tongue of another person is defined as sexual abuse. The intentional touching of the genitals or intimate parts of a child, clothed or not (including the child touching the perpetrator), for the purpose of sexual gratification or arousal is considered sexual abuse. Masturbation in the presence of a child is also included in this definition. Sexual exploitation includes preparing, selling, or distributing child pornography, child prostitution, and live obscene sexual performances (Legislative Counsel of California, 2005).

Child neglect is characterized by failure to provide for the child's basic needs. It can be physical, educational, or emotional (U.S. Department of Health and Human Services, 2003). It is generally divided into two categories, general and severe. General neglect includes the parent or guardian's negligence in providing adequate food, clothing, shelter, medical care, or supervision where no physical injury has occurred. It includes educational neglect, which is allowing chronic truancy, failure to enroll a child of mandatory school age, and failure to attend to a special education need. Severe neglect includes the parent or guardian's negligence in preventing a child's severe malnutrition as well as having a child diagnosed with nonorganic failure to thrive. Severe neglect also includes a parent or guardian endangering a child's health or placing the child in a situation in which his or her health is endangered, which includes failing to provide adequate food, shelter, clothes, or medical care (Crime and Violence Prevention Center, 2000).

Emotional abuse or risk of emotional abuse includes acts or omissions by the parents or caregivers that have caused or could cause serious behavioral, cognitive, emotional, or mental disorders. It includes evidence of severe anxiety, depression, withdrawal, or aggressive behavior toward self or others, as the result of the parent or guardian's conduct. It also includes those children who have no parent or guardian able to provide appropriate care. This definition of abuse, however, excludes parents or guardians who withhold mental health treatment based on their religious beliefs and if another means of support is available (Crime and Violence Prevention Center, 2000).

CHILD WELFARE SERVICES COMPONENTS AND FUNCTIONS

Just as specific child welfare policies vary from state to state, so too do the components of the CWS. Despite its variations in providing services, its function is the same nationwide: *to protect children and assist families.* Typically it carries out this function by providing intervention programs for abused, neglected, and exploited children. If you are counseling children who have been abused, they are likely to be involved with some form of child protective services in your state. Thus it is critical that you understand the components of this system and their functions and processes in order to anticipate the child's needs and provide skilled case management. For example, if a family is participating in family reunification services, the court has likely ordered (mandated) them to participate in some form of counseling. However, if the family has been offered family maintenance services, they may have the discretion to accept or deny the social worker's referral for counseling. Each case requires some level of case management that will include contacting the family's assigned social worker to ensure regular attendance. Reunification depends on the family completing counseling services and a court mandate may improve compliance. Family maintenance may be considered voluntary, thereby depending on the family's motivation and willingness to participate in counseling.

It is also necessary to have an understanding of the various roles of each service provider in CWS, specifically the county social worker. For example, when children enter the family reunification level of CWS, they are made dependents of the court and the county social worker acts as their guardian. It is important to develop a strong working relationship with the county social worker, who is the gatekeeper for the family and who provides recommendations to the court regarding whom the child should live with and what other services should be provided. A collaborative relationship will allow exchange of information regarding the child's treatment and family stressors, which can directly affect the social worker's recommendation of services and resources for a family.

Different divisions within CWS perform these various functions. The exact type and number of divisions vary from state to state, but looking at the system in California will provide a general overview (California Department of Social Services, 2001) (see Figure 2.1). In California, CWS includes the following nine components:

Emergency Response
Family Support Services / Family Maintenance
Family Preservation / Family Reunification / Foster Care
Permanent Placement / Independent Living / Adoptions

FIGURE 2.1. Child Welfare System

1. *Emergency response.* The emergency response system is designed to provide an immediate response to reports of abuse, neglect, or exploitation twenty-four hours per day. Its purpose is to investigate and determine if intake services and crisis intervention are necessary to maintain the child safely in the home or to protect the safety of the child through emergency shelter care. When a report of suspected child abuse is received, the information is collected by an intake worker. The intake worker does several things, including (1) assessing whether the report will be assigned to an emergency response worker or just taken for documentation purposes and (2) assigning a response time from twenty-four hours to ten days for a social worker to investigate the allegation.

The emergency response worker performs a structured decision-making process that involves a safety assessment, risk assessment, and family strengths and needs assessment. Some questions include: What is the present danger to the child and what interventions are necessary? What is the risk of recurrence of abuse? What are the strengths and needs of the child and family? Can allegations be sustained in court? Should a family maintenance or reunification plan be considered? Is the parent suffering from a disability that prevents him or her from benefiting from reunification services? If after a thorough assessment the allegations of abuse are substantiated, the child's case may go before the courts and the child will be made a dependent of the state.

2. *Family support services.* Family support services are primarily community-based prevention activities designed to alleviate stress and promote parental competencies. Parents are taught behaviors that will increase their ability to successfully nurture their children and enable them to use other resources and opportunities available in the community.

3. *Family maintenance.* Family maintenance consists of time-limited services that are designed to provide in-home protective services needed to prevent or remedy neglect, abuse, or exploitation. These services are intended to prevent the separation of children from their families. Family maintenance services can be offered to children who have been declared dependents of the court or when a child has the potential to be declared a court dependent.

In the latter case, services are considered voluntary and the parent or guardian is asked to sign a family maintenance agreement requiring certain conditions in order for the child to remain in the home. If the family abides by the agreement for six months, no further action is taken by the county or court. If another report of neglect or abuse is filed on the children, or if the family fails to abide by the agreement, the children can be removed from the home and a petition may be filed with the juvenile court.

4. *Family preservation.* Family preservation focuses intensive services on families whose children, without such services, would be subject to out-of-home placement, would remain in existing out-of-home placements, or would be placed in a more restrictive out-of-home placement.

5. *Family reunification.* Family reunification is a time-limited service to families and their children who are in out-of-home care. The aim is to remediate problems that prevent these children from returning home. This often involves individual counseling, family therapy, parenting classes, academic assistance, and so forth. Reunification services include a case plan. The case plan clearly outlines what the child's parents must do (e.g., parenting classes, securing housing) before their child is returned home.

6. *Foster care.* The foster care system is designed to serve and protect those children who cannot remain in their homes safely. Foster care includes payments to cover the cost of providing food, clothing, shelter, daily supervision, school supplies, a child's personal incidentals, and reasonable travel, including travel for purposes of visitation with biological parents. Placement options include family homes (relatives or licensed foster family homes), certified homes of foster family agencies, and group homes. Children in family reunification and permanent placement generally are in foster homes, at least for some time.

7. *Permanent placement.* Permanent placement consists of providing a family with whom the child can stay until he or she reaches young adulthood (e.g., eighteen years of age in California). These services are provided when the court has decreed that the child will never return to the parents.

8. *Independent living.* Independent living consists of education and services for foster youth age sixteen years and older based on an assessment of needs. It is designed to help the youth transition successfully from foster care to living independently. These services are provided to enhance basic living skills as well as job career development skills.

9. *Adoption.* Adoption includes services related to the recruitment of potential adoptive parents, financial assistance to adoptive parents to assist in the support of special needs children, and independent adoption services. Potential adoptive families participate in required classes for licensing, and children who are placed cannot return to their families of origin.

JUVENILE DEPENDENCY PROCEEDINGS

A review of the court system is helpful to the clinician working within the CWS system because the goals of treatment will often depend on the type, nature, and context of maltreatment (physical, sexual, emotional, and/or neglect). In addition, the focus of treatment can be impacted by the court's decision regarding placement of the child and services to the family. For example, if reunification efforts fail, the major focus of therapy will be on helping the child cope with the loss of his or her parents and adjusting to long-term placement or adoption.

We remind the reader that various states differ with regard to the court systems that make decisions about placement of maltreated children. The following, taken from the California court system, will serve as a good example of how the judicial process moves forward. In California, the Juvenile Dependency Court is a branch of the Superior Court. It hears cases involving neglected and/or abused children under eighteen years of age. The juvenile court becomes involved in a child's life when a social worker places a child into protective custody.

Protective Custody

Juvenile court dependency hearings often begin with children being removed from their parents and placed in protective custody. Children are taken into protective custody when the court determines they are at imminent risk of being injured because the parents are unable or unwilling to protect them. The law allows law enforcement or social workers to detain children for up to seventy-two hours for their protection if there is a risk of neglect or abuse. Law enforcement or social workers will immediately attempt to inform the children's parents (or guardians) that their child has been taken into protective custody.

When children are placed in protective custody and removed from the home, there must be an investigation to decide whether the children can safely return. As discussed previously, the initial investigation is led by a social worker in the intake unit of the Department of Social Services. The Department of Social Services and child protective services is responsible for receiving reports of suspected child abuse and neglect and evaluating these reports to determine if the reported information meets the statutory and agency guidelines for child maltreatment. The name of the service and its other functions may differ in your state, but this step in the process will still occur in some form.

If the social worker determines the children are not significantly at risk for abuse or neglect, the children can be released to the parents. No court action is taken, but the parents may be requested to sign a family maintenance agreement, agreeing to certain conditions in order to keep the children in their care. This can occur when the social worker responding to the initial allegation of abuse or neglect found evidence of risk sufficient to warrant the child's removal, but further inquiry reveals a less dangerous situation.

However, if it is determined that the children are at risk, they will remain in out-of-home care pending a court hearing. Typically there will be a time limit (e.g., forty-eight hours) within which a petition must be submitted to the courts telling why a dependency proceeding is considered necessary for the safety of the child.

Detention

In the event a child is removed from the home, the first court hearing will be a detention hearing. The detention hearing advises the involved parties (usually the parents) of the allegations, appoints counsel if needed, sets a future hearing, and addresses the custody status of the child pending the jurisdictional hearing (the next step in court). If children are not returned to their parents at this time, they remain in their current placement, usually with a relative or in foster care. After meeting with the parents and investigating the facts of the case, the court investigator prepares a report for the court hearing. The report will include an evaluation of the case, a plan for reunification, and recommendations to the court regarding placement of the children. If the court approves, visits will also be arranged between the parents and their children. Moreover, the social worker will develop a case plan for services to be provided to the parents and children. These services may include referrals to parenting classes, anger management classes, counseling, drug and alcohol testing, or whatever services would be appropriate.

Jurisdiction

At the jurisdictional hearing, a decision is made as to whether the evidence supports the allegations of abuse or neglect and to determine if the children need the court's protection (e.g., do they need to be placed in protective custody or become a dependent of the court?). This hearing provides the basis for state intervention in a family, addresses where the child will live, and identifies the services to be offered to the child and the parents.

Disposition

Following the court's decision that a child needs court intervention, a dispositional hearing is conducted. The judge decides who will have custody and control over the child. In some cases, the court may order the child to remain in the parents' care if the parents are willing to participate in a program of services which is determined by the county social worker. Furthermore, the judge will define the extent of control that will be exercised over the child by any parent or guardian.

In order for a child to be removed from the parents' care, one of the following criteria must be found by clear and convincing evidence (Legislative Counsel of California, 2005, Section 361, subd. (b):

- There is substantial danger to the physical health, safety, protection, or physical or emotional well-being of the minor and there are no reasonable means to protect the child in the home.
- The parent or guardian is unwilling to have physical custody of the child.
- The minor is suffering severe emotional damage and there are no reasonable means to protect the child's emotional health.
- The minor has been sexually abused by a parent, guardian, or member of his or her household or other person known to his or her parent and there are no reasonable means to protect the child from further sexual abuse.
- The minor has been left without any provisions for his or her support, or a parent who has been incarcerated or institutionalized cannot arrange for the care of the minor, or a relative or other adult custodian with whom the child has been left by the parent is unwilling or unable to provide care or support for the child and the whereabouts of the parent is unknown and reasonable efforts to locate him or her have been unsuccessful.

Concurrent Planning/Expedited Permanency

In an effort to preserve families and uphold the paramount consideration of a child's health and safety, the state requires concurrent planning. When a child is in out-of-home placement, the plan must include both reunification services and services necessary to achieve legal permanence should reunification efforts fail. The status of such services is also required to be documented in court reports. To assist the social worker, the court may order the parents to disclose the names of relatives whom the social worker may then contact about possible placement and, if needed, kinship adoption (Assembly Bill 1544, Chapter 793, Statutes of 1997).

Review Hearings

The status of every dependent child in foster care must be reviewed regularly to reevaluate the child's circumstances and determine whether the placement is still necessary and appropriate, whether the case/service plan is being properly and adequately followed, and the degree of progress that has been made toward reunifying the family. In addition, an estimated date for the child's return home, adoption, or some other permanent placement is set at these reviews.

The social worker working with the family prepares a report for the court's review. The report includes the services offered to the parent to correct the difficulties that resulted in the child becoming a dependent of the court, parent's progress and cooperation in these services, the continuing necessity of supervision (if the child is with the parent or guardian), whether the child can be returned to the care of the parent or guardian (if the child is in out-of-home care), or the development of an alternative permanent plan if the child is unable to be returned. This is also an opportunity for the child's therapist to submit a report to the court in order to make recommendations regarding the child's placement, issues related to visitation, and other concerns that may have arisen during the child's treatment.

If the reports indicate that the family's problems are resolved, the court may terminate dependency at this time. If it is determined that difficulties remain that require the assistance of the Department of Social Services, dependency will continue. Review hearings will occur as long as the child remains a dependent of the court. Generally, hearings occur at six months, twelve months, and eighteen months (in California).

If the child is not returned to the parent or guardian's care by the eighteen-month review, the court will develop a permanent plan. A hearing will determine whether adoption, guardianship, or long-term foster care is the most appropriate plan for the child who is not able to return home.

Termination of Parental Rights Hearing

The termination of parental rights ends the legal parent-child relationship. The child will be free for adoption without the consent of the parents, and the parents will no longer have the right to any contact with the child. In most states, the parent will have no further obligation to support the child. The grounds for termination of parental rights vary from state to state. However, the following factors are often considered: (1) parents' lack of interest in the child, demonstrated through abandonment, failure to visit, lack of cooperation to complete reunification plan, etc.; (2) prolonged and severe patterns of physical or sexual abuse or neglect; or (3) single instances of maltreatment that are so extreme as to make reform of the parent unlikely.

Parental incapacity is not grounds for terminating parental rights: proof is needed that the incapacity prevents the parent from adequately caring for the child and that the parent is unlikely to improve in the future as well. Past abuse and/or neglect may have significantly damaged the bond between parent and child. Usually, a judge will not terminate parental rights based solely on deterioration of the parent-child relationship, unless there are additional reasons that the child cannot be returned home safely.

OUT-OF-HOME CARE

A child may be placed in out-of-home care as a result of a court order secondary to physical or sexual abuse, neglect, positive toxicology test at birth, parental death, parents' illegal drug or alcohol abuse, or other situation resulting in the parents being unable to care for their children. Types of placement vary widely and include kinship care (i.e., home of a relative), a foster family home, a certified home of a foster family agency (FFA), or a group home. Placements can be thought of as falling on a continuum from least restrictive care (e.g., the home of a relative or a foster family) to more restrictive (group homes) to most restrictive (residential treatment facility).

Many counties will contract with private businesses called FFAs. FFAs are nonprofit agencies that recruit, certify, and train foster parents as well as provide professional support to foster parents. These agencies also find homes or other placements (temporary or permanent) for children who need intensive care. Children who require more intensive services than are usually provided by the county may be placed in an FFA group home. A group home setting is one of the more restrictive out-of-home placements. All group homes are intended to provide a higher level of care for children with significant emotional or behavior problems. Facilities differ according to what level of structure and supervision they can provide a child. There are large residential treatment centers, private homes within the suburban community, cottages clustered on campuslike grounds with each home having a "house parent," and so forth. Some group homes provide specialized treatment such as alcohol or substance abuse recovery, psychological counseling, and vocational training.

THE ADOPTION AND SAFE FAMILIES ACT OF 1997

Children in foster care numbered more than 532,000 in September 2002, with about 126,000 waiting to be adopted (U.S. Department of Health and Human Services, 2004a). The Adoption and Safe Families Act of 1997 established explicitly for the first time in federal law that a child's health and safety must be the paramount consideration when any decision is made regarding a child in the nation's child welfare system (Public Law 105-89; stat. 2115). The purpose of this act is to promote stability and permanence for abused and neglected children. To accomplish this purpose, the legislation imposes timely decision making in proceedings that determine whether a child can safely return to the family or whether he or she should be moved into an adoptive home. One way this act ensures this is by requiring states to terminate the parental rights of parents whose children have resided in foster care for fifteen of the last twenty-two months. The legislation also includes the following provisions:

1. Requires reasonable efforts be made to preserve and reunify families
2. Permits concurrent planning for reunification of a child with his or her family or an alternative permanent placement
3. Requires criminal record checks for prospective foster or adoptive parents before final placement approval if a child is eligible for federal subsidies
4. Precludes individuals from becoming foster or adoptive parents if they have a felony conviction for child abuse or neglect, spousal abuse, crimes against children (including pornography), or crimes involving violence
5. Precludes individuals from becoming foster or adoptive parents if they have a felony conviction for physical assault, battery, or drug-related offenses committed within the last five years
6. Offers financial incentives to states to quickly move children out of the foster care system and into adoptive families
7. Requires that states cannot delay or deny an adoptive placement of a child when an approved family is available outside the jurisdiction of the agency responsible for the child

SUMMARY

Child maltreatment is a growing epidemic that requires increased involvement and advocacy by various professionals. As a clinician providing treatment for abused children, having an understanding of the purpose, function, and process of the CWS is critical to your work. CWS exists to protect children who have suffered maltreatment by assisting families in remediating the problems that led to the child's removal or by providing the child a safe long-term home if the family cannot rectify these problems. The services provided by CWS are guided by the court system in each state. Although the components of the CWS and laws governing child maltreatment vary from state to state, we have provided a general overview to assist professionals working with abused children. Many variables impact the type, duration, and length of services provided to abused children and their families. The significant difference in delivering services to children involved in CWS is the level of case management required by the therapist. The key is to establish a collaborative relationship with the county social worker, who is the gatekeeper and decision maker in the process. Having an understanding of the decision-making process and your role in it will help you provide the most effective treatment for children and families involved in CWS.

REFERENCES

California Department of Social Services, Children and Family Services Division (2001). http://www.childsworld.ca.gov/.

Crime and Violence Prevention Center, California Attorney General's Office (2000). *Child Abuse Prevention Handbook and Intervention Guide*. Sacramento, CA: Author.

Legislative Counsel of California (2005). California Law: California Welfare and Institutions Code. http://www.leginfor.ca.gov/cgi-bin/calawquery?codesection= wic&codebody=&hits=20.

U.S. Department of Health and Human Services, Administration for Children and Families, Children's Bureau (2003). Child Abuse Prevention and Treatment Act. http://www.acf.hhs.gov/programs/cb/laws/capta/.

U.S. Department of Health and Human Services, Administration for Children and Families, Children's Bureau (2004a). The AFCARS Report. http://www.acf .hhs.gov/programs/cb/publications/afcars/report9.htm.

U.S. Department of Health and Human Services, Administration for Children and Families, Children's Bureau (2004b). Child Maltreatment 2002. http://www .acf.hhs.gov/programs/cb/publications/cm02/index/htm.

Chapter 3

Medical Diagnosis
of Child Abuse and Neglect

Angela J. Rosas

INTRODUCTION

A comprehensive history and physical examination is important for all children who are suspected to have been abused, whether it be physical abuse, sexual abuse, or neglect. A complete medical evaluation by a forensic pediatric specialist will best distinguish between accidental and inflicted injury and effectively search for additional occult injuries. In addition to his or her own medical examination, the forensic specialist will rely on previous medical evaluations and studies, family history, and social history. Suspicious injuries can be documented by photograph and on a written report, either of which may be used later for evidence in criminal or juvenile hearings. For many children, a nonthreatening physical examination may be the first step to regaining their self-esteem as the medical provider reassures them of a healthy body or at least their body's ability to heal completely.

The forensic pediatric specialist, however, will only be able to evaluate patients who are referred for suspicious injuries. Many of the initial reports for child abuse originate from nonmedical professionals. This chapter reviews the various physical findings of child abuse and neglect in nonmedical terms as a guide to the professionals who see these children on a day-to-day basis.

PHYSICAL ABUSE

Children are physically abused in a variety of ways, and one child may suffer several types of injury. Children under five years of age are the most vulnerable to physical abuse because they are often hidden from the public eye and the school system. Children under two years of age carry the highest risk for serious injury or death from physical abuse. Case studies have shown that many child abuse victims with serious injuries present to mandated reporters (sometimes nonmedical reporters) with suspicious injuries prior to their final injury or death (Jenny, Hymel, Ritzen, Reinert, & Hay, 1999). It then becomes imperative that all mandated reporters develop some clinical skills in detecting physical abuse injuries. Suspicious injuries from bruises, abrasions, burns, fractures, and head injuries, as well as findings that mimic abuse, are discussed in this section.

Bruises and Abrasions

Several important concepts assist in distinguishing inflicted from accidental bruises and abrasions (Table 3.1). Patterned injuries are commonly seen in physical abuse cases and consist of bruises or abrasions that match the object with which the child was hit. These patterns may be an outline or an impression of the object or both (Figure 3.1). For example, a hand slap may leave a handprint on the child's face as if the hand had been dipped in paint and an impression left behind on the cheek. In other cases, a hand slap may leave an outline bruise as if a line had been drawn around the hand as it lay across the child's skin. Thin objects such as wire hangers and cords may leave the impression of a solid line or an outline with a double "train track" bruise.

The distribution of the bruises on a child's body may also cause suspicion of abuse. When ambulating children play actively, they may accidentally injure the parts of the body that protrude and that overlie bony prominences. For example, the forehead, chin, elbows, buttocks, knees, and shins are all areas of the body that protrude and may be injured when the child falls or runs into an object. The buttocks, however, are well padded in most young children and rarely bruise. The shins are prone to repeated bruises because there is so little padding over the bone (Carpenter, 1999; Sugar, Taylor, & Feldman, 1999). Intentional injuries may appear as bruises and abrasions over the soft tissue areas such as the ears, neck, underarms, abdomen, and extensive bruises across the buttocks and back of the legs.

TABLE 3.1. Common Qualities of Accidental and Inflicted Injuries

Accidental	Inflicted
Nonspecific bruises/abrasions	Patterned injuries
Over bony prominences	Over soft tissue
Over protruding body parts	Hidden body areas
Active older children	Noncruising infants

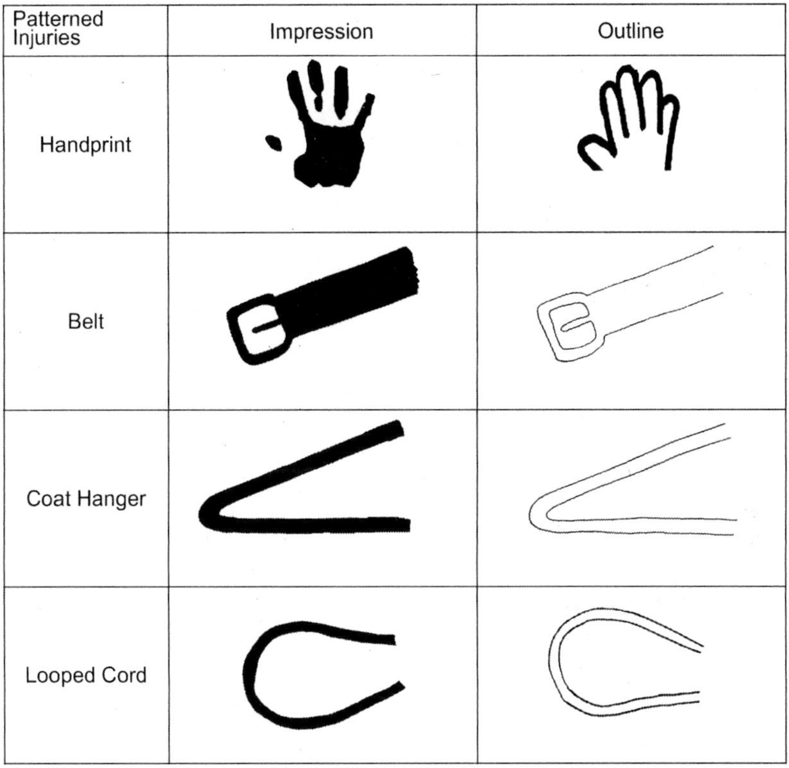

Patterned Injuries	Impression	Outline
Handprint		
Belt		
Coat Hanger		
Looped Cord		

FIGURE 3.1. Patterned Injuries of Physical Abuse

The age of the child also determines the distribution of accidental bruises expected. A large study of small children presenting for routine exam helped to show that "those who don't cruise rarely bruise," meaning that infants who are not yet up and mobile rarely have any bruises at all (Sugar et al., 1999). In the rare case of accidental injury to a small infant, the parent or caregiver can almost always give a detailed history of exactly how the injury occurred.

Even when the bruise pattern appears nonspecific and perhaps accidental, the history may point to suspicion of abuse. Accidental injuries, such as falls, must match the developmental capabilities of the child or infant. For example, children under three months of age rarely roll over and would be unable to fall off a diaper-changing table under their own power. Such a case would be suspicious for abuse, even if the infant had mild facial bruising that matched a four-foot fall. In assessing the developmental capabilities of a particular child, one cannot assume that all babies fall into the normal range. An objective developmental history and/or a developmental examination would be a more accurate assessment. Some "incredible" accidents have occurred when an older sibling assists the younger child to climb higher and fall with greater force.

Large studies have also shown that dating bruises by color is inaccurate (Schwartz & Ricci, 1996). Previous work suggested that all bruises pass through a process of healing with immediate red and blue coloring, then yellow and green, and finally brown with complete resolution in two weeks. The newer studies demonstrated so much variation in the healing process that this color dating is now considered obsolete. The studies did show, however, that if yellow is detected in the bruise, the injury is at least eighteen hours old. Unfortunately, yellow is one of the most difficult colors to detect on some children's skin, and one cannot state that the absence of yellow confirms an injury within the last eighteen hours.

Some conditions mimic the bruises of physical abuse. Mongolian spots or slate-gray spots about the buttocks and lower back are commonly seen in children of color. When these lesions occur in fair-skinned children, they can mimic bruises. The color of the slate-gray spot is homogeneous and never speckled or mottled. The spots are present at birth and fade over the first months of infancy. Occasionally the spots last beyond the first year of life or are found over other areas of the body.

Bleeding disorders can also mimic abuse because they cause easy bruising. These disorders may be congenital or acquired and the diagnosis may have not been made prior to the unusual bruises. All children with bruises suspicious for abuse should undergo blood studies for bleeding disorders.

Burns

Burns can be severe, disfiguring injuries, whether accidental or inflicted. Burns occur by scalding liquid, flame, electrocution, or contact with a hot object or caustic chemical. Patterned injuries, a clear understanding of expectations for accidental injuries, and an understanding of the developmental capabilities of the child again distinguish inflicted injuries from accidental ones.

Inflicted burns are more commonly caused by contact with a hot object or scalding with hot water. The severity of the burn is directly related to both the temperature of the hot liquid or object and the length of time of exposure to the heat. The depth of the burn is described by degrees. A first-degree burn is the most mild, with only sustained redness, such as sunburn. A second-degree burn goes partially through the skin and may include blisters or bloody abraded skin. The third-degree penetrates the full thickness of the skin and may require skin transplant to heal. Burns are also described by the extent of body surface area they cover. Body maps are used to calculate the percentage of total body surface area that is burned.

Nonaccidental contact burns are usually cigarette or iron burns. Cigarette burns quickly cause a third-degree or full-thickness burn on contact, since the end of a lit cigarette can reach 700 degrees Fahrenheit. The burn is exactly 8 mm in diameter, which is an impression of the end of a cigarette. The edges are raised with a deep crater in the center. Inflicted cigarette burns are commonly seen on the hands or feet, but can occur anywhere. Once fully healed, cigarette burns may be difficult to distinguish from other scars such as chicken pox or excoriated insect bites. Occasionally, accidental burns occur when a child runs into an adult holding a lit cigarette. Accidental burns tend to be more shallow since the contact is brief, and the 8 mm round burn may have a tail shaped like a comet.

Inflicted steam iron burns may show an impression of all or a large part of the base of the iron. The skin that comes in contact with the metal tends to burn deeper than the skin under the steam holes. As the burn heals, the steam hole areas seem to be spared of scarring. Accidental steam iron burns tend to show less of the impression of the base of the iron and appear on areas of the body that are exposed during a fall. In mobile infants, accidental iron burns can be seen on the parts of the body used for exploration, such as the hands. If the history suggests that the child pulled the iron down or climbed up to the iron, the developmental capabilities of the injured child must match the history.

Curling iron burns occur in similar ways, except the burn pattern is usually elongated over a flat or concave surface such as the forearm. The location of accidental burn injury is the same as for steam irons. Inflicted injury is distinguished by burns on unexposed areas of the body or by a clear history from the child or witness.

In child abuse cases, scald burns are usually caused by hot water from the faucet. Most water heaters are set at 140 degrees Fahrenheit at the factory and can cause a serious burn with only five seconds of exposure time. Accidents do happen, but usually with splash burns as the child attempts to get out from under the water. Even infants will kick their feet and move their arms. A lack of splash burns indicates that the child was held down during the forced immersion. Two patterns of scalding burn injury are indicative of inflicted injury. One type is a circumferential burn on the arm or leg that burns down to the hand or foot, such as the part of the body covered by a glove or stocking. The inflicted nature of the stocking or glove burn is confirmed when no splash marks are seen above the burned extremity. The second pattern of inflicted burn injury is the "doughnut" burn, which is caused by a child being held down in a sink or tub of scalding water. As the perpetrator holds the child down, the central portion of the buttocks are in continuous contact with the basin and do not burn as deeply as the surrounding skin in contact with the scalding water. The burn injury has a round spared area in the center of the buttocks, much like the center of a doughnut. Again, there are no splash marks on the trunk in such an inflicted injury.

Fractures

Much like bruises and abrasions, the frequency of accidental fractures goes up as the child ages, and it is very unusual for infants under one year of age to suffer any accidental fractures. In addition, the caregiver usually is fully aware of how and why any accidental fracture occurs, because the child cries out immediately. Even in the case of a nonverbal child, the caregiver can usually locate the area of discomfort quickly and obtain immediate medical care. In contrast to accidental injuries, infants are common victims of nonaccidental fractures. The caregivers may deny any symptoms of pain and have no history of trauma or a fictitious history of trauma. There is often delay in seeking medical attention for the fracture, or the injury is stumbled upon during a visit for another medical problem. Some fractures, particularly in the arms and legs, can be dated based on their appearance on X-ray. Finally, the most important factor in distinguishing accidental from nonaccidental fractures is matching the given history to the type and age of the fracture.

Independent of the child's history, there is a short list of fractures that are always indicative of physical abuse:

- Metaphysis
- Posterior rib
- Scapula
- Spinous process
- Sternum

These fractures occur only when a child has been physically abused and are not attributable to accidental injury. A metaphyseal fracture occurs in a specific area of the ends of the long bones in the arms and legs. Metaphyseal fractures are difficult to see on X-ray immediately after the injury. They begin to heal after two weeks and appear as a "corner chip" or "bucket handle" on X-ray. Metaphyseal fractures are caused by a violent shearing force to the extremities from repeated pulling and twisting or during violent shaking of an infant. By understanding the nature of the fracture, we can understand the mechanism of the abuse that caused it.

Posterior rib fractures are likewise difficult to find on X-ray immediately after injury. These fractures become more apparent as they heal, forming a small "baseball" of callus on the otherwise straight rib. "Posterior" refers to the position close to where the rib attaches to the spine. Posterior rib fractures are caused by forceful squeezing of an infant's chest, such as occurs during violent shaking when the perpetrator grabs the infant about the chest. Fractures of the scapula, spinous processes (part of the vertebrae), and sternum (breastbone) are uncommon child abuse fractures, but they are even more rare as an accidental injury. Any other type of fracture could occur accidentally given a plausible history, including a spiral fracture in the long bones of the arms and legs.

The history surrounding the fracture injury is crucial to distinguishing an accident from abuse. No history in the face of a fracture of an infant or small child is probably the most suspicious situation. For accidental injury, the history must be plausible considering the child's developmental capabilities (Table 3.2). The history must also match the fracture in the timing and force of the injury. Multiple studies have shown that babies rarely suffer accidental fractures in falls under four feet (Helfer, Slovis, & Black, 1977; Chadwick, 1991), so a history of rolling off the couch would not match any serious fracture in an infant. Furthermore, X-ray can date fractures with some accuracy within weeks or months of the injury. A history of falling on the same day that the X-ray is taken would not match a collarbone fracture with bony callus formation. When considering the developmental capabilities of an infant, a one-month-old would not be able to roll off a diaper-changing

TABLE 3.2. Gross Motor Developmental Milestones

Age (Months)	Motor Skill
3-5	Roll over
7-9	Crawl or scoot
9-12	Stand and walk with support ("cruise")
11-14	Walk independently
15-20	Climb stairs, run

Note: This table can be used as a general guideline to match the age at which the average child attains the corresponding motor skill. It must be noted, however, that some children do not fit into these guidelines. The best indicator of gross motor ability would be to perform a standardized developmental exam such as the Denver II (Frankenburg, Dodds, & Archer, 1996) close to the time of injury.

table alone, and such a history would not match a one-month-old with a broken arm.

In the case of a fracture that is suspicious for abuse, the medical provider may order a skeletal survey to search for additional occult fractures. Skeletal surveys are performed on children under two years of age with suspicious injuries, including bruises, burns, and fractures. Young infants with severe neglect may also warrant a skeletal survey. The skeletal survey consists of detailed X-rays of the child's entire body, usually about twenty films. A repeat study may be ordered two weeks later in some cases to pick up on any healing fractures that would have been missed when they were acute. The incidence of finding hidden fractures on skeletal survey decreases as the child ages. Even so, the older child may undergo limited X-rays based on the history and physical examination.

Some rare diseases may cause brittle bones that fracture with little force and thereby mimic child abuse. Osteogenesis imperfecta is one such disease that occurs in one in 1 million children born in the United States. The diagnosis can almost always be made by a complete history and physical examination. When in doubt, a skin biopsy makes the final diagnosis. Children with metabolic bone diseases also have bones that appear different on X-ray. In addition, when a child with brittle bones suffers a fracture, the child also will cry out in pain and localize the discomfort. The caregiver will know when the injury occurred because of the child's response, and there will be no delay in care.

Abdominal and Chest Trauma

Trauma to the chest or abdomen is the second leading cause of death in child homicide cases. The injuries to a child caused by a fist blow or foot stomp to the abdomen and chest are identical to those of an adult driver in a head-on collision who is thrown into the steering wheel without the protection of a safety belt. Both types of injuries cause blunt trauma to the chest and abdomen that directs a great force down the middle of the torso, often without leaving any injury on the skin. The organs in the upper abdomen, such as the liver, pancreas, and small bowel can be torn and may bleed. A large tear of the liver can cause rapid life-threatening hemorrhaging. A tear or bruise of the pancreas causes severe irritation to the surrounding organs. A tear or blood blocking the small bowel can cause life-threatening infection or bowel obstruction. A forceful blow to the chest can result in tears and bleeding in and about the heart and lungs. The survival rate of motor vehicle accident victims has improved dramatically with immediate advanced care at the scene and rapid referral to trauma centers that specialize in screening for occult injuries. In contrast, child abuse victims with severe injuries to the chest and abdomen are not recognized rapidly. Without the history of trauma, medical providers may consider other causes of the loss of consciousness or shock well before entertaining the possibility of child abuse trauma.

Head Injuries

Head injuries are the leading cause of child homicide, and child abuse head injuries are frequently seen in the pediatric intensive care units of children's hospitals across the country. Shaken baby syndrome is one type of abusive head trauma. The clinical features of shaken baby syndrome include a particular type of brain injury, subdural hematoma, and retinal hemorrhages. Commonly, victims also have metaphyseal fractures from the violent swinging of the arms and legs and posterior rib fractures from forceful squeezing of the chest. Occasionally, there may be suspicious bruises, but many victims of shaken baby syndrome have no bruises whatsoever.

The brain injury of shaken baby syndrome can be devastating. During violent shaking, the infant's head swings back and forth but also rotates from side to side. This rapid movement generates chaotic rotational forces on the brain tissue that shear the individual nerve cells. Studies with mechanical models suggest that the forces on the brain are greatest at the time of impact, when all the rotating forces come to a sudden halt (Duhaime et al., 1992). If the impact is against a hard surface, the infant may suffer a skull fracture or, certainly, bruises and swelling over the impact area of the scalp. If the impact is against a soft surface, such as a bed, there may be no detectable injury over the scalp, but the brain injury will be devastating. Once the nerve cells are torn or injured, they quickly swell. If the infant survives the initial shaking, he or she may still die from massive brain swelling a few days later. Several studies have suggested that during violent shaking, infants lose consciousness immediately and do not have a prolonged period of normal behavior called a lucid interval. These types of studies have aided in the timing of injury and discovery of the true perpetrator.

During violent shaking, the baby's brain also slides around within the skull and tears off the blood vessels that overlie the brain. This results in a subdural hematoma, which can expand quickly and place additional pressure on the brain. Subdural hematomas are seen in accidental brain injury also, but only in high-force injuries such as severe motor vehicle accidents or two-story falls. In contrast, retinal hemorrhages are really only seen in shaken baby syndrome. They have been described in severe accidental head injury and birth trauma, but the hemorrhages are less extensive and form a different pattern than those of shaken baby syndrome. Minor head trauma, bleeding disorders, cardiopulmonary resuscitation, or seizures do not cause retinal hemorrhages.

Skull fractures wherein the history does not match the type of fracture or the child's developmental capabilities gives another clue that abuse has occurred. The most common history for household causes of skull fracture in infants is a fall. Skull fractures are rare in falls less than four feet (Helfer et al., 1977; Chadwick, 1991). An infant who is dropped by a standing adult or falls from a high diaper table occasionally may suffer a simple linear skull fracture. A linear skull fracture forms a straight or slightly curved line that does not split widely, nor cross over to another bone in the skull. A simple linear skull fracture is also not depressed or pushed in. These qualities of a skull fracture would require much greater force than is usually seen in accidental injury to infants in the home.

The prognosis of abusive head injury is poor. Various studies have shown that 10 percent of children die and 50 percent are left with significant disabilities. Still more have visual problems or developmental delays (Bonnier, Nassagone, & Evrard, 1995; Ewing-Cobbs et al., 1998).

SEXUAL ABUSE

Studies have suggested that approximately 1 percent of children experience some form of sexual abuse each year, resulting in the sexual victimization of 12 to 25 percent of girls and 8 to 16 percent of boys by age eighteen (American Academy of Pediatrics, 1999; Finkelhor, Hotaling, Lewis, & Smith, 1990). As prevalent as this problem may be, the majority of children never disclose, and an even larger portion never undergo forensic medical examination. Nonetheless, forensic examination of sexual abuse victims offers the opportunity to recover physical evidence to substantiate a case for law enforcement or child protection agencies. Examination also permits medical treatment for injuries, sexually transmitted diseases, and pregnancy prophylaxis. Forensic examination may also provide the reassurance or verification that a child needs to begin healing emotionally (American Academy of Pediatrics, 1999).

Clinical Presentation

Sexually abused children who are referred for forensic medical examination present under a variety of circumstances. A child may disclose a history of abuse to a parent or relative who then calls the regular doctor or on-call triage system or brings the child into an urgent care facility. Another child may disclose to a trusted adult who is a mandated reporter. The local child protection agency or law enforcement agency would be contacted and a forensic anogenital examination may be requested. Medical providers may encounter a finding on physical examination such as anogenital warts or a suspicious history of sexualized behavior without any specific disclosure from the child. The medical provider may contact the local child protection agency or law enforcement first, or may refer directly to a center that performs forensic examinations. Last, an adolescent rape victim may be picked up by law enforcement and brought into a hospital emergency department for treatment. In each of these cases, the referring source may question whether and when a forensic medical examination is indicated.

Triage of Cases

Triage of sexual abuse and sexual assault cases for forensic evaluation or evidentiary examination is based on protocols designed by the multi-disciplinary teams that investigate such cases. In general, children are referred for acute evidentiary examination when there is reason to expect that body secretions and debris left by the perpetrator may be recovered, or that the victim has an injury that can be documented on medical examination. Acute exams are usually performed within seventy-two hours of the last sexual contact, which must include sexual acts that pass bodily secretions (Table 3.3). The acts may be anal, genital, or oral sexual contact. Cases using DNA typing, however, have shown that semen can be recovered from the vagina up to seven days after the last vaginal penetration, so in some cases assault victims will be referred for examination beyond the first seventy-two hours (Green, 2000). Cases in which the sexual contact is limited to fondling or digital penetration would only be referred for acute examination if the child complains of pain or bleeding.

TABLE 3.3. Criteria for Referral for Evidentiary Exam

Acute Exam	Nonacute Exam
<72 hours since last sexual contact (may be extended to 7 days in some cases)	Delayed disclosure past 72 hours (may be extended to 7 days in some cases)
and	
Sexual contact involves passage of body secretions	Sexual anogenital contact that causes pain or bleeding
or	
Anogenital pain or bleeding	Anogenital discharge or lesions suggestive of a sexually transmitted disease

Nonacute forensic examinations are also important to recover evidence of healed anogenital trauma in children. In children and adolescents who are not sexually active, healed anogenital trauma can be linked to past episodes of sexual abuse, when the victim or other witnesses can identify a perpetrator. Studies have shown that children who disclose a history of penile to vaginal contact often have physical findings of healed hymen trauma on subsequent examination (Kerns et al., 1992). Although injuries to the external genitals and the anus commonly heal quickly and completely, penetrating hymen trauma will sometimes heal with residual tears and clefts that can be seen under colposcopy.

Overview of the Examination

The acute or nonacute medical evaluation of a child sexual abuse victim should not be painful, uncomfortable, or forced. The case history is first reviewed with the referring agency, so as not to repeat the interview unnecessarily. A standard medical history is obtained from the parent or guardian if available, and the child may be asked some additional open questions regarding any current symptoms. The child is given as much control during the exam process as possible to avoid any feelings of coercion and the child is informed of each step beforehand. Throughout the exam, the child is reassured that his or her body is normal and healthy, or at least that it has the ability to heal completely. For many children, this is an important therapeutic step in the rebuilding of their self-esteem following victimization.

The child is allowed to explore the examination room guided by the medical examiner and a trusted adult. The exam process may be modeled on a stuffed toy. Most children will find the exam equipment familiar, but the colposcope will be new. The colposcope is a microscope mounted on a mobile stand. The examiner looks through the colposcope at various levels of magnification to view the child's anogenital area. The child's body is always ten to twelve inches away from the colposcope so it can never hurt the patient. Colposcopes may be adapted for videophotography or still photography, and the photos are handled with the utmost confidentiality. The child is told that photographs will be taken to be able to have the rest of the medical team and agencies involved with the case see how the child's body is doing. When a second opinion is requested by the court, the photographs can be submitted for review in place of repeating the examination. The child may play at assuming the role of the examiner by looking through the colposcope and practicing taking pictures with a remote shutter release. The child then chooses the adult who will stay in the exam room or whether to continue the examination with only medical professionals and himself or herself present. Once the child feels comfortable in the examination room, the examiner leaves while the child undresses.

The child undergoes a complete head-to-toe physical examination. This allows the child to recognize the process as a checkup, and gives the examiner the opportunity to screen for occult trauma or unknown medical conditions. In acute cases, the child's skin is scanned with an ultraviolet light, under which body secretions can be detected as areas of fluorescence. Swabs of the secretions or debris may be collected from the skin and any bruises are documented and photographed.

The anogenital examination is performed last. The child is asked to lay on his or her back with the knees splayed apart or with the feet in stirrups. The various exam positions can be demonstrated with a stuffed toy, and the child is asked to mimic the position. The child is never forced or held down in position by the examiner or the parent. The colposcope is brought into position approximately twelve inches from the anogenital area, and the child is reassured again that the machine will not touch him or her. Throughout the anogenital exam, the child is distracted by pushing the shutter release button or carrying on a conversation with the examiner. The child will be asked to roll over into the facedown knee-chest position for examination of the anus and the female genitalia upside-down. Again, the stuffed toy is used for modeling the position and the child is not restrained. In prepubertal girls, the examiner may rinse the genitals externally with warm water to assist in visualizing the hymen. This technique is not painful, but must be demonstrated with the child before using it during examination. Examination of prepubertal children does not involve insertion of any instruments or swabs into the vaginal orifice, penis, or anus. During the acute exam of young patients, when it is important to recover evidence from the anogenital area, swabs may be gently touched to the area just outside the vagina and anus. In skilled hands, the anogenital exam may take only ten to fifteen minutes.

Interpretation of Findings

To recognize and understand the physical findings of sexual trauma, one must first understand normal anogenital anatomy. Figure 3.2 shows female external genitalia, which can easily be seen without much manipulation. The labia majora overlie the clitoris and the labia minora. When the labia majora are gently separated, the hymen, posterior fourchette, and the fossa navicularis are exposed. When the labia majora are gently retracted, the hymen relaxes and the hymen edges can be seen well in prone or supine position. The perineum is the skin that lies between the genitals and the anus. In

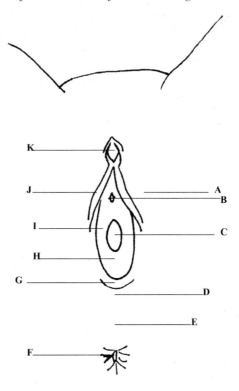

FIGURE 3.2. Anatomy of the Prepubertal Girl (*Note:* A = labia majora, B = urethra, C = hymen orifice (vagina), D = posterior fourchette, E = perineum, F = anus, G = fossa navicularis, H = hymen, I = hymen, J = labia minora, K = clitoris.)

addition, as a child enters puberty, the genitals are described by a system called Tanner stages based on pubic hair distribution and texture and enlargement of the testicles, penis, and female genitals. Tanner I means there are no signs of puberty. The other stages include Tanner II, sparse pubic hair, on up to Tanner V, with pubic hair across the pelvis. There are also Tanner stages for breast development.

During penetrating injury to the genitals, the areas of injury are usually the lower or posterior portion of the genitals. If a clock face is used for orientation with twelve o'clock at the urethra, most penetrating injuries occur between three and nine o'clock. In girls, the injuries may be abrasions, bruises, or lacerations to the hymen, posterior fourchette, or fossa navicularis. Genital injuries often heal completely, but the hymen may retain a deep cleft or tear between three and nine o'clock. Penetrating injury of the anus may cause lacerations or fissures about the edge of the anus, which heal quickly and usually completely.

Even with the best exam techniques, the majority of sexually abused children have normal examinations (Adams et al., 1994). There are various explanations for this important finding. Longitudinal case studies of anogenital trauma from sexual abuse show that injuries heal very quickly (McCann, Voris, & Simon, 1992; Heppenstall-Heger, McConnell, & Ticson, 2003). This finding, paired with the fact that young children often delay disclosure, suggests that most injuries would heal completely before a forensic examination is performed. Also, child sexual abuse often involves sexual acts on the external anogenital area that may be described by children as painful, yet the injury heals completely. Children may associate the pain with full penetration and give a history of how the perpetrator "went inside." It is important to note that whether there is genital penetration of the labia or vaginal penetration beyond the hymen, the criminal offense is the same for both acts. Certainly, the psychological trauma to the child is also equivalent.

Although anogential examination reveals a great deal of information, it is important to note that some vital information cannot be gathered by this kind of examination. The following is a list of what examinations will not reveal:

- Exactly what object caused an injury
- When it occurred once an injury has healed
- How many times it happened
- Identification of the perpetrator (unless there is DNA evidence)

Adolescent Sexual Assault

Adolescent sexual assault victims differ in many ways from prepubertal girls and adults in clinical presentation, methods of forensic examination, interpretation of physical findings, medical treatment, and outcome.

Although many adolescents never disclose their victimization, adolescents are more likely to disclose acutely than prepubertal girls. Because of this disclosure pattern, all adults close to teens must know that they should refer assault victims immediately for medical treatment and forensic examination. Adolescent sexual assault is also often associated with alcohol or drug intoxication, and the perpetrator is more likely to be an older peer. Common scenarios include teens who may voluntarily begin drinking alcohol or using recreational drugs but are then assaulted while they are intoxicated. A teen may also engage in consensual kissing or fondling but then be forced to progress to sexual acts. Two other scenarios are becoming more common in the United States. One is the use of "perpetrator drugs." An adolescent is given a drug unknowingly, often in an alcoholic beverage, by another person who plans to sexually assault him or her. Gamma hydroxybutyric acid (GHB) is a clear, tasteless, liquid illicit drug that causes short-acting hypnosis and is a popular recreational drug at "rave parties." The victim who is drugged with GHB can be coaxed into extraordinary sexual acts, yet has no memory of the events when the drug wears off. Rohypnol is a tasteless sedative drug related to Valium that is illegal in the United States but imported from Mexico to metropolitan areas along the border. Rohypnol causes the victim to fall asleep and have no memory of the assault. Last, more teens are being lured into sexual encounters with adults they meet on the Internet in chat rooms or on teen chat telephone lines.

The adolescent female medical exam differs somewhat from the exam of the young girl and the adult woman. The hormones of puberty cause the tissues of the genitalia to become larger and redundant, so additional techniques are needed during the examination. The hymen, which is very sensitive before puberty, is now more elastic and less sensitive to touch. This change allows insertion of a swab or small speculum into the vagina without discomfort to the victim. Because the hymen is so large and redundant in adolescent girls with little to no sexual experience, sexual assault will often cause acute trauma to the hymen that can be detected on colposcope examination. Several techniques are used during examination to better visualize the hymen and adolescent genitalia. A moistened swab may be inserted into the vagina to gently unfold the hymen tissue. A Foley catheter, which is usually inserted into the urethra, may be inserted into the vagina, and the balloon at the tip of the catheter is inflated. This technique is painless and helps view the hymen. Last, a dye called toluidine blue may be applied to the area outside the vagina to stain and outline any genital abrasions. Because adolescent sexual assault often involves full vaginal penetration and ejaculation, it is important to recover evidence from the cervix and inside the vagina using a small, narrow speculum. In experienced hands, the speculum exam should not be painful and never forced.

Physical findings of sexual trauma may also be interpreted differently in adolescents compared to prepubertal girls. When teens present for examination immediately after sexual assault, the fresh injuries and recovered evidence may point directly back to the perpetrator of the assault. When a teen delays disclosure and is examined much later, the healed trauma of a sexual assault cannot be distinguished from the hymen trauma of consensual intercourse or a previous molestation. In the case of adolescents, it is also quite possible to have full vaginal intercourse without any anogenital trauma at all.

Male Victims

Only a small proportion of children who disclose sexual abuse are boys, but population studies indicate that it is a prevalent problem (Finkelhor et al., 1990). Holmes and Slap (1998) conducted a comprehensive meta-analysis of the literature to date on sexually abused boys and found the greatest risk factors for male sexual victimization to be age less than thirteen years, minority race/ethnic group, poverty, and not living with the natural father. The perpetrator was usually an unrelated acquaintance, and the abuse often occurred outside the child's home. The sexual acts commonly included anal penetration and oral copulation.

Boys may present with clinical symptoms of anogenital pain and bleeding or sexualized behavior much like females. The examination for male victims differs only in that the male genitals are often examined in a sitting position. In acute cases, evidence may be collected by taking a swab sample from the area over the tip of the penis as well as the area around the anus. Acute physical findings include bruises and abrasions on the penis or fresh tears about the anus. Boys may also suffer physical abuse injuries to the genitals because of kicking or punching. The physical injuries seen in acute cases of sexually abused boys heal very quickly and usually completely. For this reason, boys who delay disclosure will have a normal exam by the time they are evaluated. Clearly, the only evidence of abuse may be their disclosure and perhaps nonspecific behavioral changes.

NEGLECT

Child neglect is a broad topic, but in general it can be defined as the caregiver's failure to provide for the major needs of a child. The term includes the failure of caregivers to provide food, shelter, clothing, health care, education, love, and nurture to a child in their care; the exposure of children to potentially harmful situations that can or do result in injury or harm; and child abandonment, including leaving a child unattended, abandonment with physical needs filled by others, adolescent "throwaways," parental custody refusal, or serious lack of supervision.

Many children who are neglected will fall into several of these categories, and many will have histories, symptoms, or medical findings of physical and sexual abuse. To focus on the medical findings associated with neglect, failure to thrive and skin problems caused by poor hygiene are discussed.

Failure to Thrive: Making the Diagnosis

The medical diagnosis of failure to thrive is defined as a child with delayed growth secondary to undernutrition. Failure to thrive is most common in infants and young children, who are completely dependent on their care providers in the home to provide nutrition. The growth pattern of failure to thrive is specific enough to make the diagnosis based solely on the child's growth measurements over time. Normally, all children grow in weight, height, and head circumference, which are measured at every well-baby checkup. After three years of age, only the weight and height are followed. The child's growth parameters are plotted over time on a standard growth chart. There are separate charts for boys and girls and separate charts for children under and over three years of age. A single growth chart will document the growth pattern of a child's height and weight over time. On the standard growth chart, the growth percentile lines at various intervals (5 percent, 10 percent, 25 percent, 50 percent, etc.) are highlighted. A normal growth pattern is described as one in which a child falls between the normal growth percentile lines (5 to 95 percent) and deviates up or down two growth percentiles over time. Some children, who come from families that are extraordinarily small, will have growth lines that normally run parallel to the fifth percentile. Overall, it is important to note that a normal infant has rapid growth in weight, height, and head circumference.

A pediatric medical provider is well versed in the patterns and variations of normal childhood growth. Such a health professional will be alerted to a growth problem when weight gain slows down, well before actual weight loss occurs. A growth line indicative of failure to thrive drops down two or more percentage points on the weight curve, usually over several weeks to months. In addition, in the case of a child with failure to thrive, weight will be most severely affected; the height will be moderately affected or normal; and the head circumference will often increase normally. It is difficult to make a clear diagnosis of failure to thrive with only one set of measurements, unless the condition is profound.

Failure to Thrive: Organic versus Inorganic

Once the diagnosis of failure to thrive is made by using growth curves, attention is turned to the cause of the delay. The cause is often described as "organic" when a medical condition is causing the growth delay. "Inorganic" failure to thrive is that caused by psychosocial problems. Certainly, intentional withholding of food does occur and accounts for some cases of failure to thrive, but the majority of the underlying cases are associated with overwhelming psychosocial family issues that place the child's nutrition at risk. The primary caregiver may be a substance abuser, suffer from incapacitating mental illness, or be mentally retarded. The primary caregiver may also be socially and physically isolated from extended family or community resources that would recognize the infant's growth problem and intervene early on. Despite an apparently appropriate caregiver, the child may be emotionally neglected or physically abused, causing the child to become depressed and withdrawn. Much like adults, infants and children can lose their desire to eat when they become depressed. Such infants will refuse a bottle or food even when they are severely underweight.

Although less common, there are literally hundreds of medical conditions that can also cause failure to thrive. These organic causes include chronic, profound diseases that reduce the appetite long-term, affect the ability to digest and process nutrition, or that increase the need for calories beyond what children can normally ingest. Such diseases include cancer and its treatment, severe and chronic anemia, cystic fibrosis, AIDS, tuberculosis, severe congenital heart disease, diabetes, kidney failure, and severe cerebral palsy. Some of these organic causes may present with poor weight gain as the first symptom. It is important for all infants and children with suspected failure to thrive to be thoroughly evaluated for medical causes of their poor growth, but still, the most common etiology is parental neglect.

The last confirmatory step in clarifying the cause of failure to thrive as organic versus inorganic is to change the child's environment enough to provide nutrition for catch-up growth and a warm and nurturing relationship with at least one adult. In a substantially improved environment, a child with failure to thrive from parental neglect (inorganic) will show rapid weight gain and normalization of all the growth parameters. In the case of medical cause (organic), the child's growth will not be affected by the change in environment. In past decades, this proof of psychosocial failure to thrive was made when the child was hospitalized and gained weight on an adequate diet with close attention and care. In today's health care system, the busy nurses and medical staff do not dote on a hospitalized infant. Today, the most nurturing environment for a baby with failure to thrive may likely be a specialized foster home or the original home with the addition of further resources for the care of the child, including, perhaps, another experienced adult caregiver.

Once sustained in a nurturing home with adequate nutrition, children who suffer a short or moderate period of failure to thrive generally recover normal growth patterns and appear physically well. Studies have shown, however, that children who suffer severe and prolonged malnutrition are at significant risk for permanent delays in physical growth and cognitive development (Grantham-MacGregor, 1995).

Skin Problems

Many neglected children also live in overcrowded conditions with poor hygiene, which leads to various medical problems of the skin and hair. Head lice, scabies, impetigo, fungal infections of the skin and scalp, and wound infections are all more common in child neglect cases, but one such episode is not indicative of neglect. Many schools will send children with skin problems home until they are treated, leaving the neglected child with poor access to health care out of school for prolonged periods.

Drug-Endangered Children

Children suffer neglect and physical harm when exposed to drugs and alcohol in various situations. Prenatal drug and alcohol exposure can cause birth defects and premature birth with various medical sequelae. Maternal drug addiction can cause the fetus to be similarly addicted so that shortly after birth the infant begins to experience withdrawal symptoms, much like adults who suddenly stop using drugs. Children can accidentally ingest alcohol or drugs that are negligently left out in the home, or they may be exposed to toxic chemicals used in home drug production labs known as meth labs.

Alcohol is the most common substance of abuse that pregnant women ingest and has been linked to serious birth defects (Eyler & Behnke,1999; Wagner, Katikaneni, Cox, & Ryan, 1998). For example, prenatal alcohol exposure may cause congenital heart disease, mental retardation, and facial anomalies that are symptoms of fetal alcohol syndrome. The stimulant drugs of abuse, mainly cocaine and methamphetamine, can induce preterm labor and birth. Premature infants are at much greater risk for low birth weight, cerebral palsy, hydrocephalus (water on the brain), blindness, chronic lung disease, overwhelming infection, and generally increased mortality in the first year of life. Heroin and methadone use during pregnancy can cause the fetus to have growth retardation and physical addiction to the narcotic. When these medically fragile babies exposed to alcohol and drugs in utero go home to a mother who is still using drugs, there is an increased risk for physical abuse and life-threatening neglect of medical problems.

Because the maternal drug supply to the newborn is suddenly cut off at birth, severe symptoms of drug withdrawal may rapidly develop in the newborn. The infant may show symptoms of tremor, irritability, seizure, temperature instability, feeding difficulties, vomiting, and diarrhea described as neonatal abstinence syndrome (Wagner et al., 1998). The symptoms of neonatal abstinence syndrome may last hours to months after birth. In severe cases, the newborn may require prolonged hospitalization and treatment with narcotic medication. Pediatricians and foster parents have described "tox" babies as having the worst colic they have ever seen, which may last for several months. Such severe symptoms would certainly challenge the parenting skills of a substance-abusing mother isolated from supportive resources.

Drug exposure in utero can be confirmed by a urine toxicology screen for illicit drugs or a blood toxicology screen for alcohol. However, a positive toxicology screen only reflects substance use in the few days or hours prior to the sample being given. Certainly, a pregnant woman could use drugs throughout the pregnancy, then abstain for a few days and never be caught. Many babies are probably exposed to harmful illegal drugs and alcohol throughout pregnancy and may even show the effects of drug withdrawal, but never be identified as tox babies. The identification of tox babies in itself is controversial. Pregnant women using drugs may fear incarceration or losing their children if their drug problem is identified, and they may avoid essential prenatal care and delivery in a hospital. For this reason, many hospitals and advocates for women's health care are opposed to universal drug screening for all pregnant women. However, identifying the drug problem may also open important resources for both the mother who needs drug rehabilitation and high-risk prenatal care and for the medically fragile fetus and newborn.

Reviews of long-term longitudinal studies have also suggested the detrimental effects of prenatal exposure to drugs and alcohol (Wagner et al., 1998; D'Apolito, 1998). Clearly, fetal alcohol syndrome is associated with a high prevalence of multiple birth defects that can leave a child with physical disabilities as well as mental retardation and learning disabilities. Studies on the long-term effects of opiates and cocaine exposure during pregnancy suggest mild to severe developmental and cognitive problems. When evaluating for the specific effects of drug exposure, these studies are fraught with comorbidity from poor prenatal care and nutrition and subsequent environmental factors seen in the home of substance-abusing families.

For children raised in homes with substance-abusing parents, the effects of neglect are profound. Substance abuse in adults is often associated with mental illness, homelessness, domestic violence, criminal activity, incarceration, lack of education, and unemployment. The effects on the child include neglect of basic needs such as food, shelter, and good hygiene, but most important, a nurturing environment. Children from substance-abusing homes are often underweight, developmentally delayed, and suffer from various skin problems. Their lack of nurturing places them at risk for attachment disorder, while their lack of supervision places them at risk for serious accidental injury. Some children accidentally ingest their parents' illegal drugs when they crawl around on the floor or get powder on their hands. Other parents will actually drug their infants to silence their crying. When the parent is intoxicated, he or she may physically or sexually abuse the children. Substance-abusing parents may also abandon their children with other abusive adults.

Children can also be exposed to illegal drugs and toxic chemicals when their parents manufacture drugs in the home. Across the United States, there is a rising number of home drug labs for methamphetamine production, which can now be found in both rural and urban areas. The chemicals used in producing the drug, such as lye, phosphorus, sulfuric acid, and hydrochloric acid, are highly toxic and place children at risk for caustic burns and damage to the intestines, liver, kidneys, lungs, eyes, and nervous system (Oishi, West, & Stuntz, 2000). Children exposed to these chemicals most commonly present symptoms of skin irritation and burns, vomiting and abdominal pain, headache, cough and difficulty breathing, and eye irritation and burns. Children may also be exposed to high concentrations of the synthesized drug and present with clinical symptoms of methamphetamine toxicity that have been described in adults to include tremor, agitation, high blood pressure, and seizures (Albertson, Derlet, & Van Hoozen, 1999).

SUMMARY

Therapists and forensic medical examiners need to collaborate to best treat child abuse victims. Forensic examination may detect other forms of abuse or document a more severe form of abuse, which may affect the therapist's approach to treatment. During therapeutic sessions, therapists may detect symptoms or visual signs of ongoing abuse, which may necessitate an immediate referral to the local child protective services agency or a forensic examiner. Last, understanding the physical outcomes of various child abuse injuries may help guide the therapist's treatment plan and help distinguish physical symptoms from psychological symptoms.

As powerful and compelling as physical findings of abuse may be in a criminal case or juvenile hearing, forensic examination does have its limitations. Children from abusive and neglectful homes may have suffered several forms of abuse, only some of which may be detected by physical examination. A medical examination usually cannot document the complete extent or severity of the abuse suffered by a child. The lack of physical evidence on forensic exam does not refute that abuse has occurred. Ultimately, the child's history and behavioral symptoms are the more important and sensitive indicators of child abuse and neglect.

REFERENCES

Adams, J.A., Harper, K., Knudson, S., & Revilla, J. (1994). Examination findings in legally confirmed child sexual abuse: It's normal to be normal. *Pediatrics, 94,* 310-317.

Albertson, T.E., Derlet, R.W., & Van Hoozen, B.E. (1999). Methamphetamine and the expanding complications of amphetamines. *Western Journal of Medicine, 170,* 214-219.

American Academy of Pediatrics, Committee on Child Abuse and Neglect (1999). Guidelines for the evaluation of sexual abuse of children. *Pediatrics, 103,* 254- 260.

Bonnier, C., Nassogone, M., & Evrard, P. (1995). Outcome and prognosis of whip-lash shaken infant syndrome: Late consequences after a symptom-free interval. *Developmental Medicine and Child Neurology, 37,* 943-956.

Carpenter, R.F. (1999). The prevalence and distribution of bruising in babies. *Archives of Diseases in Childhood, 80,* 363-366.

Chadwick, D.L. (1991). Death from falls in children: How far is fatal? *Journal of Trauma, 31,* 1353-1355.

D'Apolito, K. (1998). Substance abuse: Infant and childhood outcomes. *Journal of Pediatric Nursing, 13,* 307-316.

Duhaime, A.C., Alario, A.J., Lewander, W.J., Schut, L., Sutton, L.N., Seidl, T.S, Nudelman, S., Budenz, D., Hertle, R., Tsiaras, W., et al. (1992). Head injury in very young children: Mechanisms, injury types, and ophthalmologic findings in 100 hospitalized patients younger than 2 years of age. *Pediatrics, 90,* 179-185.

Ewing-Cobbs, L., Kramer, L., Prasad, M., Canales, D., Louis, P., Fletcher, J., Vollero, H., Landry, S., & Cheung, K. (1998). Neuroimaging, physical, and developmental findings after inflicted and noninflicted traumatic brain injury in young children. *Pediatrics, 102,* 300-307.

Eyler, F.D. & Behnke, M. (1999). Early development of infants exposed to drugs prenatally. *Clinical Perinatology, 26,* 107-150.

Finkelhor, D., Hotaling, G., Lewis, I.A., & Smith, C. (1990). Sexual abuse in a national survey of adult men and women: Prevalence, characteristics, and risk factors. *Child Abuse & Neglect, 14,* 19-28.

Frankenburg, W., Dodds, J., & Archer, P. (1996). *The DENVER II technical manual.* Denver, CO: Denver Developmental Materials, Inc.

Grantham-MacGregor, S. (1995). A review of studies of the effect of severe malnutrition on mental development. *Journal of Nutrition, 125,* 2233s-2238s.

Green, W.M. (2000). Clinical forensic medicine: Sexual assault and semen persistence. In J.A. Siegel (Ed.), *Encyclopedia of Forensic Science* (pp. 397-403). San Diego: Academic Press.

Helfer, R.E., Slovis, T.L., & Black, M. (1977). Injuries resulting when small children fall out of bed. *Pediatrics, 60,* 533.

Heppenstall-Heger, A., McConnell, G., & Ticson, L. (2003). Healing patterns in anogenital injuries: A longitudinal study of injuries associated with sexual abuse, accidental injuries, or genital surgery in the preadolescent child. *Pediatrics, 112,* 829-837.

Holmes, W.C. & Slap, G.B. (1998). Sexual abuse of boys. *JAMA, 280,* 1855-1862.

Jenny, C., Hymel, K.P., Ritzen, A., Reinert, S.E., & Hay, T.C. (1999). Analysis of missed cases of abusive head trauma. *JAMA, 281,* 621-626.

Kerns, D.L., Ritter, M.L., & Thomas, R.G. (1992). Concave hymenal variations in suspected child sexual abuse victims. *Pediatrics, 90,* 265-272.

McCann, J., Voris, J., & Simon, M. (1992). Genital injuries resulting from sexual abuse: A longitudinal study. *Pediatrics, 89,* 307-317.

Oishi, S.M., West, K.M., & Stuntz, S. (2000). *Drug endangered children healthy and safety manual.* Los Angeles: Drug Endangered Child Resource Center.

Schwartz, A.J. & Ricci, L.R. (1996). How accurately can bruises be aged in abused children? Literature review and synthesis. *Pediatrics, 97,* 254-257.

Sugar, N.F., Taylor, J.A., & Feldman, K.W. (1999). Bruises in infants and toddlers: Those who don't cruise rarely bruise. *Archives of Pediatrics & Adolescent Medicine, 153,* 399-403.

Wagner, C.L., Katikaneni, L.D., Cox, T.H., & Ryan, R.M. (1998). The impact of prenatal drug exposure on the neonate. *Obstetric & Gynecology Clinics of North America, 25,* 169-194.

PART II:
THE PSYCHOLOGICAL ASSESSMENT
OF CHILDREN FOR THERAPY

Chapter 4

Speaking with Children: Advice from Investigative Interviewers

Thomas D. Lyon

THE THERAPIST'S DILEMMA

Imagine that you are treating a child suffering from the effects of neglect. You do not suspect sexual abuse and do not directly question the child about abuse, but she makes what sounds like an abuse disclosure. Or you hear from another source (a sibling, for example, or a caretaker) that the child has made statements hinting that she was abused. What should you do? If you decide to question the child, you may inadvertently suggest information. Even if you are careful to avoid leading questions, you may later be attacked for contaminating the child's story, given the inherent polarization of the legal process. Unless you record the disclosure, the suggestiveness of your interviewing will be subject to question.

On the other hand, if you drop the subject, you may be missing a unique opportunity to elicit important information. You can simply report your suspicions of abuse and let a social worker or police officer question the child, but the child is likely to be less forthcoming with a stranger than with a trusted therapist, particularly if the investigator lacks sensitivity or training. Moreover, from a legal perspective, the statements the child makes in therapy are much more likely to be admissible in court than what she says to an investigator.

Child therapists are often faced with this dilemma, because children often disclose abuse in the course of therapy for other problems. If the disclosure leads to a battle in court—whether it be family court, dependency court, or criminal court—the defense is sure to attack the interviewing practices of the therapist, and for good reason: a large amount of research over the past ten years has documented the suggestibility of young children to leading questioning (Ceci, Bruck, & Battin, 2000; Saywitz & Lyon, 2002).

Child sexual abuse cases will be carefully scrutinized for signs that the child's testimony was contaminated by pretrial influences, and a leading candidate for such influence is the professional who first heard the child disclose. If that professional is you, you must either sharpen your interviewing skills or be prepared for a very unpleasant day in court. Moreover, even if you believe it unlikely that suggestive questioning produces false allegations of abuse (Lyon, 1999), another good reason to improve your interviewing skills is to reduce the likelihood that a true allegation will look false because of poor questioning. If you inadvertently suggest false information to a truly abused child, the child's story may start to sound incredible or simply inconsistent.

The goal of this chapter is to provide you with basic information about developmentally appropriate investigative interviewing. The emphasis is on techniques that have been proven by field and laboratory research to both decrease the suggestibility and increase the productivity of child witnesses. I draw heavily on work by Michael Lamb, Kathleen Sternberg, and their colleagues at the National Institute of Child Health and Development (NICHD). I also rely on my experience using a version of the NICHD interview protocol working with Astrid Heger, Mary Morahan, Catherine Koverola, and a team of interviewers at the Los Angeles County–USC Violence Intervention Program. If you use these methods, you will maximize the amount of useful information obtainable from children while also avoiding the risks of creating a false allegation or of making a true allegation look false. The methods discussed work best with grade school children. Very young children will benefit less because of their innate immaturity, and older children are not as needful of special treatment. However, this is not an excuse to ignore either younger or older children; the best rule is to learn to speak simply and clearly with any child.

THE PROBLEM WITH INTERVIEWING
CHILDREN ABOUT ABUSE

Abused children often find it difficult to discuss abuse. Anything dealing with nakedness and genital touch is potentially embarrassing (Saywitz, Goodman, Nicholas, & Moan, 1991)—even more so if the child recognizes that the touching is wrong. Sexual abuse is secretive. Abusers frequently warn or threaten their victims not to tell (Smith & Elstein, 1993), and even without warnings, the secrecy surrounding the abuse teaches the child not to tell. Sexual abusers are often violent toward the child and the child's mother, reinforcing a reluctance to disclose (Sas & Cunningham, 1995). On the other hand, perpetrators often seduce their victims, making the child reluctant to tell for a different reason. If, for example, a girl or her family have positive feelings about the abuser—most likely if he is a family member or a friend of the family—she will be reluctant to get him into trouble and to hurt others who love him (Sauzier, 1989). Fear, loyalty, and embarrassment are disincentives to disclosure (for a review, see Lyon, 2002).

Even if a child is highly motivated to tell, cognitive immaturity may make it difficult to do so. Young children often provide more information when asked recognition questions than when simply asked to tell "what happened" (e.g., Baker-Ward, Gordon, Ornstein, Larus, & Clubb, 1993). In free recall, one has to generate the information to be remembered on one's own, whereas with recognition one simply confirms or denies. Children also have limited understanding of what details are important, and limited ability to estimate time or number.

The solution to children's difficulties with disclosing abuse might seem simple: the interviewer can ask very direct questions in order to elicit a report and, if the child refuses to disclose, apply pressure on the child. However, pressure has some obvious problems. First, one does not know ahead of time which children have been abused. Pressure on a nonabused child may lead to a false allegation. Researchers have demonstrated that a number of coercive interviewing techniques can produce false reports, particularly in preschool children. These techniques include peer pressure (telling the child what other children have said), selective reinforcement (rewarding desired responses and punishing undesired responses), stereotype induction (telling the child that the suspect is a bad person), the use of authority (telling the child what the parent has said or what the interviewer believes), and the use and repetition of suggestive questions (for a review, see Ceci et al., 2000). Second, pressure may taint truly abused children's reports and make them look incredible or inconsistent. Finally, pressure conflicts with many clinicians' perceptions of their role as helping professionals.

The solution is more complicated than direct questions and pressure on the child. Interviewers must search for a middle ground between a hands-off approach (any question is a potentially leading question) and a highly coercive approach (every child is an abused and frightened child). Fortunately, such a middle ground often exists.

QUESTION TYPES

Everyone knows that they should not ask children leading questions, but few agree about what a leading question is. I find it useful to think of questions as lying along a continuum. On one end of the continuum the interviewer supplies details, and on the other end of the continuum the child supplies details. Consider the distinction between free recall and recognition. With free recall, the interviewer simply asks "What happened?" and the child supplies the details. With recognition, the interviewer provides choices and the child picks the correct choice. Hence, the interviewer supplies details that the child merely affirms or denies.

It is easy to understand why questions that move toward interviewer-supplied details increase the dangers of suggestion. If the interviewer supplies details, many of the details are likely to be incorrect—the product of the interviewer's presuppositions or biases. If children are susceptible to suggestion because they trust the interviewer, because they wish to please the interviewer, and because they may doubt their own memory, interviewer-supplied details are going to taint the child's report, and possibly the child's memory for the event. Moreover, if children are inclined to guess, it will be easier for them to guess in response to questions with interviewer-supplied details.

Fortunately, some questions fall between free recall and recognition. These include wh- questions (what, where, when, who, why, and how), which are often classified as either general or specific. As wh- questions become more specific, the interviewer supplies more of the details. Compare "What was the man wearing?" (more general) with "What color were the man's shoes?" (more specific). Note that with a wh- question, unlike a free recall question such as "What happened?" the interviewer is focusing on particular aspects of the event to be remembered. This is helpful to the child who has difficulty in generating details. However, as wh- questions become more specific, two dangers increase. One danger is that the interviewer's beliefs about the event will affect the child's report (e.g., the interviewer assumes the man was wearing shoes). Another danger is that a child who is inclined to guess will come up with a plausible response, one that is incorporated into the child's report.

Recognition questions can also vary in how leading they are. The simplest sort of recognition question is a yes/no question, which is any question that can simply be answered "yes" or "no." Like wh- questions, yes/no questions can also be either general ("Did he say anything?") or specific ("Did he tell you to keep a secret?"). Yes/no questions are not highly leading but can be problematic if a child has a response bias (a tendency to answer all questions "yes" or "no"), or is reluctant to say "I don't know." The research is mixed on whether young children do indeed exhibit a yes-bias to yes/no questions (cf. Greenhoot, Ornstein, Gordon, & Baker-Ward, 1999 [no yes-bias detected]; Peterson, Dowden, & Tobin, 1999 [yes-bias detected]). However, there is quite good evidence that young children are reluctant to answer "I don't know" to yes/no questions (Poole & Lindsay, 2001; Walker & Lunning, 1998). Moreover, children's responses to yes/no questions are less accurate than their responses to open-ended questions (Baker-Ward et al., 1993).

Yes/no questions can be made more leading by turning them into negative-term questions (e.g., turn "Did he tell you to keep a secret?" into "Didn't he tell you to keep a secret?") (Whipple, 1915) or tag questions (e.g., "He told you to keep a secret, didn't he?") (Greenstock & Pipe, 1996). Negative-term questions and tag questions are most likely to affect the responses of preschool children, who are more vulnerable to interviewer pressure.

Another kind of recognition question that is potentially problematic is the forced-choice question, in which the interviewer gives the child a series of choices from which the child chooses the correct response (e.g., "Was his shirt red or blue?"). Like yes/no questions, forced-choice questions assist the child in generating details but may also supply erroneous details. Because of their reluctance to answer "I don't know" to recognition questions, young children feel compelled to choose one of the options even if they don't know the correct answer, and even if neither answer is correct. When children do choose randomly, they tend to chose the last option (Walker & Lunning, 1998).

Interviewers often feel compelled to ask forced-choice questions, even when an open-ended question will elicit more details and be less subject to misunderstanding. For example, interviewers I train at the Violence Intervention Program often wish to ask "Were your clothes on or off?" because this detail affects the seriousness of the abuse and is often omitted by children describing abuse. One recent interview illustrates how dangerous this question is: my interviewer, doing her best to avoid such a question, instead asked, "Where were your clothes?" and the child responded, "Around my ankles." The detail was much more informative than "on" or "off." Indeed, if the child had picked one of the options, the interviewer would have an inaccurate picture of the abuse.

Interviewers also often rephrase wh- questions as yes/no questions, by prefacing the wh- question with "Can you tell me . . ." Although one could argue that prefacing wh- questions in this way reduces the likelihood that a child will guess a detail (because he or she can instead answer "no"), "no" responses are ambiguous. If a child says they "can't" tell you, do they mean they don't know or they don't wish to talk? It is preferable to ask a wh- question that is sufficiently general so that children will feel comfortable answering "I don't know."

Although it is surely difficult to keep all the types of questions straight in one's head, particularly during a sexual abuse interview, it is easy to remember three rules: (1) keep questions as general as possible; (2) use wh- questions; (3) and avoid recognition questions. Wh- questions start with: what, where, when, who, why, and how. Recognition questions start with: did, was, and were. Let the child supply the details.

It is important to reiterate that the use of wh- questions is not only a means to avoid a negative—the dangers of suggestibility. It is also a means of eliciting details that you would never hear were you to limit yourself to recognition questions. If you ask a series of yes/no questions, you will receive a series of yes/no answers, and the information will only be as good as your ability to imagine the details. If you ask wh- questions, children will often mention idiosyncratic details of the abuse that lend their reports credibility and rebut claims of coaching. Moreover, the likelihood of logically inconsistent responses is reduced if your questions are wh- rather than yes/no, and in most cases consistency increases the credibility of a child's report.

Further guidance in the use of nonleading questioning can be found in the interview protocol developed by Michael Lamb and his colleagues at the NICHD (e.g., Sternberg, Lamb, Esplin, Orbach, & Hershkowitz, 2002). Of course, the NICHD protocol is not the only protocol (see, e.g., Devoe & Faller, 1999), but it has received the most research support and incorporates the best elements of a number of other protocols.

The NICHD protocol provides interviewers with two different types of prompts that elicit information from children without suggestion. The first type are time segmentation prompts, in which the interviewer asks the child to fill in the timeline of events (e.g., "What happened next?"). The second type are cue questions in which the interviewer refers to details mentioned by the child and asks the child to elaborate (e.g., "You said he put some cream on his finger. Tell me more about that") (Sternberg et al., 2002).

In addition to being nonleading, an advantage of cue questions is that they clearly specify the topic of interest. When interviewers use pronouns (such as "he" and "she") or deictics (such as "that" or "there"), children may become confused regarding the intended referent. Walker (1999) recommends that interviewers replace pronouns with names (e.g., replace "he" with "Steve") and specific nouns for deictics (e.g., replace "there" with "in the garage").

If an interviewer asks a specific wh- question, or a yes/no or forced-choice question, he or she should follow up with an open-ended question, a technique the researchers call "pairing" (Sternberg et al., 2002). This minimizes the suggestiveness of the specific question.

Before asking the child to describe abuse, it is helpful to ask nonleading questions about innocuous events. Doing so teaches the child to provide narrative responses, allows the interviewer to assess the child's developmental level and ability to provide a coherent narrative, and puts the child at ease. In the NICHD protocol, the interviewer asks the child about things he or she likes and does not like to do, and the interviewer prompts the child with cue questions so that the child elaborates his or her responses. For example, if a child responds, "I like to play soccer," the interviewer says, "Tell me more about soccer." The interviewer then asks the child about a recent holiday and follows up with time segmentation cues. The interviewer can determine if the child understands questions about what happened "just before" or "after" an event. Sternberg et al. (1997) found that when sexual abuse interviewers used open-ended prompts rather than option-posing questions in the rapport-building phase of the interview, children provided longer and richer responses to the first substantive question about abuse, and longer responses to free recall questions throughout the interview.

The protocol also provides clear guidance for introducing the topic of abuse in an investigative interview. The first question is, "Tell me why you came to talk to me." The researchers have found that most children understand the purpose of the investigative interview and are ready to disclose (Sternberg, Lamb, Orbach, Esplin, & Mitchell, 2001). This is probably attributable to the fact that most reports of sexual abuse are due to disclosures by the victims, so that most children questioned about abuse have previously disclosed. If the child does not mention abuse, the interviewer says, "It is important for me to understand why you came to talk to me." If the child remains unresponsive, the interviewer works through a series of increasingly focused questions, which are based on the child's previous disclosure (or the reason abuse is suspected), but avoid directly suggesting that a particular suspect has performed a specific act. The questions include:

- "I heard that you saw a policeman [social worker, doctor, etc.] last week [yesterday]. Tell me what you talked about."
- "As I told you, my job is to talk to kids about things that might have happened to them. It's very important that I understand why you are here. Tell me why you think your mom [dad, etc.] brought you here today."
- "Is your mom [dad, etc.] worried that something may have happened to you? Tell me what they are worried about."
- "I heard that someone has been bothering you. Tell me everything about the bothering."
- "I heard that someone may have done something to you that wasn't right. Tell me everything about that, everything that you can remember."

In addition to the questions in the NICHD protocol, there are other ways of approaching the topic of abuse, some of them even less leading. In our interviews at the Violence Intervention Program, a number of children who disclosed abuse did so in response to a "feelings task," in which we asked children to tell us about the time they were the most happy, the most mad, the most sad, and the most scared (Lyon, Koverola, Morahan, & Heger, 2002). Faller (1996) recommends that the interviewer ask the child about different people in the child's life and what the child likes and does not like about each individual. If the interviewer asks about a number of people other than the perpetrator, questions about the perpetrator would not be unduly leading. Another example of a good introductory question would be to ask children whose residence has changed because of the abuse allegations about their move and the reasons for it.

INTERVIEW INSTRUCTIONS

It may be possible to reduce misconceptions children have about interviews through instructions. Young children are accustomed to speaking to authoritative adults (teachers, parents) who already know the answers to many of their questions. Given a strongly worded question, they may agree, not because of what they believe, but because of their desire to please the interviewer and because of their reluctance to appear ignorant. On the other hand, children who have been abused but who are afraid to reveal may need nonleading encouragement to do so. Researchers have examined instructions that will reduce children's tendency to defer to authoritative interviewers, to increase children's willingness to say "I don't know" or "I don't understand," and increase children's willingness to disclose negative experiences.

1. *Tell the child you do not know what happened.* It is helpful to tell the child, "I don't know what's happened to you. I won't be able to tell you the answers to my questions." Children often assume that interviewers are knowledgeable, even though the interviewer did not witness the event to be remembered (Saywitz & Nathanson, 1992). Children are more suggestible when they believe the interviewer knows what occurred (Ceci, Ross, & Toglia, 1987; Kwock & Winer, 1986; Lampinen & Smith, 1995; Toglia, Ross, Ceci, & Hembrooke, 1992). Informing children that one does not know has been shown to reduce suggestibility to misleading questions (Mulder & Vrij, 1996).

This instruction has its limitations. Young preschool children (three and younger) are not likely to benefit because of their limited ability to reason about the knowledge states of others (Welch-Ross, 2000). Highly suggestive questions will still increase error, and children may forget the instruction.

2. *Tell the child it is okay to say "I don't know," but important to answer when he or she does know.* The NICHD protocol recommends that the interviewer say the following: "If I ask you a question and you don't know the

answer, then just say 'I don't know.' So, if I ask you, 'What is my dog's name,' what do you say? Okay, because you don't know. But what if I ask you, 'Do you have a dog?' Okay, because you do know."

Children are often reluctant to answer "I don't know," particularly when asked yes/no questions (e.g., Poole & Lindsay, 2001) or specific wh- questions (e.g., Memon & Vartoukian, 1996). A number of studies have found that instructing children that "I don't know" answers are acceptable reduces children's suggestibility to misleading questions (Endres, Poggenpohl, & Erben, 1999; Gee, Gregory, & Pipe, 1999; Saywitz & Moan-Hardie, 1994; Walker & Lunning, 1998; Warren, Hulse-Trotter, & Tubbs, 1991).

This instruction has its limitations as well. Unless the interviewer emphasizes answering when one does know as much as refusing to answer when one does not, children may overuse the "I don't know" response, and thus answer non-misleading questions less accurately (Gee et al., 1999; Saywitz & Moan-Hardie, 1994; Warren et al., 1991). Furthermore, if children already feel comfortable answering "I don't know," the instruction may be unproductive (Moston, 1987). Children are more likely to answer "I don't know" without instruction if asked wh- questions in a comfortable atmosphere (Moston, 1987).

3. *Tell the child that it is okay to say "I don't understand," and that if he or she does, you will ask an easier question.* Based on the NICHD protocol, our interviewers at the Violence Intervention Program tell children the following: "If I ask you a question and you don't know what I mean or what I am saying, you can say 'I don't know what you mean.' I will ask it in a different way. So if I ask you, 'What is your gender,' what do you say? Good, because gender is a big word. So then I would ask, 'Are you a boy or a girl?' Okay because 'boy or girl' is an easier way to say 'gender.'"

Children rarely ask for clarification of questions they do not understand (Carter, Bottoms, & Levine, 1996; Perry et al., 1995; Saywitz, Snyder, & Nathanson, 1999). Children are less adept than adults at monitoring their comprehension. Even if they recognize incomprehension, they are more reluctant to let the interviewer know.

Telling children that it is permissible to say they do not understand and that doing so will lead the interviewer to reword the question reduces the likelihood that grade-school children will attempt to answer incomprehensible questions (Saywitz et al., 1999). More extensive training and reinforcement improves performance still further (Saywitz et al., 1999) and even has some effect with preschool children (Peters & Nunez, 1999).

As with the other instructions, the efficacy of permitting "I don't understand" is likely limited by the age of the child: very young children will be incapable of detecting anything but the most obvious complexities. Moreover, children underutilize the option, instead attempting to answer the most difficult questions (Peters & Nunez, 1999; Saywitz et al., 1999).

4. *Elicit a promise from the child to tell the truth.* Ask the child, "Do you promise that you will tell me the truth?" Then ask, "Are you going to tell me any lies?"

Although children are unlikely to understand adult versions of the oath, they recognize the significance of promises by grade school, and still younger children understand that when one says one "will" do something, one is likely to do it (Lyon, 2000). Research with both maltreated and nonmaltreated children has found that eliciting a promise to tell the truth increases children's honesty (Lyon, 2000; Talwar, Lee, Bala, & Lindsay, 2002).

The promise must be worded carefully, however. It is a good idea to mention both "promise" and "will," because children understand the meaning of "will" before they understand "promise." Following up with "Are you going to tell me any lies?" will ensure that the child is not simply assenting to questions he or she does not understand (because the appropriate answer is "no"), and the question is easier than asking the child to promise not to tell any lies (Lyon, 2000).

In sum, interview instructions are easy to administer and will improve the performance of many children. They will have the greatest effect on older children, and when highly suggestive questions are asked. However, given the limitations of instructions, the optimal solution is to ask simple nonleading questions. The best way to improve children's performance is to improve the questions we ask.

DIFFICULT CONCEPTS: NUMBER AND TIME

Interviewers often wish to know when and how many times abusive acts occurred. In the literature, one often reads that children understand a particular concept at a certain age. However, discussion of the ages of acquisition can be misleading in deciding how to question an individual child.

When developmental researchers state that children achieve some competence at a particular age, it is fair to assume that in an interview, much older children will often have difficulty exhibiting such competence. This is so for several reasons. First, the research usually refers to the youngest age at which a competency first appears in the most supportive context. For example, children's understanding of language is usually tested in a non-stressful environment using visible materials, rather than in a stressful context involving events to be remembered. Second, much of the research examines the ability of healthy children from enriched home environments, with little effort to sample children with diverse backgrounds. This is in large part because developmental psychologists are often more interested in the order in which abilities appear rather than the precise age at which they appear. Children with different abilities will acquire skills in the same order (generally speaking), but obviously not at the same time. Third, the fact that an age group shows evidence of understanding does not mean that an individual within that group will. Indeed, it is possible for a group of children to perform above chance on a task based on the good performance of a small proportion of children.

In addition to potentially overestimating children's abilities, age guides may sometimes underestimate what children can do. The history of developmental psychology is filled with research demonstrating good performance by preschoolers on tasks once believed to be mastered only by second or third grade. Part of the problem is that the tasks were difficult for reasons unrelated to the competencies being tested. This is the flip side of the point about supportive contexts: a highly supportive context may overestimate abilities, but a confusing context may underestimate abilities.

A final problem with age guides is that they focus attention on the competency of the child rather than on the abilities of the interviewer. It is rarely the case that a child lacks competency essential to communication. It is more often the case that a child lacks understanding of an unnecessarily complex form of speaking preferred by adults.

Number

In general, it is a mistake to ask a child how many times an event occurred, because of the likelihood that a child will arbitrarily pick an inherently incredible or arbitrary number ("a million," "thirty-eight"), and because the number will change from interview to interview. A moment's reflection highlights what a difficult task it is to estimate how many times something has occurred. Either one imagines each event and mentally counts, or one estimates the number by multiplying the frequency the events occurred in a particular time span (e.g., "every weekend") by the total time span over which the events occurred (Bradburn, 2000).

It is easy to misjudge a child's ability to make such an estimate. Children can often recite numbers before they know how to count, and can count objects before they can count events in memory (Walker, 1999). What constitutes an "event" is also open to question—does the child enumerate abuse by reflecting on particular acts or on times when a series of acts occurred? Legally, enumeration is not necessary. If the child's case ever goes to court, he or she can be asked about specific events, and questions about number should be disallowed as developmentally inappropriate.

The NICHD protocol recommends that after the child has first disclosed abuse and described an episode, the interviewer should ask, "Did this happen one time or more than one time?" If the child says "more than one time," the interviewer then inquires about the "last time" the abuse occurred, the "first time" the abuse occurred, and the time the child remembers "the most." The interviewer follows up by asking if there are "any other times" the child remembers. For each narrative, the interviewer asks the time segmentation prompts and cue questions described previously.

Time

Similar to number skills, children learn how to tell time before they can tell what time an event occurred. Unless one looks at a watch or calendar during an event, subsequent recall of the time requires inferential skills (e.g., "it was shortly before New Year's, so it probably was December") (Friedman, 1993). Although many children will fail to make such inferences, the interviewer can often elicit information from the child about contemporaneous events, which enables the interviewer to estimate the time. For example, children can often tell you where others were at the time of the abuse (e.g., "my mother was at church"), or what the child had been doing (e.g., asleep at night, taking a nap after school), in order to estimate clock time, and where the child was living or staying in order to estimate the year. Legally, exact dates and times are not necessary, particularly if the abuser had frequent access to the child and the abuse occurred on multiple occasions over a period of time (Myers, 1997).

Some temporal terms can be confusing for the young child. "Yesterday" and "today" are difficult for young children, in part because of their shifting meaning (today is tomorrow's yesterday). Moreover, the amount of time segmented by the words is initially unclear; for the young child "yesterday" often refers to anything in the past, and "tomorrow" refers to anything in the future (Harner, 1982). Obviously, the interviewer should not assume that the child understands weeks and months or can estimate time using these intervals.

The practice narrative in which the child describes a recent holiday enables the interviewer to determine if the child understands terms that are essential for providing a chronology. Most important is understanding of "next," "before," and "after," because these words are used extensively when providing the child with time segmentation cues. Because younger children will often describe events in the order in which they occurred, regardless of whether one asks about what happened "before" or "after" another event (Carni & French, 1984), the safest course is to ask "what happened next" questions as much as possible.

However, even children who understand "before" and "after" can be confused by the order in which events are mentioned. Young children "may assume the order in which events are mentioned in a sentence is the same as the chronological order in which the events occurred" (Richardson, 1993, p. 111). For example, Richardson (1993) cites a sexual abuse case in which the child was asked, "Before your father took you to the hospital, where were you?" Because "where were you" was asked after "before your father took you to the hospital," the child responded to "where were you" by stating where she was after she went to the hospital. The child might not exhibit the same confusion if asked, "Where were you before you went to the hospital?" A child's apparent confusion regarding chronology may be attributable to the interviewer's questions rather than the child's failing memory.

CONCLUSION

I have attempted to provide the reader with a brief overview of developmentally appropriate interview strategies (see Exhibit 4.1). The goal of these strategies is to maximize the amount of information one obtains from children while minimizing errors and misunderstandings attributable to

EXHIBIT 4.1.
TEN TIPS FOR INTERVIEWING CHILDREN

1. Begin with instructions.
2. Ask for a practice narrative.
3. Keep questions as general and open-ended as possible.
4. Use wh- questions (what, where, when, who, why, how).
5. Ask time-segmentation questions (e.g., "What happened just after he . . .") and cue questions (e.g., "You said he . . . Tell me more about that").
6. Avoid recognition questions (did, was, were). If you ask a recognition question, follow up with an open-ended question.
7. Replace pronouns with names (e.g., "Steve" instead of "he").
8. Replace deictics with nouns (e.g., "in the garage" instead of "there").
9. Don't ask how many times an event occurred, but whether it happened once or more than once. Follow up by focusing on individual episodes.
10. Do not ask what time or what date an event occurred, but about concurrent events that enable you to estimate the time.

poorly worded and suggestive questions. I have focused on techniques that are supported by laboratory and observational research on investigative interviewing, which was inspired by concerns over children's suggestibility.

Much more should be done. The "new wave" of research on children's suggestibility (Bruck, Ceci, & Hembrooke, 1998) emphasized the dangers of false allegations and suggestive techniques, and generated a list of techniques to be avoided. I predict that the next wave will acknowledge the risks of false denials and emphasize techniques for overcoming reluctance and minimizing developmental limitations. Researchers developing structured protocols have already taken important steps in this direction.

REFERENCES

Baker-Ward, L., Gordon, B.N., Ornstein, P.A., Larus, D.M., & Clubb, P.A. (1993). Young children's long-term retention of a pediatric examination. *Child Development, 64,* 1519-1533.

Bradburn, N.M. (2000). Temporal representation and event dating. In A.A. Stone, J.S. Turkhan, C.A. Bachrach, J.B. Jobe, H.S. Kurtzman, & V.S. Cain (Eds.), *The science of self-report: Implications for research and practice* (pp. 49-61). Mahwah, NJ: Erlbaum.

Bruck, M., Ceci, S.J., & Hembrooke, H. (1998). Reliability and credibility of young children's reports: From research to policy and practice. *American Psychologist, 53,* 136-151.

Carni, E. & French, L.A. (1984). The acquisition of before and after reconsidered: What develops? *Journal of Experimental Child Psychology, 37,* 394-403.

Carter, C.A., Bottoms, B.L., & Levine, M. (1996). Linguistic and socioemotional influences on the accuracy of children's reports. *Law and Human Behavior, 20,* 335-358.

Ceci, S.J., Bruck, M., & Battin, D.B. (2000). The suggestibility of children's testimony. In D.F. Bjorklund (Ed.), *False-memory creation in children and adults: Theory, research, and implications* (pp. 169-201). Mahwah, NJ: Erlbaum.

Ceci, S.J., Ross, D.F., & Toglia, M.P. (1987). Suggestibility of children's memory: Psycholegal implications. *Journal of Experimental Psychology: General, 116,* 38-49.

Devoe, E.R. & Faller, K.C. (1999). The characteristics of disclosure among children who may have been sexually abused. *Child Maltreatment, 4,* 217-227.

Endres, J., Poggenpohl, C., & Erben, C. (1999). Repetitions, warnings, and video: Cognitive and motivational components in preschool children's suggestibility. *Legal and Criminological Psychology, 4,* 129-146.

Faller, K.C. (1996). *Evaluating children suspected of having been sexually abused.* Newbury Park, CA: Sage.

Friedman, W.J. (1993). Memory of the time of past events. *Psychological Bulletin, 113,* 44-66.

Gee, S., Gregory, M., & Pipe, M.-E. (1999). "What colour is your pet dinosaur?" The impact of pre-interview training and question type on children's answers. *Legal and Criminological Psychology, 4,* 111-128.

Greenhoot, A.F., Ornstein, P.A., Gordon, B.N., & Baker-Ward, L. (1999). Acting out the details of a pediatric check-up: The impact of interview condition and behavioral style on children's memory reports. *Child Development, 70,* 363-380.

Greenstock, G. & Pipe, M.-E. (1996). Interviewing children about past events: The influence of peer support and misleading questions. *Child Abuse and Neglect, 20,* 69-80.

Harner, L. (1982). Talking about the past and the future. In W.J. Friedman (Ed.), *The developmental psychology of time* (pp. 141-169). New York: Academic Press.

Kwock, M.S. & Winer, G.A. (1986). Overcoming leading questions: Effects of psychosocial task variables. *Journal of Educational Psychology, 78,* 289-293.

Lampinen, J.M. & Smith, V.L. (1995). The incredible (and sometimes incredulous) child witness: Child eyewitnesses' sensitivity to source credibility cues. *Journal of Applied Psychology, 80,* 621-627.

Lyon, T.D. (1999). The new wave of suggestibility research: A critique. *Cornell Law Review, 84,* 1004-1087.

Lyon, T.D. (2000). Child witnesses and the oath: Empirical evidence. *Southern California Law Review, 73,* 1017-1074.

Lyon, T.D. (2002). Scientific support for expert testimony on child sexual abuse accommodation. In J.R. Conte (Ed.), *Critical issues in child sexual abuse* (pp. 107-138). Newbury Park, CA: Sage.

Lyon, T.D., Koverola, C., Morahan, M., & Heger, A. (2002, March). *Disclosure patterns with a structured sexual abuse interview.* Paper presented at the biennial meeting of the American Psychology and Law Society conference, Austin, Texas.

Memon, A. & Vartoukian, R. (1996). The effects of repeated questioning on young children's eyewitness testimony. *British Journal of Psychology, 87,* 403-415.

Moston, S. (1987). The suggestibility of children in interview studies. *First Language, 7,* 67-78.

Mulder, M.R. & Vrij, A. (1996). Explaining conversation rules to children: An intervention study to facilitate children's accurate responses. *Child Abuse and Neglect, 20,* 623-631.

Myers, J.E.B. (1997). *Evidence in child abuse and neglect cases* (3rd ed., Vol. 2). New York: Wiley Law Publications.

Perry, N.W., McAuliff, B.D., Tam, P., Claycomb, L., Dostal, C., & Flanagan, C. (1995). When lawyers question children: Is justice served? *Law and Human Behavior, 19,* 609-629.

Peters, W.W. & Nunez, N. (1999). Complex language and comprehension monitoring: Teaching child witnesses to recognize linguistic confusion. *Journal of Applied Psychology, 84,* 661-669.

Peterson, C., Dowden, C., & Tobin, J. (1999). Interviewing preschoolers: Comparisons of yes/no and wh- questions. *Law and Human Behavior, 23,* 539-555.

Poole, D.A. & Lindsay, D.S. (2001). Children's eyewitness reports after exposure to misinformation from parents. *Journal of Experimental Psychology: Applied, 7,* 27-50.

Richardson, G.C. (1993). *The child witness: A linguistic analysis of child sexual abuse testimony.* Doctoral dissertation, Georgetown University.

Sas, L.D. & Cunningham, A.H. (1995). *Tipping the balance to tell the secret: The public discovery of child sexual abuse.* London, Ontario: London Family Court Clinic.

Sauzier, M. (1989). Disclosure of child sexual abuse: For better or for worse. *Psychiatric Clinics of North America, 12,* 455-469.

Saywitz, K., Goodman, G., Nicholas, G., & Moan, S. (1991). Children's memory of a physical examination involving genital touch: Implications for reports of child sexual abuse. *Journal of Consulting and Clinical Psychology, 59,* 682-691.

Saywitz, K.J. & Lyon, T.D. (2002). Coming to grips with children's suggestibility. In M.L. Eisen, J.A. Quas, & G.S. Goodman (Eds.), *Memory and suggestibility in the forensic interview* (pp. 85-113). Mahwah, NJ: Erlbaum.

Saywitz, K.J. & Moan-Hardie, S. (1994). Reducing the potential for distortion of childhood memories. *Consciousness and Cognition, 3,* 408-425.

Saywitz, K. & Nathanson, R. (1992, August). Effects of environment on children's testimony and perceived stress. In B. Bottoms & M. Levine (Chairs), *Actual and perceived competency of child witnesses.* Symposium conducted at the annual convention of the American Psychological Association, Washington, DC.

Saywitz, K.J., Snyder, L., & Nathanson, R. (1999). Facilitating the communicative competence of the child witness. *Applied Developmental Science, 3,* 58-68.

Smith, B.E. & Elstein, S.G. (1993). *The prosecution of child sexual and physical abuse cases: Final report.* Washington, DC: National Center on Child Abuse and Neglect.

Sternberg, K.J., Lamb, M.E., Esplin, P.W., Orbach, Y., & Hershkowitz, I. (2002). Using a structured protocol to improve the quality of investigative interviews. In M.L. Eisen, J.A. Quas, & G.S. Goodman (Eds.), *Memory and suggestibility in the forensic interview* (pp. 409-436). Mahwah, NJ: Erlbaum.

Sternberg, K.J., Lamb, M.E., Hershkowitz, I., Yudilevitch, L., Orbach, Y., Esplin, P.W., & Hovav, M. (1997). Effects of introductory style on children's abilities to describe experiences of sexual abuse. *Child Abuse and Neglect, 21,* 1133-1146.

Sternberg, K.J., Lamb, M.E., Orbach, Y., Esplin, P.W., & Mitchell, S. (2001). Use of a structured investigative protocol enhances young children's responses to free recall prompts in the course of forensic interviews. *Journal of Applied Psychology, 86,* 997-1005.

Talwar, V., Lee, K., Bala, N., & Lindsay, R.C.L. (2002). Children's conceptual knowledge of lying and its relation to their actual behaviors: Implications for court competence examinations. *Law and Human Behavior, 26,* 395-415.

Toglia, M.P., Ross, D.F., Ceci, S.J., & Hembrooke, H. (1992). The suggestibility of children's memory: A social-psychological and cognitive interpretation. In M.L. Howe, C.J. Brainerd, & V.F. Reyna (Eds.), *Development of long-term retention* (pp. 217-241). New York: Springer-Verlag.

Walker, A.G. (1999). *Handbook on questioning children: A linguistic perspective* (2nd ed.). Washington, DC: ABA Center on Children and the Law.

Walker, N.E. & Lunning, S.M. (1998). *Do children respond accurately to forced choice questions?: Yes or no?* Manuscript in preparation.

Warren, A., Hulse-Trotter, K., & Tubbs, E.C. (1991). Inducing resistance to suggestibility in children. *Law and Human Behavior, 15,* 273-285.

Welch-Ross, M. (2000). A mental-state reasoning model of suggestibility and memory source monitoring. In K.P. Roberts & M. Blades (Eds.), *Children's source monitoring* (pp. 227-255). Mahwah, NJ: Erlbaum.

Whipple, G.M. (1915). *Manual of mental and physical tests: Part 2. Complex processes* (2nd ed.). Baltimore: Warwick and York.

Chapter 5

Psychological Evaluations
and the Child Welfare System

Anthony J. Urquiza
Dawn M. Blacker

With the advent of the juvenile court system, which is designed to administer juvenile court law and provide for the safety and protection of children when necessary, mental health professionals have offered their expertise and knowledge in various ways. Typically, psychologists and mental health professionals who furnish services for the juvenile criminal court address usual criminal forensic questions (e.g., competency to stand trial), determine the juvenile's amenability to treatment, and provide consultation (Melton, Petrila, Poythress, & Slobogoin, 1997). When psychologists provide services to the juvenile court system (child welfare system), they also offer consultation, expertise in the area of child maltreatment and parenting issues, and address questions that the court wants answered in relation to the dependent child and family. This chapter provides information about the process of conducting a psychological evaluation for the juvenile court system. It is our intent to provide information about necessary elements of a psychological evaluation. Therefore, after a discussion of some foundational information (e.g., purpose of psychological evaluations, qualifications to complete a psychological evaluation), information is presented roughly in the order in which an evaluation is conducted (e.g., referral question, clinical interviewing, observational data, test administration, conceptualization, and recommendations). For clarity, several case examples are included. Although the cases are adapted from actual cases evaluated by the authors, all potentially identifying information has been removed.

PURPOSE

A request for a psychological evaluation is typically made by the dependent child's social worker or presiding judge. On occasion, the child's or parent's attorney may request a psychological evaluation as well. The nature of the referral question varies depending on the status of the child's case and current situation. Often, the case involves mental health issues that require a psychologist to address. For instance, the child's social worker may have concerns regarding the parents' mental health, emotional functioning, and/or cognitive functioning, which may be impacting their ability to complete the reunification plan and safely and adequately parent their child. In addition, cases referred for evaluation frequently involve complex parenting, parent-child, and child maltreatment issues requiring an expert in these areas. Other cases are referred because state statutes specifically require an opinion from an experienced mental health provider (e.g., terminating parental rights due to a mental health problem that is not responsive to intervention [California Juvenile Laws and Regulations, 2001, Family Code 7827]). Other requests may pertain to an evaluation of appropriate intervention and case management because of differences of opinion by parties involved. Second opinions regarding a child's diagnosis, treatment plan, and placement plan are also reasons to request a psychological evaluation.

QUALIFICATIONS

Although there are many psychologists with a diverse set of skills and abilities, the process of conducting psychological evaluations for child welfare systems may not be suited for most clinical psychologists. Many skills, foundations of knowledge, and abilities require expertise not commonly found in graduate programs or through postgraduate training. Psychologists conducting psychological evaluations need a thorough understanding of child, adult, and family development and functioning (Turner, DeMers, Fox, & Reed, 2002). Further, they need to have knowledge of the statutes governing children and families involved in the child welfare system for their jurisdiction (although child welfare cases are managed through county personnel, they reflect state statutes). It is also necessary to have full command of psychopathology for both children and adults. This includes familiarity with the *Diagnostic and Statistical Manual of Mental Disorders,* Fourth Edition, Text Revision (American Psychiatric Association, 2000), as well as common mental health problems that may interfere with safe and adequate parenting.

As the field of child abuse and neglect is constantly changing, it is important to understand the dynamics in maltreating parent-child relationships, as well as current research related to treatment associated with abusive parents and/or abused children. Current research indicates that a large percentage of parents involved in the child welfare system have chronic problems with substance abuse. This requires individuals involved in evaluating these parents to have an understanding of the etiology and course of additive behaviors, as well as various outpatient and residential treatment approaches. Finally, although state statutes govern specific appropriate and inappropriate behaviors, it is possible that child, parent, and family cultural characteristics may have an impact on the way specific behaviors are interpreted and how treatment programs are developed (Terao, Borrego, & Urquiza, 2000). Therefore, it is incumbent on the evaluating psychologist to understand basic principles of cultural diversity, the limitations of standardized testing on different cultural groups, and development of reunification/ treatment plans that may be culturally acceptable. Clearly, the process of conducting psychological evaluations for the child welfare system should not be undertaken lightly. It is suggested that after an extensive course of graduate and postgraduate training, individuals choosing this area of clinical practice should seek extensive supervision from an experienced clinician/evaluator. Further, this is an area of practice that should not be undertaken unless the psychologist is licensed or working under the close supervision of a licensed professional.

RIGHTS, RESPONSIBILITIES, AND GUIDELINES

A number of professional organizations have developed ethical principles and guidelines for clinical practice (American Psychological Association, 1992) and for psychological evaluations related to child maltreatment (American Academy of Child and Adolescent Psychiatry, 1997; American Professional Society on the Abuse of Children, 1996; American Psychological Association, 1998). Although adherence to ethical principles, practice guidelines, and best practices is the hallmark of a competent mental health professional, the process of conducting psychological evaluations for the child welfare system contains many intersecting policies, statutes, guidelines, and standards for practice. These require substantial attention from the psychologist in carefully assessing when there may be conflicting directions for the practitioner and/or to understand the limits imposed by different disciplinary rules and legal statutes.

For these reasons, certain potentially problematic ethical and legal issues merit special attention during the process of psychological evaluations. These are discussed in the following material.

Informed Consent

The process of informed consent is a legal and ethical requirement for the delivery of services to a client (American Psychological Association, 1992). Founded in a perspective that recognizes and respects an individual's autonomy, informed consent addresses the individual's right to exercise control of his or her body. It is important to note that failure to acquire informed consent at the initiation of clinical service (i.e., at the beginning of the first appointment) may constitute maltreatment and expose the evaluator to liability. The informed consent process should address the competence of the individual to consent to treatment (or in this case, to participate in a psychological evaluation); consent must be voluntary; the client should be informed of the purpose of the clinical service (e.g., to the best of the evaluator's ability, why is the evaluation being conducted? What are the referral questions?) and notified of the right to refuse or withdraw consent. Two issues within this process are often difficult for the evaluator; the determination regarding whether the client is sufficiently competent to provide consent and whether the client's consent is voluntary. For the first issue, the evaluator may have concern about whether the client has the capacity to provide consent because of age or mental health status.

For the second issue, situations in which the psychologist is conducting an evaluation that has been ordered by the court often cause confusion. A court order that identifies a specific psychologist to perform the evaluation places this psychologist in a situation in which he or she is "directed" to conduct the evaluation by the court. Therefore, it is incumbent on the psychologist to conduct the evaluation, but it is not the responsibility of the psychologist to ensure that the client participates in the evaluation. The psychologist should ensure that clients understand both that they have the right to voluntarily participate in the evaluation and that the evaluation is ordered by the court. This provides clients with information necessary to make decisions about their care (e.g., participate in the evaluation, return to court to address their concerns with the judge, request the court appoint another evaluator).

Throughout the course of the evaluation, the psychologist may make many contacts with individuals who have information about the client (e.g., teachers, therapists, home visitors). The evaluator should make an effort to assess informants' ability to provide consent to participate in the evaluation, and they should also be informed about their right to participate in the evaluation.

Limits of Confidentiality

Like most mental health services, psychological evaluations are confidential, and the evaluator has a legal and ethical responsibility to protect confidential client information. However, the purpose of the evaluation is typically to acquire information and to disclose this information to the referring party, the court, or other agency. Therefore, it is essential that the evaluator specifically address issues of confidentiality with the client and describe the limits of this confidentiality (see Meyers, 2001, for an excellent review of client confidentiality and privilege). For example, it is important for the client to understand that a product of most psychological evaluations is a written report—which will be disseminated to the court (and indirectly to attorneys and county social service agencies). In addition, the client should know that both clinical interview information and all test results (in both raw data and computer-generated interpretive form) and any work product (e.g., interview notes) may be disclosed in a psychological evaluation report or through subpoena and court testimony. Also, information acquired from others (i.e., collateral contacts) may also be disclosed if included in the report. Finally, it is the responsibility of the evaluator to inform the client that child abuse reporting law overrides privilege and confidentiality (indicating that if the client should divulge reasonable suspicion of child maltreatment, then the evaluator is responsible to report this information. Finally, because of the complexity of the legal and ethical issues, it is strongly recommended that evaluators develop a relationship with an attorney and seek consultation on any complex legal and ethical issues.

Clarification of Professional Roles

It is likely that most people participating in a psychological evaluation have a limited understanding of the process of being evaluated and the different types of professional roles a psychologist may assume. It is incumbent on the evaluator to provide a clear description of the responsibility of the psychologist in the evaluation and the limits of their role. Mannarino and Cohen (2001) describe many of the problems inherent in professional role conflicts. For example, evaluators should be aware of the relationship between child abuse reporting laws and their ethical duty to maintain confidentiality. In the state of California, child abuse and elder/dependent abuse reporting laws override issues of confidentiality. That is, should an evaluator have concern about the safety of a child or adult/dependent, or have information about past abuse, then the evaluator is mandated to report this information. It should be noted that the evaluator should disclose only sufficient information necessary to make the report. It is incumbent on the evaluator to disclose the responsibility to report suspicion of child maltreatment and adult/dependent abuse at the beginning of the evaluation.

FOCUS OF THE EVALUATION

Referrals for a psychological evaluation are usually framed in the form of a question. Typical questions may include the following:

- What services need to be provided to the parent and/or child to facilitate reunification?
- Do the child's current mental health problems necessitate transition to a higher level of care?
- Is there a significant bond between the parent and child?
- Given the existing behavioral and/or mental health problems of a set of siblings, it is possible (or in their best interests) to be placed in separate homes?
- Is the parent able to benefit from reunification services?
- Is the parent able to safely and adequately care for the child at this time?

As most psychological evaluations conducted for child welfare systems are done for the court and/or with the permission of the court, it is important to have a clear understanding of the exact referral question. Further, it is uncommon for evaluators to speak directly with judges regarding the evaluation and the specific question (this information is often communicated through social workers or attorneys for the parties involved in the case—parent's attorney, children's attorney, or the attorney for the county). For this reason, it is essential that evaluators request the referral question be provided to them in writing. Should there be a concern about the scope of the evaluation, the evaluator should contact the referring party.

Often, the referral question provided by the court is founded in a specific state statute, but the statute may not be readily apparent to the evaluator. Therefore, it is essential that the evaluator have an understanding of the relationship between the referral question and the pertinent state statutes related to the case. For example, in California, a case may be referred with a question of determining if there is a bond between a parent and child. First, it is necessary to understand at what point the case is within the reunification process. In this specific case, the parent had repeatedly failed or refused all efforts at reunification with the child (e.g., refused mental health treatment, failed to complete residential drug treatment). As a result, the county was no longer providing any reunification services and had terminated re-unification efforts. The child had been placed in a foster home in which there was a strong desire to adopt him. The California Child Welfare and In-stitutions Code states that a child cannot be available for adoption if he or she has a bond with a parent. Therefore, the referral question in this case, to determine if there is a bond between a parent and child, would also deter-mine whether the child would be available for adoption. Should there be a determination of a bond between the parent and child (presumably a signifi-cant positive affiliative relationship), then the child would remain as a foster child or the foster parents may become guardians.

Another important issue related to the focus of the evaluation involves the limits of the evaluation. It is necessary that the evaluator carefully assess the scope of the referral question and be able to appropriately and ade-quately provide an opinion. In some instances, the evaluator may not have the skills or expertise to adequately respond to a certain question. For exam-ple, an evaluator with limited experience in substance abuse treatment should not accept a referral question related to this topic. Further, some re-ferral questions are outside the scope of any psychological evaluation. An example of this would be a referral question that expected the evaluator to provide an opinion regarding whether a child had been sexually abused and/or whether a specific person had sexually abused a child. Such ques-tions are the domain of the criminal court and judicial determination.

Finally, during the course of the evaluation, it is important that all of the contacts (parents, children, and all sources of information) have a complete understanding of the referral question and the reasons for the evaluation. This process, which should be part of an informed consent procedure, al-lows clients and sources of information to be fully informed about the eval-uation and understand the implications of the information they provide.

ASSESSMENT

No single assessment measure will provide the type of information needed to respond to referral questions in a child welfare evaluation. Test and measurement development is typically most successful when the test developers can identify specific constructs that they want to assess (e.g., de-pression, anxiety) and are able to exclude constructs that may interfere with the identified construct (e.g., trauma symptoms may confound the assess-ment of hyperactivity). This contrasts with the process of making decisions related to a child welfare psychological evaluation. Typically, the process of conducting a psychological evaluation involves acquiring a substantial amount of diverse information from different sources (e.g., standardized test data, clinical interviews, collateral contacts, court records, and client history), weighing the importance of these data, then developing an opinion based on current theoretical foundations and related to the pertinent state statutes. That is, the psychologist's opinion should be derived from many sources, and should rarely depend on a single piece of information or data (e.g., a standardized test). Although certain tests may provide information that can serve as a substantial foundation for the psychologist's opinion (e.g., administration of an intelligence test in which a parent scores in the "severe mental retardation" range), these are atypical situations.

As there is no specific or single test that will address the referral question, it is necessary for the psychologist to be aware of a number of psychological measures that assess different parent, child, and family domains. The appendix at the end of this chapter contains a list of several domains that need to be measured and some common standardized assessment measures. This list is not intended to be exhaustive, but is only an overview of some of the more common areas (i.e., domains) assessed as part of a psychological evaluation and some measures of assessment for each domain (several texts provide an overview of many standardized assessments currently in use, including Groth-Marnat, 1999; Maruish, 1999; Sattler, 1998). It is incumbent on the evaluator to have a thorough understanding of the uses and limits for each test. This understanding may come as part of the evaluator's graduate training and/or participation in continuing education. In either case, it is essential that there be a period of practice using each assessment measure while under the guidance of a skilled supervisor.

Aside from having a solid foundation on the use of standardized assessment measures, there are several additional issues with which an evaluator should be familiar in the use of such measures.

Test Familiarity and Protocol

Most standardized tests have different instructions and different response formats (e.g., true/false, ranking responses, rating severity of symptoms, agree/disagree). The evaluator should be thoroughly familiar with the test and be able to quickly and easily respond to questions by the client. With some tests, especially tests that must be administered in an interactive format with the client (e.g., intelligence tests), it is essential that the evaluator be fully trained in administration of the test. Evaluators should have had both didactic training in test administration and several opportunities to be observed and supervised in administration of the appropriate test protocol. It is essential that prior to test administration, the evaluator have a mastery of the administration protocol.

Reading Ability

Any written test requires that the client have a minimum level of reading ability. Typically, test developers provide an estimate of the reading level necessary to validly take each test. Administration of any test in which the client does not have an ability to read and comprehend each of the items (or has substantial difficulty in understanding the items) undermines the validity of the test. During the course of the evaluation, it is important to assess the client's reading ability (e.g., inquire about past school performance, identify any subject areas of difficulty). In some cases where there is a clear concern about the subject's ability to comprehend the written word, it may be necessary to administer a test of reading ability. Finally, as part of the process of giving test instructions, the evaluator can explain that clients should identify any items that they have difficulty understanding. In some cases, the test developer may have provided a means to administer the test with the assistance of an audiotape (i.e., the client marks responses after hearing the question and choices on an audiotape).

Validity Scales

Because individuals participating in many types of psychological evaluations may commonly misrepresent their responses in an effort to create an exceptionally positive or negative impression of themselves (typically, parents involved in child welfare evaluation tend to overemphasize positive attributes and limit any negative attributes or characteristics), the presence of validity scales is vital. Validity scales are present on many well-used standardized assessment measures (e.g., Minnesota Multiphasic Personality Inventory–II, Personality Assessment Inventory, Child Abuse Potential Inventory). These validity scales can provide information about a pattern of unusual or distorted responses that may invalidate the test administration. One of the initial steps in interpreting any test should be a careful assessment of the validity scales.

CLINICAL OBSERVATIONS

During the past thirty years, much has been written about the use of informal and formal observation methods. Consistently, a pattern of research has highlighted the value of clinical observation strategies (see Sattler, 1998, for a review of clinical observation methods). These strategies include both informal and formal observation strategies.

Informal Observation Characteristics

One of the more important and often overlooked aspects of any evaluation is the process of making use of the many informal observations made during the course of an evaluation. As a clinician, it is important to be aware of the subtle as well as the more obvious physical characteristics, behavior, and physical changes that occur during the course of the evaluation.

Observing Nonverbal Behavior

During the course of clinical interviews, evaluators will have the opportunity to observe many types of behavior presented by their clients. These nonverbal behaviors can be extremely informative in regard to an individual's general lifestyle, level of functioning, alertness and attentiveness to the environment (i.e., the presence of intoxication and/or drug-induced altered consciousness), and willingness to communicate. Some have argued that certain nonverbal behaviors may provide a way for the evaluator to interpret an underlying meaning (e.g., tapping of the foot means the client is impatient or anxious; not sitting upright in a chair may mean the client is sad or discouraged) (Cormier & Cormier, 1979). Although this may be true, it is also important not to overinterpret nonverbal behavior. For example, staring intently during a clinical interview (especially staring at the evaluator) may be perceived as confrontational. However, it may also be a cultural manifestation in communication, or simply an idiosyncratic behavior for clients when they are concentrating. Examples of potentially informative nonverbal behaviors include these:

- Vocal and speech qualities: loudness, fluency, responsiveness to questions, spontaneity, organization (Are clients able to respond coherently to specific questions?), pace, clarity (Are they able to clearly articulate words?)
- Gestures and mannerisms: moving rapidly, rocking, hyperactivity or hypoactivity, agitation, prolonged staring, yawning, unusual tics or tremors
- Facial expressions: direct or indirect eye contact, flat affect (e.g., no facial expression, even when discussing distressful events), dropping eyelids
- Body posture: Do they have an open and relaxed body posture (e.g., sitting upright and comfortably in the chair, arms uncrossed)? Do they have a closed and more tense body posture (e.g., arms crossed, sitting rigidly)? Do they maintain an appropriate distance in communication?

Observing Verbal Behavior

Although much information can be gained from observing nonverbal behaviors, it is important to attend to characteristics of verbal behavior (i.e., the style or manner in which a client uses language to communicate ideas and thoughts). Clients' pattern of verbal behavior may reflect their perceptions of the world and the way they organize their thoughts (Garrett, 1982). Some examples of important verbal behavior include the following:

- Shifts in conversation: Pay attention to a pattern of shifting the conversation away from specific topics (e.g., failing to respond to certain questions), and/or directing the conversation back to a specific topic (e.g., obsessively wanting to discuss an issue).
- Attempts to control the interaction: During the course of an evaluation, it is typical for the evaluator to be the person asking questions, to which the client responds. Further, it is reasonable for some clients to have legitimate questions of the evaluator. However, certain clients may attempt to control or dominate the evaluation by repeatedly asking questions of the evaluator or dictating specific areas of inquiry that are off-limits.
- Avoiding responsibility or externalizing blame: Throughout the course of life, all individuals make mistakes, have failures, and make poor decisions. One indicator that an individual has the potential to learn from past mistakes is recognizing and accepting responsibilities for past problems. The manner in which a client describes past problems may indicate willingness to acknowledge past mistakes and accept responsibility.
- Overemphasizing positive attributes and underemphasizing negative attributes: Often in an evaluation setting, clients may wish to present themselves in a positive light. However, it may be important to attend to clients who may substantially distort past events, abilities, and skills—this may raise questions related to their veracity.

Further, in some cases, careful observation of verbal behavior may indicate more significant psychopathology. Concern about certain psychiatric diagnoses (e.g., brief psychotic disorder, schizophrenia, delusional disorder) should be raised whenever a client demonstrates atypical patterns of speech and communication (e.g., disorganized speech, loose associations). The following is an excerpt from a clinical interview with a twenty-nine-year-old mother who had been severely physically and sexually assaulted by an ex-husband.

EVALUATOR: Can you tell me how you met your current husband?

MOTHER: (speaking rapidly) Why are you asking me that? What do you want to know? Well . . . he works at a restaurant near where I work. I met him on a Thursday, you know. Today is Thursday, isn't it? I have laundry to do tomorrow. It's at the cleaners now. That's where I work, at a motel right next to the restaurant. I can't keep my children there. They have their own bedroom. That's what my social worker told me that I have to do. Place them in a place where they'll be safely placed. That's what she said. Because I work starting in the morning and continuing until about when they get out of school. I try to take care of them, but now they're in foster care, so I'm trying to get them back.

This pattern of rapid and tangential responses to questions was consistent throughout the clinical interview and was supported in conversations with a home visitation worker (who indicated that this was the mother's typical style of communication). After ruling out a problem with substance abuse, this means of communication is indicative of a parent with substantial problems in organizing her thoughts—a characteristic that would impair her ability to safely parent her children.

Mental Status Examination

Modeled after the physical medical exam, administration of a mental status examination (MSE) provides a brief means to review the major systems of psychological functioning. Because many of the areas covered in an MSE are addressed in more depth during a psychological evaluation (i.e., standardized assessment of intellectual ability), it has become relatively infrequent for evaluators to use an MSE. However, the basic areas of functioning assessed with an MSE (e.g., general appearance and behavior, feeling/affect and mood, perception, thinking) may be a way for an evaluator to structure the acquisition of basic information about the client.

Timeliness for Appointments

Throughout the course of caring for a child, many appointments occur that are an important part of caregiving and contribute to the child's perspective that his or her parents are a reliable and available resource. One of the more tangible ways in which parents can demonstrate their ability to care for their child is to attend to common schedules. This would involve issues such as whether the clients are early, on-time, or late for appointments, and whether scheduling problems are common (e.g., forgetting the date/time of the appointment or arriving on the wrong day). A parent who has difficulty attending appointments (or making appointments on time) may also have difficulty in scheduling and attending appointments related to the child's immunizations, parent-teacher conferences, special education meetings, picking up a child from the babysitter, and so on.

General Hygiene

One relatively easy informal observation involves the assessment of the physical appearance of the parent and child. Typically, an individual participating in a formal evaluation should be dressed and groomed appropriately. This should involve being recently bathed, wearing clean clothes, and having a neat appearance (e.g., hair combed, shaved, free of foul body odor). Through observation, the evaluator can assess parents' ability to engage in appropriate hygienic care both for themselves and for their children. It is important to distinguish issues related to a limited ability to care for themselves from other confounding factors. For example, children attending appointments in the late afternoon may be dirty from a day playing at school. Similarly, families with severe poverty may be well groomed, but not have the resources to clean their clothes on a regular basis. Finally, children with encopresis or enuresis may have hygiene problems related to these disorders.

Physical Health

Part of the process of caring for children involves being able to consistently meet the physical demands of parenting. As a result, in some cases it may be necessary to assess the parent's physical capabilities. It is important to note that the formal assessment of an individual's medical condition is outside the scope of a psychologist's expertise. However, it may be appropriate for the evaluator to arrange to have a client referred for a medical evaluation. For example, a prospective adoptive parent with a recent history of cancer may be asked to provide a medical determination of the prognosis or status of remission for his or her disease. Similarly, the daily demands of parenting may be difficult for individuals with more fragile medical conditions.

A paternal grandmother was being evaluated to be able to adopt her two young grandsons and a young granddaughter (ages five, three, and two years, respectively). As a result of prior maltreatment and trauma, both boys had serious problems related to aggression, overactivity, and defiance. During the course of a structured observation, the paternal grandmother demonstrated little ability to manage the boys' aggressive and defiant behavior.

They were repeatedly aggressive to each other, and both boys were aggressive to their younger sister. Early into the structured play session, the grandmother became red in the face and began breathing heavily as a result of moving about the room rapidly. When the grandmother appeared to begin to hyperventilate and the boys began hitting their younger sister together, then the evaluator intervened and stopped the observation. During the course of the debriefing, the grandmother acknowledged her difficulty in controlling her grandsons, but asserted that she would rely on the assistance of her husband (the stepgrandfather) in child care. In a later interview with the stepgrandfather, he explained that he worked most of the day, that he was not interested in raising young children, and that the care for these three children was "Her thing, not mine. I already raised my family." The grandmother had recently had open-heart surgery and this had impaired her ability to maintain employment. When asked to sign a release so the evaluator could speak with her doctor, she refused. When asked to provide a letter from her doctor explaining that she possessed the physical abilities to care for three young children, she was unwilling or unable to provide any such letter. As a result, the evaluator held concerns about this grandparent's ability to physically meet the demands of caring for three young children.

As many children in the child welfare system have special needs, sometimes it is necessary for the evaluator to assess the health status of the child. Again, it is important to note that a formal medical assessment is outside the scope of a psychologist's practice. However, it may be possible to acquire a medical examination or opinion as a means to incorporate medical information in the psychological evaluation. For example, children with problems related to chronic medical conditions (e.g., diabetes, seizures) may require special attention but limited additional physical care. Children with more physically debilitating health problems (e.g., cerebral palsy, ambulatory handicaps) may require special attention to their medical condition and may make a number of physical demands on the parent (e.g., physically moving the child). These issues should be addressed as part of the psychologist's evaluation of the child, combined with an assessment of the availability of any supportive resources (e.g., assisted home care, physical therapists).

Formal Observation Paradigm

Assuming that parents and children engage in predictable and repetitious patterns of behavior when they have (or have had) an ongoing relationship, the use of a formal observation paradigm can be very valuable in identifying some of the common behavioral themes within these dyads. With this perspective as a foundation, during the last thirty-five years, a rich literature has developed on observation of parent-child dyads in a structured social context (Boardman, 1962; Wahler, Winkel, Peterson, & Morrison, 1965). Typically, formal parent-child observational paradigms provide a parent-child dyad with an opportunity to interact within a specific social context (e.g., playing in a room with age-appropriate toys) while the evaluator observes this interaction (often from a separate observation room). The instructions for the parent-child dyad tend to focus on three separate tasks—child-directed play (i.e., instructing the parent to play with the child and allow the child to direct the play while the parent follows the child's lead); parent-directed play (i.e., instructing the parent to determine the activity and get the child to play along according to the parent's rules); and clean up (i.e., instructing the parent to get the child to clean up the toys/room without assistance). The objective of the observational paradigm is not to determine if the parent and child can play together or to see if the child can clean up the room. Rather, the goal is to observe a number of bidirectional strategies each individual employs in the interaction and the response of the other to the initial strategy. For example, observe the strategies the parent uses to get the child to clean up the toys (clear, direct commands; threatening; begging; whining). Further, observe the child's response to the parent's appropriate (e.g., direct commands) or inappropriate (e.g., whining, threats) efforts.

Roberts (2001) argued that child clinicians need parent-child interaction data to confirm interview and questionnaire information and to provide some specificity to the more global perspectives offered by informant-based sources of information. Some of this information can include the type and frequency of maladaptive or coercive actions on the part of the parent or child (e.g., threats, aggression, whining), effectiveness of the parent in acquiring compliance, response of the parent to the child's compliance (e.g., Does the parent provide praise for child compliance?), use of physical affection (e.g., hugs, pats on the back, kisses) or physical coercion (e.g., slaps, holds, shoves) during the interaction, and so on. Under most circumstances, it can be reasonably assumed that if a parent-child dyad exhibits a pattern of interaction during the course of the observational paradigm, then this is a stable representation of the behavioral expectations of the relationship on the part of the child and/or parent. Taking this effort one step further, children who are placed in foster care often have a limited and maladaptive model for involvement in a parent-child relationship. For example, research has reported that physically abused children commonly have behavioral problems—including aggression and defiance (see Kolko, 1992, for an excellent review of the behavioral characteristics of physically abused children). When they are removed from a physically abusive parent-child relationship in which they were aggressive and defiant, then placed in a foster home, it is likely that they will use the only parent-child model they have experienced and understand. As a result, physically maltreated children enter foster care with a predetermined set of problem behaviors—originating from their involvement in a coercive and hostile relationship with an abusive parent. Often, through the use of an observational paradigm with a maltreated child and a foster parent, it is possible to observe the child's parent-directed strategies when engaged with a foster parent.

However, the use of formal observational paradigms is not without its limitations. Observational data is susceptible to situational variations that may bias or alter "typical" behavior of the parent and/or child. These variations can include current health status (e.g., being sick or not feeling well), problems in other areas of life, decreased mood as a result of placement of a child in foster care, and so on. Additionally, it is important for the parent to have had relatively recent ongoing contact or visitation. A prolonged period of no contact between the parent and child may alter the typical pattern of the interaction between parent and child. If there has been a period of no contact between the parent and child, it may be important to arrange for a few visits before attempting a formal observation (although it should be recognized that certain case management safeguards prevent parent-child visits from occurring).

CLINICAL INTERVIEWS

Points of Consideration

It is strongly recommended that several important considerations be assessed in the process of conducting clinical interviews. Some considerations include the number of interview sessions to hold, who should (or should not) be present during interviews, and the degree of structure in conducting the interviews.

Multiple Interviews

Generally, it is best to conduct multiple interviews during the course of an evaluation. There are several practical reasons for using a multiple interview strategy. First, a comprehensive evaluation requires that the evaluator acquire a large amount of information about the parent, child, and family. It is often necessary to acquire specific information about events that may affect the case, including family constellation and history (e.g., number of children, family medical and mental health history) and other historical information (e.g., graduation from high school, work history). Practically, it is difficult to acquire all of the information necessary in a single interview session. In addition, having multiple interviews allows an opportunity to vary the family members being interviewed and conduct a more in-depth interview on critical topics. A multiple-interview format allows the evaluator to assess parents and children over several sessions. It may be possible for parents or children to present themselves in an artificially positive light during a single clinical interview, but not to sustain this positive façade over time. Conversely, situational factors may result in a child or parent being distracted or anxious during an interview. Relying on multiple interviews allows the evaluator to avoid making clinical decisions or judgments related to situational factors, thus increasing the validity of the information acquired.

Conducting multiple interviews allows the evaluator to directly address with the parent or child any discrepancies the evaluator has noticed since the first interview. For example, if a parent declares during an initial interview that he has successfully completed a residential drug treatment program, an information release can be acquired and the drug treatment program can be contacted to assess progress in the program, relapse risk, and verify completion. Should the drug treatment program state that the individual failed to complete the program, a subsequent clinical interview can be used to specifically address this discrepancy and reassess issues related to substance abuse.

Individual, Joint, and Family Interviews

Many mental health professionals prefer not to interview parents about child and family matters while the child is present. One argument for this is that there are certain topics that are not appropriate for the child to know, the child may not understand, and for which the child may not have any substantive information to contribute (e.g., parental sexual history, mental health problems of other family members, occupational or financial concerns). In addition, some children may possess a level of behavioral disruption (e.g., impulsivity, short attention span, aggression) and/or psychopathology (e.g., autism, severe mental retardation) that prevents them from participating in the clinical interview and may impede the evaluator's efforts to acquire information.

A third concern about joint or family interviews is that if parents present information about problems they perceive or experience with the child, then this would reinforce the child's position as the "problem child," identified patient, or source of the problems. This is a reasonable and likely to be accurate representation of many families. However, this concern may reflect a limited view of family relationships. If a parent provides a negative opinion of the child during a clinical interview (e.g., "This is all her fault. She never listens to me. Never, never, never!"), then this is likely an opinion that has been heard many times previously by the child. Although it may be true that another negative representation by the parent could be emotionally harmful to the child, structuring interviews with the parent and child apart impairs the ability of the evaluator to observe a much more valuable source of information—the interchange between the parent and child. Clinical interviewing with the parent and child together enables the evaluator to acquire information about the parent's perception of the child (and perception of the relationship with the child, as well as the parents' perception of their contribution to presenting problems), the child's perception of family problems, and each individual's responses to the presentation by another family member. In this way, families not only provide an opinion of family members, problems, and symptoms, but also may engage these problems in the process. An example of the benefits of a family interview is the following clinical interview with four family members: biological mother, stepfather, fifteen-year-old daughter recently placed in an inpatient psychiatric facility because of a serious suicide attempt (Amy), and ten-year-old daughter (Beth).

EVALUATOR: Could someone explain to me why Amy is no longer living in your home?

(Amy scoots back in her chair, folds her arms across her chest with a sullen facial expression.)

MOTHER: Well, I guess I could start.

FATHER: Yes, my wife is the one who takes care of the children most of the time. I guess it would be best if she said what happened.

MOTHER: Last week I came home from work and . . .

FATHER: I drive a truck. I'm gone most of the time during the week. I'm mostly only home on weekends.

MOTHER: Yes, my husband's a truck driver, so I take care of the girls most of the time.

FATHER: Sometimes I drive a long haul, so then I'm even gone on the weekends.

MOTHER: Well, occasionally Beth has a Junior Miss beauty pageant.

FATHER: When that happens, we have Amy stay at my mother's house and my wife and I go to the beauty pageant together. My mother lives just across the street, so it's no problem for Amy to stay there. No problem with school or nothing.

MOTHER: Beth has done very well at several beauty pageants. Would you like to see some pictures? (Before the evaluator can respond, the mother has produced several photographs of Beth at beauty pageants with trophies.)

EVALUATOR: (Reviews the photographs presented) Yes, these are very nice pictures. But I would like to get back to the question I asked earlier. I understand that Amy is no longer living at home and was wondering if someone could explain to me what happened?

During this interaction, neither parent was willing to respond or comfortable with the issue of Amy's psychiatric hospitalization or recent serious suicide attempt. Amy had withdrawn to a corner of the interview room, appeared angry, and resisted talking. The focus of the parents' attention was their younger daughter (which was one of the reasons for Amy's problems). With the second effort by the evaluator to readdress the question, the parents again failed to respond to Amy's psychiatric hospitalization or her suicide attempt. When their apparent avoidance of Amy's problems were directly raised by the evaluator, Amy became very angry and an argument ensued between the mother and Amy. The focus of the argument was Amy's perception that her parents preferred Beth and that the mother was not listening to Amy's allegations of sexually inappropriate touching by her father. Conversely, the mother complained that Amy was unruly, was involved with drugs, and had been caught lying many times (she perceived the allegations of inappropriate sexual behavior as additional lies by Amy).

Finally, there may be important information that a parent or child may feel uncomfortable (or unsafe) in disclosing in the presence of another family member. For example, a spouse may be unwilling (or unsafe) to discuss the marital relationship in front of an abusive or easily angered partner. Similarly, children may feel more comfortable discussing sensitive or highly personal issues without the presence of their parents (e.g., describing details of past abusive events, providing an opinion about reunification, describing concerns they may have about their safety).

Therefore, although it may be necessary to conduct interviews with the parent or child individually, it is also strongly recommended that conjoint or family interviews also be conducted. The benefit of these interviews is that not only can the interview be used to acquire information from parent and child, but the evaluator can observe interactions between family members while addressing important family problems.

Structured versus Unstructured Interviews

In conducting the clinical interview, an evaluator may often find that specific information is needed (thus requiring specific questions), while also wanting the parent and child to provide information in their own words. This may simply be an issue of asking open-ended versus specific questions. However, it may reflect a more complex approach to conducting clinical interviews. For certain categories of inquiry, specific questions are appropriate and the most expedient means to acquire information. For example, asking questions about specific symptoms is necessary to confirm a diagnosis of depression (e.g., How long does it take you to get to sleep at night? Has your appetite changed recently? Do you often feel down, moody, or sad?). Unfortunately, the process of asking specific question directs the parent or child to respond in a specific manner and may inhibit providing richer clinical information. A less structured clinical interviewing style allows the parent or child to be more comfortable, relaxed, and free to disclose information on a broad range of topics. Some of these topics (or the manner in which they are disclosed) become an important source of information for the evaluator. Furthermore, the evaluator can use information provided by the client to follow up with additional questions and explore previously unknown areas of inquiry. In addition, a less structured interviewing style allows greater opportunity for the client to act in a manner that is more consistent with their typical behavior, rather than adopting a position of only answering questions.

A benefit of structured interviews is that they provide a systematic and comprehensive means to address domains of functioning. For example, during the last ten years there have been substantial improvements in structured diagnostic interviews for both adults and children. These interviews often parallel the DSM-IV-TR (American Psychiatric Association, 1994) in providing specific questions that aid in the determination of a specific mental health diagnosis. For children, there are many excellent structured diagnostic interviews, including the Schedule for Affective Disorders and Schizophrenia for School-Age Children (K-SADS) (Ambrosini & Dixon, 1996), Diagnostic Interview for Children and Adolescents–Revised (DICA-R) (Reich, 1996), and Diagnostic Interview Schedule for Children (DISC-IV) (Shaffer, 1996). Similarly, several excellent structured diagnostic interviews have been developed for adults, including the Schedule for Affective Disorders and Schizophrenia (SADS) (Endicott & Spitzer, 1978), Structured Clinical Interview for the DSM-III (SCID) (Spitzer, Williams, & Gibbon, 1987), and Diagnostic Interview Schedule (DIS) (Robins, Helzer, Cotler, & Goldring, 1989).

It is not necessary to learn how to administer all of these structured clinical interviews. However, it is suggested that understanding the process of administering a systematic diagnostic interview will enable greater reliability and validity in diagnosing than relying solely on clinical judgment. At times, it may be necessary to administer one of these structured diagnostic interviews to acquire a complete diagnostic impression of the client. However, more informally, a thorough knowledge of psychiatric diagnoses and the questions needed to confirm or rule out a diagnosis (which can be gleaned from these interview measures) may be sufficient when determination of a specific diagnosis is needed.

Collateral Contacts

Although it is always important to acquire information directly from parents and children who are being evaluated, it may also be necessary to acquire information from people with whom they have past associations. There are many benefits from interviewing collateral contacts, including acquiring a different (hopefully unbiased) perspective, assessing responses and results from prior intervention efforts, verifying information provided by clients during clinical interviews, and exploring discrepancies in information provided by the client.

Acquiring Additional Information

In conducting an evaluation, it is best to rely on multiple sources of information before making any determinations. Relying on only one source increases the risk that the evaluator's opinions will based on biased and/or distorted information. Also, it may be necessary to acquire information from many sources to assess multiple domains and problems in a client's life. This may require conducting clinical interviews with individuals such as the following:

- School personnel (current and former schoolteachers, teacher's aides, school counselors)
- Mental health providers (current and past therapists, psychiatrists, prior evaluators)
- Social service personnel (social workers, transporters, visit supervisors)
- Extended family members (extended kin caregivers, siblings, stepparents, former spouses)
- Medical personnel (family practitioners, medical specialists)
- Caregivers (previous foster parents, daycare providers, babysitters)

Assessing Progress in Prior Intervention Efforts

It is common for individuals participating in a psychological evaluation to have prior experience with mental health services. As a frequent referral question may include an individual's response to treatment, contacting prior treatment providers may be beneficial in addressing this type of question. Whenever you contact a therapist, it is important to provide information about the reason for the evaluation and a description of the type of information that you are seeking. When contacting a therapist, determine some baseline information about clients and their involvement in treatment (e.g., How long have they been in treatment? What is the primary type of treatment provided? What is the frequency of services? Did clients attend sessions regularly? How many total sessions did they attend?). It is also often helpful to begin the interview with a description of the treatment objectives agreed upon by the client and the mental health provider. After a period of initial assessment, all treatment should have clearly stated goals or objectives that have been reviewed and agreed upon with the client. Therapists who state that they do not have any treatment objectives may be limited in their effectiveness and may do a disservice to their client. For example, a client who is referred to treatment for issues related to anger management should have appropriate treatment objectives (e.g., to be able to express unpleasant emotions without physical aggression; to engage a plan of relaxation, and to verbally mediate emotions in stressful situations). If a therapist reports that the client has successfully completed treatment but cannot describe specific treatment objectives or a method of assessing completion of these objectives, then this raises serious questions about any benefits the client may have received from treatment. Further, it is important to assess any resistance to treatment and how this resistance was overcome. In addition, it is often important to inquire about the therapist's conceptualization of the client's problems. Although there may be many differing theoretical conceptualizations about the client's problems, it is essential that the therapist be able to articulate at least one theoretical orientation that provides an explanation regarding the client's presenting problem and process in treatment. As the therapist is likely to have been involved with the client longer than the evaluator, the therapist should have an opinion related to the evaluation referral question that could be valuable (e.g., Is the parent able to safely care for their young child? Should visitation between parent and child be extended? Is it appropriate to initiate a trial reunification placement?). Although some therapists prefer to avoid such questions, for fear that this may impair the therapeutic relationship with the client, if therapists are willing to answer such a question they should be able to provide a rationale for their opinion.

Verifying Information

It is typical during the course of a psychological evaluation that clients may distort, omit, and/or even lie about events to tilt an evaluation in their favor. This may include omitting relevant negative information (e.g., past incarcerations, continued substance abuse) or distorting accomplishments (e.g., regularly attending Alcoholics Anonymous meetings, parents describing wonderfully positive visits with their children). One way to address this client-report bias is to interview additional individuals (i.e., collateral contacts) who can provide supplemental information. Whenever contacting a collateral informant, it is especially important to consider (and if possible, assess) the truthfulness of the informant. Although there should always be concern that an informant's perspective may be biased or distorted (both positively and negatively), evaluators should be cautious of informants (e.g., friends, ex-spouses) who may purposefully misrepresent information.

Exploring Discrepancies in Reports

During the course of the evaluation, it is likely that the evaluator will acquire inconsistent information. A client may provide information that is not consistent with written social services reports; a child may describe household activities that differ substantially from a parent's description; teachers may provide information about a child's attendance which is different that that of the parent. In some cases this may reflect a minor distortion in perspective and not result in any questioning of the client (e.g., a parent may say the child is a "good student" whereas a teacher may identify this same student as having many academic problems in the classroom). However, the evaluator should be alert to more substantive discrepancies, which are not easily explained by differences in opinion or different perspectives. The most appropriate means to deal with these discrepancies is to address them directly with the client, explaining the information provided by the collateral contact and asking if the client has an explanation. For example:

During an initial clinical interview, a mother was asked, "Have you ever had any problems with any type of substance abuse?" She responded that she had never had any such problems. When the evaluator discussed this with the referring social worker, it was learned that the parent had a long-standing alcohol problem, that she had been arrested three times for driving under the influence of alcohol, and that her driver's license had been suspended. The evaluator asked for a copy of the police reports and an arrest record (verifying the accuracy of this information and providing dates of the incidents). When the parent was interviewed again, she was again asked if she had ever had any problems with substance abuse. She again denied any such problems. When the evaluator presented copies of the police reports and arrest records to the parent, the parent became upset. When asked to explain this discrepancy, she said that she had forgotten these events. The evaluator then suggested that it would be difficult to forget three such serious incidents, especially one incident that resulted in the parent having to go to court and losing her license. In response, the parent asserted that she did not want to talk about this issue any further. Although it is possible that the parent genuinely forgot these incidents, it is much more likely that she was unwilling to disclose negative information and may have believed that she could proceed through the evaluation without this information coming to light. In this situation, the parent's likely denial (i.e., lie) of her substance abuse history not only highlights a serious problem, but it also raises questions about her willingness to be truthful in the rest of the evaluation.

CASE CONCEPTUALIZATION AND RECOMMENDATIONS

Conceptualizing Cases

It is generally most appropriate to respond directly to the referral questions presented at the beginning of the evaluation. Although you may include additional comments, opinions, and recommendations, the case was referred for an evaluation because of a specific referral question. Therefore, it is suggested that it is essential to develop the conceptualization of the case in a manner that directly responds to the primary referral question. Although there may be additional issues the evaluator may wish to address, failure to adequately respond directly to the referral question may do disservice to the client.

Often, during the course of the evaluation, the evaluator may need information to serve as a foundation for addressing the referral question. For example, a case referred to address issues related to an individual's ability to safely and adequate parent a child raises many clinical issues that need to be addressed before specifically commenting on the referral question. Although it is important to examine parents in relation to their parenting ability, it is also necessary to examine their current mental health status (e.g., psychopathology, substance use, benefit from treatment). Further, it may also be necessary to describe the current functioning of children. Children with relatively few emotional or behavioral problems are easier to parent than children who are aggressive, defiant, and noncompliant. Therefore, an issue related to parenting must incorporate the child's functioning. As a result, a common foundation for addressing the referral question is to provide a description of the current psychological and social functioning of all pertinent parties directly related to the referral question. This is usually parents and/or children, but may also incorporate stepsiblings, stepparents, and so forth.

The description of current psychological and social functioning should include direct references to standardized assessments, observations made during the course of the clinical interviews, and information acquired from collateral contacts and social service records. These forms of data should be used to develop a framework or description of the individual's functioning—which will be the source of information for the referral question. For example, if the referral question involves determining whether a child has a psychiatric diagnosis, then during the course of the evaluation the evaluator should acquire broad information about the child's mental health symptoms. In the description of current psychological and social functioning, the evaluator might provide information about past life events (e.g., traumatic experiences), responses to psychological tests (e.g., elevated scores on a trauma symptom checklist), and reports of current mental health symptoms (e.g., nightmares, hypervigilance) to make a determination that the child meets diagnostic criteria for post-traumatic stress disorder. All of the information to support this diagnostic determination would be incorporated within the body of the report and summarized in the section describing the child's current psychological and social functioning.

The evaluator's use of current psychological and social functioning for the pertinent participants in the evaluation becomes the foundation by which the referral questions are directly addressed. One of the important aspects of responding to the referral question is to ensure that there is specific information (or evidence) to support any opinions. Regardless of any belief, inference, or intuition held by the evaluator, it is essential to have supporting documentation for opinions. For example, providing a diagnosis of depression in the absence of evidence of depression would be misleading and inaccurate. In addition, sometimes the evaluator may have an opinion and some information to support this opinion, but may also possess data that do not fit into this perspective. In such cases, it is important to include this discrepant information and attempt to provide a rationale for it (e.g., why a therapist would have a diagnosis that is different from that of the evaluator).

Ultimately, opinions provided by the psychologist should be framed within a theoretical foundation, grounded in a combination of facts from the case and supportable assertions, and contribute to the reader's (e.g., social worker, attorney, judge) greater understanding of the case. It is insufficient to simply restate information accrued from social service reports or to tabulate scores from standardized testing. The value of a psychological evaluation is that its total is greater than the sum of its parts. That is, the evaluator is able to acquire and compile information in a manner that makes new meaning for the reader and assists the reader to make decisions about a case and to manage it.

Recommendations

One common product of a psychological evaluation is a recommendation (or set of recommendations) about the client or the management of the case. In many instances, this is one of the more important components of the evaluation because it provides the referring parties information about what should occur next. Two issues are essential in providing valuable recommendations. First, all recommendations should be supported by information acquired during the evaluation, summarized and conceptualized within the report, and should lead the referring party to a clear and precise understanding of the next steps to take regarding the case. Second, all recommendations should be as specific possible. It is insufficient to simply assert that individual therapy is indicated. Evaluators should provide guidance on the implementation of interventions, plans, and procedures based on their current understanding of the case. This means that recommendations provide clarity on issues such as these:

Treatment	Type of treatment/intervention needed
	Specific treatment goals/objectives
	Frequency of sessions and estimated duration of treatment
	Who should be involved in treatment sessions
	Suggested theoretical foundations for treatment
Placement	Description of placement initiation plan
	Concerns and protocols for problems with placement
	Establishment of concurrent therapeutic involvement
Visitation	Frequency and duration of visitations
	Presence of a visit supervisor
	Who the supervisor should be
	Responses to problem contacts or visits

After expending a substantial amount of time, resources, and effort to provide a comprehensive and objective psychological evaluation of a child and/or parent, it is important that evaluators be able to articulate clearly their understanding of each case and how it should be managed. One of the best methods by which evaluators can advocate for the appropriate use of their evaluation is to be as specific as possible within the framework of recommendations.

APPENDIX: PSYCHOLOGICAL TESTS AND MEASURES

Child Tests

Behavior Assessment System for Children

The Behavior Assessment System for Children (Reynolds & Kamphaus, 1992) is an integrated system designed to facilitate the differential diagnosis and classification of a variety of emotional and behavioral disorders of children and to aid in the design of a treatment plan. Any score in the clinically significant range suggests a high level of maladjustment. Scores in the at-risk range identify either a significant problem that may not be severe enough to require formal treatment or a potential problem that needs careful monitoring.

Child Behavior Checklist/Teacher Report and Parent Report

The CBCL-Parent Report and Teacher Report Forms are standardized instruments that list 113 problem behaviors that children between the ages of two to eighteen may exhibit. The two versions are completed by a parent or by a teacher. Separate norms are provided for boys and girls in four age groups (two to three, four to five, six to eleven, and twelve to sixteen years). The CBCL includes two broad-band scales (internalizing) and a range of narrow-band scales for each age group and sex (e.g., Depressed, Somatic Complaints, Hyperactive, Aggressive, etc.). In addition, the CBCL-Parent provides a social competence score.

Children's Depression Inventory

The Children's Depression Inventory is a twenty-seven-item self-rated symptom-oriented scale normed for children ages seven to seventeen years. Each CDI item consists of three choices with higher scores indicating capacity, vegetative functions, self-evaluation, and interpersonal behaviors.

Eyberg Child Behavior Inventory

The ECBI (Eyberg & Pincus, 2000) measures behavioral problems exhibited by children ages two to sixteen years. Parents indicate the frequency of behaviors (intensity score) and whether they are considered to be problematic (problem score). The published cutoff scores for child deviancy are an intensity score of greater than 127 or a problem score of greater than 11.

Peabody Picture Vocabulary Test–Revised

The PPVT-R is an individually administered, norm-referenced, wide-range power test of hearing vocabulary. Norms and age-equivalent scores are provided for individuals from thirty months through forty years.

Sutter-Eyberg Student Behavior Inventory

The SESBI (Eyberg & Pincus, 2000) is a thirty-six-item teacher report inventory of classroom conduct problem behaviors. Teachers indicated how often each behavior currently occurs, yielding the intensity score, and also whether the behavior is currently a problem, yielding a problem score.

Trauma Symptom Checklist for Children

The Trauma Symptom Checklist for Children (Briere, 1996) is a fifty-four-item self-report symptom inventory designed to assess current psychological symptom patterns. Each item is a brief description of a psychological symptom which is rated on a three-point scale (0 = never to almost all the time = 3). Scales on the TSC-C include: Anxiety, Dissociation, Depression, Dissociation (Overt), anger, Dissociation (Fantasy), Posttraumatic Stress, Sexual Concerns, Sexual Preoccupation, Sexual Distress.

Wechsler Intelligence Test Series

The Wechsler test series provides a means for intellectual assessment of children and adults. These tests include the Wechsler Primary Preschool Scale of Intelligence (approximately three to six years), Wechsler Intelligence Scale for Children–III (approximately six to sixteen years), and the Wechsler Adult Intelligence Scale (approximately fifteen years and older) (Wechsler, 1991). All of the Wechsler series intelligence tests provide information about intellectual ability in two broad band scores (Verbal Intelligence Quotient, VIQ, and Performance Intelligence Quotient, PIQ), as well as a total IQ score (Full Scale Intelligence Quotient, FSIQ).

The Verbal subtests measure how well an individual can think and solve problems with words. Information is a measure of general information/facts, whereas Similarities is a measure of verbal abstract concepts, classifying and categorizing concepts. Vocabulary is an indication of an individual's language development and learning ability while Comprehension is a measure of commonsense judgment and social awareness. Arithmetic and

Digit Span is a measure of concentration or sustained attention and short-term auditory memory.

The Performance subtests measure how an individual can think and solve problems using objects, such as blocks and puzzles. Picture Completion is a measure of perceptual and conceptual visual recognition or understanding of what one sees while Picture Arrangement measures visual sequencing and social functioning. Block Design is a measure of problem solving utilizing perceptual analysis and synthesis or patterning while Object Assembly measures organizational skills and relating parts to a whole.

Adult Tests

Beck Depression Scale Inventory

The Beck Depression Scale Inventory is used to assess a client's current level of depression. The inventory has twenty-one items, each of them being a different aspect and/or diagnostic criterion of depression. These items are inclusive or vegetative (e.g., sleep disorders, appetite disruptions, weight fluctuations) and other clinical signs of depression (e.g., feelings of sadness, helplessness, apathy, anhedonia, indecisiveness, and low self-esteem). The twenty-one items are summed up and the subject is said to be not depressed or to be mildly, moderately, or severely depressed.

Marital Stress Inventory

The Marital Stress Inventory is a standardized self-report measure of marital interaction. This instrument is capable of identifying specific sources of conflict across a broad spectrum of marital interaction. There are eleven scales of the MSI, including one validity scale, one global affective scale, and nine additional scales measuring specific dimensions of marital interaction. Except for the validity and role-orientation scales, all scales are scored in the direction of discontent so that high scores indicate high levels of dissatisfaction with the specific area. The eleven MSI scales are as follows: Conventionalization, Global Distress, Affective Communication, Problem-Solving Communication, Time Together, Disagreement About Finances, Sexual Dissatisfaction, Role Orientation, Family History of Distress, Dissatisfaction with Children, and Conflict over Childrearing.

Millon Clinical Multiaxial Inventory–III

The Millon Clinical Multiaxial Inventory–III (MCMI-III) (Millon, 1994) provides a measure of an individual's personality style. The instrument is a

175 item, true/false self-report psychological inventory. The MCMI-III contains scales clustered into four groups that measure personality style, severe personality patterns, clinical syndromes, and severe syndromes.

Minnesota Multiphasic Personality Inventory–2

The Minnesota Multiphasic Personality Inventory–2 (MMPI-2) (Grahma, 1990) is a standardized measure of adult personality characteristics. It possesses several validity scales and several clinical scales which reflect dimensions of an individual's character. The primary clinical scales include: Hypochondriasis, Depression, Conversion Hysteria, Psychopathic Deviate, Masculinity/Femininity, Paranoia, Psychasthenia, Schizophrenia, Hypomania, Social Introversion. Typically, interpretation of the MMPI-2 involves examining the elevated clinical scales and combinations of scale elevations. In addition, many supplemental scales have been developed by clinical researchers.

Minnesota Multiphasic Personality Inventory–Adolescent

Similar to the Minnesota Multiphasic Personality Inventory–II, the Minnesota Multiphasic Personality Inventory–Adolescent is a standardized measure of adolescent personality characteristics. It possesses validity scales and several clinical scales which reflect dimensions of an individual's character.

Personality Assessment Inventory

The Personality Assessment Inventory (PAI) (Morey, 1991) is a well-standardized measure of adult personality. It possesses four validity scales (Inconsistency, Infrequency, Negative Impression, Positive Impression), eleven clinical scales (Somatic Complaints, Anxiety, Anxiety-Related Disorders, Depression, Mania, Paranoia, Schizophrenia, Borderline Features, Antisocial Features, Alcohol Problems, Drug Problems), five treatment scales (Aggression, Suicidal Ideation, Stress, Nonsupport, Treatment Rejection), and two interpersonal scales (Dominance, Warmth).

Substance Abuse Subtle Screening Inventory

The Substance Abuse Subtle Screening Inventory (Miller, 1988) is a paper-and-pencil questionnaire with two main scales, Face Valid Alcohol

(FVA). The higher the score on either scale, the more the clients are acknowledging use, consequences of use, and/or loss of control.

Symptom Checklist–90 Revised

The SCL-90-R is a ninety-item self-report symptom inventory designed to assess current psychological symptom patterns. Each item is a brief description of a psychological symptom which is rated on a five-point scale (0 = no discomfort to 4 = extreme discomfort). The SCL-90-R derives nine symptom subscales: Somatization, Obsessive-Compulsive, Interpersonal Sensitivity, Depression, Anxiety, Hostility, Phobic Anxiety, Paranoid Ideation, and Psychoticism. In addition, there are three indices of general distress: Global Severity Index, Positive Symptom Distress Index, and Positive Symptom Total.

Parenting-Related Tests

Child Abuse Potential Inventory

The Child Abuse Potential Inventory (Milner, 1986) is a standardized measure of an adult's potential to physically abuse a child. In addition, it provides a validity scale and factor scores on several aspects of parent functioning (e.g., distress, rigidity, unhappiness) and parent-child relations (e.g., parent-child problems, problems with family members, problems with others). The CAPI abuse scale is employed in conjunction with evaluation data from additional sources such as an interview, a case history, direct observations, or other test data.

Parenting Stress Index

The Parenting Stress Index (Abidin, 1990) is a standardized measure designed to identify parent-child dyads who are experiencing stress or may be at risk to develop dysfunctional parenting and child behavioral problems. The index consists of thirteen subscales grouped into a Child Domain (i.e., Adaptability, Acceptability, Attachment, Restrictions of Role, Sense of Competence, Social Isolation, Relationship with Spouse, and Parent Health), a Life Stress Scale, and a Total Stress Scale. The normal range is between the fifteenth and eightieth percentile rank, with the higher percentile reflecting a high degrees of stress. The total stress score is assumed to be of primary importance in guiding professional judgments as to whether professional intervention might be necessary or appropriate for a given parent-child system.

Other Tests

Kaufman Brief Intelligence Test

The K-BIT is a brief measure of intellectual ability. It can be administered to people between the ages of thirty-six months and ninety years. The K-BIT is composed of two parts: a Vocabulary subtest (indicative of crystallized thinking) and a Matrices subtest (indicative of fluid thinking). In addition, there is an overall score, a K-BIT IQ Composite score.

Vineland Adaptive Behavior Scales

The Vineland Adaptive Behavior Scales (VABS) assesses the personal and social sufficiency of an individual. The areas of communication, daily living skills, and socialization are measured.

Wide Range Achievement Test–Revision 3

The Wide Range Achievement Test–Revision 3 (WRAT) is designed to assess academic achievement. Reading is a measure of an individual's ability to recognize letters and decode words. Spelling is a measure of an individual's ability to write letters dictated to him or her, write letters representing beginning sounds, and spell words. Arithmetic is a measure of the individual's ability to solve pencil-and-paper mathematical calculations and to write numbers.

Woodcock-Johnson Psycho-Educational Battery

The Woodcock-Johnson Psycho-Educational Battery is a comprehensive, individually administered set of twenty-seven tests that assesses three areas of functioning: cognitive ability, achievement, and interest. The tests of cognitive ability in Part I are composed of twelve subtests that cover vocabulary, spatial relations, memory, quantitative concepts, and concept formation. The tests of achievement in Part II cover ten achievement areas, including reading, spelling, capitalization, punctuation, and knowledge of science, humanities, and social studies. The tests of interest level in Part III cover interest in five areas: reading, mathematics, language, physical activities, and social activities.

A Few Notes on Understanding Standardized Tests and Assessment Measures

In developing psychological tests, test developers acquire a probability sample from a broad range of individuals with varying demographic characteristics (age, gender, ethnicity). Many test developers limit these demographic characteristics in order to be able to provide more accurate information about the index group (e.g., the MMPI-II omits children under the age of eighteen years, to provide more accurate information about adults). Some test developers provide specific norms which are referenced by subgroup (e.g., the Child Behavior Checklist provides separate norms for boys and girls, and separate norms for children of different ages).

Most standardized tests utilize a normal distribution to provide information about where a specific individual performs in relation to the normative sample. Theoretically, on most tests, most individuals fall close to the mean (68 percent are within one standard deviation of the mean; 95 percent are within two standard deviations of the mean), with the number of individuals decreasing with greater distance from the mean.

The T Distribution

Most psychological tests use a *T* score to aid in description of where an individual scores in relation to the sample distribution. In a *T* distribution, a score of 50 is the mean, with ten points for each standard deviation (a *T* score of 60 is one standard deviation above the mean; a *T* score of 40 is one standard deviation below the mean). Many psychological tests somewhat arbitrarily use a *T* score of 65 as indicating clinical significance (a *T* score of 65 is 1.5 standard deviations above the mean). This means that an individual who achieves a score of 67 is in the clinically significant range, whereas if they achieve a score of 55, they are in a normal range.

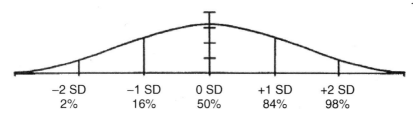

Standard Deviations
and Their Relationship
to Percentile Ranks

Standard Scores

Most intelligence tests utilize standard scores (which are based on a z score—you don't want to go there) with a mean of 100 and a standard deviation of 15. For example, the Wechsler intelligence tests provide an intelligence quotient (an IQ score). This is a value which has a mean of 100:

Standard Score	Percentile	Description
69 and below	1%	Mentally impaired
70-79	2-8%	Borderline intelligence
80-89	9-24%	Low average
90-109	25-74%	Average
110-119	75-90%	High average
120-129	91-97%	Superior
130 and above	98%	Very superior (gifted)

Percentile Scores

This is a distribution figure that provides information about where an individual's score is in relation to other individuals in the sample. For example, an individual receiving a percentile score of 50 would score above half of the individuals and below half of the individuals in the sample. Additionally, a percentile score of 95 would mean that 95 percent of the individuals in this sample score less than this individual (with 5 percent of individuals scoring above this individual).

Reading Ability

Most test developers provide information about the minimum level of reading ability necessary to read and comprehend each test item. If there is a concern about the client's reading ability (e.g., expresses difficulty reading, failed to graduate from high school), it may be necessary to administer and score a brief reading test to ensure that the client is able to read and comprehend test terms.

Test Format

Many psychological tests are developed in a multiple-choice format (e.g., yes/no, true/false; slightly/occasionally/often/rarely/never). This format can occasionally be confusing for clients, especially clients with limited reading ability, with below average intelligence, and who may not be fluent in English. It is often valuable for the test administrator to inquire if any of the questions were confusing or did not make sense.

Clinical Cutoff Scores

Although many test developers provide information about clinical cutoff scores, it is important to recognize that these are not dichotomous scales. Most scales represent a level of severity of a problem, rather than simply the presence or absence of a problem. For example, if the clinical cutoff score for a depression scale is a *T* score of 65 (1.5 standard deviations above the mean), this may be a good indicator that the individual has problems with depression. However, an individual who has a score of 64 and is below the clinical cutoff score may still have significant problems with depression. It is important to understand that the individual with a *T* score of 64 and a *T* score of 65, may have a similar pattern and severity of depressive symptoms—except one is above the clinical cutoff score and one is below the clinical cutoff score.

REFERENCES

Abidin, R.R. (1990). *Parenting Stress Index manual* (3rd ed.). Charlottesville, VA: Pediatric Psychology Press.

Ambrosini, P. & Dixon, J.F. (1996). *Schedule for Affective Disorders and Schizophrenia for School-Age Children (K-SADS)*. Philadelphia: Allegheny University of the Health Sciences.

American Academy of Child and Adolescent Psychiatry (1997). Practice parameters for the forensic evaluation of children and adolescents who may have been physically or sexually abused. *Journal of the American Academy of Child and Adolescent Psychiatry, 36,* 423-442.

American Professional Society on the Abuse of Children (1996). *Guidelines for psychosocial evaluation of suspected sexual abuse in children.* Chicago: American Professional Society on the Abuse of Children.

American Psychiatric Association (2000). *Diagnostic and statistical manual of mental disorders* (4th ed., text revision). Washington, DC: American Psychiatric Press.

American Psychological Association (1992). *Ethical principles of psychologists and code of conduct.* Washington, DC: American Psychological Association.

American Psychological Association (1998). *Guidelines for psychological evaluations in child protection matters.* Washington, DC: American Psychological Association.

Boardman, W.K. (1962). Rusty: A brief behavior disorder. *Journal of Consulting Psychology, 26,* 293-297.

Briere, J. (1996). *Trauma Symptom Checklist for Children manual*. Odessa, FL: Psychological Assessment Resources.

Cormier, W.H. & Cormier, L.S. (1979). *Interviewing strategies for helpers: A guide to assessment, treatment, and evaluation*. Monterey, CA: Brooks/Cole.

Endicott, J. & Spitzer, R.L. (1978). A diagnostic interview: The schedule for affective disorders, and schizophrenia. *Archives of General Psychiatry, 35*, 837-844.

Eyberg, S. & Pincus, T. (2000). *Eyberg Child Behavior Inventory & Sutter-Eyberg Student Behavior Inventory—revised professional manual*. Odessa, FL: Psychological Assessment Resources.

Garrett, A.M. (1982). *Interviewing: Its principles and methods* (3rd ed.). New York: Family Service Association of America.

Graham, J.R. (1990). *MMPI-2—Assessing personality and psychopathology*. New York: Oxford University Press.

Groth-Marnat, G. (1999). *Handbook of psychological assessment* (3rd ed.). New York: John Wiley.

Kolko, D.J. (1992). Characteristics of child victims of physical violence: Research findings and clinical implications. *Journal of Interpersonal Violence, 7*(2), 244-276.

Mannarino, A.P. & Cohen, J.A. (2001). Treating sexually abused children and their families: Identifying and avoiding professional role conflicts. *Trauma, Violence, and Abuse, 2*(4), 331-342.

Maruish, M.E. (1999). *The use of psychological testing for treatment planning and outcomes assessment* (2nd ed.). Mahwah, NJ: Lawrence Erlbaum.

Melton, G.B., Petrila, J., Poythress, N.G., & Slobogoin, C. (1997). *Psychological evaluations for the courts: A handbook for mental health professionals and lawyers* (2nd ed.). New York: Guilford Press.

Meyers, J. (2001). Legal issues. In M. Weinsterstein and B. Scribner (Eds.) *Mental health care for child crime victims. California Standards of Care Task Force Guidelines* (pp. 1301-1452). Sacramento: California Victim Compensation and Government Claims Board.

Miller, G.A. (1988). *The Substance Abuse Subtle Screening Inventory manual*. Spencer, Indiana: Spencer Evening World.

Millon, T. (1994). *MCMI-III manual*. Minneapolis, MN: National Computer Systems.

Milner, J.S. (1986). *The Child Abuse Potential Inventory manual* (2nd ed.). Webster, NC: Psytec.

Morey, L.C. (1991). *Personality Assessment Inventory professional manual*. Odessa, FL: Psychological Assessment Resources.

Reich, W. (1996). *Diagnostic Interview for Children and Adolescents–Revised (DICA-R) 8.0*. St. Louis, MO: Washington University.

Reynolds, C.R. & Kamphaus, R.W. (1992). *Behavior Assessment System for Children manual*. Circle Pines, MN: American Guidance Service.

Roberts, M.W. (2001). Clinic observations of structured parent-child interaction designed to evaluate externalizing disorders. *Psychological Assessment, 13*(1), 46-58.

Robins, L.N., Helzer, J.E., Cotler, L.B., & Goldring, E. (1989). NIMH Diagnostic Interview Schedule, Version III–Revised. *Archives of General Psychiatry, 38,* 381-389.

Sattler, J.M. (1998). *Clinical and forensic interviewing of children and families: Guidelines for the mental health education, pediatrics, and child maltreatment fields.* San Diego, CA: Sattler Publications.

Shaffer, D. (1996). *Diagnostic Interview Schedule for Children (DISC-IV).* New York: New York Psychiatric Institute.

Spitzer, R.L., Williams, J.B., & Gibbon, M. (1987). *Structured Clinical Interview for the DSM-III (SCID).* New York: State Psychiatric Interview.

Terao, S.Y., Borrego, J., & Urquiza, A.J. (2000). How do I differentiate culturally based parenting practices from child maltreatment. In H. Dubowitz & D. DePanfilis (Eds.), *Handbook for child protection practice,* Thousand Oaks, CA: Sage.

Turner, S.M., DeMers, S.T., Fox, H.R., & Reed, G.M. (2002). APA's guidelines for test user qualifications: An executive summary. *American Psycholoogist, 56* (12), 1099-1113.

Wahler, R.G., Winkel, G.H., Peterson, R.F., & Morrison, D.C. (1965). Mothers as behavior therapist for their own children. *Behavior Research and Therapy, 3,* 113-124.

Wechsler, D. (1991). *Wechsler Intelligence Scale for Children manual* (3rd ed.). San Antonio, TX: Psychological Corporation.

PART III:
THERAPY FOR ABUSED
AND NEGLECTED CHILDREN

Chapter 6

Foundations of Clinical Work with Children: The Therapeutic Relationship

P. Forrest Talley
Michele Ornelas Knight

THE IMPORTANCE OF ONE

A young man walking along
the beach at dawn noticed an old man
ahead of him picking up starfish
and flinging them into the sea.
Catching up with the man the youth
asked what he was doing.
The answer was that the stranded starfish
would die if left until the morning sun.
"But the beach goes on for miles
and there are millions of starfish,"
countered the young man,
"How can your effort make a difference?"
The old man looked at the starfish in his hand
and then threw it to safety in the waves.
"It makes a difference to this one," he said.

Author unknown

INTRODUCTION

One of the principle tasks of childhood is to learn about the world. This learning runs the gamut from simple to complex, and from the superficial to the profound. How to stand, the meaning of the words a mother and father speak, how to respond to these words, how to feed oneself, what to expect when someone smiles, how to share, how to control feelings, where to go for comfort, how to tie a shoe, clean one's room . . . the list goes on. What

123

concerns us here is that learning which informs the child about the nature of relationships and oneself. Learning that is interpersonal. Following common sense, and the commonsense ideas of interpersonal theory (Sullivan, 1953; Carson, 1969; Wiggins, 2003; Benjamin, 1993), we recognize that it is within the earliest relationships of children that they come to know who they are, how others view them, and what to expect of others. Bowlby (1988) coined the term "internal working model" to describe these experiences stored in memory of the interactions between self and others. Children develop a view of themselves and the world through these interactions. Conclusions are written in children's minds as a result of the questions they ask and the responses of others. Most often these questions are posed unwittingly through some action a child has taken, and the caretaker's responses provide the answer. "Am I valued, worth taking care of?" "Is it all right to explore and be inquisitive?" "Will my mistakes meet with mild corrections or calamitous outrage?" "Do my thoughts and wishes make a difference to others?" "Does anyone care if I succeed?" "Do others think I can succeed?" "Can others be counted upon to help me when I'm hurt?" "Will they celebrate if I succeed?" The questions are endless and the classroom remains open twenty-four hours each day. School is never out when it comes to this type of teaching for the child, and the central teachers are the parents.

In healthy families, children receive answers that contribute to their successfully navigating the developmental hurdles. They develop a template of themselves as worthy and competent and one of others as responsive and safe. There are, of course, no perfect parents, but by and large the responses of most parents move children forward and promote healthy development. In children from abusive and neglectful homes the opposite occurs, leading to entrenched misperceptions and the encrusted defenses that children develop to protect the psychological wounds they have suffered. Often these children develop a perception of themselves as inferior, unworthy of love and protection. To cope with the abuse, they learn strategies to avoid or escape negative emotions, or they become overstimulated by the environment and have difficulty modulating their emotions.

There are many ways to help these children. One way is by helping them build better social skills or removing as many of the stressors that trigger maladaptive reactions as possible. As a counselor, you might focus on resolving the emotional trauma associated with past abuse.* Although the possible avenues for intervening are numerous, inherent within almost all of them is the need to establish a solid relationship with the child. Just as the

---

*Counselor and *therapist* are used interchangeably in this chapter, as are *counseling* and *therapy*.

lessons that created these problems originated from the crucible of early relationships, so too can they be remedied in large part by another relationship. The role of the counselor is to develop a relationship that is appropriately supportive of the therapeutic work taking place, while also challenging the child's distorted view of self and others. In the pages that follow we discuss some of the main components that comprise this sort of relationship: trust, affection, understanding, interest, and hope. We make no pretense of being exhaustive in the dimensions listed: certainly other qualities could be nominated for inclusion. Those mentioned, however, are what we have found to be most important and pervasive.

TRUST

Trust is an essential part of the therapeutic relationship. A child who is able to trust a counselor has developed a perception of stability: there is someone in the world to count on. In evaluating the place of trust, consider Erikson's (1950) stages of development. Children's first year is occupied with the building of trust before moving on to develop greater autonomy and exploring the world around them. Often children who have suffered abuse and neglect learn from infancy that the world is untrustworthy and consequently lack the secure foundation needed for later development. The therapeutic relationship serves to repair this disruption in earlier development. Just as stability is foundational for the growth of a healthy relationship in infancy, this perception by the child that the counselor is a trustworthy adult is also foundational to the therapeutic relationship. The child's trust of the counselor is also important in that it reflects a willingness to rely on and believe in another: vital parts of being human. These aspects, although human, are vulnerable steps for an abused child to take. Once taught, however, the child has learned that change is possible and has developed a newfound confidence in healthy perceptions of self and others.

Each of us daily interacts with others whom we have little need to trust, or at least to trust beyond the most superficial level. The superficiality of this trust is not an indictment of the person we are dealing with but is most often a result of the type of exchange we have with that person—the operator who gives us a telephone number, the store clerk who rings up our purchase, the parking lot attendant who points to an empty parking space. Some small measure of trust is involved in each of these exchanges, but it requires little of us to give, and certainly does not tax our capacity to rely on another. But the mountain climber who depends upon his partner's securing the rope above him, the soldier in the foxhole counting on his buddy who is standing watch, and the child who is unable to care for himself but knows his mother will feed and comfort him: all these are examples of trust that require great reliance and belief in another and go to the heart of human intimacy.

Lasting marriages, deep friendships, and mature parental love all rest on a bedrock of trust. Trust, however, is nuanced and if we are to make the most of this aspect of the therapeutic relationship, we need to have a better understanding of its different meanings. Looking at the Koine Greek translation of *trust,* we find at least three different meanings that are applicable to therapy. These are *empistosyni* (affiance, confidence), *pisti* (belief, loyalty, faith), and *empistevomai* (entrust). We briefly examine each and how they apply.

Empistosyni

This form of trust is captured by the idea of having confidence in someone. That is, the child with this type of trust believes in your ability, in your capacity, to be of help. To promote this belief, therapists must be sure not to unwittingly undermine their position of authority. Many therapists, in their efforts to reassure their patients that they are gentle and mean no harm, end up inadvertently making this error. "How so?" you ask. It begins by the initial approach to engaging the child. They become overly solicitous. Although it is very well and good to be patient, kind, and friendly, beware of the slide into solicitation. It is important for the counselor to recognize the difference between following a child's lead in therapy and being solicitous. There is a balance between providing the necessary therapeutic support and presenting as a person of authority through setting limits that promotes the child's safety and security in the relationship. Donovan and McIntyre (1990) give a good example of this difficulty arising in a somewhat different context. They describe a police officer who has been summoned to interview a child regarding physical abuse. To paraphrase from their example, the officer arrives with all the accoutrements of authority: police uniform, badge, firearm, and so forth. Smiling kindly and bending down eye to eye with Jimmy, we hear the following: "Hi, I'm Officer Brannon and I've come to talk with you about some of the things that have happened to you. Would it be okay if we talk for a little while?"

One of two things is likely to happen here. First, the child is likely to feel compelled to answer in the affirmative. This is a common reaction of children when asked this type of question by an adult. Consequently, Jimmy's initial compliance in no way reassures us that he will be forthcoming during the interview that follows. Second, the authority that the officer possessed when entering the room may dissipate as a result of his overly solicitous style. The child who was ambivalent about discussing the abuse becomes even more hesitant. He knows his father is larger than life and appears unstoppable. After all, he beats up anyone he likes within the home. Who can stand up to him? Surely not someone who has to ask for a little boy's permission to talk. Consequently, the child reasons, talking to the "nice" police officer carries lots of risk with little guarantee that the nice policeman will keep anyone safe.

Therapists frequently make the same mistake, and the building of confidence by their patients suffers. Consider how often you hear colleagues say "Let's go back to the playroom now, okay?" Or perhaps you find yourself telling a child it is time to end, but the session goes on another ten minutes because the child does not want to leave. Even more common is the counselor telling a child he or she will meet with the parent for just ten minutes, and then the counselor returns to fetch the child twenty minutes later. Being permissive undermines the child's sense of security. Avoid these struggles and increase the confidence *(empistosyni)* of the child by taking the stance of a benevolent dictator who has few rules, but the ones that do exist are clear and consistently enforced. These rules primarily focus on the beginning and ending of the session, limit setting, and the ability to introduce strategic interventions (i.e., to sometimes structure the play or conversation). Each is pursued in the interest of the child, not for the benefit of the therapist. Most often these demands are easily accepted by children and teach important lessons about adults who use control in a kind rather than harsh manner and encourage freedom without becoming neglectful.

Another aspect of building a child's confidence in you has to do with being reliable. If you are not reliable, it will be difficult for any patient to have confidence in your ability to help. Fortunately, being seen as reliable is a very simple thing to accomplish: start and end sessions on time, show up for the appointments every week, give plenty of notice and reminders to the child when you will be absent, give advance notice if you are to meet in a different play therapy room, and so forth.

Pisti

Loyalty and faith are at the heart of *pisti*. It is a term that is used to describe the compact of marriage, a pledge, or a solemn promise. *Pisti* is the trust that imbeds an allegiance to another and speaks to an oath of fidelity. Not all children will develop this profound sense of trust in you—if they do, you have achieved much in that this will be a new and remarkable experience for the abused and neglected child.

To encourage this form of trust, you want to let children know you will be their champion. Through thick or thin, you will stick by them and fight for them. You are on their side. Of course, difficulties with taking this stance are bound to arise inasmuch as children's best interests are not always what they wish to pursue. If you were to always strive to achieve what children want (i.e., their perspective of being on their side) you would invariably end up placing them in danger from time to time. In working with abused children, you will discover that their struggle to preserve the parent-child relationship is at the sacrifice of their safety. Many abused children, for example, would very much like to return to their abusive parents, despite the fact that their parents have not changed and may continue to victimize them. Refusing to go along in these instances does not necessarily forestall the development of *pisti*. By denying what the child wants and doing instead what is called for in order to help, you may also build increased trust *(pisti)*. If you are clear and confident in conveying the reasons for your actions, you may even build increased trust *(pisti)* when denying children what they want and doing instead what is called for in order to help and keep them safe. An example of this comes from a fourteen-year-old girl seen at our clinic at the request of our nurse practitioner.

Jane was referred for counseling after her girlfriend disclosed that she knew Jane had been raped by her stepfather. Interviews with Jane corroborated the allegation, and the medical exam found substantial findings of sexual abuse. Sitting alone in the clinic, without any comfort from family (her mother refused to believe the charge, and her stepfather adamantly denied it), Jane accepted the offer of counseling that was made. During our first two meetings, she was talkative, candid about the distress she felt and her fears about not being able to trust me (it was only because of her profound distress that she was willing to risk being so open). She then made reference to having always been able to maintain good grades in school despite the abuse, even back in grammar school. This was new information. The original allegation was of abuse at present and made no reference to past abuse. When I pointed this out, she looked stunned, then confided that her stepfather had started raping her when she was ten years old. As this disclosure created a new allegation of abuse, I reminded her that I would need to report it to the social worker. Of course the problem with this is that it guaranteed a rupture in the therapeutic relationship, but as a mandated reporter and a responsible adult, I had little choice in the matter. The question in these cases is not so much what to do but how to do it. I decided to capitalize on the inevitably negative reaction she would have and use that to underscore my commitment to her. Consequently, I reminded her of what I had said in our first meeting, that she could count on me to stand up for her. This included standing up for her even when it meant that she would be angry and might decide to stop the counseling.

This reminder was received with a dismissive glare holding an edge of both contempt and hurt. She reminded me that her mother did not believe her, and if I reported a new allegation, she would surely be disowned by all of her family: brothers, grandparents, aunts, uncles, everyone. I emphasized that as much as I would like to avoid causing more heartache for her, this information needed to be told to her social worker in order to better make the case for keeping her safe from her stepfather. Once again I reminded her that my commitment to her was to do everything I could to keep her safe and help her get better. There was no wish on my part, I explained, to have her disowned by her family, but her well-being was more important than maintaining her place within a family that willingly turned a blind eye to her being raped. Did she respond with heartfelt emotion and overflowing gratitude by saying, "Thank you, Doctor! Never have I seen the wellspring of human kindness so clearly as when you put my safety first." No. Something a few steps removed from that took place. The only thing she was ready to do right away was to leave and never return. But a few more minutes of talking, this time focusing on negotiating the future of therapy, brought her to agree that she would meet with me three more times before ending the work we had just started.

Although her family did in fact largely disown her, Jane continued counseling for three years. All was not smooth sailing. It took nearly two years to come to a point where she could speak with me in a spontaneously candid manner. But during this time she developed a profound sense of trust in me, *pisti* trust, wherein she knew absolutely that I was on her side, even when she would wish that I were not. Jane is, by the way, in college now, lives on her own, and occasionally sees her family although they continue to believe she made up stories about her stepfather.

Empistevomai

Empistevomai refers to the willingness to entrust another with something of yours that is of value. That is, a giving over for safekeeping. When considering this form of trust, we recognize that there are many things that one can assign to the care of others. The greater the value, the greater the trust that is needed. (The exception being that the greater the distress, the less the trust that is needed. For example, a mother on a sinking ship will give her infant to a complete stranger if that stranger has a seat on the only lifeboat aboard the ship. Prior to the ship taking on water, that same mother may have objected to the stranger merely touching her child. Again, we counselors can use moments of patient distress to build trust that might otherwise be a long time coming.)

If a counselor demonstrates impatience, disappointment, or frustration regarding the pace of the therapeutic process, children may perceive this behavior as rejecting and view themselves as failures (Bow 1993). Attunement is demonstrated by the therapist accurately responding to what the child does in the counseling hour. You will never have a perfect score for understanding and reflecting what the child does. Understanding children's perspectives of themselves and others and how your relationship influences those perspectives takes time. Aim high, get it right most of the time, do not say things that mortally offend, and you will succeed. The little girl who comes in and with a broad smile takes care to dress the dolls and feed them requires no more than hearing, "It makes you happy to take care of the babies," and "Babies need a mommy to care for them. They cannot do it for themselves." This is an accurate reflection of affect and a gentle reminder of the reality of the roles of children and parents—a lesson many abused and neglected children do not learn from their parents. One would not respond to this child by saying, "You like to play with the dolls in here," or worse, "Is that doll really you?" The former misses the deeper precipitant of the child's happiness (not just playing with dolls but the meaning attached to the play) and the latter destroys the pretext upon which fantasy play is built and rudely introduces the director working behind the scenes. If you stick with what you are sure of, and keep within the context of the child's play fantasy, the trust of *empistosyni* gradually builds.

AFFECTION

When we look for healthy intimacy in relations, affection is always present. We are not referring to the maudlin displays of affection that we counselors sometimes see as people try to convince us of their love for a spouse or child. We are interested instead in the simple clear signs that two people enjoy being in the company of each other. Affection given by the counselor to the child acts as a welcome mat to a closer relationship. It signifies something about the child's importance inasmuch as what is important is cared about. Moreover, what people care about is also what they take care of.

Research with adults clearly shows the importance of affection to the outcome of counseling. For example, Strupp (1980a-d) has found that one of the best predictors of success in psychodynamic psychotherapy with adults is patients' perception by the third session of whether their counselor genuinely liked them and cared about them. This should not surprise us, as most therapy (other than the strictest of behavioral interventions and even these might be argued about) is anchored within a relationship. This is no different for the young child than it is for the adult, and both are reassured when the relationship contains genuine affection.

How do you build this part of the relationship? To underscore the obvious, it is necessary, to begin with, that you feel some affection for the child with whom you are working. This will not always be the case, and when it is not you need to examine the possible reasons. Perhaps the child reminds you of someone you do not care for, or it may be that the child possesses a certain quality that you find particularly unpleasant, or raises feelings within you that are uncomfortable. The reason for your antipathy may be more straightforward yet: the child may be so thoroughly obnoxious that it is difficult to have any affection for him or her. Do what you can to overcome this reaction. That may involve consulting with colleagues, rescheduling to a different time of day when you are fresher, taking a more structured approach to counseling, better understanding the reasons for the child's unpleasantness, and so forth. If these approaches do not change how you work with and feel toward the child, the therapeutic process may be jeopardized and the ethical decision is to transfer the child to another therapist. Of course you would want to discuss this thoroughly with the transferring counselor prior to making the change. It would not help to transfer the child to another counselor who has the same response to the child as you— although you may feel validated, it will have a distressing effect on the child, not to mention the next therapist.

Assuming that you do feel some natural affection for the child who has come into your office, then the task of building this sense of affection is simplicity itself. It is simple because it comes so naturally. What stands in the way are the old dictums in psychotherapy about being a "blank screen," warnings not to "contaminate the transference," and the ever-present concerns about countertransference—all good in their place, just as stop signs, "yield for oncoming traffic" signs, and "merging traffic" signs are appropriate on the streets and highways. You would not, however, find them helpful if posted every few yards down the roadway. They would add little more than distraction and end up slowing your progress. So too when it comes to showing children affection and balancing this with the old dictums. For the majority of therapists, the dictums just get in the way of building a strong relationship with the abused child. Tell children you are glad to see them when they come each week. Let them know that you were thinking of them this past week when you remembered their school outing. Laugh some in the hour when the child has made a joke, or the two of you are playing a game. Tell them you really like spending time with them, and show them small kindnesses such as writing a note, or giving a little gift for their birthday. If they are having a school staffing because some problem has arisen, show up for the meeting. The examples are endless.

Although the old dictums have been overstressed, common sense and clinical perspicacty are still required to guide you in how you express yourself (regarding affection and all other aspects of counseling). Going back to the previous example, although the street may be littered with many stop signs, this does not mean there are no intersections at which it is wise to take note and stop. Obviously you will work differently with the child who sees acts of kindness as signs of weakness than you will with a child who is starved for affirmation. Both children will benefit from your finding a way to show affection, but how it is conveyed will differ with each. Likewise for the sexually abused child. Whereas a pat on the back will be fine with some children, the child who has been sexually abused may find many types of touch to be disturbing.

This leads to the question of whether counselors should let their child patients hug them. Opinions divide sharply here, but as is often the case in our field, the answer requires more than a simple yes or no. Many maltreated children do not have experience with healthy touching by a parent figure. Conversely, most maltreated children have a wealth of experience with destructive touching, either sexually or physically abusive. To say that these children should not receive the experience of healthy touching by way of a friendly hug given to their counselor is shortsighted. The counselor, as teacher, is ideally suited to help the child understand the reassurance of a parental touch. We must exercise this role with the recognition that for many abused children, the touch of an adult is a confusing experience. Moreover, some of our patients will unwittingly use hugs as a means to reduce their anxiety, just as they did as a matter of survival in placating abusive parents. That means we approach with caution. It does not mean we fail to approach at all. Under most circumstances, in working with these children you should still feel comfortable letting them give you a hug and returning their embrace. You will, however, need to be particularly aware of any patterns that go with these embraces (e.g., do they hug you after having misbehaved, or on days when you are distracted, etc.). When these patterns appear, you need not stop the child from giving you an embrace, but you will need to intervene to change the thinking and perceptions that drive those patterns.

Last, while we are on the topic of affection, many children tell their counselor that they love them. Conversely, the counselor may be asked if he or she loves the child. How to respond? Many counselors feel flummoxed by this situation, not wanting to hurt the child's feelings by truthfully responding that they do not love them but they really are awfully fond of them. Another camp of counselors does not want to confuse the children by saying "And I love you too," thereby giving the impression that love is so easily gained, and so lightly expressed, as spending fifty minutes in play.

The sentiments of each camp have merit, and the wise counselor keeps these considerations in mind.

The best response will usually be an expression of gratitude for the child's affection (i.e., it is a gift to you, so be gracious: if it is a defense, then treat it as a gift anyway). Frequently this statement of the child's affection for you is also an implicit inquiry by the child about his or her own worth. The statement "I love you" begs a response, and even the reply of silence sends an answer to the inquisitor. We suggest that you unloose those inhibitions and without fanfare or maudlin displays affirm your affection for the child. If, on the other hand, you do not have much affection for the child, he or she will already know that, and it may be the reason for the question. In this case, it is better to say, "I sure do like you. And as I get to know you more and more that feeling keeps growing. That's the way love works. It builds up over time." Although this can be a useful response, it is infrequent that one cannot respond to the child's question with an affirmation, "I love you also." If you are concerned that this distorts the meaning of love, we refer you to *The Four Loves* by C. S. Lewis (1960): you will see there are qualities of love that clearly fit most relationships counselors have with children. None of this means that the child's statement of affection should be taken only at face value. Clearly the meaning may extend beyond what the child feels for the counselor, and this must be determined and responded to as well.

CONTROL

To help a child, the counselor must be in control when they meet together. By control, we do not mean controlling children's play and undermining their need to guide the pace of therapy. We mean that you are an authority figure with an awareness of what you bring into the relationship and the child's perspective of that relationship. You do not need to exercise your authority continuously, but you must possess sufficient control in the first place to exercise it when needed. The child may require a certain form of play, need to be redirected, or brought up short when a tantrum is escalating. In all these instances the counselor needs to be able to take control. Some counselors, however, are uncomfortable asserting any more control than is necessary to keep the child from grossly acting out. Their reasoning is that maltreated children have been so thoroughly abused by brutal means of control that minimal direction and limit setting are called for by the counselor in order to avoid recapitulating the trauma. (Of course some counselors will take this approach because of their theoretical orientation, but that is a discussion that must be saved for another time.) What is missed in this thinking is the distinction of how control is asserted, and its purpose. Fromm (1956) makes this point clearly by comparing the uses of control by a slave master and teacher. Whereas the slave is controlled in order to further the good of the master, with little regard for the slave's well-being, the student is controlled in order to further his or her own good, with great regard for the student's well-being. This same type of contrast applies to the control exerted by the abusive parent versus the counselor. The child's experience of control within intimate relationships cannot be restricted to its abusive exercise. How much better for the child to also experience the benevolent use of control within the intimacy of the counseling relationship, where the child's perceptions are given primary consideration.

Control not only allows the counselor to be effective and provide a corrective experience for the child, but it is also essential for providing a sense of safety. Safety is created by setting up a routine in the playroom that is predictable because of standard rules. Children then understand you will keep them safe and then they can direct their energies to self-expression. To maintain control, keep your treatment goals in mind, both the goals for the counseling and the goals for each session. You want to work to promote these goals at every opportunity, and this means creating conditions for learning and knocking down barriers that prevent this advance. When beginning counseling, tell children what the basic rules are (cannot hurt themselves, you both stay in the playroom for the hour, and so forth). Do not give a long list of rules; the child will not remember them. Moreover, the oppositional child will rise to the challenge of circumventing them.

Sometimes battles for control begin at the very first meeting. Often during intake you will meet with the parents and child. In this arrangement, there is no problem with getting the child to the playroom. When the situation requires, however, that a child come back to the room separately from the parent, the child may show some hesitancy. It is best if you have had the parent or foster parent tell the child about the meeting ahead of time and describe you as "a special type of teacher who is also very nice." This will go a long way toward reducing the child's anxiety. The reluctant child in the waiting room must be told, "It is time to go back to the playroom now. Your mother will be here while we are meeting." A look at the mother at that moment is usually enough to prompt her to say, "Yes, you go along now and I'll wait here." If that does not suffice, take the child's hand and start for the door. Only once have we seen this result in the child still refusing to go to the playroom. Now it will not do to drag children to the playroom, nor are we suggesting you avoid dragging them by hefting them over your shoulder. If you get the rare child who continues to refuse to comply, then take another tack, for even were you to drag the child to the room he or she would not cooperate, and you would have pretty well ruined any trust you were hoping to build. In these cases see the child and parent together, at least for a couple of sessions, then start to taper the amount of time the parent is in the room with you. Even in this situation, however, you have achieved your goal and maintained control while also recognizing the child's emotional limitations. That, of course, is the whole idea.

UNDERSTANDING

Among the many dimensions that describe we humans, two are poignantly opposed to each other but intimately related to the enterprise of counseling. The first of these is that people are social creatures, social to our core. Upon birth the baby is suckled, taken into the family fold, raised among parents, siblings, grandparents, aunts, and uncles. Independence is gained slowly as children master skills that enable them to become successful participants in society, often culminating in parenthood and eventually grandparenthood. Yes, we are social through and through and this is possible because we possess the capacity to understand others and be understood in return. What is key is the type of social reciprocity we experience. Both healthy and hurtful social interactions influence development, and the pattern of reciprocity determines our developmental path.

The other dimension of being human, diametrically opposed to our social being, is that each of us is fundamentally alone, separated at birth. Without this separation there can be no full development of the self, and when we see adults who have not adequately achieved this separation, we counselors rightly view them as being emotionally stunted. Clinging to their dependency on others, recoiling from independent action and parasitically absorbing the ideas, attitudes, and sentiments of others, these individuals evoke strong sentiments in most people. Their struggles are a moving reminder of the pathology and heartache that ensue when one does not face the inherent separateness and aloneness of life. This quality of our existence, which prompts distress, is also essential for health. It shadows us through life, at times offering the comfort of solitary reflection and contentment, at times offering the anguish of unbearable isolation.

These two dimensions are often unbalanced and distorted for the child who has suffered maltreatment. The child's healthy social needs often go unmet and are replaced with confusing or painful experiences. The necessary balance of separation for normal development is often equated with rejection, and the periods of loneliness are associated with neglect, not independence. To be misunderstood, to have one's worth and purpose unrecognized, to be dismissed as a caricature of some stereotype, all of these responses enforce a sense of isolation and create searing distress to the individual who has no one to counter the message.

This pain, however, is greatly blunted when another person clearly understands the child and in understanding continues to accept and have affection for the child. Every reader will be able to produce numerous examples of this dynamic—it is as common as a barber's chair. How often have you sat with a friend and, after listening to a tale of woe, commenting just enough to show that you understand, are then told how much better your friend now feels? How often have you experienced the same thing when confiding an embarrassing event to someone close to you? The experience is ubiquitous: draw back the curtains of your everyday face presented to the world, be seen for who you are but valued all the same, and then feel relief. Perhaps the exchange draws its potency from its relation to confession and forgiveness, but whatever the source it is both common and cogent, allowing the counselor to bring it into the relationship often and with great effect.

Not only do experience and logic lead us to these conclusions about the importance of the child feeling understood, but psychotherapy research lands us in the same spot. Strupp (1980a-d) notes that in addition to the counselor's affection, being understood by the counselor is a major predictor of successful outcome. This can be seen as early as the third meeting between patient and counselor. Those patients who feel better understood by their counselors end up at the conclusion of therapy having made more gains than those who felt less understood.

As you will see in Chapter 8, "Individual Therapy and the Abused Child," building a sense of understanding is one of the primary goals in working with these children. Abused children tend to feel strange and different, left out and not a part of their peer group. As these children grow older, their cognitive abilities grow sufficiently to allow them to reflect on their situation and compare themselves to their normative age group. The conclusions they draw often leave them struggling even more profoundly with a sense of singular peculiarity. This is most pronounced, and least admitted to, in adolescence when feelings of peculiarity and inadequacy rule the emotional landscape.

In the beginning of counseling, you will mostly be concerned with conveying your understanding of simple themes and the affect associated with individual acts. You will not be revealing new insights to the child, but merely underscoring that with which the child is already at least vaguely familiar. With younger children, this is done through comments about their play, but not necessarily referencing the child. For example, imagine the child who builds a fort under the table and crawls in holding a plastic dinosaur who barks out commands to imaginary comrades who are warned to "watch out." The counselor notes, "There are lots of dangers out there. Dinosaur has to be careful if he is going to stay safe." This is nothing more than making explicit what is implicit in the play. Could we argue that the counselor has missed the true meaning of the child's play when stating the obvious? Yes, but we will not. The counselor may have missed the true meaning when stating the less-than-obvious as well (one of the most common reasons for making erroneous interpretations in counseling comes from the desire to be clever). Use your best judgment regarding the experience the child is referencing in play, refrain from being clever for its own sake, and stay with the obvious, especially when counseling is in the earliest stages. Follow this guideline and you will do fine.

By way of example, we mention an eight-year-old boy who came to the clinic because he was bullying children at school, and his county social worker wished for this to stop. He was in the third grade and weighed 120 pounds. Bullying others was a niche well suited to his size and fueled by the anger he felt due to the murder of his younger brother earlier in the year. Every meeting at the clinic began with this boy taking a large plastic lizard off the shelf and pummeling it into the floor. "Pile drivers," "dead man drops," "bone crusher slams," and a variety of other wrestling tortures were applied with vigor for ten minutes without pause. In the beginning it was enough for the therapist to emphasize, "He really makes you angry," or "You'll beat him till he drops," or "You want to keep hurting him and hurting him." Nothing subtle, just lifting out the obvious and noting it frequently enough to convey that the therapist was understanding something about his play and himself.

Or there was the child who, having grown up in a neglectful, drug-dealing family, entered the play therapy room and immediately began playing with the dollhouse. She took all the furniture, beds, chairs, tables, rockers, dressers, refrigerator, counters, and so forth and crammed them into one room. She then took several child figures and an assortment of adult figures and squished them into the same room. As she went on to play with these figures, no pattern or themes emerged, just chaos. The counselor pointed to a little girl figure and observed, "I'll bet she is confused. So many people doing different things and no grown-up who takes care of her." Again, a simple statement that holds up the obvious.

This same principle applies to older children as well, adolescents included, the difference being that you will be responding to how and what they talk about, rather than their play. In time, as the counseling and your knowledge of the child progresses, you will have more subtle insights to convey and can do so more effectively because you have established credibility with these earlier statements of understanding. The opportunity to help the child feel understood comes up outside of play as well. Comments about the child's desires and feelings related to limit setting and changes in counseling structure are common ways to do this. For instance, a child does not want to leave at the end of the hour. You tell him, "You like being here and would like to stay. I also like it when we get together, but now it is time to end until next week." Or a teenager shoplifted after her mother failed to come for a scheduled visit. You may say, "You felt rotten. So rotten that you decided it didn't matter if you stole something." Obviously, the teen may have stolen to get back at her mother, to fill needs that her mother was not filling, to get herself in trouble thereby validating the worthlessness she felt in relation to her mother, and so on. These conjectures are fine to speak about with the youngster, and following up with some of them may produce new insight, but only the comment, "You felt rotten. So rotten . . ." is needed to get the job done and help the teen feel understood.

The variety of situations that afford a chance to convey understanding abound. The problem is not with finding these opportunities but limiting how often you use them.

INTEREST

To be of interest is to be of importance. Of what importance is under-stood by how this interest is expressed. Abused children are familiar with being on the business end of perverted interest. Neglected children, on the other hand, are familiar with living in the emotionally arid plains of receiv-ing no interest at all. Maltreatment seldom includes these pure forms and consequently the children seen in our clinics typically have experienced pe-riods of neglect punctuated by episodes of abuse. Some of these children have also known times of appropriate parental interest, but in most cases their history of maltreatment is so chronic that these healthy experiences will have been thoroughly corrupted by the times of abusive interest or cal-lous neglect (i.e., you don't purify a poisoned well by adding just a few buckets of sweet water). The counselor's interest, given consistently and without expectation of personal gain, offers something new for the child— a simple but clear affirmation of worth. This affirmation is necessary to cor-rect the child's ingrained self-perceptions of being not good enough or un-worthy of love.

Counselors show interest in their patients in a number of ways, but the thread that connects each of them is sustained attention on the child throughout the hour. Children must capture your full attention. They must be the very center of your concentration, and what they say and do must be shown to matter to you. At the bare minimum, this requires that you be free from outside distractions during the hour (e.g., turn off the phone, no inter-ruptions for messages, etc.). Your comments to the child convey this attitude clearly and concisely, without patronizing or slipping into maudlin displays of affection. The child who has built a Tinkertoy contraption is told, "Neat. Show me how you make it work," rather than, "This is the best whatchamacallit I've ever seen. You've got some brain sitting on those shoulders!" This last statement is not genuine and the child will question your sincerity in other aspects of the relationship. When told by parent or foster parent that Jane will miss next week due to a change in the family's schedule, tell the child, "I'll miss seeing you next week but we'll keep this same time and same room ready for us the week after that." If you say this, you have hit the mark. You have conveyed that you would like to have met because you enjoy seeing her. Moreover, you have reassured her, without fanfare, that she is not easily forgotten—you are keeping the room and time open because the two of you will be meeting again. This is powerful reassurance of your interest in this child.

Not surprisingly, much of what helps to advance the development of the other aspects of the counseling relationship also enhances the child's sense of your taking an interest. The consistency that builds trust also demonstrates interest; the gesture that furthers a sense of affection will do likewise, and the effort applied toward understanding will carry with it the message that this child is of interest. The counselor's eye contact, posture, and accurate statements about the child's play are also important in creating a child's sense of worthiness.

Some children will find your interest in them to be extraordinarily uncomfortable. With their history of abuse, they are familiar with adult interest in the same way as a mouse is familiar with the attention of a cat—it bodes ill. For these children, you will want to temper your expressions of regard to match their limited capacity to receive it. Over time they will become more comfortable, but at first they may show anxiety and at times even mild dissociation. Structured games, crafts, and shortened sessions are some of the ways in which these children can be helped to contain their anxiety while they become accustomed to your attention.

As with affection, you must find something of interest in the child you are seeing for this aspect of the counseling relationship to grow. When this is not happening, you must determine the cause. For instance, is a boy so guarded that he is terminally boring? Perhaps he is not guarded but indifferent to himself, having absorbed the neglect of his parents into his own attitude of self-awareness. Whatever the reason, you as the counselor must find that which is of interest about this child, and in so doing you will be able to hold this up in counseling like a mirror, reflected in your demeanor and manifest through your relationship, confirming that the child offers something of value.

HOPE

Hope is essential to life. This is true for both our physical and our mental well-being. Frankl (1959), during his years in a German concentration camp, noted that those prisoners who maintained hope for the future were most likely to survive. Those who gave up hope quickly succumbed to disease and malnutrition. Hope, however, is not for the faint of heart—at least not when the stakes are high. Allowing oneself to hope requires taking a risk. You cannot have hope without wagering something of yourself. These wagers are what unrealized dreams are made of.

Despite the risks involved, hope and optimism are ubiquitous among the very young. Consider, for example, what occurs in any kindergarten class when the teacher asks the children if any of them are good artists, good at singing, good at sports, good at helping around the house, and so forth. In response, every child in the class raises a hand in affirmation to each of these questions. These children feel sure of all they can do and this is reflected not only in their answers to these questions but also to the question, "What will you be when you grow up?" Doctor, lawyer, astronaut, scientist, and teacher are the answers one hears, and they are given because children at this young age have a natural tendency to be optimistic about the future. Despite the seemingly omnipresent character and obdurate nature of hope, a number of children in our clinics have a view of the future that is uniformly bleak. Years of abuse and privation have stolen away such optimism and left in its place a void where the future is not imagined at all, or if thought about is viewed with oppressively consistent pessimism.

Part of our job as counselors for these children is to rekindle hope, tempered with reality and driven by a sense of purpose. This goal may seem lofty and impractical given the day-to-day problems these children have that require your attention. If they are lofty, however, they are lofty in just the right way. A cow needs no higher goal than to find the next green clump of grass to chew upon, but humans need something more, and the pursuit of this will invariably require the capacity for hope. Helping to instill that capacity in children is the type of lofty endeavor all adults should put their energies into. Moreover, far from being an impractical goal, it is one of the most practical goals of all. Building a ship, planking its hull, and sewing its sails are practical efforts, but they amount to little if the ship remains moored in the harbor because the captain has no hope of ever sailing beyond the anchor line. The ship serves no practical use unless it is going about the business for which it was built. It flounders because the captain lacks hope. Curing enuresis and building social skills are important practical goals for many children, but a child who remains without hope will be easily discouraged by the first set of difficulties that befall him, and return to the familiar ways of handling problems that were practiced before the counseling began.

Hope is a great motivator that must be cultivated. The process is similar to what occurs in successful families as parents, over the course of eighteen years, instill an attitude of hopeful expectation in their children. This attitude, built on common experiences and parental confidence, acts as a bulwark against the anxiety of an uncertain future or momentary failures. During counseling it is built up in a similar way, albeit in a more minor key, when the other aspects of the therapeutic relationship are in place. Beyond attending to those elements, it is vital that the counselor demonstrate a clear belief in the child; that is, a belief in the child's ability to overcome the problems that face him or her, a conviction that the child can succeed at the tasks of childhood, and a recognition of the child's potential. The counselor's belief in children is essential for stimulating their belief in themselves, thus correcting the misperception of worthlessness. You can demonstrate belief in children by recognizing their accomplishments, pointing out the cause and effect of their ideas and behavior in session, and commenting on their creative problem solving. The key is to note, even in the smallest degree, the difference the child makes in the world and in you. A simple example of this comes from a seven-year-old boy named Jake.

Jake was referred to the clinic after his father kicked him in the stomach and hit his brother in the head. The child's mother had frequently been beaten by the father and was even more frequently immobilized by having taken any number of recreational drugs. Neglect and violence regularly visited this little boy's life. He responded to this distress by misbehaving at school and getting into fistfights with other children. When removed from the care of his parents and placed in foster care, complaints of his defiance continued. The foster parents tried punishing him, reasoning with him, and occasionally rewarding him, but these efforts brought only momentary change.

Jake began group counseling to help him develop better social skills, and during the course of this time we decided to intervene by naming the group the Never Give Up Kids. The children were greeted each week with a reminder of their group name: "Good to see you again. I always enjoy Thursdays because I get to spend time with the Never Give Up Kids." Seven months later, Jake graduated from group and entered individual counseling. The next year was difficult for him as he continuously came close to being removed from his foster home. But then fortune smiled on Jake. His grandmother petitioned the court to allow her to adopt him and within a short time he had moved in with her on a trial basis. Jake knew that this was his only chance to leave foster care and grow up with family. It would be difficult, because he was not used to accepting limits, and those that were imposed upon him were thoroughly tested.

As expected, the following year was challenging for Jake and his grandmother. The months alternated between times of harmony and times of conflict. But eventually, the periods of cooperation and happiness started to come more frequently and lasted longer until it was clear that Jake had turned the corner. We needed to plan an end to his counseling. During one of the last meetings, his grandmother joined us for the first few minutes. She looked back on the past year and spoke with affection about all that Jake had accomplished, the closeness they had formed, his improved behavior at home, and the good grades he was now earning at school. When she left the room, Jake and I were by ourselves and he busied himself shuffling a deck of cards. Then he turned to me and said, "It's been hard." I replied, "Yes, I know. But you did it. Your grandma is sure proud of you. And you know what? So am I." Jake paused and then, looking up from the cards, said, "You always told me that I'm a never give up kid. So I just didn't give up. I just kept trying."

The faith you express in children will grow within them as faith in themselves, in others, and hope for the future.

SUMMARY

Life is lived through relationships, and these experiences, both healthy and hurtful, shape our development and our view of ourselves and the world around us. Children who have grown up with abusive or neglectful parents begin to view the world, and themselves, through the prism of abuse and neglect. This view, while accurate for their family, creates distortions in other relationships. We see this manifest in many ways: the benign actions of others are seen as menacing, the intent of a friendly overture is dismissed as self-serving, the good-natured jest by a friend brings anger and hurt rather than a smile. One of the correctives for this ailment is the establishment of a healthy relationship, and one of the places such a relationship can grow is within counseling. Fundamental to this process is building a solid foundation from which the child can develop the necessary safety and security to take the vulnerable step of self-exploration. The counselor showing interest, affection, and understanding for the child, while also instilling a sense of trust and hope for the future, builds this foundation. Moreover, just as a teacher is only effective when maintaining control of the classroom, control of the session must reside with the counselor. The prospects for success in working with maltreated children are very good when these elements of the relationship have been firmly established.

REFERENCES

Benjamin, L. S. (1993). *Interpersonal diagnosis and treatment of personality disorders*. New York: Guilford Press.

Bow, J. N. (1993). Overcoming resistance. In C. Schaefer (Ed.), *The therapeutic powers of play* (pp. 17-40). Northvale, NJ: Jason Aronson.

Bowlby, J. (1988). *A secure base*. New York: Basic Books.

Carson, R. C. (1969). *Interaction concepts of personality*. Chicago: Aldine.

Donovan, D. M. & McIntyre, D. (1990). *Healing the hurt child: A developmental-contextual approach*. New York: Norton.

Erikson, E. H. (1950). *Childhood and society*. New York: Norton.

Frankl, V. E. (1959). *Man's search for meaning: An introduction to logotherapy*. Boston: Beacon Press.

Fromm, E. (1956). *The art of loving*. New York: Harper.

Lewis, C. S. (1960). *The four loves*. New York: Harcourt, Brace.

Strupp, H. H. (1980a). Success and failure in time-limited psychotherapy: A systematic comparison of two cases (Comparison 1). *Archives of General Psychiatry, 37*, 595-603.

Strupp, H. H. (1980b). Success and failure in time-limited psychotherapy: A systematic comparison of two cases (Comparison 2). *Archives of General Psychiatry, 37*, 708-716.

Strupp, H. H. (1980c). Success and failure in time-limited psychotherapy: A systematic comparison of two cases (Comparison 3). *Archives of General Psychiatry, 37*, 831-841.

Strupp, H. H. (1980d). Success and failure in time-limited psychotherapy: A systematic comparison of two cases (Comparison 4). *Archives of General Psychiatry, 37*, 947-954.

Sullivan, H. S. (1953). *The psychiatric interview*. New York: Norton.

Wiggins, J. S. (2003). *Paradigms of personality assessment*. New York: Guilford Press.

Chapter 7

Cognitive-Behavioral Interventions with Neglectful Parents

Sandra T. Azar
Linda R. Cote

More than half of the 2.9 million official reports of child maltreatment in 1999 were substantiated for neglect (54.7 percent, NCCAN, 2001) and once it is identified, recidivism appears to be high. As a group, neglected children have many negative outcomes. Despite these facts, relatively little research attention has been paid to neglect compared to other forms of maltreatment. It includes a heterogeneous group of conditions affecting children, making its study difficult and developing a one-size-fits-all intervention problematic. Also, neglect falls under the purview of many professions (physicians, nurses, juvenile system), further diffusing work. It is also linked to poverty, adding a sociopolitical element. This may make its study as a "person-based" disorder less palatable to the scientific community. Neglect also tends to be seen as chronic, with perpetrators seen as more dispositionally disturbed. Intervention may, therefore, be viewed as more futile than with other forms of abuse and thus, model building and doing research as a foundation for intervention less productive. Finally, neglect may be viewed as the least compelling type of maltreatment (only in extremes is its impact visible) and it may not arouse the same societal outrage.

Consequently, describing one unified intervention approach is a daunting task. This chapter begins by reviewing the ways in which neglect has been defined and the child outcomes that have been associated with it. This will help focus clinicians' attention in intervention on a set of parental skill deficits and child outcomes, which are key in formulating a cognitive-

This chapter was written while the first author was a Liberal Arts Fellow at Harvard University Law School in Cambridge, Massachusetts, and the second author was an adjunct assistant research professor and lecturer at San Diego State University. The writing of this chapter was in part supported by funds from the Center for Adoption Research to the first author.

behavioral treatment plan. With this background, an assessment framework and treatment strategies for selected portions of the "territory" that is neglect are described, along with a sample case.

NEGLECT: A DISORDER OF PARENTING
WITH MANY POSSIBLE ELEMENTS

Unlike other forms of child abuse, neglect is an act of omission. It involves failures in actions that lead to harm or endangerment of children's health or well-being, including a failure to provide minimal caregiving in medical care, education, nutrition, supervision, emotional contact, and safety, as well as providing inadequate environmental stimulation and structure (Wolfe, 1987; Zuravin, 1991). Recent definitions also add emotional neglect (a marked indifference to child needs for affection and attention), exposure of children to spousal abuse, and permitted substance abuse and other maladaptive behavior by a child (e.g., assaultiveness) (Gershater-Molko & Lutzker, 1999). Clearly, these elements can occur in combination with each other and with other forms of abuse.

The diversity of behaviors labeled as neglect has made model building and developing interventions particularly difficult. There is no consensus on the level at which these problems become neglectful (e.g., What is adequate supervision? How does it change with children's development? How chronic must the parental omission be?). Behaviors labeled neglectful for infants may not be for adolescents. Chronic neglect may have different causes than neglect that occurs in the context of an acute stress (e.g., job loss). The relevance of intent is also at issue.

Further complicating matters is the difficulty posed by measuring acts of omission in care. Who is labeled the "neglecter" is also open to debate. Mothers are often charged, even if another caretaker is present and/or provides a contributing factor (e.g., spends food money on drugs).

Clinicians' first task is to identify which forms are present, their antecedents, and the consequences for children and family life. Only with a clear idea of what led to the child protective services (CPS) concerns can treatment planning occur. Also important are the outcomes seen in neglected children and substantiating links to either parents' behavior or other sources. For example, lack of supervision may be due to parental substance abuse, depression, or mental retardation or, with older children, attentional problems that lead to impulsivity and wandering from home.

IMPACT OF NEGLECT ON CHILDREN'S DEVELOPMENT

Although a terrible pun, the outcomes of neglected children have been neglected by researchers. Studies often combine abused and neglected children, making it difficult to outline outcomes specific to neglect. Although often co-occurring, when distinctions are made, outcomes differ. Also, studies vary as to which types of neglect are a focus. Some make physical, medical, and emotional neglect one group; others do not. Others make physical neglect its own category, yet combine emotional abuse and neglect. Finally, substance abuse, domestic violence, and poverty often accompany neglect and play a role in outcomes.

Five areas of development may be negatively affected by neglect and deserving of clinical attention (Azar, Lauretti, & Loding, 1998):

1. Physical health and well-being
2. Cognitive functioning and academic performance
3. Emotional and social development
4. Stress management
5. Anger control and other self-regulation capacities

Although it seems intuitive that neglect, and medical neglect in particular, might negatively affect child physical health and well-being, little research has examined this. One review of research indicated that neglected children may show lower levels of a growth hormone, which may lead to delays in physical growth (e.g., Kaplan, Pelcovitz, & LaBruna, 1999), and another reported delays in motor development (e.g., Wright, 1994). Failures in health care may exacerbate existing health problems. Dubowitz (1991) gives the example of asthma, which if treated properly may keep a child free of symptoms and out of the hospital. Lack of supervision may account for burns and deaths due to house fires. Poor school performance may result from anemia, causing apathy (poor nutrition). Clearly, child health requires screening, and parental skills in this area may need intervention.

Research on cognitive functioning in early childhood and academic performance for school-age and adolescent neglected children has consistently found lower IQ scores (e.g., Perez & Widom, 1994; Widom, 1998), verbal intelligence (e.g., Wright, 1994), reading and math scores (e.g., Perez & Widom, 1994), language development (Cahill, Kaminer, & Johnson, 1999) and memory (e.g., Wright, 1994). Neglect is more strongly associated with poor achievement than abuse (e.g., Cahill et al., 1999; Kaplan et al., 1999). More school behavior problems occur among neglected or abused children than matched controls (e.g., truancy, suspension, or expulsion) (Perez & Widom, 1994; Powers, Eckenrode, & Jaklitsch, 1990). These issues appear to persist into adulthood (Perez & Widom, 1994). In adulthood, neglect is associated with significantly fewer years of schooling, lower employment rates, and higher levels of menial and semiskilled occupations (e.g., Widom, 1998). Careful cognitive and academic assessment is crucial. Academic remedial work and work on increasing school attendance and decreasing behaviors leading to school suspensions may all be targeted in treatment.

The most research has focused on emotional and social difficulties. During infancy and early childhood, maltreated children show greater dependency, tend to have insecure attachment relationships, and show little concern for their peers' distress (Wright, 1994). Rutter (1979) found that children deprived of primary caregivers in infancy (emotional neglect) were overly friendly with strangers, sought attention and were clingy toward adults, and were inept in social behavior at school (i.e., attention seeking, restlessness, disobedience, unpopularity). Neglected children also engage in less interaction with peers (Cahill et al., 1999) and have more conflictual relationships with friends and fewer reciprocal friendships than controls (Kaplan et al., 1999). Also, they have difficulty in identifying appropriate interpersonal affective responses and in social problem solving (Kaplan et al., 1999). Problems persist to adulthood (e.g., depression, isolation, loneliness, higher divorce/separation rates; Cook, 1991; Loos & Alexander, 1997; Melchert, 2000; Powers et al., 1990; Widom, 1998).

Children's stress and anger management and other self-regulation capacities also require attention. Neglected children show more negative emotions (i.e., anger, fear, or physical attack), more avoidance and noncompliance (Wright, 1994), and more conduct disorder (Rutter, 1979) than their peers. Their play shows more developmental delays and more antisocial, disruptive, aggressive, and conflict themes (Wright, 1994). Neglect has been linked to delinquent behavior, including fighting, stealing, skipping school, and traffic violations, among adolescents (Brown, 1984; Mak, 1994). Adults neglected or abused as children are more likely than controls to be arrested as a juvenile or adult, to be arrested for violent crimes, and to be diagnosed with antisocial personality disorder (Cahill et al., 1999; Widom, 1998).

Other self-regulation problems occur. Neglect has been associated with attentional difficulties and heightened risk-taking behaviors (e.g., early sexual activity and teenage parenthood) (Kaplan et al., 1999; Wright, 1994), and, in adulthood, with an increased risk of alcohol abuse (Widom, 1998).

MODELS OF NEGLECT: A CONCEPTUAL RATIONALE
FOR A COGNITIVE-BEHAVIORAL INTERVENTION

The positing of neglect-specific models has been limited, with models often combining all forms of maltreatment. Even when neglect is considered separately, type of neglect is typically not taken into consideration. Etiology may vary with the subtype. Neglect of health care and hygiene may result from parents' basic knowledge deficits (e.g., how to take a child's temperature), whereas abandonment could originate from other factors (e.g., substance abuse). Some argue for a focus on the types of outcomes seen. For example, neglect can be an antecedent of failure to thrive and, thus, has been considered under the category of feeding problems in some discussions, whereas failure to attend to medical care may be seen as treatment noncompliance. The former might lead to models regarding parent-infant transactional problems; the latter might focus on models of parental motivation or organizational skills deficits. Thus, in searching for intervention ideas, the clinician must be resourceful and knowledgeable about ways of viewing a family's problems.

Causes for neglect have been suggested at all levels of analysis. These include biological (e.g., mental retardation), personality-emotional (e.g., ego deficiency), experiential (e.g., poor attachment during the first year of life), and sociocultural (e.g., poverty, isolation) (see Azar, Povilaitis, Lauretti, & Pouquette, 1998, for a review of models). Each is unsatisfactory as a sole basis for comprehensive treatment planning. For example, although stress has been linked to maltreatment, not all stressed parents neglect their children. The mediators of risk need to be identified for intervention purposes (e.g., the impact that stress might have on moment-to-moment parenting). Similarly, parental cognitive limitations, substance abuse, and poverty have been implicated, but again not all such parents maltreat their children.[1] Only recently have all forms of maltreatment been seen as resulting from a complex interaction of factors (see the social ecological model by Belsky, · 1980), but even then the resulting models are often too global to act as frames for treatment.

In developing a cognitive-behavioral model of child maltreatment and parenting risk to guide treatment, Azar and her colleagues (Azar & Twentyman, 1986; Azar, 1986, 1989, 1998, 2002; Azar & Siegel, 1990) argue that since the negative impact on children's development is of most concern, theory should isolate those factors that are most closely linked to such outcomes. Also, although theories that see neglectful parents as distinct from other parents make sense in contexts where categorical classification is crucial (e.g., the legal system), treatment does not typically involve families where such sharp distinctions are needed. Thus, a model might best begin with a continuum view. These criteria suggest that such a model needs to be one of parenting competency.

The model they posit includes both parent-based cognitive disturbances and behavioral skill deficits, as well as disrupting socioenvironmental conditions. These are considered in the context of children's needs at each developmental stage and the parenting tasks that each stage presents (adult/family development; Azar, 2003). The model posits five general domains of parent disturbance:

1. Cognitive disturbances
2. Parenting skill problems
3. Impulse control problems
4. Stress management problems
5. Social skill problems (Azar & Twentyman, 1986)

Exhibit 7.1 provides subareas within these domains that might manifest themselves in any given case and be targets for intervention. Each of these general areas of disturbance is seen as playing a role in both parenting problems and systemic difficulties that foster further child risk. For example, poor social skills would lead to fewer friends, perceptions of low intimacy, marital problems, greater distress and negative arousal, poorer life adjustment, and a lower mood state, all of which have been linked to child neglect, parent-child interaction problems, and poor child outcomes. These disturbances may originate in parents' own childhood (poor modeling by adult caregivers), but may also evolve under situational strain (e.g., mood disorder, marital violence).

This model argues for a developmental perspective in viewing neglect. As children develop, the parental demands shift and the environmental supports needed also change. For example, the parent of an infant must have a high tolerance for crying and must problem solve to arrive at appropriate care. The parent of a newly mobile toddler must have the capacity to anticipate and monitor safety in the home, along with the ability to marshal a cadre of friends and relatives to support these capacities (e.g., provide wider solutions, auxiliary monitoring). The level and type of frustration tolerance and monitoring skills needed for infants and toddlers, however, are different than those needed for teens.[2] At this later point in development, good communication skills and understanding of teens' need for autonomy, as well as monitoring (e.g., rule setting), are needed to provide an optimal environment for development. The quality of verbal communication (e.g., modeling of negotiation skills) may be important for teens, whereas, for infants,

EXHIBIT 7.1.
Sampling of Skills Areas Required to Parent

Parenting Skills

Problem-solving abilities
A repertoire of child management skills (balance of positive and negative strategies, discipline skills)
Medical care and physical care skills (e.g., ability to identify needs for medical assistance; capacity to select nutritious foods)
Safety and emergency response skills
Capacities for warmth and nurturance (e.g., affective recognition/ expression skills)
Sensitive and discriminant interactional response capacities

Social-Cognitive Skills

Perspective taking
Problem-solving capacities
Appropriate expectations regarding children's capacities
Cognitive reflectivity/complexity
Balancing short- and long-term socialization goals
Positive attributional style
Perceptual/observational skills
Self-efficacy

Self-Control Skills

Impulse control
Accurate/adaptive perceptions
A positive interpretive bias
Self-monitoring skills
Assertiveness

Stress Management

Self-care skills
Relaxation skills
Recreational capacities
Ability to marshal and maintain social support network
Positive appraisal style
A breadth of coping capacities (problem-focused coping, emotion-focused coping, avoidant coping)
Financial planning skills

(continued)

(continued)

Social Skills

Interpersonal problem-solving skills
Empathy
Affective recognition/expression skills
Assertiveness
Social initiation skills
Capacities to respond effectively to a breadth of individuals (e.g., family, friends, employers, social workers, children's teachers)

the amount of communication (e.g., verbal stimulation) may be more crucial. Parental flexibility and skill are required to make these transitions.

This model also argues that contextual factors influence the occurrence of neglect. Parental tasks may be more difficult to carry out if parents are under environmental stress. For example, in poverty, it may be more difficult to reduce environmental risks (e.g., preventing lead paint poisoning because of limits to available housing quality). Skills must be of an even higher quality than is typical in more benign contexts. Also, cognitive processing narrows under stress and thus, an already limited cognitive and behavioral system may be further taxed, resulting in further detriments to functioning.

Using the five deficit areas noted previously, Azar and Siegel (1990) posit a framework for parent risk that specifies unique tasks they must accomplish during each era of development, as well as ones that cut across stages. They also outline period-specific child-based and contextual obstacles to completing these tasks and interactional and child outcomes to be expected with failures. This view is outlined briefly as a frame for thinking about assessment and treatment of neglect.

A foundational disturbance in this approach is an information processing one. Given that low intellectual functioning[3] and social-cognitive problems have been associated with neglect, this model has particular utility for work with neglect (see also Crittenden, 1993). Difficulties at this fundamental level would short-circuit all subsequent responses parents would make and may explain the wide-ranging areas of parental failures in caregiving. That is, if one misperceives or misinterprets child or situational cues, then responses that follow would by definition be maladaptive or dissynchronous with children's needs. Effective parents are seen as approaching interactions with their children with developmentally sensitive schemata (role expectations) (Azar, Robinson, Hekimian, & Twentyman, 1984; Azar, 1986, 1989). That is, such parents have accurate perceptions of their children's capabilities, as well as what their own role should be in moving them forward developmentally. These standards need to be flexible and complex enough to act as frameworks for the variety of parenting tasks required across development and the special needs certain children may have. Such expectancies (e.g., believing children should take care of parents) have been linked to both maladaptive parenting (less use of explanation, coercion) and neglect (Azar et al., 1984; Barnes & Azar, 1990) (see Exhibit 7.2).

EXHIBIT 7.2.
The Makings of an Abusive Incident:
A Four-Stage Process

Stage 1

The parent holds unrealistic standards for appropriate behaviors in children.

Stage 2

The parent encounters a child behavior that fails to meet those standards.

Stage 3

The parent misattributes negative intent to the behavior and does not question this interpretation or blames herself or himself when the interventions do not change the child's response.

Stage 4

The parent overreacts, perhaps after making some poorly skilled effort to change the child's behavior, and punishes the child excessively.

Note: Movement through the stages may feel automatic and the process is more likely to occur under perceived conditions of stress.

Along with appropriate standards, effective parents also have a wide enough repertoire of child-rearing strategies and problem-solving skills to adapt their responses to any given situation and the skill level of their children. For example, parents must recognize that verbal explanations regarding safety risks may be very effective with an adolescent, but will be less so with a toddler. Neglectful parents possess a narrow repertoire of child-rearing skills, as well as poor problem-solving ability (Azar et al., 1984; Hansen, Pallotta, Tishelman, & Conaway, 1989). Thus, they are more likely to fail at parenting tasks. Lower perceptions of control in parenting are related to more depression and less effective interactions (Donovan & Leavitt, 1989).

Effective parents also have a positive bias in their interpretations of events involving their children that, together with sensitive schemata and parenting skills, allows them to maintain a relatively positive affective state and to make adaptive and positive responses, even when aversive child behaviors are involved. For example, when such parents find that their three-year-old has spilled milk, they recognize that three-year-olds have trouble holding onto objects and make attributions to developmental factors (e.g., "She's only three") or factors outside both their own and their child's control, thus reducing stress and frustration. Neglectful mothers have a negative bias, often attributing their children's mishaps to spitefulness or their own inadequacy to get them to "mind" (Azar, 1995; Larrance & Twentyman, 1983). This leads to their not persisting in child-rearing efforts, finding child care aversive, feeling ineffective in encounters with children, and withdrawing from the role. Indeed, neglectful mothers show significantly low levels of interaction with their children (Bousha & Twentyman, 1984). Also, lower efficacy has been shown to relate to less involvement in parenting (Swick, 1988) and psychological unavailability has been linked to the worst child outcomes (Egeland & Erickson, 1987).

Thus, appropriate schemata, adaptive attributions, and a wide repertoire of child-rearing strategies and problem-solving skills combine to produce a situation in which parents are attuned to the developmental needs of their children and can discriminate situations where intervention is required and where it is not. They are more engaged in their role and are capable of meeting parenting tasks more calmly, flexibly, and successfully. Lack of complexity in cognitive processing may contribute to dissatisfaction in their role as parents, inept parenting more generally, and poor child outcomes. Some examples of phrases that might be heard in parents' narratives regarding their children that may signal social-cognitive problems are provided in Table 7.1. Formal assessment strategies (e.g., questionnaires) are provided in the next section.

TABLE 7.1. Parental Narratives with Infants/Toddlers and Young Children That May Signal the Need for Cognitive Work with Neglectful Parents

Phrase	Example Statements	Distorted Underlying Assumption/ Expectation/ Cognitive Problem
"He/she knows" (with an infant/toddler)	He knew I was tired. He knows his father had a bad day. She knows I don't let her do that.	Assumption of mind reading/ perspective-taking capacities
A string of personality-based explanations for aversive child behavior	He's a sneak. She's vicious.	Stable negative internal attributions
Evidence of a power struggle	She thinks she's boss! I can't let her get away with this! He thinks he can put one over on me!	Low self-efficacy
Overly personalized explanations of causality with strong language	He knew it would get to me. He knew people were watching and he did it anyway. She was trying to destroy me.	Misattributions
Self-deprecatory statements	He must think I'm stupid. She must really think I'm dumb!	Negative self-schema
Explanations that are similar to descriptions of others in the parent's life	He's just like his father— no good! She looks at me just like my mother did when I did something wrong. When she does that, she reminds me of me.	Discrimination failure

Because contextual stress may interfere further with cognitive processing, a positive affective state, and parents' capacity to enact optimal responses, parents who are effective also have skills that help them to handle stress well when it does occur, to develop buffers for themselves against its negative consequences (e.g., social support), and, when possible, to anticipate and prevent stressors from occurring in the first place (e.g., anticipate an impending financial strain and adjust their budget accordingly). Having social support, for example, provides information to fine-tune parental schemata and introduce new behavioral strategies (e.g., feedback, role modeling). Maltreating parents are more impulsive in their responses (Rohrbeck

& Twentyman, 1986), which together with their poor problem-solving capacities and poor social skills result in many life stressors befalling them and fewer social supports to help them (Salzinger, Kaplan, & Artemyeff, 1983). Skills in each of these areas also promote positive child outcomes. For example, parents are a major early source of children's ability to form social supports themselves and develop various social capacities such as empathy.

Overall, this model explains both parental maladaptive behaviors and poor child outcomes. It provides a preliminary set of potential targets for assessment, which then, using functional analytic strategies, can be further explored and be targeted for intervention.

Caution is necessary in applying this model in treatment. Differences in values between cultures may result in practices that might be labeled neglectful (e.g., the importance placed on education; views on how independent children should be; placing children in charge of siblings) (Azar & Benjet, 1994; Azar & Cote, 2002; Korbin, 1994). Mismatches between practices acceptable in one culture and not in another may explain some situations labeled as neglectful (see Azar & Cote, 2002, for a discussion of sociocultural issues).

ASSESSMENT

Careful assessment is crucial in neglectful families, given that they are often multistressed, chaotic, and heterogeneous in their difficulties. Although responses to the crises of the moment will still be necessary (e.g., evictions, no food in the house), having a set of clear goals as a frame for intervention keeps work consistent. For example, if problem-solving capacities are a concern, then this skill can continue to be targeted no matter what befalls the family. For this reason, more time is spent on frameworks for thinking about assessment in this chapter than in other chapters of this volume. Assessment should focus on risk factors, parent and child factors, family interaction, and the nature of the context in which the family lives (e.g., available resources) (Azar & Wolfe, 1998). The heterogeneity of possible parental deficits and child outcomes makes giving a single assessment strategy difficult, if not impossible. The model posited previously and the deficits observed in neglected children do suggest areas that commonly require exploration. Given space constraints, discussion focuses on neglect-specific evaluation even though other forms of maltreatment co-occur. See other chapters in this volume for assessment in these other areas.

Risk assessment should involve an examination of current level of risk in areas noted in past CPS reports. This narrows the areas to be assessed in depth, with a broader screening in other areas. Consultation with others regarding child health and school attendance and performance also is useful. Repeated failures to make appointments or small cues that emerge in interacting with the family need follow-up (e.g., a young child answers the phone and repeatedly reports the parent is not available to talk). Although some efforts at developing risk assessment protocols have occurred in physical abuse (e.g., Child Abuse Potential Inventory, Milner, 1986), less work has been done in neglect. Immediate risk must be determined and monitored throughout treatment (if necessary, foster care may be required to ensure child safety and allow treatment to proceed). Assessment with the parents should include direct observation of parenting judgment and behavior (e.g., handling of emergencies) and indirect choices they make regarding the environment in which they raise their children (e.g., home safety). For the latter, caution must be used. Poverty often determines whether parents do in fact have choice in such matters.

Global frameworks designed to assess parenting skills and family functioning provide a starting point for devising an assessment strategy for parents. Tymchuk's (1998) model covers basic child care needs in the following four areas:

1. Fundamental knowledge and skills (including effective coping strategies, grooming and hygiene skills, meal planning and finance management, ability to create and maintain a support network)
2. Health-related knowledge and skills (e.g., knowledge of common health problems, illnesses, and medicines, ability to recognize and evaluate severity of symptoms, ability to recognize and prevent life-threatening emergencies)
3. Safety-related knowledge and skills (e.g., knowledge of potential dangers in the home and community)
4. Mutual parent-child enjoyment capacities (e.g., playing together, reading to the child)

Assessment of family functioning can also be guided by the McMaster's model (Epstein, Bishop, & Baldwin, 1982). It argues for three levels of tasks families must accomplish: (1) basic tasks, which involve fundamental survival needs (food, shelter); (2) developmental tasks, which involve adjusting to family members' shifting development needs and fostering their progress; and (3) emergency tasks, which involve capacities to handle emergencies. Neglectful families often have difficulties in all three areas. To meet these tasks, capacities in six areas are needed: problem solving, behavioral control, affective responsiveness, affective involvement, communication, and adequate distribution of family roles. The cognitive behavior model just described argues for a slightly different approach and for an evaluation of more general cognitive processes and behavioral skills that pervade all areas of adult functioning, with the most fundamental being ones in the social-cognitive realm (Exhibit 7.1) (Azar & Twentyman, 1986; Azar et al., 1998).

Central to assessment in neglect should be the use of behavioral performance-based evaluation including: task analyses, live role plays, and use of visual prompts to solicit cognitive and behavioral responding capacities (e.g., enactment of a grease fire and parents' response to it to assess emergency skills). Many of the areas to be assessed (e.g., cleanliness) are personal, and care must be taken in the timing and attitude with which assessment is done. Evaluation needs to occur in a trust- and relationship-enhancing manner ("If any of these questions feel too personal, please let me know"; see Azar & Soysa, 2000). Parents also prefer assessment that focuses on their skills rather than deficits. Literacy is a problem for this group. Use of self-report measures requires reading items to ensure understanding and education in how to use Likert scales. Finally, variation in cultural practices and tolerance for the intrusion of outsiders in family life also needs to be considered.

Measures

Global neglect measures have begun to be developed that examine factors specified in the frameworks described above. Polansky, Chalmers, Buttenwieser, and Williams (1981) developed the Childhood Level of Living Scale (CLLS) to assess children's home environment in areas of concern for their minimal health, safety, and stimulation requirements (e.g., state of repair of house, quality of household maintenance, parental encouraging of competence, inconsistency of discipline, and coldness). Preliminary normative data exists with cutoff scores indicating neglectful, adequate, and good child care. Two other similar instruments of this type exist: the Child Well-Being Scales (CWBS; Magura & Moses, 1986) and the Home Observation for Measurement of the Environment scale (HOME; Bradley & Caldwell, 1979; Bradley, Mundfrom, Whiteside, Casey, & Barrett, 1994). Each is completed in unstructured home visits via casual observations and a few questions, with the former requiring more extensive knowledge of the family. For example, the HOME is a well-researched criterion checklist that reflects the quality of the preschool child's environment in terms of stimulation (aspects of the quantity and quality of social, emotional, and cognitive support available to a young child). Six subscales include emotional and verbal responsivity of the mother, avoidance of restriction and punishment, organization of the physical and temporal environment, provision of appropriate play materials, involvement with the child, and opportunities for variety in stimulation. The HOME is sensitive to child outcomes (e.g., receptive language) (Harrington, Dubowitz, Black, & Binder, 1995). Based on criticism regarding bias in items, versions of the HOME are now available for lower SES parents. Feldman (1998) also developed task analyses of basic capacities for caring for children from birth to age three, including feeding babies, washing hair, and bathing, which list component responses required to do each successfully.

Once specific neglect areas have been identified, narrow-band assessment can take place. For example, the Home Accident Prevention Inventory (HAPI) is a checklist completed by a home observer and measures safety hazards in the home (Tertinger, Greene, & Lutzker, 1984) including fire and electrical hazards, suffocation and poisoning risks, and drowning hazards. A similar measure exists for home cleanliness, the Checklist for Living Environments to Assess Neglect (CLEAN; Watson-Perczel, Lutzker, Greene, & McGimpsey, 1988). Each area of a home is rated for cleanliness, objects not belonging, and the presence of cleaning materials (sponges, mops). These instruments lead directly to behavioral treatment (i.e., the identification process used is taught to parents).

Use of medical care can be assessed through medical record checks and observing availability of common medicines/health supplies in the home. Measures of medical and emergency capacities (e.g., taking a temperature) have been developed by Delgado and Lutzker (1988) and Tymchuk (1990).

Core social-cognitive capacities can be assessed via structured interviews (Table 7.1) and instruments. For example, to assess unrealistic expectations of children, the Parent Opinion Questionnaire (POQ) has been found to distinguish abusive and neglectful mothers from controls (Azar et al., 1984). It assesses expectations around self-care, help and affection to parents, family responsibility and care of siblings, leaving children alone, proper behavior and feelings, and punishment. The Adult/Adolescent Parenting Inventory (Bavolek, 1984) is a common measure of attitudes (e.g., expectations of children, empathy toward their needs, belief in physical punishment). Because parental judgment is often poor, problem-solving and decision-making skills require evaluation. Instruments include ones by Wasik, Bryant, and Fishbein (1981), Hansen et al. (1989), and Tymchuk, Yokota, and Rahbar (1990), covering child-rearing and life issues (e.g., money).

Assessment of supervision has received less attention, except in adolescence. Protocols exist for examining parental monitoring of older children (Dishion & Andrews, 1995) that solicit daily parental reports about their knowledge of children's whereabouts, activities, homework completion, and friends. Child management and parent-child interaction levels and qualities need to be assessed. Neglectful parents have been shown to interact less frequently with their children, providing them with less stimulation. Direct observations of parents and children interacting with each other in common daily activities should be done, as well as in structured tasks in which parental stress level can be varied. Structured tools for examining such interaction can identify areas needing refinement (e.g., Dyadic Parent-Child Interaction Coding System by Eyberg, Bessmer, Newcomb, Edward, & Robinson, 1994; Behavioral Coding System by Forehand & McMahon, 1981), including difficult child behavior and parental teaching/management skills. For infants, acts such as smiling, affection, and eye contact are useful to examine (Lutzker, Lutzker, Braunling-Morrow, & Eddleman, 1987).

These can be supplemented by further client-specific assessment on unique targeted problems (e.g., child cleanliness can be rated by day care staff). School and social services records also provide risk antecedents. Neglect occurring at the end of the month may indicate economic triggers, whereas at the beginning of the month, when welfare payments are made, may reflect alcohol or drug problems.

The individual functioning of parents should be examined using traditional cognitive, academic, and personality evaluations to rule out psychiatric disturbances that may act as obstacles to treatment. Screening instruments can determine the need for more extensive evaluation (e.g., global screening for symptoms, Symptom Checklist-90-R; Derogatis, 1983), depression (Beck Depression Inventory; Beck & Steer, 1993), alcoholism (Michigan Alcohol Screening Test; Selzer, Vinokur, & van Rooijen, 1975), and drug abuse (Skinner, 1982). Literacy is needed for parenting tasks (e.g., to read prescription labels) and to utilize parent education materials. Thus, screening for reading and writing skills is important (e.g., word and reading comprehension lists) (Tymchuk, 1998) and subscales from achievement tests (Wide Range Achievement Test–Revised; Jastak & Wilkinson, 1984), Diagnostic Screening Test (DST; Gnagey & Gnagey, 1982), and Passage Comprehension (Woodcock, 1987).

Evaluation of critical contextual factors is needed. Stress and social support have both been linked to neglect (DePanfilis, 1996; Egeland, Breitenbucher, & Rosenberg, 1980). The number and type of stressful events (e.g., daily hassles, life events) and perception of the intensity of these events needs to be considered, as well as parents' coping strategies. Selecting instruments that fit parents' social class and life circumstances is crucial. Assessing support includes collecting data on the size of parents' social networks, amount of contact, its valence (positive or negative), and satisfaction with the support provided. Potential instruments include these:

- The Parenting Stress Index (Abidin, 1983; Lloyd & Abidin, 1985)
- The Life Stress Scale (Egeland et al., 1980)
- Ways of Coping Checklist–Revised (Folkman & Lazarus, 1985)
- Perceived Social Support from Family and Friends (Procidano & Heller, 1983)
- Social Support Inventory (Cyrnic et al., 1983)

Assessment of the partner relationship may also be useful (e.g., Dyadic Adjustment Scale, Spanier, 1976; Marital Adjustment Scale, Locke & Wallace, 1959) and should include an assessment for domestic violence.

Because neglect occurs as an interaction of person-based factors and environmental ones, resources in the community may need improvement (e.g., medical care, respite care for special needs child). Family resource scales are useful here (Dunst, 1986; Magura & Moses, 1986).

A thorough assessment of the child's functioning is required along with assessing the match of parental skills to their needs. This can focus on the five child areas outlined earlier. Given the heterogeneity of outcomes, assessment might start with a standard assessment and include screening issues related to specific forms of neglect (e.g., examining school records for attendance; lead paint poisoning screening). Screening can lead to referrals for more detailed evaluations. Broad-spectrum and narrow-band (e.g., attentional problems, trauma) screening instruments are available. Given that parents may distort their child difficulties, it is best to get reports of others familiar with the child (foster parents, teachers). For older children, self-report instruments may also be administered.

A multidisciplinary approach is essential (Azar & Wolfe, 1998; Hansen & Warner, 1992), including medical, behavioral, neurological, educational, and speech evaluations with children. Since health status is not something that is typically part of mental health professional's training, a discussion of screening instruments is warranted. Dubowitz (1991) describes three health screening measures, including two developed for the RAND Health Insurance Study (one for children age four and under and one for ages five to fourteen; Eisen, Donald, Ware, & Brook, 1980); Functional Status Measure (Stein & Jessop, 1982); and the Child Health and Illness Profile (CHIP; Starfield, 1988). If specific areas of deficit are identified, more focused assessment can occur (e.g., for nutritional neglect, growth pattern). Subscales of the Child Well-Being measures (Magura & Moses, 1986) are also useful.

An assessment of special needs should be done. Child skills and contextual stresses might be examined both directly and through parents' and others' reports (e.g., teachers). Instruments such as the Child Behavioral Checklist (CBCL; Achenbach & Edelbrock, 1983) or the Eyberg Child Behavioral Inventory (Eyberg & Ross, 1978) might provide insight into parenting difficulties.

The child's functioning needs to be considered across contexts. For example, discrepancies in functioning may hint at environmental contingencies that negatively affect the child and which, if the parent is unable to protect against them, may bode poorly for the child's development. For example, for children with attentional problems, a highly chaotic environment would be detrimental to performing adequately. Areas to consider include the following:

- The consistency, quality, and content of the care required (e.g., does the child have special psychological or medical needs, such as care and monitoring of a chronic illness requiring regular injections, medication, dietary restrictions?)
- Special safety needs (e.g., does the child engage in self-injurious behaviors requiring constant monitoring?)
- Needs for stability and structure
- Needs for higher than typical caregiver patience and responsiveness (e.g., where the child exhibits high rates of oppositional behavior or, in contrast, is highly passive) (Azar et al., 1998)

This highlights the need to evaluate parent-child match. The level of a parent's capacities might not place a well-functioning child at risk, but would endanger a child who has intensive medical care or other special needs. For instance, an asthmatic child needs a cleaner home than the average child. Parenting children with disabilities requires adaptations including efforts to understand the child's disability, behaviors, and needs; continuing behavior management; and long-term cooperation with medical and educational caregivers. Parents must advocate for a child in multiple settings (e.g., with schools to provide an optimal learning setting). Teachers, pediatricians, and child therapists are sources of data regarding parents' advocacy ability.

TREATMENT

Cognitive and behavioral interventions in neglect have the strongest empirical support, although most studies have involved single case designs and thus, conclusions regarding efficacy must be made cautiously. Strategies employed include the following:

- Cognitive restructuring
- Problem-solving training
- Token and other reinforcement strategies (e.g., for engaging in more competent child care)
- Modeling
- Rehearsal and feedback
- Didactic instruction
- Use of technology (e.g., pictorial presentations of material, use of in-ear transmitter for live coaching from behind a one-way mirror)

Accessing support systems is also crucial, as these can act as a safety net in times of difficulty. Other professionals with whom the family has contact can be involved. For example, Heller and Fantuzzo (1993) found that specific, neutral, and regularly provided information by schools regarding attendance, homework, and class behavior can greatly enhance parents' ability to monitor and support child school engagement. Such strategies might be incorporated into treatment of neglect.

Brief descriptions are provided below of empirically supported efforts in this area, and interventions that have not yet been evaluated, but are promising. More information is provided for cognitive restructuring and work on attributions, which have not been described in great detail elsewhere. As the reader will see, these interventions require intensive work with the family and the provision of resources that may or may not be within the reach of an individual therapist working alone or in an agency setting where time is more limited. Given the depth of problems within such families, such intensive work, however, may be crucial and efforts to combine forces with other agencies involved with them to provide comprehensive services or the development of specialized treatment teams targeting neglectful families may be necessary.

In beginning work, Tymchuk (1998) provides the following helpful hints:

1. Identify factors that may affect the success of the approach you choose (e.g., motivational issues, stressors, poor literacy) and implement procedures to address these (e.g., provide pictorial instructions for illiterate clients).
2. Determine parents' specific needs, their priority, and baseline functioning.
3. Develop a parent-specific plan, and tailor materials to their needs, style of learning, and the optimal learning setting.
4. Start easy and in small chunks for initial success.
5. Use coaching and positive reinforcement.

Cognitive Restructuring and Problem-Solving Training

Based on the cognitive-behavioral model, parenting requires thinking capacities. Thus, no matter which skills are targeted, cognitive work is required to ensure that preconceived assumptions do not interfere with skill use ("he knows what he is doing") and there are improved processing capacities that otherwise would be obstacles to generalization of skills (e.g., poor problem solving, attributional style). First, one goal should be to increase knowledge regarding developmental norms and basic care (e.g., identifying when rashes need a doctor's care). This is best done through concrete demonstrations (e.g., an exercise in which parents are asked to do a task they cannot do, such as fix a carburetor, and then are badgered, to help them understand what it is like for children; role-playing emergencies).

A second goal should be to identify and challenge unrealistic parental expectations and misattributions regarding children (see Table 7.1 for an example), using cognitive restructuring, which includes teaching parents the following:

- To recognize that their thoughts about situations and others affect their mood or behavior (e.g., believing their child is "out to get them" makes it harder to stay calm and teach their child).
- To generate their own "personalized" cognitions in problem situations, using role-plays and questioning (e.g., "All moms find tantrums hard, but what about them is the most upsetting for you? What goes through your head?").
- To challenge dysfunctional or self-defeating cognitions ("Is he really doing this on purpose?" "Do you really think other mothers can do this?"). Demonstrating children's lower capacities can also be useful (the first goal).
- To replace them with more appropriate self-talk such as: "He's only two—he doesn't know any better" or "I am doing the best I can."

Third, because their role schemas for parents and children may be distorted, parents need work on seeing their role in children's learning and growth (e.g., explaining the impact of modeling, reinforcement, and punishment on child behavior). It is important to cover the idea that parental attention actually increases negative behaviors (e.g., giving in to tantrums in the grocery store) and increases appropriate behaviors (e.g., "Why did he learn to be toilet trained? Because you gave him attention when he tried. Your attention is his paycheck!"). Modeling helps (e.g., therapists' clapping or praising reports from parents that their child has achieved a developmental milestone). This is very powerful in group settings, as a sense of pride is a natural reinforcement for parents. Finally, it is crucial to train parents in the steps of problem solving, including problem identification, alternative solution generation, and evaluating outcomes. Again, modeling is useful here.

Behavioral Skills Training

A number of studies have shown the effectiveness of behavioral approaches to problems common in neglectful families. Targets include basic care skills with infants and toddlers (e.g., diapering, taking babies' temperatures, providing cognitive stimulation) (Wolfe, Edwards, Manion, & Koverola, 1988); parent-child interaction capacities (e.g., Planned Activities Training, Lutzker, Huynen, & Bigelow, 1998; PCIT, Urquiza & McNeil, 1996); home safety, hygiene, and emergency skills (Tertinger et al., 1984; Tymchuk, 1990); nutrition, meal planning, and budgeting (Sarber, Halasz, Messmer, Bickett, & Lutkzer, 1983); and medical care skills (Delgado & Lutzker, 1988). A good example of common components of such work is a report by Feldman, Case, and Sparks (1992) of work with mentally retarded mothers of newborns and infants. They successfully trained them in basic child care (e.g., proper diapering, feeding). They first assessed baseline skill level using functional analysis-derived observation measures (e.g., bottle feeding had nine components, such as "props bottle" and "checks temperature"). Components with deficits were then targeted for intervention using verbal instructions, specially designed picture books depicting each step in the task analysis, modeling of each step by a trainer, and feedback on the mother's actual performance during and following the training sessions. Mothers received coupons (exchangeable for small gifts) contingent on scoring 80 percent correct on trained skills in weekly sessions ranging from two to twenty-nine weeks depending upon their acquisition (sessions last from ten to sixty minutes). Child involvement was maximized during training, or a doll was used to train some skills (e.g., dealing with a diaper rash). Time was spent in visits on advice, support, and problem solving on other life issues (e.g., finding an apartment). When compared to controls, trained mothers did significantly better than a nontreated control group on trained skills and did not differ significantly from comparison mothers (low and middle SES mothers of children similar in age). Further, the treated group maintained skills at follow-up (mean of twenty-eight weeks). Although this study's design had some limitations (e.g., variability in follow-up), it suggests effectiveness of such targeted training.

Although it has not targeted neglectful parents, work on supervision (monitoring child behavior) has also occurred with parents of older children to reduce potential for involvement in antisocial behavior (Dishion, Andrews, Kavanaugh, & Sobermann, 1996). Techniques developed by Patterson (1982) where the focus is on prosocial fostering, limit setting, and problem solving may be adapted.

Some researchers in this area highlight special features of this work. Although not specifically directed at neglect, Peterson and Gable (1998) outline childhood injury prevention strategies. They highlight two elements of injury prevention: removing the child from the hazard and removing the hazard from the child's environment. Although their views echo the approach already discussed (e.g., removing environmental hazards), they add other elements. First, they argue that parents expect children to control their impulses, which may lead parents to believe children require less supervision (e.g., they will check before crossing the street; will stay away from hot objects such as stoves and heaters). They also cite the fact that parents rely excessively on family rules (e.g., "He knows he's not supposed to play in the street"). Parents in general underestimate how much supervision is necessary for children and overestimate the effectiveness of their rule instructions. Targeting these elements fits with the cognitive model. These schemas need to be challenged and replaced with more realistic ones (e.g., "The child will not remember rules, and I will need to walk him home from school"). These researchers also argue that parents fail to provide enough consequences for rule breaking (e.g., either no consequences or weak ones, such as lectures). Children need to make a firm connection between risky behavior and an immediate negative outcome.

Along with skills building and challenging beliefs about children and their supervision needs, attention is needed to factors that decrease parental attention and vigilance (e.g., substance abuse, depression, neurological problems that may decrease their awareness of children's risky behavior). Child factors that make supervision of their behavior more difficult might also need intervention. Further reducing parental engagement may be parents' own basic need deprivation and low sense of self-worth and efficacy. Interventions aimed at improving parental efficacy in all domains might have spillover effects in their monitoring of their children. Factors beyond their control must also be considered. Economic status may make only poor housing available to parents (e.g., lacking window screens) and require case management (e.g., employment help, economic supports, work with landlords).

Also, Tymchuk (1998), in working with developmentally disabled parents, emphasizes the need to determine the best learning environment for their capacities and providing prosthetic materials (e.g., picture books) to compensate for deficits where needed. Delgado and Lutkzer (1988) provided parents with basic health supplies and training in medical care, and Sarber et al. (1983) provided safety materials (e.g., child locks for cupboards, outlet covers). Language barriers and literacy also require attention (Delgado & Lutzker, 1988, provided training scenarios in Spanish and/or read them to clients).

Neglect may occur when parents are overwhelmed with child management issues and fail to supervise children (e.g., withdraw from the role when they feel less success). Parents' repertoire of positive management strategies (e.g., use of reward) need to be widened and they need to be provided with alternatives to harsh and coercive punishment (e.g., use of distraction, time out), as well as reshaping their cognitive responses in the midst of using strategies. Such work has been shown to be effective (see review by Azar & Wolfe, 1998). Because of cognitive limitations, use of parenting manuals and didactic instruction may be less effective. Case studies have supported the use of technology (coaching parents through a one-way mirror using a radio transmitter that fits into the ear) and the use of a board game to train them in appropriate verbal responses to child-rearing situations (Crimmins, Bradlyn, St. Lawrence, & Kelly, 1984; Fantuzzo, Wray, Hall, Goins, & Azar, 1986).

Anger and stress management training are often needed for parents to calmly carry out other parenting strategies. This needs to be supplemented with direct efforts to decrease contextual stresses that act as setting events (e.g., financial help; marital work). Such training involves three steps. First, parents need to identify triggers for anger and stress. Through questioning their examples of stressful times (e.g., What caused the stress or anger? How did you feel? What were you thinking? What did you do? How did your child or others react?), a pattern of "hot" issues or events that set off a parent can be identified, as well as his or her unique set of warning signs. The latter can include physical responses ("I feel a tightening in my stomach") and cognitive responses ("I say to myself, 'Why me? It's not fair!' or 'He's doing this on purpose! He wants me to look bad.'"). Relaxation skills can then be taught (e.g., deep muscle relaxation) or helpful self-talk (e.g., "It feels like he's trying to get to me, but he's just tired"). Self-talk can be trained through the in-ear transmitter, with the trainer coaching parents through child-rearing situations. (See Exhibit 7.3 for an example of cognitive work with parents.)

EXHIBIT 7.3.
Transcript of Cognitive Work

THERAPIST: Can you give me a recent example of Johnny's difficulties?

PARENT: Take yesterday. I was trying to get the kids dressed for school and he threw a fit.

THERAPIST: A fit?

PARENT: Yeah . . . he had to wear his blue shirt but I couldn't find it. He started screaming and wouldn't get dressed and I lost it (obviously frustrated).

THERAPIST: That sounds awful—in the middle of trying to get the kids off to school. . . . Tantrums are awful for moms, but I have found it's awful in different ways for each mom. What about it is so hard for you?

PARENT: I don't know—he has this look on his face . . . augh!

THERAPIST: Look?

PARENT: Yeah . . . like he thinks he's boss.

THERAPIST: Like he thinks he's boss . . . mmmm. That must feel terrible. What does it feel like to have a kid who thinks he's boss?

PARENT: Like I don't matter . . . like he thinks I am stupid or something.

THERAPIST: Stupid. . . . Does he remind you of anybody when he does this?

PARENT: He looks just like his father. He used to call me stupid all the time. Johnny has the same look on his face . . .

THERAPIST: So Johnny looks like his father and when he gets mad—he reminds you of his father.

(Parent nods)

THERAPIST: How is he like his dad and how is he different?

PARENT: Well, he has his dad's eyes and chin . . . but Johnny is more cuddly and affectionate.

THERAPIST: So even though he looks like him, your relationship with Johnny is different.

PARENT: Yeah . . . he's softer.

THERAPIST: I wonder, when Johnny has a tantrum, whether he makes you think of his dad and that gets mixed in with how you feel.

PARENT: Mmmm . . . maybe.

(continued)

(continued)

THERAPIST: Lots of moms I talk to say that happens to them. I wonder if Johnny really thinks he's boss or maybe that just because he looks like his dad—you feel that way.

PARENT: It's possible. He's only two. He isn't the boss. I am. It is just when I am mad . . . I don't know.

THERAPIST: One thing that helps moms in those moments is to say to themselves . . . he's only two.

CASE EXAMPLE

The following case illustrates many of the treatment issues encountered in neglectful families.[4] More detail is given about the cognitive elements of intervention, as these have not been described elsewhere.

Case Description

M. was a twenty-year-old single mother on welfare who had a son (age three) and an infant daughter (age nine months). There were multiple reports of neglect, including failure to provide adequate care. (Her younger child had severe diaper rash. The older child often came to day care filthy and unfed and was often absent.) Supervision of the children was also lacking (e.g., the little boy was found wandering the streets unattended at night and was seen standing on the sills of open windows).

M. did not complete high school and had been in special education classes throughout her schooling. She had her first child as a teenager and lived with her mother during his early years. She had no further contact with the baby's father. She describes her mother as continually finding fault with her parenting. Shortly after meeting her daughter's father, they moved in together. When seen, however, she was no longer living with him, although he visited regularly.

Assessment

Assessment was conducted in two home visits for observation and two agency visits for more formal evaluations. Because M. had difficulty keeping appointments, she was transported by her social worker to the office for the evaluation. A systems evaluation indicated difficulties with basic tasks (e.g., difficulty maintaining a residence, clothing the children, and providing them with food). The family had lived in a homeless shelter periodically. Although she was eligible for subsidized housing and food stamps, she had failed to apply for them. She drew on her mother and her daughter's father for financial help. Meals were unpredictable and poor in nutrition. There were many problems with developmental tasks. M. failed to provide age-appropriate guidance and supervision. There was no standard bedtime for the children and they stayed up all night watching televison. She did not supervise their outdoor play (e.g., on one early visit, the three-year-old was found alone in an unfenced front yard on a busy street). She failed to acknowledge her son's mastering tasks (e.g., he would attempt to show her pictures he drew and she did not even look at them). Response to emergencies was minimal (e.g., did not identify the severe diaper rash as a problem and seek help).

These problems suggested difficulties in problem solving (failure in the identification stage) and inadequate behavioral control in the family system. On the other hand, there was some evidence of affective responsiveness (e.g., M. was affectionate with the children, although less so with her son). Her communication with them was quite direct, but often consisted of yelling. Affective involvement was also not adequate (failure to initiate behaviors showing interest in the children). As with most single mothers, M. experienced role overload and had little support.

M.'s social contacts were problematic. She often had conflicts with her family of origin and had almost no relationships aside from occasional visits with her younger child's father and other men she met. These relationships were also conflict ridden and often involved her being verbally abused. Social capacities were identified as a problem area.

Traditional assessment of the mother indicated some strengths and a large number of skill deficiencies. Her intellectual ability placed her in the borderline mentally retarded range. Specific life capacities were missing (e.g., ability to read well, budgeting). No major psychiatric problems were found, although she showed mild signs of depression. Alcohol abuse was denied, but, over time, it unfolded that she would drink small amounts of beer to "make" herself "feel better."

Cognitive and developmental assessment of the three-year-old indicated low average cognitive ability and delays in language, motor skills, and pre-academic skills. He was highly distractible during testing and showed signs of attention deficit disorder. Maternal and teacher reports indicated aggressive behavior and poor impulse control. The nine-month-old had similar developmental delays.

The cognitive-behavioral assessment done with M. showed problems in each of the five areas described earlier. An assessment of her expectations regarding children indicated many unrealistic beliefs. She agreed to statements such as: "Parents can expect even a child as young as two and a half to be able to comfort them when they are sad and crying"; "A three-year-old child usually knows when his mom or dad is upset and that he should stay out of the way at those times"; and "It's okay to leave a three-year-old who is soundly sleeping in a bed alone in the house or apartment while the parent walks a friend to the corner bus stop." She also evidenced beliefs that children are able to meet parents' needs for affection and attention. Her solutions to hypothetical parenting problems indicated a narrow repertoire of child-rearing strategies that were often not age appropriate (e.g., talking to a two-year-old to get him to stop hitting his infant brother, instead of moving him out of range of the baby). Her parenting was further assessed using daily phone calls in which she was asked a series of questions about her monitoring of the children and her interaction with them (e.g., discipline) to identify and establish baselines for targets of intervention. Her responses indicated a high rate of coercive responses and a negative attributional bias toward her son. For example, she described one incident in which he spilled milk. When asked why this happened, she said, "He's a brat. He never listens. He likes to make work for me." Her response was "screamed at him—told him how stupid he was." Little time was spent with the infant daughter who typically was "put down for a nap" or in a playpen.

Observations of the parent-child interactions further indicated that M. had a poor ability to give clear commands and confirmed a high frequency of coercive responses (e.g., threats, yelling, and criticism). Her son responded with high rates of noncompliance and negative behavior. For example, when M. was asked to get him to pick up toys, he failed to comply in a "clowning" manner and elicited mother's laughter in the midst of her attempts to get him to comply. Given the mother's negative bias toward him, M.'s positive response was a very powerful reinforcer and increased the noncompliance. At a certain point, however, M. without warning attempted to "get serious" and became angry. The boy tried harder to elicit his mother's laughter, which infuriated her and led her to threaten him with a spanking. Most of the time, however, M. ignored the boy's misbehavior. Since it was often designed to elicit attention, the behavior would escalate until she responded.

M.'s interaction with the nine-month-old was observed in daily care activities (diapering, feeding, and play). She made almost no eye contact with the child during these activities and did not verbalize much. In play, M. was awkward and not able to pace her actions to those of the child and was at times overly intrusive. For example, when told to get the child to take a block from her, rather than gently coax her, M. grabbed the baby's hand and roughly tried to move her fingers around the block. During feeding, she took a bottle and squirted the baby's face with water. This initially made the baby laugh. However, she continued to do this, even when the baby was obviously irritated by it. The mother did not attend to the cues provided by the child. When questioned regarding the baby's fussing, the mother's interpretation was that she was fine. "She likes it."

Maternal anger control was poor and she described herself as "having a short fuse," with no specific triggers to her anger, saying, "I just lose it." However, questioning revealed that incidents typically occurred in the context of other life stressors (e.g., after a negative transaction with her boyfriend). Maternal stress was found to be significant on a life event scale. Many of the events, however, were controllable (e.g., arguments with family members).

Thus, mother's interpersonal skills played a role. M. reported few social contacts and dissatisfaction with the ones she did have. While alcohol use was a concern, it was secondary to depression. It had a strong cognitive base (i.e., marked by negative and self-deprecatory statements) and centered on her worth as a parent and social isolation. It was felt alcohol use might lessen if these issues were addressed.

Treatment Selection

A multimodal treatment was planned. Since the agency in which M. was seen used a number of treatment modalities, over the course of the nine months in which she was seen, she and her children received multiple forms of help. These included the following:

- Placement of the younger child in a day care program to reduce M.'s stress and to work on her delays
- Behavioral work with day care providers of the older child to decrease his impulsivity (e.g., a Velcro board was placed on his desk and intervals when he was sitting in his seat and on task were rewarded with a colorful Velcro sticker that was exchanged for extra healthy snacks, congruent with his need for more nutritious foods)
- Rewards to M. by school staff for her son's attendance and his coming to school clean and clothed appropriately for the weather (e.g., phone calls providing social contact; cards were sent home complimenting her that did not have lots of words and illustrated praise with pictures)
- Individual and group work on parenting and social skills

Because of M.'s cognitive limitations, the group she attended was small. Socialization was enhanced by providing lunch and efforts were made to promote social skills. Active social skills work was done. Verbal initiation was trained using a board game (Fantuzzo et al., 1986) and time was spent on how to make friends (e.g., role-plays). To train mothers in cognitive stimulation, they were provided with colorful "exercise" cards with activities to do with their children (e.g., illustrations of playing peek-a-boo) and were provided with materials to do the exercises. Coaching occurred to provide feedback and perspective-taking training. Training also took place in child management (clear commands, praise) and stress management. Each was taught in small steps and adapted where necessary. Cognitive restructuring was directed at unrealistic expectations of children and the inappropriate use of them as a source of social support (see Table 7.1).

Individual home visits helped M. apply the new parenting skills and make modifications where needed. This home treatment later took a broader focus, working on other intrapersonal (depression) and interpersonal (social) problems, as well as continuing to fine-tune parenting. Goals included decreasing unrealistic expectations and negative bias, increasing parenting skills (child management, hygiene, supervision), and increasing her ability to modulate anger and her social network.

Treatment Course and Problems in Carrying Out Interventions

During cognitive parent training, problems with children elicited should be explored for their meaning. Even commonly cited child difficulties may be associated with misattributions that must be changed before the parent will be willing to use new strategies. For example, as is typical, M.'s three-year-old on occasion became oppositional. Cognitive techniques were utilized to elicit her attributions, which often were: "He's trying to get to me . . . to tell me he's the boss." When this was questioned, she responded with a self-deprecatory response (e.g., "He thinks I'm stupid"). When asked if there were others in her life who felt this way, she responded by listing her mother or the boy's father. She elaborated on the latter: "He's just like his dad, always trying to push me. . . . He thinks I'm dumb and laughs at me." This internal dialogue indicated some discrimination training was needed before training in parenting. That is, before she could choose an appropriate response, she had to view her child as in need of education, rather than malevolent in intent and indistinguishable from critical adults in her life. This negative attributional style may be limited to parents' children, but in this case seemed more generalized. For example, vocational training was set as a goal for the mother as an alternative source of self-efficacy (to decrease depressive symptoms). The first step in achieving this goal was enrollment in a GED program. Unfortunately, M. wanted to quit the program after only a week despite an initial positive response. The teacher had used a mistake she'd made on a quiz for illustrative purposes in class and M. felt she was being "made fun of" and ridiculed.

As cognitive responses were challenged, strategies for child management were instituted. For example, alternatives to physical punishment were taught (e.g., time out, response cost), as well as positive strategies. Video feedback and role-plays helped M. formulate clearer commands and avoid delivering mixed messages (e.g., laughing when trying to solicit compliance).

Lack of supervision was the hardest to treat. Such situations required anticipatory skills that seemed lacking in this client's repertoire. The first element in such skills is a recognition of children's limited capacity to anticipate risks. M. clearly believed that the children knew what they were doing and "could take care of themselves" and only got into difficulties because they were "being stupid" or "trying to get her in trouble." Cognitive challenging was undertaken. This was done in a number of ways. First, discussions took place regarding M.'s own childhood. For example, children's different conception of time was illustrated by asking her to reflect upon how long she felt she had to wait for Christmas when she was very young and how it seemed to come so quickly for her now as an adult; or how far away her school seemed to her as a child and how in reality it was quite close. "Experiments" were also undertaken. Piagetian conservation tasks were done with the boy to illustrate the fact that children think differently and make errors due to this. M.'s own needs for safety and security were discussed. Once elicited, these feelings were linked to her children's needs. Examples from her own childhood where she did not feel safe were accessed to reinforce this issue.

M.'s "short fuse" was also targeted (anger management). Cognitions that might "fan the fire of anger" were elicited first. As noted, M. denied signs that she was about to "lose it." Guided imagery and role-plays were useful in identifying cognitive, physiological, and situational anger cues. These cues then became prompts to engage in strategies to dampen the response (e.g., calming self-statements, anticipatory relaxation responses prior to high-risk situations, and avoidant responses such as counting to ten).

M. indicated a desire to increase social contact (although ambivalent—"friends hurt you"). She indicated a desire to make friends with a mother she saw each day as she waited for the bus with her son. Problem solving took place as to how she might begin such an acquaintance. The therapeutic relationship was itself used as a model (e.g., "It was tough at first for us to talk. What did I do that made it easier for you to talk to me?"). The therapist also modeled cognitive strategies to decrease obstacles (e.g., dealing with fears that the other person will not talk). Initial contact was role-played and various possible outcomes considered. M. then made an attempt to make contact (invited this person for coffee). The therapist reviewed with the client what occurred and they together identified areas for further skill development. This was repeated with other interpersonal difficulties.

Many problems arose during the course of treatment that interfered with treatment gains but presented opportunities for further skill building. At one point, M. was evicted from her home, and parenting gains disappeared as she dealt with this crisis. The episode was utilized to reinforce new interpersonal skills (stress coping). There appeared to be some capriciousness on the landlord's part and so problem solving was used to generate potential ways to change his decision. The therapist happened to be present on one of his visits and could utilize this transactional information to fine-tune M.'s social skills. For example, M. became passive when he set an unreasonable date for her departure. Work on assertiveness was undertaken. Also, this episode acted as an antecedent to irritable and coercive child-rearing responses. The therapist pointed out this spillover and this example was resurrected in other such situations (e.g., M. would become enraged with her child after having difficult conversations with her mother on the phone).

Over the course of treatment, M. made steady improvements in interactions with the children (increased her positive interactions, basic care, and supervision). Her involvement with CPS was terminated by the end of treatment and maintained at one year follow-up. She increased her social supports and completed the GED program. The alcohol use decreased, as did her depression. Her relationship with her daughter's father continued to be conflicted, but he refused treatment. M. became involved with another man.

This relationship, while far from perfect, was an improvement over her previous ones. Her son's speech and pre-academic skills improved significantly. Unfortunately, his behavior problems continued. When he entered kindergarten, behavioral work in the classroom was done and he was placed on medication. The daughter made good progress.

CONCLUSION

Cognitive-behavioral work is one strategy to combat the pervasive difficulties often seen in neglect. Clearly, the presence of substance abuse and other problems needs attention either simultaneously with such work or prior to beginning it. Cognitive-behavioral strategies, however, have shown the best outcomes with this population and should clearly be considered for such cases.

NOTES

1. In de-emphasizing the role of severe disorder in this discussion, we do not mean that attention to such disorder is not necessary as part of treatment planning, but rather that it is the outcomes that follow from the disorder that affect the child. Clearly, if severe disorder is present, it requires attention prior to, or simultaneously with, intervening in parenting (e.g., medication, cognitive-behavioral therapy for depression) or may require adaptations in the intervention (e.g., developmentally disabled parents).

2. Although more infants and toddlers may be seen within child protection caseloads for neglect, the abuse and neglect of teenagers should not be overlooked. Certain forms of neglect may be common among this age group (e.g., lack of supervision, educational neglect) and may have just as negative an impact upon their development.

3. Note that we see intellectual functioning as a proxy for more specific cognitive deficits (which may or may not be seen in all intellectually functioning parents and which also occur in higher IQ parents as well, although perhaps less frequently).

4. This case is a hypothetical one illustrating many of the strategies discussed.

REFERENCES

Abidin, R. (1983). *Parenting Stress Index—manual.* Charlottesville, VA: Pediatric Psychology Press.

Achenbach, T. & Edelbrock, C. S. (1983). *Manual for child behavior checklist and revised child behavior profile.* Burlington: University Associates in Psychiatry.

Azar, S. T. (1986). A framework for understanding child maltreatment: An integration of cognitive behavioral and development perspectives. *Canadian Journal of Behavioral Science, 18,* 340-355.

Azar, S. T. (1989). Training parents of abused children. In C. E. Shaefer & J. M. Briesmeister (Eds.), *Handbook of parent training* (pp. 414-441). New York: Wiley and Sons.

Azar, S. T. (1995, April). *Is the cognitively low functioning mother at risk for maltreatment?* Presentation at the biannual meeting of the Society for Research in Child Development, Indianapolis.

Azar, S. T. (1998). A cognitive behavioral approach to understanding and treating parents who physically abuse their children. In D. Wolfe & R. McMahon (Eds.), *Child abuse: New directions in prevention and treatment across the life span* (pp. 78-100). New York: Sage.

Azar, S.T. (2002). Parenting and child maltreatment. In M. Bornstein (Ed.), *The handbook of parenting* (Vol. 4, 2nd ed., pp. 361-388). Mahway, NJ: Lawrence Erlbaum Associates.

Azar, S.T. (2003). Adult development and parenting. In J. Demick (Ed.), *Adult development* (pp. 391-415). New York: Sage.

Azar, S. T. & Benjet, C. L. (1994). A cognitive perspective on ethnicity, race and termination of parental rights. *Law and Human Behavior, 18,* 249-268.

Azar, S. T. & Cote, L. R. (2002). Sociocultural issues in the evaluation of the needs of children in custody decision-making: What do our current frameworks for evaluating parenting practices have to offer? *International Journal of Law and Psychiatry, 25,* 193-217.

Azar, S. T., Lauretti, A., & Loding, B. (1998). The evaluation of parental fitness in termination of parental rights cases: A functional-contextual perspective. *Clinical Child and Family Psychology Review, 1,* 77-99.

Azar, S. T., Povilaitis, T., Lauretti, A., & Pouquette, C. (1997). Theory in child abuse. In J. Lutzker (Eds.), *Child abuse: A handbook of theory, research and treatment* (pp. 3-30). New York: Plenum.

Azar, S. T., Robinson, D. R., Hekimian, E., & Twentyman, C. T. (1984). Unrealistic expectations and problem solving ability in maltreating and comparison mothers. *Journal of Consulting and Clinical Psychology, 52,* 687-691.

Azar, S. T. & Siegel, B. (1990). Behavioral treatment of child abuse: A developmental perspective. *Behavior Modification, 14,* 279-300.

Azar, S. T. & Soysa, K. (2000). How do I assess a caregiver's parenting attitudes, knowlege, and level of functioning? In H. Dubowitz & D. DePanfilis (Eds.), *The handbook of child protection* (pp. 308-313). New York: Sage.

Azar, S. T. & Twentyman, C. T. (1986). Cognitive-behavioral perspectives on the assessment and treatment of child abuse. In P. C. Kendall (Ed.), *Advances in cognitive-behavioral research and therapy* (Vol. 5, pp. 237-267). New York: Academic Press.

Azar, S. T. & Wolfe, D. A. (1998). Child abuse and neglect. In E. G. Mash & R. A. Barkley (Eds.), *Behavioral treatment of childhood disorders* (2nd ed., pp. 501-544). New York: Guilford Press.

Barnes, K. T. & Azar, S. T. (1990, August). *Maternal expectations and attributions in discipline situations: A test of a cognitive model of parenting.* Paper presented at the annual meeting of the American Psychological Association, Boston.

Bavolek, S. J. (1984). *Handbook of the Adolescent-Parenting Inventory*. Park City, UT: Family Development Resources.

Beck, A. T. & Steer, R. A. (1993). *Beck Depression Inventory: Manual*. San Antonio, TX: Psychological Corporation.

Belsky, J. (1980). Child maltreatment: An ecological integration. *American Psychologist, 35*, 320-335.

Bousha, D. & Twentyman, C. T. (1984). Abusing, neglectful, and comparison mother-child interactional style: Naturalistic observations in the home setting. *Journal of Abnormal Psychology, 93*, 106-114.

Bradley, R. H. & Caldwell, B. M. (1979). Home observation for measurement of the environment: A revision of the preschool scale. *American Journal of Mental Deficiency, 84*, 235-244.

Bradley, R. H., Mundfrom, D. J., Whiteside, L., Casey, P. H., & Barrett, K. (1994). A factor analytic study of the infant-toddler and early childhood versions of the HOME inventory administered to white, black, and Hispanic American parents of children born preterm. *Child Development, 65*, 880-888.

Brown, S. E. (1984). Social class, child maltreatment, and delinquent behavior. *Criminology, 22*, 259-278.

Cahill, L. T., Kaminer, R. K., & Johnson, P. G. (1999). Developmental, cognitive, and behavioral sequelae of child abuse. *Child and Adolescent Psychiatric Clinics of North America, 8*, 827-843.

Cook, D. A. (1991). College students from emotionally neglectful homes. *New Directions for Student Services, 54*, 77-90.

Crimmins, D. B., Bradlyn, A. S., St. Lawrence, J. S., & Kelly, J. (1984). A training technique for improving the parent-child interaction skills of an abusive-neglectful mother. *Child Abuse and Neglect, 8*, 533-539.

Crittenden, P. M. (1993). An information processing perspective on the behavior of neglectful parents. *Criminal Justice and Behavior, 20*, 27-48.

Cyrnic, K. A., Greenberg, M. T., Ragozin, S. A., Robinson, N. M., & Basham, C. (1983). Effects of stress and support on mothers and premature and full term infants. *Child Development, 54*, 209-217.

Delgado, A. E. & Lutzker, J. R. (1988). Training young parents to identify and report their children's illnesses. *Journal of Applied Behavior Analysis, 21*, 311-319.

DePanfilis, D. (1996). Social isolation of neglectful families: A review of social support assessment and intervention models. *Child Maltreatment, 1*, 37-52.

Derogatis, L. R. (1983). *SCL-90-R administration, scoring, and procedures manual-II*. Townson, MD: Clinical Psychometric Research.

Dishion, T. J. & Andrews, D. W. (1995). Preventing escalation in problem behaviors with high risk young adolescents: Immediate and 1 year outcomes. *Journal of Consulting and Clinical Psychology, 3*, 538-548.

Dishion, T. J., Andrews, D. W., Kavanagh, K., & Sobermann, L. H. (1996). Preventive interventions for high risk youth: The Adolescent Transition Program. In R. D. Peters, & R. J. McMahon (Eds.), *Preventing childhood disorders, substance abuse, and delinquency* (pp. 184-214). Thousand Oaks, CA: Sage.

Donovan, W. L. & Leavitt, L. A. (1989). Maternal self efficacy and infant attachment: Integrating physiology, perception, and behavior. *Child Development, 60,* 460-472.

Dubowitz, H. (1991). The impact of child maltreatment on health. In R. H. Starr & D. A. Wolfe (Eds.), *The effects of child abuse and neglect* (pp. 278-294). New York: Guilford Press.

Dunst, C. H. (1986). *Family resources, personal well-being, and early intervention.* Unpublished manuscript. Family Infant and Preschool Program, Western Carolina Center, Morganstown, NC.

Egeland, B. R., Breitenbucher, M., & Rosenberg, D. (1980). Prospective study of the significance of life stress in the etiology of child abuse. *Journal of Consulting and Clinical Psychology, 48,* 195-205.

Egeland, B. R. & Erickson, M. F. (1987). Psychologically unavailable caregiving. In M. Brassard, R. Germain, & S. Hart (Eds.), *Psychological maltreatment of children and youth* (pp. 110-120). New York: Pergamon.

Eisen, M., Donald, C. A., Ware, J. E., Jr., & Brook, R. H. (1980). *Conceptualization and measurement of health for children in the Health Insurance Study.* Santa Monica, CA: RAND Corp.

Epstein, N. B., Bishop, D. S., & Baldwin, L. M. (1982). McMaster model of family functioning. In F. Walsh (Ed.), *Normal family processes* (pp. 115-141). New York: Guilford Press.

Eyberg, S., Bessmer, J., Newcomb, K., Edward, D., & Robinson, E. (1994). *Dyadic parent-child interaction coding system II: A manual.* Unpublished manuscript, University of Florida, Gainesville, Department of Clinical/Health Psychology.

Eyberg, S. M. & Ross, A. W. (1978). Assessment of child behavior problems: The validation of a new inventory. *Journal of Clinical Child Psychology, 7,* 113-116.

Fantuzzo, J. W., Wray, L., Hall, R., Goins, C., & Azar, S. T. (1986). Parent and social skills training for mentally retarded mothers identified as child maltreaters. *American Journal of Mental Deficiency, 91,* 135-140.

Feldman, M. A. (1998). Parents with intellectual disabilities. In J. R. Jutzker (Ed.), *Handbook of child abuse research and treatment* (pp. 401-420). New York: Plenum Press.

Feldman, M. A., Case, L., & Sparks, B. (1992). Effectiveness of a child-care training program for parents at-risk for child neglect. *Canadian Journal of Behavioral Science, 24,* 14-28.

Folkman, S. & Lazarus, R. S. (1985). If it changes it must be a process: Study of emotion and coping during three stages of a college examination. *Journal of Personality and Social Psychology, 48,* 150-170.

Forehand, R. & McMahon, R. (1981). *Helping the noncompliant child: A clinician's guide to parent training.* New York: Guilford Press.

Gershater-Molko, R. M. & Lutzker, J. R. (1999). Child neglect. In R. T. Ammerman & M. Hersen (Eds.), *Assessment of family violence* (pp. 157-183). New York: Wiley and Sons.

Gnagey, T. & Gnagey, P. (1982). *DST: Reading Diagnostic Screening Test.* East Aurora, NY: Slusson.

Hansen, D. J., Pallotta, G. M., Tishelman, A. C., & Conaway, L. P. (1989). Parental problem-solving skills and child behavior problems. *Journal of Family Violence, 4,* 353-368.

Hansen, D. J. & Warner, J. E. (1992). Child physical abuse and neglect. In R. T. Ammerman & M. Hersen (Eds.), *Assessment of family violence* (pp. 123-147). New York: Wiley and Sons.

Harrington, D., Dubowitz, H., Black, M. M., & Binder, A. (1995). Maternal substance use and neglectful parenting: Relations with children's development. *Journal of Clinical Child Psychology, 24,* 258-263.

Heller, L. R. & Fantuzzo, J. W. (1993). Reciprocal peer tutoring and parent partnership: Does parent involvement make a difference? *School Psychology Review, 22,* 517-534.

Jastak, S. & Wilkinson, G. (1984). *Wide Range Achievement Test–Revised.* Wilmington, DE: Jasmak Associates.

Kaplan, S. J., Pelcovitz, D., & LaBruna, V. (1999). Child and adolescent abuse and neglect research: A review of the past 10 years. *Journal of the American Academy of Child and Adolescent Psychiatry, 38,* 1214-1222.

Korbin, J. E. (1994). Sociocultural factors in child maltreatment. In G. B. Melton & F. D. Barry (Eds.), *Protecting children from abuse and neglect* (pp. 182-223). New York: Guilford Press.

Larrance, D. T. & Twentyman, C. T. (1983). Maternal attributions in child abuse. *Journal of Abnormal Psychology, 92,* 449-457.

Lloyd, B. H. & Abidin, R. R. (1985). Revision of the parenting stress index. *Journal of Pediatric Psychology, 10,* 169-177.

Locke, H. & Wallace, K. (1959). Short marital-adjustment and prediction tests: Their reliability and validity. *Marriage and Family Living, 21,* 251-255.

Loos, M. E. & Alexander, P. C. (1997). Differential effects associated with self-reported histories of abuse and neglect in a college sample. *Journal of Interpersonal Violence, 12,* 340-360.

Lutzker, J. R., Huynen, K. B., & Bigelow, K. M. (1998). Child neglect. In V. B. VanHasselt & M. Hersen (Eds.), *Handbook of treatment protocols for children and adolescents* (pp. 467-500). Hillsdale, NJ: Erlbaum.

Lutzker, S. Z., Lutzker, J. R., Braunling-Morrow, D., & Eddleman, J. (1987). Prompting to increase mother-baby stimulation with single mothers. *Journal of Clinical and Adolescent Psychiatry, 4,* 3-12.

Magura, S. & Moses, B. S. (1986). *The Parent Outcome Interview.* Washington, DC: Child Welfare League.

Mak, A. S. (1994). Parental neglect and overprotection as risk factors in delinquency. *Australian Journal of Psychology, 46,* 107-111.

Melchert, T. P. (2000). Clarifying the effects of parental substance abuse, child sexual abuse, and parental caregiving on adult adjustment. *Professional Psychology: Research and Practice, 31,* 64-69.

Milner, J. S. (1986). *The Child Abuse Potential Inventory* (2nd ed.). Webster, NC: Psytec.

NCCAN (National Center on Child Abuse and Neglect) (2001). *Child maltreatment 1997. Reports from the states to the National Center on Child Abuse and Neglect*. Washington, DC: U.S. Department of Health and Human Services.

Patterson, G. R. (1982). *Coercive family processes*. Eugene, OR: Castalia Publishing.

Perez, C. M. & Widom, C. S. (1994). Childhood victimization and long-term intellectual and academic outcomes. *Child Abuse and Neglect, 18,* 617-633.

Peterson, L. & Gable, S. (1998). Holistic injury prevention. In J. R. Lutzker (Ed.), *Handbook of child abuse research and treatment* (pp. 291-318). New York: Plenum Press.

Polansky, N. A., Chalmers, M. A., Buttenwieser, E., & Williams, D. P. (1981). *Damaged parents: An anatomy of child neglect*. Chicago: University of Chicago Press.

Powers, J. L., Eckenrode, J., & Jaklitsch, B. (1990). Maltreatment among runaway and homeless youth. *Child Abuse and Neglect, 14,* 87-98.

Procidano, M. & Heller, K. (1983). Measures of perceived social support from friends and from family: Three validation studies. *American Journal of Community Psychology, 11,* 1-24.

Radloff, L. S. (1977). The CES-D Scale: A self report depression scale for research in the general population. *Applied Psychological Measurement, 1,* 385-401.

Rohrbeck, C. A. & Twentyman, C. T. (1986). A multimodal assessment of impulsiveness in abusing, neglectful, and nonmaltreating mothers and their preschool children. *Journal of Consulting and Clinical Psychology, 54,* 231-236.

Rutter, M. (1979). Maternal deprivation 1972-1978: New findings, new concepts, new approaches. *Child Development, 50,* 283-305.

Salzinger, S., Kaplan, S., & Artemyeff, C. (1983). Mother's personal social networks and child maltreatment. *Journal of Abnormal Psychology, 92,* 68-72.

Sarber, R. E., Halasz, M. M., Messmer, M. C., Bickett, A. D., & Lutzker, J. R. (1983). Teaching menu planning and grocery shopping skills to a mentally retarded mother. *Mental Retardation, 21,* 101-106.

Selzer, M. L., Vinokur, A., & van Rooijen, L. (1975). A self-administered Short Michigan Screening Test. *Journal of Studies of Alcohol, 36,* 117-126.

Skinner, H. A. (1982). The Drug Abuse Screening Test. *Addictive Behavior, 7,* 363-371.

Spanier, M. A. (1976). Measuring dyadic adjustment: New scales for assessing the quality of marriage and similar dyads. *Journal of Marriage and the Family, 38,* 15-28.

Starfield, B. (1988). Measuring health status in children. *Quality of Life and Cardiovascular Care*, Winter, 147-150.

Stein, R. E. & Jessop, D. J. (1982). A non-categorical approach to chronic childhood illness. *Public Health Reports, 97,* 354-362.

Swick, K. J. (1988). Parental efficacy and involvement: Influences on children. *Childhood Education*, Fall, 37-42.

Tertinger, D. A., Greene, B. F., & Lutzker, J. R. (1984). Home safety: Development and validation of one component of an ecobehavioral treatment program for abused and neglected children. *Journal of Applied Behavior Analysis, 17,* 150-174.

Tymchuk, A. J. (1990). Assessing emergency responses of people with mental handicaps. *Mental Handicap, 18,* 136-142.

Tymchuk, A. J. (1998). The importance of matching educational interventions to parent needs in child maltreatment. In J. R. Lutzker (Ed.), *Handbook of child abuse research and treatment* (pp. 421-448). New York: Plenum.

Tymchuk, A., Yokota, A., & Rahbar, B. (1990). Decision-making abilities of mothers with mental retardation. *Research in Developmental Disabilities, 11,* 97-109.

Urquiza, A. J. & McNeil, C. B. (1996). Parent-child interaction therapy: An intensive dyadic intervention for physically abusive families. *Child Maltreatment, 1,* 134-144.

Wasik, B. H., Bryant, D. M., & Fishbein, J. (1981, November). *Assessment of parent problem solving skills.* Paper presented at the annual meeting of the Association for the Advancement of Behavior Therapy, Toronto.

Watson-Perczel, M., Lutzker, J. R., Greene, B. F., & McGimpsey, B. J. (1988). Assessment and modification of home cleanliness among families adjudicated for child neglect. *Behavior Modification, 12,* 57-87.

Widom, C. S. (1998). Childhood victimization. In D. P. Dohrenwend (Ed.), *Adversity, stress, and psychopathology* (pp. 81-94). Oxford: Oxford University Press.

Wolfe, D. A. (1987). *Child abuse: Implications for child development and psychopathology.* Newbury Park, CA: Sage.

Wolfe, D. A., Edwards, B., Manion, I., & Koverola, C. (1988). Early intervention for child abuse and neglect. *Journal of Consulting and Clinical Psychology, 56,* 40-47.

Woodcock, R. (1987). *Woodcock Reading Mastery Test–Revised.* Circle Pines: AGS.

Wright, S. A. (1994). Physical and emotional abuse and neglect of preschool children: A literature review. *Australian Occupational Therapy Journal, 41,* 55-63.

Zuravin, S. J. (1991). *Research definitions of child physical abuse and neglect* (pp. 100-128). New York: Guilford Press.

Chapter 8

Individual Therapy and the Abused Child

P. Forrest Talley

INTRODUCTION

This chapter describes individual therapy with maltreated children. Of all the different approaches to working with children, individual therapy is the most popular (Kazdin, Siegel, & Bass, 1990). It would be more accurate, however, to speak about individual therapy modalities, to speak in the plural, rather than describe this approach as if it were a singular monolithic enterprise. The individual work that takes place with a fourteen-year-old, for example, has significant differences from that which occurs with a five-year-old. Play therapy differs dramatically from cognitive therapy, and the behavioral contracting that can be done with an eleven-year-old looks very different from the hypnotherapy that might have been used with the same child. Each enterprise is approached through individual work with the child, but each brings a different tool to bear on the task of change. In this regard, it is helpful to make a distinction between working modalities and schools of thought. The same tools for making interventions are often used by professionals who hold very different ideas on what animates a child's problems and what underlying causes require change. Counselors holding a psychodynamic view will frequently use play as a tool for change, as will their colleagues who work from a social learning perspective. Each may also use reframing, behavioral consultation with parents, structured games, and so forth. Their tools are similar, but the conceptual foundations for using these tools, and sometimes the specific goals attached to their use, are very different. Individual therapy refers, then, to an array of interventions that are harnessed by a variety of conceptual orientations. The combination of interventions, driven by a particular theoretical engine, is what distinguishes one approach from another.

We can see that a clear conceptual foundation is necessary for the effective selection of interventions. Without such a foundation, the counselor becomes like the carpenter who wields a hammer, saw, and plane with little notion of what he is supposed to build. He may, through his innate gifts, create a masterpiece of craftsmanship, or he may, through his ignorance, do great damage and destroy the materials with which he is working. But most probably he will accomplish neither of these extremes, and instead spend much time and effort accomplishing very little. Conceptualization is crucial. It steers the counseling to its destination. The conceptual approach to individual work that is discussed in this chapter relies on some core principles derived from interpersonal theory. These principles apply to adults as well as children, from preschoolers to adolescents. Whether you choose play, parent consultation, or cognitive-behavioral interventions as the tools to bring about change, the interpersonal principles guiding their use will be the same.

I begin with a brief overview of interpersonal theory and its application to sexually and physically abused children. I recognize that the treatment of children suffering from these two types of abuse is most often discussed separately within clinical literature. But inasmuch as children who are sexually abused are very often physically abused as well (Urquiza, Wirtz, Peterson, & Singer, 1994), the child you see in the clinic is very likely to have experienced both types of trauma. This does not deny that specific sequelae are often found with each type of abuse, and there are some fine resources to turn to when addressing these specific concerns (Friedrich, 1995; Gil, 1991; James, 1994). It is also true, however, that there is much common ground in how children respond to each form of abuse, and the approach described herein has broad enough application to profitably inform the work of therapists helping with many types of children.

After reviewing interpersonal theory, I discuss the clinical assessment of these children and then look at the different stages of counseling and how to keep progress moving at each stage. A case history exemplifying the major points of the chapter concludes the discussion.

EVERY CHILD HAS A STORY

With myriad considerations that each counselor must keep in mind when working with a child, it is easy to forget that the child has a story. Not just a history. Not just a collection of symptoms. Not just a list of caregiver complaints. There is a story that every child presents with, and presents from within. The child is the main protagonist, there are supporting characters with different roles, plots and subplots. Within each story are acts of bravery and cowardice, virtue and sin, hopes that drive the child forward and fears that stifle the child's potential. The story is the child's life, and we counselors are much like the reader who picks up a book several chapters into the tale. If we are to help, we must understand the children placed in our charge as well as we understand the characters in the novels we read. This requires that we integrate what we know of children's strengths, weaknesses, current problems, fears, wishes, and relationships with their history in order to develop an understanding of their stories. Too often we work to learn something of each of these facets of the children we see but never take the next step of integrating them to form a story. This leaves the job only half done. It would be similar to describing a play by saying that there is a primary male lead, a primary female lead, and each loves the other. The man is often driven by pride, the woman devoted and lovely, and the play ends with tragic death. We have component parts, but we do not have the story. For that, we need to know what plots are woven throughout the play, what goals each character strives for, what animates each person's behavior, and so forth? If we knew the answers to these questions, we would know whether the story was *Othello* or *Romeo and Juliet.* The story makes a difference.

FINDING THE STORY

Interpersonal Theory

How can we go about discerning the child's story? The core concepts of interpersonal theory act as a helpful guide in this regard. Familiarity with these concepts makes it easier to identify some of the major thematic threads running through a child's life. Consequently I review these concepts before going on. From Sullivan's (1953, 1954, 1962) nascent attempts to develop an interpersonal theory of psychology, numerous refinements and theoretical offshoots have emerged. Just a few examples include Leary (1957), Wiggins (2003), and Benjamin's (1974) work on circumplex models, all of which trace their lineage to Sullivans's original ideas, as does the work of Bateson (1958), Haley (1959), and Jackson (1968) on the relationship between schizophrenia and disordered family communications. Although the areas where interpersonal theory is now applied are quite diverse, Kiesler (1982) suggests that the following four assumptions are common to them all.[1]

1. The "self-system" is central to an individual's personality and must be taken into account when attempting to understand interpersonal behavior.

Broadly defined, the self-system refers to one's self-concept and the unconscious mechanisms that help maintain it. Stepping away from the dry mechanistic terminology of self-systems, we can simply refer to this as "self." Sullivan (1953) suggested that the development of self is strongly influenced by personal evaluations voiced from important others early in a child's life. Such evaluations are thought to be internalized (often called "introjected") and subsequently form the basis of the emerging self. Successfully maintaining this sense of self provides the individual a degree of intrapsychic stability, albeit for the psychologically maladjusted a frequently painful one. How such stability is accomplished leads us to the next assumption of interpersonal theory.

2. It is within the context of social interactions that personality becomes manifest and can be best understood.

A stable self-concept depends on social interactions that confirm its veracity. For example, the ten-year-old who sees herself as competent and independent for her age will have this self-concept confirmed if her peers, teacher, and parents treat her in a manner consistent with competency and age-appropriate independence. If one day, however, her classmates begin to ridicule her behavior on the playground, her teacher ignores her contributions in the classroom, and her parents begin to treat her as though she were a preschooler, the child's self-concept would be challenged. If the situation continued, or escalated, she would feel threatened and as a result unconsciously increase her efforts to engage in interactions that confirm her sense of self (Talley, Strupp, & Morey, 1990). If these efforts persistently failed, then a change in self-concept from independent/competent to dependent/incompetent would begin to occur.

In sum, individuals tend to seek out interactions that confirm their self-concept and find social encounters that challenge them to be uncomfortable. Within this context, it can be seen that personality becomes manifest through the interpersonal transactions by which one's sense of self is maintained or perturbated to change. The medium through which these transactions take place is the focus of the next assumption.

3. Interpersonal transactions are a form of communication that occur through verbal and nonverbal channels.

This relates to prior assumptions in that self-concept develops from, and is maintained by, communicative acts. Interpersonal communication obviously depends on the interactions between two or more people, with one person attempting to convey a message that he hopes the other will understand. Yet it is the listener who acts as the final arbitrator of what message is actually received. The strength of the self-concept and the personality functions that support it reside in its ability to selectively (and unconsciously) distort and screen out information that is inconsistent with it. In short, listeners are thought to actively attempt to construct meaning from a speaker's message that will be consistent with their self-concept.

4. Interpersonal behavior is best understood in terms of circular, not unidirectional, causality.

Unidirectional models of causality tend to describe social interaction as the result of one person's behavior causing a reaction in another person. This form of description is inadequate because it fails to take into account the reciprocally evoking behaviors of each participant. For example, albeit an overly simplified one, consider the sort of interaction that occurs between a physically abusive mother and her little boy. In these sorts of relationships, we often see the child being convinced that he is fundamentally bad, and the mother is just as often convinced that she is fundamentally a failure. The little boy's misbehaviors are seen by the mother as one more proof that she is a failure, perhaps evoking a sense of humiliation and impotency within the context of all her previous failures. She lashes out at her child and the boy receives this abuse as proof of the unarticulated fear he holds that he is worthless. This perception is further fueled by the periods of neglect by his mother (the father being absent altogether) and eventually this fear breaks through in further acts of gross defiance. The mother becomes engaged with the boy in one more angry act of abuse that both substantiates his worthlessness and, paradoxically, reassures him that he is not so worthless as to be altogether abandoned and forgotten.

It is necessary to use a circular model of causality to capture the dynamic chain of events in this relationship wherein each act is the result of both participants' reciprocally evoking interpersonal styles.

The foregoing discussion of interpersonal theory emphasizes how children's view of others is largely colored by the quality of their early formative relations. A study by Ken Dodge (Dodge, Pettit, Bates, & Valente, 1995) provides a telling example of this point. Two groups of children were compared. In one group, every child had a substantiated history of physical abuse. In a comparison group, there was no evidence that any of the children had been abused. Dodge had each child watch a brief video, and afterward they were interviewed. The video showed two boys sitting next to each other at a table, with a box of crayons lying on the edge of the table between the two boys. One youngster turns to the other and in the process knocks the box of crayons to the floor. End of video. The researchers then asked the child who just viewed this scene to tell why the crayons fell off the table and what they would do if they were the other child.

The answers each group gave are instructive. For the most part, the children who had no history of abuse responded that the boy had accidentally knocked the crayons off the table. Moreover, the only response they would have would be to continue coloring, or to help pick up the crayons. The abused children, however, viewed the interaction in a very different light. They knew that the boy had intentionally knocked the crayons off the table. You can almost hear them respond, if pressed by the interviewer: "Accident? Right. Let's talk reality. The kid was trying to cause some grief. Don't be a sap with all that accident stuff." What would this group of children do about the fallen crayons were they in that situation? Let them lie there, not be the other child's friend, be sure to keep an eye on the offending child, and so forth. Not the sort of response that engenders friendships, but goes miles toward cultivating animosity and conflict.

The lesson is straightforward. Children's histories will influence how they make sense of the world and this in turn will affect how they behave. Keep in mind, however, that children with similar views of the world may have vastly different ways of coping with what they perceive.

A brother and sister were referred to our clinic after their father stuffed an infant sibling into the kitchen trash can. Prior to this act of brutality, the father had assaulted their mother, breaking her nose and leaving her thoroughly beaten and bloodied. The children had seen their mother beaten in this way many times during their young lives. The girl was four years old. I will call her Jane. The boy was six years old. Call him Jack. They met me in the waiting room of the clinic, whereupon Jane gave me a big smile and took my hand while we walked to the playroom. Jack crossed his arms over his chest and slowly followed with a scowl on his face. Once in the room, Jane asked what I would like her to draw for me. After I reassured her that she could draw whatever she liked, and I would enjoy seeing it when she was through, Jane sat herself down at the table and began earnestly working on her new project. She was a pretty little girl with an engaging manner and a bright smile beneath worried eyes. She wore a new sundress and the colorful ribbons in her hair bobbed up and down as she walked. Jack stomped into the room and began to examine a shelf that spanned the entire side of the room and was filled with toys. He picked up the first of these toys, a Velcro Mr. Potato Head. They briefly exchanged glances. Jack's eyes narrowed. He glared, muttered an epithet, and sent the soft-sided spud sailing across the room. He then went on to scrutinize the next toy. It met a similar fate. Jack was an impressive sight. Small for his age, he stood ramrod straight and wore a black cowboy hat, black T-shirt, black shorts, and black boots. Not once during these executions did Jack look over to where I was standing. Then, after dispatching the last toy on the shelf, he turned in my direction and swaggered across the room. Glaring up at me, hands on his hips, Jack slowly drawled, "You want a piece of me?"

Jack responded to the ambiguity and anxiety of the interview in a way that is consistent with the Dodge study just examined. Having learned that the world is full of angry and threatening people, he prepared himself to respond in kind. His sister Jane, with a similar history, responded to the anxiety and ambiguity of the initial interview with acts of submission and supplication. If she could only make people like her enough, they would not harm her. We understand from their differences something of how they view themselves: Jack is a fighter, one who can make his way in a threatening world by attacking those who would hurt him. He will not easily concede control, and in fact he is ready to fight at the first sign that someone may try to do him harm (we see in this encounter an unfortunate tendency for the first sign of trouble to arise from this little boy's imagination rather than the real world). Jane, however, is one who would rather appease, who will endear herself to others so that they find no reason to hurt her. If the tension rises, and hostility becomes more blatant, Jane's recourse will be to focus on something else—perhaps her efforts to please the source of her anxiety. Jack responds to his perception of hostile control with hostile control. Jane responds to her perception of threat (we assume hostile control from her history) with submissive friendliness. Each of these could serve as the start, the kernel, of Jack's and Jane's stories, the beginning of a motif that would be better established as the counseling went on.

Intake

A good therapist must also be a good investigator. Effective therapy depends upon knowing both the details of a child's life and the relation of those details to one another. The goal of the intake is to acquire these pieces of knowledge. Your purpose in this process is much like that of the biographer. Recognize this as a central fact: you are constructing a biography, and the more solidly you hit your mark here, the more help you will be to the child. The information you need for completing this task comes from several sources and includes the following:

- Social worker reports that give detailed accounts of the child's history and family
- Parent/foster parent reports of the child's behavior
- Teacher observations
- Further observations of the child in counseling, focusing both on play themes and the quality of the relationship the child builds with you

Social Worker Reports

The social worker report should be thoroughly studied so that you know what type of abuse occurred, when and to whom, for how long, and what reaction others had to knowing about this abuse (did they ignore it, effectively end it, ineffectually try to stop it, etc.). From reading these reports, you will also be able to get a sense of the broader quality of the relationship between your patient and the parents. Was it almost purely hostile abuse? Was it abuse under the guise of love and protection (most often seen in incestuous abuse by a father), or was it unvarnished abuse meted out during times of parental rage or drunkenness? It may have been neglect punctuated by abuse, or it may have had a premeditated sadistic quality (e.g., as in the parent of a youngster I saw who put hot peppers under his son's tongue until blisters would form). The point is that we cannot stop our inquiry simply because we know what type of abuse occurred. The meaning this abuse has to the child is central and is greatly influenced by the relationship within which the abuse took place. Keep this distinction in mind or you will fall short in understanding your patient.

Observations from Parents, Foster Parents, and Other Caregivers

You will also want to obtain as much information as possible from the child's caregivers. Your goal is to determine what this child is like under a number of circumstances. By delving into this question, you will be able to discover the child's status in regard to emotional, social, cognitive, moral, and physical development. Moreover, you will begin to discern patterns of behavior, affect, and thought that repeat themselves and present as chronic difficulties. For example, you may have a boy who tries extraordinarily hard to please the caregivers by obeying every household rule, and then when he is reprimanded ever so slightly for some infraction, he becomes explosive and difficult to control. This is an important pattern, suggestive of a child who believes he must meet every demand of his caregivers in order to be accepted, and who once finding that his best efforts fail, lashes out in anger at those he was attempting to please. This germ of a storyline begs further questions that will be answered through more intensive interviews with caregivers or through observations of the child's play in counseling. These questions include what he experienced in trying to meet these demands (e.g., fear, anger, comfort, humiliation, competency, etc.) and likewise what he experienced when perceiving that he had fallen short (e.g., humiliation, failure, fear of rejection, anger at having his efforts fail, etc.).

These are the patterns that you will work with in constructing the story of the child, part of the plot that you will attempt to change. If this pattern occurs with the boy's foster parents, you can assume that it will eventually manifest itself in the therapeutic relationship. Although this does not always occur, even in successful therapies, it does so often enough to warrant your looking for it. Within interpersonal and psychodynamic schools this is referred to as working within the transference, and within more cognitive-behavioral schools it is thought of as a generalized response. In either event, when you find this type of pernicious interpersonal pattern, it is your job to alter it to a more constructive pattern.

To develop an effective understanding of the child, your interview of the parents needs to provide information on the patient's functioning in several key domains, including physical, cognitive, social, emotional, and moral development. It is beyond the scope of this chapter to discuss how each of these areas of the child's life is best assessed. Some specific things to look for, however, can be briefly mentioned.

Physical. Ask about medical illnesses, what sports the child is involved in, and his or her skill in each. Also note whether the child is large or small, strong or weak, fast or slow, and so forth. Are fine motor skills as well developed as gross motor skills, and are both as developed as is expected for a child of that age (referring to developmental charts is helpful)?

Cognitive. Much of the information on cognitive functioning will come from your inquiry into school performance, discussed later. Clearly, however, there is more to learn about cognitions than just academic success. Do children have concentration appropriate for their age, and are they able to change the focus of their attention from one topic to another without becoming distracted? Do they organize information well? Are they tentative, quick, or bold in their thinking? How creative are they and are they adept at making connections between events? Is there a tendency toward ruminative thinking, or does it go well beyond this to obsessively dwelling on certain topics? All of these aspects of children's cognitions will be important in your counseling.

Social. When assessing the child's social functioning, look at the quality of relationships with peers, adults, and younger children. Also make note of differences in how the child relates to the opposite sex. More generally, does the child have many, few, or no close friendships, and what is the basis for the friendships that do exist? Keep in mind that it is natural for friendships to be based upon different criteria at different ages (Asher & Gottmann, 1981; Selman, 1980). For example, the three-year-old bases most friendships on physical proximity, whereas the early school-age child will be more influenced by activities that are mutually enjoyed. Also examine how children enter friendships. Do they make the first overture or do they usually respond to the overtures of others? Are they selective or indiscriminate, leaders or followers? Are these tendencies the same across settings and even with younger children? Although distinctly different, the quality of the relationship the child develops with you can shed much light on these topics.

Emotional. Understanding patients' emotional development is key to making effective interventions. Do children modulate affect well, and are they able to sustain a sense of affective tension without being overwhelmed? Is the comfort offered by others sufficient to compose them once they become distressed, or does it require long periods of solitude, acting out, or regression before reestablishing a sense of equilibrium? It may be that one or two emotional states predominate, often in relation to each other. These patterns of affective relation are important to detect as they create much havoc in children's lives. Being able to identify them and trace their situational and cognitive origins is a great help toward developing interventions that will break the pattern.

Moral. Although moral development has long been studied by developmental psychologists (Kohlberg, 1984; Piaget, 1965), most counselors are loath to go near the subject (refer here to their work with patients, not their personal lives). The message is most impressively drummed into the heads of young students in psychology, social work, marriage and family counseling, and related disciplines that we must not judge our patients. Examine, diagnose, and analyze yes, but do not judge their behavior, their goals, their passions and feelings. To judge would be "to pass judgment on" and that would be, one hates to say, judgmental. This approach to your work will not do. It is farce to think that we will listen to the stories of our patients and not have judgments regarding what we hear. Show me a counselor who has no judgments about parents who scald their babies, men who rape little girls, mothers who leave their children to wander the street and find meals from trash cans, and I will show you a counselor who should be in another profession. The examples I have used are painted boldly, and we are unlikely to disagree because of that. But the point is the same whether stated in stark contrasts or more subtle shades: morals provide a compass that influences the direction of one's life. The children we see are better off if they have developed a sense of values, a perspective on life that includes what is right and wrong, of what is virtuous and what is base. It has been my experience that those children who identify themselves with these virtues are most likely to overcome the trauma of their past. These convictions help a child persevere during difficult times and can sometimes buffer them from behaving exceedingly poorly when they are most stressed. By no means do they guarantee angelic behavior: the storms of childhood are too severe, and the additional forces added by trauma and foster care too great to ever hope for that. But in the midst of all this a handful of simple virtues, heartfelt by the child, may act as a polestar for the youngster to steer by.

When looking at children's moral development, you should begin by inquiring whether they ever show themselves to suffer from a guilty conscience. We hope the answer is yes. Guilt, and its cousin shame, have their place. If they run wild they do much damage, but their absence in an individual is even more chilling. We can compare them to fire. When contained it is productive, but when not contained it destroys. If fire were absent altogether . . . You see what I'm driving at. Guilt and shame are among the great social brakes that cause us to refrain from doing what we ought not do, and to stop doing what we have already begun but know we should not do.

The problem that most often occurs with abused children is that they either have a pervasive sense of guilt or shame, or almost no sense of it whatsoever. The former is much more common than the latter. Ask parents what makes their child feel guilty, when this last occurred, and how they and the child responded. Was it ever resolved? Unresolved guilt is a horrible oppressor. It must be dealt with for counseling to be effective. Shame, the feeling that there is some entrenched and deeply embarrassing flaw within oneself, is just as oppressive and harder to eradicate.

Make inquiries into children's sense of honesty; do they respect others' property or is pilfering an occasional avocation? You will also understand something about their sense of fair play and honesty when you play your first game of cards, checkers, or a board game. Likewise you will want to look at loyalty, responsibility, acts of kindness, and a sense of responsibility. This list is not exhaustive. Other virtues need to be examined as well. The main point is to make sure you consider this domain of the child's life, gather as much information as you can and use it as a vital part of your understanding the child.

Teacher Observations

Teachers are another source of information that must be tapped. Keep in mind that children of school age spend as much nonsleeping time at school as they do at home. Consequently, it is important that you make a careful assessment of children's behaviors and relationships at school. The best way to do this is to make a school visit and watch your patient in the classroom and on the playground. Very few counselors are able to do this. Second best is to have an assistant go and make these observations for you. But again, few counselors are able to do this as well. A third option that every counselor can do is to speak to the teacher over the telephone and send a standardized questionnaire (e.g., the Child Behavior Checklist [CBCL] or the Behavior Assessment System Children [BASC]) to complete. It is necessary that you secure copies of the child's report cards, any academic or intellectual testing that has been performed and, if the child has academically struggled, all records of school interventions aimed at remediating those difficulties. One of the greatest hardships on a child is to go to school six to seven hours a day, five days each week, and perpetually fail. The child's failure is usually on public display inasmuch as classmates know who is struggling and who is learning the material. Children who lag behind are daily reminded of their status as failures. One of the most effective interventions you can perform for children in this position is to assist them in getting the academic help they need.

The parents will also have information regarding the child's performance at school, and this must be carefully reviewed. Ask parents if children like school and talk appreciatively of classmates, how many friends they have at school, is homework done regularly, and how much help is solicited from parents. Also inquire about recess activities (do they join other children or sit alone), what the teacher has said about them during parent/teacher conferences, and how children respond to "open house" nights when their work is on display. Do they look forward to the evening, show pride in what they have done, acknowledge other children from class that evening, greet the teacher, respond with pride to compliments about their work, and so forth?

Clearly the answers to these questions assess more than the children. It is the parents (biological parent, foster parent, guardian, etc.) who must satisfy your curiosity. Do they seem knowledgeable, or have they missed all parent/teacher conferences and had conflicts on open house nights? Have they ever spoken to the teacher about the child? Do they notice whether homework is done and are they also curious to know how their children spend recess time? The parent who is not involved in children's school life is a parent who is largely uninvolved in the child's life altogether. If the desire is there on the part of the parents, then you may be able to improve their involvement by driving home the importance of taking an active interest, and helping to figure out ways to get around obstacles that have stymied their involvement thus far.

Unmotivated parents are more problematic. Efforts must still be made to get them involved, but successfully doing so is less likely. Sometimes when this occurs with a foster parent you will be able to see it as one example of a pervasive pattern of detachment that is not limited to the child's school, but occurs with regard to medical needs (e.g., not being attentive to regularly scheduled dental appointments), physical needs (e.g., the child consistently comes to your office in dirty clothes, uncombed hair, or with the smell of urine), and emotional needs (e.g., scheduled visits with siblings are canceled on a whim, or counseling sessions are frequently missed). Under these circumstances the social worker must be informed, and you should insist that the foster parent receive a plan of corrective action that specifically details what changes are required. If this fails to bring about the desired result, or the social worker refuses to provide the corrective action plan, you should inform the social worker's supervisor of what the child needs. This is often a good time to discuss changing foster homes. Unless the child has a particularly strong bond with the negligent foster parent (unlikely), this option is often your best recourse. Because most county social workers labor under overly large caseloads, they will not look forward to taking on the extra work of finding a new foster family. You must give them a good reason to do so and continue to prompt them to act. This course of action on your part will undoubtedly impair your working relationship with the current foster parents, but the option of having the child continue to languish under their care is not a viable one. As a final resort, you should look up the department within social services that licenses foster care parents and lodge a complaint detailing how the child's needs are being neglected. This may result in that foster parent's license being revoked and the child being moved to a new home.

The child has a wealth of information regarding school performance as well. Although the next section includes a more detailed account of how to obtain information directly from the children you see, it is worth noting here that the questions you had of the teacher and parent apply equally to the child. It works best if they are asked in a more conversational style, woven into your more general discussion of the child's life. For example, if you are speaking about friends in the neighborhood it is quite natural to ask if they go to the same school. You would then find it interesting to know if your patient has any other friends at school. The answer is invariably yes and you will want to know their names, just so you can get a clear idea of the important children at school. Here isolated children often falter, not sure of the names of the numerous friends they have just claimed to possess. No matter. Do not leave them with this anxiety. Note to yourself that they wanted to impress you by claiming to have friends, but they have very few, and then move on to say, "I'll bet you and your friends have fun during recess. Tell me what you do." This tells you what they would like to be doing, and you have gotten all of this information without appearing to interrogate them.

The main point of all these efforts needs to be remembered: to discern the child's strengths, weaknesses, and repetitive patterns of behavior. The end result of your efforts may look like the following:

Vickie was an eight-year-old third grader who frequently bullied other children during recess. Although she had a history of doing this at home, her foster parents had effectively responded with appropriate limits and support so that it was no longer a problem. Prior to the third grade, the bullying had not occurred during school at all. In fact, Vickie was a particularly bright child who had done well academically and although somewhat of a loner she had not gotten into any significant trouble with teachers or peers. She prided herself on being smart. Her intelligence was a source of great comfort to her. This was important, for she was often the target of cruel remarks by peers because she was a large, ungainly girl. Moreover, her history of abuse had thoroughly inculcated within her a sense of being flawed in almost every way. So this one ability that provided her a sense of competency was of special importance.

Dramatic fluctuations in a patient's behavior always require that we ask what changes have occurred in the child's life that could create distress, and subsequently the troubling behavior that is manifesting. A careful review of Vickie's third grade year revealed that she had been written up for bullying about twice a week. Moreover, her grades had fallen somewhat, and in particular she was struggling with a new addition to the curriculum—biology. This was the first year the school had introduced the biology curriculum in the third grade, and despite Vickie's excelling at so many other topics, she struggled just to do passing work in this domain. As the teacher reviewed the preceding months of the school year, she noted that Vickie's acting out usually occurred on the same days that the class studied biology. The connection was clear. On those days when she felt most besieged, she struck out against others. Whether this was because her psychological resources were so depleted that she had no wherewithal to hold back her anger, or whether it was due to the sense of power and competency it gave her when bullying others, was not clear. Further work within play therapy would provide those answers. The important point is that a pattern had been discovered, leading the counselor to know where to look for more specifics that would ultimately allow for a fuller understanding of the child, and more effective interventions.

Observations of the Child

Greenspan (1981) makes an important point about clinical assessment when he notes that children not only have a story, what he calls a "drama," but they also have a stage upon which it is played out. The larger the drama, the larger the stage should be if chaos is to be avoided. The smaller the drama, the smaller the stage may be. Obviously a large drama played out on a small stage creates large problems (it is hard to enact *Ben Hur* on a stage meant for dinner show entertainment). Neglected and abused children are known for having large dramas. What Greenspan refers to as the stage is the child's abilities across the various domains of functioning reviewed earlier (i.e., cognitive, social, etc.).

These domains and their assessment were briefly discussed in the previous two sections, including cognitive, academic, physical, emotional, social, and moral development. Taking their measure is no less important when meeting face to face with the child than it is when speaking to the parents and teacher. I do not go into detail here on how to approach this task, partly due to my desire to keep this chapter from becoming obese, and partly because the assessment of these abilities is mostly straightforward. For instance, you cannot help but notice whether a girl cheats when playing a game with you, what her frustration tolerance is for losing, or how well she perseveres when having to work hard to win. Likewise it is clear whether the youngster is able to warmly engage you in an age-appropriate manner, whether she is constantly oppositional and bossy, or is shy and withdrawn. Assume that what you see during your hour with the child every week is a valid aspect of who that child is and what she is like with others. Personalities do not come in "snap on" varieties: children do not leave their personalities in the car while they go in to see you. They always bring their personality with them. Of course they sometimes behave differently around adults, especially counselors, than they do with peers. But because their problems are often with adults, this is not a major concern. Moreover, even when they act differently with you than with their peers, similar trends almost invariably arise after a short time. The bossy child becomes bossy in counseling, the pouter starts to pout, the friendly engaging fellow leaves the counselor glowing with self-satisfaction, and so forth.

The relationships children establish with you will provide great insights into how they relate to others. It sometimes happens that a youngster who is a tyrant at home and school is docile and friendly with the counselor. Typically this does not last long, and the problems seen elsewhere crop up in counseling as well. When that is not the case, one of two dynamics is typically at work. The first, and most favorable, is that the child is showing a capacity for healthy relationships when the stresses present at school or home are absent (as they are in counseling). You then go about finding ways to decrease those sources of stress and increase the child's ability to respond effectively to what stressors remain. More frequently the child is not demonstrating a potential for healthy relationships but instead is trying his very best to avoid the work of counseling. This will become apparent in that his relationship to you will not change much. There will be no growing sense of engagement, trust, or rapport. Your questions are often returned with a listless remark, "I don't know," and your comments about the problems that continue to boil up at home and school are met with blank stares and adamant denials. When this occurs you are witnessing an enactment of how this child behaves with others.

How you structure the initial interview with the child will be important. If the child you are starting to see is below the age of ten years, it is desirable to see the parent alone for the first session. This allows you to candidly discuss the youngster's problems, history, and the parent's response to the stresses resulting from these difficulties. Older children are likely to be made more suspicious if you see the parent alone for the first meeting, and consequently it is advisable to see both the parent and child in these instances. Explain when they first sit down that you will be speaking with both of them together at first, and later with each of them alone. Then move on to discuss what brings them to see you and observe whether they agree on what is the problem. If not, discuss how they disagree, specific examples, and so forth. If the parent becomes unrelentingly critical, have the child leave while you spend a few minutes alone with the parent. Use this time to assess whether the parent is aware of the intensity of this criticism and the effect this has on the child. Briefly gather further information about the problems as the parent sees them, and how life in the home would be different if counseling were successful. Then move on to see the child alone.

The first time you meet with the child alone, whether this be with a school-age or latency-age child, it is recommended that you be nondirective for the first fifteen to twenty minutes. This allows you to view how the youngster responds to an ambiguous situation that has minimal demands. Be attentive, and comment on the child's play, but remain nondirective. If the child asks you to play, respond, "Thank you, but I'll just sit here and be with you while you play." Note how children investigate the playroom (cautious, reckless, joyful, afraid, methodically or disorganized, with interest or apathy), what they play with (is it appropriate for their age and sex, what symbolic significance might it have), and their engagement with you while they play (do they invite you to talk, to admire what they have done, or are they indifferent to your presence). You wish to note as comprehensibly as possible all the relevant aspects of the child's behavior, just as if you were performing a school observation in a classroom.

With about a half hour left in the meeting, call the child over to you and say that you have something fun to do using his or her imagination. You are about to ask some questions that shed light on what and who is important in the patient's life. To get a better understanding of what is important, ask the little tyke what three wishes he or she would want a genie to grant. But you must not ask the question in that straightforward kind of way. This evokes very little from a child. Dull questions bear the fruit of dull answers. Begin by asking, "Have you ever been to the beach?" "Never, you say? How about the river or lake?" "Not that either? Rats. Playground?" Yes, you hear, everyone has been to the playground. Now you move on. "Pretend you are at the playground. You can feel the warm sun on your shoulders and the wind against your face. You're walking across the sand going to your favorite part of the playground when—bump—your toe hits something. You look down and see a green, red, gold, and blue bottle sticking out of the sand. Picking it up, you take it to the grass and start to wipe off the sand when all of a sudden smoke comes pouring out. BAMMO! A genie, ten feet high, is standing in front of you." The child by this time is thoroughly enjoying the idea of this genie, and because you have taken the time to develop the scene through guided imagery, the child feels like part of the story. "The genie tells you he is glad to be out of the bottle. Far too cramped after all these years. He is so thankful that he is going to give you three wishes. You say, I know I can't ask for anyone to die, come back to life, or fall in love with me. But the genie tells you, not at all. You can ask for anything your heart desires—except for more wishes." With that you are ready to hear what is important to the child.

Move on to inquire who is the most important person in the child's life. If this question is asked directly, however, you are unlikely to get as candid an answer as when you ask the question in story form. Approach the question as follows. "Now the genie gave you these wishes and that was all very well. You enjoyed what these wishes brought you and a short while later you decided to go to the beach for a little relaxation. Once there you decided to take a little boat out on the ocean to do a little exploring. This turned out to be a lot of fun but all of a sudden a terrible storm came up and pushed your boat farther and farther from shore until it crashed on a little island. The boat sank, but you were safe on shore. The storm ended. You looked around the island and found that no one else lived there. Once upon a time there must have been someone on the island though because there was a little cabin with a warm bed, and in the cupboards lots to eat and drink." For neglected children especially, it is important to add this to the story to dampen anxiety that is aroused by the thought of hunger. "One morning you are fishing on the beach, there is a big tug on the fishing line, and you start to reel in what feels like a huge fish. You get it to shore and . . . it's a bottle. You take it to the beach, wipe it off, and smoke starts to come out. Wow. The genie again! You say, 'I know, I know, I get three wishes' but the genie says, 'Nice try. That was a one-time offer. But I do appreciate you getting me out of the bottle again, so I'm going to do you a favor. I know you'll be rescued from the island before the year is over, but in the meantime I'll bring anyone you want to stay with you on the island. Who do you want it to be?'" If the child chooses two people, that is fine. You are not primarily interested in making sure the child abides by the rules, but instead you want to know who in all the world the child wants to be with.

You will ask many other questions of the child, and perhaps use specific tasks and questionnaires. The House-Tree-Person task is often helpful, as is Sentence Completion with older children. The CBCL should be standard with all children during assessment and every six months thereafter (only those eleven years and older will be able to fill out the form for themselves; parents of younger children will complete the form). The Roberts Apperception Test should also be administered as it provides rich insights into children's views of themselves and their relationships. Use any or all of these as the situation permits. In addition, a simple question should always be added. That is, what sort of animal does the child think he or she is most similar to? Include also what type of animal is most like each member of the family.

I will not try to interpret here what the selection of various animals suggests about the child. Some choices, in light of the child's history and family dynamics, are easily understood whereas others are opaque. What is most important about the child's answer is that it gives you a clear map of what animals are associated with the child and various family members. Having this knowledge allows you, later in the counseling, to craft story interventions that use these animals. Knowing children's associations gives you more confidence that they will make the associations that you wish them to make within the story. For example, a child who said during the assessment interview that he would be a dog can pretty well be counted upon to identify with the dog in a story you tell three months later in counseling.[2] That story may have a very important point about how some source of difficulty was eventually overcome, some point that the child is not ready to hear directly but could benefit from by hearing indirectly. You will want to do everything possible to make certain your story hits the mark, and knowing the answer to this question about animals will help you to accomplish this.

One of the most informative pieces of information comes from the stories children tell about their lives, and the play they engage in during counseling. Older children, due to their greater language skills and better insight, are more adept at relating informative stories from everyday life. Nevertheless they need help from you by way of prompting. The ten-year-old girl who tells you she got in trouble for hitting a little boy at school needs your help in telling this story fully. You will want to know what occurred before she hit the boy, what he was doing, what meaning your patient attached to this boy's behavior, how she felt, and what transpired afterward (at home and school). It will also be necessary to know what conclusions the child draws from this whole conflict. Using the questioning method described by Tom Lyon (see Chapter 4) will get you started. Specific questions interposed in a conversational style will fill out the details. Collect these stories for each child you see. After a short time patterns will appear, and these patterns point to the more general plot that is interwoven throughout the child's life.

A useful way of discerning these patterns is provided by Dahl's work with adults (Dahl & Teller, 1994; Hoelzer & Dahl, 1996; Hoelzer, Dahl, & Kaechele, 1998). This method is called FRAMES (Fundamental Repetitive and Maladaptive Emotion Structures) and begins with a transcription of a patient's description of various events in his or her life. The transcription is then broken into basic parts and each part identified by the theme it reflects. After collecting several descriptions of the patient's relationships, the patterns within each narrative are compared to other life stories the same patient has told. Frequent repetitions of themes are looked for and then sorted into similar groups. An example of the final product of these efforts could be as follows: the appearance of unexpected romantic involvement followed by inexplicable loss followed by the patient feeling aggrieved and depressed and concluding that he is doomed to go through life alone. The final segment might bring the events full circle by showing that in this patient's life there are several instances where a new romantic love suddenly appears during this time of despair. This FRAME would be given a title— "Inexplicable Loss," for example. Other FRAMEs, with different themes, would also invariably emerge. These are the patient's life stories, and the method works similarly well for children. It is not necessary to transcribe audiotapes of sessions to get this information. Jot down the major points of the child's description of events at home and school. Soon enough you will have a wealth of information to review and to make note of the repetitive themes that arise. This will prove an invaluable key to understanding your patient.

Younger children will be able to give similar information through their play. The ambiguity inherent in play makes it a more time-consuming process to garner these patterns, but they are there nonetheless. To make sense of a child's play, begin by looking at themes, not specifics (of course you will have already familiarized yourself with the patient's history). For example, the youngster who comes in and carefully places every available item of furniture in the doll house before having a dinosaur crash through the home leaving it in shambles is similar to the little tyke who meticulously sets up toy army men only to have both sides blown into chaos. The theme is of the intransigence of order and the sudden disruption of predictability by powerful uncontrolled forces. If either of these children next turns to the container of pretend food and begins to have a meal, you note that nurturance follows disruption. The FRAME would be

> Trying to establish order/safety
> Uncontrollable forces creating chaos
> Searching for nurturance/consolation—but not by turning toward
>   people

You could label this FRAME "Chaos." To simplify the process of identifying the component parts of the FRAME you may use preassigned categories to describe the various aspects of the child's narratives and play. This approach is briefly noted in a later section, Using Play to Change the Child.

Your questions multiply as each piece of a pattern begins to emerge. Is the child desirous of nurturance, or even more desirous of giving nurturance? If the latter, who is the receiver, and if the former, does it matter who is the provider? After several meetings with the child, some patterns will continue to repeat. This will be clear if you have written down the major themes at the end of each meeting. Once the general patterns begin to emerge, you will be able to focus on the specifics of each play pattern. You may begin to see details that lead you to conclude, for instance, that the child who placed the furniture in each room so carefully is primarily oriented toward securing a safe and supportive home. On the other hand, you may conclude that the child who played with the army men is primarily oriented toward fighting those he feels are threatening, but never seems capable of succeeding.

Continuing in this way, you develop a solid understanding of how your patient views the world. With this information in hand you have the basics of the child's story. You, as counselor, become part of that story and as a participant can help to change its plot, characters, and ending.

THE STAGES OF COUNSELING

Counseling invariably progresses through stages. There are no discrete markers indicating when one stage has been completed and another entered, but there are signs that show a qualitative change in the counseling process. The change is often gradual, frequently subtle, and most often begins by a shift in what is emphasized within the counseling. It is helpful to conceptualize the different emphases, and consequently stages, by breaking them into three parts: foundation building, strategic changes, and leave-taking. As each of these three parts blends one into the other, you will find yourself doing two, sometimes three, at once. I now consider each in turn.

Stage One: Foundation Building

The first stage of counseling has a number of objectives. A major aim, as discussed in the previous section, is to complete an assessment of the child. Another objective is to orient both the child and the parents to counseling. After goals are agreed upon, the parents should be told by the therapist how counseling works. This discussion outlines the practical aspects of the work (frequency and length of meetings, the role of parent involvement, etc.) as well as its conceptual aspects. Too often the latter topic is ignored. This is a mistake as it can easily weaken the parents' trust in the process. When this trust is shaken, so too is their resolve to continue with the work during hard times. Consider an example: Junior's difficulties are continuing to cause much grief at home even after two months of therapy. After one especially exasperating week the little tyke tells his mother, on the way home from counseling, that he spent the last hour playing with a small sandbox. If no orientation has occurred, his mother is likely to conclude that there are better ways to spend her time and money. The lesson: be sure to discuss the conceptual underpinnings of counseling with the parents. Make this conversation a practical one. For example, when talking about play therapy, note that adults use language to talk with others when trying to make sense of traumatic experiences and to work out the problems that ensue. Likewise, young children use play in a similar way. Because their language abilities are not as developed as those of adults, they turn to play to serve the same function. As such, you tell the parent ahead of time that on the drive home Junior may talk about all the playing he did. The parent should understand this to mean that he spent his time talking, through the medium of play, about that which is important to him. He was working on solving his problems. Likewise, you let the parent know that it is going to take time to see changes. You are teaching Junior new skills, perhaps a new way of viewing himself and others. This takes time, just as learning in other areas takes time. Here you bring in analogous examples of learning new skills in order to drive the point home: developing fluency in a new language, mastering a domain of mathematics, becoming proficient in playing some musical instrument, and so on.

Keep in mind that children's orientation to counseling starts from the moment their parents tell him they are going to meet with you. When setting up the appointment, it is best to tell parents to describe you as a special type of teacher. This avoids many of the negative connotations associated with going to the doctor to receive a shot or some sort of disgusting medicine. Latency-age children will benefit from your telling them a little bit about the counseling process, but no lectures are necessary. If you end up explaining your explanation, you have gone too far. Just stop in midsentence and move on. Telling the child that counseling is a way that children are helped to solve problems that make them feel bad is sufficient. Sometimes you will want to add that children who have had bad things happen to them often have yucky feelings that are hard to get rid of, and you are good at helping to make those types of feelings go away. It takes some time, but it can be done. That usually takes care of the need to explain. There are exceptions, but don't worry about them until you have first tried the basics.

In the process of getting to know you, the child will usually start to test your limits regarding acceptable behavior. It is good to be explicit regarding the basic rules of the counseling hour: play with whatever you like (if you are using nondirected play), say whatever you like, and so forth. Make sure the list is short, not exhaustive. Counselors who recite a litany of regulations have the intention to be fair with the child, not wanting their charge to run afoul of the law without forewarning. Children, however, will not remember a long list of rules, and by giving a litany of regulations counselors quickly start to portray themselves as legislators and playroom police rather than helpful adults. Soon enough your charge will test the rules, spoken or unspoken, and you will then be able to instill a clear idea of the limits in your time together. This topic is more thoroughly discussed in Chapter 6.

It is important to note that children will sometimes throw tantrums in the counselor's office. They do this at home and school, so there is no reason for the tantrum-throwing child to consider the clinic off limits. If nothing is harmed, no materials broken, no danger to the child is posed, then no limits need be set. Depending upon the child, it may be best to calmly let the storm pass, redirect the tantrum to more constructive outlets, or talk to the child in ways that advance your goals (this might be furthering the child's sense of being understood, making connections between the frustration and the precipitating event, noting what the child expects of you as a result of the tantrum, and so forth). Tantrums, however, should not be encouraged just for their own sake. It is a mistake to think that this type of regressive behavior is, in itself, helpful to the cause of counseling. It is only helpful when harnessed in the service of your goals for the child. Ginott (1961) puts it well:

> [I]t cannot be overemphasized that acting out per se has no curative effects beyond pleasure and release. Acting out in children does not usually lead to self-evaluation, recognition of motivation, guilt, and attempts to alter behavior. This is true for all persons with inadequate superegos, but it is especially evident in young children, in whom a weak superego and strong narcissism make acting out just fun. . . . Acting out is of value only when it represents working out of the child's core difficulties. (pp. 244-245)

Building rapport, a strong relationship with the child, is certainly one of the most important elements in this phase of counseling. (As that is discussed in an earlier chapter, I do not review it again here.) Related to rapport building, however, is sparking the child's interest in counseling. For younger children, latency-age and below, it is especially important to have some fun during their time with you. If a child leaves the hour with you and has not laughed or giggled some, has not smiled or acted silly, you need to question whether this part of the foundation building is moving ahead. Counseling abused children is a serious endeavor, but it should not be a relentlessly somber one.

Throughout the initial stage of counseling, you will be trying to make sense of what the child tells you, through both play and words. It will be tempting at times to rush to interpretation, but this is to be forestalled. Instead you should use this time as an opportunity to highlight certain aspects of what the child reveals to you, then drawing attention to connections between various events, thoughts, and feelings. Your goal at this point in counseling is to wipe away much of the confusion that children have lived with regarding the abuse and the painful relationships they have experienced. For example, a little girl who takes the farm animal set and spends five minutes pairing the young animals with adults of the same kind needs to be told, "There is a mommy and daddy for every little baby animal." A description. No frills. When she comes in two weeks later and starts to feed one of the dolls a bottle, then hurriedly goes to the next doll and gives it a bottle before collapsing in a chair, you simply note, "It's important for the babies to be taken care of. They cannot do it themselves. But it sure makes you tired." The statement crafts a description, and connection, between feeding and being tired. Could she be communicating something about her own mother's struggles to keep up with the demands of caring for her children? Absolutely. Could she be conveying how much pressure is being put on her, the parentified child in the family, to care for siblings? No doubt. Perhaps she is engaged in wish-fulfilling play and displaying what she has never had but yearns for. All of these are possibilities, and the answers to these questions will help move counseling forward inasmuch as they direct you to more specific interventions. But in the first stage of your work, it is enough to highlight that which is most salient and obvious. By so doing you help clarify for the child the main elements of his or her experience and the relation of these elements to one another. This has the same salubrious effects as when an adult, who is distressed and confused, is offered support and a clearer perspective that dispels confusion. Confusion is a hobgoblin of despair, creating a mental fog that makes it difficult to find a clear path out of the troubles that plague a person. The clarity afforded by an understanding counselor helps to burn off the fog of confusion, reassuring children that they are not alone in their struggle, and providing a sense of hope that life can get better. If their lot in life is to improve, however, this important starting point must be followed by challenging the way children view themselves and others.

Stage Two: Strategic Changes

There are many approaches to helping children change, and each approach has several variants. The number of intervention strategies available is so vast that it can lead to confusion unless a sober view of goals and steps toward reaching those goals is kept clearly in mind. One of the best ways of securing this sobriety is to work within a clear and simple conceptual framework that allows you to add complexity as the clinical picture emerges with the unfolding of therapy. Helpful in this regard is the framework discussed earlier, and expounded upon by Greenspan (1981), wherein the clinician's conceptualization is divided between an understanding of the child's resources and a recognition of the dynamics of the child's world. Resources include cognitive abilities, affective skills and deficits, social support, and so on. The patient's dynamics, on the other hand, refer to the story that is lived out by each child: the hopes and fears that animate behavior, expectations of others and beliefs about oneself, and so on. I turn now to look at making changes in each of these domains.

Changing the Stage

If you wish to shore up the stage upon which the child's drama is being acted out, you might easily turn to any of the following: case management, medication, family counseling, and skill building.

Case Management. Case management takes many forms. For example, if the foster home placement is a poor fit, you may need to advocate that the child be moved to a different home. Likewise, if academics are a problem, then the child would be experiencing considerable stress in that area of life. Working within the school system to secure tutoring, a different classroom, and so forth would go a long way to reducing this stress that was depleting needed psychological resources. A youngster who is living in a home and neighborhood without many suitable playmates can be directed into community activities such as scouting, church groups, 4-H, and so forth. Case management is an extremely powerful means of affecting the child's life, and because social workers often feel overburdened by their caseloads, it is a part of patient care in which the clinician must participate. My experience from working with abused children, and supervising the work of others, is that the success of counseling is directly related to the time spent in case management.

Referral for Medication. The psychotherapeutic purist, one who believes that medication has no place in the treatment of abused and neglected children, needs to work with a different population of patients. If you see maltreated children, you will need to refer some of them for medication. Of course medications are not a cure by themselves. But not infrequently they are a great benefit. Children who have been unable to think clearly or to remain sufficiently calm to engage in counseling can be brought to a state where therapy is possible. Others who have struggled with emotional lability, making peer relations perpetually stressed, can be relieved sufficiently of these emotional storms to allow the development of more meaningful relations. The importance of medication is such that Chapter 16 is devoted to it.

Family Counseling. Family counseling can be one of the most effective means for shoring up the child's resources (of course it is also frequently used to change the child's perception of relations by changing the quality of the most intimate relations—those with mother, father, and siblings). Three of the most helpful areas on which to focus when family therapy is used to increase the patient's resources are building supportive relationships, reducing unrealistic expectations, and establishing consistency within the home. Supportive relationships may come from unexpected quarters. For example, it may be that although the child's parents are stubbornly unsupportive, a sibling relation can be nurtured. Likewise it may be a grandparent, an aunt, or an uncle who affords the best opportunity to build a nurturing relation for the child within the family. If so, you will need to get that individual involved in the family therapy and find practical ways to increase the scope of his or her participation in the child's life.

As regards expectations placed upon children in the home, there is usually no one but the parents with whom to work. Certain types of expectations need to be looked for. Some are unrealistic because they are a poor match for the child's abilities, even though they would be realistic for most children of a similar age. Others are unrealistic because they require greater independence than can be expected, or conversely they demand too much dependency from the child who is developmentally ready for more freedom. Another form of unrealistic expectation has a goal of adherence to very reasonable standards but demands unbending perfection from the child in always living up to these standards. One last type of expectation places the child in either a caretaker position or in the position to provide emotional intimacy that is either inappropriate or beyond the patient's abilities.

Consistency within the home is a wellspring of reassurance for children undergoing rapid developmental changes. Family therapy will quickly reveal whether the home has reasonable consistency or persistent uncertainty. If inconsistency is a problem, look to see when and how it becomes manifest (e.g., all the time, only around discipline, primarily when parents are angry with each other, etc.). Once pinpointed, you will need to discuss this with the parents and develop a plan to resolve the problem. The parents' response will be revealing in regard to how they approach problems more generally.

Skill Building. The skills that children must learn to be successful adults are poorly taught in homes in which abuse and neglect shadow the parent-child relation. How to properly express anger, for instance, is not role modeled by domestic violence, and personal hygiene skills are not encouraged by acts of neglect. Consequently, most children who present with these histories of maltreatment often have significant deficits in one or more major skill area. Sometimes these difficulties are adequately handled by the foster parent and only a small amount of guidance is needed on your part to push the process of remediation in the right direction. Other times you will find these deficits so pervasive that they need to be made the focus of counseling for a period of time. When skill building takes a major role in the treatment plan, and the child also requires more traditional play therapy, it is best to refer the family to a colleague to pursue one of these modalities while you tackle the other.

The most important types of skills to assess include social, affective, problem solving, and self-care. Many approaches can help children improve their abilities in each of these areas (see McGinnis, 1984, for a particularly good example). Rather than reinventing the wheel, it is much preferable that you follow the approach outlined in a manual. Once you have mastered the standardized procedure you will be prepared to use your personalized innovative procedures when necessary.

Changing the Story

I now examine how to alter the story itself. Several main approaches exist, including any of the interventions used to change the stage inasmuch as they lead children into new experiences that challenge their view of their interpersonal world; working within children's play; and intervening within the therapy relationship.

Changing the Stage to Change the Play. To carry the stage/play analogy further, it should be clear that by changing certain aspects of the stage, one makes it much more likely that the story will likewise change. That is because various healthy opportunities become available when the stage is expanded, and the pressure to engage in particularly destructive aspects of a story are reduced. Although this can occur with changes in any of the domains, it is most likely to occur with skill remediation, and in particular social skill building that includes improvements in affective control. This is because it is primarily through relationships that children and adults find fulfillment, self-definition, security, and sense of purpose. Building skills that make relationships deeper and more enduring opens opportunities for the child to realize these benefits. The building of social skills and affective control should be a central part of many therapies and is often best pursued by including group therapy during some part of the treatment process.

When taking this approach, look for social skills that are central to disrupting the pathological story that you have discerned through your assessment. Finding the right set of social skills to strengthen is the key to being successful. Different skills unlock different aspects of one's interpersonal life. The child that is inhibited is very likely to need a different set of social skills than the one who is boisterous and aggressive. Each will have a personal story within which these qualities are to be understood. For example, consider the child who is being aggressive as a reaction to feeling overwhelmed by her failure to meet the academic demands of school. These failures evoke a sense of distress that is similar to that which occurred when her parents rejected her as a failure and neglected to care for her. In this circumstance, anger management clearly would not suffice. In addition, you would want to intervene with academic remediation and be certain that the child's social skills were sufficient to allow the development of close relationships that provide an antidote to the earlier pathological relationship she had with her parents.

On the other hand, consider the child who has a history of multiple abandonments by his parents. If we found that he was being aggressive as a reaction to the anger that was arising from his fears of being abandoned by his new foster parents, we would want to teach him how to better communicate these concerns to the foster parents, as well as teaching anger management. Again, intervening with the focus on skill development can be a powerful and efficient means for bringing about change in the child's story. Success, however, requires that the counselor have a strategic plan for building skills based upon the specific dynamics that animate the child's behavior.

Therapy Relationship. Most often when working with abused children, it will not be sufficient to simply change their level of skill in some domain. You will also need to change their view of the world. The principle idea is that some of the greatest opportunities for shifting a child's perspective occur when his or her story begins to unfold within the counseling hour and is acted out within the therapy relationship. This is because it is a lived experience and not an abstraction that is discussed or played out with toys. Another way to think about this is to recognize that the process of making sense of one's relationships is a skill, and as such children learn best when engaged in the practice of that skill. This is not surprising. It is common sense. Just as a violinist learns best not by reading or talking of Bach but picking up the violin and playing Bach, so too do children learn best by experiencing a new type of relationship. They enter the relationship, however, expecting to repeat what they have found in previous relations. So when a child, for instance, becomes angry at his counselor, he may well expect that the good doctor will crumple under his heated onslaught just as his mother did, or lash back as his father did. The response from the counselor that prompts change is one that fulfills neither of these expectations but challenges them instead. A sense of perplexity is a good thing to stir up in the child at these points in therapy.

There are three things to do when the child's story becomes manifest within the therapeutic relationship. One, be sure not to respond in the expected pathological manner. Two, determine what response would be most conducive to challenging the child's negative expectations of you at that moment. Three, sometimes, not always, comment on what the child is doing, what the child expects, and what you will do. Do not lecture, and do not comment every time the child invites you to engage in a repetition of maladaptive themes—once every two or three occasions is sufficient.

A brief example will help to show how this works.

Julie is an overly compliant child who tries to endear herself to everyone she meets and never met a demand with which she was unwilling to comply. But Julie also experiences considerable rage that is expressed, on rare occasions, when she is feeling frustrated. Knowing her history, you recognize that she witnessed her father pummel her mother into submission when he was in a drunken rage. You surmise from this, and other information, that the child is compliant because she fears reprisals for even mild disobedience, and also fears for the safety of others were she to unleash her own anger (i.e., identifying with her father). You also recognize that both her compliance and anger will powerfully manifest themselves in therapy as you become an important part of her life.

Sure enough, in time, the child becomes frustrated with some limit you have set and begins to throw toys against the wall. A fire truck sails gracefully across the room before crashing near your newly framed diploma. A quick grab at the second shelf snags Mr. Potato Head and he too is launched into a flight that is cut short when the little spud hits the wall. Eyes, ears, and moustache fall asunder. You clearly need to stop Julie from breaking the toys, and mindful of what she expects, you respond by setting limits without giving any appearance of pleading or angry retribution. You do not go into lengthy expositions on why you are setting the limit, or how you wish you did not have to set this limit. That would be too close to the pleading and submissiveness she expects from her mother. It is also entirely unnecessary. Nor do you start off by threatening with the consequences that will rain down upon her should the misbehavior continue. Instead, in a measured and authoritative manner, you declare what the rule is. Simple. Then, if this does not suffice to curb her appetite for breaking toys, you go on to give her the option of ending the meeting by persisting in throwing toys at the wall, or continuing your time together by doing what you have said.

Having established control again, and with it greater reassurance for Julie's safety (remember, children feel safer when a kindly, strong adult is in charge), you move on to acknowledge her anger and the reason for it:

THERAPIST: You are really very angry with me because I won't let you throw the toys at the wall.

PATIENT: I hate you.

THERAPIST: You feel so angry you hate me. But I don't hate you—and later on you won't be so angry with me.

What have you done in this encounter that furthers the goal of challenging Julie's distorted view of relationships? With your words and demeanor, you have rebutted her expectation of a whimpering response (like her mother), or angry counterattack (like her father). The power of her anger to overcome others, or provoke them to destructive rage, has been called into question. She has been shown that acceptance can be held secure even when she fails to be overly compliant. By acknowledging her affect and its cause, you have provided the seeds of insight. Last, you have given a dose of realism that the painful state of frustration she feels will not last forever. Not bad for a start. Repeated many times during the course of your work together, and enriched through similarly challenging relationships at home, school, and play, the child's view of the world changes in powerful ways.

Using Play to Change the Child. Play is an expression of the child's inner life, and as such it is informative. For play therapy to be effective, however, the child must have the ability to use play in a communicative fashion that permits both the expression and reception of ideas even if the communication is unintentional on the child's part. Thus play interventions can be used for many purposes, just like verbal communication. Do not make the use of play more difficult than necessary by assuming it possesses some magical or mysterious qualities. We should appreciate that it can be vexingly opaque, wonderfully subtle, and profoundly powerful, but we cannot lose sight that it is, for us as counselors, first and foremost an avenue of communication. Keeping this in mind, it is easy to see the various ways in which play can be used to advance our goals with the child patient (Schaefer, 1992). We can assess, reassure, motivate, console, and inspire with play, just as one does with words. For our purposes we will focus on how play can be used to change the pathological ways in which maltreated children view the world.

Once again it bears emphasizing that you must be able to discern the major themes within a child's view of relationships to effectively intervene. You will want to pay attention to what themes are most prominent and how they are temporally ordered. Using the FRAMES method is very helpful in this regard. First define the major themes, the ones that are most clearly apparent, then fill in details after this framework has been established. To simplify the process, you may want to use predetermined categories for describing the child's play. The following domains correspond to those used in Benjamin's (1993) interpersonal circumplex model (Structural Analysis of Social Behavior, or SASB), a highly developed system for describing interactions within a relationship:

Protecting
Ignoring/neglecting
Friendly/loving
Attacking
Abandoning/leaving/separating from
Controlling/bossing/demanding
Praising/accepting
Blaming/sulking

When reviewing the child's play, identify which of these themes occurred and in what sequence. Jot this down in your progress notes. Over the course of several meetings patterns will start to emerge. For example, consider the child who comes in and gives a puppet show of a puppy who has lost her mother, searches for her, and in the process makes a new friend who in turn introduces her to others whom she befriends. She then ends the show by declaring that the mother was never found and so the puppy stays forever with her friends. The themes are

Separation	The mother is absent from the main character's life.
Control	The main character's seeking the mother is an attempt to gain control. You could also label this a seeking theme to be more specific.
Acceptance	The other animal befriends the main character. Depending on the specific qualities of the story, you might include the theme of consolation.
Continued separation	The mother is not found.
Continued acceptance	Friends remain.

Here you have the beginning of a coherent theme, certainly one you can work with. It goes: separation→control→acceptance→continued separation→continued acceptance. Now you can change the descriptors to better fit the particulars of the puppet play and it would look like the following:

Loss of loved one (separation)
Seeking that which is lost (effort to control)

Finding and accepting comfort/friendship during the adventure
    (friendly acceptance)
Failure to find, or be found, by loved one (continued separation)
Sole source of comfort now from friends (continued acceptance)

This would be labeled the "Lost" theme or FRAME. With this theme in mind, you would look for other play that, although different in the particulars, was thematically parallel (you would also expect to find several other prominent sequences of themes throughout the child's play). As this process of substantiating the major story lines within the child's play continued, you would also find answers to a number of questions that naturally arise. For example, why does loss occur? Is it predictable and can it be prevented? What is the affective reaction to such loss? How is comfort forthcoming: Is it by chance or a result of seeking comfort? Is it accepted selectively or without regard for who offers the comfort? Why do efforts at seeking the one who is lost succeed or fail (is it a matter of chance, one's own efforts, the good will of others, etc.)? Answers to these questions may come spontaneously from the child's play, or from your entering the play and introducing a new character or questions (i.e., one character making comments to another, or one character asking another a question).

Once you know the major themes it is possible to challenge the view that animates them. Keep in mind that there will be times when the child's playing out these themes in the safety of the therapeutic relationship, and with the clarity of the therapist's observations, suffices to bring about the desired changes. But when this does not occur, the therapist needs to push progress forward by other means. Do this by introducing a contradictory theme within the chain of themes you have discovered. Using the previous example, you could build the friendship theme into a long-lasting central relationship for the main character, and then introduce the inevitable threat of this relationship also being lost. All this would be very familiar to the child, who then expects loss to occur in this relationship as well. With your guiding the play, however, that threat begins to materialize but does not come to fruition. This counters the child's expectation.

Specifically, the interaction could take the following form:

Terry, the little girl with the puppet show, comes in on another day. You know the major story lines involved in her play and she enacts the "Loss/Search/Consolation/Failure to Find" theme again in her play. As usual, she wants you to participate in the puppet show. This affords you an opportunity to interject a correcting theme into her play as it unfolds, but you decide to wait and let the intensity of her affect build with her play. After she finishes the play you comment how hard it is for the tiger (the main character) to try so hard but not get his mother back. (You are engaging in consolation, a major theme of the story line.) Terry agrees and then you tell her that now you and she will play the squiggle game (see Winnicott,1971). She draws a squiggle, you take it and draw an animal, then tell a story about this animal losing his mother, and finding friends with whom he grows very close. Eventually the tiger is separated from these friends, believes he will never see them again, but in fact is reunited due to the efforts of both the friends and himself. You then give the moral of the story: "When everyone tries very hard, it can sometimes work out that they do stay together."

Upon making this intervention, do not expect the child to stare open-mouthed in wonder and exclaim how his or her world has changed. If you see an affective response, you know that your story has some immediate importance to the child. Most likely, however, the little tyke will not have a strong reaction. These corrective counterresponses will need to be given in many different contexts over the course of time. Then you will begin to see changes. But you must pace the delivering of the counterresponses. Giving too many counters or giving them when the child is particularly agitated and feeling misunderstood will only cause frustration. Pace them over time, picking key components of the child's story lines to focus on, and you will increase the power of this intervention.

A caveat is in order at this point. When choosing what aspects of the child's distorted worldview you wish to target for change, keep in mind that very often what we view as a distortion served the child very well in his or her past home life. This is due to the fact that this "distortion" predicted events pretty well within the pathological family. It is a distortion only inasmuch as it continues to be applied where it does not belong—in normal relationships. Consequently, in forming our goals we must be cognizant of where the patient is living at present, and where he or she is likely to be living in the future. If reunification is planned, then we should be particularly careful to help the patient be judicious in applying the new expectations and behaviors that emerge as a result of our challenging old perceptions. It will not do to send a child back into a pathological home life expecting healthy interactions. Feeding lambs to the wolves comes to mind. If the child is headed toward reunification within a persistently pathological family, and you do not think he or she can learn to make the distinctions necessary to selectively apply these newfound skills, it is better not to challenge the distortions in the first place.

The other caveat is to select the themes within the story line that will be challenged according to what is most problematic and amenable to change. Do not select these themes because they cause you to feel uneasy. This is a common trap that must be avoided. Many clinicians find working with maltreated children to be particularly evocative. Do not let your responses to these children be the barometer by which you judge what is to be changed. To be sure, your reaction to a child provides helpful clinical information. These visceral reactions can also be misleading—the proverbial red herring all gussied up as a gut-twitching truth. When following this lead, it is not uncommon for clinicians to intervene at the point of their own discomfort rather than the point of opportunity for the child.

Stage Three: Leave-Taking

There will come a time when the goals of therapy have been reached, and barring the advent of new goals, it is clearly time to start winding down your work with the child. It is best to be thorough in your assessment of the child at this point, making sure not only that the goals have been reached but also that the resources necessary to support the continued maintenance of these gains are also in place. This includes the parents possessing the skills necessary to adequately respond to the youngster's needs, the establishment of support outside of the family (school-based counseling, affiliation with church groups, etc.), continuity of psychiatric care, and so forth. In some instances, the goals of therapy have not yet been reached but the child's gains thus far show that they eventually will be even without further therapy. This is most likely to occur when there is a rich network of support already in place for the child, and the parents are particularly well equipped to respond to the child's needs. In these instances one should look to see that the parents, and other sources of support, have been consistently able to respond to the child's needs. If all looks good in this regard, you can end therapy before the goals are reached because progress will continue under the influence of healthy relationships and supportive institutions that act to both support the child and challenge old views of the world.

In either case, when you make a determination that it is time to end therapy, it will be best to do so in a graduated manner. Most maltreated children have not had good experiences with separations: the nature of abusive relationships works against stability and trust, two qualities that are central to making good transitions. Abrupt endings in therapy create unnecessary hardships on children who have grown to count on a therapist. Plan to end with the child over the course of several months. Taper the frequency of meetings from every week to every other week, and then to every third or fourth week. But do not end there. Plan at least two follow-up meetings occurring two months apart. If parents forget to attend these (this can be a propitious sign) then be dogged in your pursuit of having them come in nonetheless. The child needs to experience saying good-bye in a way that is planned and agreed upon. For most abused and neglected children, this is a novel experience: their home life has been chaotic, with people who are important to them leaving abruptly for no apparent reason, and the child's time in protective custody is likewise often marked by abrupt changes from one foster home to another. You have an opportunity to introduce the child to something different, and since this plan was something you had already worked out with the parent and explained to the child, it needs to be followed. Most parents are willing to abide by their prior agreement if you are willing to pursue it.

When you decide it is time to end therapy, your first step should be to discuss the plan with the child's parents, and then, that same day, with the child. If the parents are uncertain about ending therapy, you will want to carefully assess the source of their concerns. Sometimes it is only after the subject of ending your work comes up that parents decide to mention problems that had heretofore gone unspoken. I recall the parent of a youngster with whom I had just ended counseling calling me to say that we really should continue inasmuch as the little girl was soliciting elderly neighbors with the promise of her "favors" in exchange for a little money. Inexplicably, this had not been mentioned before.

More commonly, parents do not wish to end because they are uncertain of their ability to help the child on their own. When this is the case, and you are confident that the parents are up to the task, you need to reassure and remind them that this is a gradual process whereby they can slowly operate independently of you. It is also helpful to remind them that you are available for consultation, if needed, after ending therapy. It is not at all unusual to have parents call you after ending your work together. Problems crop up from time to time and on occasion these difficulties are stubborn enough to resist the parents' best efforts, even efforts that had been very effective in the past. When this happens, it is best to give some advice over the phone and have the parents call you back in a week or so (unless the situation is high risk). This conveys the message that you have confidence in the parents' ability to handle the situation with no more than modest assistance from yourself. If these efforts fail to resolve the problem then you will need to see the child.

Those with particularly busy caseloads should think carefully before referring a past patient to someone else in these circumstances. The bond that develops between therapist and child, and between parent and therapist, can be very powerful. This bond is of huge benefit when the family is in need. Likewise, it can be a tremendous disappointment when they are turned away after having developed what they thought was a personal relationship with you. Consequently, if the telephone consultation fails to bring about the desired results, have the child return to your office. Do not assume that this signifies the need to start a lengthy course of therapy. Most likely, if you respond effectively, it only signifies the need for a brief refresher before ending once again. This next ending need not be protracted, as the first ending was, but it does require that you have a follow-up appointment or two after the problem is in hand, and that you again reassure the patient and the parents of your continued availability if needed. More important still, it requires your clear display of confidence in their ability to move forward.

Not infrequently, children who had been doing very well start to slip back into old troubling patterns once you begin to end counseling. Do not be alarmed at this. In fact it is helpful to mention this possibility when first discussing termination. Sometimes I will predict it, and thus if it does occur it surprises no one and causes less concern. If my prediction is wrong, then it is of little matter. Both the parents and I are pleased that my prognostication was no better than that of the astrologers. If a relapse does occur, however, it is best to review what has changed in the child's life, other than your plans to end therapy. Sometimes unanticipated events arise that create stress for the child that, in addition to therapy ending, prove too much for the youngster to handle. If this is the case, then respond by helping the child and family deal with these stresses, reassess whether the timing is right for ending therapy, and proceed from there. More likely than unexpected events are those that we could have anticipated but did not think important, or simply failed to take into account. This includes the beginning and ending of the school year, anniversary reactions, court hearings that influence the child's dependency, major illnesses in the family, new members entering the family (e.g., newborns, adoptions, etc.), and members of the family leaving (e.g., older children leaving for college, divorce, other children moving to another residence, etc.). In either event, your plan is the same: reassess and proceed according to your findings.

The focus of your work while ending will be determined by the focus that was developed during the middle phase of therapy. It will often, however, not match the image you have in mind, especially if you are an inexperienced therapist. After thirteen years of providing clinical supervision, I can emphatically say that therapists and children have vastly different views of what this stage of therapy should look like. In the therapist's imagination, these meetings are filled with a concentrated look at the work done in the preceding months (perhaps years) and the child's deeply felt expressions of sadness at the loss of this important relationship. For the child, however, these meetings are filled with attempts to soak in those activities that were most enjoyed in the first place and keep them clean of the contamination of the sadness, anxiety, and anger associated with ending therapy.

After traveling down the same road for so long together, working hand in glove to achieve this happy ending wherein the goals of therapy have been reached, the two parties find themselves at a crossroads, each wanting to go in a different direction. The solution is for the therapist to afford children a chance to express whatever thoughts and feelings they may have about ending, but not to force the issue. Your patients may choose to express themselves, just as they did throughout the therapy, with words or play. Be perceptive enough to know when they are doing so, as children are often subtle when voicing these feelings. Be persistent enough so that when the last meeting comes at least you have had the opportunity to clarify for the quiet child what feelings he or she is likely to be having. Be revealing enough so that children go away knowing they have been important to you, that you have confidence in their ability to do well after therapy is completed, and they will not be forgotten even though your meetings have come to an end.

CASE STUDY

Mac was seven years old. Built like a miniature tank. Made me want to look for treads under his feet whenever he came to the clinic. Not only did he look like a tank, Mac had the demeanor of a tank: all business, no smiles, no complaints. But by seven years of age he had gathered up more heartaches than most grown men could claim. Born to a single mother, his father was not only uninvolved but unknown. By the time Mac was two years old, his mother was prostituting for drug money and regularly exchanging one abusive boyfriend for another.

Mac was a free spirit, and when he started to walk, his mother, Ms. Tratsdab, bought a playpen within which to corral him. That was where he spent most of his day, and as best as could be determined, quite a few nights when his mother did not return home. From his playpen he watched his mother take drugs, entertain men, sleep off drug binges, and whimper as she was beaten by a succession of boyfriends. Mac was still being housed in the playpen at three years old when Spike, the most recent man in his mother's life, came home tired from a day of selling drugs. Mac's crying irritated him more than usual that evening. Spike roughly picked the toddler up to get the momentum needed to even more roughly toss him back down. The crying turned to a persistent scream. Mac's right arm was broken. Spike stormed out of the apartment but it was not until the next morning that Ms. Tratsdab took the child to the emergency room. Her story of Mac falling off the kitchen chair did not seem plausible to the physician who looked at the boy, especially after noting the pattern of bruising on each arm as a result of being violently plucked out of the playpen. When the physician asked Mac how he got hurt, he received only a scowl for his efforts. That was Mac, an impenetrable little tank.

Mac went to the receiving home that same day, and then to his first foster home later that week. He was assaulted by older boys in the foster home, but kept the assaults secret for many months. Eventually they were revealed by another child. The boys who had attacked him were moved, and Mac stayed in the home for another year. Then, when he was five years old, parental rights were terminated as his mother had not met the demands set out by the court for getting her son back. Mac then went into a foster/adoptive home where he was cared for by a middle-aged husband and wife, the Epohtsebs, whose children were already grown and successfully on their own. No other children lived in the home, leaving Mac once again in the familiar situation of being an only child.

He did reasonably well the first year or two. Stoic, generally uncomplaining, he fit in well with the family. Although Mac did not really warm up to anyone, seeming always to keep his distance, neither did he cause problems. The Epohtsebs figured that eventually this little boy would become more engaging, start to smile and laugh a little more, not be quite so stiff when they went to give him a hug, and come to them once in awhile for comfort or help instead of always remaining distant. Their biggest concern, the thing that truly bothered them, was Mac's occasional tendency to go into a rage. This happened rarely, once every two or three months. But when it did occur, he was just as stubborn in persisting in his misbehavior as he was most times in being stoic. When this point was reached, Mac would shout, cuss, threaten, and break objects (always his own possessions). This too his parents thought would eventually change with the passage of time.

By the age of seven, Mac was in the second grade, doing fine academically, displaying an interest and skill in rock collecting (a recent hobby) and skateboarding. He also showed an unusual fascination with taking apart all things mechanical (his parents told of him taking apart broken clocks, toy cars, and other items—putting them back together was another matter). He continued, however, to struggle with the problems that his parents had hoped would fade away with time. Moreover, he was now starting to have frequent difficulties with peers. What had been a minor social problem in kindergarten was now a major difficulty that brought notes from the school to his parents every week. With advancing age, there was increasing pressure for Mac to fit in with peers. His style of avoiding others was no longer as effective as it had been upon entering school. Children in the second grade had definite social groupings they belonged to, and Mac stood out starkly from the other children. This made him the target of jokes and pranks. With typical Mac stoicism, he would endure these insults for long stretches of time, not showing any reaction at all. Then, without warning, he would respond to the proverbial "straw that broke the camel's back" and attack the child who had the misfortune of having drawn that straw. He was now midway through the second grade and his parents were hearing from the school for the third time that there had been a fight. Mac's problems were becoming worse, not better. His foster parents decided to call the social worker and request counseling.

After reviewing his current status and history with the parents during an initial meeting, Mac came in for our first session together. He entered the playroom quietly and sat at the table, keeping a blank expression on his face. I let him know that he could play with whatever he liked. A minute later he got up and started to look around the room. His attention was focused, his exploration methodical, but without any manifest pleasure or excitement. Eventually Mac started to play with the farm animals, grouping them according to kind, and then situating the groupings in various places around the floor of the room. As I commented on his play, he would glance toward where I was sitting. Mac did not talk during his play, nor did he invite me to join his project. After having arranged the farm animals in their groupings he moved on to do likewise with the jungle animals, and then too with the dinosaurs (clearly lacking a firm foundation in paleontology, his groupings of dinosaurs were less precise than those he performed on nonextinct animals). I called him over to the table where I sat and began speaking about topics that are of interest to most seven-year-old boys. During all of our talking together that first day, his responses were brief, even laconic. I did note, however, that he smiled and appeared engaged during one exchange, and that was when we spoke about his interests in skateboarding and rock hunting.

Mac's demeanor remained august as I asked him the standard questions regarding what is important (three wishes), who is important (who would he take to an island), and how he views the important people in his life (what animal others would be). In response to the question about three wishes Mac said he would ask for a castle to live in, a room full of gold, and a dog (his parents did not allow pets). If stranded on an island he would have taken both his parents (adoptive), and if turned into animals he would be a lizard, his father would be the sort of sheepdog seen on a popular cartoon, and his mother would be a deer.

Conceptualization: General Considerations

There was much to make of these responses. Mac's answer to the three wishes question suggested that his desire for protection is very strong (the wish to live in a castle). There is also the desire for greater power or prestige (gold) and a yearning for companionship, affection, and the opportunity to nurture (the dog). These inferences were drawn, of course, as conjectures in light of other presenting information. That he would take his parents, if stranded on an island, indicated the existence of a stronger parent-child bond than they may have imagined from his detached demeanor. It was also consistent with his wish to have a dog inasmuch as both converge on the theme of desiring a relationship. The responses to the question regarding what animals he and his parents would be were ambiguous, as is often the case. The one theme they did bring out, however, was his perception of himself as being very different from his parents. This is something I most often see in homes where the child is estranged from the parents, or in homes where there is domestic violence. There was no domestic violence in this little boy's current home, and if there was a sense of estrangement between Mac and his parents it was being expressed passively. Nevertheless, the juxtaposition of sheepdog and deer with a lizard does not suggest a cozy cadre of four-legged creatures. A discordant note was struck here and I noted it as one more indication that this boy had not yet found his place in life. The additional questions that this raises, such as whether Mac identified himself as loathsome, fearsome, and so on, were left to be looked at more closely as therapy progressed.

An additional meeting was scheduled so that I could make a more thorough assessment of Mac's play. Again he spent much time sorting animals and expanded this to sorting small plastic doll figures into family groups—he kept children with parents, showing an appreciation for how families should be constituted despite his history of having no father or siblings. Toward the end of the hour he played with the army men, taking a few green figures and having them face hordes of beige-suited, battle-hardened warriors. The green figures were hidden behind a fortress of blocks that were further sequestered behind a row of Play-Doh containers. As the enemy advanced, the green army lay down and hid. This strategy proved of no avail as the beige phalanx marched forward, crushing Play-Doh and laying siege to the building-block haven. Then, with the suddenness of a thunder clap on a summer day, the green army began to return fire: a vicious fight ensued. When the battle was done, only the green army remained standing. Mac then turned to the task of rebuilding the fortress.

This play sequence was jotted down and then thematically traced in the manner described earlier. It is as follows:

Hiding/self-protection—green army in the fortress
Impending threat—beige army on the move
Continued self-protection
Attack—beige army finds its mark
Counterattack (self-protection)
Foe demolished
Rebuild hiding place in preparation for further threats

As a FRAME I could have labeled this the "Hunkering Down" theme, but it was more descriptive to say that as one of Mac's primary stories it described his sense of being "alone in my castle with barbarians at the gate." In either case it nicely captured an essential part of Mac's interpersonal perspective.

Taking in what I had learned so far, it struck me that this boy wanted to be left alone, although he did not necessarily want to be alone. He wanted to be distant enough from others to be free of their demands, and free from the threats he felt would inevitably come from others. This was the primary animating force in his life. It was the refuge to which he had escaped during the years of neglect and abuse. It felt secure and was well-known territory. To become meaningfully involved with others risked being hurt or disappointed. Mac had many experiences early in his life upon which to draw this conclusion. There was very little evidence, on the other hand, that would challenge this perception of the world. Of course, since his placement in a loving home, there had been many experiences with his foster parents that were nurturing and responsive to his needs. These had failed, however, to shake loose the encrusted view laid down in the first three years of this little boy's life.

Conflicting with Mac's desire for isolation was the natural hunger that each of us has to relate to another person. Mac's upbringing had not completely extinguished this desire. As mentioned earlier, this was seen in his responses to assessment questions (wanting his parents on the island with him, or wishing for a dog). Consequently, Mac was in a situation wherein he wished to be left alone but not to be perpetually alone.

Why did he wish for this interpersonal separation from others? My conjecture was that this was due to his first three years of life consisting of daily lessons teaching that it is painful to be in a relation to others. He experienced the pain firsthand of what happens when you want something from someone else. Mac knew from the scenes that unfolded in front of his playpen how violent relationships invariably become. He also knew that he was most likely to be disappointed within a relationship, just as he had early on been taught that no one could be counted upon. By the age of seven his self-concept was of a boy who is able to weather almost any storm, but who is fundamentally unacceptable and must constantly brace himself for the inevitable affirmation of this truth. He reminded me in this respect of a man on the deck of a ship at sea in a storm, constantly bracing himself for the next wave.

Did Mac intellectually understand these things about himself? No, they were tacitly understood, lessons taught early on creating impressions laid down deep. He had adapted to these lessons by retreating into himself. The limitations of his playpen had thwarted his natural desire to explore and accentuated his tendency to turn inward. When others tried to befriend him, Mac responded with outward indifference or lukewarm interest. This did little to engender further interest by peers. After awhile his parents also accepted this as an inevitable aspect of their son and no longer pushed for a more intimate relation.

This was the core dynamic that emerged from the intake. Many questions remained, which would be answered as therapy progressed, but the basics were clear. What of the stage upon which this story was being played out? Here there was good news. Mac's progress across most developmental domains was good. That is, the stage was, for the most part, large and solid enough to sustain the action.

Cognitively Mac was able to pay attention, organize his thoughts, reason, and otherwise think at a level appropriate for his age. His interest in rock collecting, an unusual and intellectually challenging hobby, demonstrated strength in this area.

Emotionally Mac was more constricted than expected of a boy his age, but nevertheless showed good control over his emotions—most of the time.

The predominant affect that broke through this barrier of stoicism was anger, although his most persistent affect was curiosity.[3] This was expressed in his intense interest in rock collecting and attempts to figure out how mechanical devices work.

Physically Mac's development was on target. His coordination, agility, strength, speed, and general health were well within the expected range.

Mac's moral development was likewise within the expected range. There were no exceptional problems with lying or stealing. He did not persistently bully other children even though he did periodically respond violently to the teasing he received at school. Although he never showed remorse for these outbursts (this would be a bit much to expect), neither did he express delight in the other children being hurt. Indeed, he approached it as a matter of economics: they had gotten what they paid for with the currency of teasing. On the other hand, he showed sympathy for animals he saw that were hurt or lost and expressed occasional remorse with a terse "Sorry 'bout that stuff" for the times he acted out at home.

Socially Mac was clearly delayed. He had no friends and displayed little interest in making any. When pushed to "go play with other children," he would stand to the side and mutely stare at their game. On the rare occasions when another boy would invite him to join in an ongoing game, Mac would shuffle. over, scowling and silent, then half-heartedly engage in the play. He did not know how to initiate play with others, resolve conflicts that arose, engage in the give-and-take of teasing that is an integral part of boys' play, lend help when needed, nor give or receive a compliment. The information given by his parents told also of a little boy who, as is often the case with abused children, misconstrued the benign comments and actions of other children as being critical of him.

Treatment

With this formulation in mind, it became clear that the focus of our work would need to be two-pronged: challenging the primary plot of Mac's story, and increasing certain aspects of the stage upon which it was being played out. His ability to deal with strong affect needed to be shored up, as did his social skills. Mac had for so long relied upon his maladaptive responses to distress that his emotional and social functioning had withered, like the muscles of a leg that are no longer used because a crutch has taken their place. These functions now needed to be rehabilitated in order for him to successfully form new and meaningful relationships. It was these relationships with parents, teachers, classmates, and neighbors that I would count on to both enhance and sustain the gains made within individual therapy. Even with improved skills, such relationships were most likely to form only after his view of the world began to change. His perception of others as being invariably indifferent or hostile had to be challenged, as did the image he held of himself as broken and defective.

Because Mac played productively during assessment, I concluded that we could begin the work of relationship building through nondirected play therapy. This would also help circumvent arousing any oppositionality, which could have become a significant obstacle in light of his very stubborn nature. As usual my focus in the early work was on lifting out the primary themes of his play through observations and reflections. Mac continued the play of grouping animals and gradually elaborated this play so that the animals needed to move from one place to another in the playroom to escape the dangers of hunters, predators, and other threats. This elaboration was a sign that Mac was coming to trust me more (i.e., the same as when adults in counseling begin to disclose more about themselves) and in return I began making more causal connections when commenting on his play, and taking liberties in ascribing certain motives and feelings to the animal figures he used. The two figures of colts were not just running from the lion, but were frightened and wondering why their parents did not rescue them. Mac's responses, which were to concur with this comment by grunting "Yeah," or intensify his play, showed he was ready to hear more. My making comments directly to the characters Mac played with, and using personal pronouns when describing their situation or state ("You are really starting to get mad now") was also responded to well. So it went throughout this period of time, with Mac gradually coming to trust me more, to engage in more elaborated play, and to be responsive to more pointed comments.

As the therapy developed in this regard, so too did the therapeutic relationship. When it became clear that Mac enjoyed coming to the clinic and that this hour of his week was now important to him, I introduced a change in the structure of our time together. We started to save the last fifteen minutes of every meeting for us to engage in an activity that I chose beforehand. The purpose of this was to help sharpen the focus of therapy and thereby expedite progress. Although there are times when the length of therapy is not a primary concern, this is rare, and more often financial considerations dictate that gains be made in an expeditious manner. So it was with Mac. For directed play to be effective, however, I knew that whatever we did would need to capture Mac's interest and have personal meaning. Consequently, I decided that together we would build a castle. A castle was where he wanted to live (the first of three wishes), and I took it to be an apt metaphor for the stoic defensiveness that he had built up over the years. By constructing a castle together, we could help give some life to that wish, and determine who could live in the castle with him and whether it was possible for Mac to leave the castle and venture into the world.

The following months were devoted to just this exercise. The castle began on paper as we carefully drew out the location of massive outer walls, the various rooms within, and even a skateboard park somewhere behind the gardens. We spoke at length about what kinds of rocks would work best in building the castle, some selected for strength, others for the visual appeal.

His knowledge of rocks gave Mac an opportunity to feel competent within a relationship—rare for this boy. Eventually the castle on paper started to take form as a structure of blocks and other materials from the playroom. With this transformation into three dimensions, Mac's imagination became even more vivid. We began to discuss where in the castle the most valuable possessions were kept, and this we called the "heart of the castle." Special protections needed to be taken to keep this room safe. As this play developed, it allowed us many opportunities to talk about what was important to Mac, how "important stuff" is kept safe, and how it could be shared with others. Mac responded well to these brief discussions, and in the process of talking to me he was challenged, within the therapeutic relationship, to be less guarded. His self-perception of being defective was pressed to change by the interest I showed in him, even as he revealed more of himself, and his sense of others as hostile or indifferent was also being challenged by our building this type of supportive and safe relationship.

The castle building also offered a convenient segue to storytelling about the woods that surrounded the castle. Not surprisingly, these stories involved a sheepdog, a deer, and a lizard, who banded together and faced many adventures. Each story had a purpose: to convey understanding of Mac's perceptions of the world and to afford alternative ways of viewing himself and others. Most stories were told entirely by me, but at times Mac would respond to my encouragement to make up a story together. When he did so it became a helpful means of making ongoing assessments about his relationships, hopes, and fears.

The changing quality of the therapeutic relationship was demonstrated particularly strongly within the free-play portion of our meetings. Sometime during our sixth month of work he began to take the chairs in the playroom and make "hideouts." As this play developed, Mac elaborated more and more about the theme. He was hiding from "the bad guys" who were out to get him. He would crouch behind his chair fortress for long periods of time, whispering to an invisible companion, and clearly being menaced by the scoundrels who were pursuing him. I spent this time continuing to comment about major themes (affective and content) and connections between them. The similarities between Mac's play of hiding from bad guys and what I had learned of his early history as a playpen detainee caused me to speculate that he was replaying an old trauma. My suspicions were further raised by the increased level of affect that accompanied these periods of play. All of this was evidence that therapy was moving forward.

I told Mac that I wanted to join him in his hideout, and he readily agreed. (Had he said no, then of course I would have needed to go along with that inasmuch as it is difficult to effectively persuade someone to look at the world differently when your presence is resented.) Being in the play with Mac provided a powerful counterexperience to what he had known during the original trauma. Moreover, it allowed me to eventually help him see that adults could be counted upon for protection, as he saw me do battle with these imaginary hooligans and send them scurrying for cover.

As therapy progressed, other elements were added to the treatment plan to support the changes that had already started to take place. I referred Mac for group therapy where the focus was on learning social skills (see Chapter 9 for a description of a model group therapy program). As mentioned before, Mac needed the basic skills of how to make and keep friends so that once he was less inhibited about establishing relationships he would have the where-withal to successfully engage in them. To support our gains, I had the parents begin to enroll him in peer group activities that would build a sense of interpersonal competency in Mac. This was done gradually, and only after he had been in the social skills group for some time. These activities included Cub Scouts, and later on, Little League baseball. Had there been skateboarding teams, or a junior rock club, I would have very much wanted to have him involved in at least one of these as they matched an already existing interest. It is important, however, to be careful not to enroll a child in more than one activity at a time as this can be overwhelming to the little tyke. Once the child has successfully entered one activity, and given the family can assume the burden of enrolling him in another, it is then acceptable to have him join something else. No more than two activities should be taken on at any one time (e.g., Cub Scouts and baseball, soccer and 4-H, etc.).

The transition to group, while continuing individual therapy, was more difficult than expected. Mac initially responded with a quiet belligerence toward other members, a quality new to his presentation, and I took it to be a result of his anger at me for making this change in his therapy. Support for this conjecture came from his becoming more withdrawn and reverting to some of his past stoicism in individual therapy. I was struck by the change inasmuch as the group Mac had gone to was not particularly challenging. It was small, having only four children in it, and was led by a woman who was friendly, quick to respond to the children's needs, and engaging. Reviewing the facts and his core interpersonal pattern (his story), I concluded that Mac thought this move to be a rejection on my part, and subsequently I worked to clarify for him that this was just another part of our work together. We used the castle to help with this idea, adding structures onto it but pointing out that we did not have to throw out the rest of the castle just because new parts were added. Mac was unimpressed. He had to stifle a yawn when I gave him that analogy, so great was his interest. Other efforts met with similar levels of success. Mac the tank—for better or worse this was his style, not easily dissuaded once he set a course. What a wonderful virtue for a child to possess as long as he could use it wisely.

His obdurate nature met my persistence, and so it went for several weeks as Mac worked out his anger. At times like these you try what seems reasonable in order to remove the obstacle in your path, but when that does not bring about the results you want, and several successive similar efforts fail, it is usually best to stop and reconsider whether you have properly analyzed the problem. If you conclude that your analysis is on the mark, and your efforts to intervene are consistent with the analysis but still not bringing about the desired change, stop making these sorts of interventions and go back to the fundamentals of therapy. That is, show up every week, remain interested and attentive, and continue to respond as appropriate for the stage of therapy within which you are working. Persistence and a steady hand on the helm will usually see you through these times until you are back on course. This was the approach I used with Mac after he was unresponsive to my other efforts, and within a few weeks the anger had subsided, his work in individual therapy became productive again, and he had settled into group as an increasingly productive member. It is worth noting that his effectively working through this response to perceived rejection was likewise productive. His response was typical of the crystallized pattern he had developed over the years. What was not typical was the demand that he remain interpersonally engaged with the person with whom he was angry. This allowed him the chance to experience what it was like to be angry with someone from whom he expected rejection (remember, part of his core dynamic) and resolve those feelings without his needing to hide, nor receiving angry retribution in return.

Progress continued uneventfully for Mac. His parents noted that he was more affectionate at home and had shown an interest in pursuing the activities they had enrolled him in (scouting and baseball). Four months had passed since a letter of reprimand was sent home from the school, and Mac's teacher observed that he was often seen playing with other children during recess. He was still much more of a loner than other children, but no longer the butt of jokes as had been the case before. The parents even told of Mac being invited to another child's birthday party. The outbursts at home had also ceased, although Mac clearly became more angry than expected over minor incidents. Indeed, this began to occur with greater frequency, consistent with a youngster who was now more willing to express himself spontaneously. Overall he had improved greatly, and even though there was still more progress to be made, he was solidly headed in the right direction.

Within his weekly therapy, Mac was also changing. His interest in constructing hideouts was waning. When he did engage in this play it now invariably ended with Mac vanquishing the villains. The castle play had also run its course. We now had a fortress that allowed some people in and kept others out. The surrounding woods had been thoroughly investigated, and the initial population of lizard, dog, and deer had expanded to include a number of other inhabitants, each of whom had an uncanny resemblance to some important person in Mac's life. It was time to end therapy: our goals had been accomplished, and the support he needed to make further gains was now in place at home, in school, and in the community.

We cut back to every other week for three months, and then to once monthly for another three months. This gave Mac time to acclimate to the change and time for his parents to adjust to less frequent opportunities for consultation. Mac's group also ended during these first three months of termination. Because he had established better peer relationships elsewhere this ending was not difficult for him, and the ease with which he made the transition out of group was another sign that termination was progressing successfully. The last three months continued to progress uneventfully. His parents called on two or three occasions to ask advice on how to handle situations that had arisen. This is typical and when parents are motivated, and previous consultations have gone well, these calls most often require only that reassurance be given that the parents are on the right track in their response to whatever event prompted the call.

Our last meeting took place in the late afternoon. Mac was smiling, clearly pleased to see me again. Throughout our work he had not wanted to talk directly of the difficulties that beset him, and thus I knew that there was no point in having him talk directly about how it felt to end therapy after fifteen months of working together. I reminded him that this would be our last time to meet and invited him to choose how he would like to spend the time. Mac asked to play with the castle again, saying it was his turn to help build one for me. We began to construct one anew out of blocks and sticks. When it was complete he looked it over carefully, running his fingers along the outer walls, adjusting a block here and there, peering through the various openings. I admired his design and handiwork, and then commented that this castle did not have a moat or large drawbridge as had all the others we had made. Mac took his time, impassively surveying the sweep of this kingdom, the tall turrets and solid walls. Then he looked up to say, "Nope. This is a strong castle. That stuff, we don't need it anymore."

NOTES

1. Kiesler (1982) enumerates six assumptions of interpersonal theory, but I focus on the four that are most relevant to the topic of this chapter.

2. Clearly these same associations may be used for ongoing assessment, and throughout the counseling, by using the animal figures in story stems that the child completes. The particulars of the story stem that you, as the counselor, construct will influence the sort of information obtained.

3. Some will argue that curiosity is not an affect and therefore should not be included. A little reflection, however, clearly reveals that it is an affective state, but one that finds its expression through cognitive functioning. It is this close relationship that causes the confusion. Other affective states are more independent of cognitions for their expression, and therefore easier to identify as belonging to the affective realm. Curiosity, on the other hand, is an affective engine that propels certain cognitions and behaviors leading to its momentary diminution. Anyone who has spent time exploring questions, practical or theoretical, recognizes the difference between the pursuit of answers driven by curiosity versus those driven by demands of school, work, or practical expediency. Curiosity requires an answer to be sated, and even then one can count on it returning, like hunger requiring a meal, demanding further answers later on. It is a peculiar property of curiosity that the more successfully it is satisfied the more intense it becomes.

REFERENCES

Asher, S. & Gottmann, J. M. (Eds.). (1981). *The development of friendships*. New York: Cambridge University Press.

Bateson, G. (1958). *Naven*. Stanford: Stanford University Press.

Benjamin, L. (1974). Structural analysis of social behavior. *Psychological Review, 81*, 392-425.

Benjamin, L. (1993). *Interpersonal diagnosis and treatment of personality disorders*. New York: Guilford.

Dahl, H. & Teller, V. (1994). The characteristics, identification, and applications of FRAMES. *Psychotherapy Research, 4* (3-4), 253-276.

Dodge, K. A., Pettit, G. S., Bates, J. E., & Valente, E. (1995). Social information-processing patterns partially mediate the effect of early physical abuse on later conduct problems. *Journal of Abnormal Psychology, 104* (4), 632-643.

Friedrich, W. N. (1995). *Psychotherapy with sexually abused boys: An integrated approach*. Thousand Oaks, CA: Sage.

Gil, E. (1991). *The healing power of play: Working with abused children*. New York: Guilford.

Ginott, H. G. (1961). *Group psychotherapy with children: The theory and practice of play therapy*. New York: McGraw-Hill.

Greenspan, S. I. (1981). *The clinical interview of the child*. New York: McGraw-Hill.

Haley, J. (1959). An interactional description of schizophrenia. *Psychiatry, 22*, 321-332.

Hoelzer, M. & Dahl, H. (1996). How to find FRAMES. *Psychotherapy Research, 6* (3), 177-197.

Hoelzer, M., Dahl, H., & Kaechele, H. (1998). Identification of repetitive emotional structures via the FRAMEs method. *Psychotherapie Psychosomatik Medizinische Psychologie, 48* (8), 298-307.

Jackson, D. D. (Ed.). (1968). *Communications, family and marriage*. Palo Alto, CA: Science and Behavior Books.

James, B. (1994). *Handbook for treatment of attachment-trauma problems in children*. New York: Lexington Books.

Kazdin, A. E., Siegel, T. C., & Bass, D. (1990). Drawing on clinical practice to inform research on child and adolescent psychotherapy: Survey of practitioners. *Professional Psychology: Research & Practice, 21* (3), 189-198.

Kiesler, D. J. (1982). Interpersonal theory for personality and psychotherapy. In J. C. Anchin and D. J. Kiesler (Eds.), *Handbook of interpersonal psychotherapy* (pp. 274-295). New York: Pergamon Press.

Kohlberg, L. (1984). *Essays on moral development, Vol. 2: The psychology of moral development*. San Francisco: Harper and Row.

Leary, T. (1957). *Interpersonal diagnosis of personality*. New York: Ronald Press.

Mancini, C., Van Ameringen, M., & MacMillan, H. (1995). Relationship of childhood sexual and physical abuse to anxiety disorders. *Journal of Nervous and Mental Disease, 183* (5), 309-314.

McGinnis, E. (1984). *Skillstreaming the elementary school child: A guide for teaching prosocial skills.* Champaign, IL: Research Press.

Piaget, J. (1965). *The moral judgment of the child.* New York: Free Press.

Schaefer, C. E. (1992). What is play and why is it therapuetic? In C. E. Schaefer (Ed.), *The therapeutic powers of play* (pp. 1-15). Northvale, NJ: Jason Aronson.

Selman, R. L. (1980). *The growth of interpersonal understanding.* New York: Academic Press.

Sullivan, H. S. (1953). *The interpersonal theory of psychiatry.* New York: Norton.

Sullivan, H. S. (1954). *The psychiatric interview.* New York: Norton.

Sullivan, H. S. (1962). *Schizophrenia as a human process.* New York: Norton.

Talley, P. F., Strupp, H. H., & Morey, L. (1990). Therapist-patient dimensions and their effect on process and outcome. *Journal of Consulting and Clinical Psychology, 58,* 182-188.

Urquiza, A. J., Wirtz, S. J., Peterson, M. S., & Singer, V. A. (1994). Screening and evaluating abused and neglected children entering protective custody. *Child Welfare, 73* (2), 155-171.

Wiggins, J. S. (2003). *Paradigms of personality assessment.* New York: Guilford Press.

Winnicott, D. W. (1971). *The technique of psychotherapy.* New York: Grune and Stratton.

Chapter 9

Group Therapy with Children
Who Have Experienced Maltreatment

Jane F. Silovsky

Group treatment has long been considered a particularly beneficial modality for children who have been maltreated (Lynn, 1989). The positive interactions and companionship of other children from similar circumstances directly impact the sense of social isolation and sense of being different found in children who have been maltreated (Finkelhor, 1984; Mannarino, Cohen, & Berman, 1994; Reeker, Ensing, & Elliott, 1997). Problematic interpersonal relationships frequently develop in children who have experienced chronic abuse, and group therapy provides the opportunity to learn different patterns of interaction with other children and with adults. Mistrust, beliefs that the world is dangerous, and a sense of hopelessness can be replaced with more adaptive attributions about people and the world. Children who have been severely abused may find individual therapy, in which they are alone with a new adult, to be intimidating and overwhelming. These children may cope better with and thus benefit more from group therapy initially (Steward, Farquhar, Dicharry, Glick, & Martin, 1986). Thus, clinicians often find group therapy to be the treatment of choice for many children affected by maltreatment.

Group treatment has other advantages. More children can be treated in less time, thus group treatment is considered both cost effective and less labor intensive (Steward et al., 1986). School-age children and adolescents are naturally focused toward their peers and may respond better to positive

I would like to acknowledge the significant contributions, advice, support, and guidance of Barbara L. Bonner, PhD, and Mark J. Chaffin, PhD, from the Center on Child Abuse and Neglect, University of Oklahoma Health Sciences Center, and of Linda Ann Valle, PhD, of Northern Illinois University and Larissa Niec, PhD, of Central Michigan University. This work was supported in part by grants from the National Center on Child Abuse and Neglect (90CA1633) and from Children's Medical Research Institute, Oklahoma City, Oklahoma.

social pressure and modeling from peers in the group than to information provided only by adults. Being with other children their age may enhance their motivation and interest in the group. Experiencing positive interactions and receiving feedback from peers about progress can have a powerful impact on the children's self-perception (Friedrich, 1996). Further, given the need to address interpersonal skills, group therapy provides the opportunity to practice skills through role-plays as well as in less formal ways through interactions during group. In addition, therapists can more readily assess the children's social perceptions and skills by directly observing the youngsters as they negotiate social interactions (Stark, Swearer, Kurowski, Sommer, & Bowen, 1996).

Support for the efficacy of group therapy is noted in meta-analyses of treatment outcome research on child and adolescent group therapy (Hoag & Burlingame, 1997; Weisz, Weiss, Han, Granger, & Morton, 1995). Weisz et al. (1995) found an overall effect size of .50 for group therapy with children and adolescents when analyzing ninety-two group treatment outcome studies, all of which included a control group. Hoag and Burlingame (1997) conducted meta-analyses using fifty-six studies of group therapy, forty-nine of these studies including a placebo or wait-list control group. An overall effect size of .52 was found for the studies using control group comparison data and of .72 when comparing posttreatment scores to pretreatment scores.

To examine the effectiveness of group treatment for sexually abused children, Reeker et al. (1997) conducted a meta-analysis of the fifteen treatment outcome studies available and found an overall mean effect size of .79, supporting the usefulness of this modality. Limitations on these conclusions were noted because most of the studies used a pretest-posttest design, few had control groups, and the sample size for the studies tended to be low. These initial results evaluating group therapy for children who have been sexually abused are promising. Unfortunately, the research on group treatment for children who have been physically abused and/or neglected is quite limited. However, group therapy may be particularly useful for this population, who are often characterized by poor peer interactions, social withdrawal and/or aggression, and social isolation.

This chapter discusses information about types of group therapies appropriate for children who have been maltreated. After a brief description of important assessment considerations, specific types of group treatments for identified areas of concern are discussed. Abuse-specific and abuse-related group treatment topics and activities for group programs are provided. Issues related to the characteristics of the group program and the children selected (e.g., age, gender, size of group) are important when planning group programs and are discussed. Qualifications of the therapist, challenges and concerns when providing group therapy, and developmental considerations are presented. Finally, the involvement of caregivers in the group therapy process is briefly described and a case example is provided.

For many children who have experienced child maltreatment, group therapy is only part of the family plan for treatment and is not utilized exclusively, particularly in cases of chronic abuse and neglect. Other chapters provide information about individual, family, and parenting interventions important when working with families. There is an abundance of written material for sexual abuse, though little material on physical abuse and neglect, a need that is addressed with this chapter.

TREATMENT OF WHAT?
THE IMPORTANCE OF ASSESSMENT

In the early and mid-1980s, sexual abuse was being widely recognized. A plethora of group therapy programs for children were developed (Silovsky & Hembree-Kigin, 1994), and since then numerous books, workbooks, and articles have been written on group therapy designed for children who have been sexually abused. Group programs that covered a wide range of topics (including self-blame, sex education, safety skills, feeling identification skills, coping with anger toward the perpetrator) were considered the treatment of choice for most if not all children who have been sexually abused. The assumption behind these groups was that all children who have been sexually abused are negatively affected in similar ways. Research has since elucidated that children who have been sexually abused, physically abused, and/or neglected may present with internalizing problems, externalizing problems, social problems, sexual behavior problems, all of these problems, or present as resilient with no notable difficulties or negative attributions (Kendall-Tacket, Williams, & Finkelhor, 1993; Kolko, 1996). As we better understand the complexities of the impact of child maltreatment on children, therapies specifically targeted to the troubled areas (such as aggressive behavior, depression, and traumatic symptoms) have been developed, implemented, and evaluated. Rather than a generic group for all children who have experienced maltreatment, it is critical to assess needs and strengths of the children and design the treatment plan to address areas identified as interfering or potentially interfering with the children's normal functioning.

Children who have been maltreated may present with a wide range of difficulties and strengths. Areas found to be problematic in maltreated children and areas important to assess for group treatment programs are

- internalizing problems, including symptoms of depression, post-traumatic stress disorder (PTSD), separation anxiety, and other anxiety disorders;
- externalizing behavior problems, including symptoms of attention-deficit/hyperactivity disorder (ADHD), oppositional defiant disorder, conduct disorder, and aggression;
- sexual behavior problems, not limited to children who have been sexually abused;
- attributions and self-perceptions, including attributions about the abuse experiences, global attributions, and self-esteem;
- social skills and relationships with peers;
- social support and connection with healthy, supportive adults;
- coping strategies and skills;
- cognitive and language development;
- other sources of strengths;
- severe psychiatric disorders, such as a thought disorder; and
- suicidality and intent to harm others.

Thorough assessment of the areas to be targeted in treatment helps to determine if the program is appropriate for the child and provides a baseline of functioning against which to measure progress. Screening of other areas in the list may assist in determining if other services may be more warranted, or if collaborative individual or family therapy is needed. For example, a group treatment program designed to target PTSD may thoroughly evaluate PTSD symptoms with self-report measures and diagnostic interviews with the child and caregiver, but then also screen for behavior problems by administering a caregiver-report behavior checklist. A child may be identified as having PTSD symptoms, but also be demonstrating moderate behavior problems that are not severe enough to exclude her from the group, but are interfering with her functioning enough to warrant a referral for a program to address the behavior problems, such as behavioral parent training.

Initial evaluations help to determine the fit between the children's needs and program goals, to identify other areas of need for the children and family, and provide a baseline against which progress can be measured. When developing an overall treatment plan for the child and his or her family, comprehensive assessments are essential. Focused assessments may be warranted for group therapy. A thorough discussion of the assessments of children who have been maltreated is provided in Chapter 5 and in Bonner, Kaufman, Niec, and Logue (2001).

TYPES OF GROUPS AND GOALS OF GROUP

When developing the group treatment program, goals for the group must be clearly defined as must the areas to be targeted for treatment or prevention. Group programs can be designed to be preventive, supportive, educational, and/or to intervene with specific problems or disorders (Lynn, 1989). The following sections first describe emotional or behavioral problem-specific interventions for problems in children affected by maltreatment. Next, abuse-specific and abuse-related areas for treatment are discussed.

Group Treatment Topics and Activities for Specific Emotional and Behavioral Problems

Post-Traumatic Stress Disorder and Other Anxiety Disorders

Trauma-specific psychotherapy uses a cognitive-behavioral approach to treat posttraumatic stress symptoms including reexperiencing the trauma, numbing, nightmares, sleep disturbances, hypervigilance, and poor concentration. Cognitive-behavioral exposure-based treatments for PTSD have been found to reduce anxiety symptoms and improve children's functioning (Deblinger, Steer, & Lippmann, 1999; Saunders, Berliner, & Hanson, 2000). The process of this therapy is to have the children experience the event through gradual exposure by telling their stories of their traumatic experiences, with additional work on changing maladaptive attributions and teaching coping strategies, including relaxation. This process helps the children learn to tolerate memories and reminders of the abuse without distress or avoidance reactions (Deblinger & Heflin, 1996). Gradual exposure and teaching coping strategies may be components of a larger group program that also addresses other issues related to the trauma. When treating PTSD symptoms in a group therapy format, often the children selected have experienced similar traumas (e.g., sexual abuse).

Children are often initially reluctant to talk about the abuse experience in much detail. The use of relaxation strategies can reduce distress initially. Relaxation skills, including controlled breathing, progressive relaxation, and imagery, may be taught in a variety of ways for children. Ultimately, it is most therapeutic for the children to express their thoughts and feelings about the abuse and endure the emotional distress until it diminishes naturally, such that the children experience reduced fear and a sense of relief and control (Deblinger & Heflin, 1996). Children may more readily express their experiences in group than in individual therapy. Hearing other children model talking about the abuse experience may allow more open and detailed expression of thoughts and feelings (Swenson & Brown, 1999).

Before asking the children to tell their own stories of abuse, the group first provides education about trauma, such as defining physical abuse (or sexual abuse or domestic violence) and discussing who is abused, who abuses, reasons for abuse, and reasons children may not tell (Deblinger & Heflin, 1996). Allow the children to discuss their ideas before providing corrective information as needed. A group activity that can help the children begin to discuss their own experiences is to have each child draw a picture of the family when the abuse was ongoing and next to it draw a picture of the family now (Silovsky & Valle, 1997b). When describing the pictures and the differences between them, children express their thoughts and feelings about the abuse, the changes in their family, their placement in another home (if that occurred), the causes of the abuse and changes, and their future. Figure 9.1 shows the pictures from a ten-year-old boy who was attending a children's group therapy program that was part of a treatment program for parents who have been physically abusive and their children. His pictures illustrate many of his feelings and thoughts about his experiences. He expressed some degree of hopefulness, with the "before" picture showing anger and threats of violence (the father is screaming, "I'm going to get you a good whoopin'.") and the "now" picture depicting the father apologizing for past threats ("I [am] sorry [for] all [the] things I said bake [back] then."). Tentativeness in the stability of the change was expressed in his discussion of his picture and in the picture itself, which included no people. This youngster's self-expression encouraged the other group members to open up about their own thoughts and feelings.

Swenson and Brown (1999) describe an activity for children who have been physically abused, designed to facilitate self-expression and reinforce the message of the adult's responsibility for behavior. The first step of the activity is to have the group members make a puppet of the person who abused them out of a paper bag with markers, paints, and other craft materials. Each child tells about the abuse experience, with the puppet indicating what he or she did. During the recounting of what happened, the therapist and group members provide support through encouraging the use of relaxation skills and cognitive restructuring.

Treatment of PTSD with gradual exposure is a specialized approach that requires comprehensive training and supervision. Listening to distressing accounts of abuse is also naturally distressing for the therapist, who may respond in ways that inadvertently encourage avoidance by the child (Deblinger & Heflin, 1996). Specialized training and supervision is required in gradual exposure and the mechanisms of action so that the therapist may be able to facilitate the process of exposure and address the negative cognitions of the children. Methods to address negative cognitions are discussed in more detail later.

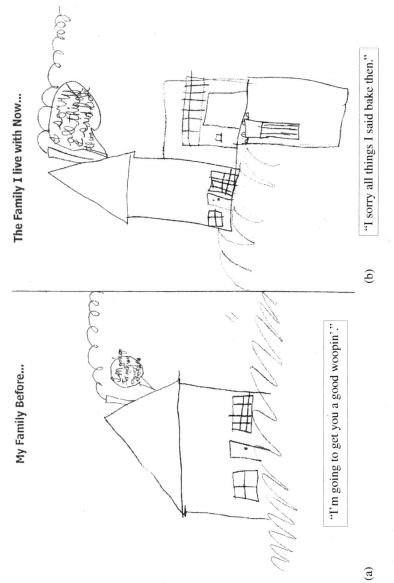

My Family Before...

"I'm going to get you a good woopin'."

(a)

The Family I live with Now...

"I sorry all things I said bake then."

(b)

FIGURE 9.1. Drawing by Ten-Year-Old Abused Boy (a) before Treatment and (b) after Treatment

Depression

Treatment for depression has been researched less extensively than treatment for PTSD, though some promising approaches are available. Similar to adults, depressed children are thought to have negative schemas (negative beliefs about themselves, the world, and their future) and attributional style (that is, believe that negative outcomes are due to internal, stable, and global causes, whereas positive outcomes are caused by external, unstable, and specific causes) (Gladstone & Kaslow, 1995; Kazdin & Weisz, 1998). Commonalities of treatment for depression across childhood and adolescence are strategies to identify a range of feelings, identify and modify maladaptive schemas and attributions, improve social interactions, increase positive, mood-enhancing activity, and reduce tension (Kazdin & Weisz, 1998; Stark, Swearer, et al., 1996). When planning the group, it is important to include children with mild depressive symptoms or use an open-ended group format so that peers can model some motivation and positive thinking, which would be challenging if all group members were severely depressed.

Group therapy for depression often begins with activities geared at affect education; children gain the skills and language to identify and label their feelings and learn the associations among feelings, thoughts, and actions. An aspect of depression is to perceive the world in extremes and to not recognize a range of feelings, thoughts, intentions, and actions. Thus, children who are depressed may begin treatment only labeling feelings as "bad," "sad," and "good," with some children failing to recognize experiencing the latter in themselves (Stark, Swearer, et al., 1996). A variety of activities can be used to facilitate affect education in an enjoyable manner that is engaging and enhances the children's interest and motivation for group. The Second Step Curriculum (Committee for Children, 1996) provides large cards picturing ethnically diverse children demonstrating feelings through their facial and body expressions. Children can be prompted to identify the feeling for each card and discuss what may have happened to cause the feelings. Charades may be used in which the children take turns picking a feeling name and then demonstrating the feeling while the other group members guess which feeling it is.

Identifying feelings requires attention to not only facial expression and body language, but also physiological responses or what is "happening inside" such as heart racing, stomach tight, becoming hot, and so on. Children may be asked to draw a picture of themselves showing what is going on inside of them when they are feeling an emotion, particularly anger. Because children who are depressed often have difficulty managing anger, specific attention to this feeling is recommended (Stark, Swearer, et al., 1996).

Identifying a variety of pleasant and unpleasant feelings and sensing the intensity of feelings in themselves and others are goals for the group. Skills at identifying feelings of other people may be especially important for children who have been maltreated. The group members can be taught to "look, listen, ask" so that they begin to look for visual cues of feelings, listen for words and tone of voice clues, and ask others about their feelings (Deblinger & Heflin, 1996). Typical child interactions (e.g., situations at school) as well as interactions associated with the abuse and disclosure of abuse should be discussed, beginning with less threatening examples.

The next level of affect education is to begin to associate experiences with feelings and understand how thoughts, feelings, and actions interact. Second Step (Committee for Children, 1996) provides additional cards picturing children interacting in a variety of potentially conflictual situations that can be used to elicit discussions about causes of feelings and thoughts associated with feelings. Questions can be asked by the therapist to prompt critical thinking about how different thoughts are related to different feelings and actions. Knowing that they can have some control of their feelings by controlling their thoughts can be empowering for the children. Example questions include, "What is this child thinking? How is he feeling? If he thought _____, how would his feelings change? What would he do differently? What are other ways that he could think about the situation?" Depending on the level of depression and the skills of the children in the group, the therapist may have to initially provide answers to the critical questions and begin to reduce their extreme thinking. Charades, drawing, role-play, and game sheets may be used for other active learning experiences (Stark, 1990, 1996).

Scheduling positive activities into the children's day is a primary tool in the treatment of depression in children (Stark, Swearer, et al., 1996). Engaging in enjoyable events helps to activate them and distract them from negative thoughts. Activities that are goal directed and include mastery experiences can directly challenge negative self-thoughts by providing evidence of success and accomplishment (Stark, Swearer, et al., 1996). These activities could include hobbies (e.g., collecting, building a model, craft activities), home and school projects, and cooperative group activities (e.g., with Boy Scouts, Girl Scouts, or school clubs). Stark, Kendall, et al. (1996) provide a variety of worksheets and activities to utilize with the group to plan, schedule, and monitor pleasant events. When planning the implementation of the pleasant activities, care is needed to address potential challenges, break down the task into reasonable steps, and provide motivating statements to counter the pessimism and negative thinking of the children (Stark, Swearer, et al., 1996).

After the group members have demonstrated skills in feeling identification and association of feelings, thoughts, and behaviors, and have increased their level of positive activities, they can directly address their negative, maladaptive cognitions and replace them with more adaptive, positive thoughts. During the first and subsequent sessions, the leaders listen for and record negative thoughts to utilize as examples for this later stage of the group. The group members may be taught to think out loud and become "Thought Detectives" to catch the negative thoughts (Stark, Swearer, et al., 1996). Props, such as pretend magnifying glasses, can be used with young children to enhance interest (Niec, personal communication, March 1998). The Thought Detectives are taught to look for thoughts that contain negative or critical words, include extremes (e.g., never, always), generalize from a small negative event to think that everything is bad, ignore positive aspects, justify conclusions with negative emotions, and blame themselves (Rosselló & Bernal, 1996). The Thought Detectives then evaluate the evidence for the thoughts, consider alternative interpretations, evaluate if the alternative explanations are plausible, adaptive, and realistic, and think about what really would happen if the undesirable event occurred (Stark, Swearer, et al., 1996). Changing the children's negative cognitive patterns is difficult, but considered to be critical for treatment of depression in children.

Sexual Behavior Problems

Sexual behavior in children is defined as problematic when it

1. occurs at a greater frequency or much earlier than would be developmentally expected,
2. interferes with children's development,
3. occurs with the use of coercion, intimidation, or force,
4. is associated with emotional distress (in the child demonstrating the sexual behavior or the other children involved), and/or
5. reoccurs in secrecy after intervention by caregivers (adapted from Hall, Matthews, Pearce, Sarlo-McGarvey, & Gavin, 1996).

Sexual behavior problems have consistently been found to be more prevalent in children who have been sexually abused than nonabused children (Kendall-Tackett et al., 1993). However, sexual behavior problems are not exclusively found in children who have been sexually abused. Neglect, physical abuse, and witnessing interparental violence histories are notable in children with sexual behavior problems (SBP) (Bonner, Walker, & Berliner, 1999a; Silovsky & Niec, 1999). Children with SBP have often been exposed to situations that lead to confused rules about their bodies and interactions with others. These children may have been exposed to sexualized materials in their home, neighborhood, or other environments (including on television, videos, magazines, video games, or the Internet), lived in a home that has little privacy, lived in a situation without supervision, been sexually abused, and/or been exposed to physical violence.

Topics in SBP treatment programs often include

1. rules about sexual behavior,
2. acknowledging the sexual behaviors (except with preschoolers),
3. boundaries,
4. sexual education,
5. impulse-control/self-control strategies,
6. abuse prevention/safety skills,
7. social skills,
8. emotional regulation skills, and
9. coping strategies.

Group treatment is often considered the treatment of choice for children with SBP. Further, a concurrent group for the caregivers is critical for treatment of sexual behavior problems in children.

Simple, clear rules about interacting with others are important for children with SBP to learn. Bonner, Walker, and Berliner (1999b) provide specific rules to teach the group members, called the sexual behavior rules, which consist of the following:

- It's not okay to touch other people's private parts.
- It's not okay for other people to touch your private parts.
- It's not okay to show your private parts to other people.
- It's okay to touch your own private parts when you are alone (p. 8).

To establish common language, private parts are defined for the children. A picture with male and female children in bathing suits can be utilized in this discussion and is especially useful with preschoolers. The rules are explained to the children. The children are prompted to think of examples and exceptions to the rules. The group therapists correct misunderstandings and describe scenarios to discuss (e.g., "Is it okay to touch your own private parts when you are alone in the living room, but there are other people in your home?"). For the second rule, exceptions due to hygiene and health are discussed. Further, it is explained that if someone else touches a child's private parts, then they are breaking the sexual behavior rules. Families vary on their acceptance of the final rule regarding touching private parts in private. The caregivers' acceptance of this rule may change as the caregivers learn about normal sexual development and healthy rules for children. For preschool children, the rules may be reworded to simpler language and labels, such as "private parts rules" (Silovsky & Niec, 1998). The children recite and memorize the rules, which are then applied to a variety of situations to enhance skills designed to prevent breaking the sexual behavior rules. Problem-solving skills and impulse-control strategies are taught to facilitate following the rules and are described in detail in the section on treatment for other externalizing behavior problems.

Children with SBP by definition have exhibited poor interpersonal boundaries. Preschool children in particular may be indiscriminate and hug, touch, and even crawl into the laps of people they do not know. The concept of boundaries is quite abstract for young children. One strategy to make boundaries more concrete is to use a hula hoop to demonstrate that each individual has personal "space." Exhibit 9.1 describes group therapeutic activities using hula hoops to teach and apply the concept of boundaries (Silovsky & Niec, 1998). The term "hula space" can be used as a cue for young children during group to remind them to respect one another's space, and also taught to caregivers to use at home and in the community. The children can also be taught to greet others with a handshake, rather than hugs, to further reinforce boundaries.

Externalizing Behaviors

Children who have been maltreated are at risk for developing externalizing behavior problems, including oppositionality, aggressiveness, delinquency, and other conduct problems (Kolko, 1996). Parent management training is often the treatment of choice for oppositional and aggressive behaviors in children, particularly evidence-based parent training models such as those developed by Eyberg (Eyberg & Boggs, 1989; Hembree-Kigin & McNeil, 1995), Webster-Stratton (1996), and Forehand (Forehand & McMahon, 1981). However, cognitive-behavioral group treatment programs addressing social problem-solving skills have been found to reduce antisocial and aggressive behaviors (Kazdin & Weisz, 1998) and a combination of problem-solving skills training and parent training has been found to lead to more marked improvements than either treatment provided in isolation (Kazdin, 1996). These problem-solving skills programs are designed to address areas of cognitive processing deficits found in children with aggressive and other externalizing behaviors (Crick & Dodge, 1994; Kazdin

EXHIBIT 9.1.
Teaching Boundaries to Preschool Children

Explaining Hula Space

Have the children pick out a hula hoop and try to "hula" with it. Then have each child choose a place where he or she can place the hoop on the floor and sit in it. Explain to the children that the area inside the hoop is called "your space." Tell the children, "No one is allowed to enter the space unless he or she has permission from you. The hoop represents the boundaries for your space. Our hula space is always with us even though we can't see it. While we are here we will use the hula hoops to help us remember that our hula space is with us and that everyone else here has hula space also. You may also be able to tell if someone is too close to you by how you feel. If it feels yucky or scary, you may be too close." (This is not necessarily true for children who have trouble with boundaries [e.g., those who have been sexually abused], so we need to reinforce the concrete ways of defining personal space, as well as the uncomfortable feelings. For example, being one giant step away is about a hula hoop space and a good distance).

Demonstrating Hula Space

Have two therapists stand in front of the group. Therapist B stands in the middle of a hula hoop. Therapist A stands a distance away from Therapist B and holds out a large doll. Therapist B should explain that there is an amount of space that people are most comfortable having between them. Therapist B tells the children that he or she will raise a hand when the doll is too close. Therapist A slowly moves the large doll toward Therapist B. Therapist B raises his or her hand when the doll is about a hula hoop space away.

Have the children practice this activity with a therapist. This can be done one at a time in front of the group, or the children can break up into groups with therapists, depending on the number of large dolls. Praise and reinforce the children for raising their hand when the doll is less than hula hoop space away from the children.

(continued)

(continued)

Using Hula Space

Teach assertive responses. After talking about how they may feel if someone is too close, teach assertive responses. "What is something we can say if someone is entering our hula space (getting too close) and we don't want them to?" Give examples of situations. "Pretend you were playing with the Play-Doh at the table and Johnny came over to play with you. He stood so close to you he was almost stepping on your feet. What could you say or do?" (e.g., "Please step back" and take a step away from Johnny). Discuss other things to say, for instance, "I don't like being so close," or "Please move back."

Teach greeting with a handshake. To teach children to respect others' hula space and to prevent children from greeting strangers and acquaintances with hugs and climbing on their lap, children can be taught to shake hands when greeting others. Special handshakes can be developed with special people, such as the therapists.

& Weisz, 1998; Spivack & Shure, 1982). Furthermore, children who have been physically abused are more likely to have hostile attributional biases, generate more aggressive responses, and perceive aggressive responses as leading to successful outcomes (Dodge, Pettit, & Bates, 1997). Relatively neutral events (e.g., an accidental brush on the shoulder when walking by a child) may be more likely to be interpreted as signs of hostility and responded to with aggression. Thus, changing aggressive and problematic interpersonal behavior may require changing how the child perceives and processes the events and actions of others (Kazdin, 1996).

To address these deficits, social problem-solving group treatment programs help children to identify problematic and potentially problematic situations; generate alternative solutions to problems; understand possible consequences; consider possible sequences of events; recognize and predict feelings and reactions of others; and use nonviolent active responses to problems (Kazdin, 1996; Kazdin & Weisz, 1998; Spivack & Shure, 1982). Often videotaped scenarios and pictures of children interacting in a variety of situations are utilized as teaching tools (e.g., Second Step; Committee for Children, 1996; Webster-Stratton & Hammond, 1997). These tools are used to prompt discussion of the areas to address and facilitate active problem solving and role-playing activities. The children are asked to identify what is happening (i.e., what is the problem), the thoughts and feelings of those involved, and possible reasons for these feelings. The steps for effective problem solving are taught (see Table 9.1) and the children practice the steps in a variety of situations. For younger children, self-control and problem-solving skills may be taught through the "turtle technique" (Schneider & Robin, 1976), which involves stories about turtles who use their shell as a safe place to calm down (and use relaxation strategies), think about possible options, choose one, then go out of their shell to do it (Bonner et al., 1999b; Silovsky & Valle, 1997a). Because high emotions can interfere with the problem-solving process, the turtle technique adds strategies to help calm the children and enhance their level of self-control. The turtle technique has been successfully taught to children as young as four years old. One method to encourage home practice of the skills is to videotape the individual group members telling the steps of the turtle with cards picturing each step, and then demonstrating the use of the turtle in a role-play situation. Using scenarios that the caregivers had identified as problematic may enhance the caregivers' expectation of the strategy and teach the child to use the turtle when needed most (Silovsky & Niec, 1998).

Another tool that encourages children to develop alternative solutions to problems and evaluate the consequences is the Problem-Solving Book series (e.g., Crary, 1983). Each book begins with a problem particularly challenging for children with behavior problems (such as being called a name, wanting to play with others, and having problems waiting) and asks the children to brainstorm about alternative responses to the situation. Each subsequent page discusses one of the options and the consequences. Questions to encourage the children to identify the feelings of the characters, generate other alternatives, and understand consequences of actions are provided throughout the book. Adaptive and maladaptive responses and their consequences are provided.

TABLE 9.1. Comparison of Steps for Effective Problem Solving

Problem-Solving Steps	Turtle Technique
Identify the problem and the goal.	Identify strong feelings/problem.
	Stop and go into the shell.
	Relax and calm down; take three deep breaths and give positive self-statements.
Brainstorm possible solutions.	Think; generate alternatives.
Evaluate the alternatives and consider the consequences.	Think about consequences and choose one option.
Decide and implement a plan.	Do it.
Evaluate the plan.	How did you do?

ADDITIONAL GROUP TREATMENT TOPICS FOR CHILDREN AFFECTED BY CHILD MALTREATMENT

Because children affected by child maltreatment may present with a combination of internalizing and externalizing symptoms, group therapy protocols may in turn utilize a combination of treatment strategies. Topics considered to further ameliorate distress and prevent future problems (such as sexual education, safety skills, and addressing attributions about the abuse) are often also integrated into the curriculum (Karp & Butler, 1996). Further, coping skills and methods to enhance social networks are taught to facilitate resiliency and long-term adjustment. Care must be taken when conducting groups that are abuse-specific to avoid inadvertently reinforcing a self-perception and identity wrapped around the abuse experience. Rather, it is critical to provide support and skills needed to move away from a preoccupation with the abuse and toward feeling, being, and acting like a typical kid. Additional discussion of cautions when conducting groups with children affected by maltreatment is provided later in the chapter. The following sections describe goals and activities for groups designed to address problems commonly found in children affected by child maltreatment, enhance coping skills, prevent future emotional and behavioral problems, and teach safety and prevention skills. The topics are ordered in sequence for group therapy programs.

Introduction and Orientation

The first session for groups naturally begins with orientation to the purposes and procedures of the group and introductions of the therapists and child group members. This session provides the groundwork and tone for the group. A well-implemented initial session helps the development of a sense of safety and trust among the members and interest in the sessions and activities. The individual assessments conducted before starting the group can inform the planning for the pace of the initial group sessions designed for introductions and to facilitate building trust (Bonner et al., 2001).

In the introduction session, the purpose of the group and the commonality of the group members (e.g., everyone who is there has experienced violence in their family) is described and confidentiality and the rules for the group are established (Silovsky & Valle, 1997a,b,c). Group rules are important to develop a sense of safety for the children, which may be most critical for boys who have been sexually abused (Friedrich, 1995). Describing the purpose of the group and providing clear and specific information about confidentiality in the beginning of the first session sets expectations for the group. Given sensitivity to and harm related to secrets in abusive experiences, when defining confidentiality the group leader can distinguish between keeping information private and keeping secrets. Rather than being a secret group, which means no one can tell anyone about the group, the groups sessions are private, which

> means neither you nor I can tell anyone what other kids in group say.
> . . . *but,* if anyone in group tells me you are thinking about hurting yourself or someone else or that someone has hurt you, that information will not be kept private. Just remember that if you tell me about abuse of you that has already been reported, I will not report it again.
> (Swenson & Brown, 1999, p. 215)

After reviewing confidentiality, establish the rules about behavior in the group, including rules about physical contact, to develop a sense of safety (Friedrich, 1995). Brainstorming rules for the group with members can improve a sense of fairness about the rules and set the tone of direct involvement of the members in group activities. Integration of the group members' ideas for the group name and rules also establishes a sense of ownership for the group (Peled & Davis, 1995).

Members can learn more about each other through a variety of activities. Group members may pair off and complete an interview worksheet on each other asking about school, friends, interests, and activities. After returning to the whole group, the paired members introduce their partner to the group using some of the information they learned in the interview. Mandell et al. (1989) provide a number of useful worksheets for this and other activities. Another activity is to give a list of items that children may enjoy and explain that their task is to talk with group members and find at least one person who likes each item (e.g., chocolate, Pokémon, pepperoni pizza, playing baseball). This activity also provides the therapist with an opportunity to evaluate the children's social skills. To start the group encouraging self-affirmations, the group members could also introduce themselves using a positive word with the same first initial as the child's name (e.g., Cool Carlos, Fun Frances) (Peled & Davis, 1995).

Feeling Identification and Expression Skills

Children who have experienced chronic abusive and neglectful experiences often have limited vocabulary for emotions. Activities for feeling identification and expression skills can be fun, engaging, and nonthreatening, which further develops interest and cohesion of the group. The activities chosen will depend on how well the group has been able to understand the concepts of feelings. For feeling identification skills, the children should be able to identify basic feelings of children in pictures; to identify feelings in themselves; to identify situations that often cause specific feelings in children; to understand that people may feel more than one feeling at once; and to know that how one thinks about situations can affect how one feels and acts. Many feeling identification activities are provided in the section on treating depression. Additional feeling identification activities for older children are found in Berman (1994).

Relaxation Skills

An important coping skill for children affected by maltreatment is to be able to calm down, relax their muscles, release tension, and regain a sense of control. Preschool children respond to practices of control breathing paired with visual cues (e.g., using bubbles or balloons) and to body tension and release activities (e.g., practicing being a "robot" and tensing one's body and then being a "rag doll" and relaxing; Pertik & Senter, 1990). Older children can respond to more progressive relaxation, especially when paired with visualization exercises. Koeppen (1974) provides a detailed guided script for progressive relaxation with older children.

Social Skills and Problem-Solving Skills

Children who are raised in families characterized by violence and/or neglect have had models of maladaptive methods for interacting and solving problems. Responding to conflict with aggression or withdrawal may be the only options in the children's repertoire. Learning how to identify, analyze, and appropriately respond to interpersonal problems are critical skills for the children to learn. Further, skills at identifying individuals with whom to interact, initiating activities with peers, and developing friendships are important to improving patterns of interaction with peers (Silovsky & Valle, 1997c). *Group Exercises for Enhancing Social Skills and Self-Esteem* (Khalsa, 1996) and *Social Skills Lessons and Activities for Grades 1-3* (Begun, 1995) are a couple of the many group activity books geared at teaching social skills.

Attributions About Abuse

How children think about the abuse experience and the changes that have occurred since disclosure (e.g., family members moving, forensic interviews, court procedures) can influence their self-perceptions and adjustment. Initial programs designed for children who have been sexually abused formerly focused on eliminating self-blame. More recently this single focus has been thought to be incomplete, as children who have been sexually abused may not blame themselves for the abuse but have other maladaptive attributions. Sexual-abuse awareness and prevention campaigns could have contributed to reducing the likelihood of self-blame for sexual abuse. However, thoughts of shame, guilt about the impact of disclosure on the family, and negative beliefs about themselves (e.g., damaged goods) may be prevalent (Mannarino et al., 1994). Further, beliefs that the world is dangerous, unjust, and that people should not be trusted are notable.

Group therapy may be ideal for addressing maladaptive attributions, as peers can provide different and adaptive interpretations of events. Addressing the topic of attributions can begin with discussing abuse in general as a group, with members contributing ideas about definitions, causes, and consequences. Confused and ambiguous feelings about the person who abused them may be expressed. When providing feedback to the group regarding their descriptions and definitions of physical abuse, "care [should be] taken to avoid placing any child in a loyalty conflict. The maltreating caregiver's behavior [can be] framed as 'against the rules' rather than as a personal flaw" (Swenson & Brown, 1999, p. 215), particularly when physical abuse appears to have been exclusively excessive physical discipline and the child remains in the home with the caregiver. Delicate balances are required to prevent children from self-blame when they have externalizing behavior problems and are beginning to take responsibility for their own behavior (i.e., that they need to follow reasonable rules). The following is a dialogue from a group session discussing the roles and responsibilities of the caregiver who was abusive and the children who were involved.

THERAPIST A: What has changed in your family, C?

CHILD C: My mom is much calmer now. She asks me to do things now. She used to yell and hit me because I used to mouth off at her.

THERAPIST B: Is it okay to mouth off at adults?

CHILD C: No, I'm learning to respect myself and others.

THERAPIST B: Was it okay for your mom to hit you?

CHILD C: No . . . but I think Mom doesn't want me to talk that way to people and she was teaching me.

THERAPIST A: Your mother wants to help you (reflecting positive beliefs about Mom). (Looking around the group) Was hitting the best way to teach?

CHILD D: She could have talked with you and explained and showed you how to talk to adults.

THERAPIST B: And it sounds like C's mom is learning to interact with C in a calm way. C, how do you feel about what happened?

CHILD C: Sad . . . and guilty for making my mom go to court.

THERAPIST B: (To the group) What do you think about her mom going to court? Is C to blame?

CHILD E: No! Her mom made her choice—and if she didn't hit C she wouldn't be in trouble. She should have calmed down.

THERAPIST A: What would you suggest that C think to herself when she starts to feel sad and blame herself?

CHILD E: You weren't the one who hit; it's *not* your fault.

CHILD D: You could think about your mom is now getting help and that things will get better.

CHILD F: C, were you pushing your mom's buttons? Did you get in the middle of her business? 'Cause if you did, then maybe it is your fault you got hit, but not your fault for the court stuff.

THERAPIST A: Is it ever okay for a parent to hit a child?

CHILD F: Oh, no. But it was not safe for her to get in her mom's business.

CHILD D: Her mom should have asked her to please leave and be calm—like she's doing now.

THERAPIST B: So, it's never okay for parents to harm their children. C can remind herself that she is not responsible for what has happened, including going to court. She can also think about how her mother does care about her and is learning better ways to teach her.

CHILD C: Yep. And I'm learning to listen to Mom better.

Roles and responsibilities may be further distinguished by having the members brainstorm on the responsibilities of parents/caregivers and those of children. Young children use cutout magazine pictures of adults and children doing typical activities to prompt discussion of their roles (Silovsky & Valle, 1997b). The caregivers' jobs are to work, provide food, pay the bills, play with the children, and keep the children safe, whereas the children's responsibilities are to do their homework, complete chores, play with friends and family members, and follow rules at home and school. Placing responsibility where it belongs can strongly impact children who have experienced chronic neglect and children who take on adult roles, such as care of their younger siblings. These discussions can lead to addressing reasons caregivers do not meet the needs of the children, including depression, substance abuse, and so on. Therapists should be attuned to the level of anxiety and distress experienced by the group members when talking about their attributions and past experiences.

Sex Education

Age and developmentally appropriate information about sexual development and sex education may be included in the group curriculum, particularly with children who have been sexually abused, exposed to sexualized material, or who have sexual behavior problems. In the group format, preschool children at a minimum need information about parts of their bodies being private, differences between boys and girls, and basic information needed for sexual abuse prevention skills. School-age children are often ready to learn about conception and where babies come from. Groups for adolescents prepare children for the process of puberty, changes in their bodies, and developing healthy relationships (Deblinger & Heflin, 1996). The therapists may ask children and adolescents to write questions for the therapists anonymously on strips of paper, which are then collected, reviewed, and discussed in the session to provide corrective information. The books *Where Did I Come From?* (Mayle & Robins, 1975) and *What's Happening to Me?* (Mayle, 1975) provide clear, accurate information in a manner that children and young adolescents have responded well to.

Abuse Prevention and Safety Skills

In addition to information about their bodies, children are taught to understand boundaries and their right to protect themselves and their bodies. Signs of risky situations are identified as a group. Safety skills are not limited to protecting self from strangers, but also discussing that children who are abused often know the abuser. Safety rules are discussed, such as that it is not okay for other people to touch children's private parts and it is not okay for people to harm children. Responses when other people may try to break safety rules are taught and role-played. A safety plan integrating a social network can be developed. For each risky situation, people who can be helpers, including family members, community members, and organizations, are identified and their specific roles and helping skills discussed. Educating about secrets and knowing when not to keep secrets is critical for children to effectively utilize safety people. Community safety people include police officers, firefighters, teachers, coaches, neighbors, foster parents, caseworkers, and friends, among others. It is important to identify multiple people as helpers. Children may also identify people who have been abusive in the past as helpers, particularly parents. Completion of safety plan worksheets provides children with lists of names and numbers of the helpers. Helpers who can help the children when they need someone to talk with are designated. If caregivers give permission to contact them, calling and preparing these safety plan members can help them respond to the child's calls in a manner that may facilitate the child's coping (Kolko & Swenson, 2000).

Clearly, protection against abuse and safety is the responsibility of children's caregivers and other adults. However, children can benefit from safety information, which can also reinforce knowledge about identifying abusive behaviors. Care must be taken to avoid provoking thoughts of self-blame for not telling about the abuse sooner. Reasons why children do not tell may be repeated during this time.

Coping Strategies

Chronic maltreatment and traumatic experiences can lead to a limited range of skills to adjust to ongoing negative life events. Children may respond to stressful events by completely withdrawing from the situation, experiencing emotional outbursts, or demonstrating aggression. An adaptive range of coping strategies includes active problem solving and implementation, assertiveness skills, using emotional and instrumental social support, positive reappraisals, distraction, and humor (Causey & Dubow, 1992). Implementation of active strategies may be most useful in situations in which the children can exert control and change, and may in turn expand the children's sense of accomplishment and self-efficacy. Although distraction has been interpreted as a sign of denial, this may be effective in coping with uncontrollable events, particularly after reappraising the situation. Adaptive coping for children may involve the ability to distinguish controllable from uncontrollable stressful events, to actively cope with events that they can affect, and to positively reappraise and reduce distress in situations that are out of their control. Group activities include having children designate situations as controllable or uncontrollable, brainstorm on strategies to cope with each, and develop a plan for implementation (Rose & Edleson, 1987). Worksheets may be used to identify personal stressful events and plans for coping.

Ending Therapy and Graduation Session

Children who have experienced chronic abuse and other traumas often have had many losses and changes in their lives. Supportive ways to experience and understand change can be provided during the last sessions by supporting positive ways to say good-bye, remembering positive experiences, and acknowledging success and progress. For groups that have a set number of sessions, being reminded each week of the number of sessions left helps prepare the child for change at the end of the group. Children can make a book to help express their feelings about ending the group and missing other children and the therapists (Silovsky & Niec, 1998). Depending on their age, children may draw pictures, write statements, or write poems or stories that express their feelings and indicate what was learned during groups, what they will miss, and what memories they will want to keep. Formal graduation ceremonies help reinforce the children's sense of success, and can include graduation certificates, statements of progress from the therapists and other children, and food.

GENERAL RECOMMENDATIONS FOR GROUP THERAPY

Age and gender of members and the size of the group are important to consider while planning a group. To facilitate learning and reduce frustration, it is preferable to have some limitations on the age range for the group (e.g., three- to six-year-olds, seven- to nine-year-olds, ten- to twelve-year-olds). Consideration of maturity, verbal skills, and social skills is needed in addition to the age of the child. Six to eight members is large enough to allow for interaction, while small enough to enable individual needs to be met (Lynn, 1989). Severity of behavior problems of members impacts decisions on the size of the group and number of cotherapists. Group members should be able to communicate with other children and the therapist in their primary language.

Children's sense of safety and security is benefited from a consistent routine for each session, which in turn improves group cooperation and reduces disruptive behaviors. For example, each group session may have the same schedule: check-in procedures (such as noting attendance by the child placing a sticker on an attendance chart, stating something positive that happened in the past week), review the rules, briefly review what was taught at the previous session, conduct new activities, and have snack time). Praise and tangible reinforcers for following group rules are often essential for success of groups for preschool and school-age children.

Point systems are often beneficial when the points are provided frequently, fines are not used, and rewards are based on group behavior, rather than separate rewards for each individual (Friedrich, 1995). For example, for a preschool group each child can have a small clear tub with his or her name on it placed in view of the children. When the therapists "catch" a child following the rules, a large, colorful wooden bead is placed in the child's tub paired with praise that includes the child's name and labels the appropriate behavior. At the end of the group, each child pours the beads into one clear group bottle. If the group earns enough beads, then the children have a special prize at the end of the group (Silovsky & Niec, 1998). Some preschoolers require immediate primary reinforcement, and small crackers and cereal (e.g., a couple of Cheerios) have been effective.

When children's behavior needs to be corrected, get down to the child's level and speak softly, tell the child what to do (instead of what not to do), and shift the child's attention to the task (Peled & Davis, 1995). The therapists should keep their minds open to creative solutions that minimize disruption and model effective problem-solving skills (Peled & Davis, 1995). A plan for managing severely disruptive behaviors is necessary, although we have found it rarely requires implementation if preventive strategies are in place. The plan may include time-out in the room, time-out in the waiting area, and for out-of-control behavior, a plan to remove the rest of the group from the room with a therapist remaining with the child to facilitate regaining self-control, illustrating the need for cotherapists.

Selecting children who vary in verbal skills and active/passive responses to stress can facilitate participation of group members. Another area that is important to balance in the group is social skills, as children are likely to benefit from live peer models of adaptive social skills. Exclusionary criteria should include severely challenging behaviors, thought disorders, or other behaviors that would hinder their response to a group therapy approach and distract from the therapeutic experiences of the other members.

Groups may have a set number of sessions, in which all the children start at the same time, also referred to as close-ended groups. Close-ended groups are beneficial to the development of trust between group members. However, children may have to wait a period of time before enough new children have been assessed and determined appropriate for the group before starting. Open-ended groups in which children join and graduate from the program at different times allow children to enter without a wait, as long as there is an opening in the group. Another advantage of the open-ended group format is that children who are close to graduating can model adaptive behaviors and responses for the new members.

Most group programs for children who have been maltreated provide snacks as part of the group schedule. Food may be provided as a reinforcer for following group rules, particularly in preschool groups. However, snacks not contingent on the group behavior are integrated in the group schedule to facilitate group cohesiveness and experiences of nurturance for the children. Further, when groups are conducted during typical mealtimes or with group members residing in homes with limited resources, providing the snack early in the group session reduces hunger, which in turn allows the children to better focus and participate in later group activities.

CHARACTERISTICS AND QUALIFICATIONS OF THE GROUP THERAPISTS

The qualifications, training, and experiences of the group therapists that are required depend in part on the type of group treatment provided. Training in mental health issues related to child maltreatment, child clinical issues, child development, and experience in working with children who have been maltreated are minimum requirements for lead therapists. Many of the types of treatment described in this chapter (e.g., abuse-focused exposure therapy for PTSD) require additional specialized training and supervision.

Although more costly, conducting the group with cotherapists is advantageous. Therapists can be more flexible and actively involved by using the support and shared leadership. Choosing cotherapists who balance each other's strengths enhances the group, such as pairing one therapist who is enthusiastic and engaging with another who is well-organized and calming (Trounson-Chaiken, 1996). When the cotherapists verbalize their problem solving and demonstrate other effective communication skills, they model the skills taught to the group. With cotherapists, the children's behavior, reactions, and social interactions are more readily observed and behavior problems can be more efficiently monitored and managed, which in turn reduces the feeling of a loss of control (Lynn, 1989). Given the children's need for consistency and reliability, sessions can continue to occur regularly and not be interrupted by absence of one of the therapists, due to illness, for example.

Consideration of the gender of the cotherapists may be made when developing the group and after completing the initial assessment of the children. A mixed-gender combination models nonviolent male-female communication, particularly important for children who have been exposed to interparental violence. Children demonstrating high levels of fear toward those who are the same gender as the perpetrator (for example, fearing men) may not respond well to group leaders of that gender initially, but may benefit from positive interactions with group therapists of the same gender in future groups.

DEVELOPMENTAL CONSIDERATIONS

Session format, structure, activities, and composition are impacted by developmental considerations. As expected, addressing issues with preschool children is dramatically different than with adolescents.

Preschool children are particularly sensitive to the need for structure and routine. Repeating the rules and session sequence each week reduces the children's anxiety as well as disruptive behaviors. Length of activities must match their attention span, which for young children is often not longer than five to ten minutes. Activities that promote participation and movement and enthusiastic presentation of materials improve attention to and learning from the therapy experiences. Preschoolers learn through active experiences and repetitive presentations of information in a variety of methods. Puppets and storybooks build on preschoolers' natural make-believe and fantasy play. Songs with hand and body movements can promote preschool children's motivation and reinforce concepts taught in group sessions. For example, the Hokey Pokey dance can help the children identify main body parts. Lengthy discussions, sedentary activities, and disorganized sessions are to be avoided. Preschool children vary tremendously in communication skills. Integrating children who have good verbal skills with children who are more limited verbally can encourage the latter children's communication. Snacks are often part of preschool children's daily routine and may be particularly valuable. Preschool children's cognitive development limits their ability to be able to generalize skills to a variety of life situations, and they may not know when to apply the skills. This increases the importance of caregivers' direct involvement in treatment, such as in a parallel group with time at the end of each session in which the children and caregivers are together practicing skills they learned during the session (Silovsky & Niec, 1998).

Another important mode of group therapy for preschool children is therapeutic child care and play groups (Bonner et al., 2001; Brady, 1991; Moore, Armsden, & Gogerty, 1998). Therapeutic child care for preschool children who have experienced chronic abuse and neglect is designed to provide an enriching, nurturing, safe environment with services for developmental, social, psychological, educational, and medical needs (Becker et al., 1995; Moore et al., 1998). Therapeutic child care programs are often part of a range of family services, including parenting education, support groups, and community outreach programs, such as Childhaven (Moore et al., 1998), which has impressive twelve-year outcome data.

School-age children guide their behaviors through rules in the community. Use of clear rules can facilitate children's behavior in group as well as help their understanding of the abuse experiences, such as that the adult who abused them "broke the rules." School-age children often interact through playing games. With this in mind, several therapeutic games have been developed to encourage children's motivation and interest. The Talking, Feeling, and Doing Game (Creative Therapeutics, 1973) and the Ungame (1975) elicit expressions of feelings, beliefs, and understanding other people's feelings. The Stop, Relax, and Think Game is designed to have children practice problem-solving and self-control skills, using a turtle theme (Childwork/Childplay, 1990), which fits the teaching of the turtle technique. School-age children often respond well to role-play and dramatic activities. In role-play experiences, the group members should be placed in the role of practicing adaptive behaviors, rather than demonstrating past behavior problems.

Depending on the severity of problems, goals of the program, and topics of the group, children may be grouped within three or four years of each other. Six-year-olds and twelve-year-olds may have difficulties interacting in the same group. Children begin to orient toward children who are the same sex and who have similar interests during the elementary school-age years and thus may respond better in same-gender groups, particularly at the upper end of the age range and for adolescents.

Adolescents are most typically in same-gender group programs, particularly groups that address sexual abuse and sexuality. Higher levels of mutual support and discussion are possible. Discussions, worksheets, and handouts are more frequently used. Adolescents may demonstrate greater resistance to group participation initially, particularly groups geared toward reducing behavior problems. Further, they may respond better to feedback from peers than from the adult therapists. An open-ended group format enhances the likelihood that peer leaders who have progressed in group can provide productive feedback. External motivation (e.g., requirements from family court) may also be necessary to treat delinquent behavior.

PARENTAL INVOLVEMENT IN TREATMENT

Parental level of support, emotional distress related to the abuse, and beliefs about the abuse influence the psychological effects of maltreatment on children, as well as the children's responsiveness to treatment. As reported in a review of the research on treatment for sexually abused children and adolescents, "working with caretakers in one form or another appears to be essential" (Saywitz, Mannarino, Berliner, & Cohen, 2000, p. 1045). Thus, plan parallel groups for the parents/caregivers or concurrent parenting or family therapy when developing group treatment programs. For details of effective parenting interventions, see the chapters on neglect and physical abuse (Chapter 11), and on sexual abuse (Chapter 12).

The children and their caregivers may have difficulty trusting the therapists of the group program. Caregivers' beliefs about the purpose of the group and faith in the leaders have direct impact on the children's response to the group, ranging from hindering the children's cooperation and motivation to supporting the children's use of skills and changing the parents' behavior and emotional responses to their children's behavior. Behavior changes in preschool children may be dependent on the caregivers' cueing and supporting use of the skills between sessions. Caregiver active participation is considered essential for reducing disruptive and aggressive behaviors.

Caregiver groups (for nonoffending parents) may address and provide information parallel with the topics addressed in the children's group. The caregivers are provided information to facilitate their own adjustment to their child's abuse as well as skills to support their children. Mothers' emotional adjustment, belief in their children, and supportive response has been found to have a dramatic impact on the children's adjustment following disclosure of abuse. Involvement of the caregivers may contribute to the generalization and maintenance of the changes by encouraging the child to continue to use more adaptive coping strategies. Further, the caregivers may change environmental events that could contribute to the children's distress and maladaptive behaviors (Stark, Swearer, et al., 1996).

PROBLEMS AND CHALLENGES

Group therapy poses unique problems. Confidentiality is handled in a manner somewhat different from individual and family therapy. Group members may attend the same school or see each other in public, especially in small communities. Rules to enforce confidentiality must be explained and ways to manage interactions outside of group can be taught. However, there cannot be the same level of control of information as is found in individual and family therapy. Further, ethical responses to new disclosures of abuse and family issues become more challenging in the group setting.

Groups will often include sessions in which the children describe their abuse experiences. Concerns are raised about possible secondary traumatic effects on children when hearing details about other children's traumatic experiences. Inclusion and exclusion criteria for group member selection must consider the range of severity of their abuse experiences. Children who are having a mild reaction to a single incident of abuse by a non–family member may be negatively impacted when hearing details of chronic, severe abuse experienced by another child. Children who present with no emotional, social, or behavioral problems may benefit from prevention-oriented psychoeducational group, rather than more intensive therapy approaches designed to treat clinical levels of symptoms and disorders. At a minimum, the group therapy participation must do no harm.

In a group, children may respond to each other in ways that aggravate behavior problems and negative interaction. Group size and composition should be selected to minimize the likelihood of out-of-control behavior. Clear rules and routine can further reduce the chances of disruptive behavior. Skills in de-escalating potentially provoking peer interactions are essential, particularly in groups of school-age boys.

Scheduling can pose another challenge. Families' lives have become more hectic, with children involved in a variety of after-school activities. Finding times in which families and therapists are available can be difficult, and meetings often end up occurring during evening mealtimes.

CASE EXAMPLE

Cherie was a ten-year-old who lived with her mother, Ms. A, and twelve-year-old sister, Tina. Ms. A and her family were referred to the treatment program after child protective services confirmed physical abuse of Cherie and removed her and her sister from Ms. A's home and placed them in a foster home. Ms. A reported that Cherie was defiant and hostile at home and school. Cherie was suspended from school for fighting, and Ms. A "disciplined" Cherie with an extension cord, leaving welts on her back and legs, resulting in the confirmation of physical abuse. Initial assessment of Cherie revealed significant aggressive behaviors and conduct problems, as reported by her mother and teacher. Cherie's self-report also suggested low self-esteem and hostile perceptions of others' intentions. An observation of Ms. A and Cherie interacting revealed that Ms. A tended to give multiple commands, with very limited use of positive statements or praise. Ms. A held strong beliefs about the importance of using corporal punishment, having a good education, and keeping her family together. She expressed that she found Cherie's behavior very challenging to manage. Ms. A and the school-teachers reported that Tina was well-behaved. However, Tina self-reported depressive symptoms and confused feelings associated with blaming her sister and with fear of losing her mother.

Cherie and her sister Tina attended a group therapy program designed for children affected by physical abuse and family violence. The goals of the group therapy for Cherie were to improve her interpersonal problem-solving skills, address maladaptive attributions about the abuse, improve her coping skills and impulse control, and enhance her peer relationships and self-esteem. Goals for Tina were to provide education about the abuse and the impact on family members, address negative and maladaptive attributions, reduce symptoms of depression and anxiety, and improve her sense of stability and relationship with her family. Their mother attended a parenting group designed to enhance motivation to change parenting behaviors and later attended parent behavior training. Initially, Ms. A was reluctant to have her children participate, voicing concerns regarding "what would be talked about" in the group. Each week parents were provided with a handout summarizing the topics addressed in that session, with suggestions on how to help their children between the sessions. The handouts helped Ms. A become more comfortable and supportive of her daughters' work within the group.

Cherie responded well to the structure and reinforcement provided during group counseling. She initially demonstrated limited skills at identifying feelings and problem solving. Rather quickly, however, she expanded her emotional vocabulary and expressed her confused feelings about both the abuse and being removed from her mother's home. Her sister had blamed Cherie for their move to foster care. The group members and therapists were able to provide corrective feedback about causes of the abuse and removal and responsibilities of the parents and children. The children were returned to their mother's home while they were attending group, and the group provided an opportunity to discuss their mixed feelings and anticipations. Tina became more supportive of Cherie and at times helped Cherie remember to use the turtle technique and problem-solving skills at home. Cherie began using better problem-solving strategies at school, with noted improvement in her relationships with peers, which in turn raised her self-esteem.

Cherie's improved self-perceptions, emotional adjustment, and behavior were supported by changes in her mother's parenting skills. Ms. A began to recognize that corporal punishment was not effective with Cherie and actually worsened her behavior. Cherie and Tina benefited from having a regular routine at home in the evening, with some short time alone with their mother each day to talk and play individually with their mother and together. Ms. A indicated at the end of treatment that praise and consistency with rewards and punishments worked well with Cherie. At six-month follow-up, Ms. A reported that Cherie continued to do well at home and at school and was participating in after-school activities. Ms. A indicated that she had not returned to using corporal punishment.

CONCLUSION

Group therapy is an important and often preferred modality for children who have been maltreated. As part of a family service plan, group therapy can effectively address many of the issues and concerns in children affected by child maltreatment. Careful attention to specific children's needs and vulnerabilities is needed in the selection of children for the group and to effectively monitor progress throughout the group.

REFERENCES

Becker, J. V., Alpert, J. L., BigFoot, D. S., Bonner, B. L., Geddie, L. F., Henggeler, S. W., Kaufman, K. L., & Walker, C. E. (1995). Empirical research on child abuse treatment: Report by the Child Abuse and Neglect Treatment Working Group, American Psychological Association. *Journal of Clinical Child Psychology, 24* (Suppl.), 23-46.

Begun, R. (Ed.) (1995). *Social skills lessons and activities for grades 1-3.* West Nyak, NY: Center for Applied Research in Education.

Berman, P. (1994). *Therapeutic exercises for victimized and neglected girls: Applications for individual, family, and group psychotherapy.* Sarasota, FL: Professional Resource Press.

Bonner, B. L., Kaufman, K. L., Niec, L., & Logue, M. B. (2001). Child maltreatment. In C. E. Walker & M. Roberts (Eds.), *Handbook of clinical child psychology* (3rd ed.). New York: John Wiley & Sons.

Bonner, B. L., Walker, C. E., & Berliner, L. (1999a). *Children with sexual behavior problems: Assessment and treatment.* Final Report, Grant No. 90-CA-1469. Washington, DC: Administration of Children, Youth, and Families, DHHS.

Bonner, B. L., Walker, C. E., & Berliner, L. (1999b). *Treatment manual for cognitive behavioral group therapy for children with sexual behavior problems.* Grant No. 90-CA-1469. Washington, DC: Administration of Children, Youth, and Families, DHHS.

Brady, G. L. (1991). A group-work approach for sexually abused preschoolers. *JGPPS,* 174-183.

Causey, D. L. & Dubow, E. F. (1992). Development of a self-report coping measure for elementary school children, *Journal of Clinical Child Psychology, 21,* 47-59.

Childwork/childplay (1990). Stop, Think, and Relax Game. (Available from Childwork/childplay, 135 Dupont Street, Plainview, NY, 11803.)

Committee for Children (1996). *Second Step: A violence prevention curriculum.* Seattle, WA: Author.

Crary, E. (1983). *My name's not dummy.* Seattle: Parenting Press.

Creative Therapeutics (1973). The Talking, Feeling, and Doing Game: A psychotherapeutic game for children. (Available from Creative Therapeutics, 155 County Road, Cresskill, NJ, 07626.)

Crick, N. R. & Dodge, K. A. (1994). A review and reformulation of social information processing mechanisms in children's social adjustment. *Psychological Bulletin, 115,* 74-101.

Deblinger, E. & Heflin, A. (1996). *Treating sexually abused children and their nonoffending parents.* Thousand Oaks, CA: Sage.

Deblinger, E., Steer, R. A., & Lippmann, J. (1999). Two-year follow-up study of cognitive behavioral therapy for sexually abused children suffering post-traumatic stress symptoms. *Child Abuse and Neglect, 23,* 1371-1378.

Dodge, K. A., Pettit, G. S., & Bates, J. E. (1997). How the experience of early physical abuse leads children to become chronically aggressive. In D. Cicchetti & S. L. Toth (Eds.), *Developmental perspectives on trauma: Theory, research and intervention* (pp. 263-288). Rochester, NY: University of Rochester Press.

Eyberg, S. M. & Boggs, S. R. (1989). Parent training for oppositional-defiant preschoolers. In C. F. Schaefer & J. M. Briesmeister (Eds.), *Handbook of parent training: Parents as co-therapists for children's behavior problems* (pp. 105-132). New York: John Wiley & Sons.

Finkelhor, D. (1984). Four preconditions: A model. In *Child sexual abuse: New theory and research* (pp. 53-68). New York: Free Press.

Forehand, R. & McMahon, R. J. (1981). *Helping the noncompliant child: A clinician's guide to parent training.* New York: Guilford Press.

Friedrich, W. (1995). *Psychotherapy with sexually abused boys: An integrated approach.* Thousand Oaks, CA: Sage.

Friedrich, W. (1996). An integrated model of psychotherapy for abused children. In J. Briere, L. Berliner, J. A. Bulkley, C. Jenny, & T. Reid (Eds.), *The APSAC handbook on child maltreatment* (pp. 104-108). Thousand Oaks, CA: Sage.

Gladstone, T. R. & Kaslow, N. J. (1995). Depression and attributions in children and adolescents: A meta-analytic review. *Journal of Abnormal Child Psychology, 23,* 597-606.

Hall, D. H., Matthews, F., Pearce, J., Sarlo-McGarvey, N., & Gavin, D. (1996). *The development of sexual behavior problems in children and youth.* Ontario, Canada: Central Toronto Youth Services.

Hembree-Kigin, T. L. & McNeil, C. B. (1995). *Parent-child interaction therapy.* New York: Plenum Press.

Hoag, M. J. & Burlingame, G. M. (1997). Evaluating the effectiveness of child and adolescent group treatment: A meta-analytic review. *Journal of Clinical Child Psychology, 26,* 234-246.

Karp, C. L. & Butler, T. L. (1996). *Treatment strategies for abused children: From victim to survivor.* Thousand Oaks, CA: Sage.

Kazdin, A. (1996). Problem solving and parent management in treating aggressive and antisocial behavior. In E. Hibbs & R. Jensen (Eds.), *Psychosocial treatments for child and adolescent disorders* (pp. 377-408). Washington, DC: American Psychological Association.

Kazdin, A. E. & Weisz, J. R. (1998). Identifying and developing empirically supported child and adolescent treatments. *Journal of Consulting and Clinical Psychology, 65,* 19-36.

Kendall-Tackett, K. A., Williams, L. M., & Finkelhor, D. (1993). Impact of sexual abuse on children: A review and synthesis of recent empirical studies. *Psychological Bulletin, 113,* 164-180.

Khalsa, S. S. (1996). *Group exercises for enhancing social skills and self-esteem.* Sarasota, FL: Professional Resource Press.

Koeppen, A. (1974). Relaxation training for children. *Elementary School Guidance and Counseling,* October, 14-21.

Kolko, D. (1996). Child physical abuse. In J. Briere, L. Berliner, J. A. Bulkley, C. Jenny, & T. Reid (Eds.), *The APSAC handbook on child maltreatment* (pp. 21-50). Thousand Oaks, CA: Sage.

Kolko, D. & Swenson, C. (2000, July). *Psychosocial evaluation and treatment of physically abused children.* Presented at the 8th Annual APSAC Colloquium. Chicago, IL.

Lynn, M. (1989). Group treatment. In S. M. Goldstein, E. G. Goldstein, L. Goodman, & J. Seinfeld (Eds.), *Clinical social work with maltreated children and their families: An introduction to practice* (pp. 79-103). New York: New York University Press.

Mandell, J. G., Damon, L., Castaldo, P., Tauber, E. S., Monise, L., & Larsen, N. (1989). *Group treatment for sexually abused children.* New York: Guilford Press.

Mannarino, A. P., Cohen, J. A., & Berman, S. R. (1994). The children's attributions and perceptions scale: A new measure of sexual abuse-related factors. *Journal of Clinical Child Psychology, 23,* 204-211.

Mayle, P. (1975). *What's happening to me?* Toronto, Ontario: Carol.

Mayle, P. & Robins, A. (1975). *Where did I come from?* Toronto, Ontario: Carol.

Moore, E., Armsden, G., & Gogerty, P. (1998). A twelve-year follow-up study of maltreated and at-risk children who received early therapeutic child care. *Child Maltreatment, 3,* 3-16.

Peled, E. & Davis, D. (1995). *Groupwork with children of battered women: A practitioner's guide.* Thousand Oaks, CA: Sage.

Pertik, M. & Senter, S. (1990). *Stress management and me: Participation activities to brighten each student's day.* Nashville, TN: Incentive.

Reeker, J., Ensing, D., & Elliott, R. (1997). A meta-analytic investigation of group treatment outcomes for sexually abused children. *Child Abuse and Neglect, 21,* 669-680.

Rose, S. & Edleson, J. (1987). *Working with children and adolescents in groups.* San Francisco: Jossey-Bass.

Rosselló, J. & Bernal, G. (1996). Adapting cognitive-behavioral and interpersonal treatments for depressed Puerto Rican adolescents. In E. Hibbs & R. Jensen (Eds.), *Psychosocial treatments for child and adolescent disorders* (pp. 157-186). Washington, DC: American Psychological Association.

Saunders, B. E., Berliner, L., & Hanson, R. (2000). *Guidelines for psychological treatment of intrafamilial child physical and sexual abuse: Draft report.* Washington, DC: Office for Victims of Crime.

Saywitz, K., Mannarino, A., Berliner, L., & Cohen, J. (2000). Treatment for sexually abused children and adolescents. *American Psychologist, 55,* 1040-1049.

Schneider, M. & Robin, A. (1976). *Turtle manual.* Unpublished manual. State University of New York, Stony Brook, NY.

Silovsky, J. F. & Hebree-Kigin, T. L. (1994). Family and group treatments for sexually abused children: A review. *Journal of Child Sexual Abuse, 3,* 1-20.

Silovsky, J. F. & Niec, L. (1998). *Group treatment for preschool children with problematic sexual behavior: Program manual.* Unpublished treatment manual. Oklahoma City: University of Oklahoma Health Sciences Center.

Silovsky, J. F. & Niec, L. (1999, January). *Assessment and treatment of preschool and primary aged children with sexual behavior problems.* Paper presented at the San Diego Conference on Responding to Child Maltreatment, San Diego, CA.

Silovsky, J. F. & Valle, L. (1997a). *Group treatment for 4 to 7 year olds who have experienced or witnessed family violence.* Unpublished treatment manual. Oklahoma City: University of Oklahoma Health Sciences Center.

Silovsky, J. F. & Valle, L. (1997b). *Group treatment for 8 to 12 year olds who have experienced or witnessed family violence.* Unpublished treatment manual. Oklahoma City: University of Oklahoma Health Sciences Center.

Silovsky, J. F. & Valle, L. (1997c). *Social skills group for 8 to 12 year old children who have experienced or witnessed family violence: AFF program follow up group.* Unpublished treatment manual. Oklahoma City: University of Oklahoma Health Sciences Center.

Spivack, G. & Shure, M. B. (1982). The cognition of social adjustment: Interpersonal cognitive problem solving thinking. In B. B. Lahey & A. E. Kazdin (Eds.), *Advances in clinical child psychology* (Vol. 5, pp. 323-372). New York: Plenum.

Stark, K. D. (1990). *Childhood depression: School-based intervention.* New York: Guilford Press.

Stark, K. D. (1996). *Treating depressed children: Therapist manual for "ACTION."* Ardmore, PA: Workbook.

Stark, K. D., Kendall, P. C., McCarthy, M., Stafford, M., Barron, R., & Thomeer, M. (1996). *ACTION: A workbook for overcoming depression.* Ardmore, PA: Workbook.

Stark, K. D., Swearer, S., Kurowski, C., Sommer, D., & Bowen, B. (1996). Targeting the child and the family: A holistic approach to treating child and adolescent depressive disorders. In E. Hibbs & R. Jensen (Eds.), *Psychosocial treatments for child and adolescent disorders* (pp. 207-208). Washington, DC: American Psychological Association.

Steward, M., Farquhar, L., Dicharry, D., Glick, D., & Martin, P. (1986). Group therapy: A treatment of choice for young victims of child abuse. *International Journal of Group Psychotherapy, 36,* 261-277.

Swenson, C. C. & Brown, E. (1999). Cognitive behavioral group treatment for physically abused children. *Cognitive and Behavioral Practice, 6,* 212-220.

Trounson-Chaiken, D. (1996). From chaos to cohesion: Group therapy with preschool-aged children. *Journal of Child and Adolescent Group Therapy, 6,* 3-25.

The Ungame Co. (1975). The UNGAME. Anaheim, CA: Author, 1440 South State College Blvd., Building 2-D, Anaheim, CA 92806.

Webster-Stratton, C. (1996). Early intervention with videotape modeling: Programs for families of children with oppositional defiant disorder or conduct disorder. In E. D. Hibbs & P. Jensen (Eds.), *Psychosocial treatment research of child and adolescent disorders: Empirically based strategies for clinical practice* (pp. 435-474). Washington, DC: American Psychological Association.

Webster-Stratton, C. & Hammond, M. (1997). Treating children with early-onset conduct problems: A comparison of child and parent training interventions. *Journal of Consulting and Clinical Psychology, 65,* 93-109.

Weisz, J., Weiss, B., Han, S., Granger, D., & Morton, T. (1995). Effects of psychotherapy with children and adolescents revisited: A meta-analysis of treatment outcome studies. *Psychological Bulletin, 117,* 450-468.

Chapter 10

Child Maltreatment and Family Therapy

John T. Pardeck

When a practitioner works with a client experiencing problems from a family therapy perspective, the client's family is either present or pictured in the practitioner's thoughts during the treatment process. This perspective is shared by virtually all family therapists regardless of their theoretical orientation (Pardeck, 1981).

Family therapists are grounded in a number of theoretical perspectives including psychoanalytic, integrative, and interactional approaches. One common orientation shared by virtually all family therapists in varying degrees is systems theory. Pardeck (1989) concludes that one cannot effectively read most of the major family therapy theorists without having extensive knowledge of systems theory and of how this perspective applies to the family.

Systems theory moves the understanding of a client's presenting problem from an individual level to a systems level. Furthermore, the family therapy approach to treatment moves pathology from an individual to a family systems level. What is interesting about the systems approach to understanding human behavior is that it developed almost entirely outside the fields of psychology and psychiatry (Pardeck, 1988). Even though systems theory and family therapy largely emerged outside the mainstream helping professions, presently, many practitioners view family therapy grounded in systems theory as an effective approach to treating numerous client problems, including child abuse and neglect.

A BRIEF HISTORY OF SOCIAL SYSTEMS THEORY

Social systems theory emerged from nineteenth-century sociology, psychology, and biology. The concept of systems is grounded in the discipline of biology and was adapted to the social sciences by early social theorists (Timsheff, 1967). Present-day systems theory has three unique components: (1) it places great importance on interaction and interdependence of the parts of a system; change in one part of a system produces change in another part; (2) the social environment is understood to play a major role in individual social functioning; and (3) pathology is defined at a systems level, not an individual level.

These three components of systems theory offer insight into how the family functions as a social system. Through systems theory, family therapists are provided insight into the impact of factors not always considered in psychodynamic approaches, which view environmental issues, such as poverty, as not particularly relevant to the treatment process. Even though psychodynamic approaches may not be as useful as the systems-based approaches used by many family therapists for treating problems facing individual family members, psychodynamic treatment continues to be quite popular among many therapists, particularly those who work with children (Shapiro, 1989; Shapiro & Esman, 1992). Furthermore, systematic reviews of the family therapy treatment outcome research (Gurman, Kniskern, & Pinsof, 1986; Hazelrigg, Cooper, & Borduin, 1987; Shadish et al., 1993) report that family therapy appears to have a positive impact on family functioning in the following areas:

1. Family therapy appears to result in improved outcomes for clients when compared to control group subjects.
2. Family therapy appears to have a positive effect on the presenting problem of the identified patient, as well as the entire family system.
3. Improvement in family functioning appears to begin to occur in a relatively short time period, less than twenty treatment sessions.
4. When the presenting problem of a family is conflict between family members, family therapy appears to be more effective than nonfamily approaches.

OVERVIEW OF SYSTEMS THEORY

A system can be viewed as a whole composed of individual parts. When change occurs in one part of the system, other parts are affected. Systems theory focuses on linkages, transactions, and relationships that connect individuals with each other, such as those found in the family system (Pardeck & Yuen, 1997).

Systems theory offers a perspective that focuses on multiple levels of phenomena simultaneously and stresses the interaction and transaction between the parts of the system. This perspective helps practitioners understand behavior in context and illustrates how systems impact individual behavior. Systems can be viewed as open or closed. Healthy systems are generally open; closed systems are often dysfunctional (Pardeck & Yuen, 1997).

An open system is one that exchanges matter and energy with its environment. An example of a closed system would be a lighted candle that is covered with a glass jar. The candle lacks a source of oxygen and gradually goes out. Like an open system exchanging matter and energy with its environment, when the jar is removed and the candle is relit, the lighted candle exchanges oxygen and carbon dioxide with the atmosphere (Pardeck & Yuen, 1997).

Systems theory suggests that a system attempts to maintain a steady state as it transacts with its social environment. Systems are self-regulating and they have the tendency to seek equilibrium; this process may result in a functional or dysfunctional system. For example, a family living in a community that is in transition toward poverty will be affected by this change. If the family is a healthy system, the family will attempt to maintain a steady state regardless of the larger social environment. In turn, the family may develop problems because of the stressors flowing from the social environment.

The exchange process occurring between a system such as a family and its social environment is referred to as input and output. Using the family as an example of a system, families need input from the larger social environment to function effectively. Input would include resources such as money. Likewise, output refers to what the family gives to the environment, such as children who are socialized to function effectively in the larger society. The exchange process occurs in all systems and is particularly helpful for understanding how families transact and interact with their social environment (Pardeck & Yuen, 1997).

Through the input/output process, a practitioner understands the delicate balance between the family system and the larger community. The community needs to provide families with adequate supports for families to operate at an optimal level. An example of this kind of input is quality schools. If the · input flowing from the community is not supportive, families may not function effectively; dysfunctional families are characterized by abuse, neglect, and other kinds of problem behaviors. Emotionally healthy families often thrive in supportive communities; nonsupportive communities may have a negative impact on family functioning (Pardeck & Yuen, 1997).

Another important concept in systems theory is equifinality—this term means similar results can be obtained from different kinds of beginning points. An example of this process is children who might be very different in their development at the beginning of the life cycle who ultimately achieve very similar states of physical growth and development as they mature if provided nurturing support from their families and the larger community (Pardeck, 1996).

Nichols and Schwartz (1991) provided insight into some of the basic tenets underpinning systems theory and family functioning as follows. First, systems theory concludes that the whole is greater than the sum of its parts. In relation to the family system, this means that the family is more than just individual family members. The nature of the transaction and interaction between family members, the rules that govern these processes, and their repetitiveness provide important insight into family functioning. If these various processes undermine family functioning, they become the focus of treatment.

Second, a family systems approach places great emphasis on contextual elements within the family system and the influence of the larger community on family functioning. This means the practitioner must consider treating not only the family in the assessment and treatment process, but also the larger community.

Third, the concept of homeostasis is critical to understanding family functioning. This process occurs when the family system responds to internal and environmental pressures. Through homeostasis, families seek a balance between stability and change.

Fourth, the concept of circular causality is critical to understanding family functioning. Traditional models of treatment are based on linear causality; a systems approach stresses the reciprocal, interactional, and transactional pattern of behaviors that influence family functioning. Circular causality can be understood in a certain sense as a new epistemology in Western thought; however, it has been a dominant orientation of time and causality for many cultural groups. Kluckhohn and Strodtbeck (1961) and Nichols and Schwartz (1991) described the spiral and present orientation of Hispanic and African populations and the circular and past orientation of Asian populations.

Fifth, the family life cycle is an important component providing insight into predictable patterns through which all families evolve. Depending on the strengths of the family system, this movement through the family life cycle can go smoothly or result in stress and pressures on the family system.

The above points provide insight into assessing and treating families from a systems perspective. It is noted that systems theory is an important component guiding many family therapeutic approaches. Last, systems theory suggests that individual social functioning is connected to the functioning of the family system.

THREE APPROACHES TO FAMILY THERAPY

Three approaches to family therapy are psychoanalytic, integrative, and interactional. Even though systems theory is the dominant theme within the general field of family therapy, it is emphasized in varying degrees by these approaches.

Psychoanalytic Approach

Family therapists who incorporate psychoanalysis into their approach to treatment stress a number of Freudian notions. These include but are not limited to psychic determinism and the subconscious mind.

As might be expected, systems theory is not emphasized by psychoanalytic family therapists. For example, Boszormenyi-Nagy and Framo, both family therapists of the Freudian persuasion, stressed the subconscious dynamics of family members and other Freudian concepts. Each placed limited emphasis on systems theory (Pardeck, 1988). Framo (1985) provided insight into the dominant theme of the psychoanalytic orientation to family therapy:

> Nevertheless in our experiences we have seen that the family cannot undergo deep or meaningful change if the therapist deals with current immediate interaction among family members. The most powerful obstacle to successful treatment is the individual members' libidinal attachments to their parental interjects, no matter what the parents were like in real life. (p. 158)

Thus the focus on the individual family member over the family system opens the psychoanalytic approach to the same criticisms as individual-based therapeutic approaches (Pardeck, 1988).

Integrative Approach

Integrative family therapy attempts to create a balance between the individual and the family system as the focus of treatment. Nathan Ackerman was the leading advocate of this approach; he argued that family therapy encompasses the interdependent, interpenetrating relations of the individual and the family as a system (Foley, 1974). Ackerman concluded that therapy should not pit the individual against the family or vice versa. It should attempt to support both the individual and the family. Integrative family therapy is the bridge between the psychoanalytic and interactional approaches.

Even though Ackerman's work suggests that such a bridge exists, he concluded that a movement toward a total systems approach to family therapy was not possible (Pardeck, 1981).

Interactional Family Therapy

Interactional family therapy incorporates a number of assumptions that appear critical to working effectively with children and families at risk. These include the ecological and systems perspectives. Interactional family therapists also focus on communication patternings in the family system. Specifically, they focus on how messages are sent and received by family members and the paths of communication within the family system. Communication takes two forms, verbal and nonverbal. The concept of the double bind emerged from the research conducted by interactional family therapists (Bateson, Jackson, Haley, & Weakland, 1956).

Interactional family therapists de-emphasize psychodynamic theories. For example, from an interactional perspective, an individual's personality is understood to emerge from interaction and transactions within the family system and other systems. In terms of treatment intervention, the intrapsychic self is not considered important.

Haley and Satir greatly influenced the development of interactional family therapy. Haley (1977), like Satir, concluded that individual-based treatment approaches are largely ineffective because they do not consider the role of systems in human behavior. Haley (1977) argued that therapists of the psychodynamic approach are no longer using a viable treatment model because the social ecology of individuals and families are not considered when conducting assessment and intervention. Haley suggested that pathology is located in the family system, not individual family members, and concluded that psychopathology is a product of power struggles between family individuals. This shift from conflict within the self to conflict outside the self challenges the essence of mainstream psychiatric treatment (Pardeck, 2001).

Satir (1967) suggested that most human beings are involved in multiple relationship systems, and that one's self-concept and self-image emerge from the interaction and transaction with social systems, particularly the family system. Satir (1967) also de-emphasized the limitations of individual-based treatment modalities. Satir understood problems as being systems based, not individual based. She also placed great emphasis on family communication processes. Satir argued that an important goal of treatment is to change communication processes that are dysfunctional to the family system and its members (Pardeck, 2001).

Jones (1980) concluded that interactional family therapy is grounded in a holistic approach to assessment and intervention that includes the following:

- Assessment of the family structure includes parents, children, personality and education levels of family members, and information on the extended family.
- Social variables that need to be included in assessment are the socioeconomic status of the family, religion, ethnicity, and the relationship of the family to the community.
- Presenting problems are assessed from the perspective of each family member. What they feel will solve the problem is important to the assessment process. An analysis of family subsystems is critical.
- Communication processes are assessed, including who speaks to whom, when, and in what tone. Family themes and emotional climate help define how family members communicate with one another.
- Role relationships are assessed, including an analysis of coalitions, patterns of praise and criticism, triangulation within the family, and so forth.
- Family developmental history is part of the assessment process, including information on the parents' families of origin. Developmental history of children and role relationships over time in the family are assessed.

Families at risk often need help in a number of areas, including family communication, role relationships, and family developmental history (Bavolek, 1989; Kempe, Silverman, Steele, Droegemueller, & Silver, 1962; Milner, 1989). What is particularly significant to interactional family therapy is the inclusion of social variables in the ecological context that transacts with the family system.

FAMILY-FOCUSED TREATMENT

Interactional family therapy offers an effective treatment approach for working with maltreated children and their families (Pardeck, 1989). The major focus of this approach is systems theory. When using a systems approach to treatment, the first priority of the practitioner is promoting an adaptive, need-fulfilling balance between the family system and family members. The larger social environment in which the family system functions is also an integral part of the treatment process.

An important assumption of interactional family therapy is that human beings can best be understood and helped only in the context of the family system, which is an intimate and powerful influence on family members. Compared to traditional treatment approaches, using systems theory is an innovative approach to problems confronting family members. Obviously, interactional family therapy is not the sole solution to child maltreatment; however, it is an extremely effective approach for assessing and treating child abuse and neglect (Pardeck, 2001).

The following brief case example illustrates how the family therapist might formulate father-daughter incest from an interactional family therapy perspective (Pardeck, 1989). A more detailed case is offered later in this chapter. The following example is designed to provide basic insight into assessing child maltreatment in the form of incest from a systems perspective.

BRIEF CASE EXAMPLE

A father takes a sexual interest in his daughter due to the deterioration of his relationship with his spouse. He may see qualities in his daughter that he wishes his wife had; for example, she gives uncritical admiration and he can easily manipulate her to fulfill his sexual and emotional needs. There is a strong probability that he was sexually abused as a child. He may rationalize that he really loves his daughter and that the incest is preferable to having an affair. He may break down his inhibitions to committing sexual abuse through drugs and alcohol.

The mother is obviously not protective of her daughter and may deny the incest exists. The father may also cultivate rivalry and conflict between the daughter and mother. The mother in turn becomes alienated from the daughter; consequently the daughter will not confide in her about the sexual abuse.

The daughter does not fully resist the advances of the father because she trusts him. She may enjoy the attention, affection, and favored status. The daughter may feel that she is holding the family system together.

This brief example illustrates that incest can be understood as a systems-based problem and that interactional family therapy may be a useful intervention strategy (Hamilton, 1989). A goal of therapy might be to realign the family roles and to work on communication and behavior between family members (Finkelhor, 1984; Garbarino, 1977; Kadushin & Martin, 1988). The daughter will probably have to be removed from the family system for a time. All family members will need individual treatment before the family therapist can begin working with the family as a system.

THE EFFECTS OF SEPARATING THE CHILD
FROM THE FAMILY

Children who are victims of maltreatment are often removed from their families. This causes a major disruption in a child's life; the child typically has only limited input into his or her placement in substitute care (Oates, 1986, 1989).

Maltreated children are often placed in emergency shelters or foster homes. Before placement, they receive a thorough medical examination to determine the degree of physical or sexual abuse. This examination is critical because it will be used as evidence in court if the case goes to trial. Unfortunately, the sexually abused child may see the medical examination as further invasion of his or her body (Pardeck, 1989).

After the medical examination, the child moves into a temporary placement setting. Even though the support staff of an emergency shelter or foster parents reassure the child that they are there to help, the child will often be very frightened. Parents may deny that their child was abused or neglected, often due to the guilt they feel or their fears of inadequacy. This denial may mean the treatment process is lengthened; consequently the child may have to remain in extended foster care. The child may thus lose a sense of permanency, which can have a negative impact on the child's social and emotional development (Pardeck, 1983).

For example, a stepfather, foster father, or the mother's boyfriend may be the perpetrator. Obviously the child cannot return to the family until the perpetrator is out of the home. Mothers in this type of family system are often dependent and passive and may be reluctant to lose a husband or boyfriend (Pardeck, 1989).

The mother in turn may convince the child that she was at fault, thus intensifying the daughter's pain, guilt, and feelings of abandonment. Interactional family therapy cannot begin until the family system is committed to change. This means the parents will have to accept responsibility for their actions; the child will need individual counseling to become ready for family therapy. Abusive parents may try to convince their child that the child is the problem (Vondra & Toth, 1989; Wiehe, 1989). This kind of violence against the child may result in the child acting out sexually and developing more severe psychological problems. It is critical for practitioners to help the child understand that he or she is not responsible for the abusive actions of the parents (Young, 1964).

INTERACTIONAL FAMILY THERAPY AND FAMILIES AT RISK

Practitioners working with maltreated children must maintain a close working relationship with both children and parents (Helfer, 1975; Howing, Wodarski, Gaudin, & Kurtz, 1989; Sameroff, 1975; Schmitt & Beezley, 1976). Interactional family therapy will not be successful unless all family members are involved in the treatment process. A number of procedures can facilitate the intervention process (Pardeck, 1988), including the following:

- Inform the children and parents about what they can expect from treatment and what the therapist expects from them.
- Help the family identify specific problems in the family system that contribute to the abuse and neglect.
- Educate family members as to what they can do to deal with problems contributing to the maltreatment.
- Develop a written contract with the family that outlines the objectives to be achieved in treatment.
- Have family members consult with self-help groups such as Parents Anonymous. Encourage them to join one of these groups.
- Maintain a working relationship with the child welfare agency monitoring the family's case. Let the family know that you will serve as their advocate.
- Retain a systems viewpoint; it is also important to maintain objectivity and sensitivity about the family system and its members.

When working with children at risk, the practitioner will often encounter rigid family patterns and low levels of ego differentiation (Minuchin, 1967). A major goal of treatment should be to alter this rigidity within the family system. If the therapist is successful at this task, follow-up treatment is important because the family may revert to its previous state of social functioning.

Most families at risk cannot change unless they have help. Family therapists working with families at risk must be extremely skillful. Tasks on which the practitioner will have to work include the following:

- Help parents learn how to empathize with their children.
- Teach parents impulse and anger control.

- Analyze the social conditions and transactions that led to an abusive act.
- Illustrate during therapy child management techniques such as establishing limits for children.
- Teach parents time and home management techniques, including being prompt for treatment sessions and maintaining an orderly home.
- Focus on subsystems of the family, particularly the husband and wife subsystem.
- If triangulating is occurring in the family, attempting to alter this process is important. An example might include a grandparent entering into the marital relationship in an unhealthy fashion; this transaction must be changed.
- Teach children and parents how to ask for help from others.
- If the children and parents are in individual or group therapy, make sure they are attending treatment on a regular basis.
- Teach the parents that they are responsible for the maltreatment and that they can change their behavior.
- Help maltreated children understand that they are not responsible for the abuse and neglect within the family system.
- Monitor the problem of role reversal in the family and work toward changing this transaction if it does occur. (Pardeck, 1988)

The interactional family therapist may also serve as a coordinator with the various groups and agencies working with the family system. It is best that the practitioner be aware of the other services and supports received by the family. Families at risk have a tendency to be involved with many agencies and often are not sure of what services they are receiving. Many families at risk also have low incomes. Parents of low-income families typically lack education. This may mean they have limited understanding of the child development process and effective discipline techniques. If the practitioner is not sensitive to these limitations, treatment may not be successful (Pardeck, 1988).

The practitioner must be aware that very disturbed children may have to live in a therapeutic milieu for an extended period before they can reunite with their families. Given this possibility, the practitioner must be patient and engage children slowly with the family therapy treatment process. The family therapist must also realize that children at risk may fail when reunited with their families. When this occurs, the child will have to be returned to placement, thus creating additional psychological issues (Goldstein, Freud, & Solnit, 1973; Pardeck, 1988).

CASE EXAMPLE

Brief History

The S. family has been in Crenshaw County for less than one year. They have a history of being transient. They have moved five times within the county. Mr. S. has had five jobs since moving to Crenshaw County. He has a history of alcohol abuse and is physically and verbally abusive toward his wife. Mr. and Mrs. S. are both in their forties. They have children from previous marriages that are presently living with relatives in other counties. They have only one mutual child living with them, Kathy S., who is eleven years old. Mrs. S. has several health problems: she is a diabetic and has high blood pressure, anemia, and a thyroid problem. These medical conditions are all controlled by medication; however, the S. family often does not have the money to buy Mrs. S.'s medication. Mrs. S. also has an emotional disability and alleges that she was sexually abused as a child. The Department of Family Services is providing services to the S. family and requested that the family apply for Temporary Assistance to Needy Families (TANF). The S. family did apply, but the application was withdrawn when Mr. S. found employment. Mrs. S. refuses to talk to her caseworker about the withdrawn application.

The Incident

Mr. J., a friend of the family, sexually molested Kathy S. and his own daughter, age ten, while on a fishing trip with the two girls. He is presently serving two six-year terms consecutively on two counts of first-degree rape. The Department of Family Services became aware of the incident when Kathy S. told her mother about the sexual abuse.

After this incident, the family was referred to the Department of Mental Health. During the course of counseling, other problems were uncovered. It was found that Kathy had behavioral problems, which included bed-wetting, immaturity, and manipulating others. The Department of Mental Health recommended a complete inpatient evaluation of Kathy. The Department of Family Services agreed with this recommendation.

This is supposedly the second sexual abuse incident for Kathy S. Her parents allege that an uncle in another county sexually molested her before. Kathy has been in foster care previously in another county for neglect when her father was drinking heavily and was physically and verbally abusive to Mrs. S. However, he has never been physically or verbally abusive toward Kathy.

The S. family is receiving in-home services, counseling, and transportation when needed. The S. family is not very cooperative and does not follow through with recommendations from the Department of Mental Health. Mr. and Mrs. S. refuse to accept or acknowledge that Kathy has problems and feel that no outside intervention is necessary. Mr. S. totally resents outside intervention; however, Mrs. S. states that she welcomes any outside intervention but fails to cooperate when assistance is offered.

Assessment

The following assessment is based on the work of Jones (1980). According to Jones, interactional family therapy focuses on six assessment areas. The following assesses the S. family in each of these areas:

1. *Family structure.* The S. family is a blended family system. The parents have children by prior marriages who live with relatives. They have one child from their present marriage, Kathy S., who is eleven years old. Mr. and Mrs. S. are in their forties. The S. family has a history of being transient. The S. family applied for TANF; however, the application was redrawn because Mr. S. found a job.

2. *Social variables.* The S. family is a low-income family system. Mr. S. has had five jobs since moving to Crenshaw County. Mrs. S. has a number of health problems requiring medications; the family does not have enough money to purchase these medications.

3. *Presenting problem.* The S. family has a number of presenting problems. The most important problem is that Kathy is a victim of sexual abuse. She has a number of behavior problems including bed-wetting, a problem often associated with sexual abuse. She also lacks maturity and manipulates people around her.

Mrs. S. has a number of health problems but is not receiving appropriate medications. She reported that she was sexually abused as a child. She also has an emotional disability. Mr. and Mrs. S. do not recognize that their daughter needs help.

Mr. S. has a history of alcoholism and is physically and verbally abusive toward his wife. He also has a work history suggesting a lack of steady employment.

4. *Communication processes.* The most telling aspect of family communication is that Mr. S. is verbally abusive to his wife. He does not appear to be abusive toward his daughter, Kathy.

5. *Role relationships.* Mr. S. does not appear to be supportive of his wife. The parents do not appear to be supportive of their daughter because they do not recognize that she needs help. The family appears to be a closed system because it does not cooperate with the Department of Mental Health. Families that are at risk are often closed systems.

6. *Family development history.* Mr. and Mrs. S. have children from other marriages who live with relatives. Mr. S. abuses alcohol, a problem that has had an impact on the functioning of the family system. Mrs. S. reports that

she was sexually abused and currently has an emotional disability. Mrs. S. also has a number of health problems that are not being treated. Kathy S. has spent time in foster care because of her father's drinking problem. She also has a history of sexual abuse. The S. family appears to be a closed system resisting treatment intervention.

Intervention

The interactive family therapist would approach the presenting problems of the S. family from a systems perspective. The therapist also needs to be sensitive to environmental pressures on the family that contribute to the presenting problems, including poverty. Two issues need to be dealt with immediately with the S. family. One, the family needs to be encouraged to apply for Medicaid. If they are eligible for this program, Medicaid should provide the prescription drugs needed by Mrs. S. for her various health problems. Second, Kathy S., as recommended by the Department of Mental Health, needs a complete inpatient evaluation.

If the therapist determines that the S. family can begin treatment, the following treatment goals should be part of the intervention plan:

- The parents must recognize that Kathy has a number of behavioral and emotional problems that need to be treated. They need to realize that these problems are probably based on her sexual abuse.
- The parents need to be encouraged to continue to use the services provided by the Departments of Family Services and Mental Health.
- All family members need to be encouraged to join self-help groups. Mr. S. in particular would benefit from Alcoholics Anonymous.
- Family members need to work on how they communicate verbally and nonverbally with one another. Mr. S. specifically needs to change his abusive behavior toward Mrs. S.
- The parents need to learn techniques that help them to be more empathic toward Kathy.
- The family needs to learn strategies for learning how and when to ask for help.
- Kathy needs to continue individual counseling. She also needs to develop strategies for communicating more effectively with people around her. Specifically, she must change her manipulation of others.

Because the S. family has a tendency to be a closed system, ongoing interactional family therapy is important. Family systems such as the S.

family have a tendency to revert to former patterns of behavior and transaction if they are not closely monitored.

CONCLUSION

This chapter presents information on strategies for using interactional family therapy as a treatment modality for child abuse and neglect. Interactional family therapy is grounded in the assumption that pathology is not individual but rather systems based. This position is a significant departure from psychodynamic approaches that view pathology as based in the individual.

To more completely understand an individual one must understand the family system in which the individual functions. Clients benefit when the system as a whole is addressed. Stabilization within and the support from family positively affect clients' mental health and lead to more effective therapy.

REFERENCES

Bateson, G., Jackson, D. D., Haley, J., & Weakland, J. (1956). Toward a theory of schizophrenia. *Behavioral Science, 1*, 251-264.

Bavolek, S. J. (1989). Assessing and treating high-risk parenting attitudes. In J. T. Pardeck (Ed.), *Child abuse and neglect: Theory, research, and practice* (pp. 97-110). New York: Gordon and Breach.

Finkelhor, D. (1984). *Child sexual abuse: New theory and research*. New York: Free Press.

Foley, V. D. (1974). *An introduction to family therapy*. New York: Grune and Stratton.

Framo, J. L. (1985). Rationale and techniques of intensive family therapy. In I. Boszormenyi-Nagy & J. L. Framo (Eds.), *Intensive family therapy* (pp. 143-212). New York: Harper and Row.

Garbarino, J. (1977). The human ecology of child maltreatment: A conceptual model for research. *Journal of Marriage and the Family, 39*, 721-727.

Goldstein, J., Freud, A., & Solnit, A. J. (1973). *Beyond the best interests of the child*. New York: Free Press.

Gurman, A. S., Kniskern, D. P., & Pinsof, W. M. (1986). Research on the process and outcome of marital and family therapy: Progress, perspective, prospect. In S. Garfield & A. Bergin (Eds.), *Handbook of psychotherapy and behavior change* (3rd ed.) (pp. 565-626). New York: Wiley.

Haley, J. (1977). Beginning and experienced family therapist. In A. Ferber, M. Mendelshon, & A. Napier (Eds.), *The book of family therapy* (pp. 155-167). New York: Jason Aronson.

Hamilton, L. R. (1989). Variables associated with child maltreatment and implications for prevention and treatment. In J. T. Pardeck (Ed.), *Child abuse and neglect: Theory, research, and practice* (pp. 29-54). New York: Gordon and Breach.

Hazelrigg, M. D., Cooper, H. M., & Borduin, C. M. (1987). Evaluating the effectiveness of family therapies: An investigative review and analysis. *Psychological Bulletin, 101,* 428-442.

Helfer, R. (1975). *Diagnostic process and treatment programs.* Washington, DC: U.S. Government Printing Office.

Howing, P. T., Wodarski, J. S., Gaudin, J. W., & Kurtz, P. D. (1989). Clinical assessment instruments in the treatment of child abuse and neglect. In J. T. Pardeck (Ed.), *Child abuse and neglect: Theory, research, and practice* (pp. 69-82). New York: Gordon and Breach.

Jones, S. (1980). *Family therapy: A comparison of approaches.* Baltimore, MD: Brady.

Kadushin, A. & Martin, J. (1988). *Child welfare services* (4th ed.). New York: Macmillan.

Kempe, C. H., Silverman, F., Steele, B., Droegemueller, W., & Silver, H. (1962). The battered child syndrome. *Journal of the American Medical Association, 181,* 17-24.

Kluckhohn, F. & Strodtbeck, F. (1961). *Variations in value orientations.* Evanston, IL: Row, Peterson.

Milner, J. S. (1989). Applications and limitations of the child abuse potential inventory. In J. T. Pardeck (Ed.), *Child abuse and neglect: Theory, research, and practice* (pp. 83-96). New York: Gordon and Breach.

Minuchin, S. (1967). *Families of the slum: Exploration of their structure and treatment.* New York: Basic Books.

Nichols, M. P. & Schwartz, R. C. (1991). *Family therapy: Concepts and methods* (2nd ed.). Needham Heights, MA: Allyn and Bacon.

Oates, K. (1986). *Child abuse and neglect: What eventually happens.* New York: Brunner/Mazel.

Oates, R. K. (1989). Ecological perspectives on child maltreatment: Research and intervention. In J. T. Pardeck (Ed.), *Child abuse and neglect: Theory, research, and practice* (pp. 55-68). New York: Gordon and Breach.

Pardeck, J. T. (1981). The current state and new direction of family therapy. *Family Therapy, 8,* 21-27.

Pardeck, J. T. (1983). *The forgotten children: A study of the stability and continuity of foster care.* Washington, DC: University Press of America.

Pardeck, J. T. (1988). Social treatment through an ecological approach. *Clinical Social Work Journal, 16,* 92-104.

Pardeck, J. T. (1989). Family therapy as a treatment approach to child maltreatment. In J. T. Pardeck (Ed.), *Child abuse and neglect: Theory, research, and practice* (pp. 149-156). New York: Gordon and Breach.

Pardeck, J. T. (1996). *Social work practice: An ecological approach.* Westport, CT: Auburn House.

Pardeck, J. T. (2001). *Children's rights: Policy and practice.* Binghamton, NY: The Haworth Press.

Pardeck, J. T. & Yuen, F. K. O. (1997). A family health approach to social work practice. *Family Therapy, 24,* 115-128.

Sameroff, A. (1975). Transactional models in early social relations. *Human Development, 18,* 65-79.

Satir, V. (1967). A family of angels. In J. Haley & L. Hoffman (Eds.), *Techniques of family therapy* (pp. 97-173). New York: Basic Books.

Schmitt, B. D. & Beezley, P. (1976). The long-term management of the child and family in child abuse and neglect. *Pediatric Annals, 5,* 165-176.

Shadish, W. R., Montgomery, L. M., Wilson, P., Wilson, M. R., Bright, I., & Okwumasua, T. (1993). Effects of family and marital psychotherapies: A meta-analysis. *Journal of Consulting and Clinical Psychology, 61,* 992-1002.

Shapiro, T. (1989). The psychodynamic formulation in child and adolescent psychiatry. *Journal of the American Academy of Child and Adolescent Psychiatry, 28(5),* 675-680.

Shapiro, T. & Esman, A. (1992). Psychoanalysis and child and adolescent psychiatry. *Journal of the American Academy of Child and Adolescent Psychiatry, 31(1),* 6-13.

Timasheff, N. S. (1967). *Sociological theory: Its nature and growth.* New York: Random House.

Vondra, J. I. & Toth, S. L. (1989). Ecological perspectives on child maltreatment: Research and intervention. In J. T. Pardeck (Ed.), *Child abuse and neglect: Theory, research, and practice* (pp. 9-28). New York: Gordon and Breach.

Wiehe, V. R. (1989). Child abuse: An ecological perspective. In J. T. Pardeck (Ed.), *Child abuse and neglect: Theory, research, and practice* (pp. 139-148). New York: Gordon and Breach.

Young, L. (1964). *Wednesday's children: A study of child neglect and abuse.* New York: McGraw-Hill.

Chapter 11

Parent Interventions
with Physically Abused Children

Holly A. Filcheck
Cheryl B. McNeil
Amy D. Herschell

The detrimental effects of child physical abuse are well documented in the literature (cf. Becker et al., 1995). In general, children who experience physical abuse are more likely than children who do not experience physical abuse to exhibit poor school performance, disruptive behavior problems (e.g., a greater prevalence of discipline referrals and suspensions) (Eckenrode, Laird, & Doris, 1993), difficulty achieving secure attachments (Crittenden & Ainsworth, 1987), problems with peer relationships (Hoffman-Plotkin & Twentyman, 1984), social withdrawal (Azar & Wolfe, 1998), a higher prevalence of psychopathology (e.g., disruptive behavior disorders, anxiety, and depression) (Blumberg, 1981; Livingston, Lawson, & Jones, 1993; Wolfe & Mosk, 1983), and a higher number of suicide attempts and self-mutilations (Green, 1978) during childhood.

As children grow older, the effects of physical abuse are not erased. Instead, research has found that adults who were physically abused as children are likely to exhibit antisocial behavior (Pollock et al., 1990) such as aggression (Briere & Runtz, 1990). Childhood abuse also is associated with adult psychopathology (Briere & Runtz, 1988; Wolfe & Alpert, 1991), perpetrating maltreatment of children (Egeland, 1988), higher rates of unemployment, low-paying jobs, increased educational problems (Widom, 1991), and physical health problems and concerns (Moeller, Bachmann, & Moeller, 1993).

Clearly, effective prevention and intervention are needed to inhibit or remediate these detrimental effects. Unfortunately, little is known about the effectiveness of treatments for these families and children because very few high-quality, systematic, empirical examinations have been conducted to document the usefulness of specific treatments. Instead, most articles have been devoted to describing characteristics associated with abusive families and abused children (Becker et al., 1995; Oates & Bross, 1995; Wolfe & Sandler, 1981). However, some evidence suggests that behavioral and cognitive-behavioral parent training programs may be effective in treating abusive families (Azar, 1989; Azar & Wolfe, 1998), which later are discussed in detail.

CHARACTERISTICS OF MALTREATING FAMILIES

Certain parent, child, and family factors have been found to be common among abusive families. The previously mentioned literature describing these characteristics has been helpful for identifying risk factors. Awareness of these factors can help the therapist to anticipate difficulties in treatment and guide solutions to treatment barriers.

Maltreating parents commonly report that they too were abused or neglected as children (Garbarino, 1984), indicating that many of these parents learned abusive behaviors as parenting techniques. This also might explain why abusive parents are likely to lack parenting skills and knowledge of child development, two factors that often result in inappropriate discipline and expectations (Azar & Wolfe, 1998). Similarly, having been abused as children might place parents at risk for problems with emotional regulation and expression (Camras, Ribordy, Hill, & Martino, 1988; DePanfilis & Salus, 1992; Kropp & Haynes, 1987), which also are common problems in this popoulation.

Although no consistent set of personality characteristics has been identified as common among maltreating parents, these parents are likely to experience "low self-esteem, low intelligence, ego deficiency, impulsivity, hostility, isolation and loneliness, anxiety, depression and apathy, rigidity, fear of rejection, low frustration tolerance, narcissism, fearfulness, immaturity and dependency, distrustfulness, neuroticism, drug or alcohol abuse, and criminal behavior" (DePanfilis & Salus, 1992, p. 12). Studies also suggest that parents who are likely to abuse their children are more often single and economically disadvantaged (Azar & Wolfe, 1998; U.S. Department of Health and Human Services, 1996). For example, families with annual incomes below $15,000 were reportedly twenty-five times more likely than families with annual incomes above $30,000 to experience or be referred for child abuse or neglect (U.S. Department of Health and Human Services, 1996). Parents who abuse drugs and/or alcohol also are at a higher risk than non–substance-abusing parents for maltreating their children. In comparison to children with non–substance-abusing parents, those with substance-abusing parents were almost three times more likely to be abused and more than four times more likely to be neglected (Reid, Macchetto, & Foster,

1999). Further, the majority (50 to 80 percent) of substantiated Child Protective Services (CPS) cases involve parent substance abuse (U.S. Department of Health and Human Services, 1999b).

In addition to these parent characteristics, certain child characteristics (e.g., gender, age, and physical, cognitive, emotional, and social development) have been associated with risk of maltreatment (DePanfilis & Salus, 1992). For example, males are slightly more likely than families to experience physical abuse (U.S. Department of Health and Human Services, 1999a). Younger and physically smaller children are at a greater risk for specific types of abuse and neglect (Kempe, Silverman, Steele, Droegenmueller, & Silver, 1962). In 1997, the highest proportion of maltreatment victims (26 percent) were between the ages of four and seven, although the majority (59 percent) of physical abuse victims were age eight or older (U.S. Department of Health and Human Services, 1999a). Children who are perceived as different, such as children with disabilities (Soeffing, 1975), or as difficult, such as children with disruptive behavior (Garbarino, 1984), also are at a higher risk for maltreatment.

Family factors such as marital conflict, domestic violence, conflict with extended family members, employment problems, financial stress, and social isolation are highly correlated with maltreatment (DePanfilis & Salus, 1992). Daily family interactions of maltreating families are "characterized by a low level of social exchange, low responsiveness to positive behavior, and high responsiveness to negative behavior" (DePanfilis & Salus, 1992; p. 13). In comparison to nonmaltreating parents, maltreating parents have been found to display fewer appropriate caregiving behaviors (Egeland & Brunnquell, 1979), a high degree of negative affect (Crittenden, 1981), inconsistent discipline strategies, a lack of empathetic responding (Frodi & Lamb, 1980), and a lower level of emotional understanding (Shipman & Zeman, 1999). Some researchers (Starr, 1987; Urquiza & McNeil, 1996) have suggested child abuse can be conceptualized as a parent-child interaction problem with additional factors contributing. As might be expected, the likelihood of child maltreatment is even higher when families experience financial hardships, additional stress, or social isolation (DePanfilis & Salus, 1992).

PARENT TRAINING TO TREAT PHYSICALLY ABUSIVE PARENTS

Parent training programs are designed to provide parents with knowledge concerning developmentally appropriate behaviors as well as to assist parents in acquiring skills necessary to decrease negative and abusive interactions. Some parent training programs focus on child management skills, whereas others focus on stress and anger control, problem solving, or multiple treatment components. Parent training programs teach behaviors that are incompatible with abusive parenting behavior.

Azar and Wolfe (1998) suggested that physically abusive parents often are lower in intellectual functioning as well as education and could benefit from concrete, problem-focused treatment approaches. Behavioral parent training programs offer this type of approach and therefore may be more effective in the treatment of physically abusive families than insight-oriented therapies (Azar & Wolfe, 1998). A review of outcome data by Azar (1989) suggested that behavioral and cognitive-behavioral approaches demonstrate promising support for their effectiveness in treating child physical abuse. Shortly after behavioral applications began to appear in the literature (in the late 1970s), single-subject design studies conducted by Wolfe and colleagues in 1981 and 1982 provided initial empirical support for teaching parents child management skills as an effective strategy for treating child physical abuse. These initial studies spurred interest and additional support for these techniques, which are discussed later.

McInnis-Dittrich (1996) suggested that parent training programs are useful in treating physically abusive parents because they have been found to improve parental attitudes, reduce tension in the marriage, improve family management skills, and decrease social isolation by expanding social support systems. In addition, parent training programs have been shown to increase feelings of parental competence in managing children.

Behavioral parent training approaches reportedly have been perceived by the parent as more educational and less threatening (Azar & Wolfe, 1998), which may increase attendance at therapy sessions and compliance with treatment recommendations. Other noted advantages in using behavioral parent training programs include time effectiveness and practicality. Also, generalization is enhanced when parents are trained to practice techniques in both the clinic and the problem environments (Altepeter & Walker, 1992).

Issues in Parent Training with Abusive Parents

Physically abusive parents present the clinician with unique challenges. Treatment dropout rates are high (estimated 32 to 87 percent) (Azar & Wolfe, 1998) as are recidivism rates (estimated 20 to 68 percent) (Azar, 1989). In comparison, Kazdin and Wassell (1998) estimated that between 40 and 60 percent of families of children and adolescents who enter treatment end prematurely, and Eyberg (1996) estimated that 32 percent of families referred for parent-child interaction therapy (PCIT), a behavioral parent-training program, terminated treatment early.

Motivation is another concern in parent training with abusive parents (Azar, 1989; Azar & Wolfe, 1998). Even if parents attend sessions regularly, resistence typically is present. Often physically abusive parents are involuntary clients and do not recognize problems in their parenting style. Some parents are even ordered by a court to attend sessions, which has been demonstrated to increase attendance at sessions (Wolfe & Sandler, 1981), but may not increase compliance with the treatment regimen. The previously discussed demographic characteristics associated with parents who physically abuse their children also contribute to difficulties in treatment (McNeil & Herschell, 1998). For example, physically abusive parents often have limited financial and social resources and experience multiple life stressors (Altepeter & Walker, 1992) that interfere with therapy attendance and success.

In addition, abusive parents have high levels of unrealistic expectations regarding the capabilities of their children and exhibit a negative attributional bias in interpreting their children's behavior. A child misbehavior is likely to be interpreted by an abusive parent as intentional or manipulative because the child is viewed as innately "bad," which leads the parent to greater frustration and aggression (Azar & Wolfe, 1998). Similarly, abusive parents are likely to make developmentally inappropriate demands of children and are unlikely to change their own behavior in response to the child's needs (Crittenden, 1981; Trickett & Kuczynski, 1986). They also have problems with engaging their children, initiating positive interactions (Bousha & Twentyman, 1984; Burgess & Conger, 1978), and understanding the importance of positive interactions.

Typical Parent Training Program Techniques

A number of therapeutic techniques have been attempted with physically abusive parents, including training in child management skills, stress and anger control, and problem solving. See Table 11.1 for a description of these parent training approaches. These strategies have been used both in isolation and in combination. Each of these techniques is taught to abusive parents because they give parents skills to use while disciplining their children rather than using physical abuse. Therefore, these techniques often are used in treating physically abusive parents.

TABLE 11.1. Parent Training Programs

Program	Skills	Training Methods	References
Child management	Reinforcement Extinction Time-out Response-cost Token economies	Modeling Role-playing Didactic instruction Videotapes Feedback	Altepeter & Walker,1989; Azar, 1989; Azar & Wolfe,1998; Becker et al.,1995; Wolfe, 1994
Stress and anger control	Risk signal identification Cognitive restructuring Self-control Systematic desensitization Progressive muscle relaxation	Didactic instruction	Azar, 1989; Azar & Wolfe, 1998; Becker et al., 1995; Wolfe, 1994
Problem solving	Problem identification Solution generation Solution evaluation Solution selection	Videotapes	Azar, 1989

Note: Descriptions of each program are nonexhaustive.

Research on Parent Training Programs

Child Management

It has been proposed that an abusive act toward a child "represents the parent's inability to deal effectively with the child's behavior due to a lack of appropriate child management skills" (Wolfe & Sandler, 1981, p. 321). Most research in the area of parent training programs for abusive parents has been conducted on child management training programs. This may be due, in part, to the consistent findings suggesting that the use of child management techniques increases parents' positive behavior, as well as decreases parents' negative behavior (e.g., Azar & Wolfe, 1998; Sandler, Van Dercar, & Milhoan, 1978; Wolfe & Sandler, 1981).

Brunk, Henggeler, and Whelan (1987) compared child management techniques to another form of treatment to determine which skills were effective in treating abusive parents. More specifically, child management parent training through a group-based approach was compared to an individual systemic family therapy approach. Child management skills were taught to parents through Becker's (1971) *Parents Are Teachers* educational book and film, and Patterson's (1973) *Living with Children* educational book. These materials commonly are used in child management training approaches. In addition, parents were taught to use positive reinforcement and noncorporal discipline strategies with their children. Results suggested that both approaches produced significant reductions in stress, mental health symptoms, and social problems. However, the individual systemic approach was effective in improving parent-child interactions, whereas the group-based approach was effective in reducing parents' social isolation (Brunk et al., 1987).

Several case studies have been conducted to determine the effectiveness of child management training with abusive parents. For example, Sandler et al. (1978) and Wolfe et al. (1982) found increases in appropriate, positive child management skills, as well as decreases in inappropriate, negative parent-child interactions. These results were maintained in Sandler et al.'s study at a three-month follow-up. Wolfe and Sandler (1981) also found decreases in negative parent-child interaction styles in their research. In addition, the results of this study showed that after treatment, children were more compliant with parental commands. These results were maintained at three-, eight-, and twelve-month follow-ups. In another case study, Wolfe, Sandler, and Kaufman (1981) found that abusive parents' child management skills had significantly increased, and their children's behavior problems decreased when a child management training program was used.

These studies used several techniques that are common in child management programs. For example, Sandler et al. (1978), Wolfe and Sandler (1981), and Wolfe et al. (1981) taught parents to use contingent reinforcement and contracting through Becker's (1971) *Parents Are Teachers* educational book and film, role-playing, homework, and feedback. In addition, Wolfe et al. (1982) used an in-ear audio device to provide immediate feedback to the abusive parent to modify the existing behavioral pattern. Also, Wolfe et al. (1981) used home-based training through modeling and vignettes in the use of problem-solving skills and self-control techniques. Thus, several case studies support the effectiveness of using child management techniques to treat physically abusive parents.

MacMillan, Olson, and Hansen (1991) conducted a single-subject-design study with three abusive parents in which child management skills were taught and results were obtained through analogue assessments in high- and low-demand situations in the home and in the clinic. In the high-demand situation, the parents were required to respond to a higher number of deviant responses to parental instructions by actors than in the low-demand situation. The child management techniques that were taught included descriptions, imitation, and praise, which were taught by rationales, modeling, and rehearsal. The results suggested that these child management skills were effective in high- and low-demand situations. When generalization training was implemented, parents' child management skills were further improved in high-demand situations. This study provides evidence that child management techniques are not only helpful to abusive parents in low-demand situations, but also in high-demand situations, which may be similar to environments in which parents are likely to become physically abusive.

Systematic training for effective parenting (STEP) was ecologically adapted to determine its usefulness with physically abusive parents (McInnis-Dittrich, 1996). This parent training program focused on the use of logical and natural consequences, which were taught through videotapes, discussion, education about noncorporal discipline techniques, and homework. McInnis-Dittrich (1996) reported that none of the parents involved in this program was involved in a child abuse report within six months of the implementation of the program, and that parents reported positive feelings concerning the program. However, this study had several limitations. For example, no data were reported to be collected before or after implementation of the program. Therefore, the evidence provided cannot lead to a decisive conclusion that effects were solely due to the treatment program. Clearly, the use of the STEP program for treating physically abusive parents needs further research to determine its effectiveness. However, it may be a promising approach to the treatment of abuse.

Stress and Anger Control

Stress and anger control techniques often are taught to physically abusive parents because of their deficits in these areas. This type of training is usually taught to parents in conjunction with other forms of treatment (e.g., child management techniques). However, Nomellini and Katz (1983) conducted three case studies in which they used anger control training exclusively. This training involved educating parents in the detection of anger arousal cues, self-monitoring of anger, cognitive restructuring, deep breathing and relaxation, and rehearsal. Through observations in the home, self-report of anger scores, and self-monitoring data, the authors found that parents' angry behaviors and urges, as well as their scores on the anger self-report scale, were significantly reduced after treatment. However, positive parent behaviors did not increase unless these behaviors were specifically targeted. Even though the authors only trained the parents in the use of anger control skills, the children's negative behavior decreased. This result may have been obtained because the parents were modeling appropriate behavior or because parents were not negatively attending to children's inappropriate behavior. In other words, the children may not have been receiving as much negative attention for disruptive behavior; therefore their negative behavior decreased. In addition, at two- to six-month follow-ups, these reductions were maintained. Thus, Nomellini and Katz's (1983) anger control treatment seems to be helpful for treating physically abusive parents.

As previously mentioned, systematic desensitization also is used in some forms of stress and anger control training. For example, Gilbert (1976) found that systematic desensitization decreased parents' level of anger arousal when their children exhibited increasingly negative (i.e., anger-producing) behavior, and increased parents' positive interactions with their children. Therefore, systematic desensitization appears to be a useful addition to stress and anger control training for physically abusive parents.

Problem Solving

Typically, problem-solving techniques are used in combination with other methods in the treatment of physically abusive parents. Although not always stated directly, it is common for parent training programs to teach problem-solving skills indirectly. For example, in child management parent training programs, parents are taught specific techniques (e.g., reinforcement, noncorporal discipline, ignoring) to use in certain situations. Parents must then learn to determine which skill to use in individual situations, which is essentially the skill of problem solving.

MacMillan, Guevremont, and Hansen (1988) conducted a single-subject-design study to assess the effectiveness of training an abusive mother in the use of problem-solving skills. Because the parent had multiple life stressors, the training focused on managing these stressors and learning to care for her child through practice with vignettes, modeling, rehearsal, and feedback. The results indicated that the problem-solving parent training program produced an increase in the amount and the quality of generating alternative solutions to problems. Improvements were shown in other areas as well. For example, a decrease in negative contacts and an increase in positive contacts with others was found. Also, as the parent learned more effective problem-solving techniques, her levels of negative affect, stress, and anxiety decreased. At one- and five-month follow-ups, all gains were maintained except the parent's stress and anxiety levels, which increased.

Multiple Components

Overall, multiple-component parent training programs seem to be more effective than single-component approaches (Egan, 1983). This may be because a greater number of problem areas are targeted for treatment in multiple-component training programs. However, in cases in which multiple-component training programs produce the same results as single-component training programs, it would be more time- and cost-effective to use single-component training, especially considering the previously mentioned issues with this population (e.g., low income, high dropout rate). Among other interventions, the multiple-component training programs discussed next typically include child management and stress management training components.

One multiple-component study of parent training conducted by Egan (1983) involved stress management training alone, child management training alone, both stress management and child management training, and a wait-list control group. The stress management training used progressive muscle relaxation and cognitive restructuring, and the child management training used reinforcement, behavioral contracting, time-out, and Patterson's (1973) *Living with Children* educational book. Measured by parent report, behavioral observation, and parent response to hypothetical interactions, differential effects were demonstrated between the components. Stress management training resulted in more positive affect in parent-child interactions, less negative affect concerning stressful events, increased parental commands, and less overall family conflict. Child management training also was effective. Parents reinforced their children's compliance more often, verbally interacted with their children more often, and were verbally negative with their children less often. However, the children who participated in the child management component of treatment were less likely to display positive affect than children who did not participate in this component.

In sum, these results led Egan to suggest that stress and anger control training alone may not be as effective in changing parents' behavior as using it in combination with child management techniques. In other words, parents may be less aggressive after stress and anger control training, but they may not have learned how to behave more appropriately with their children (Azar & Wolfe, 1998).

Another multiple-component parent training program for abusive parents was developed by Denicola and Sandler (1980). Their single-subject study focused on child management training and training in self-control skills. The child management training included educational information, positive reinforcement, problem solving, modeling, role-plays, contracting, and homework. The self-control techniques entailed deep muscle relaxation, cognitive restructuring, and exposure to stress. The results indicated, as did other single-subject studies using child management training (e.g., Sandler et al., 1978; Wolfe et al., 1982), that positive parent behavior increased while negative parent behavior decreased. In addition, the children's behavior changed in the same way as the parents' behavior (i.e., increased positive behavior and decreased negative behavior). Results were maintained at a three-month follow-up.

Another type of multiple-component training program was developed by Lutzker (1984) to prevent and treat abusive parenting using an ecobehavioral approach (i.e., treatment is in vivo in each area of concern). This program, Project 12-Ways, is comprehensive. For example, it can include stress and self-control management, basic skills training, child management, marital counseling, and assertiveness training as well as other types of social support (i.e., health and nutrition education, money management, finding a job). As compared with parents not receiving treatment, parents in this program had reduced experiences of multiple occurrences of child abuse (Lutzker, 1984) and significantly lower recidivism rates over a five-year period (Lutzker & Rice, 1987).

In conclusion, in some studies (Campbell, O'Brien, Bickett, & Lutzker, 1983; Egan, 1983) it appeared that the use of multiple-component training for physically abusive parents provided additional treatment gains that support the use of more than one component despite the possible increase in the amount of time and money that may be required. In contrast, other studies (Denicola & Sandler, 1980; Koverola, Elliot-Faust, & Wolfe, 1984) provide some evidence that of multiple-component programs provide little more than a single-component program would provide. Clearly, additional research is needed to determine the relative effectiveness of multiple-component versus single-component programs.

PARENT-CHILD INTERACTION THERAPY

PCIT (Eyberg & Calzada, 1999; Hembree-Kigin & McNeil, 1995; Herschell, Lumley, & McNeil, 2000), a parent training program developed by Eyberg in the 1970s, has demonstrated considerable success in teaching parents developmentally appropriate skills to manage disruptive behavior in children between the ages of two and seven. Currently, PCIT is being evaluated in the treatment of physically abusive families through two federally funded grants (Urquiza & McNeil, 1996). The results so far appear positive and indicate that PCIT may be a promising new approach for the treatment of these families. During the course of treatment, focus is on the child's behavior (e.g., parents learn child management skills and developmental appropriateness of behaviors) as well as on the parents' individual needs (e.g., stress and anger control, parent self-care).

Goals of PCIT

Some of the goals in PCIT for physically abusive parents include the following: providing them with knowledge of developmentally appropriate behavior; enhancing the parent-child relationship; acquiring nonaggresive behavior management skills; and obtaining child behavior that is within normal limits (see Table 11.2). In addition to these goals that apply to every family that participates in PCIT, individualized goals that apply specifically to each family are developed. For example, an individualized goal for a specific family may be to increase the child's sharing behavior or improving positive communication between the parents.

Structure of PCIT

Similar to other parent training programs (e.g., Barkley, 1987; Forehand & McMahon, 1981; Webster-Stratton, 1984, 1994), PCIT is structured such that two sets of skills are taught in two discrete treatment phases (see Table 11.2). The first phase, child-directed interaction (CDI), focuses on relationship-enhancing strategies by teaching play therapy skills to parents. The second phase, parent-directed interaction (PDI), concentrates on parents learning effective, nonaggressive discipline skills. PCIT is unique among other programs in its strong emphasis on enhancing the parent-child relationship and teaching developmentally sensitive parenting skills. Approximately seven sessions are devoted to parents mastering developmentally appropriate, relationship-enhancing skills. In fact, treatment cannot progress to discipline skills until a predetermined mastery level of relationship-enhancement skills is achieved. Parents learn new skills by being coached while they interact with their children.

Typically, PCIT can be conducted in twelve to fourteen weekly one-hour sessions. The first step in PCIT is to conduct one assessment session with the parent and child present so that the family's treatment needs can be determined and therapy can be tailored to fit the individual family. This evaluation involves obtaining self-report data (e.g., Eyberg Child Behavior Inventory [ECBI; Eyberg & Pincus, 1999], Child Abuse Potential Inventory [CAPI; Milner, 1980]) a comprehensive intake interview, and structured behavioral observations (coded using the Dyadic Parent-Child Interaction Coding System-II [DPICS-II; Eyberg, Bessmer, Newcomb, Edwards, &

TABLE 11.2. PCIT Components and Goals

Component	Goals
Phase One	
Intake assessment	Assessment of family functioning
	Rapport building
	Baseline measure of child behavior and parental skills
	Description and rationale of PCIT
CDI didactic	Teach and explain rationale for CDI skills
CDI coaching	Increase use of CDI skills
	Develop or enhance positive parent-child relationship
	Knowledge of developmentally appropriate behavior
	Decrease child attention-seeking behavior
Phase Two	
PDI didactic	Teach and explain rationale for PDI skills
PDI coaching	Increase use of PDI skills
	Develop nonaggressive behavior management skills
	Decrease child noncompliance
Posttreatment assessment	Assessment of family functioning
	Feedback concerning progress throughout PCIT
Booster sessions	Assessment of family functioning
	Refine use of CDI and PDI skills

Note: CDI, child-directed interaction; PCIT, parent-child interactive therapy; PDI, parent-directed interaction.

Robinson, 1994]). If PCIT is determined to be an appropriate treatment, parents are provided with educational information regarding PCIT and asked to commit to attending a specific number of sessions on particular dates. Often, a written contract between the therapist and client is developed and signed (McNeil & Herschell, 1998). This contract is an effort to enhance attendance at sessions and compliance with therapist recommendations. Wolfe and Sandler (1981) highlight the importance of using contracts with physically abusive families to increase treatment compliance.

After that initial evaluation session, parents attend a one-hour didactic session (without the child) to receive information regarding the relationship enhancement (also termed "behavioral play therapy") skills and developmental appropriateness of specific behaviors. During the didactic session, parents are provided with a rationale, model, and role-play for using each of the skills presented. Parents are asked to engage in five minutes of "special playtime" with their child each day at home. These five minutes are explained as an opportunity for the parent to practice skills learned in session as well as an opportunity for the child to receive positive attention from the parent in the home environment. In addition, the special playtime is presented as a therapeutic time for both the parent and the child, emphasizing that this is play therapy and therefore very different than other playtimes during the day. Parents are encouraged to allow the child to be in the lead as well as to use and to avoid very specific skills during special playtime so that the interaction is extremely warm, positive, and therapeutic. Often children from abusive families are not given opportunities to lead interactions. The special playtime allows the child at least five minutes a day when he or she can lead and develop decision-making and leadership skills. The specific skills that parents are encouraged to use are praise, reflection, imitation, description, and enthusiasm, which are presented to parents as "PRIDE" to facilitate easier recall (see Table 11.3). Parents are asked to avoid criticism, commands, and asking questions. In addition, parents are taught to use selective attention and strategic ignoring for appropriate and inappropriate behavior respectively (see Table 11.3).When the parent abides by these play therapy "do" and "don't" skills, the child will be the focus of the interaction. The child is in the lead and the parent follows the child's play, providing support, encouragement, and frequent praise. During the next five to six sessions, parents and their child attend sessions together. The therapist, using an in-ear hearing device and one-way mirror or in-room coaching (Rayfield & Sobel, 2000), coaches the parents with their child in the appropriate use of the skills. The parents' skills are coded using the DPICS-II coding system (Eyberg et al., 1994) for the first five minutes of each session to determine their level of skill acquisition. In addition, this assessment data guides the therapist's coaching of the parents. For example, if the data reveal that the parents are not describing the child's play, then the therapist will focus on coaching the parents to describe in subsequent sessions. Once parents' skill levels meet a predetermined set of mastery criteria, the second stage of PCIT (PDI) is initiated.

Similar to CDI, PDI begins with parents independently attending a didactic session. Parents are taught the importance of structure, consistency, predictability, and follow-through as well as specific skills such as giving good directions, determining compliance, and providing specific, appropriate consequences for compliance (i.e., praise) and noncompliance (i.e., time-out). In subsequent sessions, parents bring their child, and skills are practiced by the parent and coached by the therapist. Once compliance im-

TABLE 11.3. CDI Skills

Skill	Rationale	Example
Praise	Causes the behavior to increase Lets child know what you like Increases self-esteem Adds to warmth of the relationship Makes both parent and child feel good	"Terrific counting!" "I like the way you're playing so quietly." "I'm proud of you for being so polite."
Reflection	Doesn't control the conversation Shows child you're really listening Demonstrates acceptance and understanding Improves child's speech Increases verbal communication	Child: "I made a star." Parent: "Yes, you made a star." Child: "The camel got bumps on top." Parent: "It has two humps on its back."
Imitation	Lets child lead Approves child's choice of play Shows child you are involved Shows child how to play with others (forms basis of taking turns) Tends to increase child's imitation of what you do	Child: "I'm putting baby to bed." Parent: "I'll put sister to bed too." Child: "I'm making a sun in the sky." Parent: "I'm going to put a sun in my picture too."
Description	Allows child to lead Shows child you're interested Teaches concepts Models speech Holds child's attention Organizes child's thoughts about play	"That's a red block." "You're making a tower." "You drew a smiling face." "The boy looks happy."
Enthusiasm	Keeps the child interested Helps to distract the child when ignoring	Voice is playful with lots of inflection.
Selective attention	Attending to appropriate behavior teaches child that to receive attention, he or she must behave in an appropriate manner Causes appropriate behavior to increase	Parent leans toward child and pays attention when child behaves appropriately.
Strategic ignoring	Actively ignoring inappropriate behavior teaches child that he or she will receive no attention for inappropriate behavior Causes inappropriate behavior to decrease	Parent turns away from child and does not look at or speak to child until the child behaves appropriately.

Source: Modified from Hembree-Kigin and McNeil (1989). Parent-Child Interaction Therapy: Child Directed Interaction. In C. Schaefer & J. Briesmeister (Eds.), *Handbook of Parent Training: Parents As Co-Therapists for Children's Behavior Problems.* Hoboken, NJ: Wiley Publishers. Copyright © 1989 John Wiley & Sons, Inc. Adapted with permission of John Wiley & Sons, Inc.

proves to within normal limits, other misbehaviors are addressed (e.g., throwing toys, talking back). After child management skills have been mastered in the clinic and home, they are practiced in public situations and anticipated future behavior difficulties are discussed. Parents are taught to use problem-solving skills to match discipline skills with potential behavior problems.

Empirical Support for PCIT

Since its development, many empirical studies have been conducted documenting PCIT's effectiveness with families (see Herschell, Calzada, Eyberg, & McNeil, 2002, for a review). Studies have demonstrated improvements in parent as well as child behavior. Child behavior improvements have been reported both at home and at school (Eisenstadt, Eyberg, McNeil, Newcomb, & Funderburk, 1993; McNeil, Eyberg, Eisenstadt, Newcomb, & Funderburk, 1991; Schuhmann, Foote, Eyberg, Boggs, & Algina, 1998). Parents report PCIT not only is effective in helping them manage their child's behavior, but also serves to enhance their confidence in their parenting and decreases their distress (Schuhmann et al., 1998).

Furthermore, the effects of PCIT have been shown to generalize to the psychological functioning of parents (Eyberg & Robinson, 1982) as well as the behavior of untreated siblings of referred children (Brestan, Eyberg, Boggs, & Algina, 1997). Effects also have been found to continue over time (Newcomb et al., 2000). In terms of client satisfaction with treatment (which is often an important component of attendance and compliance), parents report high levels of satisfaction with both the content and the process of PCIT (Schuhmann et al., 1998).

PCIT was developed to treat, and has been tested with, children experiencing disruptive behavior problems such as oppositional defiant disorder, attention-deficit/hyperactivity disorder, or conduct disorder. It also has been successfully applied to treat children with developmental delays (Eyberg & Matarrazzo, 1975). Comparatively, PCIT appears less successful, as do other therapies, with parents who are actively abusing substances or who are experiencing significant psychopathology (i.e., major depression), cognitive deficits, or extreme marital difficulties.

Rationale for Use of PCIT with Physically Abusive Families

In spite of these limitations, PCIT may offer a promising method for treating physically abusive families for several reasons. First, PCIT targets specific deficits often found in physically abusive families (Urquiza &

McNeil, 1996). As previously mentioned, physically abusive parents often have cognitive limitations and may benefit from a more concrete, problem-oriented, behavioral training approach (Azar & Wolfe, 1998; Wolfe & Sandler, 1981). As noted by Bonner, Kaufman, Harbeck, and Brassard (1992), PCIT utilizes concrete training strategies by employing a direct coaching model with an in-ear device, using modeling and role-playing of specific skills, assigning daily homework, and practicing skills until mastery is achieved. A study by Wolfe et al. (1982) demonstrated support for the use of parent training in child management using an in-ear device.

PCIT is based on social learning principles and has been found to be effective with a population similar to physically abusive families, families of children with disruptive behavior. A large number of children who have been physically abused will exhibit behavior problems. Conversely, a large number of children with behavior problems have been physically abused. Some have suggested that problems underlying physical abuse (e.g., coercive parent-child interaction) are common among both groups of children (Urquiza & McNeil, 1996). If the behaviors children are displaying as well as the underlying problems are similar, it seems that a treatment designed to help children with behavior problems (i.e., PCIT) should also help children who have been physically abused. It is likely that PCIT already has been used to treat many physically abusive families, considering that physical abuse and behavior problems are commonly found together. Furthermore, a single-case study was conducted in which PCIT was used with a mother-child dyad at high risk for physical abuse (Borrego, Urquiza, Rasmussen, & Zebell, 1999). Results suggested that PCIT was effective with this dyad (i.e., increase in positive interaction, decrease in child behavior problems).

PCIT also places a strong emphasis on developmentally sensitive, positive parenting skills in an effort to increase positive interactions and decrease negative affect and control between the child and parent (Urquiza & McNeil, 1996). Typically, abusive families experience fewer positive interactions and a greater number of negative interactions than typical families (Azar & Wolfe, 1998; DePanfilis & Salus, 1992). Programs such as PCIT that are designed to increase stimulation and improve overall functioning have resulted in some positive outcomes (Bonner et al., 1992).

A criticism of other treatment approaches has been the consideration of the parent and child separately or the needs of one as more important than the other (Azar, 1989). PCIT provides a solution to this criticism by including both the parent and child in treatment sessions. The therapist monitors the progress of each and bases treatment decisions on individual as well as dyad needs. Also, since focusing on the client's individual needs has demonstrated greater success (Werba, Eyberg, Boggs, & Algina, 2000), PCIT therapists have been encouraged to devote time during each session to parents' personal emotional and behavioral needs, and additions to the PCIT protocol have reflected this change (Eyberg & Calzada, 1999). PCIT emphasizes an educational approach and training in specialized parenting skills to decrease parental resistance. This strategy may be particularly helpful for extremely reluctant families.

VIGNETTE

A case example is described in detail as an illustration of the use of PCIT with physically abusive parents who have children with disruptive behavior problems. More specifically, the intake session, CDI component, and PDI component are discussed.

Background Information

Steven Miller's Head Start teacher informed CPS that he arrived at school one morning with bruises on his face and arms. When she asked him what had happened, he stated that his father hit him and this was not the first time. This also was not the first time that she noticed bruises on Steven. After an investigation, CPS substantiated the abuse, and the Millers were court ordered to receive parent training to maintain custody of their five-year-old son.

Intake Session

Session Goals

The intake session is an opportunity for the therapist to receive information about the situation, as well as provide the family with information about treatment. The main goal of this session is to establish rapport with the family so that the remainder of treatment progresses smoothly. Other goals of this session include obtaining detailed information regarding the child's behavior and family history, determining if PCIT is the most appropriate treatment for the family, explaining the rationale for using PCIT, and addressing the parents' misconceptions concerning developmentally appropriate behaviors.

Content of Session

When the Miller family arrived at the clinic, the therapist greeted them and gave them some paperwork (i.e., consent forms, office policy, insurance information, questionnaires concerning Steven's behavior) to complete. The parents completed the paperwork haphazardly, not providing much detail in the information concerning Steven's behavior, as Steven played aggressively with toys on the floor.

The therapist proceeded to ask Mr. and Mrs. Miller questions concerning their perceptions and possible reasons for treatment as well as relevant family and individual (Steven's) history. Mr. Miller stated that the only reason that they were in treatment was because the court ordered it. They would do what they had to do to keep their son, but no more. In addition, Mr. Miller stated that he did not believe that they needed parent training because Steven was the problem and he was only disciplining Steven the way that he was disciplined. Physical discipline worked, and he did not see a reason to change his strategy.

Regarding Steven's behavior, Mr. and Mrs. Miller stated that he was a difficult child. For example, they stated that he was aggressive (i.e., hit others, threw toys), cussed, and would not do his chores (i.e., feeding the animals, cleaning his room, taking out the trash each day). In addition, they stated that the only way he would listen was if Mr. Miller threatened to "get his belt." Steven often exhibited disruptive behaviors in school also. For example, he hit other children, sassed the teacher, refused to comply with requests, and spit when angered.

During the session, Steven crashed cars together and threw toys. In addition, he often interrupted the conversation. In response, Mr. Miller would threaten to "get his belt" when they got home if Steven did not "sit down and shut up." Mrs. Miller remained relatively quiet throughout the session, allowing Mr. Miller to answer all of the questions that were not directly addressed to her. However, she would nod in agreement to Mr. Miller's statements. The CPS caseworker previously had informed the therapist that Mr. Miller had been physically abusive to his wife.

The therapist explained to the Millers that she believed that PCIT would be a helpful treatment for them because they would learn specialized parenting skills that have been found to be effective with children who are aggressive and defiant like Steven. The therapist also explained that the focus would be on using positive discipline skills that do not require corporal punishment. According to the therapist, these positive discipline skills have been found to be more effective than spanking and could help prevent future encounters with CPS. The therapist stated that she understood that they felt as if they did not need treatment, but asked the Millers if they would try the strategies that she was going to teach them to see if they worked even better.

The therapist explained that she would coach them in the use of all of the skills behind a one-way mirror through an in-ear device. This would allow her to give Mr. and Mrs. Miller direct feedback to help them learn the skills quickly. She also stated that PCIT had two phases, a relationship-enhancing phase (CDI) and a positive discipline phase (PDI). In addition, the therapist explained that treatment would progress based on how quickly they acquired skills. More specifically, she stated that the Millers would be expected to meet criteria for mastery of skills before moving on to the discipline phase, and that their skills would be coded (using DPICS-II) in each session to determine their progress. At the beginning of each session, information would be collected and advancements in treatment would be determined by that information. Therefore, if the parents worked hard by completing daily homework assignments, practicing skills taught, and attending sessions regularly, treatment would progress more rapidly than if they did not participate actively. Also, working hard in therapy would be reported to and viewed favorably by the court. The therapist emphasized that she would support their efforts.

At the end of the intake session, the therapist asked the Millers to play with Steven for five minutes just as they would at home while she stayed behind the mirror and took some notes. During this time, the therapist coded the Millers' interaction with Steven using the DPICS-II coding system to obtain baseline data regarding their parenting skills. This observation revealed that the Millers used a lot of criticism and very little praise when interacting with Steven. Therefore, the therapist decided that coaching in subsequent sessions should focus on decreasing criticism and increasing praise.

CDI Component

Goals of the CDI Component

There are several goals for the CDI component of PCIT: (1) educating parents on children's developmental levels; (2) helping parents master the relationship-enhancing skills; (3) making parents aware of their child's positive characteristics; and (4) helping parents to see that much of their child's misbehavior is an attempt to receive attention. The parents are taught to provide attention for appropriate, prosocial behavior in order to increase the child's positive behaviors, enhance the relationship, and create a more positive home environment. In addition, parents are taught to actively ignore inappropriate behavior by completely turning away from their child and providing no attention for inappropriate behavior. Together, the overriding goal of the CDI phase is to establish a healthier and more nurturing parent-child relationship.

Content of the CDI Component

During the first CDI session, the therapist taught the parents the PRIDE skills, explained strategic attention and selective ignoring, and discussed the importance of conducting five minutes of special playtime with Steven each day. For each PRIDE skill, the therapist provided an explanation, rationale, relevant examples, model, and role-play as well as eliciting comments from the parents. Mr. and Mrs. Miller listened and interacted when prompted, but challenged the therapist on her rationales. For example, Mr. Miller stated that he did not believe that Steven should be allowed to be in the lead during playtime because Steven would get out of hand. The therapist responded by acknowledging Mr. Miller's concern and then explaining that Mr. and Mrs. Miller would structure the playtime in such a way as to minimize disruptive behavior. They would choose the time, location, and toys of special playtime. In turn, Steven would be provided a special quality time with his parents and an opportunity to learn new social skills (e.g., sharing) through being allowed to lead the playtime. Furthermore, the therapist reminded Mr. and Mrs. Miller that it was only five minutes per day that Steven would be leading. The rest of the day, as parents, they would be in the lead concerning Steven's behavior and activities. They were skeptical about play therapy because it differed from their current interactions with Steven. However, they reluctantly agreed to try it if only to appease the therapist and the court.

During the first coaching session of CDI, the parents' skills were very low, in part because they had not practiced the skills as the therapist had recommended. During the five minutes of coding of the Millers' skills, Mr. Miller gave Steven commands to play with certain toys (i.e., took the lead away), and when Steven did not comply, Mr. Miller's face turned red in anger and he raised his voice at Steven (i.e., attention for inappropriate behavior). In addition, Steven played aggressively with the toys and his parents imitated the aggressive play. Steven often watched his parents for a reaction when he displayed an inappropriate behavior.

In subsequent coaching sessions, Mr. and Mrs. Miller's CDI skills increased through direct coaching. During one coaching session, Steven began throwing toys against the wall. Immediately, the therapist instructed Mr. Miller to turn, ignore Steven, and enthusiastically describe his own play. Steven, distracted by his father's talking, briefly stopped throwing toys. Mr. Miller was prompted to say, "Thank you for sitting so quietly. Because you are now playing gently with the toys, we can play together." Because of this interaction, Mr. and Mrs. Miller saw that ignoring and redirecting Steven's misbehavior worked and that he enjoyed receiving positive attention from his parents.

Mrs. Miller was extremely quiet and her play lacked enthusiasm. Steven appeared to misbehave so that Mrs. Miller would yell at him (i.e., more stimulation). Thus, the therapist coached Mrs. Miller to be more enthusiastic with Steven so that he would not have to misbehave to receive stimulating attention from her.

Mr. and Mrs. Miller began completing their homework because they realized that the therapist would ask for it and spend time talking about the importance of homework at the beginning of the session. In addition, the Millers completed their homework because they could see improvement in the clinic and wanted to speed the progress of therapy. Completion of homework helped their skills increase dramatically. Specifically, the Millers praise increased and criticism decreased, and Steven's attention-seeking behavior decreased. After a few more sessions, Steven was receiving more positive attention from his parents and his behavior was more appropriate. After seven sessions, the Millers' skills met mastery criteria (e.g., fifteen praises in five minutes), and the therapist decided to move to the PDI component of PCIT.

PDI Component

Goals of PDI Component

The main goal of the PDI component of PCIT is to teach parents to use noncorporal discipline strategies to effectively manage misbehavior. To accomplish this, treatment includes giving effective instructions, mastering the time-out procedure, increasing child compliance, showing parents that time-out is effective, training parents to remain calm while disciplining their children, and developing problem-solving strategies to aid in the management of future behavioral difficulties.

Content of the PDI Component

During the first PDI session, the therapist taught the parents how to give effective instructions and how to use a time-out procedure. Before she could fully explain the procedures, the parents stated that they understood how to give effective instructions and that time-out would never work with Steven. They had tried it before and he refused to sit in the time-out chair. The therapist explained that the time-out that she would teach them is very different from most, and that they would teach Steven to sit in the chair. She also stated that they would not end the first coaching session until Steven followed every instruction. Even though the Millers were skeptical that time-out would work for Steven, they were willing to try it while being coached.

During this session, the therapist addressed the issue of developmentally sensitive expectations. The Millers expected Steven to comply with commands that clearly were not developmentally appropriate. For example, Steven's chores included feeding the animals, cleaning his room, and taking out the trash each day. The Millers complained that when Steven took out the trash, it would spill all over the ground near the trash can, which led them to spank him. From talking with the Millers, the therapist discovered that the parents expected him to tie the trash bag securely, even though Steven could not tie his shoes by himself. This may have led to trash spilling on the ground. The therapist pointed this out and they discussed ideas about chores and other activities that were developmentally appropriate.

The therapist reminded the Millers that it was important to remain calm, "like a robot," during discipline, providing little attention to inappropriate behavior. Alternatively, when Steven behaved appropriately, the parents should reward him with enthusiastic, positive attention. Mr. Miller stated that staying calm would be hard for him because he had a short temper that often resulted in yelling and spanking. The therapist assured Mr. Miller that she would coach him through his first time-out procedure in the clinic and help him remain calm. In addition, she suggested that even though he might feel angry (e.g., heart racing), underreacting (instead of overreacting) would be more effective for managing Steven's behavior. Furthermore, underreacting would help prevent Mr. Miller and Steven from entering into coercive exchanges that eventually could escalate to physical abuse.

During the first PDI coaching session, the therapist explained to Steven that they would be practicing minding exercises and that his parents would tell him to do all kinds of things like "put the block in the box," and if he listened, then his parents would be really happy and play with him, but if he did not listen, then he would have to go to time-out. The therapist role-played the time-out procedure with Steven so that he would know what to expect. For example, she gave him a sticker for walking nicely to the chair and for sitting in the chair. Steven said that he understood that if he did not obey his parents, then he would have to go to time-out, which was no fun. In addition, the therapist role-played what would happen if Steven did not sit in the chair nicely and quietly. More specifically, she showed Steven the "backup room," which was an empty room, and explained that if he didn't sit in the chair "quietly like a mouse," then he would have to go to the backup room, and then he still would have to sit in the time-out chair.

Next, the therapist coached Mr. Miller to give a simple instruction to Steven (i.e., "Please put the hat on Mr. Potato Head"). Steven complied and Mr. Miller enthusiastically said, "Thank you for minding. When you listen, then you don't have to go to time-out, and we can play together." Then the therapist coached Mr. Miller to give a more difficult instruction to Steven (i.e.; "Please put the clay back in the box"). Steven did not comply. The therapist coached Mr. Miller to give Steven a two-choices statement, and Mr. Miller said, "Steven, you have two choices. You either can put the clay back in the box, or go to time-out." Again, Steven did not comply. Mr. Miller was beginning to look mad (i.e., his face was red); therefore, the therapist coached Mr. Miller to calmly lead Steven to the time-out chair. Instead, Mr. Miller responded by roughly grabbing Steven. The therapist quickly coached Mr. Miller to be gentle, and he calmed down somewhat. Steven sat in the chair for about thirty seconds but was screaming much of the time. Meanwhile, Mr. Miller was being coached to ignore his son's screaming and to breathe deeply. After thirty seconds, Steven jumped out of the chair. Mr. Miller began yelling, "I told you to stay . . ." The therapist interrupted, quickly coaching Mr. Miller through deep breathing exercises and instructed him to walk away from Steven. Mr. Miller did so and slowly brought his anger level down. Once he reported that he was calm, he completed the time-out procedure. Throughout the procedure the therapist spoke in a soothing voice, praising Mr. Miller for remaining calm and pointing out that it was effective in helping to maintain control over the situation. Mrs. Miller also was coached through minding exercises with Steven, and Steven complied with all of her instructions. During the session's wrap-up time, the therapist reiterated the importance of remaining calm while disciplining Steven and recommended that Mr. Miller practice deep breathing and progressive muscle relaxation throughout the week to decrease his overall stress level.

After several sessions of PDI, and with a lot of practice, Mr. and Mrs. Miller learned to use time-out appropriately (i.e., with little affect and little negative attention, so that discipline became boring to Steven). Steven learned to listen to his parents' instructions more often, and to sit in the time-out chair. In addition, he learned that he received more rewarding attention when he behaved appropriately than when he behaved inappropriately.

The frequency and intensity of Steven's misbehavior decreased during treatment. Also, because the time-out procedure used in PDI was effective in disciplining Steven, Mr. Miller no longer felt that he had to use physical punishment to manage Steven's misbehaviors. Thus, through hard work, Steven's and his parents' behavior changed. At termination, it was suggested that the Millers attend booster sessions once a month for the next six months to help ensure the maintenance of treatment gains.

FUTURE DIRECTIONS

As many have suggested (e.g., Altepeter & Walker, 1992; Azar, 1989; Becker et al., 1995; Kaufman & Rudy, 1991; Urquiza & McNeil, 1996), more systematic research should be conducted on the effectiveness of parent training programs such as PCIT with physically abusive families. As a start, data were collected by Urquiza and McNeil under a grant from the National Institutes of Mental Health (1996-1999). The study used a group of parents who were referred to Family Preservation Services because of physical abuse. These parents received either traditional Family Preservation Services or traditional services plus PCIT. When available, results of this study should help determine the applicability of PCIT for families with a history of physical abuse.

Pinkston and Smith (1998) suggested that another future direction for parent training should be increasing positive skills that abusive parents need to learn to effectively care for their children. Examples of positive skills include the PCIT PRIDE skills (praise, reflection, imitation, description, and enthusiasm) and Campbell et al.'s (1983) use of verbal descriptive praise and tactile reinforcement. In addition, special populations (e.g., developmentally disabled; Azar, 1989), as well as ethnic, cultural, economic, and gender (i.e., mothers versus fathers) considerations should be the focus of future research in this area (Kaufman & Rudy, 1991). A better understanding of cultural issues would aid therapists in matching clients to training programs or therapies that might successfully meet their individual needs. Finally, future research should be concerned with the long-term benefits of parent training programs (Altepeter & Walker, 1992; Becker et al., 1995; Oates & Bross, 1995). Much of the literature in this area describes follow-ups only a few months after treatment. Information regarding the maintenance of treatment gains long after termination is critical for determining treatment effectiveness.

REFERENCES

Altepeter, T. S., & Walker, E. (1992). In D. J. Willis & E. W. Holden (Eds.), *Prevention of child maltreatment: Developmental and ecological perspectives* (pp. 226-248). New York: Wiley.

Azar, S. T. (1989). Training parents of abused children. In C. E. Schaefer & J. M. Briesmeister (Eds.), *Handbook of parent training: Parents as co-therapists for children's behavior problems* (pp. 414-441). New York: Wiley.

Azar, S. T., & Wolfe, D. A. (1998). Child physical abuse and neglect. In E. J. Mash & R. A. Barkley (Eds.), *Treatment of childhood disorders* (2nd ed.) (pp. 501-544). New York: Guilford.

Barkley, R. A. (1987). *Defiant children.* New York: Guilford.

Becker, J. V., Alpert, J. L., BigFoot, D. S., Bonner, B. L., Geddie, L. F., Henggeler, S. W., Kaufman, K. L., & Walker, C. E. (1995). Empirical research on child abuse treatment: Report by the child abuse and neglect treatment working group, American Psychological Association. *Journal of Clinical Child Psychology, 24*(Suppl.), 23-46.

Becker, W. C. (1971). *Parents are teachers.* Champaign, IL: Research Press.

Blumberg, M. (1981). Depression in abused and neglected children. *American Journal of Psychotherapy, 35,* 342-355.

Bonner, B., Kaufman, K., Harbeck, C., & Brassard, M. (1992). Child maltreatment. In C. E. Walker & M. C. Roberts (Eds.), *Handbook of clinical child psychology* (2nd ed.) (pp. 967-1008). New York: Wiley.

Borrego, J., Urquiza, A. J., Rasmussen, R. A., & Zebell, N. (1999). Parent-child interaction therapy with a family at high risk for physical abuse. *Child Maltreatment: Journal of the American Professional Society on the Abuse of Children, 4,* 331-342.

Bousha, D., & Twentyman, C. T. (1984). Abusing, neglectful and comparison mother-child interactional style. *Journal of Abnormal Psychology, 93,* 106-114.

Brestan, E., Eyberg, S. M., Boggs, S., & Algina, J. (1997). Parent-child interaction therapy: Parent perceptions of untreated siblings. *Child and Family Behavior Therapy, 19,* 13-28.

Briere, J., & Runtz, M. (1988). Post sexual abuse trauma. In G. E. Wyatt & G. J. Powell (Eds.), *Lasting effects of child sexual abuse* (pp. 85-99). Newbury Park, CA: Sage.

Briere, J., & Runtz, M. (1990). Differential adult symptomology associated with three types of child abuse histories. *Child Abuse and Neglect, 14,* 357-364.

Brunk, M., Henggeler, S. W., & Whelan, J. P. (1987). Comparison of multisystemic therapy and parent training in the brief treatment of child abuse and neglect. *Journal of Consulting and Clinical Psychology, 55,* 171-178.

Burgess, R. L., & Conger, R. D. (1978). Family interaction in abusive, neglectful and normal families. *Child Development, 49,* 1163-1173.

Campbell, R. V., O'Brien, S., Bickett, A. D., & Lutzker, J. R. (1983). In-home parent training, treatment of migraine headaches, and marital counseling as an ecobehavioral approach to prevent child abuse. *Journal of Behavior Therapy and Experimental Psychiatry, 14,* 147-154.

Camras, L. A., Ribordy, S., Hill, J., & Martino, S. (1988). Regulation and posing of emotional expressions by abused children and their mothers. *Developmental Psychology, 24,* 776-781.

Crittenden, P. M. (1981). Abusing, neglecting, problematic, and adequate dyads: Differentiating by patterns of interaction. *Merrill-Palmer Quarterly, 27,* 201-208.

Crittenden, P. M., & Ainsworth, M. D. S. (1987). Child maltreatment and attachment theory. In D. Cicchetti & V. Carlson (Eds.), *Child maltreatment* (pp. 432-463). New York: Cambridge University Press.

Denicola, J., & Sandler, J. (1980). Training abusive parents in child management and self-control skills. *Behavior Therapy, 11,* 263-270.

DePanfilis, D., & Salus, M. K. (1992). *A coordinated response to child abuse and neglect: A basic manual.* Washington, DC: U.S. Department of Health and Human Services, National Center on Child Abuse and Neglect.

Eckenrode, J., Laird, M., & Doris, J. (1993). School performance and disciplinary problems among abused and neglected children. *Developmental Psychology, 29,* 53-62.

Egan, K. J. (1983). Stress management and child management with abusive parents. *Journal of Clinical Child Psychology, 12,* 292-299.

Egeland, B. (1988). Breaking the cycle of abuse: Implications for prediction and intervention. In K. D. Browne, C. Davies, & P. Stratton (Eds.), *Early prediction and prevention of child abuse* (pp. 87-99). New York: Wiley.

Egeland, B., & Brunnquell, D. (1979). An at risk approach to the study of child abuse: Some preliminary findings. *Journal of the American Academy of Child Psychiatry, 18,* 219-235.

Eisenstadt, T. H., Eyberg, S. M., McNeil, C. B., Newcomb, K., & Funderburk, B. (1993). Parent-child interaction therapy with behavior problem children: Relative effectiveness of two stages and overall treatment outcome. *Journal of Child Clinical Psychology, 22,* 42-51.

Eyberg, S. M. (1996, August). Parent-child interaction therapy. In T. Ollendick (chair), *Developmentally based integrated psychotherapy with children: Emerging models.* Symposium conducted at the annual meeting of the American Psychological Association, Toronto, Canada.

Eyberg, S. M., Bessmer, J., Newcomb, K., Edward, D., & Robinson, E. (1994). *Manual for the Dyadic Parent-Child Interaction Coding System–II. Social and Behavioral Sciences Documents* (Ms. No. 2897). (Available from Select Press, P.O. Box 9838, San Rafael, CA 94912.)

Eyberg, S. M., & Calzada, E. (1999). *Parent-child interaction therapy: Procedures manual.* Unpublished manuscript, University of Florida.

Eyberg, S. M., & Matarazzo, R. G. (1975, April). *Efficiency in teaching child management skills: Individual parent-child interaction training versus group didactic training.* Paper presented at the annual meeting of the Western Psychological Association, Sacramento, California.

Eyberg, S. M., & Pincus, D. (1999). *Eyberg Child Behavior Inventory and Sutter-Eyberg Student Behavior Inventory: Professional manual.* Odessa, FL: Psychological Assessment Resources.

Eyberg, S. M., & Robinson, E. A. (1982). Parent-child interaction training: Effects on family functioning. *Journal of Clinical Child Psychology, 11,* 130-137.

Forehand, R., & McMahon, R. (1981). *Helping the noncompliant child.* New York: Guilford.

Frodi, A. M., & Lamb, M. E. (1980). Child abusers' responses to infant smiles and cries. *Child Development, 51,* 238-241.

Garbarino, J. (1984). What have we learned about child maltreatment? In U.S. Department of Health and Human Services, National Center on Child Abuse and Neglect (Ed.), *Perspectives on child maltreatment in the mid 80s* (OHDS Publication No. 84-30338) (pp. 6-8). Washington, DC: Government Printing Office.

Gilbert, M. R. (1976). Behavioral approach to the treatment of child abuse. *Nursing Times, 72,* 140-143.

Green, A. H. (1978). Self-destructive behavior in battered children. *American Journal of Child Psychiatry, 135,* 579-582.

Hembree-Kigin, T. L., & McNeil, C. B. (1995). *Parent-child interaction therapy.* New York: Plenum Press.

Herschell, A. D., Calzada, E. J., Eyberg, S. M., & McNeil, C. B. (2002). Parent-child interaction therapy: New directions in research. *Cognitive and Behavioral Practice, 9*(1), 9-15.

Herschell, A. D., Lumley, V. A., & McNeil, C. B. (2000). Parent-child interaction therapy: Current practice and application. In L. VandeCreek & T. L. Jackson (Eds.), *Innovations in clinical practice: A source book* (Vol. 18) (pp. 103-120). Sarasota, FL: Professional Resource Press.

Hoffman-Plotkin, D., & Twentyman, C. T. (1984). A multimodel assessment of behavioral and cognitive deficits in abused and neglected preschoolers. *Child Development, 55,* 794-802.

Kaufman, K. L., & Rudy, L. (1991). Future directions in the treatment of physical child abuse. *Criminal Justice and Behavior, 18,* 82-97.

Kazdin, A., & Wassell, G. (1998). Treatment completion and therapeutic change among children referred for outpatient therapy. *Professional Psychology: Research and Practice, 29,* 332-346.

Kempe, C. H., Silverman, F. N., Steele, B. F., Drogenmueller, W., & Silver, H. K. (1962). The battered child syndrome. *Journal of the American Medical Association, 181,* 17-24.

Koverola, C., Elliot-Faust, D., & Wolfe, D. A. (1984). Clinical issues in the behavioral treatment of a child abusive mother experiencing multiple life stresses. *Journal of Clinical Child Psychology, 13,* 187-191.

Kropp, J. P., & Haynes, O. M. (1987). Abusive and nonabusive mothers' ability to identify general and specific emotion signals in infants. *Child Development, 58,* 187-190.

Livingston, R., Lawson, L., & Jones, J. G. (1993). Predictors of self-reported psychopathology in children abused repeatedly by a parent. *Journal of the American Academy of Child and Adolescent Psychiatry, 32,* 948-953.

Lutzker, J. R. (1984). Project 12-Ways: Treating child abuse and neglect from an ecobehavioral perspective. In R. F. Dangel & R. A. Polster (Eds.), *Parent training: Foundations of research and practice* (pp. 260-297). New York: Guilford.

Lutzker, J. R., & Rice, J. M. (1987). Using recidivism data to evaluate Project 12-Ways: An ecobehavioral approach to the treatment and prevention of child abuse and neglect. *Journal of Family Violence, 2,* 283-290.

MacMillan, V. M., Guevremont, D. C., & Hansen, D. J. (1988). Problem-solving training with a multiply distressed abusive and neglectful mother: Effects on social insularity, negative affect, and stress. *Journal of Family Violence, 3,* 313-325.

MacMillan, V. M., Olson, R. L., & Hansen, D. J. (1991). Low and high deviance analogue assessment of parent-training with physically abusive parents. *Journal of Family Violence, 6,* 279-301.

McInnis-Dittrich, K. (1996). Violence prevention: An ecological adaptation of systematic training for effective parenting. *Families in Society: The Journal of Contemporary Human Services, 77,* 414-422.

McNeil, C. B., Eyberg, S. M., Eisenstadt, T. H., Newcomb, K., & Funderburk, B. W. (1991). Parent-child interaction therapy with behavior problem children: Generalization of treatment effects to the school setting. *Journal of Clinical Child Psychology, 20,* 140-151.

McNeil, C. B., & Herschell, A. D. (1998). Treating multi-problem, high-stress families: Suggested strategies for practitioners. *Family Relations: Interdisciplinary Journal of Applied Family Studies, 47,* 259-262.

Milner, J. S. (1980). *The Child Abuse Potential Inventory: Manual.* Webster, NC: Psytec.

Moeller, T. P., Bachmann, G. A., & Moeller, J. R. (1993). The combined effects of physical, sexual, and emotional abuse during childhood: Long-term health consequences for women. *Child Abuse and Neglect, 17,* 623-640.

Newcomb, K., Eyberg, S. M., Funderburk, B. W., Hembree-Kigin, T., McNeil, C. B., Querido, J., & Hood, K. K. (2000). *Long-term effectiveness of parent-child interaction therapy: A two-year follow-up.* Manuscript in preparation.

Nomellini, S., & Katz, R. C. (1983). Effects of anger control training on abusive parents. *Cognitive Therapy and Research, 7,* 57-68.

Oates, R. K., & Bross, D. C. (1995). What have we learned about treating child physical abuse? A literature review of the last decade. *Child Abuse and Neglect, 19,* 463-473.

Patterson, G. (1973). *Living with children.* Champaign, IL: Research Press.

Pinkston, E. M., & Smith, M. D. (1998). Contributions of parent training to child welfare: Early history and current thoughts. In J. R. Lutzker (Ed.), *Handbook of child abuse research and treatment* (pp. 377-399). New York: Plenum Press.

Pollock, V. E., Briere, J., Schneider, L., Knop, J., Mednick, S. A., & Goodwin, D. W. (1990). Childhood antecedents of antisocial behavior: Parental alcoholism and physical abusiveness. *American Journal of Psychiatry, 147,* 1290-1293.

Rayfield, A., & Sobel, A. (2000, May). *Effectiveness of "in-room" coaching of parent-child interaction therapy.* Paper presented at the Parent-Child Interaction Therapy Conference, Sacramento, California.

Reid, J., Macchetto, P., & Foster, S. (1999). *No safe haven: Children of substance-abusing parents.* New York: The National Center on Addiction and Substance Abuse at Columbia University.

Sandler, J., Van Dercar, C., & Milhoan, M. (1978). Training child abusers in the use of positive reinforcement practices. *Behaviour Research and Therapy, 22,* 331-347.

Schuhmann, E., Foote, R., Eyberg, S. M., Boggs, S., & Algina, J. (1998). Parent-child interaction therapy: Interim report of a randomized trial with short-term maintenance. *Journal of Clinical Child Psychology, 27,* 34-45.

Shipman, K. L., & Zeman, J. (1999). Emotional understanding: A comparison of physically maltreating and nonmaltreating mother-child dyads. *Journal of Clinical Child Psychology, 28,* 407-417.

Soeffing, M. (1975). Abused children are exceptional children. *Exceptional Children, 42,* 126-133.

Starr, R. (1987). Clinical judgement of abuse-proneness based on parent-child interactions. *Child Abuse and Neglect, 11,* 87-92.

Trickett, P. K., & Kuczynski, L. (1986). Children's misbehaviors and parental discipline strategies in abusive and nonabusive families. *Developmental Psychology, 22,* 115-123.

Urquiza, A. J., & McNeil, C. B. (1996). Parent-child interaction therapy: An intensive dyadic intervention for physically abusive families. *Child Maltreatment, 1,* 134-144.

U.S. Department of Health and Human Services, National Center on Child Abuse and Neglect. (1996). *Third national incidence study of child abuse and neglect: Final report (NIS-3).* Washington, DC: U.S. Government Printing Office.

U.S. Department of Health and Human Services. (1999a). *Administration on children, youth and families, child maltreatment 1997: Reports from the states to the national child abuse and neglect data system.* Washington, DC: U.S. Government Printing Office.

U.S. Department of Health and Human Services, National Clearinghouse on Child Abuse and Neglect Information. (1999b). *Frequently asked questions on child abuse and neglect: Fact sheet.* Washington, DC: U.S. Government Printing Office.

Webster-Stratton, C. (1984). Randomized trial of two parent-training programs for families with conduct-disordered children. *Journal of Consulting and Clinical Psychology, 52,* 666-678.

Webster-Stratton, C. (1994). Advancing videotape parent training: A comparison study. *Journal of Consulting and Clinical Psychology, 62,* 299-315.

Werba, B., Eyberg, S. M., Boggs, S. R., & Algina, J. (2000). *Predicting attrition and success in parent-child interaction therapy.* Manuscript submitted for publication.

Widom, C. S. (1991). Avoidance of criminality in abused and neglected children. *Psychiatry, 54,* 162-174.

Wolfe, D. A. (1994). The role of intervention and treatment services in the prevention of child abuse and neglect. In G. B. Melton & F. D. Barry (Eds.), *Protecting children from abuse and neglect: Foundations for a new national strategy* (pp. 224-302). New York: Guilford.

Wolfe, D. A., & Mosk, M. D. (1983). Behavioral comparisons of children from abusive and distressed families. *Journal of Consulting and Clinical Psychology, 51,* 702-708.

Wolfe, D. A., & Sandler, J. (1981). Training abusive parents in effective child management. *Behavior Modification, 5,* 320-335.

Wolfe, D. A., Sandler, J., & Kaufman, K. (1981). A competency-based parent training program for child abusers. *Journal of Consulting and Clinical Psychology, 49,* 633-640.

Wolfe, D. A., St. Lawrence, J., Graves, K., Brehoony, K. B., Bradlyn, D., & Kelly, J. A. (1982). Intensive behavioral parent training for a child abusive mother. *Behavior Therapy, 13,* 438-451.

Wolfe, E., & Alpert, J. L. (1991). Psychoanalysis and child sexual abuse: A review of post-Freudian literature. *Psychoanalytic Psychology, 8,* 305-327.

Chapter 12

Cognitive-Behavioral Interventions with Nonoffending Parents of Children Who Have Been Sexually Abused

Lori B. Stauffer
Esther Deblinger

Research over the past two decades regarding variables that may contribute to the severity of the difficulties experienced by children who have been sexually abused has repeatedly found that supportive responses from non-offending parents are significantly associated with more positive postabuse adjustment in children (e.g., Adams-Tucker, 1981; Conte & Schuerman, 1987; Everson, Hunter, Runyon, Edelson, & Coulter, 1989; Spaccarelli & Kim, 1995; Morrison & Clavenna-Valleroy, 1998). Thus, maximizing parental support is a critical element in providing therapeutic interventions for children who have been sexually abused. Unfortunately, the discovery that their children have been sexually abused can also have a traumatic impact on parents (e.g., Deblinger, Hathaway, Lippmann, & Steer, 1993; Kelley, 1990; Regher, 1990) that may interfere with their ability to optimally respond to their children's needs both at the time of a sexual abuse disclosure and in the months and years that follow. There is evidence that greater maternal symptom distress is associated with poorer adjustment in children who have been sexually abused (Cohen & Mannarino, 1996a). Thus, to optimize children's postabuse adjustments, nonoffending parents need help in coping with their own distress as well as guidance in helping their children cope with the traumatic effects of sexual abuse (Deblinger et al., 1993; Regher, 1990).

Several studies have reported the effectiveness of individual and group cognitive-behavioral therapies for children who have suffered sexual abuse (Cohen, Deblinger, Mannarino, & Steer, 2004; Cohen & Mannarino, 1996b, 1997, 1998; Deblinger, Lippmann, & Steer, 1996; Deblinger, Steer, & Lippmann, 1999; Deblinger, Stauffer, & Steer, 2001; Stauffer & Deblinger, 1996). These studies have found decreases in children's post-traumatic stress disorder (PTSD) symptoms, externalizing behaviors, internalizing behaviors, sexual behaviors, shame, dysfunctional attributions, and/or depression as well as decreases in parental levels of general distress and/or abuse specific distress. Moreover, these empirically supported treatment approaches encourage the active involvement of a nonoffending parent in the therapy process. In addition, the findings of one treatment outcome investigation documented the critical role of the nonoffending parent in helping children who have suffered sexual abuse specifically overcome acting-out behavior problems and depression (Deblinger et al., 1996). Deblinger et al. (2001) also found greater increases in children's knowledge regarding personal safety skills when parents were involved in teaching their children these skills through behavior rehearsal, both in sessions and through homework.

IMPLEMENTING INTERVENTIONS

This chapter focuses on describing and giving suggestions for implementing cognitive-behavioral interventions with nonoffending parents that are similar to parent interventions studied by Deblinger and her colleagues (for a more detailed discussion of this complete treatment model, which includes cognitive-behavioral interventions with children, see Deblinger & Heflin, 1996). Throughout the chapter are segments in "script form" (these segments are in italics) to give readers a sense of what one could say to parents when presenting this information during therapy sessions. Although the scripts are continuous for illustration purposes, therapists are encouraged to provide the information in interactive discussions with parents.

The goals of cognitive-behavioral parent interventions are threefold: (1) to assist parents in coping with their own emotional reactions to enable them to be more supportive of their children; (2) to educate parents about ways to initiate and maintain open parent-child communication regarding their children's sexually abusive experiences and other sexual concerns, including teaching children personal safety skills to reduce the risk of future revictimization; and (3) to provide parents with behavior management skills to assist them in handling their children's abuse-related and non–abuse-related behavioral difficulties. It is recommended that as therapy proceeds, when appropriate, joint parent and child sessions are conducted to provide parents with opportunities to practice the skills they are learning and receive feedback from therapists. It is also recommended that each session include a homework exercise to encourage parents to actively practice the skills at home that you are teaching them during the therapy sessions.

Goal 1: Using cognitive coping to help parents cope with their own emotional responses to their children's abuse in order to help them be more supportive of their children.

When working with parents on coping with their emotional responses, it is important to first validate their feelings. Sometimes when the emphasis is on changing how parents think and feel, they begin to feel that the therapist does not understand them or that they are wrong for having their thoughts and feelings. Thus, prior to and throughout your discussions with parents regarding cognitive coping, it is crucial to reassure parents that there are no right or wrong feelings to have about their children's sexual abuse. Emphasize instead that some feelings and the thoughts and behaviors associated with the feelings can be very problematic and distressing both for them and for their children. Given this, they may want to change how they are feeling, not because their feelings are wrong, but because they want to feel better themselves and be better able to help their children. It is important to help parents recognize that they are coping models for their children. Encourage them to think about coping strategies (both good and bad) that their children have already learned from them. Remind them that their children will also learn coping strategies from them with respect to dealing with the sexual abuse. Thus, the better they cope with this situation, the better model their children will have to follow. Again, remind them that their feelings are natu-. ral emotional responses to discovering that a child they love has been sexually abused. However, highly distressing feelings such as intense anger or sadness can interfere with their ability to respond to their children's needs. Thus, while it is important to acknowledge those feelings, we also want to help them cope more effectively so that they can be happier and more effective parents.

Introduce cognitive coping as a skill that parents can use to change their own problematic or troubling thoughts and help themselves feel better. Present the thoughts-feelings-behaviors triangle to help parents understand ·the cognitive therapy model (Beck, Rush, Shaw, & Emery, 1979) and the relationship between their thoughts, feelings, and behaviors.

> *I want to encourage you to share all the thoughts and feelings you may be experiencing regarding your child's experience of sexual abuse. This is important because these thoughts dramatically influence how you feel and how you interact with your child. As we work together, I will help you think about the sexual abuse in more accurate and hopeful ways so that you will feel better and be a better role model for your child. Distressing thoughts about your child having been sexually*

abused are natural, but sometimes they can be overly pessimistic and inaccurate. When you are feeling very distressed, I will ask you to catch the thoughts that are, perhaps, racing through your mind so that we can examine their accuracy and productiveness. Ultimately, our goal will be to replace these distressing thoughts with more accurate, optimistic thoughts.

Begin the process of helping parents use cognitive coping by encouraging them first to share the feelings that they have had within the past week or two when something reminds them of their child's sexual abuse. Elicit as many feelings as possible before going on to the next step. Be sure to save the list for future weeks, because you probably will not have time to address all the feelings in one session. If parents have difficulty identifying their emotions, list examples including shame, guilt, anger, sadness, fear, and anxiety to help them. After you have a list of feelings, choose one feeling that seems very troubling to begin with. Ask parents to think about where they were and what they were doing when they had that feeling (this will help them get in touch with their memories and facilitate the recall of thoughts). Ask them to share with you what they were saying to themselves when they had that feeling. If parents share a self-talk question, rather than a self-talk statement, ask them how they answered that question, as the answer is often the troubling part of the thought. Next, help parents identify which thoughts are helpful and which thoughts are problematic. Seligman (1991) described three qualities that often characterize problematic thoughts: these thoughts are usually inaccurate and/or have one of the three "p-characteristics" (pervasive, permanent, too personal). It is often not easy for parents to reveal their innermost thoughts. Some thoughts, in fact, are so ingrained that parents are really not aware of what they are saying to themselves, until you gently and patiently wait for them to get in touch with these automatic thoughts. After you have helped parents identify the problematic thoughts, you will eventually help them work on changing those thoughts by providing accurate information about sexual abuse and helping them identify thoughts that have p-characteristics. In so doing, parents can begin to replace dysfunctional thoughts with more accurate and helpful self-statements. Below are definitions and examples of the three types of dysfunctional thoughts.

Permanent

A *permanent thought* says things will never change. However, few things in life are permanent, because things constantly change.

Original thought:	"My child has been permanently damaged by this experience."
Replacement thought:	"In some ways, my child has not changed at all as a result of this experience. In fact, in some ways he has shown strengths I didn't know he had. Although the vast majority of children never tell about sexual abuse, my child had the courage to tell. With my help and counseling, I think he can recover fully from this experience."

Pervasive

A *pervasive thought* says that what is true for one situation is true for every situation. However, most problems are not widespread, but are specific.

Original thought:	"Every aspect of my child's life has been negatively affected by this problem."
Replacement thought:	"Actually, my child still gets along well with her brothers and she continues to do quite well in school. Although she seems more fearful right now, I guess she will overcome some of those fears with my help and the help of our counselor."

Personal

A *personal thought* tells you to take too much responsibility for things that are not really in your control, or believe that a problem only happens to you. Many problems are not in your control and few, if any, problems happen to only one person or one family.

Original thought:	"I should have been able to prevent the sexual abuse from happening to my child."
Replacement thought:	"Even professionals in the field cannot identify sex offenders by looking at them. So there was no way for me to know that the soccer coach would do this, but as soon as my child told me about what happened, I did everything I could to keep her safe and get her the help she needs."

Sometimes parents have difficulty relating to the p-characteristics or just feel that they do not apply to their thoughts. Encourage parents to ask themselves these two questions as another way to help them determine if their thoughts are helpful or hurtful: (1) "Would I say these things to a good friend whose child was sexually abused?" and (2) "Would I express this thought out loud in the presence of my child?" If parents would not express the identified thoughts to a good friend or in front of their child, that is a good signal that it is probably a hurtful or problematic thought.

Cognitive coping will likely be the main focus of your first few sessions with parents because it is necessary to help them cope more effectively to prepare for some of the other tasks you will be encouraging them to do. Although cognitive coping becomes less of a focus after the first few sessions, it will continue to be important to regularly check in with parents on how they are coping and what types of thoughts they are having. Encourage parents to focus on their thoughts about their child's abuse between sessions. Ask them to actively change their problematic thoughts whenever they are able to and to write down and bring in troubling thoughts that they are unable to change on their own. As the weeks go by, be sure to praise parents' efforts and successes with using cognitive coping.

Goal 2: Assist parents in initiating and maintaining open communication with their children regarding sexual abuse and healthy sexuality.

Talking about sexual issues can be a very uncomfortable topic for many parents whose children have not been abused; it is often even more uncomfortable for parents whose child has experienced sexual abuse. Prior to starting this process with parents, it is very important that they understand why you will be asking them to talk about these things with their child. The better parents understand the benefits of these tasks, the more likely they will be to push on through their own discomfort and complete the tasks.

> *It is important to clarify any confusion that your child has about the experience of sexual abuse as well as sexuality in general. To do this, we will need to help your child talk about her [his] experiences so that we can hear any troubling thoughts she has about sex and so she can feel comfortable asking any questions she might have now or in the future. I will work with [child's name] to help her talk about the sexual abuse experiences and ask questions. It is important for your child to feel comfortable talking to you as well, however, because you will be in her life for a long, long time and I am only here for a relatively short time. To help you feel comfortable talking about these issues with your*

child, I will ask you to talk about your child's abuse in as much detail as possible with me first as preparation for talking to your child about the abuse and her questions about sex. In addition, we'll work together on how you can begin the process of age-appropriate sex education and personal safety skills education with your child. The joint activities we do with your child and the homework activities I ask you to do with your child will help you to develop open communication about these issues.

As part of working toward this goal with parents, it will be important to engage parents in the gradual exposure process. Gradual exposure refers to the gradual process of encouraging the child and his or her nonoffending parent(s) to confront and discuss in as much detail as possible abuse-related experiences and the associated thoughts and feelings. As these sessions can be difficult and highly emotional, much of this work is initially done with the child and parent in separate individual sessions. In the individual sessions, encourage parents to share as much about the child's abusive experiences as they can with particular emphasis on their current thoughts and feelings. Encourage parents to talk about these issues repeatedly with you and with other adults until they feel comfortable and believe they will be comfortable talking about the abuse with their child. This process usually occurs over several sessions with parents. The exact timing of gradual exposure work with parents depends upon the specific needs and distress level of the parent and the child.

Another crucial part of helping parents prepare for building open communication between themselves and their children involves giving parents specific guidelines and resources for talking to their children about sexual abuse (e.g., Sanford, 1986; Stauffer & Deblinger, 2003, 2004), personal safety skills (e.g., Stauffer & Deblinger, 2003, 2004), and age-appropriate education about healthy sexuality (e.g., Cole, 1988; Mayle, 1973).

The actual building of open communication between parents and children occurs in joint parent-child sessions and in parent-child homework activities. Whenever possible, it is important to reserve some joint parent-child time. Engaging in joint sessions and in therapy homework activities will be a new experience for parents and children and might be uncomfortable. Therefore, the sessions and activities should start off very neutral and gradually build toward more abuse-specific tasks. Non–abuse-related activities for early sessions can include self-esteem-related discussions and feelings exercises. A useful early joint activity involves simply encouraging the parent and the child to praise each other for something that they did during the past week. Helping parents and children communicate about feelings is another important part of the therapeutic process and therefore it is appropriate to spend several weeks on this issue. It is important to share information about your individual work with the child to help the parent build upon the work you are doing in the individual sessions. Thus, to parallel the work you may be doing with the child related to emotional expression, you may teach parents to encourage the child to label and express emotions through active listening, using open-ended questions to encourage discussion of feelings (e.g., how did you feel when . . . happened?), praising appropriate expression of feelings, and using role-plays to help children practice the skills they are learning.

As parents and children become more comfortable, move the joint work gradually toward more abuse-specific topics by including activities and discussions regarding the real names for private parts, then education about okay and not okay touches, then education about sexual abuse in general and ultimately discussion about the child's personal sexual abuse experiences and then personal safety skills training. Joint sessions regarding the child's personal abuse experiences should include discussions of the child's feelings toward the nonoffending parents during the abuse, during the disclosure and investigation process, and currently. Sometimes those feelings include anger, disappointment, and fear. It is important to help the parent prepare for such reactions prior to having the parent and child discuss these matters. It is preferable to offer the personal safety skills training after the discussions regarding the child's own abuse experiences. This is important because you do not want children to alter what they report about their own experiences in an effort to report what they think they should have done based upon the safety skills education. Although the goal is to have parents talk with their children about the abuse experiences, do not proceed with this step until the parent is able to do so in a calm and supportive fashion. In some cases, it may not be possible to do joint parent-child work, or you may restrict the focus of such work due to parents' distress levels. During the discussions to prepare parents for these activities, help parents understand the importance of using the terms *okay* and *not okay* rather than *good* and *bad*. Parents also need guidelines for talking with their children about sexual abuse and asking children questions about their sexual abuse.

Guidelines for Talking About Sexual Abuse

The long-range objective in encouraging children to talk about the sexual abuse is ultimately to reduce their discomfort when thinking about or talking about these experiences. However, in the short run, the discussions may be somewhat distressing and may cause an increase in behavior problems and emotional outbursts. It is important to prepare parents for that possibility and reassure them. Remind parents of the importance of their support during this process saying something like

> *Your child needs to experience these negative feelings with you there for support so that she or he will feel okay about it in the long run. These discussions are intended to help your child overcome the feelings of responsibility and self-blame or shame he or she might feel about the sexual abuse.*

It is important to help parents understand that children should not be held responsible for the abuse. Children who were abused were simply doing what we encourage all children to do—they were complying with the wishes of an authority figure (the offender). Remind parents that most children respond to abusive interactions in the same way their child did—they comply. Also alert them to the fact that most children never tell about abuse.

> *One study found that only two to six percent of the survivors of child sexual abuse ever told anyone about it in childhood. Even when asked directly, many sexually abused children initially deny these experiences.*

Guidelines Regarding Asking Children Questions About Their Sexual Abuse Experiences

Sometimes parents ask questions that unintentionally encourage children who have been sexually abused to feel as if they did something wrong. To avoid encouraging feelings of shame and self-blame, it is important to help parents ask questions in ways that are supportive and open ended. Encourage parents to avoid using words such as *should* and *let* or asking why the child did not do something. Help parents understand that telling a child they should have told sooner, or asking them why they did not tell sooner implies that the child did something wrong. Remind parents that telling at any time takes a lot of courage and children should be praised for telling. Help parents ask more therapeutic questions such as, "Why did you decide to tell when you did?" Help parents understand that using the word *let* implies that a child had power or control in the situation and therefore is responsible. For example, asking, "Why did you let him touch you?" indicates that the child is responsible for having allowed the abuse to occur. Again, help parents to ask more therapeutic questions such as, "How did you feel when he touched your penis?" or "What were you thinking when he touched your breasts?"

As mentioned, two important components of the open communication goal involve helping parents provide age-appropriate sexual education and personal safety skills training, not just as part of the therapy process but on an ongoing basis. Again, it is important to discuss in advance issues regarding sexuality with the parents to ensure that your individual work with the child is consistent with the parents' values. This will then make it easy for parents to build on your work in joint sessions as well as after therapy ends.

Sex Education

Age-appropriate sex education is important for all children, but is especially important for children who have been sexually abused. It is important that children who have been sexually abused receive accurate sex education to correct any distortions they may have concerning sex as a result of their abusive experiences. Sex education may help reduce their vulnerability to further victimization and premature or dysfunctional sexual behaviors. Sex education may also help a child begin to become comfortable talking about and distinguishing between healthy sexuality and abusive sexual contact.

The following guidelines are summarized from Deblinger and Heflin (1996).

1. *Help parents to explore their feelings about sexuality.* It is very important to deal with parents' personal feelings regarding sex and sexuality in order to help them to communicate more effectively about sex education to their children. Children may be less likely to ask questions and share concerns if they sense that their parents are uncomfortable talking about sexual issues.

2. *Encourage parents to provide developmentally appropriate sex education starting early and using natural opportunities.* Sex education can actually begin when parents teach children the proper names of the private parts and the concept of private parts in the natural course of teaching body part names. Dressing and bathing routines provide parents with natural opportunities to teach private part names. Parents can also share basic information about where babies come from when a family member or friend is pregnant. As children get older (seven to twelve years of age), they are often curious about and able to understand information regarding how babies are conceived and delivered. Preadolescents may be most interested in information regarding the changes that are happening to their bodies. Surprisingly, recent research suggests that teenagers often prefer to receive information about sexual feelings, behaviors, and relationships from parents rather than teachers or peers. Thus, it is important for parents to think through their ideas and values concerning sexual relationships in advance, so that they

can effectively convey accurate information as well as their thoughts and ideas about healthy sexuality to their teenagers.

3. *Encourage parents to use books, videos, and other resources.* It is often easier for parents to provide sex education information with the help of books and/or videos. Encourage parents to review such materials before presenting them to their child to ensure that the information is consistent with their values and attitudes regarding sexuality.

4. *Help parents approach sex education in a positive manner.* Approaching the topic in a negative or overly serious manner may communicate that sexual issues are unpleasant to discuss. Such an approach may accidentally discourage open communication and may reinforce a child's abuse-related perception of sexuality as a negative, distressing experience. It is beneficial to discuss healthy adult sexual relationships in a positive manner, using humor to lighten the mood and lessen feelings of embarrassment and anxiety. While parents may want to convey the seriousness of the consequences of inappropriate sexual behavior (e.g., sexually transmitted diseases or unplanned pregnancy, emotional turmoil), it is also important to discuss that sexual experiences within the context of the right adult relationship may be pleasant, loving, enjoyable, and fun.

5. *Help parents to be good listeners.* Providing effective sex education to children and adolescents involves listening as well as teaching. The effectiveness of sex education may be increased by engaging children and adolescents in two-way discussions rather than giving lectures. Posing questions such as, "Where do you think babies come from?" "What is sex?" or simply, "Do you have any questions about sex?" will encourage dialogue. Children who have been sexually abused sometimes have fears regarding possible exposure to the HIV virus and/or other sexually transmitted diseases. Their answers will reveal their level of information and understanding, as well as concerns or misconceptions that parents can help them address and correct.

6. *Help parents prepare in advance to discuss difficult sexual issues.* Preparation can go a long way in helping to demonstrate interest, enthusiasm, and comfort in dealing with these issues. It is not possible to anticipate every possible sexual question that may arise, however. Thus, it is important to help parents be prepared to offer a general response such as, "That's a good question. I'll have to think about it (or get some information about it) and we'll talk about it later." This sets a calm, open and positive tone and expresses a willingness to respond to the question. Remind parents to be sure to follow up later and not just let the question hang unanswered.

Personal Safety Skills

Although there are no guaranteed methods of protecting children from abuse, children can learn skills that may help them avoid further sexual abuse or tell about any other abusive experiences as soon as possible. Also, it has been found that children are most likely to learn, retain, and use body safety skills effectively if their parents have been involved in teaching the skills and if the skills were learned through repeated practice and behavioral rehearsal.

It is important to help parents understand that because their child has been sexually abused, they should clearly communicate that it is okay that the child did not use these skills before because he or she may not have known about them or may have been too young or too fearful to put them into practice. It is also important for parents to clearly communicate that it is okay if their child feels afraid in the future and is unable to use the skills as well. Remind parents that not saying no or getting away quickly does not mean that sexual abuse is a child's fault. Help parents understand that we do not want teaching these skills to make children feel responsible for allowing abuse to happen, but we do want to help them feel empowered enough to possibly say no or get away, and most important to tell about abuse as soon as they feel safe.

It is important to help parents understand the goals of personal safety skills.

1. Help children identify and learn real names for the parts of their body that are considered private.
2. Help children understand that their body belongs to them.
3. Help children understand the difference between "okay," "not okay," and "confusing" touches.
4. Help children identify situations when it is okay for someone to touch their private parts.
5. Help children understand their right to say no and practice saying "NO!" and getting away if they are touched in a "not okay" way.
6. Help children understand that if they are not able to say no or get away from a not okay touch, they can still tell someone and keep telling until someone protects them and helps stop the abuse.
7. Help children learn the difference between "surprise secrets" that are to be shared at a later time (e.g., a present) and secrets that they are never to tell (e.g., sexual abuse). It is important to let children to know that it is okay to share secrets they were told not to tell, even if they promised not to tell.

8. Help children understand that they also have the right to say no to an okay touch that they do not want or that makes them uncomfortable (e.g., sitting on someone's lap or giving someone a kiss). Parents often feel a little uncomfortable when their child refuses to give a favorite relative a kiss or hug; therefore it is very important to help parents understand this point and prepare to respect and support their child's decision not to share his or her body in that way.

9. Help and encourage children to communicate and express their affection for others with words and okay touches.

Goal 3: Help parents learn behavior management strategies to reduce their children's abuse- and non–abuse-related behavioral difficulties.

The purpose of this work is for parents to learn behavioral principles that will help them to interact more effectively with their children, thereby enhancing children's prosocial behaviors and decreasing their problematic behaviors. Behavioral work with parents is beneficial for children who have been sexually abused in several ways. As parents learn more effective strategies to manage their children's behaviors, children will experience more frequent positive interactions with their parents and less frequent negative interactions. As parents learn to provide more logical and consistent consequences for their children's behaviors, both positive and negative, they are providing an environment in which children can feel a greater sense of control. Clear rules and consistent consequences allow a child to know, even before engaging in a behavior, what the consequence of that behavior will be (e.g., mom says, "good job, I'm proud of you" or "time-out"), thereby increasing the child's feelings of control over his or her environment. The issue of control is especially important for children who have experienced a traumatic event that was beyond their control. Thus, teaching parents how to provide a consistent and generally positive environment is therapeutically beneficial to children who have been sexually abused.

Also, in the aftermath of a child's disclosure of sexual abuse it is often difficult for distressed parents to distinguish between normal and healthy behavioral changes and abuse-related difficulties. Parents of children who have been sexually abused are especially prone to misinterpret normal developmental sexual behaviors and sexual talk as abuse-related and problematic. The behavioral focus of your work with parents will help them to identify true abuse-related behavioral difficulties and find effective ways to minimize those difficulties as well as help them with general behavioral difficulties that may be exacerbated by the stress of the current situation. It is important to remember, however, that behavior management strategies can only be effective if they are implemented and thus it is important to give parents homework assignments each week to practice the parenting skills they are learning.

Behavior management strategies to address with parents include praise and the power of positive attention, gaining children's cooperation and teaching positive behaviors through the use of effective instructions, and minimizing attention to negative behaviors through the use of active ignoring, time-out, and other consequences. The behavioral strategies and how they are implemented are the same whether you are dealing with general behavior problems (e.g., sibling aggression) or abuse-related behaviors (e.g., fear of men or sexualized behaviors). Behavior management books that address general parenting practices (e.g., Patterson & Forgatch, 1987, 1989; Whitham, 1991) are useful tools for parents who are dealing with both abuse-specific and non–abuse-related behavior problems. It is useful to encourage parents to read a specific behavior management book that you will be referencing during your work with them to give them additional information and support between sessions.

The amount of time spent on behavior management and on the various parenting skills will vary depending on each child's behaviors and each family's needs. Praise is crucial to all behavior management work and it is important to introduce praise very early in treatment, in the first or second session. Initially focus on helping parents to increase positive attention and decrease negative attention. Provide additional information regarding consequences, time-out, and effective instructions as needed based upon the child's behaviors. No other behavior management strategies will be effective without the foundations of increased positive attention for appropriate prosocial behaviors and decreased negative attention for problematic behaviors.

It is important to resist the urge to skip over those pieces and jump immediately to consequences for cases where the child's behaviors are very problematic. In such cases, encourage parents to begin the praise assignments by increasing their attention to specific positive replacement behaviors. To do effective behavior management training with parents, it is important to help them look at the pattern of their parent-child interactions. Help them identify true problem behaviors as well as consequences they are currently using that may be inadvertently encouraging the behavior. For example, if a child frequently masturbates while watching television and the parent first lectures the child about how wrong that is and then engages the child in a game to distract him or her from masturbating, the attention the child is receiving will likely encourage the masturbatory behavior to continue rather than stop. It should be noted that excessive masturbatory behavior in children who have been sexually abused can be associated with anxiety and it is important for this issue to be addressed in therapy with the child as well as through behavior management with the parents.

To effectively reduce problem behaviors, it is necessary to help parents identify a problem behavior and an effective consequence for that behavior (e.g., ignoring, time-out, loss of a privilege) as well as the positive replacement behavior (i.e., the positive behavior they want to see instead of the negative behavior) and a consequence (e.g., praise, sticker reward, special playtime) for the positive replacement behavior. For example, a child who likes to pull his pants down might be praised for how nice he looks with his pants up and his shirt tucked in. Or, as in the previous example, a child who is masturbating compulsively in front of the television would be praised for sitting and watching it nicely. It is important to encourage parents to catch the child engaging in the positive replacement behavior quickly, sometimes within the first ten to sixty seconds of an activity, in order to offer praise before the negative behavior has a chance to occur.

In addition to praising the positive replacement behavior and giving an effective consequence for the problem behavior, it is also important to encourage parents to work on minimizing attention to the specific problem behaviors. You can help them be more aware of the negative attention they are giving by examining their patterns of interactions. Parents are sometimes not aware that their lengthy, loud, and sometimes dramatic reactions to problem behaviors, in fact, lead to increases rather than decreases in the behaviors. It is helpful to point this out to them and remind them repeatedly, because parents will tend to fall back into old patterns of nagging and yelling, even when they are working very hard to increase their praise and use of effective consequences. When behaviors are dangerous, it is important (even within the first session if necessary) to help parents decide how to respond and what consequences to give, but that does not mean that they do not also need to do the praising and ignoring pieces of behavior management. Negative consequences alone will not ultimately change behaviors and it is important to help parents understand that. Children need to perceive that there are alternative behaviors that can predictably gain positive parental attention before they are willing to give up their negative means of gaining their parents' attention and emotional involvement.

The case vignette that follows illustrates the use of the various strategies discussed in working with nonoffending parents both individually and in joint work with their children.

CASE VIGNETTE

Mrs. Gowen, a thirty-four-year-old homemaker and mother of three girls, was informed by a child protection worker that her husband had allegedly sexually abused their nine-year-old daughter, Nina, over the course of two years. Initially, Mrs. Gowen was convinced that there must have been some sort of mistake. She explained to the worker that Nina, her oldest daughter, was going through a difficult period. Nina had become very defiant since her baby sister was born and her father had been disciplining her more of late. Mrs. Gowen insisted that she would have known if something like this was happening, because she is so close to all her children and loves them so much. She also explained that as a high school math teacher, Mr. Gowen had a stellar reputation and was very well liked by his students as well as his colleagues.

The worker was concerned about Mrs. Gowen's reaction and spoke with her supervisor about placing Nina in a foster home at least temporarily. The supervisor suggested that before such an action was taken, the worker should arrange for a forensic medical examination and, if needed, a psychological evaluation for the child. The child protection worker escorted Mrs. Gowen and her daughter to the medical examination. Although Mrs. Gowen continued to appear skeptical, she asked appropriate questions about the examination and seemed satisfied with the doctor's responses. The doctor explained that while there was no medical evidence reflecting the abuse, he did not expect there to be any given Nina's very credible description of what happened. After the medical examination, the worker reported that Mrs. Gowen asked, "Are you okay, Nina?" Nina burst into tears and said, "I'm sorry, Mom. I just didn't know what to do. I should have told you." Mrs. Gowen wrapped her arms around her daughter and instinctively said, "NO—I'm sorry. I'm so sorry. I love you."

Mr. Gowen was arrested and charged with aggravated sexual assault and endangering the welfare of a child. His bail restricted him from having any contact with Nina. The worker informed Mrs. Gowen that there was some question as to his right to visit with his younger daughters. To the worker's surprise, Mrs. Gowen suddenly took a very protective stance and insisted that she would fight to prevent such contact even if she had to borrow money from her family to hire a lawyer. Satisfied with the mother's change in attitude, the worker informed her supervisor that she would not recommend foster placement at this time. Rather she planned to refer mother and daughter for a comprehensive psychological evaluation and counseling.

Although Mrs. Gowen, Nina, and her siblings were all referred to a specialized treatment program for families facing this type of crisis, this case vignette focuses on the individual assistance Mrs. Gowen received on behalf of Nina. The goals of Mrs. Gowen's sessions were to help her work through her own emotional distress, while simultaneously learning to effectively communicate and respond to her children's difficulties. During this time, the therapist worked with Nina and her mother individually with the goal of conducting joint parent-child sessions later in treatment. Nina's siblings were seen by another counselor for more nondirective supportive counseling. Future goals for the family included having joint sessions in which Mrs. Gowen and Nina could more openly talk about their thoughts and feelings about the abuse and having family sessions to further enhance open communication and practice personal safety skills with all the children.

After a comprehensive assessment that included individual interviews and standardized measures completed by both Mrs. Gowen and Nina, the therapist began the initial therapy session with Mrs. Gowen by explaining the findings of the assessment. The therapist explained that Nina had many strengths including her ability to maintain excellent grades and extracurricular interests, and her ability to express herself maturely and articulately. Still, Nina was experiencing PTSD symptoms and mild depressive symptoms. Mrs. Gowen was informed that these symptoms were not uncommon in children who had suffered sexual abuse. More important, the therapist reassured Mrs. Gowen that Nina would successfully overcome these difficulties. She explained that she was confident that Nina would do well because Nina already had the single most important factor influencing a child's recovery from sexual abuse: support from a nonoffending parent. In addition, the treatment approach to be utilized had been documented to be highly effective in treating the symptoms Nina seemed to be suffering.

When describing the treatment plan, the therapist noted that Mrs. Gowen seemed to be comforted by the fact that she and her daughter would initially be seen separately before any joint parent-child work would be attempted. Mrs. Gowen pointed out that she did not think her daughter would open up in front of her, because she adamantly refused to talk to her mom about anything concerning her father at home.

The therapist also took time to acknowledge the distress that Mrs. Gowen was experiencing, particularly in terms of her significant feelings of anxiety and depression. The first phase of therapy, in fact, would focus on helping Nina's mother cope with myriad emotions she was experiencing. The therapist explained that this was a place where she could share all her feelings, even those that she thought might not be acceptable. In so doing, the therapist would help Mrs. Gowen understand what thoughts might be driving these fluctuating emotions, thereby helping her to gain a greater feeling of emotional control and hopefulness. With a great deal of hesitancy, Mrs. Gowen explained that she loved Nina with all her heart, but still found herself wishing that it was all some kind of terrible mistake. Not knowing the details of what happened, she wondered if there was any possibility that Nina overreacted to an innocent gesture or behavior on her husband's part. As the tears welled up in her eyes, Mrs. Gowen expressed her worries about how the family could not get along without her husband, and how they might lose their house and she and her children would end up homeless. As the therapist listened carefully and simply reflected back the mother's thoughts and feelings, Mrs. Gowen's emotional distress turned to anger. Although she wished it was all just a bad dream, she angrily stated that if Mr. Gowen did sexually abuse her daughter, she wanted him "to rot in jail." The therapist empathized with Mrs. Gowen and explained that all her thoughts and feelings were valid and natural. Still, the therapist indicated that she would like to help her gain control over these intense emotions, not only so she could start to feel better, but so she could be more emotionally available for her children. The therapist then indicated that she would be asking both mother and daughter to complete automatic thought records that would help them keep track of what they were saying to themselves when they were feeling very distraught. In addition, Mrs. Gowen was asked to read an information sheet about child sexual abuse by the next session. Insisting that she would do anything for her children, Mrs. Gowen readily agreed to do the assigned homework.

As is customary, the therapist began the next session with Mrs. Gowen by inquiring about the homework. Mrs. Gowen indicated that she could not find the time to fill out the thought records, but she did try to read the information sheet. The therapist praised Mrs. Gowen for reading the information sheet, and she suggested that they do the automatic thought record together. The therapist asked Mrs. Gowen to go back to the last time in the past week that she was feeling particularly distraught about the allegations. She encouraged Mrs. Gowen to close her eyes if that would help her recapture her feelings and thoughts at the time.

MOTHER: Well, I'm not sure what you want to know.

THERAPIST: I'd like you to share with me the conversations that you are having with yourself. I realize this can be very difficult, because often we say things to ourselves that we would never say out loud. But these are the very thoughts that are driving the rollercoaster of emotions that you are experiencing. By sharing these thoughts, together we can gain control over them and help you to start to feel better.

MOTHER: I guess I can try. The last time I was really upset was when I overheard Nina say to a boy from the neighborhood, "Hey Tommy, what are you doing—jerking off?" I yelled at her and told the boy to go home. Then I asked Nina where she learned to talk like that and she said, "You still don't believe me, do you?" At that point, I ran into the house and started to cry. (long pause)

THERAPIST: That sounds like it was really difficult. Let's go through it together. Now you were in the house, crying. Where in the house? Were you sitting, standing, lying on the bed? What were you feeling? Try to go back there.

MOTHER: I was standing at the window staring as my children continued to play as if nothing happened. I was just feeling exhausted and scared.

THERAPIST: And what were you saying to yourself?

MOTHER: I guess I was saying—I can't believe this happened. Did this really happen in our family? In our all-American family? How could he? How could he? What has he done to our precious daughter?

THERAPIST: And how did you answer those questions for yourself?

MOTHER: I don't know. I guess I answered—yes, this did happen. In fact, reading that information sheet scared me, because it helped me to understand that this could happen in anyone's family, to anyone's daughter.

THERAPIST: And what else were you saying to yourself as you watched your children playing in the yard?

MOTHER: I should have known. How could he have done this under my nose? I failed. I completely failed as a mother. And I'm so worried about Nina. I'm worried about what this kind of behavior will lead to. I don't want her to be a prostitute! I don't want her life to be ruined. (long pause)

THERAPIST: So some of what you were saying to yourself was distressing because it was acknowledging that your daughter was sexually abused. And you know that is naturally very distressing and it is not a thought that I can dispute. But I'm not sure some of the other things you are saying to yourself are accurate or fair. First of all, you said, you should have known. Is there anything that your child said or did (before she told) that obviously pointed to sexual abuse that you missed?

MOTHER: I don't know. Well, she was getting more defiant.

THERAPIST: So you think when a child is defiant, we should immediately suspect sexual abuse?

MOTHER: Maybe.

THERAPIST: Well, I can tell you if you called in a suspicion of sexual abuse based on that kind of evidence, child protection would definitely not investigate it! In fact, it would be almost bizarre for you to jump to such a conclusion without some other reason. Kids are defiant for so many different reasons—and sometimes such behavior is a normal part of growing independent.

MOTHER: I guess I just should have known because I'm her mother.

THERAPIST: So what you're saying is all good mothers have special powers to see through walls, to detect lies, and to read minds. Because that is what you were expecting of yourself. It is important for you to know that even I would not be able to tell if someone I knew was a sex offender. With all my education and expertise in the area of child sexual abuse, I cannot identify a child who is being sexually abused nor can I identify an adult who is a child molester. And as a result we all have to rely on children to tell us when this happens.

MOTHER: But my daughter didn't tell right away.

THERAPIST: Did you know that the vast majority of children never tell? Your child is in the small minority of children who somehow get the courage to tell when they are still children. Although she was clearly quite frightened and upset when she told, deep down Nina knew that you would be there for her. You didn't fail Nina. On the contrary, you have been there for her every step of the way. You are here, it seems to me, because you want to do even more for her. A mother who has failed is not there for her child the way you are.

MOTHER: (crying) And I am. I am. I hope she knows that. I want to help her. I don't want her to have problems from this. I don't want her to become promiscuous. I feel like her life is ruined.

THERAPIST: I helped you dispute the idea that you should have known. And I hope you are beginning to see that you have not failed. But now I want you to dispute the thought that Nina's life is ruined. I certainly understand that the comment she made to the boy was distressing, but are there any other aspects of Nina's life that don't seem to be ruined at the moment?

MOTHER: (long pause) Well, she is still doing well in school. And her music teacher just told me that she is an extremely talented violinist.

THERAPIST: That's great. That certainly doesn't sound like a ruined life. In fact, it sounds like Nina is having some great success in school and in her music education. And I suspect that is only the beginning of a list of positive behaviors you could come up with about Nina. So for homework, for next week I'd like you to take home this list of thoughts you have been having—and add to this list when you're feeling particularly distressed. Then I'd like you to begin to record statements that would dispute the idea that your daughter's life is ruined. Which means you'll have to focus your attention this week on the positive things your daughter is doing, rather than the problems or symptoms. In fact, I will send you home with a handout about praise, so each time you see your daughter engaging in an appropriate positive interaction, particularly with that neighborhood boy, you can praise her effectively.

MOTHER: Okay, but I'm afraid to let her interact with that boy. I don't think she would ever do anything to him, but I'm still worried about it.

THERAPIST: To allay your concerns, for the time being, I would encourage you to supervise her interactions with Tommy. Still, the first step in addressing that concern is to give Nina a great deal of praise and positive attention when she plays and talks with him appropriately and minimize your reactions to any inappropriate comments she might make.

As the session continued, the therapist further examined Mrs. Gowen's concerns regarding Nina's sexualized talk and behaviors. It was apparent that Mrs. Gowen was reacting very strongly to Nina's sexualized remarks. However, in assessing Mrs. Gowen's attitudes and the characteristics of the "problematic" sexual behaviors, it became evident that while some of Nina's sexualized behaviors were age-inappropriate, others were well within the norm for her age. Thus, it became important to provide some education for her mom about normal sexual behavior in children, while also providing guidance concerning how to react to age-inappropriate sexual behaviors.

Over the sessions that followed, Mrs. Gowen continued her cognitive coping efforts and learned to utilize behavior management skills to more effectively respond to Nina's appropriate and inappropriate behaviors. She quickly understood the importance of praising Nina for interacting appropriately with Tommy and her siblings. In addition, Mrs. Gowen worked hard to control her tendency to yell at or lecture Nina when she perceived her to be behaving in a sexually precocious manner. It should also be noted that Nina's friends were predominantly boys and she often tended to exhibit more problematic sexual behavior in an effort to get attention from boys. Since there is some evidence that girls who have suffered sexual abuse may be more vulnerable to premature sexual relationships if they do not have healthy same-sex relationships, Mrs. Gowen was also encouraged to help Nina seek out opportunities to develop friendships with girls.

As the sessions progressed, Mrs. Gowen's emotional state seemed to stabilize. Although she cried when she first read her daughter's accounts of the sexual abuse in individual sessions with the therapist, Mrs. Gowen was able to maintain her composure when Nina reread these accounts in joint parent-child sessions. In fact, Nina's face lit up when Mrs. Gowen praised her daughter's "courage and skill" in writing a book about the sexual abuse. Mrs. Gowen was also encouraged to take a leadership role in planning and structuring the family sessions, which included personal safety skills exercises as well as more open-ended discussion. Although she was sure she had explained what was happening with Dad to Nina's younger siblings, they were more confused than she had realized. Their questions were poignant but difficult to answer (e.g., Is jail like time-out for Daddy? When will he get out of time-out? Do I have to go to jail if I do a not okay touch to my vagina?). Mrs. Gowen was simply encouraged to answer whatever questions arose by first asking the children how they would answer. This helps to provide a developmental baseline as well as some information about what the child already believes. Although we anticipated that there would be some questions that no parent could answer, Mrs. Gowen prepared herself to answer the questions she could with age-appropriate honesty as well as optimism when possible. Although these family sessions were quite emotional, they served an extremely valuable purpose in creating an atmosphere of open communication where the children could ask questions even about things that, as the youngest sibling expressed, "might make Mommy cry."

CHALLENGES IN APPLYING COGNITIVE-BEHAVIORAL THERAPY WITH NONOFFENDING PARENTS

Although recent research and clinical experience indicate that most nonoffending parents believe their children's disclosures, some parents steadfastly maintain that there has been a mistake, the child is confused, or the child is lying. In some cases it is best for the child and disbelieving parent to have separate therapists and even for the child to be placed in someone else's protective care. However, in some instances, particularly with parents who are unsure and/or ambivalent about the allegations, using this approach can be challenging but often very beneficial. The therapeutic process with ambivalent parents begins with cognitive coping, just as it does with believing parents. The guidelines about accepting a parent's feelings are crucial in these cases. The more these parents are challenged, the more they may feel the need to defend their positions and may more strongly convince themselves that their views are correct. Accepting and trying to understand a parent's disbelief may help the parent feel safe enough to share the most troubling thoughts and feelings. Gradually helping parents to share their thoughts and feelings about what it would mean if the allegations were true may help uncover the very thoughts (e.g., My marriage was a lie; I'm a failure as a mother; If he were satisfied with me he would not have done this; I'm a failure as a wife) that are interfering with the parent's ability to accept the allegations.

Working through the negative emotions and disbelief can take a very long time, as the thoughts and feelings that interfere with a parent's belief are often deeply rooted and hard to uncover and change. Support and acceptance for the nonoffending parent are key. It is also crucial to acknowledge the steps the parent has taken to care for her child (e.g., coming to counseling, not allowing the alleged perpetrator in the home) despite her feelings of disbelief. If an ambivalent mother is working in therapy with or regarding her child, it is important to give her the gift of recognizing how much she loves and cares for her child to go through all of this when she is not even sure the abuse occurred. Building on a parent's love for her child may help give the parent strength to confront the very troubling emotions and thoughts that are interfering with her belief.

Applying this approach is clearly limited to nonoffending parents who are stable. If a parent is at risk for harming self or others or is experiencing psychotic symptoms, those matters must be fully addressed before engaging in this type of treatment.

REFERENCES

Adams-Tucker, C. (1981). A socioclinical overview of 28 sex-abused children. *Child Abuse and Neglect, 5,* 361-367.

Beck, A. T., Rush, A. J., Shaw, B. F., & Emery, G. (1979). *Cognitive therapy of depression.* New York: Guilford.

Cohen, J. A., Deblinger, E., Mannarino, A. P., & Steer, R. (2004). A multisite, randomized controlled trial for children with sexual abuse-related PTSD symptoms. *Journal of the American Academy of Child and Adolescent Psychiatry, 43(4),* 393-402.

Cohen, J. A., & Mannarino, A. P. (1996a). Factors that mediate treatment outcome in sexually abused preschool children. *Journal of the American Academy of Child and Adolescent Psychiatry, 35(10),* 1402-1410.

Cohen, J. A., & Mannarino, A. P. (1996b). A treatment outcome study for sexually abused preschool children: Initial findings. *Journal of the American Academy of Child and Adolescent Psychiatry, 35(1),* 42-50.

Cohen, J. A., & Mannarino, A. P. (1997). A treatment study for sexually abused preschool children: Outcome during a one-year follow-up. *Journal of the American Academy of Child and Adolescent Psychiatry, 36(9),* 1228-1235.

Cohen, J. A., & Mannarino, A. P. (1998). Interventions for sexually abused children: Initial treatment outcome findings. *Child Maltreatment, 3(1),* 17-26.

Cole, J. (1988). *Asking about sex and growing up: A question and answer book for boys and girls.* New York: Beech Tree Books.

Conte, J. R., & Schuerman, J. R. (1987). Factors associated with an increased impact of child sexual abuse. *Child Abuse and Neglect, 11,* 201-211.

Deblinger, E., Hathaway, C. R., Lippmann, J., & Steer, R. (1993). Psychosocial characteristics and correlates of symptom distress in nonoffending mothers of sexually abused children. *Journal of Interpersonal Violence, 8,* 155-168.

Deblinger, E., & Heflin, A. H. (1996). *Treating sexually abused children and their nonoffending parents.* Thousand Oaks, CA: Sage.

Deblinger, E., Lippmann, J., & Steer, R. (1996). Sexually abused children suffering posttraumatic stress symptoms: Initial treatment outcome findings. *Child Maltreatment, 1,* 310-321.

Deblinger, E., Stauffer, L. B., & Steer, R. A. (2001). Comparative efficacies of supportive and cognitive behavioral group therapies for young children who have been sexually abused and their mothers. *Child Maltreatment, 6(4),* 332-343.

Deblinger, E., Steer, R. A., & Lippmann, J. (1999). Two year follow up study of cognitive behavioral therapy for sexually abused children suffering post-traumatic stress symptoms. *Child Abuse and Neglect, 23,* 1371-1378.

Everson, M. D., Hunter, W. M., Runyon, D. K., Edelson, G. A., & Coulter, J. L. (1989). Maternal support following disclosure of incest. *American Journal of Orthopsychiatry, 59,* 197-207.

Kelley, S. J. (1990). Parental stress response to sexual abuse and ritualistic abuse of children in day-care centers. *Nursing Research, 39,* 25-29.

Mayle, P. (1973). *Where did I come from?* Seacaucus, NJ: Lyle Stuart.

Morrison, N. C., & Clavenna-Valleroy, J. (1998). Perceptions of maternal support as related to self-concept and self-report of depression in sexually abused female adolescents. *Journal of Child Sexual Abuse, 7,* 23-40.

Patterson, G., & Forgatch, M. (1987). *Parents and adolescents: Living together, Part 1: The basics.* Eugene, OR: Castalia.

Patterson, G., & Forgatch, M. (1989). *Parents and adolescents: Living together, Part 2: Family problem solving.* Eugene, OR: Castalia.

Regher, C. (1990). Parental responses to extrafamilial child sexual assault. *Child Abuse and Neglect, 14,* 113-120.

Sanford, D. (1986). *I can't talk about it.* Sisters, OR: Multnomah Press.

Seligman, M. (1991). *Learned optimism.* New York: Alfred A. Knopf.

Spaccarelli, S., & Kim, S. (1995). Resilience criteria and factors associated with resilience in sexually abused girls. *Child Abuse and Neglect, 19,* 1171-1182.

Stauffer, L. B., & Deblinger, E. (1996). Cognitive behavioral groups for non-offending mothers and their young sexually abused children: A preliminary treatment outcome study. *Child Maltreatment, 1(1),* 65-76.

Stauffer, L. B., & Deblinger, E. (2003). *Let's talk about taking care of you: An educational book about body safety.* Hatfield, PA: Hope for Families. www.hope4families.com.

Stauffer, L. B., & Deblinger, E. (2004). *Let's talk about taking care of you: An educational book about body safety for young children.* Hatfield, PA: Hope for Families. www.hope4families.com.

Whitham, C. (1991). *Winning the whining war and other skirmishes: A family peace plan.* Glendale, CA: Perspective.

PART IV:
OTHER CONSIDERATIONS WHEN WORKING WITH MALTREATED CHILDREN

Chapter 13

The Consideration of Cultural Factors in the Context of Child Maltreatment

Joaquin Borrego Jr.
Sherri Y. Terao

INTRODUCTION

There is no question that the problem of child physical abuse (CPA) is a complex social issue. In 2000, the National Child Abuse and Neglect Data System estimated that 3 million referrals were made to Child Protective Services (CPS) concerning the welfare of approximately 5 million children (U.S. Department of Health and Human Services, 2002). Of the 3 million referrals, 879,000 were substantiated cases of child maltreatment. This translates to 12.2 out of every 1,000 children as victims of child maltreatment. In 2000, 62.8 percent of the children were victims of neglect (including medical neglect); 19.3 percent physical abuse; 10.1 percent sexual abuse; and 7.7 percent psychological abuse (U.S. Depatment of Health and Human Services, 2002).

CPA seems to be further complicated when clinicians are asked to take culture into account when working with families from ethnic and cultural backgrounds that differ from their own. Currently, a sociopolitical climate exists in which clinicians are strongly urged to be aware and understand the way culture influences certain practices (e.g., abuse, discipline strategies, attitudes about child-rearing, expectations about childhood). This, however, is easier said than done. The topics of race and ethnicity are controversial and cannot exist solely as a pure value-free scientific endeavor (Sue, 1995). Clinicians face many obstacles when working with ethnic minority populations. Unfortunately, there is relatively little data or base-rate information to guide clinicians in their work with people from culturally diverse backgrounds as it relates to the incidence and prevalence of CPA. There is also a paucity of research findings about appropriate assessment and intervention strategies in the child maltreatment field with culturally diverse populations. Though our chapter focuses on ethnic minority groups, it is assumed that many of the issues raised here are applicable to other under-served populations (e.g., social class as related to people living in poverty).

As our society becomes increasingly culturally diverse, the relevance of the consideration of cultural factors becomes paramount in the assessment and treatment of child maltreatment. Offering culturally competent services is a significant issue that continues to receive increasing attention in the field. Although there is an awareness that cultural factors should be taken into account (e.g., Abney, 1996; Yutrzenka, 1995), minimal research is available to guide clinicians who work with culturally diverse populations in the context of child maltreatment. With one exception (e.g., Terao, Borrego, & Urquiza, 2001), no decision-making model exists to help guide clinicians when responding to allegations of CPA with culturally diverse populations. We hope to highlight issues that clinicians might face when working with culturally diverse populations. We first provide demographic information related to the four major ethnic minority groups in the United States to emphasize the growing need for culturally responsive services. Next, a historical analysis of social and political movements that have led to cultural sensitivity and cultural competency movements in the United States are discussed. We use the example of CPA to demonstrate the challenges associated with introducing the concept of culture when deciding if an incident is physically abusive. We end this chapter by offering guidelines for clinicians on how best to respond to incidents of child maltreatment when working with culturally diverse populations. Our overall goal is to offer the clinician concrete and pragmatic suggestions on how to work effectively with ethnic minority families in the context of child maltreatment.

DEMOGRAPHICS

Over the past decade, ethnic minority populations have experienced tremendous growth. As of the 2000 census, Hispanics constituted 12.5 percent of the population, followed by African Americans at 12.3 percent, Asian Americans at 3.7 percent, and American Indians at 1 percent. In the very near future, ethnic minority groups will constitute majorities in many communities throughout the United States. It is estimated that by 2050, the U.S. population will increase by 48 percent to 419.9 million, and less than 53 percent of the population will be non-Hispanic white (U.S. Census Bureau, 2000). This will constitute a dramatic shift in population statistics of ethnic minority groups, with 24 percent Hispanic, 15 percent African American, 8 percent Asian, and approximately 5 percent American Indian, Eskimo, and Aleut (U.S. Census Bureau, 2000). The projected large increase in population size for Hispanics and Asian Americans is a reflection of a continuing pattern of immigration into the United States.

Before addressing ways in which we can best work with ethnic minority groups involved in the child welfare system, it is important to consider certain child maltreatment statistics. According to the National Clearinghouse on Child Abuse and Neglect, approximately half (50.2 percent) of all child victims are white. The second largest group of victims was identified as African American (25.0 percent), followed by Hispanic (14.5 percent), Native American (2.0 percent), and Asian American (1.3 percent) (U.S. Department of Health and Human Services, 2003).

Given the diversification of the United States and the involvement of ethnic minority families in the child welfare system, it is plausible that clinicians may be faced with the dilemma of how to best work with culturally diverse children and families. To understand the current climate of race, ethnicity, and cultural issues, it is important to be aware of historical events that have shaped our current views and practices regarding work with people from different ethnic and/or cultural backgrounds. Currently, a sociopolitical climate exists that promotes awareness of cultural differences. How this is translated into practice standards still remains a question. Having an understanding of significant historical events will provide a context for current practice.

HISTORICAL CONTEXT

Given the history of race relations in the United States, it is not surprising that discussing race and its related variables (e.g., ethnicity and culture) remains as controversial as ever (Sue, 1995). Historically, stereotypes and misinterpretation of data led to a view that members from ethnic minority groups were deficient in one or more important characteristics (e.g., intelligence). This *culturally deficient* model lost favor with many clinicians and researchers in favor of other models that focus on external and resilience factors such as a group's values and beliefs (Sue & Sue, 2003). In the mental health profession, awareness has increased that clinicians should competently meet the needs of ethnic minority and other culturally diverse clients (Abney, 1996; Bernal & Castro, 1994; Fontes, 1995). Because clinicians do not practice in a vacuum void of external societal influences, clinicians must also meet ethical and political responsibilities (Fontes, 1995; Yutrzenka, 1995).

In relation to the use of services, Sue's (1977) study on mental health utilization, coupled with a report by the President's Commission on Mental Health (1978), brought to the forefront issues related to U.S. ethnic minority populations underutilizing mental health services, having disproportionately high dropout rates after the first session, and not responding favorably to traditional mental health services. Due to these findings, it was suggested that *culturally responsive* services be developed and implemented with people from culturally diverse backgrounds. Almost a decade later, promising data suggested that the practices of clinicians and the mental health system as a whole were changing for the better. A study by O'Sullivan, Peterson, Cox, and Kirkeby (1989) reexamined the issues related to utilization patterns with ethnic minority groups seeking mental health services. O'Sullivan and colleagues found that culturally responsive services had made a positive impact since premature termination rates had decreased and utilization of services had increased. More recently, Sue and colleagues (e.g., Sue, Fujino, Hu, Takeuchi, & Zane, 1991) also found promising results, suggesting that a relationship exists between culturally responsive services and mental health treatment outcomes. Culturally responsive services also led to the establishment of guidelines related to assessment and treatment (American Psychological Association, 1993), the consideration of cultural factors in psychiatric diagnosis (American Psychiatric Association, 2000), and the inclusion of ethnic minority populations in research studies (National Institutes of Health, 1994).

Cultural Sensitivity and Cultural Competence

A significant movement in psychology and other mental health professions (e.g., social work, psychiatry) is the notion of offering services that are deemed *culturally sensitive* and *culturally competent*. Suggestions such as making services ethnicity-specific, hiring staff that are either of the same ethnicity as clients or bicultural, and having the therapist speak the same language as the client (e.g., Spanish) have been developed in attempts to improve cultural sensitivity and competence. Where these suggestions fall short is that they do not inform the clinician on how to provide an effective clinical response nor do they identify specific behaviors and practices that may be beneficial for the client. This ambiguity in incorporating the concepts of culture into clinical practice has led to a movement void of sufficient guidelines that have utility for the clinician. These and other issues are discussed in subsequent sections.

PROBLEMS IN STUDYING CULTURE

A host of problems arise in attempting to study or examine culture in the context of clinical practice. For one, there is conceptual confusion in assuming that culture and ethnicity are synonymous (Urquiza & Wyatt, 1994). Conceptually, *ethnicity* is used for group identity, and *culture* is the shared characteristics (e.g., behaviors, language, rituals, etc.) of that group (Dana, 1998). Unfortunately, culture is often used interchangeably with ethnicity and at times misused among mental health professionals. A logical explanation for this confusion is that when clinicians discuss culture it is usually in the context of an ethnic minority group (e.g., a cultural practice shared by Vietnamese). Erroneous assumptions can be made when we observe ethnic differences and attribute them to cultural influences. Though this might be true, the psychologically relevant cultural variable of interest fails to be identified and specified.

Another problem relates to how culture is defined. Specifically, culture is often defined as a set of different characteristics (e.g., behaviors, traditions, beliefs, values, expectations, etc.) that define a group. These characteristics are usually said to be shared by members of a specific group. Basically, it is assumed that Group X engages in Practice A. The problem with such thinking is that it is assumed that all members who fall under this category not only adhere to these practices but also adhere to that specific practice to the same extent. As can be guessed, it is a potentially dangerous practice to assume that all members of a group adhere to the same cultural practice to the same extent.

According to Betancourt and Lopez (1993), defining culture from a psychological perspective also causes problems. Though we continually reference culture and emphasize that professionals should take cultural factors into account, confusion still occurs when trying to define the construct of culture at a psychological level. Most of the time, clinicians erroneously attribute observed phenomena to ethnicity and not to a more relevant psychological variable such as a cultural practice. Difficulty arises when we study ethnicity but attribute the difference to "cultural differences" without specifying what is meant by culture and what cultural practices are being examined (Betancourt & Lopez, 1993).

More often than not, ethnicity is treated as being directly related to outcome. A more appropriate use of ethnicity is to treat it as a distal variable that works with other more proximal variables (e.g., cultural practices) that impact outcome (Alvidrez, Azocar, & Miranda, 1996). Psychologically, it might be more meaningful to measure for ethnic or cultural identity when examining ethnicity and to measure for values, norms, attitudes, and beliefs when examining culture (Phinney, 1996). Given that ethnic identity pertains to one's identification with a cultural group, gathering this information might assist clinicians in identifying factors that might explain why certain people engage in different cultural practices.

PROBLEMS WITH DEFINING CHILD MALTREATMENT IN THE CONTEXT OF CULTURE

One area where clinicians are challenged to consider both clinical and cultural issues is the field of child maltreatment. Clinicians and mental health professionals are challenged on a daily basis to balance both familial factors and the values inherent in defining child maltreatment. Numerous articles have addressed the problem of defining child maltreatment (e.g., Glachan, 1991; Kolko, 1996; Korbin, 1991, 1994; Maitra, 1996; Portwood, 1999; Rubin, 1992) and determining whether an incident falls within the realm of the definition of child abuse. Not only are clinicians required to make decisions about whether instances of behavior fall within the definition of child maltreatment but they are also faced with making the decision of whether to report an incident (Garbarino & Ebata, 1983; Van Voorhis & Gilbert, 1998). Lack of clear definitions of child maltreatment also gives rise to other questions such as the rights of children, the rights and autonomy of parents residing in the United States, and the right of authorities to intervene in the private lives of citizens. Definitions and statutes that vary by state add further confusion to an already complex situation. The problem of defining child abuse is further complicated when culture is introduced.

Although there are clear instances of child maltreatment that are reportable (e.g., a child is hit for spilling milk on the floor and is left with a bruise), many cases fall in the gray area of questionable parenting practices that leave no physical evidence of harm to the child. When one considers parental intent in the definition of child maltreatment, further definitional complications occur. For example, if the intent of a potentially harmful practice were healing, would the act be considered abusive? For example, consider whether the Southeast Asian practice of "coin rubbing" is an abusive, harmful practice. According to Rubin (1992), a number of factors may affect the decision to report an incident that falls in the gray area: societal standards of acceptable child-rearing practices, legal definitions of abuse and neglect, and an individual's own value system. As one can see, these are very subjective measures that may challenge a clinician when deciding whether to report an instance of suspected child abuse. The following section further expands on important issues to consider when examining culture in the context of child maltreatment.

CULTURAL CONSIDERATIONS

Determining an appropriate course of action may be challenging when a client has engaged in a parenting practice that is considered a crime in the

United States (e.g., physical abuse) but is acceptable in another country (e.g., striking the child on the back with a bamboo stick as a method of discipline among Southeast Asian families). Professionals working in the child maltreatment field are often faced with ethical issues when working with different child care and cultural parenting practices that might be mistaken for abuse or neglect (Dubowitz, 1997).

We speculate that for the most part, clinicians do not have clear guidelines to indicate what it means to be culturally competent in the child maltreatment field. Given this challenge, it can be assumed that there is great variability in what clinicians do and do not report regarding cases of child maltreatment involving cultural issues. To date, no models exist to guide a clinician's behavior when determining whether a parenting practice is culturally based and how best to respond. We do know, however, that a multitude of factors influence how a professional responds to a given scenario.

Variables such as the reporter's professional background (Zellman, 1992), attitudes toward the case (King, Reece, Bendel, & Patel, 1998), amount of training (King et al., 1998), knowledge of child abuse (Tilden et al., 1994), and institutional setting in which the case is seen (Gardner, Schadler, & Kemper, 1984; King et al., 1998) have been identified as strong predictors of reporting behavior. Another interesting finding is the fact that reporting behavior seems to be influenced more by profession than by actual knowledge about CPA (Tilden et al., 1994). More specifically, professional training background (e.g., social work versus medicine) was found to be more influential on reporting behavior than actual knowledge of child abuse. When examining professionals' demographic variables (e.g., age, gender, marital status, and parenthood), data have not supported the hypothesis that these variables influenced whether or not a report was made to CPS (Ashton, 1999). However, mediating variables, such as attitudes toward corporal punishment, do seem to play a role in the perception of the seriousness and likelihood of reporting a case (Ashton, 2001). Other mediating variables related to culture (e.g., degree of ethnic identity) have also been found to impact likelihood of reporting (Ibanez, Borrego, & Terao, 2003). Reporter behavior is also impacted by the degree of certainty in reporting a case (Escobar, 1995; Tilden et al., 1994), the belief that some positive effect would come of reporting a case to CPS (Escobar, 1995), and the belief that reporting may negatively impact therapy (Rubin, 1992; Tilden et al., 1994).

Many pitfalls are involved in making sound clinical decisions. When clinicians are faced with a complex problem, part of their professional responsibility is to make decisions and recommendations. How clinicians arrive at these decisions is not always clear. Literature suggests that clinicians do a poor job of integrating information that helps them make sound decisions (Garb, 1998). Further evidence suggests that racial biases occur with regard to predicting violent behavior (Garb, 1998). Another disturbing fact is that rather than testing alternative hypotheses, clinicians tend to collect information that will confirm their biases (Garb, 1998). Given this, it is safe to assume that clinicians would do a poorer job when working with people from cultures that are unfamiliar to them (Gray & Cosgrove, 1985). Thus, even though clinicians may be familiar with a particular cultural group and have knowledge of what may be collectively deemed an appropriate parenting practice, therapists must avoid attributing the practice in question solely to cultural factors.

OBLIGATION TO REPORT VERSUS RESPONSIBILITY TO RESPOND

When examining culturally based parenting practices, it is important to distinguish between reporting child maltreatment and providing an appropriate clinical response. All children, regardless of sex, race, ethnicity, or religious beliefs, should have the opportunity to be raised in an environment free of physical, sexual, and emotional abuse and neglect (Terao, Borrego, & Urquiza, 2000, 2001). Furthermore, although state statutes governing child abuse and neglect reporting vary, it is the ethical and legal responsibility of clinicians to report all instances of suspected child maltreatment. We know of no parenting practice that would supersede a clinician's legal and ethical obligation to ensure the safety of a child. Therefore, it is essential that all clinicians provide a prompt response by reporting instances of suspected child endangerment, regardless of the ethnic or cultural background of the family (Terao et al., 2000, 2001).

For the clinician faced with deciding whether to report an incident, the following simple steps can be helpful in determining a course of action. First, professionals should determine whether the child is at risk for physical, sexual, or emotional harm and/or neglect. If the answer is yes, then it is the professionals' legal (given the state statute governing child abuse reporting) and ethical responsibility to report suspected child maltreatment and harm. If the answer is no, then a report would not be made.

DECISION-MAKING MODEL FOR RESPONDING TO PHYSICAL ABUSE

The clinician's responsibility does not end once a report is made. Determining an appropriate response or recommendation for treatment becomes paramount. At this stage of the model, the cultural background of the family should be considered. The family's level of acculturation (e.g., views on parenting, language use, duration of time in the United States, ethnicity of friends, involvement in religious and cultural traditions) should be assessed. The purpose of this assessment would be to determine whether or not the family would best benefit from a psychoeducational or therapeutic response (psychosocial intervention).

Clinicians should respond differently given a parent's level of acculturation and the severity of the incident. In Figure 13.1, the upper left-hand quadrant represents parents who are highly acculturated and are considered low risk because they use acceptable parenting practices. The upper right-hand quadrant represents parents who are more acculturated but are considered high risk because they engage in parenting practices that may be harmful to their child (i.e., these parents have a working knowledge of acceptable parenting practices and know the laws regarding these practices). For these parents, a psychosocial intervention would be appropriate. As an example, the family may benefit from a treatment modality that focuses on discipline skills training.

The bottom left-hand quadrant represents parents who have a low level of acculturation and engage in parenting practices that are not harmful to their child. Lastly, the bottom right-hand quadrant represents parents who have a low level of acculturation and are engaging in dangerous or harmful parenting practices. These parents may not have a working knowledge of acceptable parenting practices in the United States and may be engaging in practices that are normative to their culture. If clients have minimal knowl-

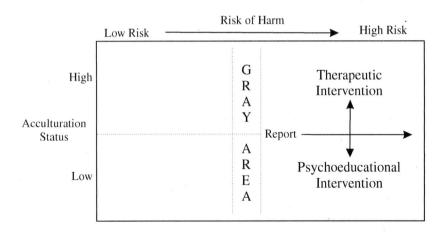

FIGURE 13.1. Risk of Harm and Acculturation Status

edge of acceptable laws and child-rearing practices in the United States, then a psychoeducational response is recommended. This program should be offered in the client's preferred language and should include an emphasis on acceptable methods of discipline and parenting. Resources would be made available to the parent as well. Once the basic psychoeducational treatment component is completed, the clinician can proceed to introduce a psychosocial intervention if it is deemed appropriate.

This model of examining parent behavior and level of acculturation can be applied to different groups, is not culture specific, and can potentially assist professionals with determining an appropriate clinical response to incidents of questionable cultural parenting practices. Assessing for acculturation is important because the process of acculturation can have a profound impact on a person's behavior, values, attitudes, and beliefs regarding parenting practices.

Though we suggest a psychoeducational focus for less acculturated parents and a psychotherapeutic approach for highly acculturated parents as a starting point for treatment, in some cases a parent may benefit from both treatment approaches. This may occur when a parent is engaging in culturally prescribed practices and has a substance abuse problem. A psychoeducational approach may be effective in educating parents regarding appropriate discipline methods and therapy may be useful in treating substance abuse problems and other psychological problems. The bidirectional relationship between these approaches suggests that the parent may benefit at some point from both types of treatments.

CLINICAL RECOMMENDATIONS

To date, a review of the literature suggests that no single approach to the assessment of ethnic minority families in the context of child maltreatment is consistently reliable and valid. Given the paucity of research and clinical guidelines, we offer some information that should be of use to clinicians working with culturally diverse clients. Given the relatively limited data available, we advocate for a multimethod and multi-informant assessment approach with ethnic minority families. This approach requires clinicians to gather information from different methods (e.g., clinical interviews, paper-and-pencil measures, and behavioral observations) and from multiple sources (e.g., parents, children, other family members, teachers, and people from the family's community) to ensure the accuracy of the assessment and to assist in offering a treatment that would meet the family's needs.

One strategy in providing culturally appropriate mental health services is to address issues related to social (i.e., ecological) validity (Wolf, 1978).

According to Wolf, the three components of social validity can be addressed separately. The first component pertains to the social significance of the goals (e.g., if mental health practitioners were to identify treatment goals, would the family agree on the same treatment goals?). The second component addresses the social appropriateness of the procedures implemented (e.g., would the family consider a specific treatment acceptable?). The third component focuses on the social importance of the outcome (is the family satisfied with the treatment provided?). Assessing for all three components will add to the cultural appropriateness of the services offered to culturally diverse populations.

It is important for clinicians to consider that, irrespective of a person's ethnic background, the professional must remain cognizant of the referral question and presenting problems. Was a family referred because of "excessive" discipline strategies (e.g., using a belt)? For example, suppose a clinician receives a referral for an African-American family that uses excessive discipline. The family claims that they do not see it as abusive because "that is the way our parents disciplined us." It is rather easy to dismiss such potentially abusive behaviors (e.g., using excessive force) in the context of a cultural practice.

As mentioned previously, clinicians have been found to minimize pathology if the practice is assumed to be culturally based (Lopez, 1989). To help guard against this bias, clinicians should ask their clients the context in which the incident occurred (e.g., child noncompliance, child brought home low grades), the topography of the behavior in question (e.g., what the parent did—use a belt, a fist, etc.), and the function of the behavior (e.g., what the parents intended to do—attempting to discipline the child, taking their frustrations out on the child, etc.). Though parents may be poor historians, the clinical interview remains the most readily available assessment tool for clinicians.

Clinicians should assess for both the frequency and duration of the parenting practice in question. Is this a new parenting practice that was acquired or has it been in the family for years? This information would assist the clinician in determining whether the parenting practice is culturally based. Mental health practitioners should be aware of the fact that because of family differences, it would be erroneous to assume that a family practice is the same as a cultural practice. Along these same lines, it is also important to gather information from other informants that might contribute to the assessment process. As an example, clinicians might want to interview close family or community members (e.g., clergy and teachers) who have contact with the family and who have observed the parent-child interactions in question.

During the interview phase, clinicians should also gather a detailed family and social history in relation to the presenting problem. If the referral is made to address excessive punishment, it would be important to gather information related to the family's attitudes toward discipline and the customs of their culture. More important, clinicians should assess for the parents' expectations for the child. Gathering information related to the family's beliefs and attitudes surrounding discipline, how they handle different discipline situations (e.g., noncompliance, being disrespectful to family members, low grades), and what they consider acceptable and unacceptable behaviors should provide very useful information for the clinician. In conjunction with identifying risk factors, a detailed assessment should also include the identification of resilience or protective factors (e.g., extended family) that the clinician might use throughout therapy.

Clinicians may also benefit from using standardized measures to assess parent discipline strategies and child behavior problems (e.g., using a behavior checklist). An assessment of child behavior problems is important since the literature suggests that most physical abuse occurs in the context of discipline (Trickett & Kuczynski, 1986; Wolfe, 1987). This becomes more difficult when working with parents who are not fluent in English. If an instrument has sound psychometric properties (e.g., reliability, discriminant validity), clinicians could use these measures to screen for potentially clinically relevant information that could be used for future hypothesis testing. Caution should be used, though, when interpreting the results since some instruments do not have normative data for ethnic groups.

The final assessment component involves using behavioral observations in assessing parent-child interactions. Behavioral observations offer a wealth of clinical information that cannot be accessed through clinical interviews and psychological instruments. The purpose of these behavioral observations would be to assess a family's strengths and weaknesses related to parent-child interactions. As previously stated, caution should be used in assuming that a deficit in one group or family would be the same in another family. This form of observer bias can lead to erroneous assumptions and conclusions about parent-child and family interactions. More than anything, these behavioral observations should be used to assess the family's strengths (e.g., family cohesion). These parent-child and family interactions can be conducted in unstructured (e.g., natural setting at home) or structured (e.g., in the clinic performing specific tasks) settings. Both assessment strategies have advantages and can add context to the understanding of current family functioning and overall patterns of interaction. Behavioral observations should provide the clinicians with specific information related to the presenting problem. As an example, if the family presents for therapy due to excessive use of discipline, the observations should include scenarios related to that specific issue. Whether conducted in a clinic or home setting, these observations contribute to the ecological validity of the assessment.

Although the use of clinical interviews, paper-and-pencil measures, and behavioral observations should give practitioners adequate information to make an informed decision regarding clinical interventions, there will still be times when information gathered is inconsistent within and across individuals. As discussed earlier, parents might either deliberately provide false information or refuse to provide any information at all. In such situations, it is important to consult with other people involved in the family's life to obtain valid and reliable information. Also, the information obtained through questionnaires and rating scales may not be valid due to social desirability issues (i.e., parents want to present themselves in a positive light) or problems with understanding the questions or format of the instrument. Under these conditions, it is best to review the questionnaire with the family in detail.

In summary, although we currently lack standardized techniques for assessing the effects of culture on different parenting practices, we advocate a multimethod and multi-informant approach when working with families from culturally diverse families. Due to the paucity of relevant research and clinical information, our approach is "the more, the better" when gathering information. Gathering information from only one source is not sufficient to make an accurate analysis of the presenting problem. Multiple assessment information (e.g., interviews, paper-and-pencil measures, and observations) should be gathered from different informants for a better understanding of different family practices that may be culturally based. Finally, clinicians need to be aware of obtaining true informed consent (e.g., the culturally different client gives consent after gaining a full understanding of procedures and does so under no conditions of coercion).

CONCLUSION

We hope that this chapter has been helpful in addressing issues related to working with ethnic minority populations, and more specifically, with those involved in the child welfare system. Part of our task is to elucidate the issues related to cultural factors in the context of child maltreatment. More specifically, we propose a model to provide clinicians with useful guidelines when working with populations who engage in different and unfamiliar cultural parenting practices. The proposed model is only meant to provide some direction in how to proceed therapeutically.

As discussed, it is important for clinicians to consider cultural factors (e.g., acculturation, attitudes toward different cultural practices) when working with ethnic minority populations in the child welfare system. Determining a person's acculturation level has clinical implications for selecting the appropriate therapeutic response. For ethnic populations who are less acculturated and not as familiar with mainstream practices and laws, a psychoeducational approach should initially be taken. Using a psychoeducational approach would help the parent and family become oriented to the expectations and goals of therapy and would also allow the clinician to provide information concerning child welfare laws regarding what constitutes potentially harmful parenting practices.

Finally, as our society becomes increasingly ethnically diverse, there is an increasing challenge for clinicians to provide culturally appropriate services in the child welfare system. One method of accomplishing this goal is through providing services that are seen as socially (i.e., ecologically) valid by the family. As mentioned earlier, attending to the social appropriateness of the therapeutic goals, measuring the family's level of acceptance regarding the intervention (i.e., treatment acceptability), and assessing for their level of satisfaction with the process and outcome of the services (i.e., consumer satisfaction) could assist clinicians in building an effective working relationship. In addition, clinicians should ensure that the family finds value in the proposed service and agrees with the intervention being implemented. Addressing these two components should lead to increased acceptance of services being provided and to better-defined services for ethnic minority families in the child welfare system.

REFERENCES

Abney, V. D. (1996). Cultural competency in the field of child maltreatment. In J. Briere, L. Berliner, J. A. Bulkley, C. Jenny, & T. Reid (Eds.), *The APSAC handbook on child maltreatment* (pp. 409-419). Thousand Oaks, CA: Sage.

Alvidrez, J., Azocar, F., & Miranda, J. (1996). Demystifying the concept of ethnicity for psychotherapy researchers. *Journal of Consulting and Clinical Psychology, 64 (5),* 903-908.

American Psychiatric Association (2000). *Diagnostic and statistical manual of mental disorders* (4th ed., text revision). Washington, DC: American Psychiatric Association Press.

American Psychological Association. (1993). Guidelines for providers of psychological services to ethnic, linguistic, and culturally diverse populations. *American Psychologist, 48,* 45-48.

Ashton, V. (1999). Worker judgments of seriousness about and reporting of suspected child maltreatment. *Child Abuse and Neglect, 23 (6),* 539-548.

Ashton, V. (2001). The relationship between attitudes toward corporal punishment and the perception and reporting of child maltreatment. *Child Abuse and Neglect, 25,* 389-399.

Bernal, M. E., & Castro, F. G. (1994). Are clinical psychologists prepared for service and research with ethnic minorities? *American Psychologist, 49,* 797-805.

Betancourt, H., & Lopez, S. R. (1993). The study of culture, ethnicity, and race in American psychology. *American Psychologist, 48,* 629-637.

Dana, R. H. (1998). *Understanding cultural identity in intervention and assessment.* Thousand Oaks, CA: Sage.

Dubowitz, H. (1997). Ethical issues in professionals' response to child maltreatment. *Child Maltreatment, 2 (4),* 348-355.

Escobar, S. F. (1995). A study of factors influencing child abuse reporting by mental health professionals. *Dissertation Abstracts International, 56,* 5-8.

Fontes, L. A. (1995). Culturally informed interventions for sexual child abuse. In L. A. Fontes (Ed.), *Sexual abuse in nine North American cultures: Treatment and prevention* (pp. 259-266). Thousand Oaks, CA: Sage.

Garb, H. N. (1998). *Studying the clinician: Judgment research and psychological assessment.* Washington, DC: American Psychological Association.

Garbarino, J., & Ebata, A. (1983). The significance of ethnic and cultural differences in child maltreatment. *Journal of Marriage and the Family, 45,* 773-783.

Gardner, G. M., Schadler, M., & Kemper, S. (1984). Classification strategies used by mandated reporters in judging incidents of child abuse. *Journal of Clinical Child Psychology, 13 (3),* 280-287.

Glachan, M. (1991). Child abuse: A social and cultural phenomenon. *Early Child Development and Care, 74,* 95-102.

Gray, E., & Cosgrove, J. (1985). Ethnocentric perception of childrearing practices in protective services. *Child Abuse and Neglect, 9 (3),* 389-396.

Ibanez, E. S., Borrego, J., Jr., & Terao, S. Y. (2003). Cultural factors in child physical abuse decision-making: Identifying reporter characteristics influencing reporting tendencies. Manuscript under review.

King, G., Reece, R., Bendel, R., & Patel, V. (1998). The effects of sociodemographic variables, training, and attitudes on the lifetime reporting practices of mandated reporters. *Child Maltreatment, 3 (3),* 276-283.

Kolko, D. J. (1996). Child physical abuse. In J. Briere, L. Berliner, J. A. Bulkley, C. Jenny, & T. Reid (Eds.), *The APSAC handbook on child maltreatment* (pp. 21-50). Thousand Oaks, CA: Sage.

Korbin, J. E. (1991). Cross cultural perspectives and research directions for the 21st century. *Child Abuse and Neglect, 15 (1),* 67-77.

Korbin, J. E. (1994). Sociocultural factors in child maltreatment. In G. B. Melton & F. D. Barry (Eds.), *Protecting children from abuse and neglect: Foundations for a new strategy* (pp. 182-223). New York: Guilford.

Lopez, S. R. (1989). Patient variable biases in clinical judgment: Conceptual overview and methodological considerations. *Psychological Bulletin, 106 (2),* 184-203.

Maitra, B. (1996). Child abuse: A universal "diagnostic" category? The implication of culture and definition and assessment. *International Journal of Social Psychology, 42 (4),* 287-304.

National Institutes of Health (NIH) (1994). *Guidelines on the inclusion of women and minorities as subjects in clinical research* (Document no. 94-5435). Bethesda, MD: NIH Office of Extramural Research.

O'Sullivan, M. J., Peterson, P. D., Cox, G. B., & Kirkeby, J. (1989). Ethnic populations: Community mental health services ten years later. *American Journal of Community Psychology, 17,* 17-30.

Phinney, J. S. (1996). When we talk about American ethnic groups, what do we mean? *American Psychologist, 51 (9),* 918-927.

Portwood, S. G. (1999). Coming to terms with a consensual definition of child maltreatment. *Child Maltreatment, 4 (1),* 56-68.

President's Commission on Mental Health (1978). *Report to the president* (4 vols.). Washington, DC: U.S. Government Printing Office.

Rubin, G. B. (1992). Multicultural considerations in the application of child protection laws. *Journal of Social Distress and the Homeless, 1 (3/4),* 249-271.

Sue, D. W., & Sue, D. (2003). *Counseling the culturally different* (4th ed.). New York: John Wiley & Sons.

Sue, S. (1977). Community mental health services to minority groups: Some optimism, some pessimism. *American Psychologist, 32,* 616-624.

Sue, S. (1995). The implications of diversity for scientific standards of practice. In S. C. Hayes, V. M. Follette, R. M. Dawes, & K. E. Grady (Eds.), *Scientific standards of psychological practice: Issues and recommendations* (pp. 265-279). Reno, NV: Context Press.

Sue, S., Fujino, D. C., Hu, L., Takeuchi, D. T., & Zane, N. W. S. (1991). Community mental health services for ethnic minority groups: A test of the cultural responsiveness hypothesis. *Journal of Consulting and Clinical Psychology, 59,* 533-540.

Terao, S. Y., Borrego, J., Jr., & Urquiza, A. J. (2000). How do I differentiate culturally based parenting practice from child maltreatment? In H. Dubowitz & D. DePanfilis (Eds.), *Handbook for child protection practice* (pp. 97-100). Thousand Oaks, CA: Sage.

Terao, S. Y., Borrego, J., Jr., & Urquiza, A. J. (2001). A reporting and response model for culture and child maltreatment. *Child Maltreatment 6 (2),* 158-168.

Tilden, V. P., Schmidt, T. A., Limandri, B. J., Chiodo, G. T., Garland, M. J., & Loveless, P. A. (1994). Factors that influence clinicians' assessment and management of family violence. *American Journal of Public Health, 84 (4),* 628-633.

Trickett, P. K., & Kuczynski, L. (1986). Children's misbehaviors and parental discipline strategies in abusive and nonabusive families. *Developmental Psychology, 22,* 115-123.

Urquiza, A. J., & Wyatt, G. (1994). Culturally relevant violence research with children of color. *The APSAC Advisor, 7,* 16-20.

U.S. Census Bureau (2000). State and county quick facts. Retrieved March 30, 2004 from http://quickfacts.census.gov/qfd/states/00000.html.

U.S. Department of Health and Human Services, Administration on Children, Youth and Families (2002). *Eleven years of reporting child maltreatment 2000.* Washington, DC: U.S. Government Printing Office.

U.S. Department of Health and Human Services, Administration on Children, Youth and Families (2003). *Child maltreatment 2001.* Washington, DC: U.S. Government Printing Office.

Van Voorhis, R. A., & Gilbert, N. (1998). The structure and performance of child abuse reporting systems. *Children and Youth Services Review, 20 (3),* 207-221.

Wolf, M. (1978). Social validity: The case for subjective measurement: How applied behavior analysis is finding its heart. *Journal of Applied Behavior Analysis, 11,* 203-214.

Wolfe, D. A. (1987). *Child abuse: Implications for child development and psychopathology.* Newbury Park, CA: Sage.

Yutrzenka, B. A. (1995). Making a case for training in ethnic and cultural diversity in increasing treatment efficacy. *Journal of Consulting and Clinical Psychology, 63,* 197-206.

Zellman, G. L. (1992). The impact of case characteristics on child abuse reporting decisions. *Child Abuse and Neglect, 16,* 57-74.

Zellman, G. L., & Bell, R. M. (1990). *The role of professional background, case characteristics, and child protective agency response in mandated child abuse reporting.* Santa Monica, CA: Rand Corporation.

Chapter 14

Legal Issues for Mental Health Professionals Treating Victims of Child Sexual Abuse

John E. B. Myers

Mental health professionals play a key role in protecting and treating sexually abused children. This chapter addresses the impact of law on mental health practice with sexually abused children. Of course, the law varies slightly from state to state, and professionals need to familiarize themselves with the law of their state.

INFORMED CONSENT

Informed consent is a legal and ethical requirement for treatment (Myers, 2001, 2002). Thus, the code of conduct of the American Psychological Association (1992) provides, "Psychologists obtain appropriate informed consent to therapy or related procedures" (Principle 4.02a). Similarly, the code of ethics of the National Association of Social Workers (1999) states, "Social workers should provide services to clients only in the context of a professional relationship based, when appropriate, on valid informed consent" (Standard 1.03a). Failure to obtain informed consent can constitute malpractice (*Cobbs v. Grant,* 1972; Smith, 1986). Consent should be obtained at the outset of treatment. During treatment, it may be necessary to revisit consent if conditions change. In genuine emergencies, treatment may be given without informed consent (Behnke, Preis, & Bates, 1998).

In addition to obtaining informed consent, therapists are encouraged to provide information regarding the therapist's education, training, and professional orientation (Behnke et al., 1998; *California Business and Professions Code,* 2003, § 4980.55).

Elements of Informed Consent

The elements of informed consent are as follows.

Voluntary

Consent must be voluntary. Consent is only voluntary if it is informed. Consent is unlikely to be informed when the consent process is viewed as a necessary evil to be dispensed with as quickly as possible. Reid (1999) writes, "When you get a formal consent, be sure it isn't merely a *pro forma* experience" (p. 64).

Purpose of Treatment

The client should be informed of the purpose of proposed treatment. It is not necessary to give the client a detailed treatment plan. Reid (1999) observes that "[r]eviewing a detailed treatment plan with the patient is generally unnecessary unless the therapy carries unusual risk or controversy" (p. 27).

Limits on Treatment

Financial or other limits on treatment should be discussed. The code of ethics of the National Association of Social Workers (1999) provides that clients should be informed of "limits to services because of the requirements of a third-party payer" (Standard 1.03a).

Length of Treatment

Inform the client of the approximate time frame of treatment. The client should understand that consent given at the beginning of treatment extends throughout therapy, unless circumstances change.

Right to Refuse and Withdraw Consent

An adult should be informed of the right to refuse consent. In addition, the client should be informed of the right to withdraw consent and terminate treatment. Children generally lack the authority to terminate treatment. However, in circumstances for which children have authority to consent to treatment (see Consent of Children to Certain Treatment), they also have the right to decline care or withdraw.

When a client is court-ordered into treatment, the client should be informed of the possible legal consequences of refusing or withdrawing from treatment. When a court-ordered client balks at treatment, it may be a good idea to advise the client to consult an attorney about possible legal consequences. Needless to say, a therapist should not give legal advice.

Risks

Inform the client of the risks of proposed treatment. It is not necessary to disclose every conceivable risk. Inconsequential risks—especially minor risks that rarely occur—do not have to be disclosed. In the context of medical treatment, the California Supreme Court wrote in *Cobbs v. Grant* (1972) that "the patient's interest in information does not extend to a lengthy polysyllabic discourse on all possible complications. A mini-course in medical science is not required; the patient is concerned with the risk of death or bodily harm, and problems of recuperation" (p. 244). Discussing mental health treatment, Reid (1999) writes that

> when speaking of adverse effects of a treatment, for example, problems that are fairly rare but very dangerous should be included; those that are very common but benign should probably be mentioned; but those that are both rare and benign may be omitted. (p. 77)

Hypnosis may adversely impact a client's ability to testify as a witness. With clients who may need to testify, consider the legal implications of hypnosis. In addition to hypnosis, techniques such the use of as sodium amytal may impact a client's testimony.

A therapist using experimental or controversial techniques should inform the client.

Naturally, psychiatrists and psychologists prescribing drugs adhere to consent procedures regarding medication.

Benefits

Discuss likely benefits of treatment.

Alternatives

Discuss alternatives to proposed treatment, including no treatment.

Limits of Confidentiality

"Unless it is not feasible or is contraindicated, the discussion of confidentiality occurs at the outset of the relationship and thereafter as new circumstances may warrant" (American Psychological Association, 1992, Standard 5.01b). The client is informed of foreseeable limits on confidentiality. The child abuse reporting law, for example, overrides confidentiality. The Committee on Professional Practice and Standards of the American Psychological Association (1995) notes that "[i]t is advisable at the outset of treatment to inform your clients that the usual rule concerning confidentiality does not apply when the duty to report child abuse arises" (p. 378).

Kremer and Gesten (1998) provide a useful approach to dealing with confidentiality in managed care:

> To ensure ethical practice under managed care, psychologists may be required to take extra steps to see that their clients are fully informed of confidentiality limits and of treatment limitations. The psychologist should be an active, but transparent, participant between the client and the managed care organization, neither hiding nor promoting requirements and restrictions. This permits managed care practices to be properly attributed to the oversight organization, rather than the psychologist, and allows clients to make informed decisions about disclosure. (p. 557)

The specific recommendations these authors propose can be summarized as follows:

1. In the first meeting, clients and therapists should engage in a discussion regarding information requirements and utilization review practices as they relate to therapy.
2. Therapists should actively question clients about these practices and requirements to help them gain a better understanding of same.
3. All paperwork related to therapy should be carefully reviewed with the client before signing.
4. Clients must be informed about the potential repercussions arising from disclosure of personal information.
5. Providers should be judicious in documentation, recording only what is necessary to secure adequate services for the client.
6. Providers should spend time working to change managed care practices that interfere with the delivery of appropriate services.
7. Carefully document conversations, letters, messages, etc., with utilization reviewers.

Fee

The client should be informed of the therapist's fee.

Status As Trainee or Supervisee

The client should be informed if the professional is a student, intern, trainee, or supervisee (American Psychological Association, 1992, Standard 4.01b).

Opportunity to Ask Questions

Encourage the client to ask questions about the consent process.

Withholding Information from a Client

In rare cases, a therapist may believe full disclosure of risks could frighten a fragile person into refusing much-needed care. Reid (1999) addresses this concern, writing that

> [u]nder special circumstances, it is permissible to keep information about adverse effects from a patient, for example, when a doctor believes a treatment is very important and the risk-benefit ratio is very favorable, but the patient would be so frightened by the discussion that he or she would not be able to judge the potential benefit rationally. Although this situation is not uncommon in severely and chronically mentally ill patients (for example, those who require antidepressants, electroconvulsive therapy, or antipsychotic drugs to alleviate morbid depression or psychosis), nonmedical psychotherapists should only rarely consider depriving the patient of information about adverse effects. (pp. 27-28)

Video or Audio Recording

Consent should be obtained to audiotape or videotape treatment sessions. Thus, the American Psychological Association (1992) code of conduct states, "Permission for electronic recording of interviews is secured from clients and patients" (Standard 5.01c; see also Standard 1.8; National Association of Social Workers, 1999, Standard 1.03f).

Informed Consent for Children

A "child" or "minor" is anyone under age eighteen. Children are legally incapable of consenting to most medical and mental health treatment (Berner, 1998a). Thus, informed consent is normally obtained from one or both parents (Brant & Brant, 1998). A parent's right to consent to treatment for a child derives from the parent's right to legal custody of the child. Generally, both parents have legal custody, and both have the right to consent to treatment for their child.

Never-married parents. Parents who never married share legal custody, unless, of course, a judge has altered the normal custodial arrangement by awarding custody to one of the parents. Assuming no custody decision from a judge, the consent of one never-married parent is usually sufficient for treatment.

Married parents. Married parents share legal custody, and each parent has authority to consent to treatment for their child. Generally, the consent of one married parent is sufficient.

Divorced parents. When parents divorce, the divorce decree determines whether they have joint custody, sole custody, or some other custodial arrangement. When divorced parents have joint custody, they generally share parenting responsibilities including decisions about treatment for their children. When the divorce decree gives one parent sole custody, that parent almost certainly has authority to consent to treatment, although the noncustodial parent may also have authority.

With divorced parents, the therapist should determine who has authority to consent for the child. If both parents consent, there is no problem. If only one divorced parent requests treatment, make sure the requesting parent has authority to consent. If in doubt, especially if divorced parents disagree about therapy, it may be necessary to examine the divorce decree, speak to the parents' lawyers, speak to your own lawyer, decline treatment, or try to help the parents reconcile their differences regarding treatment.

Married parents who are separated or divorcing. Occasionally, married parents who are separated obtain a formal legal separation, which is a court order made by a judge. Among other things, a formal legal separation determines child custody. The vast majority of separated parents, however, do not obtain a formal legal separation. Separated but married parents generally share custody and authority to consent to treatment.

Some but not all parents in the process of divorce obtain a temporary court order regarding child custody. Such temporary orders can affect who has authority to consent to treatment. Absent such an order, both parents generally have authority to consent to treatment.

With separated and divorcing parents, the professional should clarify who has authority to consent to care for the couple's children.

Who consents for abused and neglected children under authority of the juvenile court? The fact that a child is involved with the juvenile court does not necessarily mean the parents lose the right to consent to medical or psychological care. Moreover, a child's involvement with juvenile court does not automatically bestow consent authority on social workers, foster parents, or relatives other than parents. The law on this point varies from place to place. Prior to beginning therapy, the professional may wish to obtain copies of juvenile court orders regarding the child's care and custody. In some cases (e.g., parents unable or unwilling to consent; parental involvement in consent is contraindicated), it may be necessary to seek a juvenile court order authorizing a social worker or other appropriate adult to consent to the child's treatment.

Guardian. When a child has no parent willing or able to care for the child, a judge may appoint a guardian. A child's guardian may consent to medical or mental health treatment. Formal, court-approved guardianship is uncommon. Children whose parents are divorced do not need a guardian because one or both parents have legal custody of the child. Generally, children under the authority of the juvenile court do not have a formal, court-appointed guardian.

Guardian ad litem. The term "guardian ad litem" has two meanings. First, children cannot start civil lawsuits or be sued in their own name. Thus, when a child is sued or starts a lawsuit, the court appoints a guardian ad litem to pursue or defend the litigation on the child's behalf. Second, a juvenile court judge may appoint a guardian ad litem for an abused or neglected child. A guardian ad litem for an abused or neglected child is not a guardian as described in the preceding paragraph. In most states, a guardian ad litem does not have authority to consent to treatment unless the judge specifically gives that authority to the guardian ad litem.

Consent of Children to Certain Treatment

The law of every state allows adolescents to consent to certain treatment related to sexual assault, birth control, pregnancy, and communicable disease. In addition, numerous states allow adolescents to consent to certain forms of mental health care. When an adolescent is authorized by law to consent, parental consent is unnecessary. Some states (e.g., California) require parents to be notified of treatment unless the professional determines parental notification would be inappropriate. Professionals may wish to document whether and when attempts are made to contact parents. If parents are not contacted, it is useful to document why. Generally, a parent is not responsible to pay for treatment unless the parent is notified.

Emancipation

The law allows minors above a certain age to seek a court order emancipating them. An emancipated minor may consent to medical and mental health care.

The Mature Minor Doctrine

In some states, a judge may rule that a sufficiently mature minor may consent to or refuse to consent to treatment.

Informed Consent for Forensic Evaluation

Is informed consent required for purely forensic evaluation, for which treatment is not provided? Because the principle of informed consent is based on respect for autonomy, the answer should normally be yes. In certain court-ordered evaluations, however, informed consent may not be necessary. Even in court-ordered cases, professionals are encouraged to inform clients of the nature of services to be provided, and, where possible, to obtain informed consent. The American Academy of Psychiatry and the Law's (1995) Ethical Guidelines for the Practice of Forensic Psychiatry provide that "[t]he informed consent of the subject of a forensic evaluation is obtained when possible. Where consent is not required, notice is given to the evaluee of the nature of the evaluation" (Guideline III). Along similar lines, the American Psychological Association's (1991) Specialty Guidelines for Forensic Psychologists provide:

> Forensic psychologists have an obligation to ensure that prospective clients are informed of their rights with respect to the anticipated forensic service, of the purposes of any evaluation, of the nature of procedures to be employed, of the intended uses of any product of their services, and of the party who has employed the forensic psychologist. Unless court ordered, forensic psychologists obtain informed consent of the client or party, or their legal representative, before proceeding with such evaluations and procedures. (Guideline IV.E)

The American Psychological Association's (1994) Guidelines for Child Custody Evaluations in Divorce Proceedings specifically state that "[t]he psychologist obtains informed consent from all adult participants and, as appropriate, informs child participants" (Guideline III, paragraph 9).

FORENSIC IMPLICATIONS OF CHILDREN'S STATEMENTS DURING THERAPY

Children sometimes disclose abuse during therapy. The therapeutic importance of children's disclosures is described elsewhere in this book. In addition to clinical significance, children's statements describing abuse are legally relevant.

Children's statements describing abuse may be admissible as evidence in legal proceedings. Indeed, in some cases, the child's statements during therapy are the most compelling evidence of abuse. Suppose, for example, that four-year-old Beth points to her genital area and says, "Daddy put his pee-pee in me down there. Then he took it out and shook it up and down until white stuff came out." Beth's words are compelling evidence of abuse. If criminal proceedings are brought against Beth's father, the prosecutor is likely to call the therapist as a witness and ask the therapist to repeat Beth's words, and to describe her pointing gesture. When the prosecutor asks the therapist to repeat Beth's words, however, the father's defense attorney will object that Beth's words (and gesture) are hearsay. Hearsay is inadmissible in criminal and civil litigation unless the particular hearsay statement meets the requirements of an exception to the rule against hearsay.

To determine whether Beth's description of abuse is hearsay, analyze Beth's words under the following definition. A child's words are hearsay when: (1) the child intended to describe something that happened (e.g., abuse); (2) the child spoke prior to the court proceeding at which the child's words are repeated; and (3) the child's words are repeated in court to prove that what the child said actually happened. Under this definition, Beth's words are hearsay. Beth intended to describe something that happened. Beth spoke prior to the proceeding where the therapist repeats Beth's words. Finally, Beth's words are offered to prove that what Beth said actually happened.

Beth's words are not the only hearsay. Her gesture pointing to her genital area is also hearsay. The gesture was nonverbal communication intended by Beth to describe the abuse.

The judge will sustain the defense attorney's hearsay objection unless the prosecutor persuades the judge that Beth's words and gesture meet the requirements of an exception to the rule against hearsay. In this case, as in many other child abuse cases, the prosecutor's ability to convince the judge that the child's hearsay meets the requirements of an exception depends as much on the documentation of the therapist as on the legal acumen of the prosecutor. If the therapist knew what to document when Beth disclosed, the prosecutor has a much better chance of persuading the judge to allow the therapist to repeat Beth's powerful hearsay statement. Therapists should document the child's exact words. Do not paraphrase. In addition, document the questions that elicited the child's statement.

Most states have an exception to the hearsay rule for certain statements to therapists. The "treatment exception" applies when the child's statement is pertinent to treatment and the child understands the clinical reason to tell the truth. Therapists should discuss with the child the importance of providing accurate information and being completely forthcoming. The therapist might say, "When we talk about these things, it's important for you to tell me only things that really happened. Don't pretend or make things up. Part of my job is talking to children and helping them. The things you tell me help me do my job, so it is very important for you to tell me things that really happened; things that are true. Will you do that for me?"

If the child identifies the perpetrator, the professional should document why knowing the identity of the perpetrator is pertinent to treatment.

Many states have a hearsay exception that allows any reliable hearsay to be repeated in court. When a child's hearsay is offered under such an exception, the most important question is whether the statement is reliable. Professionals should document the following information:

1. *Spontaneity.* The more spontaneous a child's statement, the more likely a judge will find it reliable.
2. *Statements elicited by questioning.* The reliability of a child's statement may be influenced by the type of questions asked. When questions are suggestive or leading, the possibility increases that the questioner influenced the child's statement. It should be noted, however, suggestive questions are sometimes necessary to elicit information from children, particularly when the information is embarrassing.
3. *Consistent statements.* Reliability may be increased if the child's description of abuse is consistent over time. Consistency regarding core details is most important. Consistency regarding peripheral details is less important.
4. *Child's affect and emotion when hearsay statement is made.* When a child's emotions are consistent with the child's statement, the reliability of the statement may be enhanced.
5. *Play or gestures that corroborate the child's hearsay statement.* The play or gestures of a child may strengthen confidence in the child's

statement. For example, a child's use of dolls may support the reliability of the child's statement.

6. *Developmentally unusual sexual knowledge.* A young child's developmentally unusual knowledge of sexual acts or anatomy supports the reliability of the child's statement.

7. *Idiosyncratic detail.* Presence in a child's statement of idiosyncratic details of sexual acts (smells, tastes) points toward reliability.

8. *Child's belief that disclosure might lead to punishment of the child.* Children hesitate to make statements they believe may get them in trouble. If a child believed disclosing abuse could result in punishment, but the child disclosed anyway, confidence in the child's statement may increase.

9. *Child's or adult's motive to fabricate.* Evidence that the child or an adult had or lacked a motive to fabricate allegations of abuse impacts reliability.

10. *Medical evidence of abuse.* The child's statement may be corroborated by medical evidence.

11. *Changes in child's behavior.* When a child's behavior alters in a way that corroborates the child's description of abuse, it may be appropriate to place increased confidence in the child's statement.

Judges consider the totality of the circumstances to evaluate reliability, and professionals can assist the legal system by documenting anything that indicates the child was or was not telling the truth when describing abuse.

CONFIDENTIALITY AND PRIVILEGE

Confidentiality arises from three sources: (1) the ethical duty to protect confidential information; (2) laws that make records confidential; and (3) privileges that apply in legal proceedings.

1. *Ethical duty to safeguard confidential information.* Ethical principles of psychology, social work, psychiatry, and related disciplines require professionals to safeguard confidential information. Thus, the American Psychological Association's (1992) code of conduct provides that "psychologists have a primary obligation to take reasonable precautions to respect the confidentiality rights of those with whom they work or consult" (Standard 5.02). The code of ethics of the National Association of Social Workers (1999) provides that "social workers should protect the confidentiality of all information in the course of

professional services, except for compelling professional reasons" (Standard 1.07c).

2. *Laws that make patient records confidential.* Every state has laws that make certain records confidential. Some of the laws pertain to records compiled by government agencies, such as child protective services, schools, and the juvenile court. Other laws govern records created by professionals in private practice.

3. *Privileged communications.* In legal proceedings, confidential communications between clients and certain professionals are protected from disclosure by laws called privileges. The most well-known privileges are the psychotherapist-client privilege, the physician-patient privilege, and the attorney-client privilege.

Privileges such as the psychotherapist-client privilege apply to confidential communications between children and their therapists. Unlike the ethical obligation to protect confidential information, which applies in all settings, privileges apply only in legal proceedings. For example, a privilege applies when a professional testifies in court and is asked to reveal privileged information. Privileges also apply during legal proceedings outside the courtroom, including pretrial depositions. If questions are asked during a deposition that call for privileged information, the professional or one of the attorneys should raise the privilege issue.

Communication between a client and a professional is privileged when three requirements are fulfilled. First, the communication must be between a client and a professional with whom privileged communication is possible. All states have some form of psychotherapist-client privilege. Not all psychotherapists are covered by the privilege, however. If a client communicates with a psychotherapist who is not covered by privilege law, no privilege applies. (A privilege may apply if a therapist who is not covered by the privilege is working under the supervision of a therapist who is covered by the privilege.) Of course, the fact that a privilege does not apply does nothing to undermine the therapist's ethical duty to protect confidential information.

In legal proceedings, the presence of a privilege is important. In court, a professional may have to answer questions that require disclosure of information the professional is ethically bound to protect. By contrast, the professional generally does not have to answer questions that require disclosure of privileged information. Thus, in legal proceedings, privileges give greater protection to confidentiality, protection that is not available under the ethical duty to protect confidential information.

The second requirement for a privilege to apply is that the client must seek professional services. The client must consult the professional to obtain advice or therapy. If the client enters therapy, the privilege applies to confidential communications leading up to and during therapy. If the client does not formally enter therapy, the privilege may nevertheless apply to confidential communications between the client and the professional. For example, a person may consult a therapist who refers the person to a second professional. In most states, communication between the person and the referring therapist is privileged even though the person does not receive treatment from the referring professional.

The third requirement of privilege law provides that only communications that the client intends to be confidential are privileged. The privilege generally does not attach to communications that the client intends to be released to other people.

The fact that a third person (e.g., parent) is present when a client discloses information may or may not eliminate the confidentiality required for a privilege. The deciding factor usually is whether the third person is needed to assist the professional. For example, suppose a therapist is talking to a child client and the parent is present to participate in the session. The presence of the parent need not destroy the psychotherapist-client privilege. The important factor is whether the parent was needed to assist the professional. A privilege is not destroyed when colleagues consult about cases. Necessary release of information to third-party payers does not destroy privilege. Privileged communications remain privileged when the relationship with the client ends.

The privilege belongs to the client, not the professional. In legal parlance, the client (including a child client) is the "holder" of the privilege. As the privilege holder, the client can prevent the professional from disclosing privileged information in legal proceedings. For example, suppose a child's therapist is subpoenaed to testify about the child. While the therapist is on the witness stand, an attorney asks a question that calls for disclosure of privileged information. At that point, the child's attorney should object. The child's attorney asserts the privilege on behalf of the privilege holder—the child. The judge then decides whether a privilege applies.

If the child's attorney fails to object to a question calling for privileged information, or if the child is not represented by an attorney, the professional may assert the privilege on behalf of the child. Indeed, the professional has an ethical duty to assert the privilege if no one else does. The professional might turn to the judge and say, "Your honor, I would rather not answer that question because answering would require disclosure of information I believe is privileged." When the judge learns that a privilege may exist, the judge decides whether the question should be answered.

Confidentiality and Privilege When the Client Is a Child

Difficulties arise when the client is a child. The ethical obligation to protect confidentiality applies regardless of age, and confidential information cannot be revealed to outsiders unless consent is obtained or disclosure is required by law. But are parents outsiders? May professionals discuss confidential information with parents without the child's permission? An example illustrates why there is no one-size-fits-all answer to this question. Suppose a professional's clients are five and fifteen years of age. In the preschooler's case, it is likely the parents will be consulted regularly. The child may be informed that the therapist talks to Mommy and Daddy, but it would be developmentally inappropriate and legally unnecessary to seek the child's consent to disclose information to the parents. By contrast, it is developmentally appropriate, and perhaps legally necessary, to safeguard the teenager's confidential revelations from parents (see Mannheim et al., 2002).

The five- and fifteen-year-old clients are easy. But what about a nine- or ten-year-old? Where does such a child fit along the continuum of confidentiality? There is no simple answer. Much depends on the maturity and mental stability of the child, the reasons for treatment, and the nature of the relationship between the parents and the child.

Regardless of age, a professional's first duty is to the child. This is so regardless of who pays for treatment. The fact that a child's parents pay for therapy does not automatically entitle the parents to confidential information. A useful way to deal with potential problems concerning confidentiality is to set ground rules before therapy begins. Berner (1998b) advises that "[w]hile it is not always clear what privacy rights children actually enjoy under the law, good clinical practice requires that you work out some rules or guidelines which protect the child's confidences and the integrity of the therapy, while allowing the parents to remain appropriately involved" (p. 65). Brant and Brant (1998) add that

> [t]herapists should attempt to negotiate these "confidentiality boundaries" between parent and child at the beginning of treatment as part of the treatment contract. Arrangements will vary with the age of the child, with adolescents usually requesting and requiring more explicit contracts around confidentiality. The therapist must address the question of access to records at the commencement of treatment. (p. 76)

Reid (1999) opines,

> It is wise to discuss limitations of confidentiality with both parents and the young patient at the beginning of treatment. You may have policies

about informally keeping a child's confidences, with a broadly understood intent to keep his or her comments private; however, do not promise that "everything you say will be confidential." When the child's
safety or other important interests are at stake, bring the parents into the
picture. (pp. 92-93)

When the child is developmentally capable of participating in the process, the child's input should be obtained.

Confidentiality in Group Therapy

The ethical duty to protect confidential information applies to professionals conducting group therapy. Members of the group, however, are not
ethically bound to respect confidentiality (Roback, Moore, Waterhouse, &
Martin, 1996). It is advisable to engage the group in discussion of the importance of confidentiality. Appelbaum and Greer (1993) state that "it
seems clear that group leaders should alert their patients that the sanctity of
the communications depends on the goodwill of their fellow patient"
(p. 312). The code of ethics of the National Association of Social Workers
(1999) suggests that

> when social workers provide counseling services to families, couples,
> or groups, social workers seek agreement among the parties involved
> concerning each individual's right to confidentiality and obligation to
> preserve the confidentiality of information shared by others. Social
> workers should inform participants in family, couples, or group coun-
> seling that social workers cannot guarantee that all participants will
> honor such agreements. (Principle 1.07f)

Although relatively little law addresses the application of the psychotherapist-client privilege during group treatment, existing law suggests that
privileges do apply (see *Lovett v. Superior Court,* 1988).

Disclosure of Confidential and Privileged Information

The following sections concern disclosure of confidential and privileged
information.

Client Consent

Client consent plays the central role in release of confidential and privileged information. As Gutheil and Appelbaum (1982) observe, "with rare

exceptions, identifiable data [about clients] can be transmitted to third parties only with the [client's] explicit consent" (p. 5). A competent adult may consent to release of information to attorneys, courts, or anyone else. The client's consent should be fully informed and voluntary. The professional should explain any disadvantages of disclosing confidential information. For example, the client may be told that release to third persons may waive privileges that would otherwise apply.

A professional who discloses confidential information without client consent can be sued (*Givens v. Mullikin*, 2002). With an eye toward such lawsuits, Gutheil and Appelbaum (1982) write:

> [I]t is probably wise for therapists always to require the written consent of their patients before releasing information to third parties. Written consent is advisable for at least two reasons: (1) it makes clear to both parties involved that consent has, in fact, been given; (2) if the fact, nature or timing of the consent should ever be challenged, a documentary record exists. The consent should be made a part of the patient's permanent chart. (p. 6)

When the client is a child, parents normally have authority to make decisions about confidential and privileged information. When a parent is accused of abusing a child, however, it may be inappropriate for the parent to make decisions regarding the child's confidential information. In the event of a conflict between the interests of the child and the parents, a judge may appoint someone else, such as a guardian ad litem, to make decisions about confidential and privileged information.

Reviewing Client Records Before or During Testimony

When a professional is asked to testify, portions of the client's record may be reviewed to refresh the professional's memory. In some cases, the professional leaves the record at the office. At other times the record is taken to court. In most cases, it is not only appropriate but essential to review pertinent records prior to testifying. Professionals should be aware, however, that reviewing records before or during testimony could compromise the confidentiality of the records.

Reviewing records before testifying. While the professional is on the witness stand, the cross-examining attorney may ask whether the professional reviewed the child's record, and, if so, the attorney may request the judge to order the record produced for the attorney's inspection. In most states, the judge has authority to order the record produced. In favor of disclosure, the judge considers the attorney's right to cross-examine the professional and the extent to which the record will assist cross-examination. Against disclosure, the judge evaluates the impact on the child of disclosing confidential information. The outcome turns on which of these factors predominates.

Referring to records while testifying. When records are reviewed before testifying, the judge may or may not order the records disclosed to the attorney conducting cross-examination. If the professional takes the records to court and refers to them while testifying, however, the judge is very likely, upon request, to order the records disclosed to the cross-examiner.

Protecting records from disclosure. Whether a professional reviews a child's record before or during testimony, a judge is more likely to require disclosure of nonprivileged records than records that are protected by the psychotherapist-client privilege. In most states, the law is unsettled regarding the impact of record review on privileged communications. With the law in flux, simple steps can be taken to reduce the likelihood that reviewing records will jeopardize confidentiality. Before implementing any of these recommendations, consult an attorney.

First, when reviewing a child's record before going to court, limit review to portions of the record that are needed to prepare for testifying. Document the parts of the record reviewed and not reviewed. In this way, if the judge orders the record disclosed, an argument can be made that disclosure should be limited to portions of the record actually used to prepare for testifying.

Second, records containing privileged communications probably have greater protection from disclosure than nonprivileged records. With this in mind, professionals may wish to organize records so that privileged information is maintained separately from nonprivileged information. When a record organized in this manner is reviewed before testifying, it is sometimes possible to avoid review of privileged communications. This done, if a judge orders the record disclosed, the judge may be willing to limit disclosure to nonprivileged portions of the record. Although this approach entails the burden of separating records into privileged and nonprivileged sections, and may not persuade all judges, the technique is worth considering.

Third, if it is necessary to take the record to court, consider taking only the portions of the record that will be useful during testimony and leaving the remainder at the office.

Fourth, if the record is taken to court, perhaps the record can remain in the briefcase rather than be taken to the witness stand. Make no mention of the record unless it becomes necessary to refer to it while testifying. Once the record is used during testimony, the opposing attorney may have a right to inspect it.

Fifth, if the record is taken to court and to the witness stand, it may be possible to testify without referring to the record.

Again, legal advice should be obtained before implementing any of the foregoing suggestions. Some of the recommendations may not be permitted in some states.

Consultation and Supervision

Client information may be shared with colleagues for purposes of supervision and consultation (Reid, 1999). The American Psychological Association's (1992) code of conduct provides, however, that "in order to minimize intrusions on privacy, psychologists include in written and oral reports, consultations, and the like, only information germane to the purpose for which the communication is made" (Standard 5.03a). The National Association of Social Workers' (1999) code of ethics provides that "social workers should not disclose identifying information when discussing clients with consultants unless the client has consented to disclosure of confidential information or there is a compelling need for such disclosure" (Standard 1.07q). Hilliard (1998) states,

> Often a consultation on a difficult issue is in keeping with the standard of care. Therapists do not have to reveal the identity of their patient in order to seek a consultation. Under these circumstances, no breach of confidentiality occurs. When it is necessary to reveal the identity of a patient for a consultation, the patient's permission is necessary. A note in the patient's chart that permission was granted is usually sufficient. In all cases, whether the patient's identity is or is not revealed, a note of the consultation should be made. (p. 59)

It may be useful at the outset of treatment to inform the client that consultation may be obtained and to obtain permission. In his book on legal issues in psychotherapy, Reid (1999) notes,

> From the treater's or evaluator's point of view, when important doubts about assessment or care arise, there are almost always ways to reduce them, and one of the best is to get advice from a peer or subspecialist. You do not need the patient's permission to do this. I cringe when I hear a psychiatrist or psychotherapist try to convince a jury that he or she couldn't ask for a second opinion about a patient's suicidal behavior because of "confidentiality." No state, so far as I know, limits clinical consultation intended in the patient's interest. (p. 53)

Child Abuse Reporting Laws Override Confidentiality and Privilege

Child abuse reporting laws require professionals to report suspected child abuse and neglect to designated authorities. The reporting laws override the ethical duty to protect confidential client information. Moreover, the reporting requirement overrides privileges. Although reporting laws abrogate privileges, abrogation usually is not complete. In many states, professionals may limit the information they report to the information specifically required by law. Information that is not required to be reported remains privileged and confidential. Kalichman (1999) advises,

> The level of detail released in a report should be limited to an amount that minimizes breaches of confidentiality while maximizing child protection. It is not necessary to release information in a report unless it will assist the social service agency in making determinations of abuse or will help the agency to take action on behalf of the child and family. As stated in the *Ethical Principles of Psychologists and Code of Conduct,* "In order to minimize intrusions on privacy, psychologists include in written and oral reports, consultations, and the like, only information germane to the purpose for which the communication is made" (Standard 5.03a). In reporting suspected child abuse, the purpose of the information released is to protect children. Information should therefore be limited to the degree to which child protection will be achieved. (p. 148)

Psychotherapist's Duty to Warn Potential Victims About Dangerous Clients

In 1976, the California Supreme Court ruled in *Tarasoff v. Regents of the University of California* that a psychotherapist has a legal duty to warn the potential victim of a psychiatric client who threatens the victim. The duty to warn overcomes both the ethical duty to protect confidential information and the psychotherapist-client privilege. If the therapist fails to take reasonable steps to warn the victim, and the client carries out the threat, the therapist can be sued.

Since *Tarasoff* was decided, judges have grappled with the difficult question of when professionals have a legal duty to warn potential victims. Unfortunately, in most states, the law remains unsettled. Judges generally agree that there is a legal duty to warn potential victims, but judges have not achieved consensus on when the duty applies. In 1985, California enacted a statute on the subject, which limits the duty to warn to situations in which "the patient has communicated to the psychotherapist a serious threat of physical violence against a reasonably identifiable victim or victims" (*California Civil Code*, 2003, § 43.92).

A *Tarasoff*-style duty to warn can arise when a psychotherapist learns that a client plans to sexually abuse a particular child (*Bradley v. Ray*, 1995). Moreover, a duty to warn might exist in a case in which no particular child is targeted, but in which a sexually dangerous client has access to readily identifiable children (*Barry v. Truek*, 1990).

Emergencies

In emergencies, a professional may have little choice but to release confidential information without prior authorization from the client. The law allows limited release of confidential information in genuine emergencies.

Court-Ordered Examinations

A judge may order an individual to submit to a psychological evaluation to help the judge decide the case. Because everyone knows from the outset that the professional's report will be shared with the judge and the attorneys, the obligation to protect confidential information is limited. Privileges may not apply at all. Limits on confidentiality should be discussed with the individual.

Client Inspection and Copying of Records

Generally, clients have a right to inspect and copy their own records. A therapist may deny inspection if there is a substantial risk that seeing a record will have detrimental consequences for the client. When the client is a child, the parents may have the right to inspect and copy the child's record. The law on client inspection and copying of records varies from state to state.

OBLIGATION TO REPORT SUSPECTED ABUSE AND NEGLECT

Professionals who work with children are required to report suspected abuse and neglect to designated authorities. The list of mandated reporters includes social workers, physicians, nurses, mental health professionals, teachers, police officers, and day care providers. In most states, mandated reporters have no discretion whether to report. Reporting is mandatory, not optional.

The duty to report is triggered when a professional possesses a prescribed level of suspicion that a child is abused. The terms used to describe the triggering level of suspicion vary slightly from state to state, and include "cause to believe," "reasonable cause to believe," "known or suspected abuse," and "observation or examination which discloses evidence of abuse." Despite shades of difference, the basic meaning of the reporting laws is the same across the country: Reporting is required when a professional has evidence that would lead a reasonable professional to believe abuse is likely.

The duty to report does not require the professional to "know" abuse occurred. All that is required is information that raises a reasonable suspicion of maltreatment. A mandated reporter who postpones reporting until all doubt is eliminated probably violates the reporting law. The law deliberately leaves the ultimate decision about maltreatment to investigating officials, not reporters. Thus, Kalichman (1993) advises that "therapists should avoid acting as investigators and restrict their actions within proper roles" (p. 154). Zellman and Faller (1996) add that

> reporting laws ask professionals to be reasonably vigilant and to report their suspicions or beliefs that maltreatment occurred or is occurring. The laws are clear that no more is required: Indeed, professionals are precluded explicitly from conducting any further investigation, a prohibition reinforced by the short latency period before a report is required. (p. 365)

This does not mean that professionals should ask no questions and consider no alternatives to maltreatment. The point is that in-depth investigation is the bailiwick of child protective services and law enforcement, not reporters.

The law provides that professionals who report suspected child maltreatment are immune from liability for the report (see *Myers v. Lashley,* 2002). Again, the law varies from state to state, with some states providing greater immunity than others. Although the immunity provision is vitally important, professionals should understand that the immunity provision in a child abuse reporting law cannot prevent an angry adult from suing a professional. The immunity provision—assuming it applies—gives the professional a way out of a lawsuit, but cannot prevent the suit from being filed.

DOCUMENTATION

Documentation is important to treatment. In addition, documentation has legal implications. Failure to keep appropriate records can lead to disciplinary action by licensing authorities.

> When psychologists have reason to believe that records of their professional services will be used in legal proceedings involving recipients of or participants in their work, they have a responsibility to create and maintain documentation in the kind of detail and quality that would be consistent with reasonable scrutiny in an adjudicative forum. (American Psychological Association, 1992, Standard 1.23b)

Documentation is central to risk management. Moline, Williams, and Austin (1998) write that "if you become involved in a lawsuit, you are likely to be deemed as behaving unprofessionally if you have not kept adequate records" (p. 4). Attorneys have a maxim: "If it isn't in writing, it didn't happen" (Knapp & VandeCreek, 1996). Reid (1999) writes, "Whoever started the rumor in professional circles that 'if you don't write it down, they can't hang you with it' was dead wrong. In far more cases than not, legible notes help clinicians whose care is questioned" (p. 12). Berner (1998b) adds that "there is more than one way to assure self-destruction, and keeping no notes is one of those ways" (p. 68). Thorough, accurate, ongoing documentation is a powerful defense against charges of improper practice (see Harris, 1995; Moline et al., 1998). Consultation with colleagues and supervision should be noted in the client's file (Lewis, 2002; Rivas-Vazquez, Blais, Rey, & Rivas-Vazquez, 2001).

Do not alter records. Reid (1999) advises, "*Do not* change your notes after the fact except by adding *and dating* additional or explanatory information, or flagging inaccuracies by drawing a line through them" (p. 12). Smith (1996) adds that "[t]his is particularly true once litigation involving the records is anticipated" (p. 92). Of course, records can be corrected. Corrections, however, should be noted as such. Behnke et al. (1998) offer the following guidelines:

> It sometimes happens that you or your client discover inaccuracies or mistakes in the record. While you cannot alter the record, you also do not want to perpetuate inaccurate clinical information. If you become aware of a mistake in the record, you may make an additional entry. In the entry, note the date of the mistaken information, explain that previously recorded information is inaccurate, provide the accurate information, and then date the entry according to when it is written. You may make a notation to the entry with the mistaken information, such as "See note of September 18, 1998, for correction." Initial this notation. In this manner you are adding correct information, rather than altering the record. (p. 149)

Berner (1998b) offers equally good advice:

> *Never, ever, change a record,* is not the same as *Never, ever make a mistake.* The issue here is how to correct a mistake in the record without breaking [the principle against changing records]. Corrections should be in real time, contemporaneously labeled, and transparent. This means that you should not attempt to make the record look as if there never had been a mistake in it. When you discover a mistake, you must acknowledge it and then correct it. This [is] what we mean by "real time." "Contemporaneously labeled" means that you must write "error" in the margin of the note, to alert the reader to both the existence of the error and the subsequent correction. "Transparent" means that the correction should refer to the site of the error but not hide it. It means no whiteout and no indelible black magic marker. (p. 67)

Some professionals keep two sets of records. So-called process or private records are nevertheless part of the client's record, and are governed by the same advice not to alter records outlined above. Moreover, process and private records have to be disclosed in response to a lawful subpoena or court order. Reid (1999) writes that

> [t]he record is the record, and includes private or "process" notes that are not kept with the main file. Keeping a second, more private set of notes may be a good idea to protect the patient's revelations from the prying eyes of secretaries, medical records personnel, or other clinicians; however, the second set is no more privileged than the main file when your record is subpoenaed. Do not attempt to hide private notes. (p. 97)

RESPONDING TO SUBPOENAS

There are two types of subpoenas: (1) a subpoena requiring an individual to testify (subpoena *ad testificandum*), and (2) a subpoena requiring a person to produce records designated in the subpoena (subpoena *duces tecum*).

A subpoena is a court order and cannot be ignored. Disobedience of a subpoena can be punished as contempt of court. Although a subpoena cannot be ignored, neither should subpoenas be unthinkingly obeyed. In *Crescenzo v. Crane* (2002), the court wrote, "That a physician may find himself in a difficult position when confronted with the imposing language of a subpoena does not warrant a resolution of the problem by simply providing the records without a release or further inquiry" (p. 290). Tranel (1994) writes that "psychologists need not automatically translate the serving of a subpoena into prompt acquiescence to legal demands without regard for the ethics of the matter" (p. 36). After all, some subpoenas are invalid. Before complying with a subpoena, consider the following.

Should I contact the client before I respond to a subpoena?

A client cannot override a professional's duty to respond to a subpoena. Nevertheless, the client should be consulted before responding to a subpoena. If the client is a child, consultation occurs with the child's parent or the adult legally responsible for the child. If the child is sufficiently mature, the child should be consulted. If the child has an attorney, the attorney should be consulted.

When discussing a subpoena with a client or the client's attorney, describe what information is requested through the subpoena and by whom. The client should understand what, if any, confidential information may be released. The client should also understand that release of information that meets the requirements of a privilege could jeopardize future application of the privilege. "Following such a discussion, a legally competent client or the client's legal guardian may choose to consent in writing to production of the data" (Committee on Legal Issues of the American Psychological Association, 1996, p. 246). Getting the client's consent in writing "may avoid future conflicts or legal entanglements with the client over the release of confidential" information (p. 246).

When the client is a child, the discussion of a subpoena typically takes place with an adult. The adult's decision about a subpoena must be in the child's best interest.

As stated, professionals cannot ignore subpoenas. Yet blind obedience can cause problems. Consider the unusual case in which a psychologist was disciplined for complying with a subpoena (*Rost v. State Board of Psychology,* 1995). In this case, a psychologist supervised an unlicensed therapist who provided treatment to a child suffering chronic headaches. The headaches were allegedly caused by a fall at a community center. The child's mother sued the community center. Some time later, the attorney for the community center mailed a subpoena to the supervising psychologist demanding the child's treatment record. Without contacting the child, the child's mother, or the child's attorney, the psychologist gave the child's treatment record to the community center's attorney. Although the mother had previously given permission to disclose the child's record to the child's attorney, no permission had been given to disclose records to anyone else.

The state board of psychology disciplined the psychologist. The psychologist appealed to a court, but the judges agreed with the board of psychology. The judges wrote that the psychologist "had a duty to either obtain written permission to release the records from [the child] or challenge the propriety of the subpoena before a judge. [The psychologist] did neither. Instead, she unilaterally gave [the child's] records to [the attorney for the community center] without consulting with [the child] or her attorney" (p. 629). Moral of the story? Consult the client, the client's attorney, and, if necessary, your attorney before responding to a subpoena.

Should I get legal advice?

If you have any doubt about what to do, consult an attorney before you comply with a subpoena. Do not accept "legal" advice from someone who is not an attorney. If you work for a government agency, consult legal counsel for the agency. Hospitals and some clinics have an attorney on staff or on retainer. Professionals in private practice can retain an attorney, talk to an attorney they know, or contact their malpractice insurance carrier. If the child has an attorney, consult the child's attorney. In criminal cases, the prosecutor handling the child's case may be a good source of advice on responding to a subpoena for the child's records. In juvenile court cases, the attorney handling the child's case may be consulted. In many juvenile court cases, children have an attorney of their own.

Professional organizations such as the American Psychological Association and the National Association of Social Workers dispense useful information. So do government agencies such as the state boards of psychology. Generally, however, these organizations and agencies do not give legal advice on specific cases. Malpractice insurance carriers are often a good source of advice.

Should I talk to the attorney who issued the subpoena?

The one attorney who is not in a position to give objective advice about a subpoena is the attorney who issued it. Do not get the impression, however, that you should never talk to the attorney who issued the subpoena. Before doing so, get the client's consent. When the client is a child, obtain consent from the child's parent or the person with legal authority to consent. When the child is sufficiently mature, get the child's consent. If the child has an attorney, consult the attorney.

When you talk to the attorney who issued the subpoena, it is usually possible to avoid revealing confidential information. The Committee on Legal

Issues of the American Psychological Association (1996) recommends that discussions with the attorney who issued the subpoena "explore whether there are ways to achieve the requesting party's objectives without divulging confidential information, for example, through disclosure of nonconfidential materials or submission of an affidavit by the psychologist disclosing nonconfidential information" (p. 246). In some cases, discussion between a therapist and an attorney helps the attorney realize the therapist has nothing useful, and the subpoena is withdrawn. In other cases, discussion narrows the information requested.

What if the client does not want me to respond to the subpoena?

As stated, a client cannot override the duty to respond to a subpoena. At the same time, however, some subpoenas are invalid and can be resisted. For example, a subpoena may seek disclosure of information that is protected by the psychotherapist-client privilege. A subpoena does not override privilege.

Sometimes the client is too young to decide, yet the adults in the child's life are not making responsible decisions. What to do? If the client wants to resist the subpoena, or if resistance is in a child's best interest, the appropriate action is to file a motion in court to quash the subpoena. A motion to quash may be filed by the child's attorney, a prosecutor, or the therapist's attorney.

When a motion to quash is filed, a judge decides whether the subpoena is valid. The therapist may have to testify at a hearing on the motion to quash. If the judge quashes the subpoena, the therapist does not have to respond. The judge may decide, for example, that records sought by the subpoena are privileged. On the other hand, if the judge rules that the subpoena is valid, the therapist must comply or risk being held in contempt of court.

Instead of a motion to quash, the Committee on Legal Issues of the American Psychological Association (1996) suggests that the professional may wish to write to the judge, sending a copy of the letter to the lawyers:

> The simplest way of proceeding, and perhaps the least costly, may be for the psychologist (or his or her attorney) to write a letter to the court, with a copy to the attorneys for both parties, stating that the psychologist wishes to comply with the law but that he or she is ethically obligated not to produce the confidential records or test data or to testify about them unless compelled to do so by the court or with the consent of the client.

The purpose of this letter is multifold. It serves to protect the interests of the patient and reminds the court of the ptentially adverse effects of disseminating confidential information. The aforementioned guidelines go on to say that the psychologist may wish to suggest to the court ways in which the adverse aspects of disclosure might be reduced.

What if my client receives a subpoena and calls me for advice?

Needless to say, mental health professionals do not give legal advice. For legal advice, the client is referred to a lawyer. With the client's consent, the professional may work with the lawyer. Of course, the professional helps the client deal with the psychological implications of the subpoena.

EXPERT TESTIMONY IN CHILD ABUSE LITIGATION

Expert testimony plays a critical role in child abuse litigation. Such testimony is provided by social workers, psychologists, medical professionals, and others. For in-depth discussion of expert testimony, see Myers (1998), Myers and Stern (2002), and Stern (1997).

Who Qualifies As an Expert Witness

Before a professional may testify as an expert witness, the judge must be convinced that the professional possesses sufficient knowledge, skill, experience, training, or education to qualify as an expert. Normally, the professional takes the witness stand and answers questions about his or her educational accomplishments, specialized training, and relevant experience.

Preparation for Expert Testimony

When a professional prepares to testify, it is important to meet with the attorney for whom the professional will testify. Pretrial conferences are ethically and legally proper. Chadwick (1990) observes that "[f]ace-to-face conferences between attorneys and experts are always desirable, and rarely impossible" (p. 936).

Forms of Expert Testimony

Expert testimony usually takes one of four forms:

1. An opinion
2. An answer to a hypothetical question
3. A lecture providing background information for the judge or jury
4. Some combination of these

The most common form of expert testimony is an opinion, although expert testimony in child sexual abuse cases often takes the form of a lecture designed to help jurors understand the psychological dynamics of sexual abuse.

Opinion Testimony

Expert witnesses are permitted to offer opinions. For example, in a physical abuse case, a physician could testify that, in the doctor's opinion, the child has battered child syndrome, and the child's injuries are probably not accidental. In a neglect case, an expert could offer an opinion that a child's failure to thrive is caused by parental behavior.

The expert must be reasonably confident of the opinion. Lawyers use the term "reasonable certainty" to describe the necessary degree of confidence. Unfortunately, reasonable certainty is not easily defined. How certain must an expert be to be reasonably certain? It is clear that expert witnesses may not speculate or guess. It is equally clear that experts do not have to be completely certain before offering opinions. Thus, the degree of certainty lies somewhere between guesswork and absolute certainty.

In the final analysis, the reasonable certainty standard provides little guidance. A more useful way to assess the strength of expert testimony looks beyond reasonable certainty and asks questions that shed light on the factual and logical strength of the expert's opinion: In formulating the opinion, did the expert consider all relevant facts? Did the expert have adequate understanding of pertinent clinical and scientific principles? Did the expert use methods of assessment that are appropriate, reliable, and valid? Are the expert's assumptions and conclusions reasonable? Is the expert reasonably objective? In the end, the issue is whether the expert's reasoning is defensible, logical, consistent, and reasonably objective.

The Hypothetical Question

In some cases, expert testimony is elicited in response to a hypothetical question asked by the attorney who requested the expert's testimony. A hypothetical question contains hypothetical facts that closely parallel the facts of the actual case on trial. In a physical abuse case, for example, the attorney might say, "Now, Doctor, let me ask you to assume that all of the following facts are true." The attorney then describes injuries suffered by a hypothetical child. After describing the hypothetical child, the attorney asks, "Doctor, based on these hypothetical facts, do you have an opinion, based on a reasonable degree of medical certainty, whether the hypothetical child's injuries were accidental or nonaccidental?" The doctor gives an opinion about the hypothetical child's injuries. The jury then applies the information supplied by the doctor regarding the hypothetical child to the injuries suffered by the actual child in the case on trial.

In bygone days, expert witnesses often testified in response to hypothetical questions. Yet the hypothetical question is a cumbersome device, and it gradually fell into disfavor. Today, expert witnesses usually take the more direct approach of offering an opinion about the child in the case on trial, rather than an opinion about a hypothetical child.

In modern trials, it is more often the cross-examining attorney who resorts to hypothetical questions. The cross-examiner seeks to undermine the expert's opinion by presenting a hypothetical set of facts that differs from the facts described by the expert. The cross-examiner then asks, "Now, Doctor, if the facts I have suggested to you turn out to be true, would that change your opinion?" Chadwick (1990) observes that it is "common to encounter hypothetical questions based on hypotheses that are extremely unlikely, and the witness may need to point out the unlikelihood" (p. 967).

A Background Lecture to Educate the Jury

Rather than offer an opinion, an expert may testify in the form of a lecture that provides the jury with background information on technical, clinical, or scientific issues. This form of expert testimony plays an important role in child sexual abuse litigation when the defense asserts that a child's delayed reporting or recantation means the child cannot be believed. When the defense attacks the child's credibility in this way, judges in most states allow an expert witness to inform the jury that it is not uncommon for sexually abused children to delay reporting and recant. Equipped with this background information, the jury is in a better position to evaluate the child's credibility.

Cross-Examination and Impeachment of Expert Witnesses

Testifying begins with direct examination. During direct examination, the expert answers questions from the attorney who asked the expert to testify. After direct examination, the opposing attorney has the right to cross-examine. Cross-examination is sometimes followed by redirect examination. Redirect examination affords the attorney who asked the expert to testify an opportunity to clarify issues that were raised during cross-examination.

Cross-examination causes anxiety. The following discussion is intended to demystify cross-examination by explaining six techniques commonly used by cross-examining attorneys.

Raise Doubts About the Expert's Testimony That Will Be Emphasized During Closing Arguments

At the end of the case, attorneys present closing arguments. One goal of closing arguments is to persuade the jury to disbelieve certain witnesses. With closing arguments in mind, the cross-examining attorney uses cross-examination to raise doubts about the expert's testimony. A closing argument is used to remind the jury of those doubts.

Leading Questions

The attorney conducting direct examination is generally not supposed to ask leading questions. By contrast, the cross-examiner is permitted to do so, and some attorneys ask only leading questions during cross-examination. The cross-examiner attempts to control the expert by using leading questions that require short, specific answers; answers the attorney wants the jury to hear. The cross-examiner keeps the witness hemmed in with leading questions and seldom asks why or how something happened. How and why questions permit the witness to explain, and explanation is precisely what the cross-examiner does not want.

Limit the Expert's Ability to Explain

When an expert attempts to explain, the cross-examining attorney may interrupt and say, "Please just answer yes or no." If the expert persists, the cross-examiner may ask the judge to admonish the expert to limit answers to the questions asked. Experts are understandably frustrated when an attorney thwarts efforts at clarification. It is sometimes proper to say, "Counsel, it is not possible for me to answer with a simple yes or no. May I explain myself?" Chadwick (1990) advises that "[w]hen a question is posed in a strictly 'yes or no' fashion, but the correct answer is 'maybe,' the witness should find a way to express the true answer. A direct appeal to the judge may be helpful in some cases" (p. 967). Many judges permit witnesses to explain themselves during cross-examination if the jury needs more information to make sense of the witness's testimony.

Remember that after cross-examination comes redirect examination, during which the attorney who asked the expert to testify is allowed to ask further questions. During redirect examination, the expert has an opportunity to clarify matters that were left unclear during cross-examination.

Undermine the Expert's Assumptions

One of the most effective cross-examination techniques is to get an expert to commit to the facts and assumptions that support the expert's opinion, and then dispute one or more of those facts or assumptions. Consider, for example, a case in which a physician testifies on direct examination that a child experienced vaginal penetration. The cross-examiner begins by committing the doctor to the facts and assumptions underlying the opinion. The attorney might say, "So, Doctor, your opinion is based exclusively on the history, physical examination, and on what the child told you. Is that correct? And there is nothing else you relied on to form your opinion. Is that correct?" The cross-examiner commits the doctor to a specific set of facts and assumptions so that when the attorney disputes those facts or assumptions, the doctor's opinion cannot be justified on some other basis.

Once the cross-examiner pins down the basis of the doctor's opinion, the examiner attacks the opinion by disputing one or more of the facts or assumptions that support it. The attorney might ask whether the doctor's opinion would change if certain facts were different (a hypothetical question). The attorney might press the doctor to acknowledge alternative explanations for the doctor's conclusion. The attorney might ask the doctor whether experts could come to different conclusions based on the same facts.

Rather than attack the doctor's assumptions and conclusions during cross-examination, the attorney may limit cross-examination to pinning the doctor down to a limited set of facts and assumptions, and then, when the doctor has left the witness stand, offer another expert to contradict those facts and assumptions.

Impeach the Expert with a "Learned Treatise"

The judge may allow a cross-examining attorney to undermine an expert's testimony by confronting the expert with books or articles (called "learned treatises") that contradict the expert. The rules on impeachment with learned treatises vary from state to state. There is agreement on one thing, however. When an expert is confronted with a sentence or a paragraph selected by an attorney from an article or chapter, the expert has the right to put the selected passage in context by reading surrounding material. The expert might say to the cross-examining attorney, "Counsel, I cannot comment on the sentence you have selected unless I first read the entire article. If you will permit me to read the article, I'll be happy to comment on the sentence that interests you."

Raise the Possibility of Bias

The cross-examiner may raise the possibility that the expert is biased. For example, if the expert is part of a multidisciplinary child abuse team, the cross-examiner might proceed as follows:

Q: You are employed by Children's Hospital, isn't that correct?

A: Right.

Q: At the hospital, are you a member of the multidisciplinary team that investigates allegations of child abuse?

A: The team performs medical examinations and interviews. We do not investigate as the police investigate. But yes, I am a member of the hospital's multidisciplinary child abuse team.

Q: Your team regularly performs investigative examinations and interviews at the request of the prosecuting attorney's office, isn't that correct?

A: Yes.

Q: When you complete your investigation for the prosecutor, you prepare a report for the prosecutor, don't you?

A: A report and recommendation is prepared and placed in the child's medical record. Upon request, the team provides a copy of the report to the prosecutor and, I might add, to the defense.

Q: After your team prepares its report and provides a copy to the prosecutor, you often come to court to testify as an expert witness for the prosecution, isn't that right?

A: Yes.

Q: Do you usually testify for the prosecution rather than the defense?

A: Correct.

Q: In fact, would I be correct in saying that you always testify for the prosecution and never for the defense?

A: I am willing to testify for the defense, but so far I have always testified for the prosecution.

Q: No further questions.

Clearly, the cross-examiner is seeking to portray the witness as biased in favor of the prosecution. Notice, however, that the cross-examiner is too cunning to ask, "Well then, because of your close working relationship with the prosecution, you are biased in favor of the prosecution, aren't you?" The cross-examiner knows the answer is "No," so the cross-examiner refrains from asking directly about bias, and simply plants seeds of doubt in the jurors' minds. When it is time for the defense to give its closing argument, the defense attorney will remind the jury of the witness's close working relationship with the prosecution.

What is the antidote to this tactic? First, the witness may find an opportunity to indicate lack of bias during cross-examination itself. Second, remember that cross-examination is followed by redirect examination. During redirect, the prosecutor may ask, "In light of the defense attorney's questions about your job on the multidisciplinary team, are you biased in favor of the prosecution?"

AVOIDING DUAL ROLES

Should mental health professionals providing psychotherapy agree to perform forensic evaluations of their therapy clients? Are the therapeutic and forensic roles compatible? For example, should the psychotherapist for a child whose parents are divorcing agree to perform a custody evaluation of the entire family? Should a psychotherapist who is treating a child for the effects of sexual abuse agree to conduct a formal forensic assessment of abuse and testify in court regarding the findings of the assessment?

Although there are few pat answers to such questions, the literature sheds light on the subject. Greenberg and Shuman (1997) write that "a role conflict arises when a treating therapist also attempts to testify as a forensic expert addressing the psycholegal issues in the case" (p. 50). Melton, Petrila, Poythress, and Slobogin (1997) add that "forensic assessment differs from a therapeutic assessment on a number of dimensions" (p. 42). The American Professional Society on the Abuse of Children (1996) notes that "forensic evaluations are different from clinical evaluations in generally requiring a different professional stance and additional components."

Ethics codes emphasize the potential conflict between therapeutic and forensic roles. The code of conduct of the American Psychological Association (1992) states that "[i]n most circumstances, psychologists avoid performing multiple and potentially conflicting roles in forensic matters" (Principle 7.03). The American Psychological Association's Specialty Guidelines for Forensic Psychologists (1991) state:

> Forensic psychologists recognize potential conflicts of interest in dual relationships with parties to legal proceedings, and they seek to minimize their effects. Forensic psychologists avoid providing professional services to parties in a legal proceeding with whom they have personal or professional relationships that are inconsistent with the anticipated relationship. When it is necessary to provide both evaluation and treatment services to a party in a legal proceeding (as may be the case in small forensic hospital settings or small communities), the forensic psychologist takes reasonable steps to minimize the potential negative effects of these circumstances on the rights of the party, confidentiality, and the process of treatment and evaluation. (p. 659)

The ethical guidelines of the American Academy of Psychiatry and the Law (1995) provide that "[t]reating psychiatrists should generally avoid agreeing to be an expert witness or to perform evaluations of their patients for legal purposes because a forensic evaluation usually requires that other people be interviewed and testimony may adversely affect the therapeutic relationship" (p. xiv). The Committee on Psychiatry and Law, Group for the Advancement of Psychiatry (1991) states that "[w]hile, in some areas of the country with limited numbers of mental health practitioners, the therapist may have the role of forensic expert thrust upon him, ordinarily, it is wise to avoid mixing the therapeutic and forensic roles" (p. 44). The code of ethics of the American Professional Society on the Abuse of Children (1997) likewise provides guidance on this matter, stressing that professionals be aware of their role in the client's care and be cautious about mixing therapeutic and forensic duties. Although the guidelines acknowledge that it is not necessarily unethical for the clinician to have multiple roles in the care and assessment of a client, they do stress the need for the professional to be clear about the different responsibilities attendant with each role, to guard against conflicts that may consequently arise, and to fully inform the client and parents of the multiple responsibilities the clinician is obliged to fulfill in assuming each role.

Ethical guidelines for professionals performing child custody evaluations in divorce cases are quite specific regarding the potential conflict between forensic and treatment roles. The Model Standards of Practice of the Association of Family and Conciliation Courts (1994) provide that a person who has been a mediator or a therapist for any or all members of the family should not perform a custody evaluation because the previous knowledge and relationships may render him or her incapable of being completely neutral and incapable of having unbiased objectivity. (Principle VI.E)

The "Guidelines for Child Custody Evaluations in Divorce Proceedings" of the American Psychological Association (1994) recommend that "[p]sychologists generally avoid conducting a child custody evaluation in a case in which the psychologist served in a therapeutic role for the child or his or her immediate family or has had other involvement that may compromise the psychologist's objectivity" (Guideline II).

A child's therapist can provide useful information to the courts without crossing the line into dual roles. For example, the therapist may provide information about the child's progress in therapy, the child's current level of functioning, and the child's feelings about various adults.

CONCLUSION

The mental health and legal professions sometimes seem like ships passing in the night. Yet, if children are to be protected and assisted, mental health professionals and attorneys must put their differences aside and work together. Only genuine interdisciplinary cooperation holds realistic hope of reducing the tragic number of abused children, and ameliorating suffering.

REFERENCES

American Academy of Psychiatry and the Law (1995). Ethical guidelines for the practice of forensic psychiatry. In *Membership directory of the American Academy of Psychiatry and the Law*. Retrieved from http://www.aapl.org/ethics.htm.

American Professional Society on the Abuse of Children (1996). *Guidelines for psychological evaluation of suspected sexual abuse in young children*. Chicago: Author.

American Professional Society on the Abuse of Children (1997). *Code of ethics*. Chicago: Author.

American Psychological Association (1992). Ethical principles of psychologists and code of conduct. *American Psychologist, 47*, 1597-1611.

American Psychological Association (1994). Guidelines for child custody evaluations in divorce proceedings. *American Psychologist, 49*, 677-680.

American Psychological Association, Committee on Ethical Guidelines for Forensic Psychologists (1991). Specialty guidelines for forensic psychologists. *Law and Human Behavior, 15*, 655-665.

Appelbaum, P.S., & Greer, A. (1993). Confidentiality in group therapy. *Law and Psychiatry,* 44, 311-312.

Association of Family and Conciliation Courts (1994). Model standards of practice. *Family and Conciliation Courts Review,* 32, 504-513.

Barry v. Truek, 218 Cal. App. 3d 1241 (1990).

Behnke, S.H., Preis, J., & Bates, T. (1998). *The essentials of California mental health law: A straightforward guide for clinicians of all disciplines.* New York: W.W. Norton.

Berner, M. (1998a). Informed consent. In L.E. Lifson & R.I. Simon (Eds.), *The mental health practitioner and the law: A comprehensive handbook* (pp. 24-44). Cambridge, MA: Harvard University Press.

Berner, M. (1998b). Write smarter, not longer. In L.E. Lifson & R.I. Simon (Eds.), *The mental health practitioner and the law: A comprehensive handbook* (pp. 61-71). Cambridge, MA: Harvard University Press.

Bradley v. Ray, 904 S.W.2d 302 (Mo. Ct. App. 1995).

Brant, R.T., & Brant, J. (1998). Child and adolescent therapy. In L.E. Lifson & R.I. Simon (Eds.), *The mental health practitioner and the law: A comprehensive handbook* (pp. 72-88). Cambridge, MA: Harvard University Press.

California Business and Professions Code (2003). St. Paul: West.

California Civil Code (2003). St. Paul: West.

Chadwick, D.L. (1990). Preparation for court testimony in child abuse cases. *Pediatric Clinics of North America,* 37, 955-970.

Cobbs v. Grant, 8 Cal. 3d 229 (1972).

Committee on Legal Issues of the American Psychological Association (1996). Strategies for private practitioners coping with subpoenas or compelled testimony for client records or test data. *Professional Psychology: Research and Practice,* 27, 245-251.

Committee on Professional Practice and Standards, A Committee of the Board of Professional Affairs of the American Psychological Association (1995). Twenty-four questions (and answers) about professional practice in the area of child abuse. *Professional Psychology: Research and Practice,* 26, 377-385.

Committee on Psychiatry and the Law, Group for the Advancement of Psychiatry (1991). *The mental health professional and the legal system.* New York: Brunner/Mazel.

Crescenzo v. Crane, 796 A.2d 283 (N.J. Super. App. Div. 2002).

Givens v. Mullikin, 75 S.W.3d 383 (Tenn. 2002).

Greenberg, S.A., & Shuman, D.W. (1997). Irreconcilable conflict between therapeutic and forensic roles. *Professional Psychology: Research and Practice,* 28, 50-57.

Gutheil, T.G., & Appelbaum, P.S. (1982). *Clinical handbook of psychiatry and the law.* New York: McGraw-Hill.

Hilliard, J. (1998). Liability issues with managed care. In L.E. Lifson & R.I. Simon (Eds.), *The mental health practitioner and the law: A comprehensive handbook* (pp. 50-53). Cambridge, MA: Harvard University Press.

Kalichman, S.C. (1993). *Mandated reporting of suspected child abuse: Ethics, law, and policy.* Washington, DC: American Psychological Association.

Kalichman, S.C. (1999). *Mandated reporting of suspected child abuse: Ethics, law, and policy* (2nd ed.). Washington, DC: American Psychological Association.

Knapp, S., & VandeCreek, L. (1996). Risk management for psychologists: Treating patients who recover lost memories of childhood abuse. *Professional Psychology: Research and Practice, 27*, 452-459.

Kremer, T.G., & Gesten, E.L. (1998). Confidentiality limits of managed care and clients' willingness to self-disclose. *Professional Psychology: Research and Practice, 29*, 553-558.

Lewis, B.L. (2002). Second thoughts about documenting the psychological consultation. *Professional Psychology: Research and Practice, 33*(2), 224-225.

Lovett v. Superior Court, 203 Cal. App. 3d 521 (1988).

Mannheim, C.I., Sancilio, M., Phipps-Yonas, S., Brunnquell, D., Somers, P., Farseth, G., & Ninonuevo, F. (2002). Ethical ambiguities in the practice of child clinical psychology. *Professional Psychology: Research and Practice, 33*(1), 24-29.

Melton, G.E., Petrila, J., Poythress, N., & Slobogin, C. (1997). *Psychological evaluations for the courts* (2nd ed.). New York: Guilford.

Moline, M.E., Williams, G.T., & Austin, K.M. (1998). *Documenting psychotherapy: Essentials for mental health professionals.* Thousand Oaks, CA: Sage.

Myers, J.E.B. (1998). *Legal issues in child abuse and neglect practice* (2nd ed.). Thousand Oaks, CA: Sage.

Myers, J.E.B. (2001). Legal issues. In M. Winterstein & S.R. Scribner (Eds.), *Mental health care for child crime victims: Standards of Care Task Force guidelines* (pp. 13-1–13-52). Sacramento, CA: California Victim Compensation and Government Claims Board, Victim of Crime Program.

Myers, J.E.B. (2002). Risk management for professionals working with maltreated children and adult survivors. In J.E.B. Myers, L. Berliner, J. Briere, T. Hendrix, C. Jenny, & T. Reid (Eds.), *The APSAC handbook on child maltreatment* (2nd ed.) (pp. 403-427). Thousand Oaks, CA: Sage.

Myers, J.E.B., & Stern, P. (2002). Expert testimony. In J.E.B. Myers, L. Berliner, J. Briere, T. Hendrix, C. Jenny, & T. Reid (Eds.), *The APSAC handbook on child maltreatment* (2nd ed.) (pp. 379-401). Thousand Oaks, CA: Sage.

Myers v. Lashley, 44 P.3d 553 (Okla. 2002).

National Association of Social Workers (NASW) (1999). *Code of ethics.* Washington, DC: NASW Press.

Reid, W.H. (1999). *A clinician's guide to legal issues in psychotherapy: Or proceed with caution.* Phoenix, AZ: Zeig and Tucker.

Rivas-Vazquez, R.A., Blais, M.A., Rey, G.J., & Rivas-Vazquez, A.A. (2001). A brief reminder about documenting the psychological consultation. *Professional Psychology: Research and Practice, 32*, 194-199.

Roback, H.B., Moore, R.F., Waterhouse, G.J., & Martin, P.R. (1996). Confidentiality dilemmas in group psychotherapy with substance-dependent physicians. *American Journal of Psychiatry, 153*(10), 1250-1260.

Rost v. State Board of Psychology, 659 A.2d 626 (Pa. Commonwealth Ct. 1995).

Smith, J.T. (1986). *Medical malpractice: Psychiatric care.* New York: John Wiley.

Smith, S.R. (1996). Malpractice liability of mental health professionals and institutions. In B.D. Sales & J.W. Shuman (Eds.), *Law, mental health, and mental disorder* (pp. 76-93). Pacific Grove, CA: Brooks/Cole.

Stern, P. (1997). *Preparing and presenting expert testimony in child abuse litigation.* Thousand Oaks, CA: Sage.

Tarasoff v. Regents of the University of California, 551 P.2d 334 (Cal. 1976).

Tranel, D. (1994). The release of psychological data to nonexperts: Ethical and legal considerations. *Professional Psychology: Research and Practice, 25,* 33-38.

Zellman, G.L., & Faller, K.C. (1996). Reporting of child maltreatment. In J. Briere, L. Berliner, J.A. Bulkley, C. Jenny, & T. Reid (Eds.), *The APSAC handbook on child maltreatment* (pp. 359-381). Thousand Oaks, CA: Sage.

Chapter 15

Expert Mental Health Testimony in Child Abuse Cases

Steven N. Sparta

The subject of expert mental health testimony in child abuse determinations is timely if for no other reason than the increasing tendency for attorneys or the courts to request such testimony (Ceci & Hembooke, 1998). The tradition of helping and caring within the mental health disciplines is an insufficient basis for determining whether some mental health testimony is inadvertently doing more harm than good due to its sometimes inaccurate and/or misleading nature. The need for dialogue between the legal and mental health professions is intensified when dealing with highly contested issues such as delayed memory for reporting abuse; recantations; proffering professional opinions of abuse based upon syndromal evidence; use of techniques such as anatomically detailed dolls for sexual abuse evaluation; whether a child suspected of abuse should be seen conjointly with the suspected parent as part of an evaluation procedure; interpretations of children's drawings; the necessity for supervised visitation; validity questions about child reporting due to potential contamination secondary to suggestibility; repeated questioning; selective reinforcement for answering in a given direction; or other forms of coercion.

Mental health professionals can provide the court relevant and important information. However, the consequences of providing inaccurate and/or inappropriate testimony are potentially unethical, potentially violative of the rights and dignity of all participants, and may unwittingly betray the goal of protecting the child. This chapter discusses some of the common expert-witness situations that warrant caution before the mental health professional offers testimony in a child-protection proceeding and describes some of the essential elements of expert mental health testimony.

QUALIFICATION AS AN EXPERT

A lay or percipient witness usually has knowledge of the facts related to the litigation. Mental health professionals are usually sought to testify in their capacity as an expert witness, although sometimes parties attempt to designate the professional a lay witness to avoid payment of required expert fees. Each state codifies within its respective statutes the rules of evidence that govern expert witness testimony. On the whole there are greater similarities between these statutes and the Federal Rules of Evidence (Myers & Erickson, 1999) than there are differences. Federal Rules of Evidence (2002) (U.S. Code Title 28), Section 702, define an expert as one who is appropriate to speak about a given issue because of special "knowledge, skill, experience, training or education." The testimony of the expert is considered outside the general knowledge of a jury or judge. Opinion testimony is generally not permitted from lay witnesses, whereas expert witnesses are allowed to give opinions or to take the opinions of others into account in formulating their expert opinion (Caudill & Pope, 1995).

In child abuse cases, testimony should be offered only by those who possess the requisite knowledge, skill, experience, and education related to the child protection issues of the case. The range of problems in child protection matters is very broad. Each case may involve different stages of developmental functioning, comorbidity with different types of psychopathology unrelated to child abuse, and a recognition that child abuse involves a broad spectrum of child-endangering behavior. The expert for one type of abuse will not always possess the requisite knowledge, training, and experience for other types of child maltreatment. Many types of problems occur in child abuse cases, which can include Munchausen's syndrome by proxy, sexual abuse, physical abuse, sexual abuse accommodation syndrome, neglect of young children, various forms of psychological and emotional abuse, the detrimental effects of exposure to domestic violence, and others.

One potential problem is that the professional may have been assigned the case before the relevant issues could be identified. Thus, the expert may discover that while treatment started based upon a referral for physical abuse and neglect, sexual abuse was subsequently disclosed. If the expert did not possess sufficient knowledge in the treatment of sexual abuse, he or she should consider consultation and/or supervision for that aspect of the treatment. Testimony in such situations could involve more than one professional for different aspects of the treatment.

A witness does not automatically qualify as an expert simply because he or she possesses a mental health license. More recent cases, including the U.S. Supreme Court case of *Daubert v. Merrell Dow* (1993) refined the rules for admitting expert opinion in federal cases by conferring on the judge greater gatekeeper responsibilities regarding which type of expert testimony is appropriate for the trial. A state court can determine if the expert's opinion meets acceptable standards of reliability and accuracy, as with the California Supreme Court in *People v. Kelly* (1976), which held the same rationale as the U.S. Supreme Court case of *Frye v. United States* (1923). Each state may have its own rules of evidence regarding the admissibility of expert mental health opinion. For example, in general, the California Kelly-Frye test sets minimum standards that must be met before a technique or opinion is considered sufficiently trustworthy to be introduced into evidence. A review of many cases construing Kelly-Frye principles in California courts indicates that they fall into two major categories: (1) new techniques for developing and measuring physical evidence, and (2) the use of psychological evidence to establish a pattern of conduct or symptoms from which a conclusion as to an individual's behavioral disposition may be extracted (*People v. Cegers,* 1992).

The Cegers case discussed "homicidal somnambulism," "nocturnal confusional arousal," and "confusional arousal syndrome," and noted that the psychological community need not reach a consensus on a specific term before testimony could meet the admissibility requirements under Kelly-Frye. Part of the Cegers decision noted that a "diagnosis based on medical literature will not be viewed as a new scientific technique, but simply the development of an opinion from studies of certain types of cases" (*People v. Cegers,* 1972). Thus, for child abuse testimony, it is important to explain clearly the basis for one's opinion, including the methods used in formulating the opinion, and to articulate a logically compelling analysis that adequately incorporates the history, clinical functioning, and knowledge about the disorders in question. Child abuse testimony includes an abundance of terminology and opinions among professionals for describing similar psychological states of functioning. Experts should resist the temptation to use more complicated terminology than is needed to describe their opinion for a number of reasons, including the recognition that in legal proceedings the casual or imprecise choice of a term could lead to unintended controversies.

CHOOSING TO TESTIFY

The mental health professional should decide whether to testify only after a careful analysis of the individual factors of a given case. The decision should not be based solely upon whether he or she has qualified in the past as an expert, or possesses the requisite knowledge, training, and experience about a child maltreatment subject in general. Experts should also be alert to being asked to overreach in an opinion, because others either seduce them with feelings of importance or coerce them to testify (or not testify). Because in many child abuse cases there is little direct evidence substantiating abuse, the mental health professional's work with the child becomes a very important source of information for the court. The expert should always remain aware of these influences to maximize the potential for offering accurate and unbiased opinion.

Before testifying, consider carefully whether you have an ethical and/or legal obligation to assert a privilege on behalf of an individual involved in the proceeding. This determination can be more complicated in child abuse proceedings because often various family members are involved in the case. You may have examined some, spoken to others by telephone, possess court orders naming some but not all of the people you have contacted, and you may not have clearly defined, informed consents and written authorizations from persons potentially affected by the testimony. The American Psychological Association (APA, 1992) ethical principles for psychologists state: "Psychologists release confidential information only with client consent or pursuant to law" (Standard 5.05b). Absent a signed authorization following an informed consent from those who hold the privilege, you may reveal confidential information only under legally authorized conditions such as a valid court order. When in doubt, assert the privilege and have the legal representatives of the different parties resolve the issue before a judge. This is particularly important in child abuse cases because there may be a permissive atmosphere of discussion with county child protection investigators or legal counsel for the child. Remember that the authority that permits you to speak freely to county investigators or legal counsel for the child may not apply to other confidential information regarding a wide variety of other individuals.

In cases where you are compelled by statute to make reports of suspected child abuse or neglect, there are no legal or ethical prohibitions against communicating your evaluations or other information, so long as you do so properly within the parameters of the statute's requirements. For example, California Penal Code Section 11165-6 requires health care practitioners who have knowledge or reasonable suspicion to suspect abuse for persons under the age of eighteen to make reports as soon as possible by telephone and to prepare a written report within thirty-six hours. The statute does not impose a duty to investigate abuse but to report it. However, Caudill and Pope (1995) note that while child abuse reporting constitutes an express exception to confidentiality, the California Supreme Court has interpreted this waiver as limited in scope. In one case, although the reporter was authorized to communicate with the appropriate agencies, further communications with sheriffs seeking additional information did not constitute an equivalent situation and confidentiality was not therefore deemed waived (*People v.*

Stritzinger, 1983). By analogy, when a professional determines that some type of testimony is appropriate in a child abuse proceeding, he or she must not assume that the testimony can indiscriminately extend to all persons and all issues. For example, in preparing for testimony, you may have reviewed a privileged psychiatric hospital report about one of the child's family, and you should not disseminate the contents of that report absent a clear and appropriate authorization from the holders of the privilege to do so.

Often, when professionals are acting in the role of evaluator instead of psychotherapist, there are more clearly defined parameters about who is the client, the purpose of the assessment, the intended recipient of the results, and a documented acknowledgment of the absence of any confidentiality about the results of the assessment. When one is a treating professional, the referral can originate from the parties themselves, their respective legal counsel, the court, at the suggestion of the county agency investigating the case, an attorney or guardian ad litem appointed to represent the child, or law enforcement. The purpose for the therapy can be imprecisely articulated or may be one among a great number of possible purposes. You should not automatically assume that you can reveal information obtained within a professional relationship until you carefully analyze your particular situation. If the district attorney, law enforcement, or designated child protection investigation agency made the referral, you should not assume that you can testify simply because the referral came from an agent of society designated to investigate child abuse or protect children. Only the holder of the privilege can waive it.

Perhaps more important is the problem of practitioners who exceed the limits of their knowledge and training when offering testimony. Brodsky and Anderer (2000) note that many practitioners tend to testify beyond the scope of their competency, despite clear ethical prohibitions to the contrary, and that the responsible clinician will show restraint against such impulses. The individual who is prone to testify beyond his or her capabilities is also likely to be unaware of the testimonial prohibitions explained in the beginning of this section.

When you have treated a client, one legitimate way to deal with complex issues involving testimony is to constantly remind yourself of your role and its limitations. Thus, if you were referred a parent accused of child abuse and the therapy focused on ameliorating distress and fostering better parental decision making, you can legitimately decline to offer any opinions on parenting capacity, violence potential, or other relevant questions related to the child abuse proceeding. One of the most troublesome errors I have observed is that therapists may fail to realize how they exceed the limits of their knowledge or expertise because they confuse the absence of evidence with evidence of the absence of some problem. In other words, just because no violence-related data presented itself during the course of therapy does not mean that the therapist can opine that there is no evidence for violence potential and that the individual should not be considered violent. To do so ignores the fact that no systematic review or analysis was conducted about criteria related to violence potential, because it was not the purpose for the referral. The therapist could avoid ethical problems and more accurately report the reason for the treatment, what goals were formulated, how progress was determined, the outcome during the last point of contact, and so on. This is vastly preferable to overextending oneself by answering questions that are outside the realm of one's role. Sometimes therapists allow themselves to become overextended for unconscious motivations to protect the client. A more informed, fair, and ethical response would be to explain the limitations of one's role and allow the court to decide if an independent comprehensive evaluation is required about a specific issue.

THERAPIST OR EVALUATOR: PROFESSIONAL ROLE BOUNDARIES

Mental health professionals can become involved in many different facets of a child abuse case. Professional roles include but are not limited to therapist, evaluator, confidential consultant, marriage counselor, mediator, or consultant to legal counsel representing the parent, child, court, or department investigating the abuse. Each role has its own objectives and methods. Child abuse proceedings are often complex, partly because they include a number of different persons with competing interests and attendant points of view, and each party can retain a mental health consultant for any one of a wide variety of functions.

When offering testimony, professionals must recognize that they are acting as forensic experts. Not all professionals are acquainted with the differences in role definition and methods that distinguish the traditional clinical role from that of the forensic expert. Greenberg and Shuman (1997) provide an excellent review of these differences. In part, they note how forensic practitioners are more strongly oriented to seek and utilize external corroboration for their hypotheses, view the retaining attorney or court as the client, and are more apt to act in an objective way in interpreting the data rather than using an empathic and treatment-oriented approach. It is helpful to ask oneself what one's role is and how it might potentially affect opinions.

Legal issues often involve relevant and important questions about a variety of complex decisions, involving many interdependent factors drawn from diverse factors. Frequently, a therapist testifying on behalf of a child or parent cannot easily answer the most important question before the court. For example, for a psychotherapist for a child, the question, "Is it safe to return the child to the parent's home?" depends more on factors outside of the professional's knowledge involving information other than the child's functioning. A variety of other factors are more relevant to consider, outside the scope of purpose and methods of the child's psychotherapist, including parental functioning, community support and monitoring, and situational factors such as unemployment, substance abuse, acceptance of personal responsibility by the perpetrator, and motivation for treatment. It has long interested me how often juvenile courts continue to make separate orders for evaluation or treatment among different providers, without permitting any single professional the benefit of gathering and integrating data about all family members within the dysfunctional system that produced the child protection issue. Expert testimony requires that the expert not speculate or guess, and professional ethics demand that the professional have information sufficient to support a professional opinion. The courts are asking the right questions, but professionals should be reminded of the saying, "fools rush in where angels fear to tread." The challenge is to formulate useful, professionally justifiable opinions, recognizing the special vulnerability of victims in child protection matters. If you are asked whether it is safe to return the child to a parent, and you have only treated the child, it is strongly advised that you state that you do not know and describe what you believe to be the relevant factors to be considered if asked. In this way, you can testify ethically within the limits of your role and help the court to identify what foundational information is needed should a subsequent order be made involving another professional.

Postadjudication involvement of mental health professionals in child abuse cases frequently involves rehabilitation of the parents or psychological treatment of children. In the rehabilitative role, the professional can rely upon traditionally accepted diagnostic descriptions, describe clinical changes in mood and behavior, recommend adjunctive forms of treatment, assess relative change in functioning from different time periods, inform the court about other previously unrecognized psychological issues, and provide opportunities for family members to problem solve objectives issued by the court. When psychotherapists remain within their traditionally defined roles and perform those functions that enjoy the greatest consensus among most practitioners, the professional's opinion is more likely ethical.

SUBPOENAS AND PREPARATION FOR COURT

Complying with a Subpoena

A subpoena is an order of the court that must always be taken seriously, which means that some response is in order. One type of subpoena commands an individual to appear at a certain time and place to testify; another commands the individual to produce records *(duces tecum)*. Subpoenas may be issued by the court or attorneys who are engaging in a pretrial process known as discovery. Often, the subpoena is issued by a party whose interests are antithetical to those of your client, since it is more likely that your clients's attorney would have provided advance notice and cooperated by providing you with the necessary written authorizations prior to any release of information.

In some cases, providing information requested by a subpoena absent a clearly informed consent is unethical, and in one reported case cited in Myers and Erickson (1999) a psychologist was reprimanded for complying (*Rost v. State Board of Psychology,* 1995). Prudence would dictate consultation with one's own attorney to reach a proper decision to produce records or testimony. Mental health professionals frequently make the mistake of relying upon the advice of any available legal counsel involved in the case, whether or not such legal counsel is specifically retained to represent the interests of the mental health professional. Mental health professionals should recognize that their interests demand a legal opinion from someone specifically retained by them with no competing interests or duties. This situation often occurs when psychotherapists are employees of agencies who have legal counsel retained to represent the agency that employs the mental health professional. Attorneys other than one's own have different obligations and must remain focused on their client's interests (i.e., the agency), not those of the mental health professional.

When the mental health professional cannot clearly determine that a release of records or opinion is warranted, then it is prudent to defer the decision to the court. When a professional acts pursuant to the order of the court, he or she is more likely to enjoy immunity from actions resulting from the release, whereas there are lesser protections should the professional make the release on his or her own.

In matters where the subpoena seeks release of information that includes psychological testing data or compelling testimony, the APA (1996) has published a useful guide for protecting test security, minimizing potential misuse of testing data by others not appropriately trained to interpret such data. The guide offers strategies for coping with subpoenas or compelled testimony.

Despite the fact that one is acting as a psychotherapist, the subpoena may involve information that includes psychological testing data. In these cases, psychologists should consider other alternatives. The recently revised Standards for Educational and Psychological Testing (American Educational Research Association, American Psychological Association, and National Council on Measurement in Education, 1999) state, "Test users have the responsibility of protecting the security of the test materials at all times" (Standard 5.7). Standard 5.6 states, "Reasonable efforts should be made to assure the integrity of test scores by eliminating opportunities for test takers to attain scores by fraudulent means." The mandate to refrain from disclosing testing materials in response to subpoenas issued by lawyers or others not ethically or legally obligated to safeguard these materials is problematic. In response, the APA in 1999 published an editorial on test security that recommended the mental health professional ask the court to allow delivery of secured materials only to psychologists or other professionals who are bound by the same duty to protect them. If this is not possible, the recommendation is to seek a protective order prohibiting parties from making copies of the materials, requiring that the materials be returned at the close of litigation, and ordering that the record be sealed if test questions or answers are admitted as part of the record. These protections can be particularly important in child abuse cases, where the content is very sensitive and it is not infrequent that therapy material is intermingled with testing data. If attempts fail to limit or control dissemination or misuse, document your attempts to protect the relevant persons and allow the court to decide the matter.

Different Types of Courts

Just as the law includes diverse subjects treated in many different legal codes, mental health professionals should not view different courts as always having the same objectives, procedures, burdens of proof, and need for expert opinion. Child abuse cases may involve therapists in several different venues, including but not limited to family court hearings where contested child custody cases involve allegations of child abuse, juvenile courts that make findings of child abuse for purposes of establishing dependency protection of minors, or criminal courts that prosecute adults for various forms of child endangerment. In any of these proceedings, Melton and Limber (1989) note that courts and investigation agencies have increasingly attempted to use mental health experts in earlier phases of child abuse investigation, causing the mental health professional to be used as a surrogate investigator. When the mental health professional has been involved prior to a judicial determination of child abuse, extreme caution is warranted to avoid exceeding the limits of one's professional knowledge.

Melton and Limber (1989) noted that traditionally, mental health professionals were involved after adjudication of child abuse. During the last decades, professionals have become involved at earlier stages of the process, including the earliest investigation phase when abuse has not yet been determined in contested situations. Melton and Limber note the complexity of determining abuse and the caution that professionals should exercise against being imprudently drawn into the process. One example they offer is in cases in which an individual has a proven history of abusive acts, which cannot alone justify the conclusion that current abuse exists. To do so would be unduly prejudicial (Federal Rules of Evidence [2002], 404). Similarly, use of syndromal evidence that the suspect shares characteristics of abusers or the child shares characteristics of victims is not a defensible basis for an opinion that someone committed child abuse. When professionals are asked to offer opinions with reasonable professional certainty as to whether a particular individual has perpetrated abuse against a child, such a conclusion is better left to the court to determine after having considered a variety of information, including psychological testimony.

In yet another arena, criminal courts prosecuting penal code offenses for child abuse may appropriately involve mental health professionals in focused areas, such as supporting a child's competence to testify, explaining how delays in reporting abuse can be plausible, or discussing how it is possible to explain recantations by children.

Preparation Before Going into Court

Proper preparation for court testimony requires knowledge of the scope of inquiry, identification of the relevant issues and the questions likely to be asked, and familiarity with the rules governing the particular court's proceedings. Although you are not expected to have the knowledge of a lawyer, the mental health professional should be generally familiar with the rules of court. For example, Myers and Erickson (1999) note, professionals should know courts do not allow experts to testify that children told the truth when disclosing abuse.

What is necessary for all legal proceedings is for professionals to be honest, objective, provide a clearly logical rationale to support their opinion, and to offer such opinions only to the extent professionally supported by the data. It may be helpful for mental health professionals to conceptualize their role to explain rather than to advocate. Forensic psychologists, as opposed to clinical psychologists, sometimes note that their role is to advocate for the relevant data, not persons. The goal is to offer impartial, objective analysis of the relevant data consistent with the present state of professional knowledge.

Toward this end, it is essential that you review everything reasonably available to you before going to court. If possible, identify what you have not reviewed and why not. Bring extra copies of your curriculum vitae. Determine whether you should bring all your records and avoid relinquishing the original record without court advice. Be prepared to answer questions about the precise nature of your education, training, and experience related to child protection matters, including specific job duties related to treatment or evaluation of children and families, and your levels of responsibility. You should anticipate attempts to impeach your testimony, such as attempts to show that you have only limited experience with the issues before the court. It is helpful to prepare a list of prior cases in child abuse, how many cases have you treated versus evaluated within a particular type of abuse category, where your referrals have come from and in what proportion, and what knowledge you have of outcomes from your cases. If you appear young, you could expect questions designed to show you are inexperienced because of your limited opportunity to treat people. Remember to prepare yourself for such impeachment attempts. You should not become defensive, but instead remain objective and focused.

CONTENT OF TESTIMONY

The Limits of Professionally Supported Evidence

In many instances, the most honest, objective, and carefully considered opinion in child abuse cases is summarized as follows: "I do not know." There are limits of inference involving psychological data gathered from psychotherapy or assessment data, either retrospectively about whether specific acts were necessarily committed by certain individuals, or prospectively in terms of whether future behavior (e.g., abuse) will necessarily occur. Special care should be taken to avoid inadvertently overstepping the bounds of what is scientifically or professionally supportable.

The process of psychotherapy often involves an intensely personal alliance in furtherance of the client's goals. When the wishes of a client do not coincide with third-party judgments of a court (e.g., whether to reunify a child with a parent), the psychotherapist may experience conflicting or confused feelings. Psychologists may perceive themselves as acting ethically

. when advocating perceived client interests because they want to help their clients. However, this advocacy inherent within the helping relationship may lead one to unknowingly violate the threshold requirements for offering various opinions. This can be particularly true when treating children, because children deserve special protections due to their developmental vulnerabilities. The mental health professional may believe his or her testimony is the only thing that can save the child from repeated abuse. Parents who themselves were the victims of sexual or physical abuse can seek trust or protection from their therapists, or make coercive demands because of fears of rejection or abandonment. These influences can also affect protective identifications within therapists.

Another factor that can potentially influence therapists into making unjustified conclusions is the desire to justify one's professional usefulness or sense of competence, either to oneself or the court. The therapist can feel useless, incompetent, or lacking moral courage unless a stronger or specific opinion is provided. A not-so-subtle influence is coercion by an attorney who advances a series of questions or hypotheticals designed to get the expert to state the desired opinion. Some of the most effective techniques used by attorneys are to construct scenarios that cause the psychologist to feel it would be unethical not to adopt the attorney's viewpoint. This can be done by first getting the professional to agree with a series of respected views or authoritative texts leading up to the critical questions. When therapists are asked to go beyond reporting what was observed or stated in therapy, they should be careful to examine the underlying associations or assumptions of the hypothetical question.

Therapists also undermine undermine their effectiveness if they exceed the limits of their data by offering inferential opinions about other members of the patient's family who were not directly assessed or treated. The APA (1992) *Ethical Principles of Psychologists* and Specialty Guidelines for Forensic Psychology (APA, Division 41, 1991) specifically prohibit offering evaluative opinions about those not evaluated. The APA (1998) Guidelines for Psychological Evaluations in Child Protection Matters specifically provide: "Psychologists conducting a psychological evaluation in child protection matters provide an opinion regarding the psychological functioning of an individual only after conducting an evaluation of the individual adequate to support their statements or conclusions" (Section 14). When I served on the committee that wrote those guidelines, discussion reflected the complexity of formulating opinions that retained the focus of the child's interests as paramount, at the same time recognizing that it is easy to drift into opinions about others who have not been properly evaluated. It is defensible to raise questions or concerns about others on behalf of the child without offering conclusive opinions of others not evaluated.

Ultimate Legal versus Ultimate Psychological Opinion

Is your contemplated testimony in a child abuse case inappropriate because it exceeds the limits of professionally supported knowledge and experience? Assume you have only seen a child suspected of being sexually abused. During your evaluation, the child exhibits atypical sexualized behavior compared to known developmental norms. Furthermore, the child is anxious and fearful, representing a differential altered affective response when discussing abuse by a family member, which was not exhibited during any other times or circumstance of the interview. Myers (1992) notes that the line separating ultimate facts from questions of law is illusory, although there is universal agreement among mental health professionals that they should not be permitted to offer legal opinions. Myers cites Federal Rules of Evidence (2002), Section 704(a), that testimony should not be objectionable because it embraces the ultimate issue to be decided by the trier of fact. In an alleged sexual abuse case, an opinion can be both an opinion of fact and of law. The suggestions offered by Myers to help mental health professionals include making a diagnosis of the child and/or explaining how some aspects of the child's functioning can be compatible with sexual abuse, without stating whether it necessarily happened and/or was committed by a particular individual. Analogous to my recommendation of staying close to what is objectively learned about the child from the evaluation or therapy, avoid inferential sexual abuse conclusions based upon presumed correlations, and defer to the court for the ultimate finding. Psychological testimony can represent extremely important information for the court to consider, but is only one of a number of sources of relevant information for the court to use in making an ultimate finding.

There is disagreement among professionals about whether a professional should ever offer an opinion that a particular child was abused based upon psychological findings. Melton and Limber (1989) stated that no court should admit an opinion that a child was abused. Other mental health and legal writers (Myers et al., 1989) support such testimony in some cases.

In the context of sexual abuse cases, Myers (1996) suggested that the greatest confidence in testimony was warranted when the "expert's opinion is based on a coalescence of five types of data" (p. 331). The following five categories were suggested by Myers in the context of sexual abuse testimony:

1. Developmentally unusual sexual behavior, knowledge, or symptoms providing relatively strong evidence of sexual experience. For an ex-

cellent discussion about how to distinguish what normal and sexually abused children exhibit, see Friedrich (1993).

2. Nonsexual behavior or symptoms commonly observed in sexually abused children. Again, the research of Friedrich is helpful in this regard as well as the review of empirical research by Kendall-Tackett, Williams, and Finkelhor (1993).
3. Medical evidence indicative of abuse.
4. Convincing disclosure by the child.
5. Evidence that corroborates the abuse, such as collateral sources of information.

Regarding Myers' criterion of convincing disclosure by the child, those offering testimony should appreciate the complexity of the subject in consideration of other research, which illustrates how preschool-age children in particular can be influenced by suggestibility, selective reinforcement, coercion, or susceptibility caused by repeated interviews (Ceci & Bruch, 1995). Myers also notes that a professional should be circumspect when offering testimony about sexual abuse, as no single symptom or behavior, whether sexual or nonsexual, is pathognomonic of abuse.

Objectivity and Honesty in Testimony

All writers note the need for honesty in any testimony. The Specialty Guidelines for Forensic Psychologists (APA, Division 41, 1991) state expert witnesses must be honest with the jury, judge, attorneys, and in the final analysis with themselves. What does it mean to be honest with oneself in expert child abuse testimony?

A therapist should acknowledge the potential for narcissistically gratifying identifications with law enforcement and the district attorney's office, as these agencies are conferred deserved respect as institutions representing the law and often protecting victims. For some therapists, there is status and potential financial gain in fostering a relationship with such persons or agencies. As mental health services are sometimes neglected relative to other professional endeavors, the relationship can cause distortions in perceptions or judgments. As psychotherapy is performed in a totally private manner that is often never known to anyone other than the patient, the therapist can be more easily seduced into unconscious reinforcements for providing opinions in the desired directions of one party or the other in a legal hearing. There is a pressure, even if unconscious, to say something. Ultimately, your answer should be nothing more or less than that which you would have dispassionately decided after a careful review and reasoned interpretation of the available information. If the therapist is affected by narcissistic gratification or coercion, it is hard to state, "I do not know."

Sometimes the professional must resist intimidating or threatening actions by individuals suspected of child abuse or domestic violence. Coercion or threats can take many forms, including but not limited to threats of legal actions, ethical complaints to professional associations, or licensing board complaints. The professional must guard against compromising objectivity to minimize the risk of personal stress. To do so would betray the most vulnerable clients and compromise the integrity of the mental health professions. Professionals should also be alert to secondary forms of attack upon individuals making child abuse allegations. Sometimes the professional is asked to globally label an individual with professionally unsupported characterizations, which has the effect of undermining the child abuse allegation. Seeking multiple consultations can reinforce the professional in maintaining objectivity.

Another potential influence upon objectivity is protective overidentification with the child. This can happen for a variety of unconscious reasons, including the therapist's naturally empathic or supportive feelings toward the child or reasons related to personal unresolved childhood issues. Ongoing case consultation with colleagues on a variety of child protection matters can provide an effective, objective check about one's formulations. Over time and with the objective feedback of colleagues, the professional should become aware of any perceptual distortions or interpretive errors.

Reasonable Certainty

Myers has noted that an opinion offered with a reasonable degree of certainty is somewhere between speculation or guessing and absolute certainty. To help experts determine whether the testimony they are offering is reasonable, Myers (1992) offered the following criteria:

1. *Did the expert consider all the facts?* Was there some information the expert could have reviewed but never asked for, or never reviewed although the expert already possessed it? Even if the expert has significant information that can weigh heavily in support of his or her opinion, the failure to examine all information that was reasonably available weakens the expert's opinion. Without a review of all the available information, the expert can never be sure what effect, if any, other information might have had on the opinion. For example, children's reports can be particularly vulnerable to situational variables or strong psychological influence from family members, which manifests differently at different times and under different interview situations. If an expert did not examine the statements of a child

in contexts other than those of therapy or evaluation, many rival hypotheses can exist without reasonable explanation. My experience with child abuse allegations in the context of child custody disputes illustrates the possibility for highly contradictory representations among children depending upon the time, place, and circumstance for the disclosure.

2. *How much confidence can be placed in the facts underlying the expert's opinion?* Mental health professionals need to assess the adequacy of the information they possess. In other words, to borrow from the computer processing adage, "garbage in, garbage out." In mental health work, the risk is great if you have weak, misleading, or inaccurate data. For example, a four-year-old child is living with her mother after a protracted child custody conflict. The mother attributes to the child various troubling statements suggestive of sexually inappropriate activity. When you see the child, how do you determine whether the child's statements are a product of coercion, selective reinforcement, repeated questioning, suggestion, a blending of actual experience with distorted beliefs, or other factors introduced from other sources? The potential for coercion works in both psychological directions for a young child whose parents are going through a protracted custody battle, that is in producing inaccurate expressions of abuse or suppressing legitimate bases for child protection.

3. *Does the expert adequately understand clinical and scientific principles?* The expert should understand that there are no child symptom-specific markers that prove or disprove child abuse, nor are there empirically supported testing profiles sufficient to prove whether an individual is an abuser. The expert should also know that some empirical research exists showing the prevalence of certain types of sexualized behavior in children by different age groups, gender, and for abused and nonabused children (Friedrich, 1993; Kendall-Tackett et al., 1993). It is beyond the scope of this chapter to review the many relevant professional issues and it is incumbent upon professionals working in this area to familiarize themselves with the professional literature regarding such topics as the use of anatomically correct dolls in interviewing children who may be victims of sexual abuse; techniques for evaluating children's descriptions of abuse, including statement validity analysis and criterion-based content analysis; sexual abuse accommodation syndrome; false memory and implantation beliefs; delayed reporting and recantation; and others.

4. *Have principles or theories relied upon by the expert been generally accepted as reliable by experts in the field or recognized in peer-reviewed journals?* For example, research on the use of anatomically correct dolls for assessing sexual abuse in young children raises certain cautions and concerns. Various studies have expressed caution and concern about reliance upon these methods in sexual abuse evaluations, and the APA cited

some of these cautions in a 1991 document. The expert should become aware of the range of opinions about the strengths and weaknesses for a given technique used to formulate an opinion offered in testimony. The foregoing does not suggest that it is always inappropriate to use such methods, but simply that those offering testimony must be able to provide a professionally supportable rationale for which technique was employed and why.

5. *Did the expert employ appropriate methods of assessment?* First, did the expert do any assessment, or is the therapist simply reporting what was stated by the child during a session? I do not know of any single recognized assessment procedure or list of instruments to be used with children in child abuse cases recognized by all mental health professionals. The requirement should not be that a professional can use only one type of specific procedure, but that the expert can articulate a clearly logical and consistent rationale for what was done and why. Guidelines by professional societies are helpful in this regard and should challenge professionals as to why their procedures do not necessarily comport with such guidelines. Some guidelines have been published by various professional societies and provide an excellent reference for professionals considering giving testimony in child abuse cases. In addition to the APA practice guidelines previously cited, the reader is also referred to the practice parameters for the forensic evaluation of children and adolescents who may have been physically or sexually abused, published by the American Academy of Child and Adolescent Psy-. chiatry (1997), or the guidelines for psychosocial assessment of suspected sexual abuse of children published by the American Professional Society on the Abuse of Children (1997).

6. *Are the inferences and conclusions drawn by the expert defensible?* Sometimes therapists have not clearly articulated the factors responsible for their own opinion. If you have a faulty understanding of the history and facts of the case, or if the information upon which you base your opinions contradicts the assumptions or inferences contained in your opinion, your testimony will be compromised. If you failed to consider alternate explanations, your opinion will be further weakened. As cited in Myers (1992), Black noted that in the final analysis, the value of the expert's opinion will depend heavily upon whether the opinion is logical, consistent, explainable, objective, and defensible.

Mental Health Testimony and Syndromal Evidence

"Syndrome" as used in child abuse literature can mean different things to different people. When used as a collection of signs and symptoms that imply an exclusive existence relative to other alternative conditions, it can be misleading. For example, Summit's (1983) child sexual abuse accommodation syndrome has often been misapplied to detect sexual abuse, rather than for its intended use, to psychologically explain children's reactions to intrafamily sexual abuse and how recantation is possible in legitimate cases of abuse. In one work that discussed these concerns, Summit (1992) published a follow-up article titled, "Abuse of the Child Sexual Abuse Accommodation Syndrome." It is a significantly different matter to explain to the court how it might be possible for a sexually abused child to delay disclosing sexual abuse to others than to use this fact as a basis for detecting whether a particular individual sexually abused a given child. The accommodation syndrome explains how it is possible for a child victim of intrafamilial sexual abuse to delay reporting because of the pattern of secrecy, helplessness, entrapment, and accommodation; delayed, conflicted, or unconvincing disclosure; and retraction. In criminal proceedings, family court custody cases, or juvenile dependency proceedings where there has been no finding of abuse, it is incorrect to superimpose the features of the accommodation syndrome to prove or disprove whether abuse occurred.

No test or group of tests exists that can reliably identify the perpetrator of sexual abuse. Persons who sexually abuse children represent a heterogeneous group of people with no traits or characteristics that reliably differentiate them from persons who do not abuse children, other than the sexual abuse of children. It is inappropriate to offer such testimony, not only from a psychological perspective, but from a legal one as well. One of the basic principles underlying U.S. law prohibits the establishment of a person's guilt through attempts to show the person has particular traits or propensities.

Opinions About Those Not Directly Evaluated

The Specialty Guidelines for Forensic Psychologists (APA, Division 41, 1991) state:

> Forensic psychologists avoid giving written or oral evidence about the psychological characteristics of individuals when they have not had an opportunity to conduct an evaluation of the individual adequate to the scope of the statements, opinions or conclusions to be offered. Forensic psychologists make every effort to conduct such evaluations. When it is not possible or feasible to do so, they make clear the impact of such limitations on the reliability and validity of their professional products, evidence or testimony. (Guideline VI.H)

The APA (1992) ethical principles state: "Psychologists provide written or oral forensic reports or testimony of the psychological characteristics of an individual only after they have conducted an examination of the individual adequate to support their statements or conclusions" (Standard 7.02b). The APA (1998) Guidelines for Psychological Evaluations in Child Protection Matters state: "Psychologists conducting a psychological evaluation in child protection matters provide an opinion regarding the psychological functioning of an individual only after conducting an evaluation of the individual adequate to support their statements or conclusions" (Section III, No. 14).

The American Academy of Child and Adolescent Psychiatry notes: "Honesty, objectivity and adequacy of the evaluation may be called into question when an expert opinion is offered without a personal examination" (Guideline IV).

Although these guidelines clearly involve evaluations of those engaged in child abuse matters, all psychotherapists perform some amount of assessment as part of their treatment. Mental status examination and assessment of clinical functioning are ongoing concerns. When this information includes data furnished by a child about family members, it is easier to blur the distinctions in formal assessment of others versus inferential data presented by one's patient.

When conducting psychotherapy of a child brought by one parent from a divorced family, the other parent may not be evaluated. In child abuse cases where only the child or a parent is seen, the expert witness should be careful not to offer specific opinions about an individual who has not been the subject of history taking, interview, possible review of records, possible evaluation instruments, and other methods common to an appropriate assessment.

COMPENSATION

It is important to keep careful records for all billing matters, not only for purposes of being fairly compensated, but also to prevent a potential impeachment of your accuracy, organization, and conscientiousness. Being unable to answer questions about your billing can also create an impression of evasiveness or unprofessionalism. After you have accurately and fairly maintained a record, you need to reach an agreement prior to your deposition or court testimony as to exactly how much is to be paid, in what manner, and at what time. You can seek the help of the attorney propounding your testimony in memorializing an exact understanding, but failing that, it is incumbent upon you to satisfactorily resolve the issue.

Many mental health professionals are unassertive or avoid dealing with such matters for fear it makes them appear greedy or only secondarily interested in the welfare of the participants. You as a professional are entitled to compensation and you should not be reticent about requesting payment. It may be useful to check with your local professional society about the reasonable ranges of compensation for forensic matters by others with similar qualifications. Because many states have specific statutes that necessitate the mandatory payment of expert fees prior to testimony, beware of attempts to designate you a lay or percipient witness as a method of avoiding the payment of reasonable expert fees.

FILE CONTENTS

The expert may be required to make the entire file available to the attorney for one of the parties. Check with the attorney who retained you to determine whether any of the contents of the file contain information protected from disclosure because of attorney work-product privilege. If for any reason some part of the file is not available—for example, for size constraints some material is confidentially filed elsewhere—make a note in the chart describing the location of the stored file and date it was relocated. Having a precise record of procedures helps the expert immediately answer questions about the information relied upon in the development of the opinion. Remember that an expert can be examined on materials referred to, considered, or relied upon in arriving at his or her opinion. If the expert has reviewed such material, have a list ready at the time of testimony of all such material along with any other document that was reviewed. This will allow you to answer qustions in a more coherent and organized fashion.

Sometimes an attorney will read portions of a treatise well known in the field but not something you examined as part of the case, asking if you agree or disagree. This could represent an attempt to force you to respond without adequate time for review or without knowledge that the particular portion read is out of context with the rest of the treatise. Before answering any question, you should allow a suitable time period to permit objections if you are asked inappropriate questions. In this example, the state where you practice may not permit examination on a treatise that you did not rely on, refer to, or consider unless it is admitted into evidence. If you relied upon a particular treatise in the formulation of your expert opinion prior to testimony, then you should be thoroughly prepared to answer any questions about the treatise in relation to your opinion.

APPEARING FOR COURT OR DEPOSITION

When the professional is thoroughly prepared and satisfied that there are no legitimate prohibitions against testifying, several traits noted by various writers are considered to be desirable or undesirable.

Things to avoid include Brodsky and Anderer's (2000) suggestions that you resist redundant overexplaining, becoming defensive, or acting in an anxiously insecure manner during cross-examination. I would add to check that your opinions are not unqualified in the sense that you exhibit no appreciation for counterhypotheses or factors that possibly could be contradictory to your opinion.

Positive traits in testifying mentioned by Brodsky and Anderer include being thorough in preparation, lucid in responses, and organized in thought, knowing the limits of knowledge and saying, "I don't know," being open to admitting certain weaknesses, speaking to the whole courtroom, explaining without pontificating, and being likable, earned through an avoidance of being argumentative, caustic, or sharp.

Direct examination will begin by reviewing your qualifications. It may be helpful to have your curriculum vitae available for review and to note highlighted areas relevant to the testimony. You will then be asked questions pertaining to your knowledge of the case. Prior to testimony, rehearse with yourself and determine whether you can relate a simple story about the case. If you hear doubts or realize you are unsure of something, look it up because it will likely surface during your testimony. You will then be asked to describe what you considered in formulating your opinion. Be clear with yourself as to what was related to you as part of the history of the case versus what you judged to exist because of your professional opinion about your client.

COMMON CROSS-EXAMINATION PRACTICES

The expert in child abuse cases should be prepared to expect practices commonly used by attorneys to impeach expert testimony. These include attempts to demonstrate one is not truly an expert in the field. This can be done by extensive review of the expert's education, credentials, and experience to find weakness relative to the areas of testimony. Did the expert overstate his or her credentials? Were publications or committee assignments not relevant to the proceedings? It is not enough to have worked professionally with children. Does the expert have supervised experience, training, and experience in the assessment or treatment of abused children? At what ages? Involving what types of abuse? At what point in the investigative process?

Attorneys may also attempt to show bias. This can be attempted by asking how often you testify for one side of a type of proceeding versus the other side. Do you work for a child abuse treatment agency that only sees children brought to the facility because of contractual obligations with county law enforcement? Do you only assess accused parents at the referral of a small number of defense attorneys who regularly challenge accusations of child abuse?

A common impeachment approach is to inquire of the expert whether he or she believes that individuals involved in a case are capable of lying, malingering, or are subject to distorting motives of revenge, secondary gain, or other influences? An expert would justifiably appear to be naive and misinformed if he or she were to testify that children never lie about abuse-related matters or that one can always tell if a child is credible based upon how convincing the report was.

Does the expert have any conflict of interest that taints the objectivity of his or her testimony? Does the professional have a personal relationship with any of the attorneys? Did the professional agree to accept payment for testimony on a lien basis pending the outcome of a proceeding? This practice is considered unethical according to the Specialty Guidelines for Forensic Psychologists (APA, Division 41, 1991). Any testimony offered under such conditions cannot be considered objective if payment is in any way contingent upon the outcome of the case.

Attacks on the expert's credibility pertaining to his or her therapy or evaluation can be predicated on the paucity of time spent with the patient. This can be difficult for the professional working at an understaffed and underfunded agency that does not permit a great amount of time for each case. The expert can be asked what specifically was asked and what was omitted. This line of inquiry can also ask what the professional said in response to key answers, as a method for revealing potential biases or flaws in technique. For example, reviews of videotaped interviews of children can reveal that interviewers selectively focused on follow-up questions about one individual at the exclusion of others.

How should you handle such tricks of questioning? Do you appear defensive or embarrassed? Do you apologize for acknowledging omissions or mistakes? You should remind yourself you are not expected to know everything. A candid admission that you did not know certain things can enhance your credibility, if you are open-minded and nondefensive.

Attorneys can ask what materials related to child abuse were consulted, including books, treatises, or articles other than materials provided through counsel. Expect to be asked about what you identified as an authoritative reference. Also, expect to identify authoritative references contrary to those you mentioned. A well-prepared attorney probably has consulted with another expert about what to ask you based upon the contrary references.

Attorneys may also seek to identify what areas of your findings are consistent with the legal position of the cross-examiner. Experts should always answer honestly. When the expert is taken into this area of questioning, it is not unusual to then be asked if it would be possible or plausible for other opinions to be valid that are different from those the expert previously offered. Particularly within the complex field of child abuse testimony, many things need to be acknowledged as possible. Redirect examination by the attorney offering your opinion usually balances the testimony. Always strive to offer reasonable opinion, which should include the willingness to consider other possibilities.

CONCLUSION

Few areas of professional mental health work are as important as those related to the assessment or treatment of child abuse victims. This chapter focuses upon many areas of complexity that warrant caution by the professional prior to giving testimony. These recommendations should not inhibit honest, clear, and informed testimony. The increased numbers of requests from the court for your testimony represent both a compliment and a challenge. Anything less than our most informed involvement would reduce the mental health professions to an unscientific and unprofessional collection of opinions, but worse, would betray the very children and families deserving protection.

REFERENCES

American Academy of Child and Adolescent Psychiatry (1997). Practice parameters for the forensic evaluation of children and adolescents who may have been physically or sexually abused. *Journal of the American Academy of Child and Adolescent Psychiatry,* 36 (Supplement), 57S-68S.

American Educational Research Association, American Psychological Association, and National Council on Measurement in Education (1999). *Standards for educational and psychological testing.* Washington, DC: American Educational Research Association.

American Professional Society on the Abuse of Children (1997). *Guidelines for psychosocial evaluation of suspected sexual abuse of children.* Chicago: Sage.

American Psychological Association (1991, February 8). *Statement on the use of anatomically detailed dolls in forensic evaluations* (as adopted by the APA Council of Representatives). Washington, DC: Author.

American Psychological Association (1992). *Ethical principles of psychologists and code of conduct.* Washington, DC: Author. Retrieved from http://www .apa.org/ethics/code.html.

American Psychological Association (1994). Guidelines for child custody evaluations in divorce proceedings. *American Psychologist, 49*, 677-680.

American Psychological Association (1996). Strategies for private practitioners coping with subpoena or compelled testimony for client records or test data. *Professional Psychology: Research and Practice, 27*, 245-251.

American Psychological Association (1998). Guidelines for psychological evaluations in child protection matters. *American Psychologist, 54*, 586-593.

American Psychological Association (1999). Test security: Protecting the integrity of tests. *American Psychologist, 54*, 1078.

American Psychological Association, Division 41 and the American Psychology-Law Society. Committee on Ethical Guidelines for Forensic Psychologists (1991). Specialty guidelines for forensic psychologists. *Law and Human Behavior, 15*, 655-665.

Brodsky, S. & Anderer, S. (2000). Serving as an expert witness: evaluations, subpoenas and testimony. In F. Kaslow (Ed.), *Handbook of couple and family forensics* (pp. 189-201). New York: John Wiley.

Caudill, B. & Pope, K. (1995). *Law and mental health professionals.* Washington, DC: American Psychological Association.

Ceci, S. & Bruch, M. (1995). *Jeopardy in the courtroom: A scientific analysis of children's testimony.*Washington, DC: American Psychological Association.

Ceci, S. & Hembrooke, H. (1998). *Expert witnesses in child abuse cases.* Washington, DC: American Psychological Association.

Daubert v. Merrell Dow Pharmaceuticals, 509, U.S. 579 (1993).

Federal Rules of Evidence (2002). *United States Code,* Title 28, Sections 404, 702.

Friedrich, W. (1993). Sexual victimization and sexual behavior in children: A review of recent literature. *Child Abuse and Neglect, 17*, 59-66.

Frye v. United States, 293 F. 1013 (D.C. Cir. 1923).

Greenberg, S. & Shuman, D. (1997). Irreconcilable conflict between therapeutic and forensic roles. *Professional Psychology, 28*, 50-57.

Kendall-Tackett, K., Williams, L., & Finkelhor, D. (1993). Impact of sexual abuse on children: A review and synthesis of recent empirical studies. *Psychological Bulletin, 113*, 164-180.

Melton, G. & Limber, S. (1989). Psychologist's involvement in cases of child maltreatment: Limits of role and expertise. *American Psychologist, 44*, 1225-1233.

Myers, J. (1992). *Evidence in child abuse and neglect cases* (2nd ed., Vol. I). New York: John Wiley.

Myers, J. (1996). Expert testimony. In J. Briere, L. Berliner, J. Bulkley, C. Jenny, and T. Reid (Eds.), *The APSAC handbook on child maltreatment* (pp. 319-340). Thousand Oaks, CA: Sage.

Myers, J., Bays, J., Becker, J., Berliner, L., Corwin, D., & Saywitz, K. (1989). Expert testimony in child sexual abuse litigation. *Nebraska Law Review, 68*, 1-34.

Myers, J. & Erickson, R. (1999). Legal and ethical issues in child custody litigation. In R. Galatzer-Levy and L. Kraus (Eds.), *The scientific basis of child custody decisions* (pp. 12-31). New York: John Wiley.

People v. Cegers. 7 Cal. App. 4th 988, 9 Cal.Rptr.2d 297. (1992).

People v. Kelly. 17 Cal. 3d 24. (1976).

People v. Stritzinger. 34 Cal. 3d 505. (1983).

Rost v. State Board of Psychology, 659 A.2d 626 (Pa. Commonwealth Ct. 1995).

Summit, R. (1983). The child sexual abuse accommodation syndrome. *Child Abuse and Neglect,* 7, 177-193.

Summit, R. (1992). Abuse of the child sexual abuse accommodation syndrome. *Child Abuse and Neglect,* 16, 153-163.

Chapter 16

Medication Considerations
with Maltreated Children

Michael De Bellis

INTRODUCTION

The focus of this chapter is the use of medications for psychiatric disorders commonly associated with child maltreatment. It was written to help the treating psychiatrist and the treating clinician understand both the adverse biological effects of maltreatment and the rationale for using medications to attenuate these effects. For the purposes of this chapter, child maltreatment is defined as neglect (including emotional neglect, which is defined as witnessing domestic violence by omission [failure to protect]), physical abuse, sexual abuse, and emotional maltreatment (which includes verbal threats to the child and witnessing domestic violence by commission).

Maltreatment during childhood is a grave problem that has serious consequences for its victims and for society. Nationally, over 3 million children were referred for investigation to Child Protective Services (CPS) in 1996 (U.S. Department of Health and Human Services, 1998). Of these cases, about one-third were substantiated while only 1 percent were identified as false reports (U.S. Department of Health and Human Services, 1998). There has been a disproportionate increase in the incidence of maltreatment among young children (under twelve years of age) (Sedlak & Broadhurst, 1996). Child neglect is the most prevalent form of child maltreatment, followed in order by physical abuse, sexual abuse, and emotional abuse (National Research Council, 1993). However, for the child victim, maltreatment occurs as a chronic and stressful life condition, and various forms of child abuse and neglect tend to coexist (Kaufman, Jones, Stieglitz, Vitulano, & Mannarino, 1994; Levy, Markovic, Chaudry, Ahart, & Torres, 1995; McGee, Wolfe, Yuen, Wilson, & Carnochan, 1995; Widom, 1989).

Child maltreatment may be the single most preventable and treatable contributor to child and adult mental illness in this country. Adults with child maltreatment histories are more likely to manifest multiple health risk behaviors and serious medical illnesses (Felitti et al., 1998) and greater rates of psychiatric and medical utilization (Walker et al., 1999) than adults without maltreatment histories. Maltreated children and adolescents manifest high rates of posttraumatic stress symptoms, depression, suicidal thoughts and behaviors, aggression and antisocial behaviors, and cognitive deficits (for review see National Research Council, 1993). The causes of these high rates of mental disorders in maltreated children is both familial/genetic and environmental. Increased rates of major depression, post-traumatic stress disorder (PTSD), alcohol and/or substance abuse, and antisocial behaviors are found in parents involved in maltreatment (De Bellis et al., 2001; Famularo, Kinscherff, & Fenton, 1992; Kaplan, Pelkovitz, Saltzinger, & Ganeles, 1983; Taylor et al., 1991). However, some authors believe that child abuse is causally and independently related to this increased risk for adult psychiatric and alcohol and substance abuse disorders. For example, a study of twins discordant for child abuse exposure showed that even after controlling for family background and parental psychopathology, the exposed twin suffered from an increased risk for adult psychopathology (Kendler et al., 2000).

Despite the widespread prevalence of child maltreatment in our society, little information is available on the medical treatments of the common psychiatric disorders that are associated with (and may result from) childhood maltreatment. Psychopharmacological treatment studies of childhood mood, anxiety, and behavioral disorders have typically excluded maltreated subjects in their protocols. Therefore, this chapter focuses on psychopharmacotherapies for the psychiatric disorders that are commonly seen in maltreated children and adolescents. One method of approach for maltreatment research and treatment is the PTSD or biological stress response systems model. The traumatic stress model can help physicians utilize a rational approach for prescribing medications.

Thus, this chapter begins by using the PTSD model approach. In this model, the stressor is seen as a dysfunctional and traumatized interpersonal relationship. Thus, abuse and neglect are seen as a most extreme form of dysfunctional family and interpersonal functioning on a continuous spectrum of adverse life circumstances and dysfunctional interpersonal/family relationships. These adverse life circumstances include socioeconomic disadvantage, parental mental illness (including alcohol and substance abuse), community violence, and a lack of adequate social support.

Child maltreatment is caused by interpersonal stressors. Maltreatment trauma is likely to be chronic and more severe than noninterpersonal single-event traumas. An interpersonal stressor likely involves the maltreated child losing faith and trust in a parent or authority figure. Hence, for the maltreated child, the ability to form relationships and attachments is intact (e.g., the hard wiring is present) but traumatized (e.g., the software is programmed to distrust and fear relationships). Consequently, the maltreated child will be more difficult to treat in psychotherapy and have a harder time forming healthy social relationships. In view of this, the establishment of a therapeutic alliance will involve a process of desensitizing the maltreated individual to distrust. Hence the therapeutic alliance may be difficult to form and effective therapy will take more time to progress. In theory, the appropriate use of medications aimed at desensitizing the maltreated child's hyperaroused biological stress response systems and thus attenuating their PTSD symptoms can help foster this therapeutic alliance.

It must be acknowledged that maltreatment during childhood is a severe and chronic trauma. Abuse and neglect may impede the development of age-expected achievements in behavioral and emotional regulation and in cognitive functioning. Maltreated children usually present with multiple problems including comorbidity for both internalizing and externalizing disorders. Thus, the psychopharmacological treatments of childhood anxiety, mood, and behavioral disorders that are commonly seen in maltreated children and adolescents are reviewed. The information presented in this chapter is based on double-blind studies of psychopharmacological agents used to treat these disorders in nonmaltreated children and adolescents, published case reports regarding psychopharmacological therapies for maltreated children with PTSD, a review of double-blind studies of psychopharmacological agents for the treatment of adult PTSD, and the many years of clinical treatment experience of the author. Since adolescents with histories of maltreatment are also at an increased risk for alcohol and substance abuse or dependence, I review this area as well. Child and adolescent psychiatrists are usually not the first professionals to see these children. This chapter was written to be user-friendly to the nonphysician clinician. Information on how clinicians and psychiatrists can work together effectively is provided throughout. Last, impediments to effective treatment (or when medications do not work) are addressed.

TRAUMATIC STRESS DISORDERS

The *Diagnostic and Statistical Manual of Mental Disorders,* fourth edition, text revision (DSM-IV-TR) has four diagnoses in which a stressor precipitates the mental illness: PTSD, acute stress disorder, reactive attachment disorder of infancy or early childhood, and adjustment disorders. The essential feature (criterion A) of PTSD and acute stress disorder in the

DSM-IV-TR is exposure to an extreme traumatic stressor in which the person experienced, witnessed, or was confronted with an event or events that involved actual or threatened death or serious injury, or a threat to the physical integrity of self or others, and responded with intense fear, helplessness, horror, or, in children, disorganized or agitated behaviors (American Psychiatric Association, 2000). These include physical abuse, sexual abuse, witnessing domestic violence, or verbal threats to a child or the primary caregiver. It can also be argued that childhood neglect without physical or sexual abuse may be perceived by the neglected child as traumatic. The degree of the traumatic experience perceived by the child will depend on the age of the child at the time of neglect. For example, continuously neglected infants suffer from increased rates of infection and early death (Chapin, 1917). These high rates of infection may be associated with stress-induced suppression of the immune system (for review see De Bellis & Putnam, 1994). Infants have been known to aspirate and die from the stress of severe and continued unanswered crying. A toddler who is not fed or supervised does not develop a "secure base" and is in a chronic state of severe anxiety (Rutter, 1981). An unsupervised nonabused young child is more likely to witness interpersonal traumas or experience traumatic accidents. It is estimated that one-third to one-half of neglected children witness domestic violence (i.e., emotional neglect) (for review see Lyon, 1999). Furthermore, it is estimated that half of these neglected children will experience PTSD symptoms secondary to witnessing domestic violence (for review see De Bellis, 1997).

Although PTSD has traditionally been studied in male soldiers and combat veterans, it may arise from a variety of traumatic events in both males and females and in children, adolescents, and adults. It is now known that children are more likely to be diagnosed with PTSD, after experiencing a traumatic event, than their adult counterparts (Fletcher, 1996). The DSM-IV-TR diagnosis of PTSD is made when criterion A is experienced and when three clusters of categorical symptoms are present for more than one month after the traumatic event(s): (1) intrusive reexperiencing of the trauma(s) (criterion B), (2) persistent avoidance of stimuli associated with the trauma(s) (criterion C), and (3) persistent symptoms of increased physiological arousal (criterion D) (American Psychiatric Association, 2000). Symptoms meeting PTSD criteria must be associated with significant psychological distress or psychosocial impairments.

The clinical picture of PTSD in children is similar to that of adults (Eth & Pynoos, 1985; Goodwin, 1988; Lyons, 1987; Pynoos et al., 1987; Terr, 1991; Wolfe, Gentile, & Wolfe, 1989), with the exception of children less than four years old, for which more objective criteria based on observable behaviors are warranted (Scheeringa, Zeanah, Drell, & Larrieu, 1995). PTSD is commonly seen in maltreated children. In clinically referred samples, the reported incidence rates of PTSD resulting from sexual abuse range from 42 percent to 90 percent (Dubner & Motta, 1999; Lipschitz, Winegar, Hartnick, Foote, & Southwick, 1999; McLeer, Callaghan, Henry, & Wallen, 1994), from witnessing domestic violence from 50 percent to 100 percent (for domestic homicide) (Pynoos & Nader, 1989), and from physical abuse to as high as 50 percent (Dubner & Motta, 1999; Green, Grace, & Gleser, 1985). High rates of PTSD are also seen in non-clinically referred maltreated children. Famularo, Fenton, and Kinscherff (1993) reported a 39 percent incidence rate of PTSD in a non-clinically referred maltreated sample interviewed within eight weeks of abuse or neglect disclosure. About a third of the PTSD subjects reexamined from the original sample continued to meet PTSD criteria at two-year follow-up (Famularo, Fenton, Augustyn, & Zuckerman, 1996). McLeer et al. (1998) reported prevalence rates of PTSD of 36.3 percent in non-clinically referred sexually abused children sixty days immediately following sexual abuse disclosure.

The DSM-IV-TR categorizes disorders as an all-or-none or yes-or-no outcome. However, many traumatized individuals suffer from subclinical disorders, whose symptoms cause significant clinical distress and psychosocial impairment. When patients or clients fit this category, a diagnosis of adjustment disorder or PTSD in partial remission (if they met the full DSM-IV-TR PTSD criteria previously) is made. These individuals may benefit from therapy and/or medications. Thus PTSD may be better conceptualized as a dimensional process rather than a categorical all-or-none outcome, as complete and partial PTSD responses are usually seen in victims of childhood maltreatment (Armsworth & Holaday, 1993; Famularo, Fenton, & Kinscherff, 1994; Hillary & Schare, 1993; Mannarino, Cohen, & Berman, 1994; Wolfe, Sas, & Wekerle, 1994; Wolfe & Charney, 1991). Furthermore, physical abuse, sexual abuse, and witnessing domestic violence are traumas of interpersonal origin. This type of disorder is thought to cause more severe and long-lasting symptoms. The DSM-IV-TR states that the following constellation of symptoms occurs more commonly in association with an interpersonal stressor: anxiety, a loss of previously sustained beliefs, depression, dissociation, feeling permanently damaged, hostility, hopelessness, self-destructive and impulsive behaviors, somatization, shame, and personality and relational disturbances (American Psychiatric Association, 2000). These associated sequelae of symptoms may represent a distinct subtype of PTSD that is termed complex PTSD or disorder of extreme stress not otherwise specified (DESNOS; Herman, 1993). Complex PTSD can also be thought of as the adverse impact of childhood trauma on the development of age-expected achievements in behavioral and emotional regulation and in cognitive functioning. Thus maltreated children usually present with a diagnosis of PTSD or partial PTSD and other multiple problems including comorbidity for both internalizing (dysthymia or major depression) and externalizing (oppositional defiant) disorders.

Acute stress disorder is a new DSM-IV anxiety disorder diagnosis (American Psychiatric Association, 1994). Distinguishing between PTSD and acute stress disorder depends on the length of time of the illness. Acute stress disorder is thought to distinguish acute and severe short-term from long-term posttraumatic stress reactions. The essential features are the presence of three or more dissociative symptoms such as numbing or detachment, "being in a daze," derealization, depersonalization, and dissociative amnesia as well as symptoms seen in PTSD such as intrusive thoughts of the trauma, persistent avoidance of traumatic reminders, and increased physiological arousal. However, if a person experiences acute stress disorder symptoms for more than one month, the diagnosis is then changed to PTSD. When PTSD symptoms and their related psychological impairment are not severe enough to meet DSM-IV-TR acute stress disorder or PTSD, a diagnosis of adjustment disorder (acute or chronic) is made. However, maltreatment tends to occur as a chronic condition. Thus many maltreated children suffer from chronic PTSD, chronic PTSD symptoms, or an adjustment disorder, chronic type.

Reactive attachment disorder of infancy or early childhood is considered another traumatic stress-related diagnosis. This disorder is thought to be the result of pathogenic care including emotional and physical neglect. The essential feature of this disorder is disturbed and developmentally inappropriate social relatedness marked by persistent failure to initiate or respond in a developmentally appropriate fashion to most social interactions (inhibited type) or by indiscriminate sociability (disinhibited type) (American Psychiatric Association, 2000). The inhibited type consists of symptoms of hypervigilance (core symptoms of PTSD criterion D) including frozen watchfulness, resistance to comfort, and approach/avoidance. The disinhibited type consists of excessive familiarity with strangers and lack of selectivity in choice of attachment figures. The disinhibited type may consist primarily of dissociative symptoms (core symptoms of PTSD criterion C).

Traumatic stress disorders during childhood are associated with dysregulation of biological stress systems. This traumatic stress model is the basis for a rational approach for prescribing medications to symptomatic maltreated children and adolescents. Next I review the PTSD or biological stress response systems model.

THE PSYCHOBIOLOGY OF MALTREATMENT TRAUMA

Trauma causes activation of behavioral and biological stress response systems. This is called the "fight-or-flight reaction." Multiple densely interconnected neurotransmitter systems and neuroendocrine axes are activated during traumatic stress (reviewed by Charney, Deutch, Krystal, Southwich, & Davis, 1993). These neurobiological stress response systems significantly influence physical and cognitive development and emotional and behavioral regulation. Traumatic stress may have negative effects on the development of these systems (for review see De Bellis & Putnam, 1994). Research suggests that the overwhelming stress of maltreatment experiences in childhood is associated with alterations of biological stress response systems and with adverse influences on brain development (De Bellis, Baum, et al., 1999; De Bellis, Keshavan, et al., 1999; De Bellis, Keshavan, Spencer, & Hall, 2000). The locus coeruleus-norepinephrine/ sympathetic nervous system or catecholamine system, the serotonin system, and the hypothalamic-pituitary-adrenal axis are three major neurobiological stress response systems that significantly influence arousal, stress reactions, physical and cognitive development, emotional regulation, and brain development.

A brief review of the major biological stress response systems is important because

1. these are the major systems implicated in mood, anxiety, and impulse control disorders (for review see Charney, Nestler, & Bunny, 1999);
2. there are pharmacological treatments to target these systems;
3. alcohol and various illicit substances will also self-medicate or target these systems by damping down hyperarousal or dysregulated stress system(s); and
4. a hyperaroused or primed stress system may lead to behavioral manifestations of motor restlessness and learning and memory deficits that may be secondary to anxiety.

An understanding of the psychobiology of maltreatment may lead to early psychotherapeutic and psychopharmacological treatment. This may lead to secondary prevention of the psychiatric chronicity and comorbidity commonly seen in maltreated children and adolescents.

There is little research on the neurobiological effects of maltreatment and PTSD in developing children. Thus studies of the neurobiological effects of overwhelming stress in animal models and of the psychobiology of adult PTSD also provide comparative models. Traumatic stress is perceived by the body as overwhelming fear. Traumatic stress increases the activity of the locus coeruleus, the major catecholamine or norepinephrine-containing nucleus in the brain. Activation of locus coeruleus neurons increases norepinephrine in specific brain regions (locus coeruleus, hypothalamus, hippocampus, amygdala, and cerebral cortex). These brain regions are associated with regulation of stress reactions, memory, and emotion (reviewed by De Bellis & Putnam, 1994). Stress also results in simultaneous activation of another very basic and ancient cell body, the paragigantocellularis (for review see Aston-Jones, Valentino, Van Bockstaele, & Meyerson, 1994). The paragigantocellularis has major inputs to the locus coeruleus, but also controls and activates the sympathetic nervous system, causing the biological changes of the fight-or-flight reaction, or of life-saving responses to an acute threat. The locus coeruleus via indirect connections through the limbic system results in activation of the limbic-hypothalamic-pituitary-adrenal (LHPA) axis. During stress, the locus coeruleus stimulates the LHPA axis via indirect connections through the brain's limbic system. Intense fear or anxiety activates an important brain structure in the limbic system, the amygdala, which in turn activates the hypothalamus, and hypothalamic corticotropin-releasing hormone (CRH) or factor (CRF) is released. CRH activates the LHPA axis by stimulating the pituitary to secrete adrenocorticotropin (ACTH). These events promote cortisol release from the adrenal gland, also stimulate the sympathetic nervous system, and centrally cause behavioral activation and intense arousal (for review see Chrousos & Gold, 1992).

The serotonin system is also part of the stress response systems. Serotonin regulation is interdependent with the catecholamine system (Sulser, 1987). In animal studies of unpredictable and uncontrollable stress (e.g., inescapable shock), brain serotonin levels decrease. Drugs that increase brain serotonin (serotonin agonists) prevent stress-induced behavioral changes in animal studies (Southwick, Krystal, Johnson, & Charney, 1992). Serotonin plays important roles in compulsive behaviors, the regulation of emotions (mood) and behavior (aggression, impulsivity), and is dysregulated in individuals with major depression, impulsivity, or suicidal behaviors (Benkelfat, 1993; Siever & Trestman, 1993). Depression, suicidal thoughts, self-destructive behaviors, and aggression are commonly seen in victims of childhood maltreatment (National Research Council, 1993).

In summary, the direct effects of the fight-or-flight reaction or traumatic stress reaction include increases in catecholamine turnover in the brain, the sympathetic nervous system, and adrenal medulla. These processes lead to direct and indirect effects of the fight-or-flight reaction. These processes include increases in heart rate, blood pressure, metabolic rate, alertness, and in the circulating catecholamines (epinephrine, norepinephrine, and dopamine); as well as dilated pupils; sweating; inhibition of renal sodium excretion; redistribution of blood to the heart, brain, and skeletal muscle and away from skin, gut, and kidneys; enhanced blood coagulation by increasing platelet aggregability; increased glycogenolysis; and increased metabolic rate and alertness. Activation of the catecholamine system and CRH in animals results in behaviors consistent with anxiety, hyperarousal, and hypervigilance, which are the core symptoms of PTSD.

The prefrontal cortex may override this intense fear or stress response and thus dampen the activity of the amygdala and biological stress response systems (LeDoux, 1998). However, severe stress and its associated increased activation of catecholamines (especially norepinephrine and dopamine) can "turn off" this frontal inhibition of the limbic system (Arnsten, 1998). The prefrontal cortex subserves executive cognitive functions such as planned behaviors (Fuster, 1980), decision making, working memory, and attention (Goldman-Rakic, 1994) and is activated during novel or dangerous situations (Posner & Petersen, 1990). Thus turning off this frontal inhibition can result in inattention and inability to focus. The effective use of medications is aimed at downregulating this fear system so that the frontal cortex can effectively inhibit the fear response (hyperviligance) and thus enhance learning and therapeutic processes. Evidence to support these ideas in further detail is discussed next.

Biological Stress Response Systems and the Developing Brain

Traumatized children and adults manifest dysregulation of biological stress response systems or the fight-or-flight reaction (for review see De Bellis, 2001). Hence it is not surprising that traumatized children and adults with and without PTSD evidence this dysregulation at baseline, when confronted with something that reminds them of their trauma ("traumatic trigger") or when confronted by other life stressors. For example, in adult combat-related PTSD, elevated levels of central CRH were found (Baker et al., 1999; Bremner et al., 1997). In addition, in adult PTSD, elevated twenty-four-hour urinary excretion of catecholamines was found and provides evidence of an increase in baseline functioning of the catecholamine system (for review see Southwick, Yehuda, & Wang, 1998). Depressed women with histories of child abuse evidenced autonomic hyperarousal at baseline and hypersensitivity of the LHPA axis in response to a social stressor (Heim et al., 2000). Furthermore, serotonin turnover was decreased in adult combat-related PTSD (Arora, Fichtner, O'Connor, & Crayton, 1993).

The limited data published to date suggest that biological stress response systems are dysregulated in maltreated children who may suffer from depressive and PTSD symptoms but who may or may not have a diagnosis of PTSD. Medication-naive maltreated children with PTSD excreted significantly greater twenty-four-hour UFC (urinary free cortisol) levels than nonabused healthy controls (De Bellis, Keshavan, et al., 1999). Depressed maltreated young children failed to show the expected diurnal decrease in cortisol secretion from morning to afternoon (Hart, Gunnar, & Cicchetti, 1996; Kaufman, 1991). Depressed maltreated school-age children who were undergoing current psychosocial adversity evidenced hypersensitivity of the LHPA axis in response to human CRH infusion, compared to nonabused healthy children (Kaufman et al., 1997). Furthermore, findings of elevated baseline twenty-four-hour urinary catecholamine concentrations suggest an increase in baseline functioning of the catecholamine system in sexually abused girls, 58 percent of whom had histories of severely depressed mood with suicidal behavior (but only one of whom had PTSD) compared with demographically matched nonabused controls (De Bellis, Lefter, Trickett, & Putnam, 1994). Levels of twenty-four-hour urinary NE (norepinephrine) were elevated in male children who suffered from severe clinical depression and had a history of parental neglect (Queiroz et al., 1991). Perry (1994) found decreased platelet adrenergic receptors and increased heart rate following orthostatic challenge in physically and sexually abused children with PTSD, suggesting an enhancement of sympathetic nervous system tone in childhood PTSD. Furthermore, medication-naive boys and girls with PTSD, secondary to child abuse, excreted significantly greater amounts of urinary catecholamines (norepinephrine and dopamine) than nonabused healthy and nontraumatized anxious control children (De Bellis, Keshavan, et al., 1999).

Understanding the complexities of these dysregulated or hyperactive biological stress response systems is the key to understanding PTSD symptoms in traumatized individuals. The prefrontal cortex continues its development throughout young adulthood. The anterior cingulate region of the medial prefrontal cortex is involved in the extinction of conditioned fear responses. LeDoux (1998) has shown that the medial prefrontal cortex may inhibit activation of parts of the limbic system involved in fearful behaviors (amygdala and related nuclei and circuitry). This inhibition downregulates the fight-or-flight response. Recent neuroimaging studies provide evidence for anterior cingulate dysfunction in adult PTSD. Positron emission tomography investigations comparing women who had been sexually abused as children and who had PTSD with women with similar history who did not have PTSD found a lower level of anterior cingulate activation or blood flow during traumatic script-driven imagery (Shin et al., 1999) and during memories of sexual abuse (Bremner et al., 1999). A lower level of anterior cingulate blood flow has also been seen in Vietnam combat veterans with

PTSD compared to those without PTSD during exposure to combat-related traumatic stimuli (Bremner et al., 1999). In these studies, subjects with PTSD activated the amygdala, while subjects without PTSD did not show the same degree of limbic activation. Thus PTSD symptoms may represent an impairment of medial prefrontal cortex functioning (Zubieta et al., 1999).

New technologies, such as magnetic resonance spectroscopy (MRS), a safe and novel approach, were used to study the in vivo neurochemistry of the medial frontal cortex in the brains of living children. The N-acetyl signal in the proton (^{1}H) spectrum mainly consists of N-acetylaspartate and is considered to be a marker of neural integrity. Decreased N-acetylaspartate concentrations are associated with increased metabolism and loss of neurons (for review see Prichard, 1996). A preliminary investigation suggested that maltreated children and adolescents with PTSD have lower N-acetylaspartate : creatine ratios that are suggestive of neuronal loss in the anterior cingulate region of the medial prefrontal cortex compared to sociodemographically matched nonmaltreated controls (De Bellis et al., 2000). These results were not specific to gender. Neuronal loss in the anterior cingulate of pediatric PTSD patients agrees with the recent adult neuroimaging studies, which provide evidence for medial cortex dysfunction in adult PTSD.

As stated, exposure to mild to moderate uncontrollable stress impairs prefrontal cortical function in studies of humans and animals (for review see Arnsten & Goldman-Rakic, 1998). This impairment is catecholamine mediated (for review see Arnsten, 1998). Impairment of prefrontal cortical functioning has profound effects on thinking and decision making and may be responsible not only for PTSD symptoms but also for lower IQ and cognitive impairments seen in adults with PTSD (Macklin et al., 1998) and in maltreated children (Perez & Widom, 1994).

Understanding the complexities of dysregulated or hyperactive biological stress response systems is the key to understanding the brain development and cognitive functioning of maltreated children. Growth from birth to adulthood is marked by progressive physical, behavioral, cognitive, and emotional development. Paralleling these stages are changes in brain maturation. In the developing brain, elevated levels of catecholamines and cortisol may lead to adverse brain development through the mechanisms of accelerated loss (or metabolism) of neurons (Edwards, Harkins, Wright, & Menn, 1990; Sapolsky, Uno, Rebert, & Finch, 1990; Simantov et al., 1996; Smythies, 1997), delays in myelination (Dunlop, Archer, Quinlivan, Beazley, & Newnham, 1997), abnormalities in developmentally appropriate pruning (Lauder, 1988; Todd, 1992), and/or inhibiting neurogenesis (Gould, McEwen, Tanapat, Galea, & Fuchs, 1997; Gould, Tanapat, & Cameron, 1997; Tanapat, Galea, & Gould, 1998).

In a research study, forty-three maltreated children and adolescents with PTSD and sixty-one matched controls underwent comprehensive clinical assessments and an anatomical magnetic resonance imaging (MRI) brain scan (De Bellis, Baum, et al., 1999). Maltreated subjects with PTSD had 7.0 percent smaller intracranial and 8.0 percent smaller cerebral volumes than matched controls. The total midsagital area of corpus callosum, the major interconnection between the two hemispheres that is broadly conceptualized as facilitating intercortical communication, and the middle and posterior regions of the corpus callosum were smaller in abused subjects. In contrast, right, left, and total lateral ventricles were proportionally larger than controls, after adjustment for intracranial volume. Intracranial volume robustly correlated positively with age of onset of PTSD trauma (i.e., smaller cerebral volumes were associated with earlier onset of trauma) and negatively with duration of abuse. The positive correlation of intracranial volumes with age of onset of PTSD trauma suggests that traumatic stress is associated with disproportionately negative consequences if it occurs during early childhood. The negative correlation of intracranial volumes with abuse duration suggests that childhood maltreatment has global and adverse influences on brain development that may be cumulative. Symptoms of intrusive thoughts, avoidance, hyperarousal, and dissociation correlated positively with ventricular volume and negatively with intracranial volume and total corpus callosum and regional measures.

There was some indication that maltreated males with PTSD may show more evidence of adverse brain development than maltreated females with PTSD. A significant sex-by-diagnosis effect revealed greater total corpus callosum area reduction and trends for smaller cerebral volume and corpus callosum region 6 (isthmus) in maltreated males with PTSD compared with maltreated females with PTSD. Thus, these findings may suggest that males are more vulnerable to the effects of severe stress in global brain structures than females. However, both males and females showed findings of adverse brain development. Findings of decreased intracranial volumes and cerebral volumes in maltreated children with PTSD are intriguing. Findings of lateral ventricular enlargement that also correlated positively with abuse duration may be indicative of neuronal loss associated with severe stress. This stress-induced enhancement of neuronal loss may be the mechanism causing such pervasive problems in maltreated children and adolescents with PTSD. However, since we know that there is neurogenesis in the primate brain (Gould, Reeves, Graziano, & Gross, 1999), effective treatment of maltreatment-related depressives and anxiety disorders is an important area for future investigations regarding therapeutic reversibility.

Understanding the complexities of dysregulated or hyperactive biological stress response systems is the key to rational psychopharmacological therapies for maltreated children. Because dysregulated biological stress response systems can have profound adverse effects on brain development and cortical functioning, it is extremely important to downregulate cate-cholamines and cortisol by damping down the activity of the fight-or-flight reaction and its indirect limbic (amygdala) activation. This can be done in many ways. Obviously, the first and most important approach is to ensure the safety of the maltreated child's living environment. Effective psycho-therapy and use of antianxiety and antidepressant medications that target specific somatic symptoms can downregulate hyperaroused biological stress systems. A dampening down of stress response systems will hopefully alle-viate the adverse physiological effects of maltreatment stress on a child's development. For example, because of the maltreated child's baseline hyperarousal and history of traumatized attachments, the therapeutic alli-ance may be difficult to form and effective therapy will take more time to progress. In theory, the appropriate use of medications aimed at desensitiz-ing the maltreated child's biological stress response systems can assist in fostering this therapeutic alliance by decreasing posttraumatic stress symp-toms. Moreover, it is now known that there is a capacity for primate neurogenesis in the frontal cortex and the hippocampus (Gould, McEwen, et al., 1997; Gould et al., 1999). Environmental stress and adrenal steroids (i.e., cortisol) inhibit the rate of neurogenesis (Gould,Tanapat, et al., 1997; Tanapat et al., 1998). In theory, medications may improve global brain functioning and alleviate PTSD and depressive symptoms by removing the stress-mediated inhibition of the rate of cortical neurogenesis. This can, in theory, lead to therapeutic reversibility of the adverse brain developmental effects of maltreatment. Medications alone will not cure or heal the multiple problems associated with child maltreatment but may be an important and sometimes overlooked tool in a maltreated child's treatment.

However, before we discuss specific types of medications, it is important to understand the need for a comprehensive medical workup of all mal-treated children and adolescents who come to our attention.

The Medical and Mental Health Diagnostic Evaluations

Since PTSD and other psychiatric disorders are so common in mal-treated children, all maltreated children and adolescents, once identified, should receive a medical and mental health screening by licensed profes-sionals who specialize in child development and trauma. Typically, a child or adolescent is presented to a child and adolescent psychiatrist for episodes of acting out. These episodes can be related to PTSD or other unrelated dis-orders such as attention-deficit/hyperactivity disorder (ADHD) or bipolar disorder, or an undiagnosed medical disorder. A comprehensive medical evaluation must be done to appropriately make a differential diagnosis and before the beginning of psychotherapy and an appropriate medication trial.

The medical health and well child care of maltreated children and adolescents is usually not optimal. Maltreated children and adolescents may have significant developmental delays. Thus, all maltreated children and adolescents should undergo a physical exam for general health concerns. Sometimes, PTSD, mood, and/or disruptive behavioral symptoms are the results of physical illness, and may require more detailed medical workup and treatment. Developmental delays and symptoms of dissociation, concentration problems, attentional deficiencies, impulsivity, hyperactivity, and irritability can result from environmental toxins such as lead poisoning or a partial complex seizure disorder or, more rarely, from a brain injury (e.g., subclinical shaken baby syndrome). Some maltreated children and adolescents will need to undergo laboratory blood testing (including CBC [complete blood count] with differential, thyroid function studies, electrolytes, blood urea nitrogen levels, creatinine, urinalysis, urine toxicology screen, urine pregnancy screen), and an electrocardiogram as part of a general health assessment, to rule out medical causes for behavioral problems, and to screen for contraindications for medication. It is also important to consider screening maltreated children who are at risk from sexual abuse or prenatal exposure for sexually transmitted diseases such as HIV. Thus, more sophisticated blood tests or neurological and neuropsychiatric testing such as a neurological exam, a sleep-deprived electroencephalogram, and an MRI scan of the brain, as well as complete psychoeducational and neuropsychological testing, may be indicated for children with significant developmental delays and attentional and learning problems.

An important part of the mental health assessment of maltreated children and adolescents is an understanding of their maltreatment trauma. I now briefly review the methods of identification of traumatic triggers and specific PTSD symptoms that are targeted for treatment.

The Identification of Traumatic Triggers

Since the childhood trauma is not only the act of maltreatment itself (e.g., physical abuse or sexual abuse) but also the relationship the victim has with the perpetrator of the trauma, clinical identification of traumatic triggers may involve identification of subtleties that can sometimes be difficult to assess clinically. For example, a child who witnesses domestic violence may experience a fight-or-flight reaction and either freeze or act out every time a teacher raises his or her voice. In this case, the traumatic reminder may be shouting, yelling, or verbal aggression. A physically abused child may be hypersensitive or fearful of perceived failures. In this case, the traumatic reminder may be fear of perceived punishment. Traumatic triggers can also involve changes in facial expression, unpredictable environmental changes, or visits with the perpetrator or other family members. Maltreated children may not be aware of their traumatic triggers. Evaluators may need to identify these traumatic reminders from their understanding of the child's maltreatment, their review of multiple sources of information, and by a careful understanding of the objective events that led to a child's sudden change in feelings or behaviors. Consequently, a clear understanding of the child's maltreatment trauma and symptoms will not only foster an appropriate diagnosis but also help the child begin to trust authority figures.

The trauma consultation child interview or technique was developed by Pynoos and Eth (1986). It is highly recommended reading for individuals who treat traumatized children, and its details are beyond the scope of this chapter. This interview was developed for children and adolescents ages three to sixteen years. It is applicable for the child who has witnessed murder, suicide, rape, accidental death, assault, kidnapping, natural or human-made disasters, and school and community violence. It may be used for victims of child maltreatment or criminal assault with modifications. It differs from the usual child psychotherapy session or initial psychiatric or mental health assessment interview because it has a stated focus of discussing traumatic experiences (Pynoos & Nader, 1993). It takes one to two hours to explore the child's traumatic experiences. Prior to the interview, it is important to obtain information about the child's maltreatment, his or her behavior after maltreatment disclosure, and premorbid functioning from family members, medical and child protective service records, the police, the school, or other appropriate sources of information. The interview is intended for individual intervention and incorporates a review and reprocessing of the traumatic experiences.

Briefly, the trauma interview involves a three-stage process: opening, trauma, and closure. In the opening stage, it is the interviewer's job to establish the focus and a working relationship (therapeutic alliance) with the child or adolescent in a nonthreatening and empathetic manner. In the discussion of the trauma stage, the interviewer does not allow the child to digress from this task of mastery of the trauma. The interviewer may need to question the child to ensure that the circumstances are completely reviewed. It is important to pay attention to the details the child provides and ask their significance. The interviewer needs to observe for traumatic triggers and their relationships to current symptoms and behaviors. The last stage of this trauma consultation interview is closure. The interviewer reviews with the child or adolescent what they have discussed and emphasizes how understandable, realistic, and universal the child's feelings and thoughts are. Since chronic PTSD symptoms may provide the mechanisms for the pervasive psychopathology seen in maltreated children, it is extremely important to identify the traumatic triggers of these symptoms during the trauma interview.

Practice parameters for the treatment of pediatric PTSD have been published by the American Academy of Child and Adolescent Psychiatry (Cohen & The Work Group on Quality Issues, 1998). These practice parameters were written to aid clinicians and are a comprehensive overview of specific pediatric mental disorders. The reader is referred to them for further information on the epidemiology, assessment, use of structured interviews and rating scales, clinical course, and treatment of PTSD. Next I review specific childhood mental disorders associated with maltreatment. My major focus will be on the identification of PTSD symptoms and the use of medications.

MEDICATIONS FOR THE TREATMENT OF SYMPTOMS OF TRAUMATIC STRESS DISORDERS

Psychopharmacological treatment and psychotherapy aimed at target symptoms of PTSD criterion B, C, and D symptoms provide for the rational treatment of maltreatment-related PTSD symptoms. At this writing, it must be noted that double-blind psychopharmacological studies of PTSD in maltreated children are not available. Therefore, the information presented is based on double-blind studies of psychopharmacological agents used to treat these disorders in nonmaltreated children and adolescents, published case reports regarding psychopharmacological therapies for maltreated children with PTSD, the adult literature regarding PTSD treatment, and my many years of clinical treatment experience.

When undertaking a mental health screening and making a referral for psychiatric evaluation, it is important to identify all presenting symptoms of psychiatric disorders. Maltreated children and adolescents usually meet DSM-IV-TR criteria for PTSD symptoms and other non-posttraumatic stress psychiatric disorders and for multiple psychiatric disorders. Effective treatments will depend on appropriately identifying these disorders and being able to distinguish confusing clinical presentations within a diagnostic framework. Since the clinical identification of traumatic triggers may involve identification of subtleties that can be difficult to assess, first I review the clinical symptoms of specific PTSD criterion symptoms, other common mental disorders associated with maltreatment (major depression and ADHD), and their psychobiological basis before discussing specific types of medications for treatment.

Reexperiencing and Intrusive Symptoms

Criterion B, reexperiencing and intrusive symptoms, can best be conceptualized as a classically conditioned response. An external or internal conditioned stimulus (e.g., the traumatic trigger) activates unwanted and distressful recurrent and intrusive memories of traumatic experience (the unconditioned stimulus). Intrusive phenomena take the form of distressing intrusions such as nightmares or night terrors, dissociative flashback episodes, and psychological distress and physical reactivity on exposure to traumatic reminders. In young children, these intrusive thoughts may be part of repetitive play or trauma-specific reenactments or compulsive rituals. These compulsive rituals may resemble symptoms of pervasive developmental disorders. Intrusive symptoms such as hearing the voice of a threatening perpetrator (particularly when a child is alone or feels afraid) can be easily misdiagnosed as psychotic behavior (auditory hallucinations). Intrusive symptoms can also involve acting-out behaviors when a child reenacts the perpetrator's abusive behaviors toward himself or herself.

Intrusive PTSD symptoms most closely resemble another psychiatric disorder, obsessive-compulsive disorder, which is characterized by intrusive, recurrent, and persistent thoughts, impulses, or images. Obsessive-compulsive disorder is a disorder of serotonin regulation, and antidepressants that enhance serotonin functioning attenuate these symptoms (for review see Rosenberg & Keshavan, 1998). Because of serotonin's interdependence with the noradrenergic system, dysregulation of serotonin may not only play a major role in cluster B symptoms but also may increase the risk for comorbid major depression and aggression in maltreated children. Consequently, it has been shown that the onset of major depression is markedly increased for trauma-exposed persons who suffer from PTSD, but not in trauma-exposed persons who did not suffer from PTSD (Breslau, Davis, Peterson, & Schultz, 2000). PTSD may lead to major depression and be influenced by common genetic vulnerabilities to serotonin dysregulation and trauma-related factors in maltreated children. Thus it is not surprising that studies show strong support for the efficacy of the serotonin reuptake inhibitor antidepressant and anti-obsessive-compulsive disorder medications sertraline (Brady et al., 2000) and fluoxetine (van der Kolk et al., 1994) in adult PTSD. To date there are no published reports of serotonin reuptake inhibitors or other antidepressants for the treatment of PTSD in traumatized children. However, in double-blind studies, fluoxetine, a serotonin agent, has been shown to be very effective in decreasing symptoms of major depression in children and adolescents (Emslie et al., 1997).

Avoidant and Dissociative Behaviors

Criterion C symptoms represent both avoidant and dissociative behaviors and can be thought of as ways to control painful and distressing re-experiencing of symptoms. These include efforts to avoid thoughts, feelings, conversations, activities, places, people, and memories associated with the trauma, amnesia for the trauma, diminished interest in others, feelings of detachment from others, a restricted range of affect, and a sense of a foreshortened future. In assessing for these symptoms, one needs to learn what changes occurred in the child's premorbid personality and psychosocial functioning. Avoidance of traumatic reminders of interpersonal trauma can cause a child to have difficulty handling strong emotions such as anger, joy, or intimate relationships because strong and out-of-control emotions may have precipitated the traumatic maltreatment act. In children who have suffered multiple aversive experiences, reconstruction of their premorbid personality may be very difficult and will involve careful and detailed information on their developmental history. One must also be aware that children may deny their maltreatment or their posttraumatic symptoms or say that they do not remember an event in an effort not to talk about their trauma. It is important to clarify this with the child to ascertain whether they have avoidant symptoms.

Dissociative symptoms are commonly seen in traumatized individuals. These symptoms are defined as disruptions in the usually integrated functions of consciousness, memory, identity, or perception of the environment that interfere with the associative integration of information (Putnam, 1997). Detachment or numbing can be seen when a child has an absence of emotional responsiveness such as joy when given a favorite toy or lack of anger when insulted, teased at school, or threatened. Children with these symptoms usually have constricted affect and a limited sense of humor. Teachers may notice that children with this symptom stare into space and have difficulty paying attention in school. The therapist may notice that a child stares and becomes mute when aspects of the trauma are discussed in therapy. Derealization is a difficult symptom to elicit. Sometimes maltreated children will say that their abusive experience "did not seem real." Emotional numbing and diminished interest in others, particularly during development, may result in lack of empathy, comorbid dysthymia, and an increased risk for self-mutilation (van der Kolk, Greenberg, Orr, & Pitman, 1989), personality disorders (Johnson, Cohen, Brown, Smailes, & Berstein, 1999), and/or antisocial behaviors (Luntz & Widom, 1994).

Avoidant and dissociative symptoms are thought to be mediated by dysregulation of the endogenous opiate system (for review see Bremner, Davis, Southwick, Krystal, & Charney, 1993). However, higher concentrations of urinary dopamine are associated with avoidant symptoms in adult PTSD (Yehuda, Southwick, Giller, Ma, & Mason, 1992) and with avoidant and dissociative symptoms in maltreated children with PTSD (De Bellis, Keshavan, et al., 1999). Endogenous opiate systems and their links with dopamine systems may contribute to the constricted affect and high incidence of self-injury and violent behaviors reported in maltreated children and in adults who have experienced maltreatment as children. The dopamine system is linked with the serotonin and noradrenergic (norepinephrine) systems (Sulser, 1987). Antidepressant and antianxiety medications that dampen down the activity of these biological stress response systems should, in theory, dampen the activity of dopamine and endogenous opiates and thus decrease both avoidant and dissociative behaviors.

Persistent Symptoms of Increased Physiological Arousal and Catecholamines

Criterion D hyperarousal symptoms consist of persistent symptoms of increased physiological arousal. These symptoms include difficulty falling or staying asleep, irritable mood or angry outbursts, difficulty concentrating, hypervigilance, and exaggerated startle response. These symptoms are part of the biological stress response systems response, or the fight-or-flight reaction. These symptoms are thought to be mediated by increased activity of central CRH and enhanced sympathetic nervous system tone as discussed in detail in the Psychobiology of Maltreatment Trauma section. It is important to be specific when eliciting these symptoms, because children may minimize and caregivers may be unaware of these symptoms. For example, if you ask most children and adolescents how they slept last night, they will say "fine." It is better to ask: "What time do you get in bed and what time do you fall asleep? Do you feel rested when you wake up? Do you ever have bad dreams?" Furthermore, most children and adolescents will tell you that they feel irritable or angry or mad. They will seldom tell you that they feel bad, sad, or depressed because they tend to perceive these questions as value judgments. Symptoms of increased arousal such as anxiety, insomnia, restlessness, and poor concentration are also included as symptoms in DSM-IV-TR major depressive disorder, dysthymia, and generalized anxiety disorder. These and their shared psychobiology are some of the important reasons for these disorders to be commonly comorbid with PTSD.

Child and adolescent psychiatrists as well as other mental health professions can work together in identifying and tracking these symptoms during treatment using standardized rating scales for PTSD and depressive symptoms as well as by helping the caregiver fill out a mood and sleep/wake cycle daily activity log on the child. A list of some of these measures is included in the American Academy of Child and Adolescent Psychiatry practice parameters for PTSD (Cohen & The Work Group on Quality Issues, 1998) and depressive disorders (Birmaher, Brent, & The Work Group on Quality Issues, 1998).

IDENTIFICATION OF NONTRAUMATIC STRESS DISORDERS COMMONLY SEEN IN TRAUMATIZED CHILDREN AND ADOLESCENTS

This section includes the DSM-IV-TR criteria for nontraumatic stress disorders commonly seen in maltreated children and adolescents. The reader is referred to the DSM-IV-TR for further information (American Psychiatric Association, 2000). Table 16.1 lists the common psychiatric disorders observed in maltreated children and adolescents. This list is not a comprehensive assessment of all psychiatric disorders seen in maltreated children and adolescents.

Depressive Disorders

Maltreated children and adolescents manifest high rates of dysthymic disorder and major depression. In maltreated children and adolescents, depressive disorders usually co-occur or follow symptoms of acute stress disorder or PTSD. These disorders are commonly comorbid with PTSD throughout the life cycle (for review see De Bellis, 1997). To meet DSM-IV-TR criteria for dysthymic disorder, a maltreated child or adolescent must complain of depressed, sad, or irritable mood more days than not and have at least two of the following symptoms: poor appetite or overeating, insomnia or hypersomnia, low energy or fatigue, low self-esteem, poor concentration or difficulty making decisions, and hopelessness for at least one year.

To meet DSM-IV-TR criteria for major depressive disorder, a maltreated child or adolescent must complain of depressed, sad, or irritable mood or loss of interest or pleasure for the same two-week period and at least four of the following symptoms: weight loss or gain or failure to make expected weight gains, insomnia or hypersomnia nearly every day, psychomotor agitation or retardation nearly every day, fatigue or loss of energy nearly every day, feelings of worthlessness or excessive or inappropriate guilt nearly every day, poor concentration or difficulty making decisions nearly every day, and recurrent thoughts of death, recurrent suicidal ideation without a plan, suicidal ideation with a plan, or suicide attempt.

TABLE 16.1. Psychiatric Disorders Commonly Associated with Maltreatment

Type	Disorder	Symptoms	Commonly Used Medications
Internalizing			
Attachment disorders	Reactive attachment disorder of infancy or early childhood	Failure to initiate or respond to social interactions (inhibited type) or indiscriminate sociability (disinhibited type)	Medications used for associated PTSD
Anxiety disorders	Adjustment disorder with anxiety	Excessive situational worry	Possible use of adrenergic agents (clonidine, guanfacine, propranolol)
	Acute stress disorder		
	PTSD	Intrusive thoughts, nightmares, diminished interest in others, restricted range of affect, hopelessness, dissociation, poor sleep and concentration, worries about the future, and hypervigilance	Antianxiety or antidepressant agents (clonidine, guanfacine, propranolol, fluoxetine, sertraline, paroxetine, fluvoxamine)
	Separation anxiety disorder	Recurrent distress when separated from home or attachment figure, nightmares, worries about the future, refusal to attend school or sleep alone	Antianxiety agents (fluoxetine, sertraline, paroxetine, fluvoxamine)
	Generalized anxiety disorder	Excessive and uncontrollable worry, restlessness, difficulty concentrating, irritability, and sleep problems	Antianxiety agents (fluoxetine, sertraline, paroxetine, fluvoxamine)
Mood disorders	Adjustment disorder with depressed mood	Excessive situational sad or irritable mood	Possible use of antidepressants if chronic

443

TABLE 16.1. (continued)

Type	Disorder	Symptoms	Commonly Used Medications
	Major depression dysthymia	Persistent sad or irritable mood, loss of interest, insomnia or hypersomnia, agitation, fatigue, feelings of worthlessness, poor concentration or difficulty making decisions, and recurrent thoughts of death	Antidepressants (fluoxetine, sertraline, paroxetine, fluvoxamine, bupropion, venlafaxine)
	Bipolar disorder	Grandiosity, decreased sleep, pressured speech, racing thoughts, distractibility, increased goal-directed activity, and/or excessive involvement in reckless activities	Mood stabilizers (lithium, carbamazepine, valproate); possible use of antipsychotics if delusional
Externalizing			
Disruptive disorders	Oppositional defiant disorder	Negativistic, hostile, and defiant behavior, loses temper, often argues, blames others, and often angry or resentful	Medications for associated mood, anxiety, or ADHD disorders
	ADHD	A persistent pattern of inattention and/or hyperactivity-impulsivity prior to age seven years	Stimulants (methylphenidate, dextroamphetamine, pemoline, amphetamine)
	Conduct disorder	Persistent pattern of behavior which violates the basic rights of others (aggression, deceitfulness, theft, property destruction)	Medications for associated mood, anxiety, or ADHD disorders; possible use of antipsychotics if violent
Substance use disorders	Alcohol and substance use disorders	Maladaptive patterns of use leading to significant impairment or distress and/or tolerance or withdrawal	Medications for associated mood, anxiety, or ADHD disorders

The American Academy of Child and Adolescent Psychiatry practice parameters for the treatment of child and adolescent depressive disorders inform us that psychotherapy and serotonergic antidepressant medications are very effective in treating pediatric depressive disorders (Birmaher et al., 1998). It is recommended that all maltreated children and adolescents with significant depressive symptoms be evaluated and clinically followed by a child and adolescent psychiatrist. The reader is referred to the practice parameters for comprehensive information on the epidemiology, assessment, use of structured interviews and rating scales, clinical course, and psychotherapy and psychopharmacological treatment of pediatric depression.

Anxiety Disorders

Anxiety disorders commonly seen in maltreated children and adolescents include separation anxiety disorder and generalized anxiety disorder. The essential feature of separation anxiety disorder is excessive worry about separation from an attachment figure and the home that is beyond what is expected for an individual's developmental level. To meet DSM-IV-TR criteria for separation anxiety disorder, a maltreated child or adolescent must be under age eighteen years and complain of at least three of the following symptoms for a duration of at least four weeks: recurrent distress when separated from home or attachment figure, persistent worry about losing one's attachment figure, persistent worry about untoward events that will lead to losing one's attachment figure, persistent reluctance to attend school, refusal to sleep or to be in one's home alone, repeated nightmares involving separation from attachment figure, and repeated somatic complaints when separation from attachment figure is anticipated. The presence of PTSD does not exclude a diagnosis of separation anxiety disorder. Therefore, one can easily see how a child who is traumatized from emotional abuse (domestic violence or verbal threats to the mother) can have a diagnosis of separation anxiety disorder that may be comorbid with PTSD.

The essential feature of generalized anxiety disorder is excessive and uncontrollable worry for a duration of at least six months. To meet DSM-IV-TR criteria for generalized anxiety disorder, a maltreated child or adolescent must complain of at least one of the following: restlessness, being easily fatigued, difficulty concentrating, irritability, muscle tension, and sleep disturbance. A diagnosis of PTSD excludes this diagnosis. Sometimes a child will present with anxiety symptoms months or years after maltreatment disclosure. It is important to be aware of this and to clarify whether there was a past diagnosis of PTSD that is now in partial remission versus making a new diagnosis of another anxiety disorder such as generalized anxiety disorder.

The American Academy of Child and Adolescent Psychiatry practice parameters for the treatment of child and adolescent anxiety disorders inform us that psychotherapy and serotonergic antidepressant medications are very effective in treating pediatric anxiety disorders (Bernstein, Shaw, & The Work Group on Quality Issues, 1997). It is recommended that all maltreated children and adolescents with significant anxiety symptoms be evaluated and clinically followed by a child and adolescent psychiatrist. The reader is referred to the practice parameters for comprehensive information on the epidemiology, assessment, use of structured interviews and rating scales, clinical course, and psychotherapy and psychopharmacological treatment of pediatric anxiety disorders.

Disruptive Disorders

Disruptive disorders commonly seen in maltreated children and adolescents include oppositional defiant disorder, ADHD, and conduct disorder. Oppositional defiant disorder is a pattern of negativistic, hostile, and defiant behavior and is commonly seen in maltreated children and adolescents. To meet DSM-IV-TR criteria for oppositional defiant disorder, a maltreated child or adolescent must have four or more of the following behaviors for at least six months: often loses temper, often argues with adults, often actively defies or refuses to comply with adults' requests or rules, often deliberately annoys people, often blames others for his or her mistakes, is often angry, resentful, spiteful, or vindictive. Oppositional defiant disorder is usually not seen as a primary diagnosis. It is usually secondary to one or more of the following primary problems:

1. A severely impaired parent-child relationship
2. Irritability and negative affect secondary to unrecognized and untreated PTSD criteria D or depressive symptoms
3. Unrecognized and untreated ADHD
4. Bipolar disorder

The treatment of oppositional defiant disorder involves behavioral parent training and individual and family dynamic psychotherapy. However, in order to make an appropriate medication recommendation, it is important to understand the underlying reason for a maltreated child's oppositional behaviors.

The essential feature of ADHD is a persistent pattern of inattention and/or hyperactivity-impulsivity prior to age seven years that is above what is expected for a child's developmental level. This disorder is divided into several subtypes, predominantly inattentive, predominantly hyperactive-impulsive, and combined type. To meet DSM-IV-TR criteria for ADHD predominantly inattentive type, a maltreated child or adolescent must have six or more of the following behaviors for at least six months: difficulty sustaining attention, carelessness, not listening, failure to follow instructions, difficulty organizing tasks, avoidance of tasks that require sustained attention, often losing things, being easily distracted, and often forgetful. To meet DSM-IV-TR criteria for ADHD predominantly hyperactive-impulsive type, a maltreated child or adolescent must have six or more of the following behaviors: fidgetiness, runs or climbs excessively, often leaves classroom without permission, difficulty playing quietly, is often on the go, and often talks excessively, blurts out answers, has difficulty awaiting his or her turn, and is intrusive for at least six months. To meet DSM-IV-TR criteria for ADHD combined type, a maltreated child or adolescent must meet criteria for both subtypes during the past six months. Stimulant medications are very effective and safe when prescribed for pediatric ADHD (for review see Wilens & Spencer, 2000). This disorder is frequently observed in maltreated, particularly physically abused, children and adolescents. Rather than the popular misconception that ADHD is overdiagnosed and treated, it is a very treatable condition that is underdiagnosed and undertreated in the United States (Jensen et al., 1999). However, sometimes a traumatized child presents with severe acting-out behaviors that are context specific. These behaviors can be misdiagnosed as ADHD. It is important to get an idea of what a child's activity level, moods, and behaviors are like in different environmental situations. A child with ADHD will have symptoms of ADHD in most types of unstructured environments (home, a large classroom in school, during play periods), while a child with PTSD will only show these behaviors when they are feeling unsafe or experience a traumatic reminder. Some maltreated children suffer from ADHD and PTSD. To ensure learning and social skills development, it is extremely important to treat ADHD in a maltreated child. The American Academy of Child and Adolescent Psychiatry practice parameters for the treatment of child and adolescent ADHD (Dulcan & The Work Group on Quality Issues, 1997) provide further information concerning the diagnosis, assessment, use of structured interviews and rating scales, clinical course, and treatment of ADHD.

The essential feature of conduct disorder is a persistent pattern of behavior that violates the basic rights of others or major age-appropriate social norms. To meet DSM-IV-TR criteria for conduct disorder, a maltreated child or adolescent must have three or more of the following behaviors for at least twelve months: aggression to people and animals, destruction of property, deceitfulness or theft, and serious violations of rules. The treatment of conduct disorder is psychosocial in nature and requires multisystemic treatment (Henggeler, Schoenwald, Borduin, Rowland, & Cunningham, 1998). However, conduct disorder is frequently comorbid with ADHD (Szatmari, Boyle, & Offord, 1989) and/or PTSD (Steiner, Garcia, & Matthews, 1997). It is important to identify and use medications to treat these comorbid disorders in a maltreated conduct-disordered child or adolescent. The American Academy of Child and Adolescent Psychiatry practice parameters contain further information concerning the diagnosis, assessment, clinical course, and treatment of conduct disorder (Steiner & The Work Group on Quality Issues, 1997).

Bipolar Disorder

The hallmark feature of child and adolescent bipolar disorder is a manic episode. This is a distinct period of abnormally and persistently elevated, expansive, and/or irritable mood that represents a significant change in an individual's baseline status and lasts for at least one week. During this mood disturbance, an individual must display at least three or more of the following: grandiosity, decreased sleep, pressured speech, racing thoughts, distractibility, increased goal-directed activity, and/or excessive involvement in reckless activities. The diagnosis of bipolar disorder in children and adolescents is controversial. Pediatric bipolar disorder is frequently comorbid with ADHD, PTSD, and disruptive disorders. However, about 20 percent of all bipolar patients have their first onset during adolescence. Maltreated children and adolescents are at increased risk for bipolar disorder secondary to increased familial loading for mood disorders. Therefore, this is an important diagnosis to consider if a maltreated child or adolescent meets criteria for this disorder. The American Academy of Child and Adolescent Psychiatry practice parameters for the treatment of child and adolescent bipolar disorders inform us that multimodal treatment and mood-stabilizing medications can be very effective in treating pediatric bipolar disorder (McClellan, Werry, & The Work Group on Quality Issues, 1997). It is recommended that all maltreated children and adolescents with significant symptoms of bipolar disorder be evaluated and clinically followed by a child and adolescent psychiatrist. The practice parameters provide comprehensive information on the epidemiology, differential diagnosis and assessment, use of structured interviews and rating scales, clinical course, and psychotherapy and psychopharmacological treatment of child and adolescent bipolar disorder.

Alcohol and Substance Use Disorders

The hallmark features of child and adolescent alcohol and substance use disorders, defined as DSM-IV-TR abuse or dependence, are maladaptive patterns of use leading to significant impairment or distress and/or tolerance or withdrawal. A review of the literature suggests that childhood maltreatment and the diagnosis of PTSD are associated with an enhanced risk of adolescent and adult alcohol and substance use disorders. Physical and sexual abuse are associated with adolescent PTSD and often occur prior to alcohol and substance abuse in adolescents (Clark, Lesnick, & Hegedus, 1997; Clark, Pollock, et al., 1997; Dembo, Dertke, Borders, Washburn, & Schmeidler, 1988; Dembo, Williams, Wothke, Schmeidler, & Brown, 1992; Deykin & Buka, 1997). Physical and sexual abuse were associated with an increased likelihood of alcohol, marijuana, and other substance use in a survey of high school aged children and adolescents (Harrison, Fulkerson, & Beebe, 1997). Thus, it is important to ask about substance use when assessing and treating a child or adolescent with a history of maltreatment. Furthermore, symptoms of substance use may resemble a primary mood or bipolar disorder. The primary goal of child and adolescent substance use disorders is the achievement and maintenance of abstinence.

A complete description of child and adolescent substance use disorders is beyond the scope of this chapter. Child and adolescent substance use disorders are frequently comorbid with mood disorders, PTSD, ADHD, and/or conduct disorder. Medications are targeted at the treatment of these comorbid disorders. The American Academy of Child and Adolescent Psychiatry practice parameters give comprehensive information on the epidemiology, assessment, use of structured interviews and rating scales, clinical course, and psychotherapy and psychopharmacological treatment of child and adolescent substance use disorders (Bukstein & The Work Group on Quality Issues, 1997).

PHARMACOTHERAPY: PSYCHOEDUCATION, TYPES OF MEDICATIONS, AND THEIR SIDE EFFECTS

The majority of maltreated children with psychiatric symptoms of specific disorders would benefit from medications. Children and adolescents who have at least moderate psychosocial impairment from symptoms that have not responded to brief (two to four weeks) psychotherapy or are so severely affected as to require intensive outpatient or inpatient treatment may be helped with psychotropic medication. It should be noted that most behavioral and emotional problems in children are self-limited or situational.

Therefore, one should not start a medication unless there are specific and clear target symptoms that the medication is designed to treat.

As a general rule and before choosing a psychopharmacological treating agent, it is important to identify and describe specific target symptoms for treatment. It is also important to rule out any medical or substance use problems that may be contributing to these psychiatric symptoms. For adolescent girls who are sexually active, birth control issues and pregnancy must be addressed before beginning a medication trial. Both the clinician and child and adolescent psychiatrist can work together in identifying and documenting the duration, onset, and frequency of these target symptoms as well as documenting their improvement or any medication side effects associated with psychopharmacological treatment. For example, many maltreated children and adolescents require antianxiety or antidepressant medications to target symptoms of hyperarousal or fight-or-flight reaction biological stress response systems dysregulation such as reduced attention and learning, sleep disturbance, nightmares, restricted affect, anxiety, and/or depression. These symptoms can be monitored with specific rating scales, sleep/wake logs and diaries, or medication side effect rating scales. It is extremely important to educate the patient and family about what medications will and will not do. In this discussion, giving the patient and family a chart describing the medication, the symptoms that the medication is designed to treat, and common side effects is helpful. It is important to help families and children understand that medication alone will not take care of all the problems that lead them into treatment, nor will it change their personality, make them into docile robots, or cause them to become drug addicted. These discussions can take place during the informed consent procedure.

Physicians who prescribe medications to children and adolescents need to obtain informed consent for treatment from their parent or legal guardian. For children in foster care or state custody, informed consent may also be needed from child protective services. Adolescents age fourteen years and older may also be required to sign an informed consent form depending on state law. To obtain informed consent for medication treatment, a child and adolescent psychiatrist must discuss the following with the patient and/or decision maker in understandable language: a discussion of the psychiatric disorder and symptoms to be treated, the nature of the medication prescribed, the probability and types of side effects and the other risks of a medication trial, the possible benefits of the treatment, the fact that the physician cannot predict the results of the treatment, the likely results of no treatment, and the risks and benefits of alternative treatments. The discussion of these issues needs to be documented in the patient's medical record as well as a statement that the patient and/or the decision maker voluntarily accepts the prescribed treatment. Parents and/or adolescents have the right to refuse treatment. This discussion must also be documented in the patient's medical record.

One should take particular care when prescribing medications to children and adolescents. It is important to choose the best drug for treatment of the particular target symptoms with the best side-effect profile. It is important to start at the lowest effective dose, minimize the drug maintenance dose and frequency of administration, and avoid using multiple medications if possible. However, children and adolescents metabolize drugs faster than adults. Therefore children and especially adolescents may need a higher equivalent dose for maintenance than an adult for the drug to have a therapeutic effect. A medication trial should take six to twelve weeks before a decision can be made as to the effectiveness of the medication. The treating psychiatrist must also be aware of the mental status and ability of a maltreating parent to comply with a medication trial. One way to handle this is to have the caregiver repeat back the medication instructions to you and/or to have him or her write them out on a medication record. For example, it may not be wise to keep a child on medication if the parent has the potential to misuse it by giving a child a potentially toxic dose. When treating maltreated children who remain in their maltreating families, such issues will need to be addressed as part of a multidisciplinary team approach before beginning a medication trial.

Next I review specific classes of medication that can be helpful for the treatment of maltreatment-associated psychiatric disorders and their common side effects (see Table 16.2). I also discuss possible strategies for treating patients with complicated comorbidities in each section. This chapter is not meant to be a comprehensive assessment of all medications and their side effects. The reader is referred to a comprehensive textbook on psychoactive drugs for children and adolescents for further information (Werry & Aman, 1999).

Antianxiety Medications

Adrenergic Agents

Adrenergic agents dampen down baseline biological stress response systems (locus coeruleus-sympathetic nervous system) and are among the most commonly used antianxiety medications in traumatized children. Clonidine, a central alpha$_2$-adrenergic partial agonist, dampens catecholamine transmission centrally by decreasing the activity of the locus coeruleus. Perry (1994) reported an open-label treatment trial of clonidine at relatively low doses (0.05-.1 mg b.i.d.) in physically and sexually abused

TABLE 16.2. Medications Used in Psychiatric Disorders Commonly Associated with Maltreatment

Class	Medications	Side Effects	Special Points of Interest
Antianxiety medications	Adrenergic agents (clonidine, guanfacine)	Sedation, dizziness, and hypotension	Blood pressure and pulse rate should be monitored routinely Need to taper when ending
	Propranolol	Raynaud's phenomenon, bradycardia, bronchoconstriction, sexual impotence, and depression	Should not be given to children with asthma
	Benzodiazepines (alprazolam, clonazepam, lorazepam, diazepam, clorazepate)	Sedation, drowsiness, dizziness, and decreased mental acuity	Potentially embarrassing behavioral disinhibition Need to taper when ending
	Buspirone	Mild nausea, headache, drowsiness, and overexcitement	Relatively safe side effect profile
	Antihistamines (diphenhydramine and hydroxyzine)	Sedation, dry skin and mouth, and dilated pupils	No controlled studies evaluating their effectiveness to date
Antidepressants	Selective serotonin reuptake inhibitors (Fluoxetine, sertraline, paroxetine, fluvoxamine)	Nausea, stomach pains, restlessness, sweating, headaches, bruising, and changes in appetite, sleep, and sexual function	Relatively safe side effect profile, very low lethality after overdose, but need to taper when ending
	Selective serotonin reuptake inhibitors are also effective antianxiety agents		May cause akathisia, allergeric skin rash, or mania
	Tricylic antidepressants (imipramine, clomipramine, nortriptyline, desipramine)	Sedation, slowing of heart conduction, tachycardia, dry mouth, constipation, elevated liver enzymes	All tricylic antidepressants require comprehensive medical workup before use and are potentially fatal in overdose Blood pressure and pulse rate should be monitored routinely Need to taper when ending

Category	Drug	Side Effects	Notes
Stimulants	Bupropion Venlafaxine	Mild sedation Mild sedation	May be used for ADHD; may increase seizure risk
	Methylphenidate, dextroamphetamine, pemoline, amphetamine	Decreased appetite, sleep problems, nervousness, irritability, tearfulness, stomachaches, headaches, and increase in nervous tics	Must monitor long-term body growth Rarely fatal if taken in an overdose
Mood stabilizers	Lithium	Nausea, diarrhea, vomiting, tremor, weight gain, headache, bed-wetting, increased drinking and urination, fatigue, and dizziness	All mood stabilizers require comprehensive medical workup before use and are potentially fatal in overdose Lithium levels, kidney and thyroid function should be monitored routinely
	Anticonvulsants		Need to taper when ending
	Carbamazepine	Sedation, drowsiness, dizziness, nausea	Uncommon but serious side effects (blood and liver problems)
	Valproate	Sedation, nausea, and vomiting	Uncommon but serious side effect (fatal liver toxicity)
Antipsychotics	High potency (risperidone, sertindole, and ziprasidone)	Extrapyramidal side effects (e.g., dystonic reactions, Parkinsonian side effects, akathisia)	May cause many adverse and permanent movement disorders (e.g., tardive dyskinesia)
	Low potency (clozapine, quetiapine, olanzapine)	Sedation Dizziness Rashes Photosensitivity	Uncommon but serious side effects (seizures, neuroleptic malignant syndrome)

453

children with PTSD. Clonidine treatment was associated with general clinical improvement and decreases in the arousal cluster of PTSD symptoms and impulsivity. Harmon and Riggs (1996) reported the effectiveness of using an open trial of clonidine in the transdermal patch for effective reduction of PTSD symptoms in seven maltreated children ages three to six years. I have found that clonidine given in the evening twenty minutes before bedtime (usual dose of 0.05-0.1 mg po qhs) is particularly helpful in reducing initial insomnia and nightmares in maltreated preschool and school-age children and in adolescents. Increasing effective sleep was also associated with decreasing daytime inattention and irritability. Clonidine needs to be started slowly (initial dose of 0.025-0.05 mg po qhs) because it may cause sedation and hypotension. The maximum dose of clonidine is appropriately 3 to 5 ug/kg per day in divided doses. Some children cannot tolerate a morning dose because of this sedation and doses over 0.2 mg total per day are associated with sedation.

Guanfacine is a longer-acting central alpha$_2$-adrenergic partial agonist that is more selective and thus less likely to be associated with side effects and rebound adrenergic symptoms. Guanfacine was found to be effective in decreasing nightmares in a single case study of a seven-year-old child (Horrigan, 1996). Guanfacine has been given in regimens of 0.5 mg at bedtime increasing by 0.25 to 0.5 mg every five to seven days to a mean effective dose of 1.27 mg (0.0225 mg/kg per day) given in two divided doses. However, smaller doses can be very effective for PTSD symptoms.

Blood pressure and pulse rate should be monitored at baseline, routinely, and during dose increase of these medications. Patients may be screened with an electrocardiogram for preexisting cardiac abnormalities before starting these medications. Common side effects of clonidine and guanfacine are sedation and dry mouth. However, these side effects are unlikely when using these low doses. Abruptly stopping clonidine or guanfacine treatment can cause rebound adrenergic symptoms such as headache, anxiety, tremors, abdominal pain, sweating, and tachycardia. Therefore, these medications need to be tapered when discontinued.

Propranolol, a beta-adrenergic antagonist, also dampens down sympathetic nervous system arousal. It is frequently used in low doses for stage fright. Famularo, Kinscherff, and Fenton (1988) found that five weeks of an open treatment trial of propranolol, at a dose of 2.5 mg/kg per day, was associated with decreases in aggressive behaviors, intrusive symptoms, and insomnia in eight of eleven abused children with PTSD. Common side effects of propranolol include Raynaud's phenomenon, bradycardia, bronchoconstriction, sexual impotence, and depression. Propranolol should not be given to children with asthma.

Clonidine, guanfacine, and propranolol appear to be relatively safe at the low doses described and effective for the treatment of PTSD symptoms in uncomplicated cases in which the psychopharmacological treatment of PTSD is of primary concern.

Tricylic Antidepressants

Tricylic antidepressants (imipramine, clomipramine, nortriptyline, desipramine) act at the neurotransmitter level to increase norepinephrine, serotonin, dopamine, and acetylcholine. Patients should be screened with an electrocardiogram for preexisting cardiac abnormalities, resting blood pressure, and pulse rate before starting these medications. When using these medications, the clinician frequently needs to obtain blood levels of the drug to monitor therapeutic levels. Common side effects include sedation, slowing of cardiac conduction, tachycardia, dry mouth, constipation, and elevated liver enzymes. Withdrawal effects include a flulike syndrome with nausea, vomiting, headache, lethargy, and irritability. Tricylic antidepressants were the first drugs used to treat anxiety disorders (separation anxiety disorder or school refusal) in children. However, scientific data to support the use of tricylic antidepressants in childhood anxiety disorders are inconsistent, with the exception of the use of clomipramine for obsessive-compulsive disorder and trichotillomania. Tricyclic antidepressants are also effective in the treatment of enuresis and as a second-line drug for the treatment of ADHD. Like clonidine, tricylic antidepressants need to be started slowly because they may cause sedation, and these medications need to be tapered when discontinued. However, unlike clonidine, low doses of tricylic antidepressants are not effective. Overdosage of tricylic antidepressants carries a significant risk of cardiac toxicity and death. Therefore, we do not recommend tricylic antidepressants as a first-line treatment for maltreated children with anxiety or mood disorders. Although these drugs may be helpful in some cases, tricylic antidepressants should only be given to children under the care of an extremely responsible caregiver who can effectively partner with the treatment team.

Benzodiazepines

Benzodiazepines (alprazolam, clonazepam, lorazepam, diazepam, clorazepate) are clearly effective in treating anxiety disorders in adults. However, no studies have been conducted in childhood PTSD. Benzodiazepine receptors are functionally linked to the inhibitory neurotransmitter gamma-aminobutyric acid (GABA). This system downregulates the locus coeruleus and cortical dopamine activity (Friedman & Southwick, 1995). However, scientific data to support the use of benzodiazepines in childhood anxiety disorders are inconsistent (for review see Bernstein et al., 1997). Common side effects of benzodiazepines include sedation, drowsiness, dizziness, decreased mental acuity, and behavioral disinhibition. Behavioral disinhibition can cause a child to act in a particularly embarrassing way that may further traumatize the child (e.g., disrobing in the classroom). Because of the potential for tolerance and dependence in children and adolescents, these medications are only recommended as a short-term treatment. These drugs are sometimes used to help control seizure disorders. Benzodiazepines should not be used as a first- or second-line treatment in maltreatment-associated anxiety disorders.

Buspirone

Buspirone is an atypical anxiolytic that acts primarily at dopamine and serotonin 1A receptors. It has a short half-life and no active metabolites. Common side effects are mild and transitory and include nausea, headache, drowsiness, and overexcitement. Only a few cases and open trials of this medication have been reported, with some positive effects in decreasing Hamilton Anxiety Disorder Ratings in anxious children and adolescents. This agent may safely be used as a second-line treatment in maltreatment-associated anxiety disorders.

Antihistamines

Diphenhydramine and hydroxyzine were used to alleviate anxiety symptoms in children beginning in the 1950s. However, no controlled studies have evaluated their effectiveness. Common side effects are sedation, dry skin and mouth, and dilated pupils. These drugs have been replaced with the anxiolytics to treat anxiety disorders.

Selective Serotonin Reuptake Inhibitors

Selective serotonin reuptake inhibitors (SSRIs) are also effective in the treatment of anxiety disorders in children and adolescents (Birmaher et al., 1994). Studies show strong support for the efficacy of the SSRI antidepressant and anti-obsessive-compulsive disorder medications sertraline (Brady et al., 2000) and fluoxetine (van der Kolk et al., 1994) in adult PTSD. To date there are no published reports of SSRIs or other antidepressants for the treatment of PTSD in traumatized children. These drugs are described in the next section.

Antidepressant Medications

Selective Serotonin Reuptake Inhibitors

SSRIs act to increase serotonin at the level of the synapse. This mechanism of action may be particularly important in traumatized individuals, as the review detailed how trauma is associated with decreased serotonin levels. Low levels of serotonin may lead to depression, impulsivity, and aggression. Selective serotonin reuptake inhibitors (fluoxetine, sertraline, paroxetine, fluvoxamine) are efficacious for the treatment of major depression in double-blind studies of adults and youth (Emslie et al., 1997). These drugs have a relatively safe side effect profile, very low lethality after overdose, and easy (once a day) administration. Currently there is no indication for baseline laboratory tests before beginning an SSRI. Selective serotonin reuptake inhibitors are the first-line treatment for the maltreated child or adolescent with major depression and major depression comorbid with PTSD. One should start these medications at a low dose and go slowly because SSRIs have a relatively flat dose-response curve, suggesting that maximal clinical response may be achieved at minimum effective doses.

Common side effects are gastrointestinal symptoms, restlessness, sweating, headaches, bruising, and changes in appetite, sleep, and sexual function. Side effects are dose dependent and may subside with time or by decreasing the dose. Akathisia, a very distressing restlessness in the legs, is a common side effect of SSRIs and can be very uncomfortable. Lowering the dose, switching to a less selective serotonin reuptake agent, or adding very low doses of propranolol (10 mg po b.i.d.) may help alleviate akathisia. Some children and adolescents will not be able to tolerate this side effect and the medication will need to be discontinued. Some patients have an allergeric reaction to SSRIs and get a very red raised itchy rash on their trunk and extremities. If this happens, the medication needs to be stopped immediately and the pediatrician notified. The rash will usually subside in a few days after discontinuation of the SSRI.

Children and adolescents can become manic or hypomanic while being treated with an antidepressant. Common symptoms include a change in behavior involving silliness, impulsivity, agitation, grandiosity, and recklessness. If this happens, the medications may need to be lowered or stopped. Hypomanic symptoms will usually decrease once the medication is stopped. However, if a full-blown mania occurs, appropriate intervention such as hospitalization may be indicated. Members of the treatment team should also monitor suicidal ideation in any depressed child or adolescent during the course of treatment and take appropriate action for the child's safety.

Abrupt withdrawal from an SSRI due to discontinuation, missing doses, or too-rapid tapering can cause a short-lived serotonin discontinuation syndrome. The symptoms are dizziness, nausea, vomiting, fatigue, chills, increased anxiety, and depression. Using an SSRI with a longer half-life (e.g., fluoxetine or sertraline) or carefully tapering the medication will avoid this withdrawal syndrome. A rare effect of overdose of SSRIs is the serotonin syndrome. It has the following clinical features: confusion, agitation, myoclonus, hyperreflexia, sweating, shivering, tremor, diarrhea, incoordination, and fever. This can be fatal if not treated rapidly in a hospital or emergency room.

Selective serotonin reuptake inhibitors inhibit the cytochrome P450 isoenzymes. This means that the metabolism of a number of other medications can be affected by the concurrent administration of an SSRI. The caregiver must always let the child's physician know that the child is taking an SSRI before being prescribed another medication. Monoamine oxidase inhibitors (MAOIs) should never be given with an SSRI. Selective serotonin reuptake inhibitors can also be used with low doses of clonidine (0.025-0.1 mg po qhs) to target insomnia and nightmares during the initial course of antidepressant treatment. Selective serotonin reuptake inhibitors have been safely used with tricyclic antidepressants and stimulants when doses are adjusted (for review see Werry & Aman, 1999).

Tricyclic Antidepressants

Tricyclic antidepressants have not proven to be efficacious for the treatment of major depression in double-blind studies of children and adolescents. These agents should not be used as a first- or second-line treatment in maltreatment-associated depressive disorders.

Bupropion. Bupropion is a relatively new antidepressant with effects on dopamine. It has few sedating and minimal anticholinergic and noradrenergic effects. It has been found to be an effective antidepressant in open trials of adolescent and double-blind studies of adult depression. Because bupropion may increase the risk for seizures, it should be prescribed with caution in a patient with suspected or known seizure history. Bupropion may safely be used as a second-line treatment in maltreatment-associated depressive disorders or depressive disorders associated with ADHD.

Venlafaxine. Venlafaxine is a relatively new antidepressant with effects on serotonin and norepinephrine. It has mild sedating and minimal anticholinergic effects. It has been found to be an effective antidepressant in open trials of adolescent and double-blind studies of adult depression. Venlafaxine may safely be used as a second-line treatment in maltreatment-associated depressive disorders.

Stimulants

Stimulant medications (methylphenidate, dextroamphetamine, pemoline, amphetamine) are the most powerful and best-documented intervention for the treatment of ADHD. Stimulants are the most commonly used psychotropic drugs with children. Substantial research has shown that stimulant medications improve behavioral, academic, and social functioning of 50 to 95 percent of children treated. These are the only medications to date to demonstrate the normalization of inattention, impulsiveness, and restless behavior in children. The primary action of stimulants, which are sympathomimetic compounds, is to enhance catecholamine activity in the central nervous system. Stimulants are always given by mouth, are rapidly absorbed from the gastrointestinal system, cross the blood-brain barrier quickly, and are rapidly eliminated from the body within twenty-four hours. Dextroamphetamine and pemoline plasma levels peak within two to three hours. Methylphenidate plasma levels peak within one-and-one-half to two hours. Adderall is a new longer-acting stimulant comprising a combination of amphetamine and dextroamphetamine. Behavioral effects are noticeable within sixty minutes of taking the medication. Stimulants are metabolized by the liver and kidneys.

Initial medical workup includes baseline height and weight. Patients should be screened with an electrocardiogram for preexisting cardiac abnormalities, resting blood pressure, and pulse rate before starting these medications. Effective dosages range from 0.3 to 1 mg/kg of body weight (in divided doses). During stimulant treatment, growth rate should be measured and the side-effects questionnaire used routinely (for review see Dulcan & The Work Group on Quality Issues, 1997; Werry & Aman, 1999). Conners rating scales should be used to get an objective assessment of the medication's effectiveness. Common side effects are decreased appetite, insomnia, anxiousness, irritability, tearfulness, stomachaches, headaches, and increase in nervous tics. Side effects will increase as the daily dose increases. Patients can develop an allergic skin reaction and will need to be taken off the drug. Some children and adolescents have "behavioral rebound" in the afternoon when the medication plasma levels rapidly decrease. This severe dysphoric reaction can be lessened by using a longer-acting or sustained-release stimulant or giving an afternoon dose of medication. Stimulants are rarely fatal if taken in an overdose. Clonidine has been combined with stimulants when ADHD presents with extreme impulsivity, aggression, or PTSD symptoms. Physicians must use caution when prescribing this combination, as three cases of sudden death have been reported in children taking methylphenidate/clonidine therapy (Popper, 1995).

Stimulants are effective medications and should be used when maltreated children and adolescents suffer from ADHD. However, it should be noted that the experience of maltreatment may enhance the activity of the catecholamine system. Thus stimulants may exacerbate hyperarousal symptoms. Therefore, when using these drugs in maltreated children it is very important to obtain several objective reports of the child's behavior in different settings (e.g., classroom) before confirming the diagnosis. Sometimes teachers and clinicians confuse the restlessness and distractibility of the anxious maltreated child with ADHD. One method of distinguishing the two disorders is to evaluate symptoms in different environments. An ADHD child will show ADHD symptoms in most situations, whereas these symptoms will be context-specific in an anxious maltreated child. Even with this information, differential diagnosis can still be difficult. However, stimulants are safe and work quickly. Therefore, if a child does well with a test dose (as reported by an objective observer), these drugs should be utilized for the child's educational and social benefit.

Bupropion

Bupropion, an antidepressant, has been demonstrated to be effective in ADHD in doses of 3 to 6 mg/kg per day (Barrickman et al., 1995). A sustained-release preparation is also available for this drug. Bupropion can be effective in treating maltreated children and adolescents with comorbidity (ADHD, PTSD, and major depression or dysthymia). It can also be safely used with low doses of clonidine (0.025-0.1 mg po qhs) to target insomnia and nightmares.

Mood-Stabilizing Drugs

Mood stabilizing or antimanic medications used in adults include lithium, the anticonvulsants, carbamazepine and valproate, the benzodiazepine clonazapam, and the calcium channel blockers verapamil, nifedipine, and diltiazem. Although psychopharmacological intervention is necessary to effectively treat early onset bipolar disorder, the literature regarding the use of these medications in youth is limited. This discussion is limited to the mood stabilizers more frequently used in children and adolescents.

Lithium

Lithium is a naturally occurring alkali metal found in seawater. It is the first-choice agent in the treatment of mania. Double-blind studies and a series of case reports have found lithium to be effective in bipolar disorder of youth (for review see McClellan et al., 1997). Lithium is excreted entirely by the kidneys without undergoing hepatic metabolism. Since children generally have a higher glomerular filtration rate than adults, the lithium dose relative to weight is usually somewhat higher for this age group. As in adults, the recommended therapeutic serum level is 0.6 to 1.2 mEq/L during an acute mania. Maintenance serum levels are somewhat lower (0.6 to 0.8 mEq/L). To achieve therapeutic levels, start the medication at a dose of 300 to 900 mg per day (approximately 30 mg/kg body weight per day). Serum levels are usually measured within the first five days of steady dose administrated and titrated to therapeutic levels as necessary.

Before starting lithium, a careful medical workup including a detailed history of renal problems, cardiovascular disease, or the use of medications that interfere with sodium regulation needs to be done. Laboratory workup includes baseline complete blood count, with differential, thyroid function tests, electrolytes, kidney function tests including twenty-four-hour collection of urine for creatinine clearance, blood urea nitrogen, creatinine levels, and an electrocardiogram. These measures should be monitored routinely. Common side effects of lithium treatment are nausea, diarrhea, vomiting, tremor, weight gain, headache, polyuria, polydipsia, enuresis, fatigue, and ataxia. Lithium can be fatal if taken in overdose. Carbamazepine and neuroleptics may increase the potential for lithium toxicity secondary to drug interactions. Lithium treatment should be reserved for the treatment of mania, acute psychotic disorders with affective features, and severe aggression with affective features. Typically these patients will be very impaired and should be followed closely in an inpatient, partial hospital, or intensive outpatient setting.

Carbamazepine and Valproate

Carbamazepine and valproate are anticonvulsant drugs that are effective in the treatment of acute mania. No placebo-controlled studies have been published to date using these agents for the treatment of early onset bipolar disorder. However, these drugs are safely used in children and adolescents with seizure disorders and have been found to be effective mood stabilizers in open treatment trials. Most children and adolescents tolerate carbamazepine or valproate well. Common side effects of carbamazepine include drowsiness, dizziness, nausea, and mild ataxia. Common side effects of valproate include sedation, nausea, and vomiting. Potentially rare and serious side effects of carbamazepine are agranulocytosis, aplastic anemia, and hepatic toxicity. A potentially rare side effect of valproate is fatal hepatic toxicity during the first six months of therapy.

Prior to beginning carbamazepine or valproate, a careful medical workup including baseline complete blood count, with differential, electrolytes, liver function tests, and blood coagulation tests are recommended. Carbamazepine induces its own metabolism, which sometimes makes obtaining therapeutic serum levels difficult. Hepatic and hematological measures as well as serum drug levels should be monitored routinely to avoid toxicity. Carbamazepine or valproate can be fatal if taken in overdose. Anticonvulsant treatment should be reserved for mania, acute psychotic disorders with affective features, and severe aggression with affective features in a very impaired patient.

Calcium channel blockers have not been well studied in the treatment of early onset bipolar disorder. They should only be used after more standard regimens have been tried.

Antipsychotic Medications

Antipsychotic drugs form a large class of psychotropic agents originally called neuroleptics. They are divided into two groups, the typical and atypical types. The typical or classical neuroleptics are associated with many adverse and permanent side effects such as tardive dyskinesia. The use of classical neuroleptic drugs is not recommended in children and adolescents. Atypical antipsychotic drugs are often grouped into high- (risperidone, sertindole, and ziprasidone) and low-potency (clozapine, quetiapine, olanzapine) categories, which tends to distinguish drugs with high incidence of extrapyramidal side effects from those with atropine side effects. The use of atypical antipsychotic drugs rather than the classical neuroleptics is thought to decrease the risk of extrapyramidal and permanent side effects. Antipsychotic drugs are indicated for the reduction of positive psychotic symptoms (delusions, hallucinations, and/or a formal thought disorder), movement disorders (stereotypies and tics), or extremely severe aggression, assaultiveness, paranoia, and extreme irritability.

Prior to beginning antipsychotic drugs, a careful medical workup including baseline measures of height and weight, neurological exam for tics, stereotypies, extrapyramidal disorders and tardive dyskinesia, complete blood count, with differential, electrolytes, and liver and kidney function tests are recommended. These evaluations, including the Abnormal Involuntary Movements Scale (AIMS) should be repeated routinely.

Common and uncommon side effects include sedation, extrapyramidal side effects (acute dystonic reactions, Parkinsonian side effects, akathisia, dyskinesis, tardive dystonia, and tardive dyskinesia), seizures, neuroleptic malignant syndrome, benign tachycardia, orthostatic hypotension, hepatic dysfunction rashes, and photosensitivity. When using these drugs, it is important to maintain the lowest therapeutically effective dose.

WHEN MEDICATIONS DO NOT WORK

Caregivers may complain about ineffective doses of medications that were previously effective. It is always important to review the case and re-evaluate your differential diagnosis and the target symptoms of treatment when this happens. This circumstance can occur for several reasons.

The first is noncompliance with the drug regimen as prescribed. The second is an unrealistic expectation of what a drug will and will not do for the child. The third is an increase or new precipitating psychosocial stress, which is causing the child to feel unsafe and anxious. Sometimes agitation and acting out may be the first indication of more abuse. The fourth is that the medication is causing significant side effects. For example, the experience of akathisia can lead to restlessness and acting-out behaviors. The fifth is an overlooked medical problem that is related to the increase in psychiatric symptoms. The sixth is normal growth and development. Growth may either mean that the dose will need to be adjusted (increased) for effectiveness or that because of individual differences during pubertal development the medication may need to be changed to another type or class of drug.

SUMMARY

Maltreatment in childhood has psychopathological and developmental consequences. Developmental consequences may include biological changes in stress systems as well as failures to obtain important psychological developmental achievements. Although trauma in childhood may have a profound and long-lasting impact on development, it is always hopeful to know that individual children strive toward growth. When rescued from extremely neglectful and abusive environments, profoundly maltreated children are capable of accelerated rates of catch-up growth, including remission of severe psychopathology and normalization of cognitive function (Koluchova, 1972, 1976; Money, Annecillo, & Kelly, 1983). The appropriate use of medications is one step in this process.

REFERENCES

American Psychiatric Association (1994). *Diagnostic and statistical manual of mental disorders* (4th ed). Washington, DC: American Psychiatric Press.

American Psychiatric Association (2000). *Diagnostic and statistical manual of mental disorders* (4th ed., text rev.). Washington, DC: American Psychiatric Press.

Armsworth, M. W., & Holaday, M. (1993). The effects of psychological trauma on children and adolescents. *Journal of Counseling and Development, 72,* 49-56.

Arnsten, A. F. T. (1998). The biology of being frazzled. *Science, 280,* 1711-1712.

Arnsten, A. F. T., & Goldman-Rakic, P. S. (1998). Noise stress impairs cortical function: Evidence for a hyperdopaminergic mechanism. *Archives of General Psychiatry, 55,* 362-368.

Arora, R. C., Fichtner, C. G., O'Connor, F., & Crayton, J. W. (1993). Paraoxetine binding in the blood platelets of post-traumatic stress disorder patients. *Life Sciences, 53,* 919-928.

Aston-Jones, G., Valentino, R. J., Van Bockstaele, E. J., & Meyerson, A. T. (1994). Locus coeruleus, stress, and PTSD: Neurobiological and clinical parallels. In M. Murburg (Ed.), *Catecholamine function in posttraumatic stress disorder: Emerging concepts* (pp. 17-62). Washington, DC: American Psychiatric Press.

Baker, D. G., West, S. A., Nicholson, W. E., Ekhator, N. N., Kasckow, J. W., Hill, K. K., Bruce, A. B., Orth, D. N., & Geracioti, T. D., Jr. (1999). Serial CSF corticotropin-releasing hormone levels and adrenocortical activity in combat veterans with posttraumatic stress disorder. *American Journal of Psychiatry, 156,* 585-588.

Barrickman, L. L., Perry, P. J., Allen, A. J., Kuperman, S., Arndt, S. V., Herrmann, K. J., & Schumacher, E. (1995). Bupropion vs. methylphenidate in the treatment of attention-deficit hyperactivity disorder. *Journal of the American Academy of Child and Adolescent Psychiatry, 34,* 649-657.

Benkelfat, C. (1993). Serotonergic mechanisms in psychiatric disorders: New research tools, new ideas. *International Clinical Psychopharmacology, 8*(Suppl. 2), 53-56.

Bernstein, G. A., Shaw, K., & The Work Group on Quality Issues. (1997). Practice parameters for the assessment and treatment of children and adolescents with anxiety disorders. *American Academy of Child and Adolescent Psychiatry, 36*(10 Suppl.), 69S-84S.

Birmaher, B., Brent, D., & The Work Group On Quality Issues. (1998). Practice parameters for the assessment and treatment of children and adolescents with depressive disorders. *American Academy of Child and Adolescent Psychiatry, 37*(10 Suppl.), 63S-83S.

Birmaher, B., Waterman, G. S., Ryan, N., Cully, M., Balach, L., Ingram, J., & Brodsky, M. (1994). Fluoxetine for childhood anxiety disorders. *American Academy of Child and Adolescent Psychiatry, 33,* 993-999.

Brady, K., Pearlstein, T., Asnis, G. M., Baker, D., Rothbaum, B., Sikes, C. R., & Farfel, G. M. (2000). Efficacy and safety of sertraline treatment of posttraumatic stress disorder: A randomized controlled trial. *Journal of the American Medical Association, 283,* 1837-1844.

Bremner, J. D., Davis, M., Southwick, S. M., Krystal, J. H., & Charney, D. S. (Eds.). (1993). *Neurobiology of posttraumatic stress disorder.* Washington, DC: American Psychiatric Press.

Bremner, J. D., Licinio, J., Darnell, A., Krystal, J. H., Owens, M. J., Southwick, S. M., Nemeroff, C. B., & Charney, D. S. (1997). Elevated CSF corticotropin-releasing factor concentrations in posttraumatic stress disorder. *American Journal of Psychiatry, 154,* 624-629.

Bremner, J. D., Narayan, M., Staib, L., Southwick, S. M., McGlashan, T., & Charney, D. S. (1999). Neural correlates of memories of childhood sexual abuse in women with and without posttraumatic stress disorder. *American Journal of Psychiatry, 156,* 1787-1795.

Breslau, N., Davis, G. C., Peterson, E., & Schultz, L. R. (2000). A second look at comorbidity in victims of trauma: The posttraumatic stress disorder-major depression connection. *Biological Psychiatry, 48*(9), 902-909.

Bukstein, O., & The Work Group on Quality Issues. (1997). Practice parameters for the assessment and treatment of children and adolescents with substance use disorders. *American Academy of Child and Adolescent Psychiatry, 36*(10 Suppl.), 140S-156S.

Chapin, H. D. (1917). Systematized boarding out vs. institutional care for infants and young children. *New York Medical Journal, 105*(22), 1009-1011.

Charney, D. S., Deutch, A. Y., Krystal, J. H., Southwich, S. M., & Davis, M. (1993). Psychobiological mechanisms of posttraumatic stress disorder. *Archives of General Psychiatry, 50,* 294-305.

Charney, D. S., Nestler, E. J., & Bunny, B. S. (1999). *Neurobiology of mental illness.* New York: Oxford University Press.

Chrousos, G. P., & Gold, P. W. (1992). The concepts of stress and stress system disorders: Overview of physical and behavioral homeostasis. *Journal of the American Medical Association, 267,* 1244-1252.

Clark, D. B., Lesnick, L., & Hegedus, A. (1997). Trauma and other stressors in adolescent alcohol dependence and abuse. *Journal of the American Academy of Child and Adolescent Psychiatry, 36,* 1744-1751.

Clark, D. B., Pollock, N., Bukstein, O. G., Mezzich, A. C., Bromberger, J. T., & Donovan, J. E. (1997). Gender and comorbid psychopathology in adolescents with alcohol dependence. *Journal of the American Academy of Child and Adolescent Psychiatry, 36*(9), 1195-1203.

Cohen, J. A., & The Work Group on Quality Issues. (1998). Practice parameters for the assessment and treatment of children and adolescents with posttraumatic stress disorder. *American Academy of Child and Adolescent Psychiatry, 37*(10 Suppl.), 4S-26S.

De Bellis, M. D. (1997). Posttraumatic stress disorder and acute stress disorder. In R. T. Ammerman & M. Hersen (Eds.), *Handbook of prevention and treatment with children and adolescents* (pp. 455-494). New York: John Wiley.

De Bellis, M. D. (2001). Developmental traumatology: The psychobiological development of maltreated children and its implications for research, treatment, and policy. *Development and Psychopathology, 13,* 539-564.

De Bellis, M. D., Baum, A., Birmaher, B., Keshavan, M., Eccard, C. H., Boring, A. M., Jenkins, F. J., & Ryan, N. D. (1999). A.E. Bennett Research Award. Developmental traumatology part I: Biological stress systems. *Biological Psychiatry, 45,* 1259-1270.

De Bellis, M. D., Broussard, E., Herring, D., Wexler, S., Moritz, G., & Benitez, J.G. (2001). Psychiatric co-morbidity in caregivers and children involved in maltreatment: A pilot research study with policy implications. *Child Abuse and Neglect, 25,* 923-944.

De Bellis, M. D., Keshavan, M., Clark, D. B., Casey, B. J., Giedd, J., Boring, A. M., Frustaci, K., & Ryan, N. D. (1999). A.E. Bennett Research Award. Developmental traumatology part II: Brain development. *Biological Psychiatry, 45,* 1271-1284.

De Bellis, M. D., Keshavan, M. S., Spencer, S., & Hall, J. (2000). N-acetylaspartate concentration in the anterior cingulate in maltreated children and adolescents with PTSD. *American Journal of Psychiatry, 157,* 1175-1177.

De Bellis, M. D., Lefter, L., Trickett, P. K., & Putnam, F. W. (1994). Urinary catecholamine excretion in sexually abused girls. *Journal of the American Academy of Child and Adolescent Psychiatry, 33,* 320-327.

De Bellis, M. D., & Putnam, F. W. (1994). The psychobiology of childhood maltreatment. *Child and Adolescent Psychiatric Clinics of North America, 3,* 663-677.

Dembo, R., Dertke, M., Borders, S., Washburn, M., & Schmeidler, J. (1988). The relationship between physical and sexual abuse and tobacco, alcohol, and illicit drug use among youths in a juvenile detention center. *International Journal of the Addictions, 23,* 351-378.

Dembo, R., Williams, L., Wothke, W., Schmeidler, J., & Brown, C. H. (1992). The role of family factors, physical abuse and sexual victimization experiences in high-risk youths' alcohol and other drug use and delinquency: A longitudinal model. *Violence and Victims, 7,* 245-266.

Deykin, E. Y., & Buka, S. L. (1997). Prevalence and risk factors for posttraumatic stress disorder among chemically dependent adolescents. *American Journal of Psychiatry, 154,* 752-757.

Dubner, A. E., & Motta, R. W. (1999). Sexually and physically abused foster care children and posttraumatic stress disorder. *Journal of Consulting and Clinical Psychology, 67,* 367-373.

Dulcan, M., & The Work Group on Quality Issues. (1997). Practice parameters for the assessment and treatment of children, adolescents, and adults with attention-deficit/hyperactivity disorder. *American Academy of Child and Adolescent Psychiatry, 36*(10 Suppl.), 85S-121S.

Dunlop, S. A., Archer, M. A., Quinlivan, J. A., Beazley, L. D., & Newnham, J. P. (1997). Repeated prenatal corticosteroids delay myelination in the ovine central nervous system. *Journal of Maternal-Fetal Medicine, 6,* 309-313.

Edwards, E., Harkins, K., Wright, G., & Menn, F. (1990). Effects of bilateral adrenalectomy on the induction of learned helplessness. *Behavioral Neuropsychopharmacology, 3,* 109-114.

Emslie, G. J., Rush, A. J., Weinberg, W. A., Kowatch, R. A., Hughes, C. W., Carmody, T., & Rintelmann, J. (1997). A double-blind, randomized, placebo-controlled trial of fluoxetine in children and adolescents with depression. *Archives of General Psychiatry, 54,* 1031-1037.

Eth, S., & Pynoos, R. (1985). *Post-traumatic stress disorders in children.* Washington, DC: American Psychiatric Association.

Famularo, R., Fenton, T., Augustyn, M., & Zuckerman, B. (1996). Persistence of pediatric post traumatic stress disorder after 2 years. *Child Abuse and Neglect, 20,* 1245-1248.

Famularo, R., Fenton, T., & Kinscherff, R. (1993). Child maltreatment and the development of posttraumatic stress disorder. *American Journal of Diseases of Children, 147,* 755-760.

Famularo, R., Fenton, T., & Kinscherff, R. (1994). Maternal and child posttraumatic stress disorder in cases of maltreatment. *Child Abuse and Neglect, 18,* 27-36.

Famularo, R., Kinsherff, R., & Fenton, T. (1988). Propranolol treatment for childhood posttraumatic stress disorder, acute type. *American Journal of the Diseases of Children, 142,* 1244-1247.

Famularo, R., Kinscherff, R., & Fenton, T. (1992). Psychiatric diagnoses of abusive mothers. *Journal of Nervous and Mental Disease, 180,* 658-661.

Felitti, V. J., Anda, R. F., Nordenberg, D., Williamson, D. F., Spitz, A. M., Edwards, V., Koss, M. P., & Marks, J. S. (1998). Relationship of childhood abuse and household dysfunction to many of the leading causes of death in adults. *American Journal of Preventive Medicine, 14,* 245-258.

Fletcher, K. E. (Ed.). (1996). *Childhood posttraumatic stress disorder.* New York: Guilford.

Friedman, M. J., & Southwick, S. M. (Eds.). (1995). *Toward psychopharmacology for post-traumatic stress disorder.* Philadelphia: Lippincott-Raven.

Fuster, J. M. (1980). *The prefrontal cortex: Anatomy, physiology, and neuropsychology of the frontal lobe.* New York: Raven Press.

Goldman-Rakic, P. S. (1994). Working memory dysfunction in schizophrenia. *Journal of Neuropsychiatry and Clinical Neurosciences, 6,* 348-357.

Goodwin, J. (1988). Post-traumatic stress symptoms in abused children. *Journal of the American Academy of Child and Adolescent Psychiatry, 22,* 231-237.

Gould, E., McEwen, B. S., Tanapat, P., Galea, L. A., & Fuchs, E. (1997). Neurogenesis in the dentate gyrus of the adult tree shrew is regulated by psychosocial stress and NMDA receptor activation. *Journal of Neuroscience, 17,* 2492-2498.

Gould, E., Reeves, A. J., Graziano, M. S. A., & Gross, C. G. (1999). Neurogenesis in the neocortex of adult primates. *Science, 286,* 548-552.

Gould, E., Tanapat, P., & Cameron, H. A. (1997). Adrenal steroids suppress granule cell death in the developing dentate gyrus through an NMDA receptor-dependent mechanism. *Developmental Brain Research, 103*, 91-93.

Green, B. L., Grace, M. C., & Gleser, G. C. (1985). Long-term impairment following the Beverly Hills Supper Club fire. *Journal of Consulting and Clinical Psychology, 53*, 672-678.

Harmon, R. J., & Riggs, P. D. (1996). Clonidine for posttraumatic stress disorder in preschool children. *American Academy of Child and Adolescent Psychiatry, 35*, 1247-1249.

Harrison, P. A., Fulkerson, J. A., & Beebe, T. J. (1997). Multiple substance use among adolescent physical and sexual abuse victims. *Child Abuse and Neglect, 21*, 529-539.

Hart, J., Gunnar, M., & Cicchetti, D. (1996). Altered neuroendocrine activity in maltreated children related to symptoms of depression. *Development and Psychopathology, 8*, 201-214.

Henggeler, S. W., Schoenwald, S. K., Borduin, C. M., Rowland, M. D., & Cunningham, P. B. (1998). *Multisystemic treatment of antisocial behavior in children and adolescents.* New York: Guilford.

Herman, J. L. (Ed.). (1993). *Sequelae of prolonged and repeated trauma: Evidence for a complex posttraumatic syndrome (DESNOS).* Washington, DC: American Psychiatric Press.

Hillary, B. E., & Schare, M. L. (1993). Sexually and physically abused adolescents: An empirical search for PTSD. *Journal of Clinical Psychology, 49*, 161-165.

Horrigan, J. P. (1996). Guanfacine for posttraumatic stress disorder nightmares. *American Academy of Child and Adolescent Psychiatry, 35*, 975-976.

Jensen, P. S., Kettle, L., Roper, M. T., Sloan, M. T., Dulcan, M. K., Hoven, C., Bird, H. R., Bauermeister, J. J., & Payne, J. D. (1999). Are stimulants overprescribed? Treatment of ADHD in four U.S. communities. *American Academy of Child and Adolescent Psychiatry, 38*, 797-804.

Johnson, J. G., Cohen, P., Brown, J., Smailes, E. M., & Berstein, D. P. (1999). Childhood maltreatment increases risk for personality disorders during early adulthood. *Archives of General Psychiatry, 56*, 600-606.

Kaplan, S., Pelkovitz, D., Saltzinger, S., & Ganeles, D. (1983). Psychopathology of parents of abused and neglected children and adolescents. *Journal of the American Academy of Child and Adolescent Psychiatry, 22*, 238-244.

Kaufman, J. (1991). Depressive disorders in maltreated children. *Journal of the American Academy of Child and Adolescent Psychiatry, 30*, 257-265.

Kaufman, J., Birmaher, B., Perel, J., Dahl, R. E., Moreci, P., Nelson, B., Wells, W., & Ryan, N. (1997). The corticotropin-releasing hormone challenge in depressed abused, depressed nonabused, and normal control children. *Biological Psychiatry, 42*, 669-679.

Kaufman, J., Jones, B., Stieglitz, E., Vitulano, l., & Mannarino, A. (1994). The use of multiple informants to assess children's maltreatment experiences. *Journal of Family Violence, 9*, 227-248.

Kendler, K. S., Bulik, C. M., Silberg, J., Hettema, J. M., Myers, J., & Prescott, C. A. (2000). Childhood sexual abuse and adult psychiatric and substance use disorders in women: An epidemiological and cotwin control study. *Archives of General Psychiatry, 57,* 953-959.

Koluchova, J. (1972). Severe deprivation in twins: A case study. *Journal of Child Psychology and Psychiatry, 13,* 107-114.

Koluchova, J. (1976). The further development of twins after severe and prolonged deprivation: A second report. *Journal of Child Psychology and Psychiatry, 17,* 181-188.

Lauder, J. M. (1988). Neurotransmitters as morphogens. *Progress in Brain Research, 73,* 365-388.

LeDoux, J. (1998). Fear and the brain: Where have we been, and where are we going? *Biological Psychiatry, 44,* 1229-1238.

Levy, H. B., Markovic, J., Chaudry, U., Ahart, S., & Torres, H. (1995). Reabuse rates in a sample of children followed for 5 years after discharge from a child abuse inpatient assessment program. *Child Abuse and Neglect, 11,* 1363-1377.

Lipschitz, D. S., Winegar, R. K., Hartnick, E., Foote, B., & Southwick, S. M. (1999). Posttraumatic stress disorder in hospitalized adolescents: Psychiatric comorbidity and clinical correlates. *Journal of the American Academy of Child and Adolescent Psychiatry, 38,* 385-392.

Luntz, B. K., & Widom, C. S. (1994). Antisocial personality disorder in abused and neglected children grown up. *American Journal of Psychiatry, 151,* 670-674.

Lyon, T. D. (1999). Are battered women bad mothers? Rethinking the termination of abused women's parental rights for failure to protect. In H. Dubowitz (Ed.), *Neglected children: Research, practice, and policy* (pp. 237-260). Thousand Oaks, CA: Sage.

Lyons, J. A. (1987). Post-traumatic stress disorder in children and adolescents: A review of the literature. *Journal of Developmental and Behavioral Pediatrics, 8,* 349-356.

Macklin, M. L., Metzger, L. J., Litz, B. T., McNally, R. J., Lasko, N. B., Orr, S. P., & Pitman, R. K. (1998). Lower precombat intelligence is a risk factor for posttraumatic stress disorder. *Journal of Consulting and Clinical Psychology, 66,* 232-236.

Mannarino, A. P., Cohen, J. A., & Berman, S. R. (1994). The relationship between preabuse factors and psychological symptomatology in sexually abused girls. *Child Abuse and Neglect, 18,* 63-71.

McClellan, J., Werry, J. S., & The Work Group on Quality Issues. (1997). Practice parameters for the assessment and treatment of children and adolescents with bipolar disorder. *American Academy of Child and Adolescent Psychiatry, 36*(10 Suppl.), 157S-176S.

McGee, R., Wolfe, D., Yuen, S., Wilson, S., & Carnochan, J. (1995). The measurement of maltreatment. *Child Abuse and Neglect, 19,* 233-249.

McLeer, S. V., Callaghan, M., Henry, D., & Wallen, J. (1994). Psychiatric disorders in sexually abused children. *Journal of the American Academy of Child and Adolescent Psychiatry, 33,* 313-319.

McLeer, S. V., Dixon, J. F., Henry, D., Ruggiero, K., Escovitz, K., Niedda, T., & Scholle, R. (1998). Psychopathology in non-clinically referred sexually abused children. *Journal of the American Academy of Child and Adolescent Psychiatry, 37*, 1326-1333.

Money, J., Annecillo, C., & Kelly, J. F. (1983). Abuse-dwarfism syndrome: After rescue, statural and intellectual catchup growth correlate. *Journal of Clinical Child Psychology, 12*, 279-283.

National Research Council (1993). *Understanding child abuse and neglect.* Washington, DC: National Academy Press.

Perez, C., & Widom, C. S. (1994). Childhood victimization and long-term intellectual and academic outcomes. *Child Abuse and Neglect, 18*(8), 617-633.

Perry, B. D. (Ed.). (1994). *Neurobiological sequelae of childhood trauma: PTSD in children.* Washington, DC: American Psychiatric Press.

Popper, C. (1995). Combining methylphenidine and clonidine: Pharmacologic questions and new reports about sudden death. *Journal of Child and Adolescent Psychopharmacology, 5*, 157-166.

Posner, M. I., & Petersen, S. E. (1990). The attention system of the human brain. *Annual Review of Neuroscience, 13*, 25-42.

Prichard, J. W. (1996). MRS of the brain-prospects for clinical application. In I. R. Young & H. C. Charles (Eds.), *MR spectroscopy: Clinical applications and techniques* (pp. 1-25). London: Livery House.

Putnam, F. W. (1997). *Dissociation in children and adolescents: A developmental perspective.* New York: Guilford.

Pynoos, R. S., & Eth, S. (1986). Witness to violence: The child interview. *Journal of the American Academy of Child and Adolescent Psychiatry, 25*, 306-319.

Pynoos, R. S., Frederick, C., Nader, K., Arroyo, W., Steinberg, A., Eth, S., Nunez, F., & Fairbanks, L. (1987). Life threat and post-traumatic stress in school-aged children. *Archives of General Psychiatry, 44*, 1057-1063.

Pynoos, R. S., & Nader, K. (1989). Children's memory and proximity to violence. *Journal of the American Academy of Child and Adolescent Psychiatry, 28*, 236-241.

Pynoos, R. S., & Nader, K. (Eds.). (1993). *Issues in the treatment of posttraumatic stress disorder in children and adolescents.* Washington, DC: American Psychiatric Press.

Queiroz, E. A., Lombardi, A. B., Santos Furtado, C. R. H., Peixoto, C. C. D., Soares, T. A., Fabre, Z. L., Basques, J. C., Fernandes, M. L. M., & Lippi, J. R. S. (1991). Biochemical correlate of depression in children. *Arq Neuro-Psiquiat, 49*(4), 418-425.

Rosenberg, D. R., & Keshavan, M. S. (1998). A.E. Bennett Research Award: Toward a neurodevelopmental model of obsessive-compulsive disorder. *Biological Psychiatry, 43*, 623-640.

Rutter, M. (1981). *Maternal deprivation reassessed.* New York: Penguin Books.

Sapolsky, R. M., Uno, H., Rebert, C. S., & Finch, C. E. (1990). Hippocampal damage associated with prolonged glucocorticoid exposure in primates. *Journal of Neuroscience, 10*, 2897-2902.

Scheeringa, M. S., Zeanah, C. H., Drell, M. J., & Larrieu, J. A. (1995). Two approaches to the diagnosis of posttraumatic stress disorder in infancy and early childhood. *Journal of the American Academy of Child and Adolescent Psychiatry, 34,* 191-200.

Sedlak, A. J., & Broadhurst, D. D. (1996). *Third national incidence study of child abuse and neglect.* Washington, DC: U.S. Department of Health and Human Services.

Shin, L. M., McNally, R. J., Kosslyn, S. M., Thompson, W. L., Rauch, S. L., Alpert, N. M., Metzger, L. J., Lasko, N. B., Orr, S. P., & Pitman, R. K. (1999). Regional cerebral blood flow during script-imagery in childhood sexual abuse-related PTSD: A PET investigation. *American Journal of Psychiatry, 156,* 575-584.

Siever, L., & Trestman, R. L. (1993). The serotonin system and aggressive personality disorder. *International Clinical Psychopharmacology, 8*(Suppl. 2), 33-40.

Simantov, R., Blinder, E., Ratovitski, T., Tauber, M., Gabbay, M., & Porat, S. (1996). Dopamine induced apoptosis in human neuronal cells: Inhibition by nucleic acids antisense to the dopamine transporter. *Neuroscience, 74,* 39-50.

Smythies, J. R. (1997). Oxidative reactions and schizophrenia: A review-discussion. *Schizophrenia Research, 24,* 357-364.

Southwick, S. M., Krystal, J. H., Johnson, D. R., & Charney, D. S. (Eds.). (1992). *Neurobiology of posttraumatic stress disorder.* Washington, DC: American Psychiatric Press.

Southwick, S. S., Yehuda, R., & Wang, S. (1998). Neuroendocrine alterations in posttraumatic stress disorder. *Psychiatric Annals, 28,* 436-442.

Steiner, H., Garcia, I. G., & Matthews, Z. (1997). Posttraumatic stress disorder in incarcerated juvenile delinquents. *Journal of the American Academy of Child and Adolescent Psychiatry, 36,* 357-365.

Steiner, H., & The Work Group on Quality Issues. (1997). Practice parameters for the assessment and treatment of children and adolescents with conduct disorder. *American Academy of Child and Adolescent Psychiatry, 36*(10 Suppl.), 122S-139S.

Sulser, F. (1987). Serotonin-norepinephrine receptor interactions in the brain: Implications for the pharmacology and pathophysiology of affective disorders. *Journal of Clinical Psychiatry, 48*(March) (Suppl), 12-18.

Szatmari, P., Boyle, M., & Offord, D. R. (1989). ADHD and conduct disorder: Degree of diagnostic overlap and differences among correlates. *American Academy of Child and Adolescent Psychiatry, 28,* 865-872.

Tanapat, P., Galea, L. A., & Gould, E. (1998). Stress inhibits the proliferation of granule cell precursors in the developing dentate gyrus. *Journal of Developmental Neuroscience, 16,* 235-239.

Taylor, C., Norman, N., Murphy, M., Jellinek, M., Quinn, D., Poitrast, F. G., & Groshko, M. (1991). Diagnosed intellectual and emotional impairment among parents who seriously mistreat their children: Prevalence, type, and outcome in a court sample. *Child Abuse and Neglect, 15,* 389-401.

Terr, L. C. (1991). Childhood traumas: An outline and overview. *American Journal of Psychiatry, 148,* 10-20.

Todd, R. D. (1992). Neural development is regulated by classical neuro-transmitters: Dopamine D2 receptor stimulation enhances neurite outgrowth. *Biological Psychiatry, 31,* 794-807.

U.S. Department of Health and Human Services (1998). *Child maltreatment 1996: Reports from the states to the national child abuse and neglect data system.* Washington, DC: U.S. Government Printing Office.

van der Kolk, B. A., Dreyfuss, D., Michaels, M., Shera, D., Berkowitz, R., Fisler, R., & Saxe, G. (1994). Fluoxetine in posttraumatic stress disorder. *Journal of Clinical Psychiatry, 55,* 517-522.

van der Kolk, B. A., Greenberg, M. S., Orr, S. P., & Pitman, R. K. (1989). Endogenous opioids, stress induced analgesia, and posttraumatic stress disorder. *Psychopharmacology Bulletin, 25,* 417-421.

Walker, E. A., Unutzer, J., Rutter, C., Gelfand, A., Saunders, K., VonKorff, M., Koss, M. P., & Katon, W. (1999). Costs of health care use by women HMO members with a history of childhood abuse and neglect. *Archives of General Psychiatry, 56,* 609-613.

Werry, J. S., & Aman, M. G. (Eds.). (1999). *Practitioner's guide to psychoactive drugs for children and adolescents* (2nd ed.). New York: Plenum Medical.

Widom, C. S. (1989). The cycle of violence. *Science, 244,* 160-166.

Wilens, T. E., & Spencer, T. J. (2000). The stimulants revisited. *Child and Adolescent Psychiatric Clinics of North America, 9,* 573-603.

Wolfe, D. A., Sas, L., & Wekerle, C. (1994). Factors associated with the development of posttraumatic stress disorder among victims of sexual abuse. *Child Abuse and Neglect, 18,* 37-50.

Wolfe, J., & Charney, D. S. (1991). Use of neuropsychological assessment in posttraumatic stress disorder. *Psychological Assessment: A Journal of Consulting and Clinical Psychology, 3,* 573-580.

Wolfe, V. V., Gentile, C., & Wolfe, D. A. (1989). The impact of sexual abuse on children: A PTSD formulation. *Behavior Therapy, 20,* 215-228.

Yehuda, R., Southwick, S., Giller, E. L., Ma, X., & Mason, J. W. (1992). Urinary catecholamine excretion and severity of PTSD symptoms in Vietnam combat veterans. *Journal of Nervous and Mental Disease, 180,* 321-325.

Zubieta, J. K., Chinitz, J. A., Lombardi, U., Fig, L. M., Cameron, O. G., & Liberzon, I. (1999). Medial frontal cortex involvement in PTSD symptoms: A SPECT study. *Journal of Psychiatric Research, 33,* 259-264.

Index

Page numbers followed by the letter "e" indicate exhibits; those followed by the letter "f" indicate figures; and those followed by the letter "t" indicate tables.